TYPE-LOGICAL SEMANTICS

Language, Speech, and Communication

TYPE-LOGICAL SEMANTICS

Bob Carpenter

A Bradford Book
The MIT Press
Cambridge, Massachusetts
London, England

This book was set in Times New Roman on the Monotype "Prism Plus" PostScript Imagesetter by Asco Trade Typesetting Ltd., Hong Kong, and was printed and bound in the United States of America.

First printing, 1997.

Library of Congress Cataloging-in-Publication Data

Carpenter, Bob.
 Type-logical semantics / Bob Carpenter.
     p.   cm. — (Language, speech, and communication)
"A Bradford book."
 ISBN 0-262-03248-1 (hc). — ISBN 0-262-53149-6 (pbk).
 1. Semantics. 2. Semantics (Philosophy) 3. Language and logic. 4. Grammar, Comparative and general. 5. Computational linguistics. 6. Logic. I. Title.
P325.C324   1997
401'.43—dc21   97-863
                                                                          CIP

In memory of my grandmother, Lotus Ione Boggess (1924–1989)

Contents

Contents

This book is based on lectures given for an introductory course on natural-language semantics at Carnegie Mellon University. Although this book was developed in conjunction with a class, it contains a great deal of original work on categorial grammar and its application to natural-language semantics. Thus it should be of interest not only to students, but to anyone interested in natural language semantics. The course on which this book is based is intended for advanced undergraduates and first-year graduate students without previous exposure to natural-language semantics. As a prerequisite, students entering the course were expected to have completed at least one semester of upper-level logic to the point of understanding completeness in first-order systems. Students were also expected to have taken at least one course in linguistics, and most had taken an intensive introductory syntax course. On the other hand, our development is entirely self-contained and only presupposes a degree of mathematical sophistication and experience with sets, functions, and relations.

I should be clear at the outset that this book does not pretend to present state-of-the-art type-logical solutions to linguistic problems. Rather, my goal is to provide the reader with an introduction to type-logical grammar and to its use as an underpinning for the development of grammars with rich semantics. It is thus attempting to play the same role as a textbook on Newtonian physics. Just as it would be unthinkable to begin a physics education with the general theory of relativity, it is just as hard to imagine starting with more sophisticated type-logical grammar formalisms. But the reader should be aware that many of the problems faced by the grammar developed here have elegant solutions that are simply beyond the level of this text. I have tried to be thorough in pointing out such cases and providing references to solutions. I hope that after reading this book, the reader is inspired to delve deeper into the type-logical grammar literature. I should also point out that the ultimate type-logical grammar has not yet been developed; there are still interesting open problems in the field, and I hope this book also encourages some readers to work toward solutions.

My approach involves the stepwise development of successively more powerful logical and grammatical systems. As is standard practice in the application of logic to linguistics, there is little emphasis here on metatheoretical issues such as completeness, compactness, and so forth. Instead, students are encouraged to apply various object-level systems to particular empirical issues in natural-language semantics. On the other hand, there is more mathematical development in this book than is usually found in texts on natural language. All of our definitions, including side conditions, are completely rigorous, and many proofs are either sketched or presented in detail. Many of the exercises lead the student through further mathematical development. In spite of my linguistic orientation, I hope that this book will also be of interest to logicians and computer scientists seeking connections between logical systems and natural language.

I think of natural-language semantics as being naturally divisible into two components. The first of these, *lexical semantics*, is charged with the responsibility of adequately characterizing the meanings of lexical expressions. The second component is *compositional semantics*, the purpose of which is to explicate the meanings of arbitrarily complex linguistic expressions in terms of the meanings of their subexpressions and the way in which they are combined. Of course, compositional and lexical semantics are closely intertwined, and I do my best to explain how certain decisions about lexical and compositional semantics stem from the tight relationship between the two domains.

I begin with just enough λ-calculus and higher-order logic to allow the development of a simple categorial grammar. This grammatical formalism is then applied to simple sentences of English, with the focus on argument and adjunct structure. Next I develop a more robust categorial grammar based on type theory and its associated logic. I apply this system to some of the classical issues in logical semantics: coordination, quantifier scope, and anaphora. In addition to these topics, categorial grammars allow a natural treatment of unbounded dependency constructions. I hope that this text will be of use not only to those interested in an introduction to semantics but also to those interested in logical varieties of categorial grammar.

The remainder of the book is devoted to seeking progressively more extensive and refined analyses of lexical meanings. I begin with the noun phrase, studying the role of plurals and related notions of plural anaphora and reciprocity. I then digress to introduce modal logics, in their standard first-order form under the standard possible-worlds interpretation. Modal logics provide a more fine-grained model of the semantic content of propositions, based on the notion of truth in a possible world. I illustrate simple modal logics with an application to the semantics of counterfactual conditionals (those in which the antecedent is false). After that, I discuss tense logic as an instance of modal logic and discuss its applicability to tenses in natural language.

I then turn to possible-worlds semantics and see how it can be embedded naturally in higher-order logic through the inclusion of possible worlds and times as basic types of entities. I apply this system to propositional-attitude verbs, control verbs, the auxiliary system, and temporal modification. The final result is an extensive grammar fragment of English. This fragment, I hope, will serve as a springboard for further development of natural-language syntax and semantics.

I include an appendix with the basic mathematical definitions that are employed throughout this book. This appendix begins with basic set theory, functions, and relations. It then moves on to discuss orderings and induction. I go on to lay out the rudiments of formal languages and trees. The appendix concludes with a discussion of first-order logics and algebras.

I should perhaps provide a bit more explanation for my rather nonstandard choice of a type-logical categorial grammar as our grammatical basis. The primary reason for the choice is that I believe that syntax and semantics are closely related aspects of the same issue, namely the relation between expressions and their meanings. In this, categorial grammar is far more articulated than any other grammar formalism, primarily owing to its tight coupling of syntactic categories and their interpretations through logical types. Historically, categorial grammar was the first formalism in which a serious attempt was made to link syntax with semantics. Even though categorial grammar has progressed a long way since then, the underlying motivation to link syntax and semantics has remained. Recent attention has focused on enhancing the syntactic coverage of categorial grammar, and I believe it now rivals that of any other grammar formalism in existence. Another reason for choosing categorial grammar is its extreme perspicuity; it is straightforward to develop a self-contained presentation in the context of developing a semantic theory. While there may be those who are put off by the choice of categorial grammar, I believe the underlying motivations of categorial grammar are present in the lexical core of all well-known grammar formalisms. In particular, there are deep connections between categorial syntax and the θ-criterion and projection principles in Government-Binding syntax, and close connections between grammatical roles and their completeness and coherence in Lexical Functional Grammar. Generalized Phrase-Structure Grammar was built on a higher-order categorial semantics, whereas its successor, Head-Driven Phrase-Structure Grammar, is explicitly categorial in its subcategorization principles.

I should also provide an outline of what I do not cover in this book. In part, these decisions were made because there are many excellent sources for learning about this material that go well beyond what would be possible in the space of one book. Most important, I do not discuss the relation between semantics and pragmatics. Before beginning with the material in this book, the class usually reads two seminal works in natural-language pragmatics: Grice on implicature and Searle on speech acts. These topics, as well as their extensions, are also discussed in Steve Levinson's excellent book *Pragmatics*. I also do not discuss many of the deep issues in the philosophy of language. I know of no better introduction to this topic than the original papers collected A. P. Martinich's *Philosophy of Language* (1996). Specifically, this collection contains excellent articles on metaphor, reference and presupposition, and the ontological and epistemological foundations of natural language. As far as possible, I avoid the complications engendered by multisentence discourses and indefinite constructions. One popular approach to these issues, Discourse Representation Theory, is well documented in Hans Kamp and Uwe Reyle's textbook *From Discourse to Logic* (1993). Although I briefly discuss the role of events in interpreting natural language, a more thorough introduction to event-based semantics can be found in Terry Parsons's *Events in the Semantics of English* (1990). Another interesting branch of inquiry is that involved in the connections between natural language and cognition, a subject well beyond this study.

A student mastering the material presented here and in the textbooks previously mentioned should have no trouble in understanding most discussions of semantics in the major journals and conference proceedings. In the course of a semester, I try to cover at least one topic in greater depth, drawing material from the following sources. In any case, it is impossible to get a real feeling for a field from a textbook. Primary sources are absolutely essential, and every serious student of linguistics should become familiar with the topics and approaches discussed in the following sources. The major semantics journals are *Linguistics and Philosophy* (*L & P*), *The Journal of Semantics*, *Natural Language Semantics* (*NLS*), and *The Journal of Logic, Language, and Information* (*JoLLI*). But discussion of semantics can also be found in the major syntax journals, including *Linguistic Inquiry* (*LI*), *Natural Language and Linguistic Theory* (*NLLT*), *Language*, and the *Journal of Linguistics*. Often, discussions of natural-language semantics can be found in philosophy journals with an emphasis on logic, such as the *Journal of Philosophical Logic* (*JPL*), *Synthese*, and *Noûs*. Finally, there are often articles related to natural-language semantics from a computational point of view in journals such as *Computational Linguistics* (*CL*), *Machine Translation*, and *Artificial Intelligence* (*AI*). Besides journals, many articles can only be found in conference proceedings, which usually contain a much greater diversity of theoretical and empirical topics. The two main semantics conferences are the Amsterdam Colloquium and the conference on Semantics and Linguistic Theory (SALT). Many regional linguistics conferences also contain papers on semantics, especially the West Coast Conference on Formal Linguistics (WCCFL), and the meetings of the Chicago Linguistics Society (CLS), the Berkeley Linguistics Society (BLS), and to a lesser extent, the Northeastern Linguistics Society (NELS), and the Eastern States Conference on Linguistics (ESCOL). Finally, work on natural language semantics can be found in the proceedings of computationally oriented conferences, including the meetings of the Association for Computational Linguistics (ACL), the European Association for Computational Linguistics (EACL), Computational Linguistics (COLING), Knowledge Representation (KR), Theoretical Aspects of Reasoning about Knowledge (TARK), the American Association of Artificial Intelligence (AAAI), and the International Joint Conference on Artificial Intelligence (IJCAI). This is, of course, not an exhaustive list—many other journals and conferences also contain papers of interest to semanticists.

Acknowledgments

Starting at the beginning, I would like to thank my first instructors in logic, linguistics, and linguistic semantics: Donna Carr, Herb Hendry, and Barbara Abbott of Michigan State University. Herb's notes for a nonstandard-logic class form the basis of the discussion of tense and modal logics in chapter 10, and Donna's set-theory notes are still my standard reference in that field. In graduate school at the University of Edinburgh's Centre for Cognitive Science, my instructors and colleagues continued the excellent tradition. On the instructor side, I would like to thank Barry Richards, Mark Steedman, and David McCarty for their excellent courses and mentorship. I also benefitted tremendously from the active semantics and categorial-grammar student community, members of which included Marc Moens, Jon Oberlander, Alex Lascarides, and Glyn Morrill. During a year I spent at the Center for the Study of Language and Information at Stanford in 1988, I also learned a great deal from interacting with Bonnie Webber, Craige Roberts, Sally McConnell-Ginet, Bill Rounds, Stanley Peters, Jean Mark Gawron, and John Nerbonne. At Carnegie Mellon University, I continued learning about semantics and the philosophy of language from Teddy Seidenfeld, a philosophy professor with whom I cotaught an upper-level undergraduate philosophy-of-language course on two occasions. At the 1990 European Summer School in Leuven, I had the opportunity to take a class on generalized quantifiers from Dag Westerståhl and Frans Zwarts, the notes from which serve as the basis for section 3.3. My learning about categorial grammar improved dramatically during summer-school sessions taught by Glyn Morrill, Dick Oehrle, and Michael Moortgat, and during a four-month leave of absence at the Institute for Speech and Language at the University of Utrecht, during which time I benefitted from coteaching a class with Ivan Sag on categorial grammar and Head-Driven Phrase-Structure

Grammar, and from extensive tutoring by Michael Moortgat, Natasha Kurtonina, Koen Versmissen, Herman Hendriks, and Erik Aarts.

I would like to thank Craige Roberts and Peter Lasersohn for sharing their extensive bibliographies on plurals with me. Along similar lines, I would like to thank Ivan Sag for sharing his list of androgynous names with me.

I would also like to thank our computational-linguistics graduate students at Carnegie Mellon University. The first three batches of students, in 1990, 1991, and 1992, suffered through a sketch of these notes in very terse, handwritten form, without the benefit of a natural-deduction presentation. I would also like to thank the 1993 class, during the teaching of which I compiled these notes for the first time. I would further like to thank the 1994 class, who gave me a large amount of feedback on a partial draft. I finished a draft during the 1995 class, and the 1996 class used the notes in more or less their present form. Students and teaching assistants who provided feedback include Michael Mastroianni, Deryle Lonsdale, Haruyuki Fujii, Chris Hogan, Páraic Sheridan, Kaori Shima, Chengxiang Zhai, Hanming Ong, Marsal Gavalda, Octav Popescu, Jeff Hill, Kevin Keck, Rosie Jones, Greg Aist, and Klaus Zechner.

A number of other people have provided feedback either on these notes or on various papers and presentations I have given that are related to these topics: Chris Barker, Filippo Beghelli, Gosse Bouma, Ariel Cohen, Robin Cooper, Jaap van der Does, David Dowty, Dan Flickinger, Jean Mark Gawron, Irene Heim, Erhard Hinrichs, Mark Johnson, Esther Kraak, Manfred Krifka, Peter Lasersohn, Kiyong Lee, Hans Leidekker, Jan Tore Lønning, Hendrik Lübben, Chris Manning, Louise McNally, Alice ter Meulen, Sjaak de Mey, Philip Miller, Michael Moortgat, John Nerbonne, Fernando Pereira, Massimo Poesio, Carl Pollard, Joachim Quantz, Christian Retore, Craige Roberts, Ivan Sag, Hidetosi Sirai, Ed Stabler, Mark Steedman, Henriëtte de Swart, Shravan Vasishth, Henk Verkuyl, and Robert Westmoreland. Several people have given me feedback on complete drafts, and they deserve extensive thanks for their detailed comments: Glyn Morrill, Dick Oehrle, and Dale Gerdemann.

As is always the case with such an undertaking, the field as a whole shifted foundationally and empirically during the preparation of these notes, causing considerable reworking. Although the foundational discussions in this book remain current at the time of writing, considerable progress has been made in the syntactic dimension. For pedagogical purposes, the presentation of some material is not quite up to the state of the art at the time of writing, and other matters such as structural control for islands and locality have simply been omitted. An excellent source for developments in the type-logical framework beyond those presented here is the survey article by Moortgat (in press). One pleasant aspect about categorial grammarians is that they never lose sight of the fact that syntax exists to provide a vehicle for structuring communication. With increased participation, the categorial enterprise will, I hope, flourish on both the syntactic and semantic frontier.

One last note. The natural-deduction derivations in this book were generated directly in Latex using a portable public-domain Prolog program (see Carpenter 1994b). A technical report, along with the code and grammar, are available free of charge via the world wide web and anonymous ftp; please contact the author via e-mail at carp@research.bell-labs.com for details.

Chapter 1

Introduction

In this chapter I provide an outline of the role of semantics in linguistic theory. I begin with a discussion of the central role of truth and reference. In this book I develop a truth-conditional model of semantics, the purpose of which is to explain the conditions under which a sentence can be uttered truthfully. I carry this out by appealing to a theory of reference, which tells us how linguistic expressions can be linked to objects in the world. In the next two sections I discuss some of the primary empirical issues in semantics and pragmatics. In the final section I discuss my methodology, which involves building logical models of the meanings of expressions in terms of the meanings of their parts.

1.1 TRUTH AND REFERENCE

In this section we study the philosophical and psychological issues that motivate my decision to center our study of semantics around the notions of truth and reference. In the first subsection we consider the fundamental role of truth in developing a theory of meaning in natural language. I also lay out the general structure of a theory of truth. In the next subsection I discuss the referential nature of language, or in other words, how language relates to the world. I also discuss how a theory of reference can be employed as the foundation of a theory of truth. In the last subsection I discuss some of the philosophical and psychological positions that have been taken with respect to truth and reference. I concentrate on the conventional nature of linguistic meaning, contrasting it with conceptualist and realist theories.

Before beginning this all too brief section, I would like to point out that truth and reference are two of the most widely studied areas not only in linguistic semantics but also in twentieth-century philosophy as a whole.

This being the case, I can only provide a taste of the nature of the debates that surround these contentious issues and pointers for those interested in learning more.

1.1.1 Truth

At least since the time of Plato, the concept of truth has been seen as fundamental in understanding the nature of human language. This preoccupation with truth is reflected in Plato's *Sophist, Phaedo*, and *Thaetetus*, and is further developed in Aristotle's *Metaphysics, Categories*, and *De Interpretatione*.

One of the principal goals of linguistic semantics, as initiated in its present form by its founding fathers, Frege and Russell, has been to develop a workable theory of the conditions under which a sentence can be uttered truthfully. To *utter* a sentence is to use it in a specific context. Given the crucial role of context in natural language, it should be clear that utterances, rather than sentences, can be either true or false. Of course, some sentences are *eternal* in that their truth conditions do not depend on context, but these are few and far between in ordinary discourse. In this book we will be focusing primarily on what is known as *truth-conditional semantics*. There are certainly a wide range of uses of sentences for purposes other than conveying a truth value, and we will consider some of these in sections 1.3.1 and 1.3.2. Nevertheless, the primary focus of semantics has been on formulating truth conditions for literal uses of declarative sentences.

While the notion of truth has been central since the advent of Western philosophy, it was not until the work of Tarski (1935, 1944) that a mathematically sound truth-conditional semantics was formulated. Before we consider Tarski's semantic approach in section 1.4.3, we consider his general approach to a theory of truth. Tarski introduced the following paradigm, instances of which have come to be known as T-*sentences* (Davidson 1967c).

(1) *s* is true if and only if *P*.

The variable *s* is to be filled with a sentence, whereas the variable *P* is to be instantiated with the conditions for the truth of *s*. Ideally, we would like a general theory that gives us truth conditions for every sentence in the language. Developing truth conditions for a large fragment of English is the primary goal of this book, and of a great deal of contemporary semantic investigation.

Tarski provided the following kind of instance of a *T*-sentence.

(2) *The cat is on the mat* is true if and only if the cat is on the mat.

Such a construal of truth conditions may at first appear to be circular, tautological, or nonsensical, although this is not the case. First note that on the left-hand side of the biconditional is a claim about the truth of a particular sentence, namely $s = $ *The cat is on the mat*. In technical terms, we have what is known as a *mention* or *name* of the sentence. In the text I will italicize words that are mentioned (in the literature, quotes are often used). On the right-hand side of the biconditional in (2), however, we interpret the sentence as we would any other sentence of English. In other words, we have what is known as a *use* of the sentence. To clarify the use/mention distinction, consider the following pair of examples.

(3) a.   *Chris* is a word with five letters.
     b. #Chris is a word with five letters.

The first case, (3a), mentions the word *Chris*; it is true because the word *Chris* does in fact have five letters. The second example, (3b), involves a use of the word *Chris*; it is semantically infelicitous (a condition we mark with the symbol " # ") because Chris is an individual, not a word. Note that it is uses of sentences that refer to truth values, and uses of names that (sometimes) refer to individuals.

With this distinction in hand, notice that the left-hand side of the *T*-sentence contains a statement that a particular sentence is true, whereas the right-hand side is just a statement of English. The primary reason that *T*-sentences such as (2) seem circular is that we are using English as a metalanguage in which to develop a theory of English itself. A *metalanguage* is a language for theorizing about another language, known as the *object language*. Of course, this relationship is relative. A language $\mathscr{L}_1$ may have a metalanguage $\mathscr{L}_2$, which in turn has a metalanguage $\mathscr{L}_3$, leaving $\mathscr{L}_2$ in the position of being a metalanguage relative to $\mathscr{L}_1$ and an object language relative to $\mathscr{L}_3$. It is usual for a metalanguage to include terms that pick out elements of the object language. What is confusing about (2) is that English is acting as both the metalanguage and the object language. An alternative instance of the *T*-sentence in (2) might involve a shift in object language, say to Italian.

(4) *Il gatto é sul tappeto* is true if and only if the cat is on the mat.

In this case there is no apparent circularity because the two languages are distinct (despite some common historical antecedents); Italian is the object language, and English is the metalanguage. Certain paradoxes arise if one is not careful when using the same language for both object language and metalanguage, and we consider some of these in section 11.1.5.

Of course, for a metalanguage to be of use in explicating an object language, the metalanguage must itself be well understood. The reason that natural language is often used as a metalanguage is that it is usually assumed that readers of English understand the language. Thus it is typical to find English used as the metalanguage in discussions of the English language. English is often used in fields other than linguistics, such as history and biology. But natural languages, though quite expressive, have a number of drawbacks when employed as metalanguages. Specifically, natural-language expressions are often vague, ambiguous, prone to misconstrual, and so on. Often this problem can be rectified by employing additional words and phrases, whose meaning is carefully spelled out (usually in English). For instance, this is the strategy employed in mathematics, chemistry, philosophy, the law, and almost every other field of inquiry.

For my purposes, I will find it convenient to employ the mathematical constructions of set theory to supplement English as a metalanguage. A firm mathematical foundation was once considered at the heart of what was known as *generative grammar*. Chomsky (1957, 5) had the following to say.

Precisely constructed models for linguistic structure can play an important role, both negative and positive, in the process of discovery itself. By pushing a precise but inadequate formulation to an unacceptable conclusion, we can often expose the exact source of this inadequacy, and consequently, gain a deeper understanding of the linguistic data.... I think that some of those linguists who have questioned the value of precise and technical development of linguistic theory have failed to recognize the productive potential in the method of rigorously stating a proposed theory and applying it to strictly linguistic material with no attempt to avoid unacceptable conclusions by *ad hoc* adjustments or loose formulation.

Such sentiments engendered a major paradigm shift away from imprecise theories formulated loosely in English, to more exacting mathematical theories. Ironically, Chomsky (1990b), in a reply to Pullum (1989), has recently reversed his position. Chomsky now argues against formal methodology, claiming that it is premature to formulate explicit and mathematically precise theories about domains of which we have such a limited understanding. He claims that to make a theory fully explicit would require arbitrary decisions at fine-grained levels of detail. In the end, this debate comes down to one about whether or not to use mathematics in the metalanguage. I strongly disagree with Chomsky's present belief, apparently shared by the majority of his followers, that the state of linguistic theorizing is not precise enough so that "inquiry can proceed in a constructive way" (Chomsky 1990, 146). In this book, we will be following Chomsky's original injunction and endeavor to construct precise, mathematical theories of the structure of language.

1.1.2   Reference

A longstanding approach to formulating the meaning of a sentence is by specifying the conditions in the world under which the sentence could be truthfully uttered. In other words, a sentence is true if it corresponds to the way the world is, and it is false otherwise. Such theories have come to be known as *referential* or *correspondence theories of truth*. One of the foundations of referential theories is their assumption that the truth of an utterance depends on facts about the world, independently of the cognitive agents uttering and hearing the sentence. The goal is to provide an objective measure of the truth or falsehood of utterances based on the objects in the real world to which they refer. Such a view of language is obviously attractive when language is used in domains such as science or even politics. I consider some of the philosophical ramifications of referential theories and their rivals in the next section.

Referential theories are as venerable as theories of truth and have been part of the philosophical discourse at least since Plato's Socratic dialogues, in which he states a referential theory of truth more or less identical to the one I have just given. Aristotle reinforced this choice in his *Metaphysics*, clearing away many of the ancillary assumptions and digressions of Plato (Prior 1967b).

For an example of how a referential theory of truth may be formulated, we return to the example I introduced in (2).

(5) The cat is on the mat.

To determine whether or not an utterance of this sentence is true, we need to know the objects to which its salient constituent expressions refer. For instance, we need to know the referents of the definite noun phrases *the cat* and *the mat*. Furthermore, we need to know under what conditions one object can be said to be on another object. With these three referents from (5), two individuals and a relation, we are in a position to determine the truth of the sentence as a whole by investigating whether the referent of the subject, *the cat*, stands in the relation specified by *on* to the referent of the prepositional object, *the mat*. To determine the referents of the various expressions, we need to know how the meanings of the various expressions connect to the world, such as *cat*, *mat*, and *on*, as well as the auxiliary *is* and the definite article *the*. With such a theory, it does not really matter whether the utterer of (5) knows whether the cat is on the mat, or even whether he believes that the cat is on the mat; the truth or falsehood of the sentence only depends on the referents. Certain subtleties arise concerning the determination of the referents, which may depend on the context of utterance, a point to which we return in section 1.2.4.

A general framework for the construction of referential theories of truth was provided by Tarski (1935). In fact, this work was fundamental in establishing the very consistency of the referential enterprise. Tarski accomplished this by developing a theory of truth for first-order logic. The objects of reference in this theory were individuals and relations. The key insight provided by Tarski was a recursive procedure for combining the meanings of constituents to determine the truth of arbitrarily complex sentences. I provide an overview of Tarski's general method in section 1.4.2. The rest of this book will be devoted to developing a Tarskian theory of truth for natural language.

While it may at first appear obvious that some notion of reference to objects in the world is a necessary step in determining the truth of a sentence, this theory has not gone unopposed. A principal contender is the *coherence theory of truth*. The coherence theory determines the truth of a statement not by its correspondence with the world but rather by how it coheres within a larger collection of statements. Historically, coherence theories of truth have been closely allied to rationalist metaphysical positions, as put forward by Leibniz, Spinoza, and later Hegel (White 1967).

The other prominent position opposed to a direct, referential theory of language is *conceptualism*. Under a conceptualist theory, language derives its meaning through its relation to our mental states. Some conceptualist theories, most notably *solipsism*, go so far as to deny the very existence of a reality beyond our minds. Other, more moderate conceptualists instead assume that language refers to mental entities or *representations*, with or without elaborating on the relation between our mental representations and the world. Representationalism has been a popular theory among some linguists and philosophers, most notably Katz and Fodor (1963; Katz 1966, 1972; Fodor 1975), Jackendoff (1972), and the *generative semanticists*, as represented by Lakoff (1970a). Recent versions of conceptualism have been argued for by the proponents of *cognitive semantics* (Fauconnier 1985, Lakoff 1987, Langacker 1987). Fodor (1975) and Chomsky (1986b, 1990a) even go so far as to assume that such representations of concepts are genetically innate.

1.1.3   Conventionalism and Realism

Although I have adopted a referential theory of meaning, the specific nature of individuals, concepts, and relations among them remains in need of explanation. Furthermore, how individuals, concepts, and relations enter into a language must also be explained. In this section we consider some popular theories of reference, as well as some philosophical arguments against the possibility of developing a truly referential theory.

The approach I favor to the thorny issue of how reference is established is known under the general heading of *conventionalism*. According to such a theory, expressions derive their referential force by means of conventions established by linguistic communities. In other words, it is up to speakers of the language, either individually or collectively, to legislate the referents of expressions in their language. Conventionalism provides a natural explanation of how different communities are able to specialize their conceptual and individual categories. Under a conventionalist theory, any number of factors may influence the development of a language's basic vocabulary and structure. Specific motivations for choice may include cultural ideals, scientific knowledge, and psychological considerations. Such linguistic communities need not be separated by a great cultural divide; physicists and lawyers, for instance, have their own distinct, specialized vocabularies and usages. In a conventionalist theory, the way in which a language subdivides the world into objects and relations has come to be known as a *conceptual scheme*.

To fully specify a conventionalist theory of language, it would be necessary to understand how conventions arise and, just as important, how they can be shared among different speakers. The most important aspect of conventionalist theories is that individuals, concepts, and relations come about because we in some sense create them as cognitive agents. Recently, the linguistic-semantics community has paid a great deal of attention to the role of our psychological and physical constitutions in the determination of our conceptual schemes (Fauconnier 1985; Herskovits 1986; Jackendoff 1983; Lakoff 1987; Langacker 1987; Rosch, Gray, Johnson, and Boys-Braem 1976). To what degree our psychological makeups determine our conceptual schemes is a matter of some debate; as we noted above, Fodor and Chomsky believe that such conceptual schemes are *innate*. Proponents of the *innateness hypothesis* argue that there is no other way in which such concepts could be acquired. The innateness hypothesis is also one of the most prevalent assumptions made by the theoretical-syntax community, ever since Chomsky (1965) identified the notion of an explanatory linguistic theory with one that could adequately characterize language acquisition and speculated that language must be innate.

An alternative to conventionalism is *realism*, a theory in which individuals, concepts, and relations among them are assumed to be independent of cognitive agents. A historically significant form of realism, known as *platonism*, has its roots in the writings of Plato. Platonism is the theory that there is an extant realm of ideas, sometimes known as (platonic) *ideals* or *universals*, to which our words refer. Platonists argue that these ideas exist independently of our minds but may be discovered by cognitive agents. Only indirectly, through the connection of ideas to the world, is our language able to refer to the world. Frege's (1892) notion of senses, to which we return in section 1.2.5, is the most prominent platonic theory in linguistic semantics. More recently, Katz (1981) has advocated a platonist view of concepts.

Although thuroughgoing platonists are scarce these days, there are many who argue that at least some individuals, concepts, and relations exist in the world. This brand of realism shares with platonism the view that we discover, rather than create, concepts. For instance, many realists assume that there is a circumscribed class of real concepts, known as *natural kinds*, that form the foundation of the conceptual system of our language. Putnam (1970, 1973, 1975) has been one of the most prominent supporters of a notion of natural kinds in interpreting human language. Kripke (1972) put forward a theory of referential uses of names that directly connects them to real individuals, rather than by assuming that a name is just an abbreviation for a cluster of concepts with which to pick out an individual. We return to theories of individual reference in sections 7.8 and 7.10. Natural kinds, like platonic ideals, provide a potential explanation of how different individuals can come to share similar, or even identical, concepts, both within and across cultural and historical boundaries. An extreme brand of realism has been championed by Lewis (1973, 1986), who argues that so-called *possible worlds*, that is, other ways in which the world might have been, are just as real as any other objects (we return to the topic of possible worlds in section 1.2.5). But if a realist theory admits too many natural kinds, for instance, by positing one for every social and individual conceptual class, it becomes difficult to distinguish the theory from a conceptualist one. Some realists have actually attempted to bring realism in line with conventionalism, by stating that one way in which concepts can be real is if they are conceptualized by cognitive agents (Barwise and Perry 1981, 1983).

There is a great deal of controversy surrounding the nature of conceptual schemes and their connection to reality. The *empiricist* approach assumed that language was connected to the world through primitive observations (Russell 1940, Ayer 1946, Carnap 1947, Hempel 1950). Such a connection was taken to provide a foundation for scientific inquiry. One of the foundations of empiricism was a division between so-called *analytic* and *synthetic* truths. Analytic truths are ones that follow from logic, whereas synthetic truths require empirical verification. Mainstream philosophers of science abandoned the strict empiricism of the logical positivists, primarily due to the persuasive arguments of Nagel (1944) and Quine (1953b). Quine, for instance, argues that the notion of analyticity and attempts to explain it are inherently circular. Instead, he abandons the empiricist distinction between analytic and synthetic truths in favor of a more holistic approach, the result of which is a "blurring of the supposed boundary between speculative metaphysics and natural science" (1953b, 20). Specifically, Quine denies the objective realism of concepts, stating, "in point of epistemological footing the physical objects and the gods differ only in degree and not in kind" (1953b, 44).

But Quine did not abandon empiricism entirely. He still believed that conceptual schemes could be judged for their efficacy in formulating predictive theories about the world. Such a view is often identified with the belief that the world comes not only through physical reality; also required is a true or proper way to conceptualize it, that is, to divide it up into individuals, relations, and the like. Recently this view has been challenged by philosophers such as Rorty (1979, 1989), Davidson (1989), and Putnam (1988), who deny not only that there is a fact of the matter concerning conceptual schemes but also that humans will ever be able to evaluate conceptual schemes themselves. This latter shortcoming arises because we are forever trapped in our current conceptual scheme. While they believe we can change our conceptual schemes, as a result, for instance, of a scientific paradigm shift (Kuhn 1962), there is no way to achieve a god's-eye perspective from which to evaluate our conceptualizations, as Putnam maintains. Though these philosophers do not deny the existence of a mind-independent reality, they believe there is no way that we, as human cognitive agents, will ever be able to disentangle the dichotomy of conceptual scheme and content.

1.2   TOPICS IN SEMANTICS

In this section I provide a brief survey of some of the topics that linguistic semantic theories address.

1.2.1   Synonymy, Entailment, and Contradiction

Traditionally, natural-language semantics has been devoted to explaining several relationships that hold among utterances of sentences and smaller phrases. In this section I discuss some of these relations and their role in semantics.

One of the primary semantic relations is that of *synonymy*. We say that two phrases are *synonymous* if they have the same meaning. For instance, the following two sentences are usually taken to have the same meaning.

(6) a. Dana saw Kim.
     b. Kim was seen by Dana.

The second sentence, (6b), is merely the passive form of the first sentence, (6a). Any time that one sentence in (6) can be used truthfully, so can the other. Even though these sentences are synonymous from a semantic perspective, they do have functional differences in larger contexts. For instance, consider following each of the examples in (6) with the following sentence.

(7) He heard her, too.

It seems that this continuation is only felicitous when following the active sentence, (6a). In particular, the resolution of pronouns, such as *he* and *her*, may depend on the active/passive distinction. But such putative constraints are rather subtle. Dick Oehrle (p.c.) suggests the following dialogue.

(8) *Speaker A*: Dana saw Taylor. But he didn't see Kim.
     Speaker B:· Kim was seen by Dana. He heard her, too.

With the explicit contrast of the second speaker's contribution with the first speaker's, reversing the order of the pronouns is much more acceptable. It has become quite popular to integrate such dynamic aspects of a sentence's contribution to discourse into the meaning of a sentence (see Chierchia 1995 for an up-to-date overview). If such a dynamic approach to meaning is adopted, then the examples in (6) would not be considered synonymous.

Some cases of semantic interactions with discourse are even more subtle. For instance, consider the clefted form of the active and passive sentences in (6).

(9) It was Kim who Dana saw.

It is not so clear that the clefted sentence (9) can be applied in the same situations as the active and passive versions in (6). The clefted form seems to have a uniqueness effect in that Kim was the only person that Dana saw.

We might assume that nouns can be synonymous. Consider the classic example of *bachelor* and *unmarried man*. It seems that one can be applied to an individual just in case the other can. We can often consider the problem of synonymy of expressions smaller than sentences in terms of their substitutability in larger contexts. For instance, consider the following pair of sentences.

(10) a. Pat is not a bachelor.
      b. Pat is not an unmarried man.

It seems that the sentences in (10) are just as synonymous as their component nouns. The terms *bachelor* and *unmarried man* are the canonical examplars of terms that are said to be *analytically equivalent*. An example due to Plato is that of *featherless biped* and *human*. In Plato's experience, all featherless bipeds were human and vice-versa. If this held in the wider world, it would be an example of a so-called *synthetic equivalence*; whether the two terms refer to the same set of objects is a matter for empirical investigation to determine. But consider terms like *vampire* and *unicorn*, which apply to exactly the same set of individuals, namely none, on the assumption, of course, that there are no vampires or unicorns. In this case, we are not so hasty to conclude that *unicorn* and *vampire* are synonymous; they appear to have very different meanings. This case illustrates the difficulty of formulating definitions for terms like *synonymous*. I consider the distinction between *unicorn* and *vampire* and other, similar distinctions in section 1.2.5.

In a truth-conditional approach to semantics, we might say that two sentences are *synonymous* if they can be truthfully uttered in exactly the same situations. This reduces the problem to the nature of truth and the nature of situated utterances, topics we return to below.

Another important relationship between sentences is that of *entailment*. Informally, one sentence entails another if the truth of the first sentence guarantees the truth of the second. For instance, consider the following pairs of sentences.

(11) a. Terry is an unmarried man.
     b. Terry is a man.

(12) a. Terry is tall and handsome.
     b. Terry is tall.

(13) a. Terry ate a cake.
     b. Terry ate.

In all of these cases, (11) through (13), the first sentence entails the second. In each case, the second sentence provides strictly less information than the first. In general, two synonymous sentences will entail one another. But as with synonymy, the notion of entailment is extremely subtle, and there are borderline cases that are difficult to untangle.

Two sentences are said to be *contradictory* if they could not both be truthfully uttered in the same context. Consider the following canonical examples.

(14) a. Lee is asleep.
     b. Lee is awake.

(15) a. Lee is asleep.
     b. Lee is not asleep.

In both (14) and (15), it is not possible for both sentences to be uttered truthfully. Of course, their contradictory nature depends on their being uttered at the same time (we return to the notion of time dependence in section 1.2.4).

A sentence may also be self-contradictory, in which case we say that it is *inconsistent* or simply a *contradiction*. Consider the following examples.

(16) a. Terry is 30 years old, and Terry is not 30 years old.
     b. Pythagoras constructed a round square.
     c. My computer danced a jig.

The first example, (16a), is logically inconsistent. The second example, (16b), is inconsistent because an object cannot be both round and a square. The last example, (16c), is an instance of what is often referred to as an *anomaly*; computers simply are not the kinds of objects that dance jigs.

There is a dual notion to contradictory sentences: sentences that are true whenever they are uttered are said to be *tautologous* or *eternal truths*. Consider the following examples.

(17) a. Dana ran or didn't run.
     b. Every bachelor is unmarried.

Assuming that the time at which both clauses are interpreted remains constant, the first case, (17a), derives its truth from logic alone. The second example, (17b), is true because bachelorhood entails not being married.

1.2.2 Presupposition

Another key way in which sentences convey information is by what is known as *presupposition*. Presupposition is related to entailment, but is not expressed as a relation between sentences. Rather, a sentence is said to presuppose a piece of information when the sentence may be felicitously uttered only if the information is valid. For instance, consider the following common examples.

(18) a. My opponent supports the plan that will hurt the people.
     b. Terry has (not) stopped attending lodge meetings.
     c. The present king of France is (not) bald.

For the first sentence, (18a), to be used felicitously, there must be a plan that will hurt the people. For the sentence to be true, the opponent of the speaker must support that plan. Here the fact that the plan hurts the people is presupposed. Note that if we negate the sentence, the presupposition that there is a plan that hurts the people does not go away (unlike ordinary entailments). The second sentence, (18b), has similar behavior in that it entails that Terry was attending lodge meetings. Notice that the presupposition is not canceled when the sentence is negated. For Russell's (1905) famous example, (18c), there are conflicting opinions as to whether this sentence presupposes the existence of a present king of France, an issue to which we return in section 7.8. Presuppositions are even more insidious when embedded in questions:

(19) Has Sandy stopped drinking?

There is no way to answer this apparently simple yes/no question with a simple *yes* or *no* without committing to the proposition that Sandy drank in the past. Either answer admits the fact that Sandy was once drinking. If Sandy never was drinking, the respondent must attempt to address the falsehood of the presupposition. Often presuppositions are quite subtle to address; it is common to find presuppositions in political debates, advertisements, and other manipulative language.

1.2.3 Ambiguity and Vagueness

Another important semantic aspect of sentences is their potential *ambiguity*. Ambiguity arises from many different sources, as the following examples illustrate.

(20) a. I went to the bank.
     b. Put the block in the box on the table.
     c. At least one referee read every paper.

The first example, (20a), involves *lexical ambiguity*. The word *bank* can mean either a river bank or a savings bank (among other things, like a bank shot in pool). The second example, (20b), involves what is known as *structural ambiguity*. It can either be read as a request to take a particular block and put it in the box on the table, or a request to take the block in the box and put it on the table. The last example, (20c), involves what is known as *scope ambiguity*; it can mean that there is one referee who happened to read every paper, or that for every paper, there was at least one referee who read it.

Ambiguity can be distinguished from the closely related concept of *vagueness*. Ambiguity reflects the possibility of interpreting an expression in more than one way. For instance, the term *nut* is ambiguous among a fastener for a bolt, a kind of food that grows on trees, and more colloquially, an insane person. An utterance of *nut* means one of these things but not all of them or even the disjunction of them. Vagueness, on the other hand, arises when one expression is intrinsically underspecified but cannot be used with only one meaning among several. The term *brother-in-law* is an example of a vague term. Although it can be applied to the brother of a spouse or to the male spouse of a sibling, it cannot be uttered to include one possibility and not the other. One way to see this distinction is with the standard linguistic test of sensitivity to negation, as in the following two examples.

(21) a. Leslie is not a nut.
     b. Leslie is not Pat's brother-in-law.

If an expression is ambiguous, a use of it picks out one of its ambiguous senses, which is then negated. Negating a vague term, on the other hand, negates all of the possible meanings. In the first example, (21a), there is an ambiguity involved. An utterance of it could be false in the situation in which Leslie is insane but is not a hard-shelled fruit. But contrast this with (21b); the term *brother-in-law* is *vague* in the sense that it is equivalent in meaning to the disjunction of being a brother of a spouse or the husband of a sister. If Leslie is the husband of Pat's sister or a brother of Pat's wife, then (21b) is going to be false.

Another standard test for distinguishing vagueness from ambiguity arises in cases of verb-phrase ellipsis, wherein an elided verb phrase must be interpreted in the same way as its antecedent.

(22) a.   Robin has a brother-in-law, and Sandy does too.
     b.   #The broker went to the bank, and the riverboat did too.

The first example, (22a), allows Robin to have one kind of brother-in-law and Sandy the other. On the other hand, the second case, (22b), cannot be interpreted as having the broker visit a savings bank and the riverboat a river bank (but it could, of course, be true if the broker and riverboat both went to the bank of a river or both went to a savings bank). Similarly, coordination requires only one sense of an expression to be used.

(23) a.   #Terry is in Chicago and a good mood.
     b.   #Terry has and will score a goal.

These are examples of a phenomenon known as *zeugma*, in which two different senses of the same word are juxtaposed. Such usages are considered extragrammatical.

Unfortunately, the term *vague* is itself ambiguous. Besides meaning something like disjunctively underspecified, a term is also said to be *vague* if membership in the class denoted by the term is not precisely specified. Adjectives like *red* and *tall* are common instances of expressions that fit the second definition of vagueness. It is not at all clear at which point along the spectrum from canonical red to canonical orange an object stops being red and begins to be orange. Similarly, there is no precise height above which someone is considered to be tall. A further complication arises because so-called *comparative* terms like *tall* involve comparison to some extrinsically specified class. Consider being tall for a basketball player versus being tall for a jockey. Even with an explicit comparison class, say linguistics professors, the boundary between tall and nontall remains underdetermined. Of course, many nouns, verbs, and probably all prepositions are vague. In fact, it is rather rare to encounter terms that are not vague outside of certain scientific or mathematical sublanguages. Such considerations sparked Wittgenstein's (1953) theory of *family resemblances*, in which he assumed there were canonical exemplars or *prototypes* of terms, and other objects were gauged for inclusion in a class on the basis of their similarity to the prototype. Such theories have also found their way into psychological work on categorization (Rosch et al. 1976). Others have claimed that the classes determined by (at least some) natural-language terms are determined by a core set of simpler concepts, together with some peripheral concepts (Smith and Medin 1981, Collins and Quillian 1969). For instance, canaries' being yellow is central to canaries; their having skin is a less centrally associated concept. A taxonomic organization of terms that reflects the central and peripheral properties is clearly reflected in most dictionary definitions of concepts, although this may be simply an artifact of dictionaries being forced to explain the meanings of words in terms of other words. Others have argued for the centrality of *natural kinds* in settling issues of vagueness. For instance, Putnam (1975) argues that being composed of H_2O is central to the concept of water, which is for him a canonical instance of a natural kind, even if those who used the term *water* in 1750 had no grasp of the chemical structure of water. But even terms like *water*, at least in common usage, are vague in the sense that it is not clear at what level of impurity or pollution a body of liquid turns from water into something else.

1.2.4   Indexicality and the Situation of an Utterance

Often the meaning of an expression in a natural language depends on the context in which it is uttered. Canonical examples include first- and second-person pronouns such as *I* and *you*, temporal adverbials such as *now* and *yesterday*, and the tenses of verbs such as *ran* and *will run*. The reference of these expressions depend on facts about the *utterance situation*, such as the speaker and hearer in the case of the pronouns and the time of utterance in the temporal cases. For instance, *I* always refers to the speaker, and *you* to the hearer. As is standard in linguistics, I use the term *speaker* and *hearer* generically to refer not only to spoken communication but also to the initiator and recipient of written language, signed language, semaphores, and so on. The temporal adverbial *now* always refers to the time of utterance, and *yesterday* to the day before the time of utterance. These terms are known as *indexicals*, due to the logical theories that were proposed to explain them (Bar-Hillel 1954). These theories provided a number of *indices*, which are parameters representing the context of utterance on which expressions depend to determine their interpretations. For instance, the speaker and hearer and the time and location of an utterance are often supplied as indices. A more general class of context-determined expressions are known as *demonstratives*, which include terms such as *this, that,* and *those.* The term *deixis* has traditionally been applied to cover the whole spectrum of contextually referential phenomena.

The indexical view of meaning is slightly more sophisticated than the simple referential theory. Rather than establishing their referents once and for all, the interpretation of an expression such as *I* will depend on an index, which must be supplied by the context of utterance. Of course, the issue immediately arises as to just how many indices are necessary for the interpretation of natural language and just where the line is to be drawn, if anywhere, between indexicality and other discourse phenomena such as the resolution of other anaphoric dependencies (see chapter 9). Lewis (1970) proposed a finite set of indices, but these included several specialized indices to deal with the discourse dependency of expressions such as *aforementioned.* Cresswell (1973) then extended the notion of index to allow an arbitrary number of properties determined by the context of utterance, construed very broadly. Kaplan (1977, 1978) is usually credited with formulating the general theory of indexicality, as later put to use by Montague (1973), in which the meaning of an expression is a mapping from a context of utterance to an interpretation. The basic notion of indexicality, though, is clearly defined by Bar-Hillel (1954). In its most general form, an indexical theory of *meaning* provides a general characterization of how *interpretations* may be derived from contexts.

Barwise and Perry (1981, 1983) generalized the functional notion of meaning to a relational one in which a context does not uniquely determine an interpretation. One motivation for Barwise and Perry's relational approach to context and reference is its ability to account for many of the ways in which information can be extracted from an utterance. For instance, if someone utters a noun phrase such as *my wife* and you know from the context who the intended referent is, you will be able to extract the information that the speaker is married, and in fact married to the person in question (on the assumption that the utterance was truthful). The notion of reference is quite subtle though, and we will return to it in section 7.8.

1.2.5   Sense and Reference

Any referential semantic theory that attempts to explain the use of verbs like *believe* is immediately faced with the following puzzling examples (Frege 1892).

(24) a. The morning star is the evening star.
    b. The evening star is the evening star.
    c. The ancients believed the morning star is the evening star.
    d. The ancients believed the evening star is the evening star.

Because the terms *the morning star* and *the evening star* both refer to the planet Venus, which can be seen on the horizon both in the evening and the morning, a naive referential theory would assign *the morning star* and *the evening star* the same meaning, namely Venus. If the referent of a sentence is taken to be a truth value, as is commonly assumed in truth-conditional semantics, then (24a) and (24b) have the same meaning, because both are true. The further assumption that belief sentences express relationships between their subjects and the meanings of their sentential objects brings the theory up against the obvious counterexamples in (24c) and (24d). Even though the ancients did not realize that the morning star and the evening star were both Venus, (24c) and (24d) will have the same interpretation according to the naive theory.

As a solution to this puzzle, Frege (1892) proposed that the meaning of an embedded sentence was not its referent (*Bedeutung* in German), but its *sense* (*Sinn* in German). In other words, the two sentences (24a) and (24b) have different senses, and hence different meanings. Unfortunately, Frege never formally articulated his notion of sense. But he did clarify one aspect of the theory, namely the relation of senses to referents, by saying "the sense of a proper name is grasped by everyone who knows the language or the totality of designations of which the proper name is a part" (1892, 26). Frege was also clear to separate the notion of sense from that of our ideas of such senses, which are necessarily incomplete and can often be erroneous.

Since Frege, the notion of senses containing the complete set of their denotations has been elaborated in a number of ways. For instance, Church (1951), although he only provides an axiomatic (rather than referential) treatment of Frege's logical notions, states that an adequate model must provide a referent for each sense. Furthermore, he claims that "there is no difference in principle between this case [formal languages] and that of one of the natural languages" (1951, 110). Carnap (1947), though he disagrees with Church's approach along a number of dimensions, proposes a semantic approach to sentence meanings in which a proposition is modeled as a function from "states of affairs" to referents. He applies this perspective to *modal adverbs* such *necessarily* and *possibly*. For instance, Carnap assumes a sentence is necessarily true if and only if it is true under every interpretation of the nonlogical terms it contains (he assumed that logical terms, such as conjunction, negation, and quantification, are always interpreted the same way).

Kaplan (1964) developed Carnap's ideas and applied them to Church's language by modeling states of affairs as logical models of the underlying nonintensional language. For instance, a proposition is necessarily true if it is true in every model. Kaplan's approach suffers from a number of logical drawbacks, most notably its inability to deal with iterated attitudes such as the following.

(25) Terry knows that Chris believes that Dana runs.

The problem is that the intensional model is only one level deep, being built on top of a nonintensional model.

The philosophical and logical treatment of senses was revolutionized by the advent of Kripke's (1959, 1963a) possible-world semantics for modal logics, which cleared up a number of the more technical and empirical problems with previous approaches such as Church's and Carnap's. In Kripke's models, a *possible world* provides complete information about a possible way the world could be. It is assumed that the real world is simply one such possible world. Under such a theory, the sense of a sentence is just a function from possible worlds to truth values. In other words, a sense must determine the truth or falsity of a proposition in each of the possible worlds. Looked at the other way around, a possible world is just an abstract entity that determines the truth or falsity of every proposition. To determine whether a proposition is true in the actual world, it is applied as a function to the actual world, the result being its truth value in the actual world. The added power of Kripke's model derives from the richness of propositions in providing information in different worlds. Thus we could distinguish (24a) and (24b) if there were two possible worlds, one in which the morning star and the evening star are both the planet Venus, and one in which they are distinct. Under such a conception, the senses of (24a) and (24b) would be distinguished. If we then follow Frege in the assumption that belief is a relation between the individual denoted by the subject and the sense of its sentential object, we can also account for the different truth values of (24c) and (24d).

While this discussion has concentrated on sentences, almost all expressions of natural language display subtle distinctions in meanings beyond their immediate referents. For instance, a noun phrase such as *the president of the United States* may denote different individuals in different possible worlds or at different times in the real world. Common nouns such as *vampire* and *unicorn* might actually apply to some individuals in some possible world. Often the synthetic/analytic division is recast in possible-world semantics as one of being true in the actual world versus being true in all possible worlds.

1.2.6   Lexical Semantics

A significant amount of effort in semantics has concentrated on the classification of the words and phrases of a language. Not surprisingly, several approaches to lexical semantics have been developed. Although lexical semantics will play only a minor role in this book, in this section I will describe a few of the more popular avenues of research in this area.

Traditionally, words have been categorized by their meanings. For instance, in the construction of a thesaurus, words are grouped according to similarity of meaning. Of course, it is difficult, perhaps even impossible, to find pairs of words that are truly synonymous. Often studies are made of the different *connotations* of roughly synonymous words, such as *tall* and *overgrown*. A similar undertaking involves *antonymy*, or words with meanings that vary along a single dimension but are otherwise similar, such as *large*, *medium*, and *small*, or *hot*, *warm*, *tepid*, and *cold*. A significant portion of the basic lexicon of a language can be organized into antonym classes. In addition to thesauruses, there are antonym dictionaries.

Another way in which words are classified involves *taxonomical* relationships. For instance, we often have words for broad categories, with further words reserved for successively smaller subclasses, e.g., *furniture*, *chair*, and *armchair*, or *vehicle*, *car*, and *sedan*.

Often there are groups of words that do not stand in a taxonomic relationship but nevertheless share contexts of use and a broad similarity of meaning. Examples are the pair *husband* and *wife* and the pair *hit* and *kick*. Other examples include *he*, *she* and *it*. Such relationships are known in linguistics as *paradigmatic*. Paradigmatic relationships are roughly defined as those between elements that can occur in the same contexts. A closely related notion is that of *syntagmatic* relations, which hold among words that occur together, but not in variation with one another. For instance, consider the pair *coffee* and *beans* or the pair *cat* and *meow*. A similar pattern is that of *collocational restrictions*. For instance, it is much more natural to use the expression *strong coffee* than the seemingly synonymous *powerful coffee*. A grasp of collocation patterns is essential in generating natural-sounding utterances and is becoming increasingly important in the mechanical generation of natural-language by computers. Many researchers have attempted to link such classifications with human cognitive organization (Jackendoff 1983, Lakoff 1987). Standard word-association tests can often reveal closely related terms.

Because semantic relationships are notoriously tricky and subtle, much recent research in lexical semantics has focused on how semantic relationships are expressed in the syntactic patterns of language. One instance of this work is in the so-called *linking* of thematic roles and grammatical roles. Roughly, *thematic roles* indicate the semantic relationships between an event and its participants. For instance, in an event of Lee's hitting Pat, Lee is the instigator of the action, and Pat is the recipient. *Grammatical roles*, on the other hand, are marked by subjecthood and objecthood in a sentence, for instance. In English, the subject precedes the verb and the object follows in standard sentences, whereas in languages like Japanese, grammatical roles are reflected in morphological suffixes (or perhaps postpositional particles). In the typological pattern across the verbs of the world's languages we find instigators, often called *agents*, realized grammatically as subjects and recipients, often called *patients*, as objects. This observation formed the core of Fillmore's (1968) highly influential theory of *case grammar* and is the basis of the lexical *linking theory* of lexical functional grammar (L. Levin 1987). A semantic foundation for thematic roles was put forward in Dowty 1991, which also contains an extensive bibliography on the subject. B. Levin (1993) provided an extremely detailed survey and classification of the lexical patterns of English verbs from both a syntactic and a semantic perspective.

The relation between thematic roles and grammatical roles is only one kind of pattern that has been found to be *universal* across languages. Linguists, especially syntacticians of a typological persuasion, are usually much more concerned with universal patterns than language-specific ones. Some universal patterns simply concern the organization of language. For instance, all languages allow reference to individuals, actions, and relations, as well as methods for combining these, such as conjunction and disjunction. Universals can also be found in the possible meanings assigned to certain kinds of categories. We return to this topic in section 3.3, where we study constraints on the meanings of quantificational determiners, such as *every*, *no*, and *most*.

Another avenue of exploration in lexical semantics has been the *decompositional* approach. In a decompositional theory, primitive meaning units are presupposed, along with limited means of combining them. Such studies were at the heart of the *structuralist* theory of semantics and later were incorporated into the theory known as *generative semantics*. Such theories often attempted to link their primitives to cognition. While most of the specific assumptions of the structuralists and generative semanticists have been abandoned, to a large extent their basic approach is reflected in contemporary research on lexical semantics. Decompositional approaches commonly resurface in computational approaches to natural-language understanding, the most widely known of which are Schank and Abelson's (1977) conceptual-dependency theory and knowledge-representation schemes based on semantic networks (Brachman 1979).

1.3   TOPICS IN PRAGMATICS

The branch of linguistics devoted to studying the effects of context on utterance interpretation has traditionally been known as *pragmatics*. Semantics, on the other hand, is usually taken to refer to the literal, context-independent aspects of meaning. Of course, the location of the dividing line between literal and context-sensitive aspects of interpretations is notoriously difficult to pin down. For instance, indexicality has traditionally been considered a pragmatic phenomenon, because the interpretation of indexical elements is clearly context-sensitive. More recently, the term *pragmatics* has been narrowed to encompass just those aspects of meaning that involve more than the literal interpretation of utterances, and this is how I will use the term. In this section I briefly survey three of the main areas of pragmatics: conversational implicature, speech acts, and discourse analysis. A thorough survey of the field, including the traditional issues of indexicality, deixis, and presupposition, can be found in Levinson 1983. The survey of discourse by Brown and Yule (1983) is also a good source for further reading. I will also discuss in this section the role of metaphor in language interpretation. While the study of metaphor is generally not thought to be pragmatic in nature, I include it here because of its nonliteral nature.

1.3.1   Conversational Implicature

Entailment and presupposition are only two of the ways in which language can convey information. Another important means of conveying information by language, originally articulated by Grice (1975), is through what he calls *conversational implicature*. Roughly, Grice noted that utterances may convey information by means of their use in context and that such information goes beyond the literal content and entailments of the utterances. As a typical example, Grice provides the following dialogue.

(26) *Speaker A*: I am out of petrol.
      Speaker B: There is a garage around the corner.

Grice notes that the response of speaker *B* to speaker *A*'s request, namely that there is a garage around the corner, has the conversational implicature that speaker *B* believes the garage is open for business and sells petrol. While this latter piece of information is not explicitly entailed by the statement that there is a garage around the corner, a cooperative use of the response implicates it.

In contrast to true entailment, implicatures are *cancelable*. That is, the response of speaker *B* in (26) does not fail to be true if the garage around the corner is closed. On the other hand, if around the corner there is nothing but a convenience store, then speaker *B*'s statement is simply false. Furthermore, implicatures can be explicitly overridden. For instance, speaker *B* may have continued his response in (26) with *but it's not open, so you'll have to go further down the road.*

The cornerstone of Grice's account of conversational implicature is the view of language as just one form of cooperative behavior. Along these lines, Grice formulated his *cooperative principle* for language as follows.

Make your conversational contribution such as is required, at the stage at which it occurs, by the accepted purpose or direction of the talk exchange in which you are engaged.

Grice then observed that conversational implicatures arise due to the interaction of the cooperative principle with discourse. It should be clear how the implicature derived from the response of speaker *B* in (26) follows from the assumption that speaker *B* is being cooperative.

Under Grice's analysis, implicatures are derived from the meaning of an utterance and its interaction with the cooperative principle. The syntactic form of the utterance is irrelevant, and thus Grice claimed that implicatures are *nondetachable*. True implications are obviously nondetachable by definition. Presuppositions, on the other hand, are detachable. For instance, *The winner of the race is Sandy* presupposes the existence of a winner, whereas *Sandy won the race* does not, even though both sentences would be true in exactly the same set of circumstances.

Given his analysis, Grice drew the related conclusion that implicatures are *nonconventional*. That is, implicatures are derived from the meaning of sentences and their situations of use, rather than from conventions of language per se. Support for this claim can be found by completing exercise 2.

An equally important means of conveying information that crucially involves the cooperative principle arises when the principle has apparently been disregarded. For instance, consider Grice's example of a tutor writing a reference letter for a pupil who is a candidate for a job in philosophy, who reports only the following.

(27) Dear Sir,
     Mr. X's command of English is excellent, and his attendance at
     tutorials has been regular.
     Yours, etc.

Grice reasonably suggests that the implicature here is that X is no good at philosophy. Given the context, if X had been an excellent student, the tutor would have indicated as much. The omission of this information forms the basis of the implicature.

Grice breaks the cooperative principle down into four broad categories, which he referred to as *conversational maxims*.

(28) a. *Quantity*
        i. Make your contribution as informative as is required.
        ii. Do not make your contribution more informative than is
            required.
     b. *Quality*
        Try to make your contribution one that is true.
        i. Do not say what you believe to be false.
        ii. Do not say what you lack adequate evidence for.
     c. *Relation*
        Be relevant.
     d. *Manner*
        Be perspicuous.
        i. Avoid obscurity of expression.
        ii. Avoid ambiguity.
        iii. Be brief.
        iv. Be orderly.

Any of these Gricean maxims may be used to implicate information that is not entailed or presupposed by the literal meaning of an utterance. Grice provides examples of uses of each, as well as a more precise definition of conversational implicature and its relation to the maxims. Further examples and discussion may be found in Levinson 1983. Grice realistically admits that this list is likely to be incomplete, and in fact there have been many who have reclassified the cooperative principle into coarser, finer, or simply differently organized maxims. A currently popular approach has been to take the notion of *relevance* as central (Sperber and Wilson 1986).

1.3.2   Speech Acts

Another way in which language may be used to convey information that goes beyond its literal meaning is by the use of *speech acts*. The theory of speech acts, originally developed by Austin (1961) and further elaborated by Searle (1965, 1975), also places a great deal of importance on the role of language as cooperative behavior.

Austin (1961) introduced the notion of a *performative utterance*, and as typical instances he provided the following:

(29) a. I name this ship the *Queen Elizabeth*.
     b. I now pronounce you man and wife.
     c. I give and bequeath my watch to my brother.

Utterances of the sentences in (29) can be used to christen a ship, marry a couple, or create a will and testament. As Austin claims, "If a person makes an utterance of this sort we should say that he is *doing* something rather than merely *saying* something" (1961, 251). Thus the key fact about performative utterances is that their users are performing some sort of action with language, rather than making a true or false claim about the world. This places an analysis of performatives outside of the scope of this book, which focuses on truth-conditional semantics.

Austin noted that performative sentences, such as those in (29), derive their meaning from the conventions of a given language community. Thus they could fail to be meaningful in many of the same ways as simple declarative sentences. For instance, an utterance of (29b) will be infelicitous if the speaker does not have the authority to perform a marriage or, in some cultures, if one member of the couple in question is already married. Performatives may also fail for more mundane semantic reasons. For instance, (29c) will fail if the speaker does not own a watch or does not have a brother.

Austin (1962) generalized his approach to language as action, introducing the general term *illocutionary act* for the use of language to perform actions. The most well-known exposition of a theory of illocutionary acts is due to Searle (1965), although he referred to them using the now standard term *speech acts*. Searle provided examples of verbs that were typically used in speech acts, such as *warn, remark, command, criticize, apologize, promise,* and *welcome.* Austin claimed there were thousands of such speech-act verbs in English.

Searle stressed the following point.

> It is not, as has generally been supposed, the symbol or word or sentence, or even the token of the symbol or word or sentence, which is the unit of linguistic communication, but rather it is the *production* of the token in the performance of the speech act that constitutes the basic unit of linguistic communication. To put this point more precisely, the production of the sentence token under certain conditions is the illocutionary act, and the illocutionary act is the minimal unit of linguistic communication. (1965, 222)

In other words, Searle emphasized the speech context, including the intentions of the speaker, in the interpretation of an utterance.

Perhaps the most influential aspect of Searle's analysis of speech acts was his account of *indirect speech acts* (Searle 1975). A typical indirect speech act would be an utterance of the following sentence as a request to pass the salt.

(30) Could you pass the salt?

Interpreted literally, (30) is a yes/no question. Yet one common usage of such a polar interrogative is as a request to pass the salt. While this may seem to be an almost completely conventionalized, polite usage, consider another example due to Searle.

(31) It is cold in here.

Such a statement could also be used as a request, say to turn up the heat or close a window, depending on the context.

One of the key aspects of Searle's analysis of speech acts was his emphasis on the component illocutionary acts that make up the larger utterance. Searle argued that to understand utterances such as (30) and (31), it is necessary to understand their component speech acts, including determining the reference of definites (such as *the salt*) and indexicals (such as *you* and *here*), as well as to understand the literal meanings of the expressions (such as *in* and *pass*). Interpreting the speech act itself is a matter of cooperation among cognitive agents, rather than a process determined by the linguistic conventions adopted by a linguistic community, and is well beyond the scope of this book. I will concentrate almost exclusively on the referential and truth-conditional aspects of meaning and interpretation.

As Grice points out, in his analysis of meaning, a crucial feature of A's meaning something by x is that "A intended the utterance of x to produce some effect in an audience by means of the recognition of this intention" (1975, 51). Searle (1965) distinguishes the effects of utterances that come about by the hearer's recognition of the speaker's intentions from those that do not. The former case simply involves ordinary uses of language. As an example of the latter case, he imagines a situation where an American soldier is captured by the Italian army during World War II. The American remembers one line of German from a poem, namely *Kennst du das Land, wo die Zitronen blühen?* (literally, 'Knowest thou the land where the lemon trees bloom?'), and utters this sentence in an effort to convince his Italian captors that he is German. For the American's ploy to succeed, it is crucial that the hearers not recognize the speaker's intention in uttering the line from a German poem. The American's utterance is used for what Austin terms its *perlocutionary effect*, rather than its illocutionary effect. As another example of perlocutionary effects, he cites the case of a speaker who uses abstruse language in an effort to impress the hearer with his erudition.

1.3.3   Discourse Structure

It is evident that sentences cannot simply be randomly organized in the presentation of complicated information. Consider what would happen if all of the sentences in this chapter were put into a bag, and then extracted at random to form the text (a technique actually advocated by the beat author William S. Burroughs). Theories of discourse structure are generally centered around the organizations of written or spoken language as it occurs in narrative fiction, interpersonal dialogues, newspaper articles, television commercials, instruction manuals, classroom interaction, and just about any other conceivable occurrence of language in context. Usually such analyses focus on multisentence discourses and intersentential relationships. Brown and Yule (1983) provide a thorough survey of the field.

Of the more linguistically oriented studies, a great deal of attention has been paid to notions such as the *topic* and *focus* of a text, the role of stress and intonation on discourse structure, the theme of an exposition and its development, and the computation of the antecedents of pronouns and elided elements based on discourse structure. Various theories have been proposed, including the development of grammars for texts. Most computational implementations of discourse structuring revolve around speaker and hearer intentions (see Grosz and Sidner 1986) and around the knowledge of prototypical events and their structure (Schank and Abelson 1977). Like other aspects of pragmatics, theories of discourse structure are usually constructed using semantic analyses of single phrases, clauses, and sentences as a basis. A popular technique, embodied in recent theories of *dynamic semantics* (Groenendijk and Stokhof 1990, 1991; Chierchia 1995), has been to model the meaning of a sentence as a mapping from discourse contexts to discourse contexts. The effect of a sentence with a definite noun phrase might be to introduce an individual into the domain of discourse, whereas a sentence with a pronoun might require that the input discourse context contain an antecedent for it. This allows the effects of longer stretches of text to be modeled by composing the meanings of sentences.

1.3.4   Metaphors, Idioms, and Language Change

One of the most subtle aspects of the semantics of natural language arises in the use of *metaphor*. Intuitively, a metaphorical usage of a term involves some shift in meaning away from how the term is conventionally understood. Thus metaphorical uses of terms or phrases are often contrasted with their literal or conventional uses.

First, let us consider some examples of metaphor, drawn from Searle 1979.

(32) a. Sandy is a gorilla.
      b. I have climbed to the top of the greasy pole. (Benjamin Disraeli)
      c. Juliet is the sun.

In each of these cases, it is clear that the intended meaning is not the literal one. In each case there is a rough, literal paraphrase. For example, (32a), according to Searle, means that Sandy is fierce and nasty. The second example, (32b), means that Disraeli struggled to become prime minister of Great Britain. In the last example, (32c), there may be any number of plausible interpretations, or the speaker, Romeo, may have meant a great many things with the utterance, including that he could not live without Juliet or that she brought sunshine into his life (another metaphor).

A theory of metaphor must provide answers to a number of questions. Searle (1979) isolates the following primary issues. First, we must understand how metaphorical meaning differs from literal meaning and from other figurative uses of language. Second, a theory of metaphor should explain how it is possible for speakers to formulate and for hearers to understand metaphors. The final piece of a theory of metaphors is actually extrinsic to the understanding of metaphors per se but is of perhaps of the greatest importance, both psychologically and semantically; the issue is why speakers use metaphors rather than expressing themselves literally.

Searle (1979) argues that the key aspect of metaphorical interpretation is the divergence between *speaker meaning* and *literal meaning*. He concludes that metaphorical meaning is a kind of speaker's meaning and that it crucially depends on understanding the literal meaning of an utterance. But rather than trying to provide a unified theory of metaphorical interpretation, Searle concludes that the issue of how metaphors function reduces to the issue of how one thing or concept reminds us of another. Thus the reason that some metaphors fail is that some things simply cannot be used to remind us of other things. This intentionally vague "theory" of the interpretation of metaphors does provide an explanation of their utility. A common view is that we depend on metaphors when there is no literal usage that will convey the meaning we intend, or at least not with the same force, economy, or perspicuity.

Metaphors have often been argued to be one of the driving forces both in scientific change and in language change. An excellent discussion of their utility for the sciences and the humanities can be found in Rorty 1989. Lakoff and his colleagues (1987, 1989; Lakoff and Johnson 1980) have greatly revived interest in metaphorical interpretations of natural language, focusing on those derived from our physical makeup as humans. Such theories have been especially important in the understanding of prepositions, such as *in*, as can be witnessed by the extensive study of prepositions in Herskovits 1986. For instance, consider the following examples.

(33) a. The block is in the box.
     b. Robin is in the army.
     c. Robin is in charge.
     d. Robin is in a good mood.

All of these sentences use the preposition *in* in a different sense, ranging from physical containment to disposition. These examples are only the tip of the iceberg; there are literally hundreds of common uses of most of the simple prepositions. Most of these uses have some metaphorical relation to the notion of physical inclusion, though the connection is often tenuous.

Most theories of *idioms* treat them simply as dead metaphors. That is, an idiom is thought of as nothing more than a metaphor whose meaning has become frozen. For instance, consider the following sentences with idiomatic verb phrases.

(34) a. Sandy kicked the bucket.
      b. Sandy let the cat out of the bag.

The first example, (34a), means that Sandy died. The second, (34b), means that Sandy gave away a secret. Note the degree to which these expressions are frozen. Variants such as *boot the pail* and *allow the feline to escape*, while having very similar literal meanings to *kick the bucket* and *let the cat out of the bag*, simply do not convey the same meanings as their idiomatic counterparts (except insofar as they invoke the idiom itself).

If we follow conventional wisdom and suppose that idioms are like any other expressions with conventionalized meanings, then there is only one problem left to solve, and that is the nature of their syntactic realization. This is complicated, though, because of the phrasal nature of idioms. The pattern of allowable modifiers and inflections, the discontinuity of idioms themselves, and their seeming disregard for normal lexical constituency require special care. Recently researchers have proposed two theories of the syntax and semantics of idioms that are consistent with the semantic approach I adopt in this book (Nunberg, Sag, and Wasow 1994; van der Linden 1993).

1.4 METHODOLOGY

In this section I discuss the methodology that I will employ throughout the rest of the book to develop a theory of natural-language semantics. I begin by motivating a compositional approach to semantics. I then discuss the use of mathematical models in linguistics.

1.4.1 Productivity

One of the most fundamental aspects of natural language lies in our ability to produce and understand novel utterances. This ability is often referred to as linguistic *creativity* or *productivity*. Perhaps even more surprising is that the set of grammatical sentences in English to which a semantic theory must assign meanings is unbounded (though arguably countable). To see that this is so, simply consider the following sequence of expressions.

(35) a. The kid ran.
   b. I know that the kid ran.
   c. You know that I know that the kid ran.
   d. I know that you know that I know that the kid ran.
   ⋮

Significantly, each of these sentences has a distinct meaning. There are, of course, many other ways to construct unbounded sequences of sentences with distinct meanings.

It might be argued that there should be some upper bound to the length of a sentence, and any longer sentence should be classified as ungrammatical. After all, with only a relatively short lifespan, it would be impossible to produce a sentence with a trillion words. It is also clear that sentences of more than a few hundred words will be incomprehensible if they have a structure that is more complex than a simple conjunction of simpler sentences. With the examples in (35), it is not at all clear where to draw the line. It seems that if any sentence in (35) is grammatical, then so is the next sentence. There seems to be no principled way in which to decide at what point sentences become too long or complex to be considered grammatical. In every theory of grammar proposed to date, if *s* is admitted as a sentence, then *I know that s* is also admitted. Furthermore, it is clear how to semantically interpret each of the sentences in the sequence. Rather than choosing a length beyond which sentences are considered ungrammatical, linguists endeavor to create more general, productive theories.

The primary goal of theoretical linguistics, as opposed to psycholinguistics, is to formulate a theory of language itself, rather than the human ability to process it. Chomsky (1965) drew a distinction between linguistic *competence*, on the one hand, and *performance* on the other. Chomsky believed that our competence comprised a system of rules for the construction of utterances and their meanings, such as the one stated above, namely that if *s* is a sentence, so is *I know s*. Chomsky further assumed that the knowledge of some such rules is innate, as is the ability to use such rules. Linguistic performance is subject to the vagaries of all human cognitive activities, such as attention span, alertness, distractions, and so on. Even relatively short sentences can quickly overcome human processing limitations if their structure is too complex. For instance, consider the case of center-embedded relative clauses.

(36) a. The mouse ran.
      b. The mouse that the cat chased ran.
      c. The mouse that the cat that the dog bit chased ran.
      d. The mouse that the cat that the dog that the person owns bit chased ran.
        ⋮

Even the third example, (36c), with only two center embedded clauses, is pretty incomprehensible.

Abstracting away from performance issues, Chomsky took it to be the job of linguistics to construct a competence model. Even before Chomsky, most linguists distinguished human language itself from our ability to use it. Notable exceptions were those who took language to be determined by our use of it, such as the later Wittgenstein and the behavioral psychologists. In the last few decades there has been a tremendous amount of effort expended on the debate concerning whether humans are born with innate linguistic knowledge, or whether language, like many other aspects of our knowledge, is induced from the environment. Often these debates have been sparked by particular theories of the organization of the knowledge of language in our brains and of whether such knowledge can be separated from our presumably more procedural ability to use such knowledge. A detailed and relatively nonpartisan survey of the empirical data and various positions that have been taken with respect to language acquisition and processing can be found in Taylor and Taylor 1990.

1.4.2   Compositionality

The fundamental approach to modeling the productivity of human language has its roots in the writings of Frege (1892). He was attempting to explain how a finite system can lead to a productive grammar of language. Frege presented roughly the following theory of how such a system could be organized, which has come to be known as the principle of *compositionality*.

DEFINITION: COMPOSITIONALITY   The meaning of an expression is determined by the meanings of its parts and the way in which they are combined.

On the assumption that there are only finitely many atomic parts involved in language, say those corresponding to words, and furthermore that there are only finitely many grammatical constructions that can be employed to build larger structures, this definition shows how a finite number of building blocks can be used to generate an infinite set of sentences and interpretations. Typically, the smallest meaningful unit in language is assumed to be the *morpheme*. Morphemes can be *roots* or *stems*, such as *happy* or *run*; they can be *inflectional affixes*, such as the tense suffixes *-ed* and *-ing*, or they can be *derivational affixes*, such as the negative *un-* or the nominalizer *-tion*. The morphological structure of some languages is much less concatenative than in English. In some Bantu languages, morphological marking takes the form of tones overlayed on the stems. In other languages, such as Arabic and Sierra Miwok, stems consist of consonants and inflections of vowels, which are then merged into words. But in any case, there is typically a simple way to identify the underlying meaningful units and their compositional structure.

As Partee (1984b) points out, with a statement of Frege's principle as general as the one above, the notion of compositionality appears nearly trivial. There seems very little hope of building a noncompositional theory of meaning that would account for the productivity of language. In practice, with a rich enough collection of meanings and methods for combining them, just about any theory associating strings of symbols with meanings can be made compositional in the sense above. Thus rather than being an empirical claim, the compositionality principle has come to be a methodological principle. But strictly compositional theories are not, in fact, the only possibility; often a compositional formulation of a semantic theory may not be the most perspicuous one. For instance, consider discourse-representation theory, which has both compositional and noncompositional presentations (see section 7.10).

The theories of meaning I present will be compositional, but this statement requires some elaboration of what I mean by *meaning*. I will use the term *meaning* to denote the context-independent aspects of the semantics of an expression. I reserve the term *interpretation* for the semantic result of refining the meaning with contextual information. For instance, the meaning of the indexical expression *I* is the speaker, the interpretation of an utterance of *I* will be the speaker who uttered the expression. In what follows, I will adopt the methodology of Kaplan (1977, 1978), as discussed in section 1.2.4, and treat the meaning of an expression as a relation between contexts and interpretations. Furthermore, I follow Frege (1892) in treating interpretations as senses rather than referents, which provides an additional degree of freedom.

1.4.3   Model Theory and Grammar Fragments

The primary tool employed by contemporary semanticists is model theory, which is a branch of mathematical logic dealing with the interpretation of logical languages and theories expressed within them. Model-theoretic approaches to natural-language semantics were originally proposed by Tarski (1935). Following in the Tarskian tradition, most of the model-theoretic approaches to natural language have been devoted to truth-conditional semantics.

Logical model theory as applied to natural-language semantics has often been misconstrued as making stronger claims than its proponents are comfortable with. For instance, model theory is usually employed to produce models of a natural language itself, not our knowledge of or facility to use natural language. Logical models should rather be understood as idealizing away from speakers and thus should not be given epistemological interpretations. Along another dimension, models are rarely comprehensive, usually modeling only a small part of language. Furthermore, the objects employed in models are usually not intended to be provided with a metaphysical interpretation, though many proponents of model theory have done just that. These properties of model-theoretic semantics can be productively compared with the theory of differential equations as applied to the motion of a football. No one would claim that a football computes a differential equation, or even represents one, as it flies through the air. Nor would most physicists claim that differential equations were real in the metaphysical sense. Physicists also realize that most differential equations provide only an approximation of a football's movement, abstracting away from considerations such as turbulence, air temperature, and other details. Nevertheless, differential equations do provide useful approximations; the basic theory of differential equations and the classical theory of mechanics (as opposed to the more accurate relativistic one) formed the basis for the construction of the Apollo rockets that transported humans to the moon.

The most ambitious and influential application of model theory to natural-language semantics was carried out by Richard Montague in the late 1960s. He went so far as to write, "I reject the contention that an important theoretical difference exists between formal and natural language" (Montague 1970a, 188). While I believe this claim to be exaggerated, I draw many insights from both Montague's general grammatical framework (1970b) and his particular grammars (1973).

Chomsky (1957) pioneered the technique of building precise models of subsets of natural language, concentrating on syntactic and phonological phenomena. Montague employed logical model theory to develop semantic models in the same spirit. Since the early 1980s, Chomsky (1990b) has argued against the utility of building grammar fragments, and subsequently their use in syntax and phonology has gone out of vogue in "mainstream" linguistic theorizing. But there is still a strong community of syntacticians who employ the fragment-building technique, including those working in lexical functional grammar (LFG) (Kaplan and Bresnan 1982), generalized phrase-structure grammar (GPSG) (Gazdar, Klein, Pullum, and Sag 1985), head-driven phrase-structure grammar (HPSG) (Pollard and Sag 1994), and the formalism I adopt, categorial grammar (CG) (Morrill 1994a). The construction of grammar fragments remains prevalent in studies of natural-language semantics. One of the primary threads of this book is the construction of a semantic model of a relatively large fragment of English. In following a compositional approach to semantics, I will also need to formulate a precise syntactic model of English, though this will not be my principal concern, and I will refrain from introducing too much syntactic detail into my models.

In the next two chapters I will be developing the logical model theory I will later employ in extensional grammar fragments. This will involve developing a general theory of functions, known as the λ-calculus, which I do in the next chapter. In the chapter after that, I will build models of higher-order logic, which are built on the foundation of the λ-calculus.

Exercises

1. From a source such as a newspaper or transcribed speech, find several occurrences of metaphor. For each instance, explain what the intended interpretation is and what clues there are that it should be interpreted nonliterally. From a similar source, find several occurrences of presupposition. Why did the author or speaker choose to convey information by presupposition? From a similar source, find several instances of implicature and explain why implicature was chosen as a vehicle for conveying information.

2. Sketch a situation and an utterance in that situation where the utterance is true but its implicature is not. Next provide a situation and an utterance that is literally false but has a true implicature. Finally, provide a sentence and sketch two situations in which it would have different implicatures. (Levinson 1983)

3. Provide (the initial parts of) three or four sequences of grammatical sentences whose length is unbounded. Do not use the same grammatical pattern as in (35) or (36).

4. Choose a few contiguous sentences from some naturally occurring text and discuss the nonlinguistic knowledge necessary to interpret them. Consider both contextual information and encyclopedic information.

5. Jot down a few uses of indirect speech acts from discourses that you have recently participated in.

6. Provide an example of a linguistic community, and discuss both the motivation for and the kind of language used in the community.

7. Discuss the extent to which our language affects our culture and vice-versa.

8. Discuss the range of empirical facts that we have available to us as linguists. How are such facts interpreted?

9. Choose a short thesaurus entry and discuss how the synonyms listed vary in connotation.

Chapter 2

Simply Typed λ-Calculus

The λ-calculus provides an elegant solution not only to the vexing problem of providing denotations for the basic expressions of a language but also for productively composing these basic meanings into larger units. In this chapter I lay out the basic theory of the simply typed λ-calculus along with its linguistic motivation. I begin with the language of the simply typed λ-calculus, the most popular version of the theory for linguistic applications. I then consider a model theory and proof theory for the logical language. I discuss important issues such as normal forms, strong normalization, and the Church-Rosser theorem. I also consider combinators, which are a kind of simply typed λ-term that has been applied in several varieties of categorial grammar and that can be taken as the foundation for the semantic operations corresponding to syntactic constructions. I conclude with a discussion of the product (pairing) and sum (disjoint union) constructors, which extend the functional λ-calculus to products and (disjoint) sums.

The λ-calculus was invented by Church (1940), with the goal of providing a uniform language with which to describe functions. In mathematical notation, say in algebra, it is common to define a function f by a statement such as the following:

(1) f is the binary function such that $f(x, y) = x^2 - y^2$

At the same time, we might want to describe another similar function, say g, by stipulating that $g(x, y) = y^2 - x^2$. In general, such an ad hoc method of defining functions suffices for mathematical reasoning in most domains. We can define new functions in terms of f and g, for instance, by saying that $h(x, y, z) = f(x, y) + g(y, z)$. A drawback to this approach is that it forces us to create new names for all of our functions, defining them explicitly in terms of their behavior or in terms of functions we already have. It also becomes rather unwieldy when we begin to define higher-order functions, sometimes called *functionals* in mathematics, which themselves operate over functions. For instance, composition is an operation that takes two functions f and g and returns the function h such that $h(x) = f(g(x))$. In recursion theory, which is a traditional means of characterizing the computable functions, we need to be able to express the fact that if two functions f and g are computable, then so is f composed with g. We also want to say that if there is a computable function that returns a tuple of values, then the function that only returns a segment of the tuple, known as a *projection*, is also computable. But a quick glance at the definition of composition and projection in a recursion-theory textbook shows that it is by no means straightforward to define all of the functions that can be constructed by composition and projection in terms of more elementary computable functions. The simply typed λ-calculus provides an expressive, elegant, and uniform method of composing functions out of a set of primitive functions. By means of coding natural numbers in the λ-calculus, Kleene (1936) showed that the monotyped λ-calculus, which I discuss briefly below, is itself powerful enough by to define all of the recursively computable functions (see Barendregt 1981, 131).

In calculus, the operations of differentiation and (unbounded) integration both involve functionals mapping a function on reals into a function on reals (it is best to indicate whether a particlar function is onto, one-one, or both if known; otherwise I just say "maps into"). Thus both operations are of type $(\mathbf{R} \times \mathbf{R}) \times (\mathbf{R} \times \mathbf{R})$, where $\mathbf{R}$ is the type of real numbers. Furthermore, the $\mathrm{d}x$ notation in calculus is just an explicit way of binding variables, although this is rarely clear in complex cases expressed in standard mathematicla notation. For instance, $\int x^2\,\mathrm{d}x$ indicates that it is the function $\lambda x.x^2$ that is to be integrated, the result of which is the function $\lambda x.x^3/3$. In most calculus textbooks, the result is confusingly written as simply $x^3/3$, which can make it difficult to distinguish between bound and unbound variables, especially in the case of multiple integrals or derivatives. Explicit mathematical programming languages such as Mathematica (Wolfram 1991) use the λ-calculus directly in their representations.

A significant application of the λ-calculus is in both the operational and denotational description of higher-order programming languages such as Lisp and ML. In fact, the operation of β-conversion, which I describe in this chapter, is at the heart of the definition of the evaluation function in Lisp, whereas λ-abstraction is the essence of function definition.

My applications of the λ-calculus will be to natural-language semantics, where it will provide a formalism in which we can assign meanings to the basic expressions of a language and all of the larger constituents constructible from the basic expressions. In other words, it forms the basis of the compositional method of defining the meanings of expressions in terms of the meanings of their parts. This can be contrasted with first-order logic, which is rather impoverished in terms of being able to assign meanings to the relevant syntactic constituents of an expression. As in first-order logic, higher-order logic allows us to provide terms for the lexical items in an expression like *Sandy dazzled Chris*; *Sandy* and *Chris* are represented by individual constants, which are interpreted as individuals, and *dazzled* is represented by a two-place relation symbol, which is interpreted as a binary relation. But unlike first-order logic, we can in addition provide a term corresponding to the meaning of the verb phrase *dazzled Chris*. The closest approximation in first-order logic would be **dazzle**(x, **chris**), but this is a formula with a free variable, which is not at all the same kind of expression as **run**, a unary predicate symbol, which would be the translation of the verb phrase *run*. The λ-calculus provides a language in which we will be able to assign all of our constituents first-class logical expressions.

2.1   SIMPLE TYPES

My presentation of the simply typed λ-calculus begins with a discussion of the language of λ-terms, which is based on the notion of classifying all expressions into types. Recall that in first-order logic there are two types of expressions: terms and formulas. In the simply typed λ-calculus there are infinitely many types for expressions. These types are all constructed from a finite set of basic types. A common choice of basic types in linguistics, which we consider in the next chapter, consists of a type for propositions and a type for individuals. The full set of types is then built up hierarchically by closing the set of basic types under the construction of total function types. This is very similar to the stratified hierarchy of sets in common use in set theory, in which we begin with a set of objects and at each subsequent stage introduce sets containing only elements that we have already constructed. For now we will assume that every type is either a basic type or a functional type.

DEFINITION: TYPES   From a nonempty set **BasTyp** of *basic types*, the set **Typ** of types is the smallest set such that

a. **BasType** ⊆ **Typ**,
b. $(\sigma \rightarrow \tau) \in$ **Typ** if $\sigma, \tau \in$ **Typ**.

A type of the form $(\sigma \rightarrow \tau)$ is said to be a *functional type*, the elements of which map objects of type σ to objects of type τ. For instance, if **Ind** is the type of individuals and **Bool** is the type of propositions, then the functional type (**Ind** → **Bool**) is the type of functions from individuals into propositions, or in more familiar terms, the type of unary relations. We also get types for boolean operations, so that (**Bool** → **Bool**) is the type of unary boolean functions, which is the type we assign to the negation operator. In fact, we get not only simple functional types corresponding to the types of logical and nonlogical constants in first-order logic but also second-order types, such as ((**Ind** → **Bool**) → (**Ind** → **Bool**)), which is the type of a function mapping unary relations into unary relations, the appropriate type for adjectives in natural-language semantics. I routinely drop the parentheses from functional types, associating to the right, so that I write $\sigma \rightarrow \tau \rightarrow \rho$ for $(\sigma \rightarrow (\tau \rightarrow \rho))$. For instance, the property-modifier type, which we will assign to adjectives, prepositional phrases, and relative clauses, will be written as (**Ind** → **Bool**) → **Ind** → **Bool**.

I have adopted the notation for types that is common in mathematics and computer science. The components of a functional type consist of a pair of types. Using what is known as *abstract syntax*, we could define the set **Typ** as the minimal solution to the following equation:

(2) **Typ** = **BasTyp** ∪ (**Typ** × **Typ**)

Such a syntax is abstract in the sense that it makes no commitments about how we write down expressions in terms of their constituents. Montague depicted the type I write as $\sigma \rightarrow \tau$ as the tuple $\langle \sigma, \tau \rangle$, and he was obviously thinking purely in terms of abstract syntax. Another common notation for $\sigma \rightarrow \tau$ is $(\sigma\tau)$.

In this chapter I discuss the *simply typed* λ-calculus, which derives its name from the rather straightforward structure of types that are assumed. Since Church's original formulation of the λ-calculus, there have been a great many type systems explored, ranging from what is often referred to as the *untyped* λ-calculus, which is actually better described as the *monotyped* λ-calculus, as every object is of the same type, to very sophisticated type systems employing parametric and inheritance-based polymorphism.

An example of a *parametric type* is **List**$(\sigma) \rightarrow$ **Set**(σ), which one could think of as a function from lists of type σ to sets of type σ, where σ could be any type. Such a type might be assigned to a generic algorithm that returns the elements of a list of type σ as a set of type σ or that computes identity between pairs of terms of arbitrary type. A parametric type is said to be *polymorphic* because it represents a possibly infinite set of instantiated types (see Gunter 1992). I apply polymorphic types in our analysis of boolean coordination in section 6.1, where the meaning of *and* and *or* can be applied to an infinite variety of types.

It is also possible to enrich the type language by allowing statements such as **Int** $\subseteq$ **Real**, which tells us that the integer type is a subset of the real type. A function of type **Real** $\rightarrow$ **Bool**, such as a nonzero test, would then be polymorphic in the sense that it could also be applied to objects of type **Int**, as every integer is a real. Operations on reals can thus be *inherited* by integers. Care must be taken, though, in determining the output domain; operations such as the square root, which would be of type **Real** $\rightarrow$ **Real**, obviously can not be applied to integers with integer results, though it could be applied to integers to produce real results. Inheritance-based polymorphic types are a key component in object-oriented programming and can be found in the Common Lisp Object System (CLOS), Smalltalk, and C^{++}, whereas parametric types are at the heart of strongly typed functional programming languages such as ML. In linguistics, only the simply typed λ-calculus has been explored in any detail, though the monotyped system is coming under scrutiny for its possible applications for *nominalization*, as can be found in sentences such as the following:

(3) To study λ-calculus is fascinating.

This example, with a verb-phrase subject, can be likened to a similar example such as *Sandy is fascinating*, with a simple noun-phrase subject. Thus we might want verb phrases such as *to study λ-calculus* to share the same type as noun phrases. This approach has been studied by Chierchia and Turner (1988; Chierchia 1982, 1984a).

2.2   λ-TERMS

We build up expressions in the λ-calculus out of variables and constants of the various types. Thus we assume for each type τ that we have the following sets.

(4) a. **Var**$_\tau$: a countably infinite set of *variables* of type τ
   b. **Con**$_\tau$: a collection of *constants* of type τ

Variables will be employed as in first-order logic to allow us to express binding operations such as quantification. But variables will also be used in the construction of new function terms, in much the same way as the x and y are used in the definition of f by $f(x,y) = x^2 - y^2$. It is common practice to write a variable down with some annotation on its type, such as x^τ, if x is a variable of type τ. I will generally omit the types on variables when they can be inferred by context or are not significant but will explicitly mention them otherwise. In particular, in the same context x^τ and x will count as two occurrences of the same variable. I thus define collections of constants and variables that includes all elements of all types.

(5) a. **Var** $= \bigcup_{\tau \in \mathbf{Typ}} \mathbf{Var}_\tau$
   b. **Con** $= \bigcup_{\tau \in \mathbf{Typ}} \mathbf{Con}_\tau$

The study of precise systems of *type inference*, which show exactly when types can be inferred from context, is a rich area of computational investigation, especially for type systems more complicated than the simple one I have introduced here. For instance, the programming language ML involves a very rich type-inference system used at compile time to make sure that type errors cannot occur at run time (Milner 1978; Milner, Tofte, and Harper 1991). I also employ constants just as in first-order logic. In particular, we might have a constant **run** of type **Ind** $\rightarrow$ **Bool**. I will also employ constants for the logical operations, so that **not** will be a constant of type **Bool** $\rightarrow$ **Bool**. This is rather unlike the first-order-logic case, in which the logical connectives were defined by special clauses in the definition of the language. In general, this latter kind of rule-based approach to defining logical operators is said to be *syncategorematic*.

We build the λ-terms by recursion, in a way similar to the construction of formulas and terms in first-order logic.

DEFINITION: λ-TERMS   The collections **Term**$_\tau$ of λ-*terms* of type τ are defined by mutual recursion as the smallest sets such that

a. **Var**$_\tau \subseteq$ **Term**$_\tau$,
b. **Con**$_\tau \subseteq$ **Term**$_\tau$,
c. $(\alpha(\beta)) \in$ **Term**$_\tau$ if $\alpha \in$ **Term**$_{\sigma \rightarrow \tau}$ and $\beta \in$ **Term**$_\sigma$,
d. $\lambda x.(\alpha) \in$ **Term**$_\tau$ if $\tau = \sigma \rightarrow \rho$ and $x \in$ **Var**$_\sigma$ and $\alpha \in$ **Term**$_\rho$.

A term of the form $(\alpha(\beta))$, usually abbreviated to $\alpha(\beta)$, is said to be a *functional application* of α to β. We will have terms such as **run(lee)** of type **Bool** if **run** is a constant of type **Ind** $\rightarrow$ **Bool** and **lee** is a constant of type **Ind**. Similarly, if **quickly** is a constant of type (**Ind** $\rightarrow$ **Bool**) $\rightarrow$ **Ind** $\rightarrow$ **Bool**, then **quickly(run)** will be a term of type **Ind** $\rightarrow$ **Bool**, or in other words, the same type as **run** itself. Similarly, (**quickly(run)**)(**lee**) is a term of type **Bool**, just like **run(lee)**.

A term of the form $\lambda x.(\alpha)$ is said to be a *functional abstraction*. The λ-calculus gets its name from the original notation involving the Greek letter λ, used by Church in the original definition of abstraction terms. Application must always involve a functional type, while abstraction always produces a functional type. For instance, assuming x is a variable of type **Ind**, we have an abstraction term such as $\lambda x.(\textbf{like}(x)(\textbf{ricky}))$. We think of such a term as denoting a function from individuals to the proposition that they were liked by Ricky. The order of variables is, of course, conventional, and in the next chapter I will discuss the interpretation of such terms in higher-order logic.

To eliminate parentheses, I associate functional application to the left, writing $\alpha(\beta)(\gamma)$ for $(\alpha(\beta))(\gamma)$. Some authors simply use $\alpha\beta$ or sometimes $(\alpha\ \beta)$ for $\alpha(\beta)$. I also assume that application has precedence over abstraction, so I write $\lambda x.(\alpha(x)(y))$ as $\lambda x.\alpha(x)(y)$.

I define free variables for λ-terms in a way similar to that employed for first-order expressions, but the definition is significantly simpler and more elegant, because λ is the only binding operator, and function application is the only constructor. Compare the following definition with its first-order counterpart, in which universal quantifiers bind variables, conjunction and negation are logical constructors, and both functional and relational application are nonlogical constructors.

DEFINITION: FREE AND BOUND VARIABLES   The set Free(α) of *free variables* of the λ-term α is defined by

a. Free$(x) = \{x\}$ if $x \in$ **Var**,
b. Free$(c) = \emptyset$ if $c \in$ **Con**,
c. Free$(\alpha(\beta)) =$ Free$(\alpha) \cup$ Free(β),
d. Free$(\lambda x.\alpha) =$ Free$(\alpha) - \{x\}$.

A variable that is not free is said to be *bound*.

Note that the free variables of $\lambda x.\alpha$ include all of the free variables in α except x. In $\lambda x.\alpha$, all of the free occurrences of x in α are bound by the outermost abstraction, so α is said to be the *scope* of binding for λx in $\lambda x.\alpha$. For instance, in $\lambda x.y(x)(\lambda x.z(x))$, the scope of the outermost λx is $y(x)(\lambda x.z(x))$ and the scope of the innermost λx is $z(x)$; the occurrence of x in the subterm $y(x)$ is bound by the outer λ-abstraction, and the occurrence of x in $z(x)$ is bound by the inner λ-abstraction; both y and z remain free. A λ-term with no free variables is said to be *closed*. I write $[x \mapsto \alpha]$ for the syntactic substitution that acts on a term by replacing free occurrences of the variable x with the term α. Note that x and α must be of the same type.

DEFINITION: SUBSTITUTION   The result $\alpha[x \mapsto \beta]$ of the *substitution* of β for the free occurrences of x in α is defined by

a. $x[x \mapsto \beta] = \beta$,
b. $y[x \mapsto \beta] = y$ if $y \in \textbf{Var}$, $x \neq y$,
c. $c[x \mapsto \beta] = c$ if $c \in \textbf{Con}$,
d. $\alpha(\gamma)[x \mapsto \beta] = \alpha[x \mapsto \beta](\gamma[x \mapsto \beta])$,
e. $(\lambda x.\alpha)[x \mapsto \beta] = \lambda x.\alpha$,
f. $(\lambda y.\alpha)[x \mapsto \beta] = \lambda y.(\alpha[x \mapsto \beta])$ if $x \neq y$.

The fact that we only substitute β for free occurrences of x is guaranteed by the fact that if we try to substitute for x in $\lambda x.\alpha$, the result is simply $\lambda x.\alpha$, because there can be no free occurrences of x in α. Just as in first-order logic, it is possible to inadvertently bind variables during a substitution. For instance, consider the following case.

(6) $(\lambda x.\textbf{foo}(x)(y))[y \mapsto \textbf{bar}(x)] = \lambda x.\textbf{foo}(x)(\textbf{bar}(x))$.

Here the variable x in $\textbf{bar}(x)$ is bound by the abstraction after the substitution. We have to be careful about this case when we consider proof theory. To this end, I define the notion of a term being free for a variable in another term. In words, a term α is free for the variable x in the term β if none of the free variables in α become bound when substituting α for x in β.

DEFINITION: FREEDOM FOR SUBSTITUTION   We say that the term α is *free for* x in β, which we write FreeFor(α, x, β), if and only if one of the following holds:

a. $\beta \in \textbf{Con}$
b. $\beta \in \textbf{Var}$
c. $\beta = \gamma(\delta)$ and FreeFor(α, x, γ) and FreeFor(α, x, δ)
d. $\beta = \lambda y.\gamma$ and FreeFor(α, x, γ) and either $x \notin$ Free(γ) or $y \notin$ Free(α)

Note that this definition simply merges parts of the definition of $\beta[x \mapsto \alpha]$ and Free. For instance, **run**(y) is free for x in $\lambda z.z(x)$, but not in $\lambda z.\lambda y.z(y)(x)$.

2.3   FUNCTIONAL MODELS

Models of the simply typed λ-calculus are quite straightforward, more or less following the pattern of first-order models, only without the logical content. In particular, a model of the simply typed λ-calculus consists of a domain of objects for each type and an assignment of a domain element of the appropriate type to each constant. I proceed in two steps, first discussing the domains, which are known as *frames*, and then proceeding to the models proper.

2.3.1   Frames

In first-order logic, a model consists of a domain of individuals, along with an assignment of values to constants. Things look much the same with the λ-calculus, except that there is a separate domain for each of the types. Only the basic domains need to be specified in a model; domains for functional types are generated from the basic domains.

DEFINITION: FRAME   A *frame* for the collection **BasTyp** consists of a collection **Dom** $= \bigcup_{\tau \in \mathbf{BasTyp}} \mathbf{Dom}_\tau$ of *basic domains*. Domains for functional types are defined by

$$\mathbf{Dom}_{\alpha \to \beta} = \mathbf{Dom}_\beta^{\mathbf{Dom}_\alpha} = \{f \mid f : \mathbf{Dom}_\alpha \to \mathbf{Dom}_\beta\}.$$

In words, the domains **Dom**$_\tau$ for basic types τ are stipulated as part of the definition of a frame. Domains for functional types $\sigma \to \tau$ are taken to be functions from the domain of type σ to the domain of type τ. I assume that the elements of a functional domain are total functions. It is not at all straightforward to extend the simply typed λ-calculus to models allowing partial functions, though Muskens (1989a, 1989b) and Barwise and Etchemendy (1987) provide relational alternatives. On the other hand, when considering higher-order logic in the next chapter, we will consider frames in which the domain assigned to a functional type need not consist of all of the total functions from its argument type to its result type, although each function in such a frame is required to be total over its domain.

2.3.2 Models

Just as in the propositional and first-order models, models for the simply typed λ-calculus are built up by assigning each constant symbol to a member of the appropriate domain.

DEFINITION: MODEL OF THE SIMPLY TYPED λ-CALCULUS   A *model* of the simply typed λ-calculus is a pair $\mathscr{M} = \langle \mathbf{Dom}, [\![\cdot]\!] \rangle$ in which

a. **Dom** is a frame,
b. the *interpretation function* $[\![\cdot]\!]$: **Con** $\rightarrow$ **Dom** respects typing so that $[\![\alpha]\!] \in \mathbf{Dom}_\tau$ if $\alpha \in \mathbf{Con}_\tau$.

For example, assuming we have atomic types **Ind** and **Bool**, we might take $\mathbf{Dom_{Ind}}$ to consist of all of the members of Congress and $\mathbf{Dom_{Bool}}$ to be the set $\{\mathbf{yes}, \mathbf{no}\}$ of truth values. We could then interpret **pat** to be a Congressperson named Pat. Similarly, we could interpret **lie** as the function from members of Congress to truth values in which a Congressperson who lied would be mapped to **yes** and those who never lied would be mapped to **no**. Thus if Pat lied, then $[\![\mathbf{lie}]\!]$ would be a function that mapped the individual named Pat to **yes**.

As is standard for first-order logic, I use assignments of values to variables to extend the interpretation function $[\![\cdot]\!]$ to arbitrary terms. For the simply typed λ-calculus, an *assignment* consists of a function θ: **Var** $\rightarrow$ **Dom** such that $\theta(x) \in \mathbf{Dom}_\tau$ if $x \in \mathbf{Var}_\tau$. In words, an assignment is a function mapping variables to elements of the domain of the appropriate type. It is very important to keep in mind the distinction between assignments and substitutions. Substitutions map variables to terms, whereas assignments map variables to objects in the domain. Substitutions will play a role in the proof theory, while assignments provide the second half of the link between expressions and their denotation (with the interpretation function providing the first half).

Denotations for arbitrary terms are constructed recursively as follows:

DEFINITION: DENOTATION   The *denotation* $[\![\alpha]\!]^\theta_{\mathscr{M}}$ of a term α with respect to the model $\mathscr{M} = \langle \mathbf{Dom}, [\![\cdot]\!] \rangle$ and assignment θ is given by

a. $[\![x]\!]^\theta_{\mathscr{M}} = \theta(x)$ if $x \in \mathbf{Var}$,
b. $[\![c]\!]^\theta_{\mathscr{M}} = [\![c]\!]$ if $c \in \mathbf{Con}$,
c. $[\![\alpha(\beta)]\!]^\theta_{\mathscr{M}} = [\![\alpha]\!]^\theta_{\mathscr{M}}([\![\beta]\!]^\theta_{\mathscr{M}})$,
d. $[\![\lambda x.\alpha]\!]^\theta_{\mathscr{M}} = f$ such that $f(a) = [\![\alpha]\!]^{\theta[x:=a]}_{\mathscr{M}}$.

We take $\theta[x := a]$ to be the assignment that maps x to a and maps $y \neq x$ to $\theta(y)$. I intentionally use a notation here that is similar to an assignment statement in an imperative programming language such as Pascal or C. We can think of an assignment as a store, albeit an infinite one, that assigns values to variables, with the role of $[x := a]$ being that of updating the store. It is important to keep in mind that $\alpha[x \mapsto \beta]$ substitutes a term β for the variable x in the term α, whereas $\theta[x := a]$ updates the value of x to the object a in the assignment function θ. The last case in the definition is worth unpacking and discussing in some detail. First, note that the definition is very similar to that of the quantified formulas in first-order logic, as both definitions involve updating the assignment function and then evaluating the scope of the binding operator. Second, note that a term of the form $\lambda x.\alpha$ must be of a functional type, such as $\sigma \to \rho$. The denotation of the term $\lambda x.\alpha$ is then defined so that it is a function in this domain, mapping an element $a \in \mathbf{Dom}_\sigma$ to the element $f(a) \in \mathbf{Dom}_\rho$ that is the result of evaluating α under an assignment where x takes the value a. Intuitively, applying the denotation of a functional term $\lambda x.\alpha$ to an object a is the result of evaluating α in an assignment where x takes the value a.

We assume in the definition of denotation that we are dealing with well-formed terms, so that, in particular, for the term $\alpha(\beta)$, there are types σ and τ such that α is a term of type $\sigma \to \tau$ and β is a term of type σ. It is important to verify that this definition respects our typing, which is the point of the following theorem:

THEOREM: TYPE SOUNDNESS   If α is a term of type τ, then $[\![\alpha]\!]^\theta_{\mathscr{M}} \in \mathbf{Dom}_\tau$ for every model $\mathscr{M}$ and assignment θ.

Proof A simple induction on terms suffices. The result obviously holds for variables and constants by the definition of assignments and models, respectively. In the case of a term $\alpha(\beta)$ of type τ, we may assume that α is of type $\sigma \to \tau$ and β is of type σ, as this is the only way in which $\alpha(\beta)$ can be of type τ. By induction, we know that $[\![\alpha]\!]^\theta_{\mathscr{M}} \in \mathbf{Dom}_{\sigma \to \tau} = \mathbf{Dom}_\tau^{\mathbf{Dom}_\sigma}$ and that $[\![\beta]\!]^\theta_{\mathscr{M}} \in \mathbf{Dom}_\sigma$. Thus $[\![\alpha(\beta)]\!]^\theta_{\mathscr{M}} = [\![\alpha]\!]^\theta_{\mathscr{M}}([\![\beta]\!]^\theta_{\mathscr{M}}) \in \mathbf{Dom}_\tau$. Finally, if we assume that $\lambda x.\alpha$ is of type τ, then we must have $\tau = \sigma \to \rho$ for some types σ and ρ, with $x \in \mathbf{Var}_\sigma$ and $\alpha \in \mathbf{Term}_\rho$. Assuming by induction that $[\![\alpha]\!]^{\theta'}_{\mathscr{M}} \in \mathbf{Dom}_\rho$ for every assignment θ', we know that $[\![\lambda x.\alpha]\!]^\theta_{\mathscr{M}}$ is a function f mapping objects $a \in \mathbf{Dom}_\sigma$ to $[\![\alpha]\!]^{\theta[x := a]}_{\mathscr{M}}$, which we know by induction to be an element of $\mathbf{Dom}_\rho$. Thus f is a member of $\mathbf{Dom}_{\sigma \to \rho}$, and hence $[\![\lambda x.\alpha]\!]^\theta_{\mathscr{M}} \in \mathbf{Dom}_{\sigma \to \rho}$. $\square$

As with first-order logic, the identity of bound variables is irrelevant, and closed terms have the same value under all assignments (recall that a closed term is one with no free variables). I make this notion precise when I present a proof theory for the simply typed λ-calculus in the next section. A λ-term without constants is said to be *pure*. Thus if α is a closed pure λ-term, then its denotation depends only on the frame, because there are no constants to be interpreted by the model. Our notion of equivalence of λ-terms is the same as that of formulas in first-order logic, namely that two terms are equivalent if they take the same value in every model and assignment.

DEFINITION: LOGICAL EQUIVALENCE   Two λ-terms α and β are said to be *logically equivalent*, in symbols, $\alpha \equiv \beta$, if and only if $[\![\alpha]\!]_{\mathscr{M}}^{\theta} = [\![\beta]\!]_{\mathscr{M}}^{\theta}$ for every model $\mathscr{M}$ and assignment θ.

Of course, two terms of different types will never be logically equivalent. But note that it is possible for terms of different types to take the same denotation in some models, because nothing in our definition prevents different types from being interpreted over the same domains.

Besides logical equivalences, there are close connections between some of the functional domains. Because the λ-calculus forces arguments to be attached one at a time, some order must be chosen if there is more than one argument. But which order is merely a matter of convention. To see this, note that in general we can use the λ-calculus to define a one-to-one and onto function between the domain of type $\sigma \to \tau \to \rho$ and the domain of type $\tau \to \sigma \to \rho$ for any types σ, τ, and ρ. We take $\mathbf{perm}_{\sigma,\tau,\rho}$ to be an abbreviation defined as follows.

$$(7) \quad \mathbf{perm}_{\sigma,\tau,\rho} \stackrel{\text{def}}{=} \lambda f^{\sigma \to \tau \to \rho}. \lambda x^{\tau}. \lambda y^{\sigma}. f(y)(x)$$

Note that there is a distinct term $\mathbf{perm}_{\sigma,\tau,\rho}$ for each triple of types, but I will typically drop such type information when it can be deduced from context. Given the definition in (7), the term $\mathbf{perm}(\mathbf{like})(\mathbf{a})(\mathbf{b})$ is logically equivalent to $\mathbf{like}(\mathbf{b})(\mathbf{a})$. We will see more examples of such domain relations when we turn to products and sums. Further note that applying $\mathbf{perm}_{\sigma,\tau,\rho}$ to the result of applying $\mathbf{perm}_{\tau,\sigma,\rho}$ to a function of type $\sigma \to \tau \to \rho$ is equivalent to that function; in symbols, $\mathbf{perm}_{\tau,\sigma,\rho}(\mathbf{perm}_{\sigma,\tau,\rho}(f^{\sigma \to \tau \to \rho})) \equiv f$.

There are some other well known operations on functions that can be defined in the λ-calculus. For instance, *functional composition* can be defined as follows.

$$(8) \quad \mathbf{comp}_{\sigma,\tau,\rho} \stackrel{\text{def}}{=} \lambda g^{\tau \to \rho}. \lambda f^{\sigma \to \tau}. \lambda x^{\sigma}. g(f(x))$$

I employ the following standard infix notation for functional composition.

(9) $\beta \circ \alpha \overset{\text{def}}{=} \textbf{comp}(\beta)(\alpha)$

Thus we have $(\beta \circ \alpha)(\gamma) \equiv \beta(\alpha(\gamma))$, assuming the terms are well typed. Note that with simple types, we need a different composition function for every triple of types.

Another useful class of functions are the *identity functions*, which map type τ objects to themselves. The identity function of type τ is defined as follows.

(10) $\textbf{I}_\tau \overset{\text{def}}{=} \lambda x^\tau . x$

Clearly we have $\textbf{I}_\tau(\alpha) \equiv \alpha$.

2.4 PROOF THEORY FOR SIMPLY TYPED λ-CALCULUS

The term *calculus*, as it is employed in logic, refers to a formal system defined purely syntactically, as in standard proof theories for propositional and first-order logic. While in common use, it is not quite accurate to refer to the model-theoretic portion of the λ-calculus as a calculus. The proof theory for the typed λ-calculus turns out to be much simpler than that for first-order logic, primarily because we do not have the logical constants to contend with. The rules for the λ-calculus are somewhat different than those for first-order logic in that they involve direct proofs of logical equivalence. In particular, what we prove in the proof system for the λ-calculus is that two terms are equivalent, whereas proof theories for classical first-order logic traditionally formalize logical consequence in terms of provability. Because there is no logic associated with the λ-calculus, these notions are not even defined in this system. In the next chapter we turn to a special instance of the λ-calculus, higher-order logic, in which notions such as satisfiability, validity, and logical consequence make their first appearance.

The axioms of the typed λ-calculus have standard names, due originally to Curry and Feys (1961). Note that the axioms are directional, involving the symbol $\Rightarrow$, referred to as *reduction*. The reason for this is that if the relation $\alpha \Rightarrow \beta$ holds between λ-terms, then in a sense I define below, β is simpler than α. The reduction relation induces what is known as a *rewriting system*. I employ this rewriting system to characterize logical equivalence indirectly: two λ-terms turn out to be logically equivalent if and only if the rewriting system reduces them to a common result. We extend the basic cases of reduction in the axioms with inference rules, which I will present after the axiom schemes.

DEFINITION: AXIOMS FOR SIMPLY TYPED λ-CALCULUS   The axioms of the simply typed λ-calculus consist of all of the instances of the following three schemes:

a. $\vdash \lambda x.\alpha \Rightarrow \lambda y.(\alpha[x \mapsto y])$ (α-reduction)
   $[y \notin \text{Free}(\alpha)$ and y is free for x in $\alpha]$
b. $\vdash (\lambda x.\alpha)(\beta) \Rightarrow \alpha[x \mapsto \beta]$ (β-reduction)
   $[\beta$ free for x in $\alpha]$
c. $\vdash \lambda x.(\alpha(x)) \Rightarrow \alpha$ (η-reduction)
   $[x \notin \text{Free}(\alpha)]$

It is worth considering these schemes fairly closely, as they play a substantial role in subsequent developments. Before doing this, it is important to keep in mind that we are implicitly requiring all of the terms mentioned in our schemes to be appropriately typed. For instance, in the α-reduction scheme, x and y must be variables of the same type. For β-reduction, we require β and x to be of the same type. Finally, in the η-reduction scheme, we need α to be of functional type $\sigma \to \tau$ and x to be a variable of argument type σ. It is standard to refer to a formula on the left-hand side of a β-reduction or η-reduction as a β-redex or η-redex, and the corresponding right-hand side as a β-contractum or η-contractum.

The schemes of β-reduction and η-reduction can be used to simplify the terms on the left-hand side of the rewriting, in a sense to be made clear shortly, which is why the schemes are referred to as reductions. The α-reduction scheme, on the other hand, is provided to allow us to change the names of variables during a reduction, which allows us to avoid getting into trouble with the conditions of application for the rules, as we see below. It is important to note that while β- and η-reduction appear to be similar, in fact, β-reduction applies to terms of the form $\alpha(\beta)$ in which $\alpha = \lambda x.\alpha'$, whereas η applies to terms of the form $\lambda x.\alpha$ with $\alpha = \alpha'(x)$.

The first scheme, α-reduction, tells us that we can freely rename bound variables. In words, α-reduction states that we can replace a binding of x over α with a binding of y by replacing the free occurrences of x in α with y. To ensure that the rule is sound, we need to be careful about the two application conditions. First, we should not bind any occurrences of y that might be free in α. For instance, the rule does not hold in the case of $\lambda x.\textbf{like}(x)(y)$, which is obviously not equivalent to $\lambda y.\textbf{like}(y)(y)$. The problem is that there is a free occurrence of y in $\alpha = \textbf{like}(x)(y)$. Second, we have to make sure that the y substituted for x is not bound in $\alpha[x \mapsto y]$. For instance, y is not free for x in $\lambda y.\mathbf{like}(x)(y)$, and thus the term $\lambda x.\lambda y.\mathbf{like}(x)(y)$ is not equivalent to $\lambda y.(\lambda y.\mathbf{like}(x)(y)[x \mapsto y])$, which is $\lambda y.\lambda y.\mathbf{like}(y)(y)$. Under the application conditions, the α rule allows us to change the names of bound variables as long as no accidental bindings occur. Many authors simply identify two terms that are provably equivalent using α-reduction. I introduce a notation for equivalence of terms up to the names of bound variables, write $\beta =_\alpha \gamma$, and say that β and γ are *α-equivalent* or *alphabetic variants* if and only if β is provably equivalent to γ using only the scheme of α-reduction and the rules of inference to be presented below.

The β-reduction scheme defines the result of applying an abstraction to an argument in terms of substituting the argument for the variable abstracted. Again, we have to be careful about the application condition, which requires β to be free for x in α. Thus we cannot reduce the term $(\lambda x.\lambda y.\mathbf{like}(y)(x))(\mathbf{mother\_of}(y))$ to $\lambda y.\mathbf{like}(y)(x)[x \mapsto \mathbf{mother\_of}(y)]$, which is just $\lambda y.\mathbf{like}(y)(\mathbf{mother\_of}(y))$. Below, we will see that the α-reduction rules will, in general, allow us to rename the variables of the function term before proceeding with β-reduction. For instance, the term $\lambda x.\lambda y.\mathbf{like}(y)(x)$ will be provably equivalent to $\lambda w.\lambda z.\mathbf{like}(z)(w)$, which we can then apply to the term $\mathbf{mother\_of}(y)$ to produce $\lambda z.\mathbf{like}(z)(\mathbf{mother\_of}(y))$.

The β-reduction scheme takes on additional significance in the context of higher-order functional programming languages such as Lisp or ML, where it is used to evaluate functions. For instance, consider a Lisp definition of the squaring function.

(11) (DEFUN SQUARE(x) (TIMES x x))

This establishes the name SQUARE as an abbreviation for the following λ-term, in Lisp notation.

(12) (LAMBDA (x) (TIMES x x))

Evaluating a call to this function, such as (SQUARE 2), involves replacing SQUARE with its definition to yield the following result.

(13) ((LAMBDA (x) (TIMES x x)) 2)

This term is then β-reduced to (TIMES 2 2), at which point the built-in definition for the primitive constants TIMES and 2 are evaluated to produce a result.

The η-reduction scheme allows us to prove that applying a term of functional type to a variable of the appropriate type and then abstracting over that variable does not change the meaning of the term. For instance, it allows us to prove that $\lambda x.\textbf{like}(x)$ and **like** are equivalent as long as everything is of the right type. But we have to be careful again that no variables are inadvertently bound in the process. For example, the term $\lambda x.((\textbf{like}(x))(x))$ is not equivalent to $\textbf{like}(x)$, but this would arise from η-reduction with $\alpha = \textbf{like}(x)$ without the application condition prohibiting x from occurring freely in α.

There is a close connection between the η-reduction scheme and the notion of extensionality in the theory of functions. In general, we say that a theory of functions is *extensional* if we can derive the equivalence of f and g from the fact that $f(a) = g(a)$ for every object a in the domain. Note that the two sides of the η-reduction, the redex $\lambda x.\alpha(x)$ and the contractum α, must denote the same value because of how we have defined functions solely in terms of their input/output pairs. By the β-reduction scheme, applying either of the two terms to a term β results in $\alpha(\beta)$. We need the η-reduction scheme for a complete axiomatization of the simply typed λ-calculus, because we adopt a classical set-theoretical interpretation of functions as sets of ordered pairs describing their actions on inputs. In other versions of the λ-calculus, such as the monotyped one, it is possible to find quite reasonable models that are not extensional. Such nonextensional models are often employed in the theory of computability, where λ-terms are identified with computer programs, and only operationally identical programs (those that go through the same steps in a computation) are identified. In this way it is possible to distinguish two programs that produce the same output for every input. For instance, merge sort and insertion sort are extensionally identical but are not the same program. Nonextensional λ-calculi have potential applications in natural-language semantics in procedural interpretations of natural-language expressions and in the semantics of so-called *propositional attitudes*, which I discuss in section 11.1.2.

The rules of inference for the λ-calculus take the closure of the axioms in two ways. First, they allow reflexive and transitive application of the rules, thus allowing us to prove that a term is equivalent to itself and that if α reduces to β and β reduces to γ, then α can reduce to γ. They also allow us to take what is known as the *congruence closure* of the rules, meaning that logically equivalent terms may be freely substituted for one another in terms without a change in meaning. The final scheme introduces the relation $\Leftrightarrow$, which we refer to as *provable equivalence*. My axiomatization of provable equivalence relies on the *Church-Rosser theorem*, which states that two terms are logically equivalent if and only if they are reducible to the same result solely by the application of reduction rules.

DEFINITION: RULES OF INFERENCE   The rules of inference for the simply typed λ-calculus consist of all of the instances of the following schemes:

a. $\vdash \alpha \Rightarrow \alpha$ (Reflexivity)
b. $\alpha \Rightarrow \beta, \beta \Rightarrow \gamma \vdash \alpha \Rightarrow \gamma$ (Transitivity)
c. $\alpha \Rightarrow \alpha', \beta \Rightarrow \beta' \vdash \alpha(\beta) \Rightarrow \alpha'(\beta')$ (Congruence)
d. $\alpha \Rightarrow \alpha' \vdash \lambda x.\alpha \Rightarrow \lambda x.\alpha'$ (Congruence)
e. $\alpha \Rightarrow \gamma, \beta \Rightarrow \gamma \vdash \alpha \Leftrightarrow \beta$ (Equivalence)

I adopt the standard definition of proof in axiomatic systems.

DEFINITION: PROOF   A proof of ϕ from Ψ is a sequence $\phi_0, \ldots, \phi_n$ such that $\phi = \phi_n$ and for every ϕ_i, one of the following holds:

a. $\phi_i \in \Psi$
b. ϕ_i is an axiom
c. $\Phi \vdash \phi_i$ is an inference rule with $\Phi \subseteq \{\phi_0, \ldots, \phi_{i-1}\}$

We write $\Psi \vdash \phi$ if there is a proof of ϕ from Ψ.

Thus every step of a proof is either an assumption in Ψ, an axiom, or else follows by one of the inference rules from a subset of the formulas derived in the previous steps. We write $\vdash \phi$ as a shorthand for $\emptyset \vdash \phi$, indicating that ϕ is provable from the empty set of assumptions. If $\vdash \phi$ holds, we say that ϕ is a *theorem*. Notice that I have overloaded our notation somewhat, using the same symbol, $\vdash$, for axioms, rules of inference, and provability. But as can be seen from the definition, inference rules and axioms are just the base cases of provability. The definition of proof could be simplified by noticing that axioms, according to our notation, are simply inference rules with an empty set of antecedents.

As usual, it is important to demonstrate that the axioms and inference rules are sound. That is, I will show that two terms are provably equivalent only if they are logically equivalent. Before proceeding with this soundness result, I pause to prove a lemma that says that the denotation of a term under a substitution is not sensitive to the value of the substitution on variables not free in the term.

LEMMA: If $x \notin \text{Free}(\alpha)$, then $[\![\alpha]\!]^\theta_{\mathscr{M}} = [\![\alpha]\!]^{\theta[x:=a]}_{\mathscr{M}}$.

Proof We proceed by induction on the structure of α. If α is a constant, the result is obvious, since the denotation of a constant depends only on the model. If α is a variable y, then $y \neq x$, since $x \notin \text{Free}(\alpha)$. Hence

$$[\![y]\!]^\theta_{\mathscr{M}} = \theta(y) = [\![y]\!]^{\theta[x:=a]}_{\mathscr{M}}.$$

If $\alpha = \beta(\gamma)$, we assume by induction that the result holds for β and γ. By means of this result,

$$[\![\beta(\gamma)]\!]^\theta_{\mathscr{M}} = [\![\beta]\!]^\theta_{\mathscr{M}}([\![\gamma]\!]^\theta_{\mathscr{M}}) = [\![\beta]\!]^{\theta[x:=a]}_{\mathscr{M}}([\![\gamma]\!]^{\theta[x:=a]}_{\mathscr{M}}) = [\![\beta(\gamma)]\!]^{\theta[x:=a]}_{\mathscr{M}}.$$

There are two cases to consider if α is an abstraction. First, if $\alpha = \lambda y.\beta$ and $x \neq y$, then we assume that the result holds for β, and see that

$$[\![\lambda y.\beta]\!]^\theta_{\mathscr{M}} = f \text{ such that } f(b) = [\![\beta]\!]^{\theta[y:=b]},$$

$$[\![\lambda y.\beta]\!]^{\theta[x:=a]}_{\mathscr{M}} = g \text{ such that } g(b) = [\![\beta]\!]^{\theta[x:=a][y:=b]}_{\mathscr{M}} = [\![\beta]\!]^{\theta[y:=b][x:=a]}_{\mathscr{M}}.$$

We were able to switch the order of updating the assignment because $x \neq y$. At this point the induction hypothesis ensures that $g(b) = f(b)$. Finally, if $\alpha = \lambda x.\beta$, we have

$$[\![\lambda x.\beta]\!]^\theta_{\mathscr{M}} = f \text{ such that } f(b) = [\![\beta]\!]^{\theta[x:=b]}_{\mathscr{M}},$$

$$[\![\lambda x.\beta]\!]^{\theta[x:=a]}_{\mathscr{M}} = g \text{ such that } g(b) = [\![\beta]\!]^{\theta[x:=a][x:=b]}_{\mathscr{M}} = [\![\beta]\!]^{\theta[x:=b]}_{\mathscr{M}}.$$

Note that $\theta[x := a][x := b] = \theta[x := b]$ by the definition of updates.   □

I will use this lemma in the proof of the soundness result, which tells us that the syntactic rules we have for reducing λ-terms always reduce a term to a simpler, logically equivalent term. Recall that we write $\alpha \equiv \beta$ if α and β are logically equivalent in the sense of having the same denotation in all models under all assignments.

THEOREM: SOUNDNESS   If $\vdash \alpha \Rightarrow \beta$, then $\alpha \equiv \beta$.

Proof We begin by verifying the axioms. First consider β-reduction. To prove that β-reduction is sound, we need to show that for all assignments θ and models $\mathscr{M}$, if β is free for x in α, we have

$$[\![(\lambda x.\alpha)(\beta)]\!]^\theta_{\mathscr{M}} = [\![\alpha[x \mapsto \beta]]\!]^\theta_{\mathscr{M}}.$$

We first note that by the definition of denotation, we have

$$[\![(\lambda x.\alpha)(\beta)]\!]^\theta_{\mathscr{M}} = [\![\lambda x.\alpha]\!]^\theta_{\mathscr{M}}([\![\beta]\!]^\theta_{\mathscr{M}}) = [\![\alpha]\!]^{\theta[x:=[\![\beta]\!]^\theta_{\mathscr{M}}]}_{\mathscr{M}}.$$

Thus it suffices to show that for every term α such that β is free for x in α, we have

$$[\![\alpha]\!]_{\mathcal{M}}^{\theta[x:=[\![\beta]\!]_{\mathcal{M}}^{\theta}]} = [\![\alpha[x \mapsto \beta]]\!]_{\mathcal{M}}^{\theta}.$$

We proceed by induction on the structure of α, which involves base cases for constants and variables and inductive steps for applications and abstractions.

For $\alpha = c \in \mathbf{Con}$, we have

$$[\![c]\!]_{\mathcal{M}}^{\theta[x:=[\![\beta]\!]_{\mathcal{M}}^{\theta}]} = [\![c]\!]_{\mathcal{M}}^{\theta} = [\![c[x \mapsto \beta]]\!]_{\mathcal{M}}^{\theta}.$$

If α is a variable, we have two subcases, depending on whether or not $\alpha = x$. First suppose that $\alpha = x$, in which case

$$[\![x]\!]_{\mathcal{M}}^{\theta[x:=[\![\beta]\!]_{\mathcal{M}}^{\theta}]} = [\![\beta]\!]_{\mathcal{M}}^{\theta} = [\![x[x \mapsto \beta]]\!]_{\mathcal{M}}^{\theta}.$$

The second subcase is where $\alpha = y \in \mathbf{Var}$ but $x \neq y$, in which case

$$[\![y]\!]_{\mathcal{M}}^{\theta[x:=[\![\beta]\!]_{\mathcal{M}}^{\theta}]} = [\![y]\!]_{\mathcal{M}}^{\theta} = [\![y[x \mapsto \beta]]\!]_{\mathcal{M}}^{\theta}.$$

We now move into the inductive steps and suppose that $\alpha = \gamma(\delta)$ and that β is free for x in $\gamma(\delta)$. Consequently, β is free for x in both γ and δ by definition. Furthermore, we assume by the inductive hypothesis that our result holds for γ and δ, so that

$$
\begin{aligned}
[\![\gamma(\delta)]\!]_{\mathcal{M}}^{\theta[x:=[\![\beta]\!]_{\mathcal{M}}^{\theta}]} &= [\![\gamma]\!]_{\mathcal{M}}^{\theta[x:=[\![\beta]\!]_{\mathcal{M}}^{\theta}]}([\![\delta]\!]_{\mathcal{M}}^{\theta[x:=[\![\beta]\!]_{\mathcal{M}}^{\theta}]}) \\
&= [\![\gamma[x \mapsto \beta]]\!]_{\mathcal{M}}^{\theta}([\![\delta[x \mapsto \beta]]\!]_{\mathcal{M}}^{\theta}) \\
&= [\![\gamma[x \mapsto \beta](\delta[x \mapsto \beta])]\!]_{\mathcal{M}}^{\theta} \\
&= [\![\gamma(\delta)[x \mapsto \beta]]\!]_{\mathcal{M}}^{\theta}.
\end{aligned}
$$

The final step to consider involves abstraction and again involves two subcases, depending on whether or not the abstracted variable is x. First, suppose $\alpha = \lambda x.\gamma$. Then by the definition of abstraction and update, we have

$$[\![\lambda x.\gamma]\!]_{\mathcal{M}}^{\theta[x:=[\![\beta]\!]_{\mathcal{M}}^{\theta}]} = f, \text{ where } f(a) = [\![\gamma]\!]_{\mathcal{M}}^{\theta[x:=[\![\beta]\!]_{\mathcal{M}}^{\theta}][x:=a]} = [\![\gamma]\!]_{\mathcal{M}}^{\theta[x:=a]}.$$

Working from the other side of the equation, we have

$$[\![(\lambda x.\gamma)[x \mapsto \beta]]\!]_{\mathcal{M}}^{\theta} = [\![\lambda x.\gamma]\!]_{\mathcal{M}}^{\theta} = f \text{ such that } f(a) = [\![\gamma]\!]_{\mathcal{M}}^{\theta[x:=a]}.$$

The final subcase we need to consider is the only tricky one and involves abstracting over a variable $y \neq x$ so that $\alpha = \lambda y.\gamma$. Again we assume the result holds for γ, in which case we have

$$[\![\lambda y.\gamma]\!]_{\mathcal{M}}^{\theta[x:=[\![\beta]\!]_{\mathcal{M}}^{\theta}]} = f \text{ such that } f(a) = [\![\gamma]\!]_{\mathcal{M}}^{\theta[x:=[\![\beta]\!]_{\mathcal{M}}^{\theta}][y:=a]}.$$

Note that we have already assumed that β is free for x in $\lambda x.\gamma$, and hence it is free for x in γ. Working again from the other side of the equation we are trying to establish, we have

$$[\![(\lambda y.\gamma)[x \mapsto \beta]]\!]_{\mathcal{M}}^{\theta} = [\![\lambda y.(\gamma[x \mapsto \beta])]\!]_{\mathcal{M}}^{\theta} = g$$

such that $g(a) = [\![\gamma[x \mapsto \beta]]\!]_{\mathcal{M}}^{\theta[y:=a]}$

We now need to consider the two subcases in which β is free for x in $\lambda y.\gamma$. One way in which this can happen is if $x \notin \text{Free}(\gamma)$. Thus we can apply the definition of substitution, the lemma, and the inductive hypothesis because β is free for x in γ by assumption. So

$$f(a) = [\![\gamma]\!]_{\mathcal{M}}^{\theta[x:=[\![\beta]\!]_{\mathcal{M}}^{\theta}][y:=a]} = [\![\gamma]\!]_{\mathcal{M}}^{\theta[y:=a]} = [\![\gamma[x \mapsto \beta]]\!]_{\mathcal{M}}^{\theta[y:=a]} = g(a).$$

The other subcase in which β is free for x in $\lambda y.\gamma$ occurs if $y \notin \text{Free}(\beta)$ and β is free for x in γ. In this case, we continue our derivation as follows:

$$f(a) = [\![\gamma]\!]_{\mathcal{M}}^{\theta[x:=[\![\beta]\!]_{\mathcal{M}}^{\theta}][y:=a]} = [\![\gamma]\!]_{\mathcal{M}}^{\theta[y:=a][x:=[\![\beta]\!]_{\mathcal{M}}^{\theta}]}$$
$$= [\![\gamma]\!]_{\mathcal{M}}^{\theta[y:=a][x:=[\![\beta]\!]_{\mathcal{M}}^{\theta[y:=a]}]} = [\![\gamma[x \mapsto \beta]]\!]^{\theta[y:=a]} = g(a)$$

We are able to switch the order of our updates of x and y in θ because $x \neq y$. Furthermore, the lemma shows that we get the same result by evaluating β in θ as we do in $\theta[y := a]$, because y is not free in β, according to the assumption of the second subcase.

I leave the proof of the soundness of α-reduction and η-reduction as exercises. They are considerably simpler than the β-reduction case.

The soundness of the rules of inference are all straightforward. Reflexivity and transitivity are obvious from the definition of equality. Congruence in the case of applications and abstractions simply follows from the definition of denotation. $\square$

One of the most significant results concerning reductions in the λ-calculus is the Church-Rosser theorem, in part because of its role in establishing the completeness of the proof theory.

THEOREM: CHURCH-ROSSER   If $\vdash \alpha \Rightarrow \beta$ and $\vdash \alpha \Rightarrow \gamma$, then there is some δ such that $\vdash \beta \Rightarrow \delta$ and $\vdash \gamma \Rightarrow \delta$.

Proof   The two standard proofs can both be found in Barendregt 1981. The basic idea is to use structural induction to show that if the two terms β and γ can be rewritten using an axiom applied to a subterm in one step, then there is a further sequence of steps that can reduce them to a common term. This result is then extended to arbitrary sequences of rewritings by induction on the length of a rewriting sequence.   ☐

The importance of the Church-Rosser theorem is that it tells us that the order in which we reduce subterms of a term is not important, in that we can always return to an equivalent result by further rewritings.

The other significant theorem concerning reduction over the simply typed λ-calculus is that reduction eventually terminates with a term that can no longer be reduced using β- or η-reduction. Such a term is said to be in *normal form*.

DEFINITION: β, η NORMAL FORM   A λ-term α is in β, η *normal form* if and only if there is no subterm γ of α that has an alphabetic variant $\gamma' =_\alpha \gamma$ such that γ' is either a β-redex or an η-redex.

In other words, a term is in β, η normal form if and only if it does not have a subterm that can be reduced by either the β-reduction or η-reduction after renaming variables using α-reduction. The use of α-reduction is important; if it is not possible to apply β-reduction or η-reduction to a subterm due to a violation of the application side conditions, we can use α-reduction to rename all bound variables.

The following theorem tells us that every term is normalizable by applying a finite number of reductions. This property is known as *strong normalization*; some systems of the λ-calculus, such as the monotyped variety, have unique normal forms when normal forms exist, but not every term reduces to a normal form.

THEOREM: STRONG NORMALIZATION   There are no infinitely long sequences of terms $\alpha_1, \ldots, \alpha_n, \ldots$ such that for $i > 0$, $\vdash \alpha_i \Rightarrow \alpha_{i+1}$ and $\alpha_i \neq_\alpha \alpha_{i+1}$.

Proof   The proof of strong normalization is quite involved. The standard proof, employing a method of Tait's (1967), can be found in Hindley and Seldin 1986, Appendix 2 and Thompson 1991, 44–50. The proof proceeds by an induction over a measure defined on the structure of the types of the terms, rather than over the structure of the terms themselves.   ☐

Note that the strong normalization theorem says just that the reduction relation $\Rightarrow$ forms a well-founded ordering over the simply typed λ-terms modulo alphabetic variance.

The β, η normal form is not the only one that has been proposed for the λ-calculus. Another popular normal form involves the application of β-reduction in the standard direction and η-reduction once in the reverse direction. This results in terms that have explicit abstractions for all of their functional subterms but cannot be β-reduced.

DEFINITION: β, η LONG FORM   A λ-term α is in β, η *long form* if and only if

a. every subterm of α of type $\sigma \rightarrow \tau$ is either applied to an argument or of the form $\lambda x.\beta$,
b. α does not contain a subterm γ that has an alphabetic variant $\gamma' =_\alpha \gamma$ such that γ' is a β-redex.

For example, the terms $\lambda x.\mathbf{run}(x)$, $\mathbf{every}(\lambda x.\mathbf{kid}(x))(\lambda y.\mathbf{run}(y))$, and $\lambda y.\mathbf{yesterday}(\lambda x.\mathbf{run}(x))(y)$ are in long form, while the terms $\mathbf{run}$, $\mathbf{every}(\mathbf{kid})(\mathbf{run})$, and $\mathbf{yesterday}(\mathbf{run})$ are their corresponding normal forms, with the following types for constants and variables: x and y are of type **Ind**, **kid** and **run** are of type **Ind** $\rightarrow$ **Bool**, **yesterday** is of type (**Ind** $\rightarrow$ **Bool**) $\rightarrow$ **Ind** $\rightarrow$ **Bool**, and **every** is of type (**Ind** $\rightarrow$ **Bool**) $\rightarrow$ (**Ind** $\rightarrow$ **Bool**) $\rightarrow$ **Bool**. Long forms are sometimes clearer in that they display all of the abstractions in a term, but I will usually use normal form terms in linguistic applications simply because they are more concise.

Functional programming languages, such as Lisp and ML, evaluate programs by means of β-reduction. Even for monotyped systems like Lisp, the Church-Rosser result holds. Computations typically terminate when some language-specific reduction strategy produces a normal form. The choice of reduction strategy is of utmost importance not only for reasons of efficiency but also for termination. This is because, unlike the simply typed λ-calculus, the monotyped system underlying Lisp and the polymorphic system underlying ML do not enjoy the property of strong normalization. A language in which $(\lambda x.\alpha)(\beta)$ is reduced by first reducing β and then substituting the result for x in α is said to be a *call-by-value* language. This corresponds to the way in which Lisp evaluates function calls. Of course, not every term can be normalized by this strategy, a fact to which any programmer who has written a functional Lisp program with an infinite loop can attest. For instance, consider the following β-reduction sequence.

(14) $(\lambda x.x(x)(x))(\lambda y.y(y)(y))$
    $\Rightarrow (\lambda y.y(y)(y))(\lambda y.y(y)(y))(\lambda y.y(y)(y))$
    $\Rightarrow (\lambda y.y(y)(y))(\lambda y.y(y)(y))(\lambda y.y(y)(y))(\lambda y.y(y)(y))$
    $\Rightarrow \cdots$

Another standard evaluation strategy, known as *call by name*, involves reducing $(\lambda x.\alpha)(\beta)$ by first substituting β for x in α and then reducing the result. It is possible for the execution of a program to terminate using call by name but not terminate using call by value. For instance, consider the application of the term $\lambda w.\lambda z.z$ to the term in (14). With call by value, the execution will not terminate, but using call by name, the term in (14) will disappear when substituted for w in $\lambda z.z$, and thus no reduction of it will ever be attempted. On the other hand, if we have a term such as $(\lambda x.\alpha(x)(x))(\beta)$, the call-by-name strategy will involve extra work, because β will have to be evaluated twice in $\alpha(\beta)(\beta)$ after β is substituted for x. There are other reduction strategies as well; for discussions of reduction in the context of functional programming, see Revesz 1988, Thompson 1991.

Usually only β-reduction is involved in the evaluation of functional programs, because we are usually interested in evaluating not functions themselves, which would require η-reduction, but only function applications. For instance, Lisp evaluates the equivalent of the abstraction term $\lambda x.\alpha(x)$, namely (LAMBDA (X) (ALPHA X)), to itself, rather than to α. But compilers can take advantage of η-reduction to optimize code with redundant abstractions. Efficiency is a matter of how many steps are required to reduce a term.

As with other logical systems, we are interested in the completeness of the reduction system for the λ-calculus. Completeness is a consequence of strong normalization and the following lemma, which tells us that two normal form terms are logically equivalent if and only if they are alphabetic variants.

LEMMA: If α and β are in normal form, then $\alpha \equiv \beta$ if and only if $\alpha =_\alpha \beta$.

Proof Suppose that α and β are in normal form. Now if $\alpha =_\alpha \beta$, then obviously $\alpha \equiv \beta$. Thus we only need to show that if $\alpha \neq_\alpha \beta$ then $\alpha \not\equiv \beta$. If α and β are of different types, the result is trivial. So suppose they are of type $\sigma_1 \to \sigma_2 \to \cdots \to \sigma_n \to \tau$, with $n \geq 0$ and τ a basic type. If $x_1, \ldots, x_n$ are variables of type $\sigma_1, \ldots, \sigma_n$ not occurring in α or β, then $\alpha =_\alpha \beta$ if and only if $\alpha(x_1) \cdots (x_n) =_\alpha \beta(x_1) \cdots (x_n)$. We now proceed by induction on the number of subterms of α and β. Suppose α' is the result of applying β-reduction to $\alpha(x_1) \cdots \alpha(x_n)$ and similarly for β'. Then both α' and β' must be in normal form. Furthermore, $\alpha' = \alpha_0(\alpha_1) \cdots (\alpha_m)$ and $\beta' = \beta_0(\beta_1) \cdots (\beta_i)$, each α_j and β_j is in normal form, and α_0 and β_0 are either constants or variables; otherwise, we could carry out further β-reductions. If $\alpha_0 \neq_\alpha \beta_0$, then the result is obvious, as they can get arbitrary interpretations in a model under an assignment. So suppose k is minimal such that $\alpha_k \neq_\alpha \beta_k$. Then by induction, we must have $\alpha_k \not\equiv \beta_k$ because they are in normal form and contain fewer subterms than α and β. Because α_0 and β_0 can get arbitrary interpretations, we can find a model in which $\alpha' \not\equiv \beta'$, and hence in which $\alpha \not\equiv \beta$. $\square$

An immediate consequence is the completeness of our axiomatization.

THEOREM: COMPLETENESS   Two λ-terms α and β are logically equivalent only if $\vdash \alpha \Leftrightarrow \beta$ is provable.

Proof Suppose α' and β' are normal such that $\vdash \alpha \Rightarrow \alpha'$ and $\vdash \beta \Rightarrow \beta'$. If $\alpha' =_\alpha \beta'$ then $\vdash \alpha' \Rightarrow \beta'$, and hence $\vdash \alpha \Rightarrow \beta'$. Thus we have $\vdash \alpha \Leftrightarrow \beta$. $\square$

Thus unlike the case of first-order logic, but like the case of propositional logic, the issue of whether or not two λ-terms are logically equivalent is decidable.

THEOREM: DECIDABILITY   There is an algorithm to decide whether two λ-terms, α and β, are logically equivalent.

Proof Simply normalize α and β; this process terminates after finitely many steps, by the strong normalization theorem. Now check to see if they are alphabetic variants, which is clearly a decidable relation. $\square$

2.5 COMBINATORS AND VARIABLE-FREE LOGIC

Recall that a λ-term is pure if it does not contain any constants and is closed if it does not contain any free variables. A pure closed λ-term is said to be a *combinator*. I will make extensive use of combinators in the definitions of grammatical theories. In particular, my grammar rules will provide not only a syntactic operation but also a semantic operation that tells us how to define the meaning of the mother of a rule in terms of the meanings of the daughters. These semantic operations are often defined by means of combinators. Steedman's (1985, 1987, 1988, 1991, 1992) theory *combinatory categorial grammar* (CCG) employs combinators for the semantic component of grammars. Because of its type-driven nature, the combinatory basis has consequences in the syntax of CCG too. Combinators can also be used to provide the semantic component of lexical rules (Carpenter 1992a).

Combinators also play a significant role in the mathematical development of the λ-calculus. In particular, a small set of combinator schemes can be selected from which every pure, closed λ-term can be defined by various applications of these combinators. By adding constants to this stock of simple combinators, we can find a term formed purely by application from these combinators and our basic stock of constants that is logically equivalent to any λ-term. The interesting thing about this move is that it gives us a language for representations that are completely free of variables because only applications of combinators and constants are involved.

The theory of combinators, independently introduced by Schönfinkel (1924) and Curry (1930), actually predates the λ-calculus, which was introduced by Church (1940). Schönfinkel's motivation was to create a language for logic that was free of variables, because he believed that variables were not natural logical objects. Readers not interested in these foundational matters can skip this section; it will not be necessary for understanding my applications of combinators.

Combinators have also been used in the definition of the programming language Miranda (Turner 1986). The interest in such an application is that combinators are not only functionally complete but provide such completeness wholly without recourse to variables and variable binding, the treatment of which introduces a host of problems into the design of compilers. Very often, optimizing compilers for languages such as ML and other programming languages allowing higher-order functions make use of combinators to eliminate the need for tracking local variables. The drawback to using combinators is that often a rather large combinatory term is necessary to represent what would have been a relatively simple term in the λ-calculus.

The combinators I choose to use are commonly known as **I**, **K**, and **S**, and they are defined as follows.

DEFINITION: BASIC COMBINATOR SCHEMES   The collection **BasComb** of *basic combinators* consists of all of the instances of the following schemes for $\sigma, \tau, \rho \in$ **Typ**:

a. $\mathbf{I}_\sigma \overset{\text{def}}{=} \lambda x^\sigma.x$
b. $\mathbf{K}_{\sigma,\tau} \overset{\text{def}}{=} \lambda x^\sigma.\lambda y^\tau.x$
c. $\mathbf{S}_{\sigma,\tau,\rho} \overset{\text{def}}{=} \lambda x^{\sigma\to\tau\to\rho}.\lambda y^{\sigma\to\tau}.\lambda z^\sigma.x(z)(y(z))$

Note that I have annotated our combinators with types to indicate the types of their arguments. I have simply taken **BasComb** to be the set of all such combinators for every possible choice of types. The type of a combinator is defined just as for λ-terms, as we are treating combinators simply as closed pure λ-terms. These types can be directly read off of the definitions.

(15) a. $\mathbf{I}_\sigma$ is of type $\sigma \to \sigma$
   b. $\mathbf{K}_{\sigma,\tau}$ is of type $\sigma \to \tau \to \sigma$
   c. $\mathbf{S}_{\sigma,\tau,\rho}$ is of type $(\sigma \to \tau \to \rho) \to (\sigma \to \tau) \to \sigma \to \rho$

With the definition of combinators by means of λ-terms, we can simply import our models of the λ-calculus to interpret them. In fact, all we really need are frames, as there are no variables, free or otherwise, in combinators. The interpretation of the basic combinators is clear in the case of $\mathbf{I}_\sigma$ and $\mathbf{K}_{\sigma,\tau}$; $\mathbf{I}_\sigma$ is interpreted as the identity function over type σ objects, and $\mathbf{K}_{\sigma,\tau}$ is interpreted as a function that takes two arguments, one of type σ and the second of type τ, and returns the first. The third combinator scheme, $\mathbf{S}_{\sigma,\tau,\rho}$, is more complex. It functions as a kind of pointwise application operator. Loosely speaking, it is the only basic combinator that uses one of its arguments twice. Its application and utility should become clear when we see how to represent arbitrary λ-terms by means of combinators.

From the stock of basic combinators, I define the complete set of combinators that can be built up out of the basic combinators as follows. It should be clear that if we apply one combinator to another as a function, the result is a combinator.

DEFINITION: COMBINATORY TERM   The set **Comb** of *combinatory terms* is the least such that

a. **BasComb** $\subseteq$ **Comb**
b. $\alpha(\beta) \in$ **Comb** and is of type τ if $\alpha \in$ **Comb** is of type $\sigma \to \tau$ and $\beta \in$ **Comb** is of type σ

The primary theorem motivating the use of combinatory terms is the following, which tells us that every closed, pure λ-term corresponds to a logically equivalent combinatory term in **Comb**.

THEOREM: COMBINATORIAL COMPLETENESS   If α is a closed, pure λ-term, there is a combinatory term $\beta \in$ **Comb** such that $\alpha \equiv \beta$.

Proof We construct a combinatory term corresponding to a closed pure λ-term in two stages, following Curry and Feys (1958, section 6A). First we define a mapping AC that works on abstraction terms by recursion as follows:

a. $AC(\lambda x.\alpha) = \mathbf{K}(\alpha)$ if $x \notin \mathrm{Free}(\alpha)$
b. $AC(\lambda x.x) = \mathbf{I}$
c. $AC(\lambda x.\alpha(x)) = AC(\alpha)$ if $x \notin \mathrm{Free}(\alpha)$
d. $AC(\lambda x.\alpha(\beta)) = \mathbf{S}(AC(\lambda x.\alpha))(AC(\lambda x.\beta))$ otherwise

We then use this mapping to define a mapping LC that works on arbitrary terms by recursion as follows:

a. $LC(x) = x$ if $x \in \mathbf{Var}$
b. $LC(\alpha(\beta)) = LC(\alpha)(LC(\beta))$
c. $LC(\lambda x.\alpha) = AC(\lambda x.LC(\alpha))$

The mappings AC and LC are well defined, as the recursive calls are always applied to structurally simpler terms. The obvious structural induction suffices to show that the result is a combinatory term if the input is a closed λ-term. I leave the verification of this property, which is best carried out simultaneously with the verification of the logical equivalence of the input and output, as an exercise.   □

The system I provide here is not the only complete set of primitive combinators that may be used to define all of the closed pure λ-terms. In fact, the system remains complete even without the combinator $\mathbf{I}$, because we have the following logical equivalence.

(16) $\mathbf{I}_\sigma \equiv \mathbf{S}_{\sigma,\tau,\sigma}(\mathbf{K}_{\sigma,\tau})(\mathbf{K}_{\tau,\sigma}(\mathbf{K}_{\sigma,\sigma}))$ where $\tau = \sigma \rightarrow \sigma \rightarrow \sigma$

I leave the verification of this result, along with a specification of the types involved, as exercise 2.6. For other systems, albeit presented in the monotyped rather than in the simply typed case, the reader is urged to consult Curry and Feys 1961.

There is a straightforward axiomatization of the logical equivalence of combinatory terms in **Comb**. We merely need to take the relevant instances of β-reduction, as we do not need to worry about variables, such as those involved in α-reduction and η-reduction. I present these instances, along with the relevant instances of the rule schemes, as follows:

DEFINITION: AXIOMATIZATION OF COMBINATORY TERMS   The axioms and rules for combinatory terms are all well-typed instances of the following schemes:

a. $\vdash \mathbf{I}(\alpha) \Rightarrow \alpha$
b. $\vdash \mathbf{K}(\alpha)(\beta) \Rightarrow \alpha$
c. $\vdash \mathbf{S}(\alpha)(\beta)(\gamma) \Rightarrow \alpha(\gamma)(\beta(\gamma))$

d. $\vdash \alpha \Rightarrow \alpha$

e. $\alpha \Rightarrow \beta, \beta \Rightarrow \gamma \vdash \alpha \Rightarrow \gamma$

f. $\alpha \Rightarrow \alpha', \beta \Rightarrow \beta' \vdash \alpha(\beta) \Rightarrow \alpha'(\beta')$

g. $\alpha \Rightarrow \gamma, \beta \Rightarrow \gamma \vdash \alpha \Leftrightarrow \beta$

This logic is sound and complete over the combinatory terms, which I note as follows:

THEOREM: SOUNDNESS AND COMPLETENESS   If $\alpha, \beta \in$ **Comb**, then $\alpha \equiv \beta$ if and only if $\vdash \alpha \Leftrightarrow \beta$.

Proof Soundness is obvious from the fact that we have chosen a subset of our sound logic for the λ-calculus. Completeness also follows from the completeness of the λ-calculus after noting that every relevant instance of β-reduction is included, and η- and α-redexes never occur.   □

This section should assuage the doubts of those who are worried about the status of variables in their semantic theories. All such variables can be eliminated, in the spirit of Schönfinkel, by the judicious introduction of combinatory terms. I will not actually follow this paradigm, because variables are convenient for stating rules. For linguistic or computational applications, I could introduce additional, nonlogical constants into the combinatory framework. This would involve trivial changes in the definitions, and the resulting system remains sound and complete.

2.6 PRODUCTS

It might seem unusual at this point that all of our functions are unary in that they all apply to a single argument to produce a result, which itself might be a function. In this section I show that the introduction of tuples into the λ-calculus does not in fact increase its power to represent functions. We will see that n-ary functions of arbitrary order can be reduced to unary functions that are equivalent in a sense that I will make precise shortly.

To handle functions of more than one argument, I need to introduce tuples into our language, which I choose to do through pairing. Because I am introducing a new kind of object into our language, I need to begin by introducing a new kind of type. I will not change our assumption that there is a basic set **BasTyp** of basic types, nor the assumption that we can form arbitrary function types out of the types that we have. Instead, I simply introduce another clause into our definition of types.

(17) $(\sigma \times \tau) \in \mathbf{Typ}$ if $\sigma, \tau \in \mathbf{Typ}$

I refer to $(\sigma \times \tau)$ as a *product type*. I assume that this new clause is added to the basic clauses in the definition of types. Thus if we start with types like **Ind** and **Bool**, we get types such as $(\mathbf{Ind} \times \mathbf{Ind}) \rightarrow \mathbf{Bool}$, which will be the type of a binary relation. The argument to such a function is a pair of individuals, and the result is boolean, just as expected. As a notational convention, I assume that products bind more tightly than functions, so that $(\sigma \times \tau) \rightarrow \rho$ is abbreviated to $\sigma \times \tau \rightarrow \rho$.

Rather than introducing additional types for tuples of arbitrary arity, we can follow standard procedure in mathematics, which defines triples in terms of pairs, as follows:

(18) $\langle a, b, c \rangle \stackrel{\text{def}}{=} \langle a, \langle b, c \rangle \rangle$

This operation may be applied recursively to produce tuples of arbitrary finite length. For instance, a ternary relation would be assigned the type $\mathbf{Ind} \times (\mathbf{Ind} \times \mathbf{Ind}) \rightarrow \mathbf{Bool}$. Note that this is exactly the same method used by programming languages such as Lisp or Prolog for defining arbitrary tuples, which are often called *lists*, though compiler optimizations and syntactic abbreviations often hide this theoretical fact. I will assume that the product type constructor associates to the right, allowing us to abbreviate $\sigma \times (\tau \times \rho)$ to $\sigma \times \tau \times \rho$.

On the way to introducing a more comprehensive set of λ-terms involving product types, I introduce logical constants for product types, $\mathbf{Con}_{\sigma \times \tau}$, and assume a collection of variables for product types, $\mathbf{Var}_{\sigma \times \tau}$. Note that because I have assumed that the clauses for products are simply added to our previous definitions, we have the following:

(19) a. $\mathbf{Con}_{\sigma \times \tau} \subseteq \mathbf{Term}_{\sigma \times \tau}$
     b. $\mathbf{Var}_{\sigma \times \tau} \subseteq \mathbf{Term}_{\sigma \times \tau}$

To complete the modification of the language, I need to add the following clauses to our definition of terms, which can now be of product types.

(20) a. $\langle \alpha, \beta \rangle \in \mathbf{Term}_{\sigma \times \tau}$ if $\alpha \in \mathbf{Term}_{\sigma}$ and $\beta \in \mathbf{Term}_{\tau}$
     b. $\pi_1(\alpha) \in \mathbf{Term}_{\sigma}$ if $\alpha \in \mathbf{Term}_{\sigma \times \tau}$
     c. $\pi_2(\alpha) \in \mathbf{Term}_{\tau}$ if $\alpha \in \mathbf{Term}_{\sigma \times \tau}$

The intuition behind these terms is that $\langle \alpha, \beta \rangle$ will be interpreted as a pair consisting of the interpretation of α and the interpretation of β. The operators π_1 and π_2 are commonly known as *projection functions*; $\pi_1(\alpha)$ is interpreted as the first component and $\pi_2(\alpha)$ the second component of the tuple interpreting α.

Before adding products to our models, I need to add tuples to our frames. In particular, I add the following clause to the definition of frames.

(21) $\mathbf{Dom}_{\sigma \times \tau} = \mathbf{Dom}_\sigma \times \mathbf{Dom}_\tau$

Thus the domain of a product type $\sigma \times \tau$ consists of pairs of elements whose first component is an element of the domain of σ and whose second component is an element of the domain of τ. Note that I have overloaded the symbol $\times$ in the standard way, using it for cross-products of sets and as the product type constructor.

I assume that a model $\mathcal{M}$ for the λ-calculus with products is defined just as before. In particular, a model consists of a pair consisting of a frame, now including domains for pairs, and an interpretation function $[\![\cdot]\!]$ for the constants. I retain the requirement that a frame maps constants into the domain of the appropriate type:

(22) $[\![c]\!] \in \mathbf{Dom}_{\sigma \times \tau}$ if $c \in \mathbf{Con}_{\sigma \times \tau}$

Our assignment functions must now map variables of product types into pairs in the appropriate domain.

(23) $\theta(x) \in \mathbf{Dom}_{\sigma \times \tau}$ if $x \in \mathbf{Var}_{\sigma \times \tau}$

In considering the denotation of terms in general, we need to add clauses for the pairing and projection terms, which I do as follows:

(24) a. $[\![\langle \alpha, \beta \rangle]\!]^\theta_{\mathcal{M}} = \langle [\![\alpha]\!]^\theta_{\mathcal{M}}, [\![\beta]\!]^\theta_{\mathcal{M}} \rangle$
     b. $[\![\pi_1(\alpha)]\!]^\theta_{\mathcal{M}} = a$ if $[\![\alpha]\!] = \langle a, b \rangle$
     c. $[\![\pi_2(\alpha)]\!]^\theta_{\mathcal{M}} = b$ if $[\![\alpha]\!] = \langle a, b \rangle$

I am here overloading the tuple brackets, and it is important to keep in mind that $\langle \alpha, \beta \rangle$ is a term if α and β are terms, whereas $\langle a, b \rangle$ is an element in a frame if a and b are elements from the frame. Of course, this definition of denotations for products is type-sound in my earlier sense, as can be shown by adding three additional clauses to the proof for the pairing and projection functions. As with ordinary functions, it is common to see λ-terms such as $\alpha(\langle \beta, \gamma \rangle)$ abbreviated to $\alpha(\beta, \gamma)$.

Product types can be illustrated using a simple algebraic example. Suppose $\mathbf{R}$ is the type of real numbers. An object of type $\mathbf{R}$ can be taken to represent a point on a line. To represent a point in a plane, two real numbers are needed, and the resulting type is $\mathbf{R} \times \mathbf{R}$. Thus an object $\langle x, y \rangle$ of type $\mathbf{R} \times \mathbf{R}$ represents a location with a horizontal location of x and a vertical location of y. Now suppose we want to compute distances between points. To compute the distance between two points on a line, we simply take the absolute value of their difference (I use $|x|$ to represent the absolute value of x). Thus we can define a distance function for points on a line as follows:

(25) $\mathbf{dist_R} \stackrel{\text{def}}{=} \lambda x. |\pi_1(x) - \pi_2(x)|$

Here $\mathbf{dist_R}$ is of type $\mathbf{R} \times \mathbf{R} \to \mathbf{R}$, with input a pair of real numbers and output a single real number. Thus for a pair of points on a line, say $\langle x_1, x_2 \rangle$ of type $\mathbf{R} \times \mathbf{R}$, we apply $\mathbf{dist_R}$, with the result being $\mathbf{dist_R}(\langle x_1, y_1 \rangle) \equiv |\pi_1(\langle x_1, x_2 \rangle) - \pi_2(\langle x_1, x_2 \rangle)| \equiv |x_1 - x_2|$. To compute the distance between a pair of points on a plane, we need a function that takes as an argument a pair of such points and returns a real value according to the Pythagorean theorem, which we can define as follows.

(26) $\mathbf{dist_{R \times R}} \stackrel{\text{def}}{=}$
$$\lambda y. ((\pi_1(\pi_1(y)) - \pi_1(\pi_2(y)))^2 + (\pi_2(\pi_1(y)) - \pi_2(\pi_2(y)))^2)^{1/2}$$

Thus $\mathbf{dist_{R \times R}}$ is itself of type $(\mathbf{R} \times \mathbf{R}) \times (\mathbf{R} \times \mathbf{R}) \to \mathbf{R}$. The distance between a pair of points on a plane, $\langle x_1, y_1 \rangle$ and $\langle x_2, y_2 \rangle$, is computed as follows

(27) $\mathbf{dist_{R \times R}}(\langle\langle x_1, y_1 \rangle, \langle x_2, y_2 \rangle\rangle)$
$$\equiv ((\pi_1(\pi_1(\langle\langle x_1, y_1 \rangle, \langle x_2, y_2 \rangle\rangle)) - \pi_1(\pi_2(\langle\langle x_1, y_1 \rangle, \langle x_2, y_2 \rangle\rangle)))^2$$
$$+ (\pi_2(\pi_1(\langle\langle x_1, y_1 \rangle, \langle x_2, y_2 \rangle\rangle)) - \pi_2(\pi_2(\langle\langle x_1, y_1 \rangle, \langle x_2, y_2 \rangle\rangle)))^2)^{1/2}$$
$$\equiv ((\pi_1(\langle x_1, y_1 \rangle) - \pi_1(\langle x_2, y_2 \rangle)) + (\pi_2(\langle x_1, y_1 \rangle) - \pi_2(\langle x_2, y_2 \rangle)))^{1/2}$$
$$\equiv ((x_1 - x_2)^2 + (y_1 - y_2)^2)^{1/2}$$

I make crucial use of projection functions and pairing in the definition of the distance functions to project points in more than one dimension into their values in each dimension, and also to break the input pair down into the two arguments.

Not only can tuples be used for inputs, but we can also have functions that produce tuples of outputs. A useful function of this type might be one that takes as input a pair of street names representing an intersection and produces a resulting tuple of street names that represents the location of the nearest bus stop. An arithmetical example is vector operations in two-dimensional spaces. An operation that takes a pair of two dimensional vectors as input and produces a two-dimensional vector as output (say by vector addition), would be assigned to a type such as $((\mathbf{R} \times \mathbf{R}) \times (\mathbf{R} \times \mathbf{R}))$ $\rightarrow (\mathbf{R} \times \mathbf{R})$.

We can add a few simple axioms and the relevant congruence schemes to our proof system to produce a sound and complete proof theory for tuples. Again, I take our axioms to be directional and read them as reductions.

(28) a. $\vdash \pi_1(\langle \alpha, \beta \rangle) \Rightarrow \alpha$ (Left projection)

 b. $\vdash \pi_2(\langle \alpha, \beta \rangle) \Rightarrow \beta$ (Right projection)

 c. $\vdash \langle \pi_1(\alpha), \pi_2(\alpha) \rangle \Rightarrow \alpha$ (Pairing)

 d. $\alpha \Rightarrow \alpha', \beta \Rightarrow \beta' \vdash \langle \alpha, \beta \rangle \Rightarrow \langle \alpha', \beta' \rangle$ (Pairing congruence)

 e. $\alpha \Rightarrow \alpha' \vdash \pi_1(\alpha) \Rightarrow \pi_1(\alpha')$ (Projection congruence)

 f. $\alpha \Rightarrow \alpha' \vdash \pi_2(\alpha) \Rightarrow \pi_2(\alpha')$ (Projection congruence)

The notion of normal form is amended to include no product redexes, such as those above. In the resulting system, the Church-Rosser, strong normalization, and soundness and completeness results still hold.

Just as with the arguments of functions, the order of products is a matter of convention. For instance, the domains of type $\sigma \times \tau$ and $\tau \times \sigma$ are isomorphic, as shown by the following combinator.

(29) $\mathbf{comm} \overset{\text{def}}{=} \lambda x. \langle \pi_2(x), \pi_1(x) \rangle$

The combinator $\mathbf{comm}$ maps an element $\langle a, b \rangle$ of type $\sigma \times \tau$ to $\langle b, a \rangle$ of type $\tau \times \sigma$. As a second example of domain equivalences, consider the types $\sigma \times (\tau \times \rho)$ and $(\sigma \times \tau) \times \rho$. They are isomorphic as witnessed by the following combinator.

(30) $\mathbf{assoc} \overset{\text{def}}{=} \lambda x. \langle \langle \pi_1(x), \pi_1(\pi_2(x)) \rangle, \pi_2(\pi_2(x)) \rangle$

Continuing this line of reasoning, it is worth noting that products do not add any functional representational power to our system. In particular, there are two important combinators that allow us to map back and forth between functions defined in terms of products and unary functions.

DEFINITION: CURRYING

a. $\mathbf{curry} \overset{\text{def}}{=} \lambda x^{\sigma \times \tau \to \rho}. \lambda y^\sigma. \lambda z^\tau. x(\langle y, z \rangle)$

b. $\mathbf{uncurry} \overset{\text{def}}{=} \lambda x^{\sigma \to \tau \to \rho}. \lambda y^{\sigma \times \tau}. x(\pi_1(y))(\pi_2(y))$

These operations are commonly referred to as *currying* and *uncurrying*, after the logician Haskell B. Curry, one of the primary developers of the λ-calculus and combinators. Even though these operations were originally defined by Schönfinkel, the term *schönfinkeling* never caught on for obvious reasons. The result of currying a function is to take a function defined on pairs and convert it into a function that takes the elements of the pair one at a time to produce a result. Conversely, uncurrying takes a function of type $\sigma \to \tau \to \rho$, which applies to an argument of type σ to produce a function from type τ objects into type ρ objects, and converts it into a function which takes its arguments of type σ and τ simultaneously in the form of a pair.

The important fact to note about currying and uncurrying is that we have the following relationship, assuming all of the terms are well typed.

(31) a. **curry**(**uncurry**(α)) $\equiv \alpha$
       b. **uncurry**(**curry**(β)) $\equiv \beta$

In other words, currying and uncurrying establish a one-to-one relationship between objects of type $\sigma \times \tau \to \rho$ and those of type $\sigma \to \tau \to \rho$. Thus we can conclude that adding products to our calculus does not really provide us with any additional representational power.

Following Montague (1973), it is common in presentations of natural-language semantics for all functions and relations to be in curried form. Thus rather than treat the liking relation as a binary relation of type (**Ind** $\times$ **Ind**) $\to$ **Bool**, we curry it to produce a higher-order function of type **Ind** $\to$ **Ind** $\to$ **Bool**. The benefit of currying from a natural-language perspective is that we have a simple term in the object language, namely **like**(**terry**), to correspond to the verb phrase *like Terry*. I will exploit this fact a great deal, especially in my treatments of coordination, unbounded dependencies, and quantifiers.

2.7 SUMS

Sum types are used for combining domains by disjoint union. Sums allow us to define operations that apply to more than one type of object. Such definitions are stated using an explicit conditional on the type of the argument. Product types provide a way to model records, to which sums add the capacity to handle so called *variant records*, which are sometimes known as *union types* or *disjoint types* in programming languages like C. For natural-language applications, I will use sums to represent the semantics of lexical entries and derivations that combine different types, such as the copula, which takes arguments that are properties, individuals, or modifiers. My presentation will follow my presentation of products.

I include the following clause in the recursive definition of types in order to account for sums.

(32) $(\sigma + \tau) \in \mathbf{Typ}$ if $\sigma, \tau \in \mathbf{Typ}$

The idea is that terms of type $(\sigma + \tau)$ are interpreted in the disjoint union of the domains of σ and τ.

(33) $\mathbf{Dom}_{\sigma+\tau} = \mathbf{Dom}_\sigma \oplus \mathbf{Dom}_\tau$

Recall that $S \oplus T$ is defined to be the union of $\{\langle 1, s\rangle \,|\, s \in S\}$ and $\{\langle 2, t\rangle \,|\, t \in T\}$. That is, a disjoint-sum element is either an element of S, marked with a 1, or an element of T, marked with a 2.

Just as I did with binary products, we can extend binary sums to sums of arbitrary finite length by iteration. I often drop parentheses and assume that products bind more tightly than sums, so that $((\sigma \times \tau) + (\sigma' \times \tau'))$ would be abbreviated to $\sigma \times \tau + \sigma' \times \tau'$.

As with products, I assume that there is a set $\mathbf{Con}_{\sigma+\tau}$ of constants to be interpreted over $\mathbf{Dom}_{\sigma+\tau}$ and a set $\mathbf{Var}_{\sigma+\tau}$ of variables of type $\sigma + \tau$ to be assigned to elements of the same domain.

Again as with products, I also introduce some additional term constructors to deal with sums. Dual to the projections, I introduce constants for *injections*, with types as follows:

(34) a. $\iota_1(\alpha) \in \mathbf{Term}_{\sigma+\tau}$ if $\alpha \in \mathbf{Term}_\sigma$
      b. $\iota_2(\alpha) \in \mathbf{Term}_{\sigma+\tau}$ if $\alpha \in \mathbf{Term}_\tau$

The injections map from individual domains to sum domains. To get from sum domains back to the original domains is a bit more work. To this end, I introduce a general *choice* function, which is analogous to the if-then-else construction in computer languages.

(35) $\alpha \to \beta; \gamma \in \mathbf{Term}_\rho$ if $\alpha \in \mathbf{Term}_{\sigma+\tau}$, $\beta \in \mathbf{Term}_{\sigma\to\rho}$, and $\gamma \in \mathbf{Term}_{\tau\to\rho}$

Terms constructed by injection and choice will be interpreted as follows:

(36) a. $[\![\iota_1(\alpha)]\!]^\theta_\mathscr{M} = \langle 1, [\![\alpha]\!]^\theta_\mathscr{M}\rangle$
      b. $[\![\iota_2(\beta)]\!]^\theta_\mathscr{M} = \langle 2, [\![\beta]\!]^\theta_\mathscr{M}\rangle$
      c. $[\![\alpha \to \beta; \gamma]\!]^\theta_\mathscr{M} = \begin{cases} [\![\beta]\!]^\theta_\mathscr{M}(a) & \text{if } [\![\alpha]\!]^\theta_\mathscr{M} = \langle 1, a\rangle \\ [\![\gamma]\!]^\theta_\mathscr{M}(b) & \text{if } [\![\alpha]\!]^\theta_\mathscr{M} = \langle 2, b\rangle \end{cases}$

The notion of injection as embedded in this rule is the ordinary one. That is, $\iota_1(\alpha)$ denotes the pairing of the marker 1 and the denotation of α; the 1 simply indicates the type of α as the first component of the pair $\sigma + \tau$. The injection functions maps elements of type σ and τ into elements of type

$\sigma + \tau$; this notion is dual to the mapping of elements of type $\sigma \times \tau$ into elements of type σ and τ by the projection functions. Note that I have overloaded the symbols ι_1 and ι_2 by using them both as term constructors and as symbols in the metalanguage. The choice function works by checking whether its first argument is a left injection or a right injection. If the first argument is a left injection, the choice function applies the second argument to it, and if the first argument is a right injection, it applies the third argument to it. This allows us to define functions whose behavior is conditional on the type of input.

We saw in (25) and (26) how to define distance functions $\mathbf{dist_R}$ and $\mathbf{dist_{R \times R}}$ between points in one- and two-dimensional space. With sum types, we can define a polymorphic function that operates on either points in a line of type $\mathbf{R}$ or points in a plane of type $\mathbf{R} \times \mathbf{R}$. Thus our general distance function $\mathbf{dist}$ is assigned the type $((\mathbf{R} \times \mathbf{R}) + ((\mathbf{R} \times \mathbf{R}) \times (\mathbf{R} \times \mathbf{R}))) \to \mathbf{R}$ and is defined as follows:

(37) $\mathbf{dist} \overset{\text{def}}{=} \lambda x.x \to \mathbf{dist_R}; \mathbf{dist_{R \times R}}$

Now it is important to note that the input to $\mathbf{dist}$ cannot be a simple point of type $\mathbf{R}$ nor a pair of type $\mathbf{R} \times \mathbf{R}$ but rather must be a member of type $\mathbf{R} + (\mathbf{R} \times \mathbf{R})$. Thus a pair of points must be properly injected into the sum type. To measure the distance between points x_1 and x_2 on a line, we evaluate the following expression:

(38) $\mathbf{dist}(\iota_1(\langle x_1, x_2 \rangle)) \equiv (\lambda x.x \to \mathbf{dist_R}; \mathbf{dist_{R \times R}})(\iota_1(\langle x_1, x_2 \rangle))$
$\equiv \mathbf{dist_R}(\langle x_1, x_2 \rangle)$

To measure the distance between points $\langle x_1, y_1 \rangle$ and $\langle x_2, y_2 \rangle$ on a plane, we evaluate the following expression:

(39) $\mathbf{dist}(\iota_2(\langle \langle x_1, y_1 \rangle, \langle x_2, y_2 \rangle \rangle))$
$\equiv (\lambda x.x \to \mathbf{dist_R}; \mathbf{dist_{R \times R}})(\iota_2(\langle \langle x_1, y_1 \rangle, \langle x_2, y_2 \rangle \rangle))$
$\equiv \mathbf{dist_{R \times R}}(\langle \langle x_1, y_1 \rangle, \langle x_2, y_2 \rangle \rangle)$

In this manner, we obtain polymorphic functions that can operate on two distinct types of arguments. By iterating the formation of sums, we can extend the polymorphism to any finite number of argument types. Polymorphically typed λ-calculi, such as that underlying the programming language ML, typically allow more general definitions over infinitely diverse types.

As with products, I add a few new rules to our proof theory to deal with injection and choice.

(40) a. $\vdash \iota_1(\alpha) \to \beta; \gamma \Rightarrow \beta(\alpha)$ (Choice)

b. $\vdash \iota_2(\alpha) \to \beta; \gamma \Rightarrow \gamma(\alpha)$ (Choice)

c. $\alpha \Rightarrow \alpha' \vdash \iota_1(\alpha) \Rightarrow \iota_1(\alpha')$ (Injection congruence)

d. $\alpha \Rightarrow \alpha' \vdash \iota_2(\alpha) \Rightarrow \iota_2(\alpha')$ (Injection congruence)

e. $\alpha \Rightarrow \alpha', \beta \Rightarrow \beta', \gamma \Rightarrow \gamma' \vdash \alpha \to \beta; \gamma \Rightarrow \alpha' \to \beta'; \gamma'$

(Choice congruence)

Normalization still involves applying these schemes from left to right. Strong normalization still obtains in the presence of sums, and the resulting system is sound and complete.

Exercises

1. Normalize the following λ-terms, indicating each reduction step. Assume all of the terms are well formed. (Hint: Some may already be normalized, and some may require multiple steps. It may also help to match the parentheses and reinsert the parentheses that have been abbreviated.)

(a) $(\lambda x.\mathbf{run}(x))(\mathbf{a})$

(b) $\lambda x.\mathbf{like}(x)(y)$

(c) $\lambda x.\mathbf{like}(y)(x)$

(d) $(\lambda x.\mathbf{like}(y)(x))(\mathbf{a})$

(e) $\lambda x.\mathbf{like}(\mathbf{sis}(x))(x)$

(f) $(\lambda x.\mathbf{like}(x)(y))(y)$

(g) $(\lambda x.\mathbf{like}(x)(x))(y)$

(h) $(\lambda x.\lambda y.\mathbf{like}(x)(y))(y)$

(i) $(\lambda x.\lambda y.\mathbf{like}(x)(y))(\mathbf{a})(\mathbf{b})$

(j) $(\lambda x.\lambda x.\mathbf{run}(x))(\mathbf{a})(\mathbf{b})$

(k) $(\lambda P.P(\mathbf{b}))(\mathbf{run})$

(l) $(\lambda P.P(\mathbf{b}))(\mathbf{like}(\mathbf{a}))$

(m) $\lambda x.\mathbf{run}(x)$

(n) $(\lambda x.\mathbf{run})(x)$

(o) $(\lambda y.\lambda x.\mathbf{like}(y)(x))(\mathbf{a})$

(p) $(\lambda Q.Q(\mathbf{run}))(\lambda P.P(\mathbf{a}))$

(q) $(\lambda R.\lambda x.R(x)(x))(\mathbf{show}(\mathbf{a}))(\mathbf{b})$

(r) $(\lambda P.P(\mathbf{a}))((\lambda R.\lambda x.R(x)(x))(\lambda y.\lambda z.\mathbf{give}(z)(\mathbf{a})(y)))$

(s) $(\lambda R.\lambda y.\lambda x.\mathbf{and}(R(x))(R(y)))(\mathbf{run})(\mathbf{a})(\mathbf{b})$

(t) $(\lambda R.R(x))(\lambda y.\lambda x.\mathbf{like}(x)(y))$

(u) $\mathbf{some}(\mathbf{uni})(\lambda z.(\lambda Q.\lambda x.Q(\lambda y.\mathbf{find}_2(y)(x)))(\lambda T.T(z)))$

2. Normalize the following λ-terms involving sums and products.

(a) $(\lambda x.\mathbf{run}(\pi_1(\langle x,y\rangle)))(\mathbf{a})$

(b) $(\lambda x.\mathbf{run}(\pi_2(\langle x,y\rangle)))(\mathbf{a})$

(c) $\pi_1(\pi_2(\langle\langle w,x\rangle,\langle y,z\rangle\rangle))$

(d) $(\pi_2(\pi_1(\langle\langle\mathbf{run},\mathbf{jump}\rangle,\langle\mathbf{sing},\mathbf{dance}\rangle\rangle)))(\mathbf{a})$

(e) $(\lambda y.\pi_2(\langle\mathbf{run}(x),\mathbf{run}(y)\rangle))(\mathbf{a})$

(f) $(\lambda x.\lambda y.\mathbf{give}(\pi_1(x))(\pi_2(x))(y))(\langle\mathbf{a},\mathbf{b}\rangle)(\mathbf{c})$

(g) $(\lambda x.\lambda y.\langle\pi_1(x),\pi_2(y)\rangle)(\mathbf{p})(\mathbf{p})$

(h) $\iota_1(\mathbf{a}) \to \mathbf{run};\mathbf{jump}$

(i) $\iota_2(\mathbf{like}) \to \lambda R.\lambda x.R(x)(x); \lambda R.R(\mathbf{a})$

(j) $(\lambda x.x \to \lambda z.z; \lambda w.w)(\iota_1(\mathbf{a}))$

(k) $(\lambda x.x \to \lambda w.\lambda y.\mathbf{eq}(w)(y); \lambda P.\lambda y.P(y))(\iota_1(\mathbf{a}))(\mathbf{b})$

(l) $(\lambda x.x \to \lambda w.\lambda y.\mathbf{eq}(w)(y); \lambda P.\lambda y.P(y))(\iota_2(\mathbf{run}))(\mathbf{b})$

3. Prove that the rules of α-reduction and η-reduction are sound.

4. Show that if β and β' are logically equivalent terms, then $\alpha[x \mapsto \beta]$ and $\alpha[x \mapsto \beta']$ are also logically equivalent. (Hint: Proceed by induction on the structure of α.)

5. Consider the following tightening of the application conditions in our reduction axioms. For α-reduction, we allow $\lambda x.\alpha$ to reduce to $\lambda y.\alpha[x \mapsto y]$ if and only if y does not occur in α. For β-reduction, we allow $(\lambda x.\alpha)(\beta)$ to reduce to $\alpha[x \mapsto \beta]$ if and only if β and α have no variables in common. For η-reduction, we allow $\lambda x.\alpha(x)$ to reduce to α if and only if x does not occur in α. If we take the same rules of inference, is the resulting system still complete?

6. Verify that the terms in (16) are well typed and that the equation holds.

7. Use structural induction to verify that the mapping in the proof of the combinatorial-completeness theorem both terminates and results in a combinator that is logically equivalent to the input.

8. Prove that $\mathbf{curry}(\mathbf{uncurry}(\alpha)) \equiv \alpha$ and that $\mathbf{uncurry}(\mathbf{curry}(\beta)) \equiv \beta$.

9. Extend the definition of distance in two dimensions given in (26) to three dimensions.

10. Consider adding the type σ^* for lists of objects of type σ. What would the terms look like in this scheme and how are they interpreted and treated proof-theoretically? Is there any gain in expressive power by admitting arbitrary lists? What might we do to interpret infinite sequences?

Chapter 3

Higher-Order Logic

First-order logic is characterized by the fact that it allows quantification over individuals. A logic that involves quantification over relations is said to be a *second-order logic*. A logic that quantifies over relations over relations is said to be *third-order*. And so on. By higher-order logic, I mean a logic that involves constants and variables of arbitrary finite type, with every kind of object being a first-class citizen over which quantification and abstraction may be performed.

To be more precise, I begin with basic types for individuals and for propositions and allow variables, terms, and quantification over all of the functional types that can be constructed from these basic types. Such a logic is often said to be *ω-order*, as we allow operations over objects of arbitrarily high finite order. The utility of this move for the study of natural-language semantics is that we have types to assign to all of the intermediate meanings we will assign to phrases, as well as to complete sentences and noun phrases. For instance, adjectives modify properties, and intensifiers modify adjectives, and logical operations modify adjectives or perhaps intensifiers, as can be seen in expressions such as *not very happy camper*. Questions can involve reference to adverbs, as can be seen in *How did Pat study?* Higher-order logic provides types corresponding to propositions, properties, relations, adjectival modifiers (property modifiers), generalized quantifiers, determiners, and so on.

3.1 HIGHER-ORDER SYNTAX

I treat higher-order logic as an application of the simply typed λ-calculus. In particular, I make the following assumptions concerning the basic types:

DEFINITION: TYPES OF HIGHER-ORDER LOGIC   The types of higher-order logic are determined by taking **BasTyp** = {**Bool**, **Ind**}, in which

a. **Bool** is the type of *boolean values*
b. **Ind** is the type of *individuals*

This determines the type theory of higher-order logic. As I mentioned in the previous chapter, I will not adopt product types in our analysis here, instead choosing to curry all of our basic relations and functions in order to provide appropriate intermediate representations. Some types are worth singling out. For instance, **Ind** → **Bool** is the type of function from individuals to boolean values, which we can think of as the type of a unary property. In the case of a binary relation, we have the type **Ind** → **Ind** → **Bool**. Note that this is the type of a function from individuals into properties. Thus applying a term of the binary-relation type to an individual term results in a term of type **Ind** → **Bool**, which is just the type of properties. For instance, if **like** ∈ **Con** _{Ind→Ind→Bool} and **dana** ∈ **Con** _{Ind}, then **like**(**dana**) ∈ **Term** _{Ind→Bool}, which is the type of property constants such as **run**. Similarly, a three-place predicate in first-order logic corresponds to a constant of the type **Ind** → **Ind** → **Ind** → **Bool**.

In dealing with higher-order logic, I assume that some of the constants are of a logical nature. In the following section we will see how some of these constants may be defined in terms of each other, but I choose to simply treat them all as primitive.

DEFINITION: LOGICAL CONSTANTS OF HIGHER-ORDER LOGIC   We assume the existence of the following collection of *logical constants*:

a. **not** ∈ **Con** _{Bool→Bool}
b. **and** ∈ **Con** _{Bool→Bool→Bool}
c. **eq**$_\tau$ ∈ **Con** _{τ→τ→Bool}
d. **every**$_\tau$ ∈ **Con** _{(τ→Bool)→Bool}
e. ι_τ ∈ **Con** _{(τ→Bool)→τ}

The reason these are called logical constants has to do with their receiving fixed interpretations with respect to a frame, which we turn to shortly. The types of the logical connectives **not** and **and** should be apparent: **not** applies to a boolean term to produce another boolean term, whereas **and** applies to a pair of boolean terms to produce another boolean term. The indexed constant **eq**$_\tau$ represents equality between two type τ objects. For instance, if α and β are terms of type τ, then **eq**$_\tau(\alpha)(\beta)$ is a term of type **Bool**. In the model theory, **eq**$_\tau$ is interpreted as the equality relation between type τ objects. I also adopt a family of logical constants corresponding to universal *generalized quantifiers* of the form **every**$_\tau$ for all types τ. The idea is that a generalized quantifier **every**$_\tau$ quantifies over objects of type τ. Because λ-abstraction is the only way to bind variables, we do not treat quantifiers in higher-order logic as binding operators, as is standard for first-order logic. Instead, we treat quantifiers over objects of type τ as properties of properties of type τ. In the particular case where $\tau = \mathbf{Ind}$, we have a constant **every**$_\mathbf{Ind}$, which is of type $(\mathbf{Ind} \rightarrow \mathbf{Bool}) \rightarrow \mathbf{Bool}$. A formula $(\forall x)\phi$ in first-order logic will be rendered as **every**$_\mathbf{Ind}(\lambda x.\phi')$, where ϕ' is the translation of ϕ into higher-order logic. The truth conditions will be such that **every**$_\mathbf{Ind}(P)$ will denote **yes** $\in \mathbf{Dom}_\mathbf{Bool}$ in a model if and only if P denotes the property that is true of every individual. The same kind of truth condition will be given for quantifiers **every**$_\tau$ of arbitrary types τ. The notion of treating quantifiers as properties of properties dates back to Frege (1891) and was applied to natural-language quantifiers and definite descriptions by Russell (1905). Finally, we have a constant ι_τ, called a *description operator*, for each type τ. The description operator is used for mapping singleton sets to the single object they contain. More precisely, $\iota_\tau(P)$ picks out an element a of type τ if a is the unique element that has the property denoted by P. If P does not denote a singleton set, then $\iota(P)$ still denotes an element of type τ, but the identity of the element is unconstrained by the logic.

The type system for higher-order logic is fixed to those types generated from individuals and truth values. In addition to the logical constants, a higher-order logic may involve nonlogical constants of arbitrary type. Such constants are referred to as *nonlogical constants*, and their interpretation will depend on the particular model being employed. The higher-order approach has the benefit of providing a type for higher-order relations and functions such as quantifiers and specifiers.

3.2   HIGHER-ORDER MODELS

A model $\mathcal{M}$ of higher-order logic is a model of the λ-calculus over the logical and nonlogical constants that is constrained in the denotations it assigns to the logical constants.

The first restriction is that the frame assign the domain of truth values to the boolean type.

(1) $\mathbf{Dom}_\mathbf{Bool} = \{\mathbf{yes}, \mathbf{no}\}$

$$[\![\textbf{francis}]\!] = f \qquad [\![\textbf{brooke}]\!] = b \qquad [\![\textbf{robin}]\!] = r$$

$$[\![\textbf{laughed}]\!] = \begin{bmatrix} f & \mapsto & \text{yes} \\ b & \mapsto & \text{no} \\ r & \mapsto & \text{no} \end{bmatrix} \qquad [\![\textbf{cried}]\!] = \begin{bmatrix} f & \mapsto & \text{yes} \\ b & \mapsto & \text{yes} \\ r & \mapsto & \text{yes} \end{bmatrix}$$

$$[\![\textbf{man}]\!] = \begin{bmatrix} f & \mapsto & \text{yes} \\ b & \mapsto & \text{yes} \\ r & \mapsto & \text{no} \end{bmatrix} \qquad [\![\textbf{woman}]\!] = \begin{bmatrix} f & \mapsto & \text{no} \\ b & \mapsto & \text{no} \\ r & \mapsto & \text{yes} \end{bmatrix}$$

$$[\![\textbf{respect}]\!] = \begin{bmatrix} f & \mapsto & \begin{bmatrix} f & \mapsto & \text{no} \\ b & \mapsto & \text{yes} \\ r & \mapsto & \text{yes} \end{bmatrix} \\ b & \mapsto & \begin{bmatrix} f & \mapsto & \text{no} \\ b & \mapsto & \text{no} \\ r & \mapsto & \text{no} \end{bmatrix} \\ r & \mapsto & \begin{bmatrix} f & \mapsto & \text{yes} \\ b & \mapsto & \text{yes} \\ r & \mapsto & \text{yes} \end{bmatrix} \end{bmatrix}$$

Figure 3.1
A simple three-individual model

The domain **Dom**$_\textbf{Ind}$ is arbitrary but, of course, must be fixed to determine a frame. Nonlogical constants are interpreted over this frame. For instance, consider the simple frame determined by **Ind** $= \{f, b, r\}$, representing Francis, Brooke, and Robin. I provide some constants representing properties expressible lexically in natural language in figure 3.1. The notation indicates, for instance, that $[\![\textbf{respect}]\!](b)(r) = \textbf{no}$. By our conventions, which are based on the structure of English, this indicates that Robin does not respect Brooke. I order the arguments so that A *respects* B is translated as **respect**$(B')(A')$, where A' and B' are the translations of A and B. This is so that verb phrases receive simple translations. So *respect Francis* would be treated as **respect(francis)**, which denotes the function with action $f \mapsto \textbf{no}$, $b \mapsto \textbf{yes}$, and $r \mapsto \textbf{yes}$. This illustrates how higher-order logic provides a uniform domain for interpreting verb phrases composed either of an intransitive verb or of a transitive verb and a simple object. We can also perform operations such as passivization, by converting **respect** into $\lambda x.\lambda y.\textbf{respect}(y)(x)$, whose denotation is as follows:

$$(2)\ [\![\lambda x.\lambda y.\textbf{respect}(y)(x)]\!] = \begin{bmatrix} f \mapsto \begin{bmatrix} f \mapsto \textbf{no} \\ b \mapsto \textbf{no} \\ r \mapsto \textbf{yes} \end{bmatrix} \\ b \mapsto \begin{bmatrix} f \mapsto \textbf{yes} \\ b \mapsto \textbf{no} \\ r \mapsto \textbf{yes} \end{bmatrix} \\ r \mapsto \begin{bmatrix} f \mapsto \textbf{yes} \\ b \mapsto \textbf{no} \\ r \mapsto \textbf{yes} \end{bmatrix} \end{bmatrix}$$

I now turn to the interpretation of the logical constants. I assume that **not** is interpreted in a model $\mathcal{M}$ of higher-order logic so as to have the following behavior:

$$(3)\ [\![\textbf{not}]\!] = \begin{bmatrix} \textbf{yes} \mapsto \textbf{no} \\ \textbf{no}\ \mapsto \textbf{yes} \end{bmatrix}$$

For instance, **not**(**cried**(**francis**)) would denote **no**.

Similarly, conjunction is defined to have its usual action on truth values:

$$(4)\ [\![\textbf{and}]\!] = \begin{bmatrix} \textbf{yes} \mapsto \begin{bmatrix} \textbf{yes} \mapsto \textbf{yes} \\ \textbf{no} \mapsto \textbf{no} \end{bmatrix} \\ \textbf{no}\ \mapsto \begin{bmatrix} \textbf{yes} \mapsto \textbf{no} \\ \textbf{no}\ \mapsto \textbf{no} \end{bmatrix} \end{bmatrix}$$

Thus **and**(**cried**(**francis**))(**laughed**(**francis**)) will denote **yes**, because both **cried**(**francis**) and **laughed**(**francis**) denote **yes**.

These are simply the higher-order analogues of the usual operations of negation and conjunction. The denotations of **and**, **not**, and the other logical operators are often referred to as *truth tables*, especially when presented tabularly as above. Note that we now have a type for the intermediate term **and**(α), where $\alpha \in$ **Term**$_{\textbf{Bool}}$. Thus **and**(α) and **not** have the same type if α is a boolean term.

The equality constant is interpreted in the obvious way.

$$(5)\ [\![\textbf{eq}_\tau]\!](a)(b) = \begin{cases} \textbf{yes} & \text{if } a = b \\ \textbf{no} & \text{otherwise} \end{cases}$$

Thus equality returns the value true if it is supplied the same argument in both positions, and it returns false otherwise. For instance,

$\mathbf{eq_{Ind}(francis)(francis)}$ denotes $\mathbf{yes}$ and $\mathbf{eq_{Ind}(francis)(brooke)}$ denotes $\mathbf{no}$. At the intermediate stage, $\mathbf{eq_{Ind}(francis)}$ denotes the property of being equal to Francis, a natural-translation for the natural-language expression *is Francis*.

The final logical connective is the universal quantifier. It is given the semantics I hinted at earlier. For type τ and for $P \in \mathbf{Dom}_{\tau \to \mathbf{Bool}}$, we have the following definition:

$$(6) \quad [\![\mathbf{every}_\tau]\!](P) = \begin{cases} \mathbf{yes} & \text{if } P(a) = \mathbf{yes} \text{ for every } a \in \mathbf{Dom}_\tau \\ \mathbf{no} & \text{otherwise} \end{cases}$$

Just as we think of functions from type τ to type $\mathbf{Bool}$ as characteristic functions of properties, so the truth conditions for universal quantification amount to $P = \mathbf{Dom}_\tau$. The denotations in a two-person model are as follows:

$$(7) \quad [\![\mathbf{every_{Ind}}]\!] = \begin{bmatrix} \begin{bmatrix} a \mapsto \mathbf{yes} \\ b \mapsto \mathbf{yes} \end{bmatrix} \mapsto \mathbf{yes} \\ \begin{bmatrix} a \mapsto \mathbf{yes} \\ b \mapsto \mathbf{no} \end{bmatrix} \mapsto \mathbf{no} \\ \begin{bmatrix} a \mapsto \mathbf{no} \\ b \mapsto \mathbf{yes} \end{bmatrix} \mapsto \mathbf{no} \\ \begin{bmatrix} a \mapsto \mathbf{no} \\ b \mapsto \mathbf{no} \end{bmatrix} \mapsto \mathbf{no} \end{bmatrix}$$

Returning to our previous example, we have $\mathbf{every_{Ind}(cried)}$, a logical translation of *everyone cried*, evaluating to $\mathbf{true}$ because $[\![\mathbf{cried}]\!]$ maps every individual to $\mathbf{true}$. On the other hand, $\mathbf{every_{Ind}(laughed)}$ evaluates to $\mathbf{false}$. We can quantify over arbitrary verb phrases: $\mathbf{every_{Ind}(respect(robin))}$ denotes $\mathbf{yes}$ because $\mathbf{respect(robin)}$ maps every individual to $\mathbf{yes}$, as everyone respects Robin. We can also quantify over other positions by means of abstraction. For instance, $\mathbf{every_{Ind}}(\lambda x.\mathbf{respect}(x)(\mathbf{robin}))$ serves as the translation of *Robin respects everyone*; the quantifier applies to the property of being an x such that Robin respects x.

In first-order logic we can define the existential quantifier in terms of the universal quantifier by noting that $(\exists x)\phi \equiv \neg(\forall x)\neg\phi$. In higher-order logic, we can also define the existential quantifier in terms of the universal quantifier:

(8) $\mathbf{some}_\tau \overset{\text{def}}{=} \lambda P.\neg(\forall x)\neg P(x)$

$\equiv \lambda P^{\tau\to\mathbf{Bool}}.\mathbf{not}(\mathbf{every}_\tau(\lambda x^\tau.\mathbf{not}(P(x))))$

Just as in first-order logic, we get the appropriate existential interpretation of $\mathbf{some}_\tau$. In other words, the term $\mathbf{some}_\tau(P)$ evaluates to **yes** if and only if the property P of type τ objects maps at least one object to **yes**. Simply consider the following expansion of the definition of $\mathbf{some}_\tau(Q)$ according to the definitions of the other constants (we assume that Q is a closed term of type $\tau \to \mathbf{Bool}$).

(9) $[\![\mathbf{some}_\tau(Q)]\!]_\mathcal{M}^\sigma = \mathbf{yes}$ iff

$[\![(\lambda P^{\tau\to\mathbf{Bool}}.\mathbf{not}(\mathbf{every}_\tau(\lambda x^\tau.\mathbf{not}(P(x)))))(Q)]\!]_\mathcal{M}^\sigma = \mathbf{yes}$ iff

$[\![\mathbf{not}(\mathbf{every}_\tau(\lambda x^\tau.\mathbf{not}(Q(x))))]\!]_\mathcal{M}^\sigma = \mathbf{yes}$ iff

$[\![\mathbf{every}_\tau(\lambda x^\tau.\mathbf{not}(Q(x)))]\!]_\mathcal{M}^\sigma = \mathbf{no}$ iff

$[\![(\lambda x^\tau.\mathbf{not}(Q(x))]\!]_\mathcal{M}^\sigma(a) = \mathbf{no}$ for some $a \in \mathbf{Dom}_\tau$ iff

$[\![\mathbf{not}(Q(x))]\!]_\mathcal{M}^{\sigma[x:=a]} = \mathbf{no}$ for some $a \in \mathbf{Dom}_\tau$ iff

$[\![Q(x)]\!]_\mathcal{M}^{\sigma[x:=a]} = \mathbf{yes}$ for some $a \in \mathbf{Dom}_\tau$ iff

$[\![Q]\!]_\mathcal{M}^{\sigma[x:=a]}([\![x]\!]_\mathcal{M}^{\sigma[x:=a]}) = \mathbf{yes}$ for some $a \in \mathbf{Dom}_\tau$ iff

$[\![Q]\!]_\mathcal{M}^\sigma(a) = \mathbf{yes}$ for some $a \in \mathbf{Dom}_\tau$

The fact that Q is closed allows us to carry out the final reduction step. For example, in the model given in figure 3.1, the statement $\mathbf{some}_\tau(\mathbf{laughed})$ evaluates to **yes**, but $\mathbf{some}_\tau(\mathbf{respect}(\mathbf{brooke}))$ denotes **no**.

In dealing with quantifiers, it is crucial to have an intuitive grasp of the truth conditions for terms involving multiple quantifiers. Let us pause now to consider these conditions for the following example:

(10) $\mathbf{every}(\lambda y.\mathbf{some}(\lambda x.\mathbf{break}(y)(x)))$

In this case, the term will be true if for every object y, there is some object x such that x broke y. This is just as in first-order logic, but it is worth considering directly in terms of the definition of denotation for higher-order logic, which we do as follows:

(11) $[\![\mathbf{every}(\lambda y.\mathbf{some}(\lambda x.\mathbf{break}(y)(x)))]\!]_\mathcal{M}^\sigma = \mathbf{yes}$ iff

$[\![\lambda y.\mathbf{some}(\lambda x.\mathbf{break}(y)(x))]\!]_\mathcal{M}^\sigma(a) = \mathbf{yes}$ for every $a \in \mathbf{Dom}_{\mathbf{Ind}}$ iff

$[\![\mathbf{some}(\lambda x.\mathbf{break}(y)(x))]\!]_\mathcal{M}^{\alpha[y:=a]} = \mathbf{yes}$ for every $a \in \mathbf{Dom}_{\mathbf{Ind}}$ iff

$[\![\lambda x.\mathbf{break}(y)(x)]\!]_\mathcal{M}^{\alpha[y:=a]}(b) = \mathbf{yes}$ for some $b \in \mathbf{Dom}_{\mathbf{Ind}}$ for every
$a \in \mathbf{Dom}_{\mathbf{Ind}}$ iff

$$[\![\mathbf{break}(y)(x)]\!]_M^{\alpha[y:=a][x:=b]} = \mathbf{yes} \text{ for some } b \in \mathbf{Dom}_{Ind} \text{ for every}$$
$$a \in \mathbf{Dom}_{Ind} \text{ iff}$$

$$[\![\mathbf{break}]\!]_M(a)(b) = \mathbf{yes} \text{ for some } b \in \mathbf{Dom}_{Ind} \text{ for every } a \in \mathbf{Dom}_{Ind}$$

I adopt a standard set of abbreviations for the logical constants, as well as defining some new connectives in terms of existing ones.

(12) a. $\phi \wedge \psi \stackrel{\text{def}}{=} \mathbf{and}(\phi)(\psi)$

b. $\neg\phi \stackrel{\text{def}}{=} \mathbf{not}(\phi)$

c. $\alpha =_\tau \beta \stackrel{\text{def}}{=} \mathbf{eq}_\tau(\alpha)(\beta)$

d. $(\forall x^\tau)\phi \stackrel{\text{def}}{=} \mathbf{every}_\tau(\lambda x.\phi)$

e. $(\exists x^\tau)\phi \stackrel{\text{def}}{=} \mathbf{some}_\tau(\lambda x.\phi)$

f. $\phi \vee \psi \stackrel{\text{def}}{=} \neg((\neg\phi) \wedge (\neg\psi))$

g. $\phi \to \psi \stackrel{\text{def}}{=} (\neg\phi) \vee \psi$

The constant ι_τ denotes the description operator for properties of type τ, and it maps a property that holds of a unique individual to that individual. Thus we impose the following constraint on the interpretation of the description operator ι.

(13) $[\![\iota]\!](P) = a$, if $P(b) = \mathbf{yes}$ if and only if $b = a$

The behavior of ι is unconstrained for properties that do not hold of a unique individual. Of course, such behavior must be fixed in a particular model. This makes ι a kind of *quasi-logical operator*, as its behavior is not completely determined by the frame. In a two-element model, the description operator is constrained to behave as follows, where ? indicates that a fixed value, a or b, must be provided, but which one is not constrained logically.

$$(14) \ [\![\iota]\!] =
\begin{bmatrix}
\begin{bmatrix} a \mapsto \mathbf{yes} \\ b \mapsto \mathbf{yes} \end{bmatrix} \mapsto \text{?} \\[2ex]
\begin{bmatrix} a \mapsto \mathbf{yes} \\ b \mapsto \mathbf{no} \end{bmatrix} \mapsto a \\[2ex]
\begin{bmatrix} a \mapsto \mathbf{no} \\ b \mapsto \mathbf{yes} \end{bmatrix} \mapsto b \\[2ex]
\begin{bmatrix} a \mapsto \mathbf{no} \\ b \mapsto \mathbf{no} \end{bmatrix} \mapsto \text{?}
\end{bmatrix}$$

In a partial logic, or one with a distinguished truth value "undefined," the behavior of ι may be constrained to be undefined in cases where it is applied to a nonsingleton.

For convenience, I will also assume that we have the constants **true** and **false** such that the model interprets **true** as **yes** and **false** as **no**. These constants, and in fact all other logical constants, can be defined using only the description and equality operators. I leave the verification of this result as exercise 16.

I adopt the standard definitions of logical notions for higher-order logic. In particular, a *formula* is an expression of type **Bool**, and a *statement* is a formula with no free variables. We say that a formula is *valid* if and only if it is true in every model. Similarly, two terms are *logically equivalent* if and only if they have the same value in every model.

Although many linguists claim to have intuitions concerning which expression in a construction acts functionally and which acts as an argument, the distinction is blurred in higher-order logic. For instance, the following two terms are logically equivalent:

(15) **run(kim)** $\equiv (\lambda P.P(\textbf{kim}))(\textbf{run})$

In this example, **run** appears as either the argument or the function with the same result, which is immediate by β-reduction. Of course, we could try to argue for the function or argument status of an expression in terms of the underlying type of its constant, but I feel no need to do so. In fact, in the categorial grammars I introduce shortly, the distinction is also blurred in the syntax.

Along similar lines, we can raise the types of the logical operations. For instance, property coordination can be defined as follows.

(16) **and**$_{\textbf{Ind}\rightarrow\textbf{Bool}} \stackrel{\text{def}}{=} \lambda P.\lambda Q.\lambda x.\textbf{and}(P(x))(Q(x))$

Thus if we have two properties like **run** and **jump**, we can derive the following via β-reduction:

(17) **and**$_{\textbf{Ind}\rightarrow\textbf{Bool}}(\textbf{run})(\textbf{jump}) \equiv \lambda x.\textbf{and}(\textbf{run}(x))(\textbf{jump}(x))$

Of course, we can also produce higher-order equivalents of property negation, and so on.

3.3 QUANTIFIERS IN NATURAL LANGUAGE

The behavior of noun phrases in natural language provides our first application of type-logical methodology. I begin with an explanation of how natural language determiners and quantifiers can be treated compositionally within higher-order logic. In the next section we consider some of the properties that the generalized quantifiers found in natural language have all been found to possess.

3.3.1   A Compositional Approach to Quantifiers

The roots of this approach date back to Russell's (1905) endeavor to resolve the apparent discrepancy among the logical contributions of the subjects of the following simple sentences.

(18) a. Lee ran.   (Proper name)
      b. The kid ran.   (Definite article)
      c. A kid ran.   (Indefinite aritcle)
      d. Some kid ran.   (Existential quantifier)
      e. Every kid ran.   (Universal quantifier)
      f. No kid ran.   (Negative quantifier)

With these five examples, we see the three basic patterns of singular noun phrases in English: proper names, articles, and quantifiers. Russell was puzzled by the fact that first-order logic translations for these sentences showed a distinction not expressed by the grammatical form of the sentences. Consider the standard translations of these sentences into first-order logic:

(19) a. $\mathbf{run}(\mathbf{lee})$
      b. $\mathbf{run}(\iota(\mathbf{kid}))$
      c. $(\exists x)(\mathbf{kid}(x) \wedge \mathbf{run}(x))$
      d. $(\exists x)(\mathbf{kid}(x) \wedge \mathbf{run}(x))$
      e. $(\forall x)(\mathbf{kid}(x) \rightarrow \mathbf{run}(x))$
      f. $\neg(\exists x)(\mathbf{kid}(x) \wedge \mathbf{run}(x)) \equiv (\forall x)(\mathbf{kid}(x) \rightarrow \neg\mathbf{run}(x))$

Logically, proper names and definite noun phrases are translated as individuals to which a verbal predicate applies. The other noun phrases translate as a combination of a quantifier, a restriction on the variable, and some logical apparatus. (For the time being, I have simplified matters with respect to the indefinite article by treating it as synonymous with the existential quantifier.) Russell's (1905) solution to this puzzle, although not stated type-theoretically, was to treat all noun phrases as behaving as functions over their verb phrases (see section 7.8). Russell's semantic insight lies at the heart of the type-logical account of quantifiers.

The contemporary solution to Russell's dilemma emerged in two stages. First, the compositional contribution of the quantifier, nominal restriction, and predicate scope were isolated in higher-order logic (Henkin 1950) by means of generalized quantifiers (Mostowski 1957). We can already see the beginning of this process in the definition of **every**$_{Ind}$ in higher-order logic as being of type $(\textbf{Ind} \to \textbf{Bool}) \to \textbf{Bool}$. This allows a quantifier to apply to a property to produce a truth value. The same abstraction can be applied to the noun position. A *generalized determiner* can then be taken to be a relation between two properties, one contributed by the restriction from the noun and one contributed by the predicate supplying the scope of the quantification. As such, its type will be $(\textbf{Ind} \to \textbf{Bool}) \to (\textbf{Ind} \to \textbf{Bool}) \to \textbf{Bool}$. Thus a generalized determiner applies to a property (supplied linguistically by a noun) to produce a generalized quantifier. In higher-order logic, we can calculate the contributions of the determiners to the meaning of a sentence by finding the values for the constants **some**^{2}, **every**^{2}, and **no**^{2} in the following. I distinguish the quantifier **some** from the determiner **some**^{2} by superscripting a 2 to the determiner to indicate it takes two arguments; I will ellide the superscript when the use as a determiner is clear from context.

(20) a. $\textbf{some}^2(\textbf{kid})(\textbf{run}) \equiv \textbf{some}(\lambda x.\textbf{kid}(x) \wedge \textbf{run}(x))$
   b. $\textbf{every}^2(\textbf{kid})(\textbf{run}) \equiv \textbf{every}(\lambda x.\textbf{kid}(x) \to \textbf{run}(x))$
   c. $\textbf{no}^2(\textbf{kid})(\textbf{run}) \equiv \neg\textbf{some}(\lambda x.\textbf{kid}(x) \wedge \textbf{run}(x))$

Solving for the determiners gives the following results.

(21) a. $\textbf{some}^2 \stackrel{\text{def}}{=} \lambda P.\lambda Q.\textbf{some}(\lambda x.P(x) \wedge Q(x))$
   b. $\textbf{every}^2 \stackrel{\text{def}}{=} \lambda P.\lambda Q.\textbf{every}(\lambda x.P(x) \to Q(x))$
   c. $\textbf{no}^2 \stackrel{\text{def}}{=} \lambda P.\lambda Q.\neg\textbf{some}(\lambda x.P(x) \wedge Q(x))$

The second key step in setting Russell's fears to rest was made by Montague and lies at the heart of his "proper treatment" of quantifiers (Montague 1973). This insight raised the type of individuals so that they were treated as generalized quantifiers. That is, we apply the same trick as in (20) with simple names.

(22) $Q(\textbf{run}) \equiv \textbf{run}(\textbf{lee})$

With higher-order logic, we can solve this equation by taking $Q = \lambda P.P(\textbf{lee})$, because $(\lambda P.P(\textbf{lee}))(\textbf{run}) \equiv \textbf{run}(\textbf{lee})$. Note that the equation in (22) has another solution, namely $Q = \lambda P.\textbf{run}(\textbf{lee})$, but the vacuous abstraction is a tipoff that this is not the entry that we are after; similar trivial solutions exist for the equations in (20) too. The semantic term $\lambda P.P(\textbf{lee})$ has a natural interpretation: it is the set of all properties that Lee has. Thought of in this way, it is natural to see a subject-verb phrase as analyzed with the subject acting as a higher-order predicate over the verb phrase. The beauty of Montague's approach to proper names as generalized quantifiers is that it allows the syntactically natural category of noun phrases to be realized uniformly in the semantic dimension.

Unlike ordinary quantifiers such as the universal and the existential, type-raised names do not participate in scope ambiguities. Thus the following fails in general:

(23) $Q_1(\lambda x. Q_2(\lambda y. \alpha)) \equiv Q_2(\lambda y. Q_1(\lambda x. \alpha))$

But when one of the quantifiers is a type-raised individual, the resulting terms are the same:

(24) $Q(\lambda x.(\lambda P. P(\mathbf{lee}))(\lambda y. \alpha))$
$\equiv Q(\lambda x.(\lambda y. \alpha)(\mathbf{lee}))$
$\equiv Q(\lambda x.\alpha[y \mapsto \mathbf{lee}])$
$\equiv Q((\lambda x.\alpha)[y \mapsto \mathbf{lee}])$
$\equiv (\lambda y. Q(\lambda x.\alpha))(\mathbf{lee})$
$\equiv (\lambda P. P(\mathbf{lee}))(\lambda y. Q(\lambda x.\alpha))$

When we turn to a grammar for multiple quantifiers, this fact will explain why *Someone likes everyone* displays an ambiguity in interpretation that is absent in *Leslie likes everyone* and *Someone likes Leslie*.

3.3.2   Properties of Natural-Language Quantifiers

In this section we consider a number of properties with which we can classify natural-language determiners and quantifiers. I will also discuss some proposed universal constraints on the kinds of interpretations possible for determiners in natural languages.

Recall that generalized quantifiers take a property as an argument and return a truth value, whereas determiners take a property as an argument and return a generalized quantifier. That is, a generalized determiner takes two property arguments and returns a truth value. We have already considered truth conditions for simple existential, universal, and negative determiners. In table 3.1, I restate these conditions and introduce truth conditions for several other determiners. Note that the arguments P and Q to the determiners correspond to a pair of properties, with P being derived from the noun argument and Q being the property over which the quantifier has scope. As usual, we are moving back and forth between a conception of properties as characteristic functions and as sets. I begin by glossing the definitions for the truth of $D(P)(Q)$ for several determiners

Table 3.1
Truth conditions for generalized determiners

Determiner	Truth conditions
$[\![\mathbf{every}]\!](P)(Q)$	$P \subseteq Q$
$[\![\mathbf{some}]\!](P)(Q)$	$P \cap Q \neq \emptyset$
$[\![\mathbf{no}]\!](P)(Q)$	$P \cap Q = \emptyset$
$[\![\mathbf{three_=}]\!](P)(Q)$	$\|P \cap Q\| = 3$
$[\![\mathbf{three_\leq}]\!](P)(Q)$	$\|P \cap Q\| \leq 3$
$[\![\mathbf{three_\geq}]\!](P)(Q)$	$\|P \cap Q\| \geq 3$
$[\![\mathbf{the}]\!](P)(Q)$	$\|P\| = 1$ and $P \cap Q \neq \emptyset$
$[\![\mathbf{most}]\!](P)(Q)$	$\|P \cap Q\| > \|P - Q\|$
$[\![\mathbf{few}]\!](P)(Q)$	$\|P \cap Q\| \ll \|P - Q\|$

D. For the universal determiner **every**, the condition that $P \subseteq Q$ requires every individual in the denotation of the noun to be in the denotation of the scope. For instance, a simple sentence such as *Every kid ran* has a meaning we could represent as **every**(**kid**)(**run**), where **kid** is the representation of the noun and **run** is the representation of the verb phrase. For a sentence such as *Sandy likes every kid*, we have **every**(**kid**)($\lambda x.$**like**$(x)(\mathbf{s})$), where the property in the scope is that of being liked by Sandy. For the existential **some**, we require the intersection of the noun denotation and the scope denotation to be nonempty; in other words, some individual must be in both the denotation of the noun and the denotation of the scope. The negative determiner **no** is simply the negation of **some**. I have used $\|P\|$ to denote the cardinality of the set P (see section A.2 for a definition of cardinality). I have split the numerical determiners into three classes, corresponding to equality and lower and upper bounds. Specifically, **three**$_=$ requires the number of objects in both the noun and scope denotation to be exactly three, **three**$_\leq$ requires three or less elements in the intersection, and **three**$_\geq$ requires three or more elements. The definite determiner **the** is defined as a quantifier by requiring the noun denotation to be a singleton and requiring that singleton to be an element of the denotation of the scope. For **most**, we require the number of elements in the denotation of the noun and the scope to be greater than the number in the noun less the scope; in other words, the Ps that are Qs have to outnumber the Ps that are not Qs. The notation $P \ll Q$ employed in the definition of **few** is a standard notation taken to mean that the size of P is "much smaller" than

Q; I do not provide a precise definition because of the inherent vagueness of *few*. Other vague quantifiers include *several* and *many*.

We begin our study of quantifiers by considering some general properties that will allow us to classify them along useful dimensions. If we think of properties of type $\tau \rightarrow$ **Bool** as a set of objects of type τ, we have a natural subset ordering of properties. This classifies quantifiers with respect to their behavior as the size of their set arguments is increased or decreased.

DEFINITION: MONOTONICITY   A function α of type $(\tau \rightarrow$ **Bool**$) \rightarrow$ **Bool** is said to be *monotonically increasing (decreasing)* if and only if whenever $\alpha(T) =$ **yes** and $T \subseteq T'$ $(T \supseteq T')$, we have $\alpha(T') =$ **yes**.

Usually a monotonically increasing function is simply referred to as being *monotonic*. We can actually study the monotonicity of determiners in both of their argument positions. Determiners that are upward monotonic in their first argument are said to be *persistent*, and those that are downward monotonic in their first argument are said to be *antipersistent*. To define monotonicity in the first argument or second argument of a determiner, we consider the generalized quantifiers $\lambda X . Q(X)(A)$ and $\lambda X . Q(A)(X)$ composed from the generalized determiner Q by abstracting one argument and filling the other with a term A. For instance, **some** is monotonic upwards in both positions, because both $\lambda X . \mathbf{some}(X)(A)$ and $\lambda Y . \mathbf{some}(A)(Y)$ are monotonic for every A. Note that it is not enough to establish monotonicity for a fixed A. For instance, $\lambda X . \mathbf{some}(X)(\emptyset)$ is downward monotonic, but we do not say that **some** is downward monotonic in its first position. Next consider **no**; it is downward monotonic in both arguments. On the other hand, **every** is downward monotonic in its first argument and upward monotonic in its second. But positions need not be one or the other; **three**$_=$ is neither upward or downward monotonic in either of its arguments. I leave as an exercise the complete classification of argument positions and turn to some other properties of quantifiers.

In applications to natural language, we know that certain classes of modifiers, like prepositions and relative clauses, restrict the denotation of the element they modify. For instance, consider the following:

(25) a. Chris is a [red fish] $\vdash$ Chris is a [fish]
     b. Chris [ran in the park] $\vdash$ Chris [ran]
     c. Chris is a [kid who I know] $\vdash$ Chris is a [kid]

In each case the denotation of the modifier-noun combination is a (not necessarily strict) subset of the denotation of the noun being modified.

This general property of modifiers, when coupled with monotonicity, allows us to account for the following patterns of inference.

(26) a. Every fish swims ⊢ Every red fish swims
     b. Some red fish swims ⊢ Some fish swims
     c. No kid ran ⊢ No kid ran in the park
     d. No kid passed ⊢ No kid who I know passed
     e. Some kid who I know passed ⊢ Some kid passed

A slightly weaker notion than monotonicity is that of closure under intersection and union.

DEFINITION: CLOSURE   A quantifier Q is said to *closed under union* (*intersection*) if $Q(X)$ and $Q(Y)$ entail $Q(X \cup Y)$ ($Q(X \cap Y)$).

Trivially, every monotonic upward quantifier is closed under union, and every downward monotonic quantifier is closed under intersection. But consider the universal determiner **every**, which is upward monotonic in its second argument but is also closed under intersection: **every**$(P)(S)$ and **every**$(P)(R)$ imply **every**$(P)(S \cap R)$. The universal determiner is downward monotonic in its first argument and is also closed under union. Similarly, the negative determiner **no** is downward monotonic in both arguments but is also closed under union. The existential quantifier, on the other hand, is not closed under intersection.

Given the close correspondence between the union and intersection of sets and logical disjunction and conjunction, closures account for the following inferences:

(27) a. Every kid ran and every kid jumped ⊢ Every kid ran and jumped
     b. Every kid ran and every dog ran ⊢ Every kid or dog ran
     c. No kid ran and no kid jumped ⊢ No kid ran or jumped
     d. No kid ran and no adult ran ⊢ No kid or adult ran

The converses are also valid; they follow from the various monotonicity properties of the quantifiers.

Two additional properties have a logical motivation but can be applied to the study of quantifiers.

DEFINITION: CONSISTENCY   A quantifier Q is said to be *consistent* if and only if $Q(X)$ implies $\neg Q(\neg X)$.

DEFINITION: COMPLETENESS   A quantifier Q is said to *complete* if and only if $\neg Q(X)$ implies $Q(\neg X)$.

Note that I used a generalized notation for negation where $\neg X$ is short-hand for $\lambda y. \neg X(y)$. The terminology here is logical: a theory is *consistent* if it does not contain a formula and its negation and is *complete* if for every formula, it contains either the formula or its negation. Note that this is a different kind of completeness from the completeness of a proof theory with respect to a model theory. In particular, the set of formulas true in a model with respect to a fixed assignment forms a complete theory in the present sense.

It is clear from their definition that quantifiers corresponding to proper names, which are of the form $\lambda P.P(\alpha)$, are consistent and complete. For consistency, note that if $(\lambda P.P(\alpha))(X) \equiv X(\alpha)$ holds, then $\neg(\lambda P.P(\alpha))(\lambda y. \neg X(y)) \equiv \neg\neg X(\alpha)$ also holds. For completeness, note that if $\neg(\lambda P.P(\alpha))(X) \equiv \neg X(\alpha)$ holds, then we have $(\lambda P.P(\alpha))(\lambda y. \neg X(y)) \equiv \neg X(\alpha)$. Note that the existential quantifier is complete but not consistent, whereas the universal quantifier is neither.

Consistency and completeness provide insight into the interaction of quantifiers with negation. Several quantifiers are sensitive to the difference between verb-phrase scope and sentential scope for negation. For instance, consider the difference between the following:

(28) a. Every kid did not run.
     b. It is not the case that every kid ran.

The first sentence, (28a), has a reading in which every kid has the property of not running. This involves what is known as *verb-phrase negation*. The second sentence, (28b), has a reading in which it is not the case that every kid has the property of running. This is derived by *sentential negation*. Although the first sentence has an additional reading that is synonymous with the reading of the second sentence, our type-logical grammar allows a unified analysis of the negative particle *not* in terms of verb-phrase negation (see section 7.7). We will also be able to capture the subtleties of the interaction of contraction and negation scope (see exercise 6, chapter 11).

Sentence negation can be assigned a meaning which is just the ordinary propositional negation operator of type **Bool** $\rightarrow$ **Bool**. The type-theoretical reflection of verb-phrase negation is property negation, of type (**Ind** $\rightarrow$ **Bool**) $\rightarrow$ (**Ind** $\rightarrow$ **Bool**). It is standard to overload the negation symbol, using it for both propositional and property negation, according to the following definition.

(29) $\neg P \overset{\text{def}}{=} \lambda x. \neg P(x)$

Note that the use of $\neg$ on the left-hand side of this definition in $\neg P$ is property negation, whereas the use of $\neg P(x)$ on the right-hand side is simple boolean negation. This definition simply distributes the negation through the abstracted variable, which is known as a *pointwise* definition. Thus property negation is nothing more than the pointwise application of boolean negation. With the aid of these two forms of negation, the examples in (28) can be translated into higher-order logic as follows:

(30) a. **every**(**kid**)(**¬run**) $\equiv$ **every**(**kid**)($\lambda x. \neg$**run**(x))
    b. **¬every**(**kid**)(**run**)

Clearly these boolean terms have distinct truth conditions. In the case of the universal **every**, verb-phrase negation entails sentential negation, but in the case of **some**, the entailment is reversed (assuming a nonempty set of individuals).

Quantifiers defined from individuals, such as $\lambda P. P(\text{lee})$, are both consistent and complete, as the following shows:

(31) $(\lambda P. P(\text{lee}))(\neg\text{run}) \equiv \neg\text{run}(\text{lee}) \equiv \neg(\lambda P. P(\text{lee}))(\text{run})$

This corresponds to the equivalence of the following sentences involving sentential and verb-phrase negation:

(32) Lee did not run $\dashv\vdash$ It is not the case that Lee ran

Note that I have used the notation $\dashv\vdash$ to indicate that entailment goes in both directions.

In general, if a quantifier is complete, then a simple use of sentence negation entails the simple use of verb-phrase negation, as in the following:

(33) It is not the case that someone ran $\vdash$ Someone did not run

This result requires a nonempty domain of individuals, as we have assumed. If a quantifier is consistent, then verb-phrase negation entails sentence negation. This is because if $Q(X)$ implies $\neg Q(\neg X)$, then by contraposition, $\neg\neg Q(\neg X)$, that is, $Q(\neg X)$, implies $\neg Q(X)$.

Pointwise applying negation to the quantifier or the determiner provides the same result as sentential negation, no matter what the behavior of the quantifier by itself (assuming the quantifier has widest scope, which it must have if there is only one quantifier; we return to the notion of quantifier scope in chapter 7). That is, we can define $\neg Q \overset{\text{def}}{=} \lambda P. \neg Q(P)$

for quantifier negation and $\neg D \overset{\text{def}}{=} \lambda P.\lambda R.\neg D(P)(R)$ for determiner negation. Assuming that negating a quantifier involves quantifier negation and negating a determiner involves determiner negation, the following three sentences are synonymous.

(34) a. [Not every] kid ran.
      b. [Not [every kid]] ran.
      c. It is not the case that every kid ran.

All of these cases are analyzed as meaning $\neg \mathbf{every}^2 (\mathbf{kid})(\mathbf{run})$.

Determiners such as $\mathbf{no}^2$, $\mathbf{some}^2$, and $\mathbf{three}^2_=$ are insensitive to the order of their arguments. We have the following general definition:

DEFINITION: SYMMETRY   A determiner D is said to be *symmetric* if $D(A)(B)$ holds if and only if $D(B)(A)$ holds.

Symmetry allows us to swap information between the verb phrase and the noun phrase.

(35) a. Some kid ran ⊣⊢ Some runner is a kid
      b. Exactly three kids I know are runners ⊣⊢ Exactly three runners are kids I know

An even stronger property than symmetry is pure distributivity of information, which can also be seen in the determiners **some**, **no**, and **three**$_=$:

(36) $D(B \cap C)(A)$ if and only if $D(B)(A \cap C)$

This allows us to make the following kinds of reassociations, rendering all of the following examples truth-conditionally equivalent.

(37) a. Some kid who I like ran.
      b. Some kid is a runner who I like.
      c. Some runner who I like is a kid.
      d. Some runner is a kid who I like.

Of course, it is mathematically possible to have a symmetric quantifier that does not allow this kind of distributivity, but clearly this form of distributivity entails symmetry.

We now turn to some properties that have been claimed to hold universally not only of all determiners in English but also of all determiners in all natural languages.

DEFINITION: CONSERVATIVITY   A determiner D is said to be *conservative* just in case $D(A)(B)$ holds if and only if $D(A)(A \cap B)$ holds.

All of the determiners we have considered so far are conservative. Sometimes the property of conservativity is expressed by saying that natural-language determiners *live on their nominal argument.* In other words, the universe set up by the nominal argument is all that matters when looking at the predicate argument. In my analysis of plurals in chapter 8, I provide type-theoretical motivation for treating certain determinerlike expressions such as *three* and some uses of *few* as modifiers rather than as determiners. In these cases, because of the type mismatch between the nominal arguments, which are treated sets of sets, and verbal arguments, which are treated as sets, the notion of conservativity becomes moot.

Another key property claimed to hold of all natural-language determiners is permutation invariance. Specifically, natural-language determiners are not sensitive to facts about particular individuals but rather are concerned with more abstract properties of sets and their relations to one another. More formally, we have the following:

DEFINITION: PERMUTATION INVARIANCE   A determiner D is said to be *permutation-invariant* if for every permutation $\pi: \mathbf{Dom}_\tau \to \mathbf{Dom}_\tau$ of the domain, $D(A)(B)$ holds if and only if $D(\pi(A))(\pi(B))$ holds.

Recall that a permutation is a one-one and onto function from a set to itself. I have used the notation $\pi(B)$ in the usual way to stand for $\{\pi(b)|b \in B\}$. All of the determiners we have considered are permutation-invariant in the sense of this definition. We consider an alternative, equivalent presentation of permutation invariance in exercise 23.

A permutation-invariant determiner is often said to have the property of *quantity.* This is because with a permutation-invariant determiner D, the truth of $D(A)(B)$ only depends on the cardinalities of the sets $A \cap B$, $A - B$, $B - A$, and the entire domain $\mathbf{Dom}_{\mathrm{Ind}}$. I leave the relatively straightforward proof of this proposition as exercise 23.

Despite the relatively severe restrictions of permutation invariance, it has been further claimed that natural-language determiners depend not on the size of the domain of individuals but only the individuals in the extension of the nominal and verbal arguments, that is, A and B in $D(A)(B)$.

DEFINITION: EXTENSION   A determiner D is said to be *extendable* if the truth of $D(A)(B)$ depends only on A and B and not on any individuals in $\mathbf{Dom}_{\mathrm{Ind}} - (A \cup B)$.

This is a rather difficult condition to state formally, insofar as we tend to consider only a single domain of indivduals, and this condition is essentially metatheoretical in its comparison of different possible frames of domains.

A natural-language determiner is said to be *logical* if it is conservative, permutation-invariant, and has extension. Thus a logical determiner D has truth conditions for $D(A)(B)$ that depend only on the relative sizes of $A - B$ and $A \cap B$. The standard claim is that all natural-language determiners are logical.

An important disclaimer is in order before concluding. The universal claim of logicality is typically restricted to lexical determiners. Logicality does not hold of nonlexical determiners such as possessives, as in *Sandy's*, or compositions, as in *some tall*. I postpone discussion of these determinerlike expressions until chapter 7 and their nonlogicality until exercise 12 of that chapter.

3.4 NEGATIVE POLARITY ITEMS

There are some expressions in natural language whose distribution is sensitive to the so-called *polarity* of the context in which they occur. For example, consider the adverb *ever*.

(38) a. *Kim [ever did run]. $\lambda P. P(\mathbf{k})$
     b. *Kim did [ever run]. $\lambda P. P(\mathbf{k})$
     c.   Kim did not [ever run]. $\lambda P. \neg P(\mathbf{k})$
     d. *Kim did [ever not run]. $\lambda P. P(\mathbf{k})$
     e. *Someone [ever did run]. $\lambda P. \mathbf{some}(P)$
     f. *Someone did [ever run]. $\lambda P. \mathbf{some}(P)$
     g.   No one [ever did run]. $\lambda P. \mathbf{no}(P)$
     h.   No one did [ever run]. $\lambda P. \mathbf{no}(P)$

Ladusaw (1979) noticed that *ever* (and related polarity-sensitive expressions) can only modify verb phrases that occur in a so-called *negative polarity* context. As shown in the examples, higher-order logic allows the context of an occurrence of a verb phrase to be characterized as a function of the same type as a generalized quantifier. Ladusaw further noticed that the contexts that license negative-polarity items such as *ever* are just the downward monotonic ones.

Negative-polarity items can be found in many lexical categories. In addition to adverb *ever*, the quantifier *any* on its existential reading is only found in negative contexts.

(39) a. *Robin did have [any training].
   b. Robin did not have [any training].
   c. *Everyone had [any training].
   d. No one had [any training].

In a positive context, *any* only has a habitual reading.

(40) a. Sandy climbed [any mountain].
   b. Sandy does not climb [any mountain].

In the first example, (40a), *any* can only be understood generically or quasi universally. The second example, (40b), on the other hand, can be understood not only as the negation of the generic (40a) but also as the negation of an existential. The latter reading arises because the negative-polarity context licenses the occurrence of the existential *any*.

  Another negative-polarity item is the idiomatic intransitive verb phrase *to budge an inch*.

(41) a. *Terry did [budge an inch].
   b. Terry did not [budge an inch].
   c. *Someone [budged an inch].
   d. No one [budged an inch].

There are lexical distinctions in polarity that go beyond the logical categories of negative particles and determiners.

(42) a. Chris failed to {[ever run] / like [anyone]}.
   b. ?Chris did not fail to {[ever run] / like [anyone]}.
   c. *Chris needed to {[ever run] / like [anyone]}.
   d. Chris did not need to {[ever run] / like [anyone]}.

Here we see that the semantic negativity of the verb *fail* licenses the negative polarity item in (42a) and renders it odd in (42b), whereas the lexically positive *need* engenders the complementary distribution of negative polarity items, as seen in (42c) and (42d).

  The following examples illustrate that polarity sensitivity is not a local matter but permeates embedded contexts. The polarity of the nested item depends not only on local elements but on how they are embedded.

(43) a. {*Some / No / Every} student who has had any training could have written that.
   b. {Some / ?No / ?Every} student who has not had any training could have written that.

Recall that the generalized determiner *every* is downward monotonic in its first argument, and thus it patterns with *no* rather than *some*. The examples in (43b) marked with a question mark are more subtle because double negations cause the semantic polarity of an embedded position to be reversed. Specifically, the negative determiner *no* and the verb phrase negation *not* conspire to produce a positive polarity context for the relativized verb phrase. Nestings of polarities are rather difficult to process in general, as the following simpler examples show:

(44) a. ?Someone {didn't / failed to} win anything.
     b. ?No one {didn't / failed to} win anything.
     c. ?No one didn't {not / fail to} win anything.
     d. ?No one didn't fail to not win anything.

According to one conception of negative polarity items, they should be allowable if and only if there is some negative polarity context that licenses the negative polarity item. According to such a theory, (42b) and all of the examples in (44) would be acceptable. On the other hand, if negative polarity items required true negative polarity with respect to the entire sentence in which they are embedded, we would expect the grammer to be different, with (44b) and (44d) being ungrammatical. It is fairly straightforward in a type-logical account of grammar to mark types for their polarities (Sánchez Valencia 1991) and to provide a deductive account of their propagation (Dowty 1994); I leave the matter as exercise 16, chapter 7.

3.5   DEFINITE DESCRIPTIONS

In my survey of quantificational determiners, I deliberately avoided discussion of the definite article *the*. Historically, there have been two dominant approaches to the behavior of definites. For instance, consider the noun phrase *the best student*. On the first account, it introduces an existential quantifier with a restriction that the individual be the unique best student. The second approach takes *the best student* to be referential, with the condition that it be taken to refer to the unique individual who is the best student acting as a presupposition.

3.5.1   Quantificational Definites

Russell (1905) introduced the theory of definite descriptions in which they are interpreted quantificationally. Their quantificational force is existential. A sentence such as *The best student runs* entails the existence of a best student. Furthermore, Russell accounted for the *definiteness* of the determiner by placing a restriction on the quantifier that there be exactly one entity denoted by the noun in question. With higher-order logic, Russell's definite quantifier and its corresponding predicate can be defined as follows:

(45) a. **the** $\overset{\text{def}}{=}$ $\lambda P.\lambda Q.\textbf{some}(P)(Q) \wedge \textbf{definite}(P)$
      b. **definite** $\overset{\text{def}}{=}$ $\lambda P.\textbf{some}(\lambda y.\textbf{every}(\lambda x.P(x) \leftrightarrow x = y))$

With this definition, **the**$(P)(Q)$ is true if and only if there is exactly one member x of P and furthermore x has the property Q.

Under Russell's analysis, the entailment of a definite that the referent exists can be cancelled. For instance, Russell considers the interaction of definite subjects and verb negation. He argued that (46a) has two distinct readings, analogous to verb-phrase and sentence negation, which I represent as (46b) and (46c).

(46) a. The king of France is not bald.
      b. **the**(**king**(**fr**))$(\lambda x.\neg\textbf{bald}(x))$ (Primary)
      c. $\neg$**the**(**king**(**fr**))(**bald**)   (Secondary)

Here I have assumed that **king** is a binary relation so that **king**(**fr**) is the property of being the king of France. On the first reading, (46b), which Russell called the *primary reading*, we have verb-phrase negation, because the property applying to the verb phrase is negated. That is, we have the term $\lambda x.\neg\textbf{bald}(x)$, which denotes the complement of the denotation of the embedded verb-phrase term **bald**. We then use this negated property in the scope of the definite **the**. The resulting term, (46b), will be true if and only if there is a unique king of France and he is not bald. On the second reading, (46c), which Russell called the *secondary reading*, we have sentence negation, because the negation takes scope over the remaining content of the sentence. Note that the term (46c) is true if and only if it is not the case that there is a unique king of France that also happens to be bald. It is important to note that (46c) could be true for two reasons. In the first case, there could be a unique king of France, and he could turn out to be hirsute rather than bald. Second, there could simply be no unique king of France, either because there are none or because there are more than one. Thus, at least under the secondary reading, the truth of a sentence involving a definite does not always entail the existence of a referent for that definite.

When I introduce a grammar of quantification in chapter 7, the two readings in (46) will be generated for all sentences with subject quantifiers and negated verb phrases. We will also see how the theory of quantification extends the situation with a single subject-position quantifier to cases in which multiple quantifiers, often in complex structural configurations, interact in terms of scope. On a quantificational theory of definites, it will be clear how definites can interact with other scope-bearing expressions.

3.5.2 Referential Definites

Strawson (1950) questioned the availability of the secondary reading, (46c), in which a verbal negation scopes over an indefinite subject quantifier. As evidence, Strawson considered simple discourses such as the following, in which a question is addressed to a clerk in a hotel that does not employ a porter.

(47) q.   Is the porter on duty?
   a.   There is no porter.
   b. #No.

Strawson claimed that the first possible response, (47a), is the only felicitous one. A simple negative reply, as in (47b), should be deemed pragmatically infelicitous due to the failed reference of *the porter*.

To account for a broadly Strawsonian account of definites, we can employ the description operator ι. This move allows us to translate a noun phrase such as *the king of France* into a term of type **Ind**, namely $\iota(\mathbf{king}(\mathbf{fr}))$. Then if we translate (46a) into higher-order logic, we have a unique result:

(48) $\neg\mathbf{bald}(\iota(\mathbf{king}(\mathbf{fr})))$

The only problem is that in our higher-order logical setting, where logical connectives are translated into the λ-calculus, the behavior of the description operator ι is less than ideally suited as a translation of the definite article. The drawback is that if the property argument P does not denote a singleton set, the behavior of $\iota(P)$ is unregulated.

The proposal embraced by Strawson for such failed referents was to claim that the whole sentence should simply fail to be well formed because of a failure of the presupposition engendered by the use of the definite. Thus a sentence such as (46a) should simply receive no truth value if there is no king of France. One approach to Strawson's analysis within higher-order logic would be to admit partial functions, but partiality has dramatic logical consequences. For an introduction to the issues involved in developing a higher-order logic with partial functions, see Muskens 1989a, 1989b. A second, perhaps more promising approach would be to follow the lead of programming language semantics, in which many theories of error detection, passing, and control have been elaborated (Stoy 1977, Gunter 1992). In the simplest case, the application of a definite article to a non-singleton-denoting property would raise a so-called *exception*. Furthermore, any program receiving an exceptional input itself raises an exception. Semantically, we can add an exceptional element to each domain and return that value when an exception has been found. Preferably, the domain of errors would itself be highly structured rather than a singleton, as in the programming language ML, thus allowing information about the error to be propagated. Such a mechanism might be useful in generating cooperative responses, such as (47a), to presuppositional failures, such as (47q).

I do not attempt to settle the debate concerning the nature of definite noun phrases. Rather, I develop type-logical accounts of both approaches in section 7.8. The only truth-conditional issue that could decide between the two approaches is the status of examples such as (46).

3.5.3 Contextual Elaboration

Strawson (1950) pointed out that the meaning of the noun underdetermines the restriction supplied to quantificational and referential determiners. When a quantifier such as *every student* or *no student* is used, the quantification is typically not over every student in the world but rather over some contextually restricted subset of such individuals. The same holds of definite uses, such as *the student*, and even superlative uses, such as *the best student*. As noted by Russell (1959), the theory of contextual refinement is independent of whether definiteness is treated referentially or quantificationally.

Such contextual elaboration is always restrictive; we never find elements admitted into the quantification that do not fall into the denotation of the nominal restriction. On the other hand, we have no theory of how such referential restrictions might be constrained grammatically. In fact, we believe this is a purely pragmatic issue. With our general semantic approach to meaning, if a promising theory of contextual restrictions were to come along, it would be straightforward to incorporate it into both the general theory of quantification and into the interpretation of referential definites. One standard technique is to encode the meaning of a

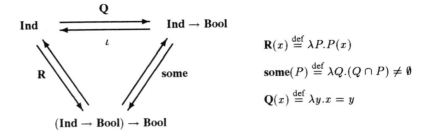

$$\mathbf{R}(x) \overset{\text{def}}{=} \lambda P.P(x)$$

$$\mathbf{some}(P) \overset{\text{def}}{=} \lambda Q.(Q \cap P) \neq \emptyset$$

$$\mathbf{Q}(x) \overset{\text{def}}{=} \lambda y.x = y$$

Figure 3.2
Nominal type shiftings

noun such as student as $\lambda x.\mathbf{student}(x) \wedge R_c(x)$, where the additional restriction R_c is determined contextually.

3.5.4   Nominal Type Shifting

After our consideration of definiteness, we are left with a tidy picture relating the principal nominal domains. We have combinators for type raising, which we write **R**, definite descriptions, and existential quantification. These operations provide the main routes for shifting types among the domains of individuals, properties, and generalized quantifiers. These mappings, along with the additional mapping **Q**, are depicted in figure 3.2. The purpose of the combinator **Q** is to map an individual into the property of being equal to it.

(49) $\mathbf{Q} \overset{\text{def}}{=} \lambda x.\lambda y.x = y$

The application of **Q** to an individual is often referred to as *quining*, after W.V.O. Quine, who originally introduced the operation.

The mappings **Q**, **R**, and **some** on the outside edges of the diagram in figure 3.2 are all total. Furthermore, these edges are said to *commute*, which means that different paths through the diagram lead to the same result. In the case of these operators, this amounts to the following (recall the definition of function composition from chapter 2, (8)).

$$
\begin{aligned}
(50) \quad \mathbf{some} \circ \mathbf{Q} &\equiv (\lambda Q.\lambda P.(Q \cap P) \neq \emptyset) \circ (\lambda x.\lambda y.x = y) \\
&\equiv \lambda z.(\lambda Q.\lambda P.(Q \cap P) \neq \emptyset)((\lambda x.\lambda y.x = y)(z)) \\
&\equiv \lambda z.(\lambda Q.\lambda P.(Q \cap P) \neq \emptyset)(\lambda y.z = y) \\
&\equiv \lambda z.\lambda P.((\lambda y.y = z) \cap P) \neq \emptyset \\
&\equiv \lambda z.\lambda P.P(z) \\
&\equiv \mathbf{R}
\end{aligned}
$$

In words, quining and then existentially quantifying amounts to the same result as raising. Similarly, we have the following relation (recall that $\mathbf{I}_\sigma \overset{\text{def}}{=} \lambda x^\sigma.x$).

(51) $\iota \circ \mathbf{Q} \equiv \mathbf{I}_{\mathbf{Ind}}$

Applying quining to an individual and then applying the description operator to the result produces the original individual. This is also a kind of commuting. Other paths cannot be guaranteed to commute because of the lack of totality of the operations. But in the case where we have a term P that denotes a singleton set, we have $\mathbf{Q}(\iota(P)) \equiv P$. The other arrows, those on the inside in figure 3.2, do not commute because the inverses of $\mathbf{R}$ and **some** are not necessarily well defined. The inverse of $\mathbf{R}$, $\mathbf{R}^{-1}$, is often called *quantifier lowering*. It maps a quantifier generated by the properties of an individual back to that individual. Of course, $\mathbf{R}^{-1}$ is not total, because not every quantifier is generated in this way from an individual. But $\mathbf{R}^{-1}$ commutes with $\mathbf{R}$ in that $\mathbf{R}^{-1} \circ \mathbf{R} = \mathbf{I}_{\mathbf{Ind}}$ in general and $\mathbf{R} \circ \mathbf{R}^{-1} \subseteq \mathbf{I}_{(\mathbf{Ind} \to \mathbf{Bool}) \to \mathbf{Bool}}$. The inverse of **some** behaves similarly, though it is of lesser interest.

These type-shifting operations have been employed by numerous linguists, most notably Montague (1973) and Partee and Rooth (1983, 1987; Rooth and Partee 1982). We will have several occasions to employ these operations in the sequel. The type-logical approach to grammar that I adopt has the benefit, over these previous analyses, of generating these operations where they are needed from the simple logic of syntactic combination.

3.6 PROOF THEORY FOR HIGHER-ORDER LOGIC

In our model theory I assumed what are known as *standard frames*, in which every total function from $\mathbf{Dom}_\sigma$ to $\mathbf{Dom}_\tau$ is an element of $\mathbf{Dom}_{\sigma \to \tau}$. This model-theoretic assumption has been standard in higher-order logics and in their application to natural language. But it suffers from the drawback that the resulting notion of logical consequence is not axiomatizable, or in other words, not recursively enumerable. In this section we consider the relaxation of the standard requirement on frames. Following Henkin (1950), I allow what are known as *general frames*, in which not every function of type $\sigma \to \tau$ is assumed to exist in the model. For these general models, Henkin provided a complete proof theory.

This situation may seem odd or even paradoxical at first glance. Although we are able to axiomatize logical equivalence in the general case of the simply typed λ-calculus, we cannot axiomatize the instance of it embodied in higher-order logic. On the other hand, by generalizing the λ-calculus notion of frame, we are able to axiomatize the resulting system. This is reminiscent of the situation in first-order logic, where Gödel's incompleteness theorem states that even though first-order validity is axiomatizable, validity in the standard model of natural numbers is not axiomatizable. In fact, the standard method of proving that higher-order logic is not axiomatizable simply demonstrates an encoding of arithmetic and applies the Gödel incompleteness theorem (Andrews 1986).

Henkin's (1950) definition of general frames, which leads to an axiomatizable version of higher-order logic, is as follows:

DEFINITION: GENERALIZED FRAME   A *generalized frame* consists of a collection of sets $\mathbf{Dom}_\tau$ for each type $\tau \in \mathbf{Typ}$ such that $\mathbf{Dom}_{\sigma \to \tau} \subseteq \mathbf{Dom}_\sigma^{\mathbf{Dom}_\tau}$.

The difference between a generalized frame and the frames I defined earlier, which are often known as *standard frames*, is that the set of functions in a generalized frame need not be complete. For instance, in a generalized frame we could take $\mathbf{Dom}_{\sigma \to \tau}$ to be the set of computable total functions from $\mathbf{Dom}_\sigma$ to $\mathbf{Dom}_\tau$. Similarly, if we were dealing with sets that formed topologies, we could take the set of continuous functions, or if we were dealing with domains that are algebras, we could take the homomorphic functions, and so on. But note that we are still assuming that every function in $\mathbf{Dom}_{\sigma \to \tau}$ is a total function.

We now have to be slightly more careful in interpreting our language over generalized frames. In particular, we have to make sure that all of the well-formed terms have a denotation. This is not so straightforward, because the λ-calculus is a powerful way of defining new functions. For instance, if α denotes a function of type $\sigma \to \tau$ and β denotes a function from $\tau \to \rho$, then $\lambda x.\beta(\alpha(x))$ denotes their composition, which is a function of type $\sigma \to \rho$. But the definition of generalized frames does not ensure that $g \circ f$ will be in $\mathbf{Dom}_{\sigma \to \rho}$ just because $f \in \mathbf{Dom}_{\sigma \to \tau}$ and $g \in \mathbf{Dom}_{\tau \to \rho}$. Thus we have to make sure that our generalized frames are populous enough to provide denotations for all of the terms we can define in the language. In moving to generalized models, all of our standard definitions remain the same. In particular, we take the same logical and nonlogical constants as before, assume that models assign values in the appropriate domain to constants, assume that assignments map variables to domain values of the appropriate type, and define denotations for terms recursively as before. We then simply require every term to have a denotation in the appropriate domain, which we state as follows:

DEFINITION: GENERALIZED MODEL   A pair $\mathcal{M} = \langle \mathbf{Dom}, [\![\cdot]\!] \rangle$ is a *generalized model* if and only if

a. **Dom** is a generalized frame,
b. $[\![\alpha]\!]_{\mathcal{M}}^{\sigma} \in \mathbf{Dom}_{\tau}$ if $\alpha \in \mathbf{Term}_{\tau}$.

The second clause here simply requires every term to have a denotation. In particular, every constant must be interpreted in the model. Further, I assume that the logical constants have the same denotations as I assumed for standard models. In particular, I adopt the basic types **Bool** and **Ind**, require that $\mathbf{Dom}_{\mathbf{Bool}} = \{\mathbf{yes}, \mathbf{no}\}$, and require that the logical connectives **and**, **not**, **eq**, and **every** are interpreted just as before. Of course, our previous models of higher-order logic are just generalized models based on a standard frame.

I now present an axiomatic system that is sound for models of higher-order logic and complete for generalized models. Just as for the λ-calculus, I axiomatize the notion of equality between terms, only this time the equality relation is in the object language. These axioms are drawn from Andrews 1986, which is based on the original complete axiomatization of Henkin (1950). Note that I have used our abbreviations and omitted types in these axioms to make them more readable. Also note that I have axiomatized only the behavior of equality and the description operator; the behavior of the other logical constants is determined by their definitions in terms of equality and description (see exercise 16).

DEFINITION: AXIOMS FOR GENERALIZED HIGHER-ORDER LOGIC   The axioms consist of all of the instances of the following schemes:

a. $\vdash P(\mathbf{true}) \wedge P(\mathbf{false}) = (\forall x)(P(x))$
b. $\vdash (x = y) \rightarrow (P(x) = P(y))$
c. $\vdash (x = y) = (\forall z)(x(z) = y(z))$
d. $\vdash (\lambda x.\alpha)(\beta) = \alpha[x \mapsto \beta]$ $[\beta$ free for x in $\alpha]$
e. $\vdash \iota(\mathbf{eq}_{\mathbf{Ind}}(y)) = y$

It is worth considering the content of these axioms. The first axiom tells us that if a property of truth values holds of truth and holds of falsehood, then it holds of every truth value. We can recover the types of the variables and constants by noting that $\wedge$ takes boolean arguments, and thus $P(\mathbf{true})$ must be boolean, and hence P must be of type $\mathbf{Bool} \rightarrow \mathbf{Bool}$. Thus *x* must be a boolean variable of type **Bool** to make the result well typed. This first axiom basically states that there are only two truth values. The second axiom states that if two objects are equal, then the result of applying a function to both of them is equal. In other words, our functions are functional in that if a single function is given two objects that are equivalent, it returns the same result in both cases. The third axiom states that the identity condition for functions is extensional: if two functions return the same result for every object, then they are the same function. Note that in this axiom, x and y must be of some type $\sigma \to \tau$ and z must be of type σ for the resulting formula to be well formed. The fourth axiom is simply β-reduction and allows us to reduce abstractions as before. Note that we do not need the η-reduction axiom because we have the third axiom coupled with β-conversion. Similarly, α-reduction is a consequence of the axioms provided. I leave the verification of these results as an exercise. Finally, the fifth axiom states that the property of being equal to an object has a unique element that is that object. Note that $\mathbf{eq}_{\mathbf{Ind}}(x)$ is the property of being equal to x, because by η-conversion, it is the same as $\lambda y . \mathbf{eq}_{\mathbf{Ind}}(x)(y)$. This property should be interpreted as true only when applied to an object equivalent to x.

Our object language is powerful enough that we can get away with only one rule of inference: substituting equals for equals in a proof.

DEFINITION: SUBSTITUTION RULE OF INFERENCE   Our rules of inference are all of the instances of $\phi[x \mapsto \alpha], \alpha = \beta \vdash \phi[x \mapsto \beta]$.

In words, this inference scheme tells us that if ϕ is true when x is α and α and β are equal, then ϕ is true when x is β. Note that we do not need any side conditions on this rule.

I define proofs as before and note without proof that the resulting system is both sound and complete. Recall that a formula ϕ is valid if and only if it is true in every model.

THEOREM: SOUNDNESS AND COMPLETENESS   The formula ϕ is valid in the class of generalized models if and only if $\vdash \phi$.

I leave soundness as an exercise. For a proof of completeness, see Andrews 1986. As a corollary of soundness, note that the axioms and their logical consequences are also sound for standard models.

Exercises

1. Expand all the terms in the axiomatization of higher-order logic to their standard syntax using the abbreviations.

2. Using the model given in figure 3.1, provide denotations for the following terms, given after their natural-language analogues. These denotations should be given extensionally by their actions, as in figure 3.1.

(a) respect Francis: **respect(francis)**

(b) respected by Francis: $\lambda x.\mathbf{respect}(x)(\mathbf{francis})$

(c) laughed and is not a woman: $\lambda x.\mathbf{laugh}(x) \wedge \neg\mathbf{woman}(x)$

(d) respects and is respected by: $\lambda x.\lambda y.\mathbf{respect}(x)(y) \wedge \mathbf{respect}(y)(x)$

(e) respects himself: $\lambda x.\mathbf{respect}(x)(x)$

(f) Robin (as a quantifier): $\lambda P.P(\mathbf{robin})$

(g) everyone respects themselves: $\mathbf{every}(\lambda x.\mathbf{respect}(x)(x))$

(h) every man cried: $\mathbf{every}(\lambda x.\mathbf{man}(x) \rightarrow \mathbf{cried}(x))$

(i) some man laughed: $\mathbf{some}(\lambda x.\mathbf{man}(x) \wedge \mathbf{laughed}(x))$

3. Verify that De Morgan's law obtains in higher-order logic:

$\mathbf{and} \equiv \lambda x.\lambda y.\mathbf{not}(\mathbf{or}(\mathbf{not}(x))(\mathbf{not}(y)))$

4. Provide a definition in higher-order logic of relational composition for binary relations R and T of type **Ind** $\rightarrow$ **Ind** $\rightarrow$ **Bool**. (See section A.2 for the standard mathematical definition of relational composition.)

Prove that a relation U is transitive (see section A.2) if and only if $U \circ U \equiv U$. Let $R^1 \overset{\text{def}}{=} R$ and $R^{n+1} \overset{\text{def}}{=} R \circ R^n$ for $n > 0$. Show that if the domain of individuals is finite, then there is a finite k such that $R^k = R^{k+1}$. Show that this R^k is the transitive closure of R (see section A.2 for a definition of transitive closure).

5. Show how the description operator ι can be used along with the equality relation to define a function inverting combinator $\mathbf{Inv}_{\sigma,\tau}$ such that if f is a one-to-one and onto function of type $\sigma \rightarrow \tau$, then $[\![\mathbf{Inv}_{\sigma,\tau}(f)]\!](x) = y$ if and only if $[\![f]\!](y) = x$. (The standard notation for $\mathbf{Inv}(\alpha)$ is α^{-1}.) What is the behavior of your definition of $\mathbf{Inv}(\alpha)$ if α is not one-to-one and onto?

6. Define a quantifier of type (**Ind** $\rightarrow$ **Bool**) $\rightarrow$ **Bool** that is true of a property P if and only if it meets the conditions on the right. (On the left is the natural-language analogue). Your definition should be in the form of a λ-term.

(a) no one: P is empty.

(b) at least three people: P has at least three elements.

(c) at most three people: P has at most three elements.

(d) exactly three people: P has exactly three elements.

(e) Francis or Brooke: P contains f or b.

(f) Francis but not Brooke: P contains f but not b.

7. Assume Q is a generalized quantifier and define the following sets.

(a) $Q^c \overset{\text{def}}{=} \{X \mid \neg Q(X)\}$ (External complement)

(b) $Q^{cd} \overset{\text{def}}{=} \{X \mid Q(\neg X)\}$ (Internal complement)

(c) $Q^d \overset{\text{def}}{=} \{X \mid \neg Q(\neg X)\}$ (Dual)

Show that $Q^c(B)$ holds if and only if $Q^d(\neg B)$ holds. Show that $Q = Q^d$ if and only if Q is consistent and complete. Show that **some** $\equiv$ **no**^{c} and **no** $\equiv$ **some**^{c}. (Westerståhl and Zwarts, p.c.)

8. Employ the definitions in exercise 7 for the following exercises.

   If Q is monotonic upward or downward in its first or second arguments, what are the monotonicity properties of Q^c and Q^{cd}?

   Define appropriate notions of internal and external complementation for determiners. How does this affect the monotonicity of the first argument position? Show that $(Q^c)^c \equiv Q \equiv (Q^d)^d$.

   Consider the following quantifiers: *no N*, *every N*, *some N*, and *not all N*. Indicate which quantifiers are internal negations, external negations, and duals of each other. This is the so-called *square of opposition* from traditional logic. Show that $Q \overset{\text{def}}{=} \lambda P. P(\mathbf{k})$ is *self dual* in that $Q^d \equiv Q$. (Gamut 1991)

9. Provide terms in higher-order logic that denote the various properties of quantifiers: monotonicity (up or down), closure (under union or intersection), consistency, completeness, symmetry, permutation invariance, and conservativity.

10. A determiner D is said to be *reflexive* if $D(A)(A)$ holds, *quasi-reflexive* if $D(A)(B)$ entails $D(A)(A)$, and *transitive* if $D(A)(B)$ and $D(B)(C)$ imply $D(A)(C)$. Show that **every** is transitive, reflexive, conservative, and permutation invariant, but not quasi-reflexive. Show that **some** is neither transitive nor reflexive, but is quasi-reflexive. Show that if a determiner D is reflexive, transitive, conservative, and permutation invariant, then it is upward monotonic in its second argument and downward monotonic in its first argument. (Westerståhl and Zwarts, p.c.)

11. Which monotonicity properties of quantifiers are preserved under generalized boolean disjunction and conjunction? Is conservativity preserved under disjunction and conjunction? What kinds of entailments does this license among utterances?

12. Show that the quantifier lowering combinator $\mathbf{R}^{-1}$ (defined as the inverse of $\mathbf{R} \overset{\text{def}}{=} \lambda x. \lambda P. P(x)$) satisfies the following relation for all quantifiers:

(a) $\mathbf{R}^{-1}(Q) \equiv \bigcap Q$

13. The constant **nand** is defined by the following action:

$$\text{(a)} \quad [\![\mathbf{nand}]\!] = \left[\begin{array}{l} \mathbf{yes} \mapsto \left[\begin{array}{l} \mathbf{yes} \mapsto \mathbf{no} \\ \mathbf{no}\ \mapsto \mathbf{yes} \end{array} \right. \\ \mathbf{no} \mapsto \left[\begin{array}{l} \mathbf{yes} \mapsto \mathbf{yes} \\ \mathbf{no}\ \mapsto \mathbf{yes} \end{array} \right. \end{array} \right.$$

Show that every binary function of type **Bool** $\rightarrow$ **Bool** $\rightarrow$ **Bool** is definable using only **nand**, function application, and abstraction. Either solve the general problem or provide all 16 cases. (Hint: Either way you approach this problem, defining unary **not** first is helpful.)

The set of simple boolean types is the least set **SimpBool** such that

(b) **Bool** $\in$ **SimpBool**,

(c) **Bool** $\rightarrow \tau \in$ **SimpBool** if $\tau \in$ **SimpBool**.

Show that every function of simple boolean type can be defined using only the constant **nand**. Show that every function whose type contains only instances of **Bool** can be defined using **nand**. Is there another binary boolean operator that is complete in the same sense as **nand**?

14. Keenan and Faltz (1985) employed the boolean elements of the following standard ordering, which was later generalized in the natural way to arbitrary domains by van Benthem (1986a). The orderings on the functional domains are said to be defined *pointwise*.

(a) **Bool**: $x \leq y$ if and only if $x = y$ or $x = $ **no**, $y = $ **yes**

(b) **Ind**: $x \leq y$ if and only if $x = y$

(c) $\mathbf{Dom}_{\sigma \to \tau}$: $f \leq g$ if and only if $f(a) \leq g(a)$ for every $a \in \mathbf{Dom}_\sigma$

We can now say that a function $f \in \mathbf{Dom}_{\sigma \to \tau}$ is *monotonic* upwards (downwards) if and only if $x \leq y$ implies $f(x) \leq f(y)$ $(f(y) \leq f(x))$.

   Show that $f, g \in \mathbf{Dom}_{\tau \to \mathbf{Bool}}$ are such that $f \subseteq g$ if and only if $f \leq g$.

   Show that if $f \in \mathbf{Dom}_{\sigma \to \tau}$ and $g \in \mathbf{Dom}_{\tau \to \rho}$ are monotonic upward (downward), then so is $g \circ f$.

   Show that if $f \in \mathbf{Dom}_{\sigma \to \tau}$ is monotonic upward (downward) and $g \in \mathbf{Dom}_{\tau \to \rho}$ is monotonic downward (upward), then $g \circ f$ is monotonic downward (upward).

   Determine whether $\lambda V. \mathcal{Q}_1(\lambda x. \mathcal{Q}_2(\lambda y. V(x)(y)))$ is monotonic upward, downward, or neither for the cases where $\mathcal{Q}_1, \mathcal{Q}_2 \in \{\mathbf{some}, \mathbf{every}, \mathbf{no}, \mathbf{three}_= \}$.

   Extend the definition of generalized ordering to products so that the currying operation is an order isomorphism. (Because we know currying is one-one and onto, the condition of order isomorphism reduces to the condition that $f \leq g$ if and only if $\mathbf{curry}(f) \leq \mathbf{curry}(g)$.)

15. Provide a term for implication and disjunction that contains only the constants **not** and **and**. Use this definition to evaluate the truth conditions for the following:

(a) $\mathbf{every}(\lambda x. \mathbf{implies}(\mathbf{kid}(x))(\mathbf{some}(\lambda y. \mathbf{and}(\mathbf{toy}(y))(\mathbf{break}(x)(y)))))$

Provide a natural-language sentence that translates as the above statement.

16. Show that all of the other higher-order constants can be defined in terms of equality and the description operator.

   We can define **true** as follows:

(a) $\mathbf{true} \overset{\text{def}}{=} \mathbf{eq}_{\mathbf{Bool} \to \mathbf{Bool} \to \mathbf{Bool}}(\mathbf{eq}_{\mathbf{Bool}})(\mathbf{eq}_{\mathbf{Bool}})$

How can we define **false**?

   Verify the following logical equivalences.

(b) $\mathbf{not} \equiv \mathbf{eq}_{\mathbf{Bool}}(\mathbf{false})$

(c) $\mathbf{every}_\tau \equiv \mathbf{eq}_{\mathbf{Ind} \to \mathbf{Bool}}(\lambda x^\tau . \mathbf{true})$

(d) $\mathbf{and} \equiv \lambda x^{\mathbf{Bool}} . \lambda y^{\mathbf{Bool}} . \mathbf{eq}_{(\mathbf{Bool} \to \mathbf{Bool} \to \mathbf{Bool}) \to \mathbf{Bool}}(\lambda f^{\mathbf{Bool} \to \mathbf{Bool} \to \mathbf{Bool}} . f(\mathbf{true})(\mathbf{true}))$
$(\lambda g^{\mathbf{Bool} \to \mathbf{Bool} \to \mathbf{Bool}} . g(x)(y))$

17. Show how to define an arbitrary description operator ι_τ of type τ that maps singleton sets (represented as unary functions from type τ objects to truth values)

onto their single elements, in terms of the individual description function ι_{Ind} and equality.

18. Provide a mapping from first-order logic into higher-order logic. First, map the syntax. Then show how first-order models can be translated into higher-order models. Finally, show that for propositional and individual terms, the denotations in both models are the same.

19. Do the following principles of Leibniz's hold in standard models? In general models?

(a) $x^\tau = y^\tau \rightarrow (\forall P^{\tau \rightarrow \textbf{Bool}})(P(x) = P(y))$ (Indiscernibility of identicals)

(b) $(\forall P^{\tau \rightarrow \textbf{Bool}})(P(x) = P(y)) \rightarrow x^\tau = y^\tau$ (Identity of indiscernibles)

20. Prove that our axioms for higher-order logic are sound over generalized models.

21. Prove that α-reduction and η-reduction follow from the axiomatic presentation of higher-order logic. (Hint: Use the extensionality axiom scheme and β-reduction.)

22. Consider the meaning of sentences such as the following involving nominal comparatives.

(a) More linguists than psychologists study syntax.

(b) Linguists study syntax less than psychologists.

(c) More linguists study syntax than psychologists.

(d) More linguists study syntax than mathematicians study algebra.

Provide a definition of **more** as a ternary generalized determiner, that is, one that takes three property arguments of type **Ind** $\rightarrow$ **Bool**. Provide a definition in higher-order logic. (Hint: Cardinalities can be compared by considering the existence of one-one functions between the two sets; see section A.2.)

What are the monotonicity properties of **more**? Does it live on any of its arguments?

Show that as a generalized quantifier, the meaning of the expression *more linguists than psychologists* is not permutation invariant. Show that as a term, **more** is permutation invariant. (Keenan and Stavi 1986)

23. Show that a determiner D is permutation invariant if and only if the truth value of $D(A)(B)$ depends only on the cardinality of the sets $A \cap B$, $A - B$, $B - A$, and $\textbf{Dom}_{\text{Ind}} - (A \cup B)$. (Gamut 1991)

24. A determiner D is said to have *variety* if for every A, there exist a B and B' such that $D(A)(B)$ holds and $D(A)(B')$ does not. Provide examples of natural-language quantifiers that have variety and examples of those that do not. (Hint: For the latter, consider numerical quantifiers and finite domains of individuals.) (van Benthem 1986a)

25. A ternary quantifier Q of the following type:

(a) $(\textbf{Ind} \rightarrow \textbf{Bool}) \rightarrow (\textbf{Ind} \rightarrow \textbf{Bool}) \rightarrow (\textbf{Ind} \rightarrow \textbf{Ind} \rightarrow \textbf{Bool}) \rightarrow \textbf{Bool}$

can be defined by composing two binary generalized determiners Q_1 and Q_2 of type $(\mathbf{Ind} \rightarrow \mathbf{Bool}) \rightarrow (\mathbf{Ind} \rightarrow \mathbf{Bool}) \rightarrow \mathbf{Bool}$ as follows:

(b) $Q \stackrel{\text{def}}{=} \lambda P.\lambda R.\lambda V.Q_1(P)(\lambda x.Q_2(\lambda y.V(x)(y)))$

Show that not every ternary determiner can be defined by means of a pair of binary determiners. (Hint: Consider the cardinality of the domain of ternary determiners and the cardinality of the set of pairs of binary determiners.)

Explain informally why the ternary determiner **more** (defined in exercise 22) is not reducible to a pair of binary determiners. (Hint: Consider the conservativity properties of reducible quantifiers.) (Keenan 1987)

Chapter 4

Applicative Categorial Grammar

Syntax determines how expressions of various categories can be assembled to form larger constituents. Under the assumption of compositionality, syntactic constructions provide a vital link in determining semantic structure. Because I want to present a compositional theory of how expressions in natural languages correspond to meanings describable in some logic, I need to be specific about my syntactic assumptions. The approach I adopt to syntax is that of categorial grammar. Categorial grammars have an established connection to the higher-order logics through type theory. Originally, categorial grammars were developed to provide a precise syntactic structure for logical expressions by Ajdukiewicz (1935), on the basis of ideas of Lesniewski (1929). Only later were categorial grammars applied to the study of natural-language syntax, first by Bar-Hillel (1950) and then by Lambek (1958, 1961). Montague (1970b) put forward a theory of *universal grammar* in which there was an intimate connection between syntactic categories and semantic categories. Montague's (1970a, 1973) subsequent use of higher-order logic naturally accommodated a type-logical view of syntactic categories. The essentially categorial nature of Montague's grammars led to a renewed interest in the application of categorial grammar to natural language. On the syntactic side, Geach (1972) independently argued for a number of rewriting rules that turned out to be theorems of Lambek's associative calculus. Categorial grammar has always been popular among semanticists, primarily due to its type-theoretical elegance (see, for instance, Dowty 1978, 1979a, 1979b; Bach 1983a, 1983b, 1984). But it was Ades and Steedman (1982) who revived interest in categorial grammar as a mainstream paradigm for developing unified grammars for syntactic and semantic phenomena. Steedman (1985, 1987, 1988) moved this program forward by employing combinatory rules that fine-tuned the kinds of rules employed by Geach, introducing novel analyses of several important syntactic and semantic phenomena across several languages.

In categorial grammar, every linguistic category corresponds to some higher-order type, with the assumption being that expressions of such categories can be assigned meanings of the appropriate type. In this chapter we will be concerned not with the fine-grained details of the meanings of particular phrasal categories but rather with seeing how the compositional aspects of meaning can be cast in a setting combining categorial grammar with higher-order logic. In subsequent chapters I present more appropriate logics and more elaborate categorial-grammar systems, but my basic approach remains constant.

When applying categorial grammars to the study of natural languages, it is traditional to assume a *universal* collection of phrase-structure rule schemes. Not only are these phrase-structure schemes applied cross-linguistically, but a compositional approach to meaning driven by the types of categories is usually assumed to be determined solely on the basis of syntactic structure. It follows from these strong semantic and syntactic restrictions that all language-specific generalization must be lexically determined in a categorial grammar; once the lexicon is established for a language, universal rules of syntactic and semantic combination take over to completely determine the set of grammatical expressions and their meanings.

4.1 THE CATEGORY SYSTEM

The categories of categorial grammar are built up much like the types of the λ-calculus. In particular, we assume some fixed finite set **BasCat** of *basic categories* from which other categories may be constructed. For the time being, it will suffice to assume that our collection **BasCat** of basic categories contains the following:

(1) *Category*   *Description*
     np   noun phrase
     n   noun
     s   sentence

My uses of these categories are the ordinary ones. We later turn to categorial grammars that distinguish plural from singular nouns and noun phrases, as well as discriminating between aspectual categories of sentences, among other things.

The finite set of basic categories is used to generate an infinite set of functional categories, each of which specifies a (possibly complex) argument and result category. The fundamental operation in applicative categorial grammar is that of concatenating an expression assigned to a functional category to an expression of its argument category to form an expression of its result category, with the order of the concatenation being determined by the functional category. For example, a determiner will be specified as a functional category that takes a noun complement to its right to form a noun-phrase result.

DEFINITION: SYNTACTIC CATEGORY   The collection of *syntactic categories* determined by the collection **BasCat** of basic categories is the least set **Cat** such that

a. **BasCat** $\subseteq$ **Cat**,
b. $(A/B), (B\backslash A) \in$ **Cat** if $A, B \in$ **Cat**.

A category $B\backslash A$ or A/B is said to be a *functor* category and to have a *domain* or *argument* category of B and a *range* or *result* category of A. A functional category of the form A/B is said to be a *forward functor* and looks for its B argument to the right, while the *backward functor* $B\backslash A$ looks for its argument to the left. With our choice **BasCat** of basic categories, the following are categories in **Cat**.

(2) $n, np/n, (n\backslash n)/np, np\backslash s, (np\backslash s)/(np\backslash s), ((np\backslash s)/np)/np$

For instance, np/n would be the type of a determiner: it looks forward for a noun to produce a noun phrase. Similarly, the type n/n would be the category of prenominal adjectives: they look forward for nouns to produce nouns. The category $n\backslash n$, on the other hand, is used for postnominal modifiers, and thus the category $(n\backslash n)/np$ is the category of prepositions because a preposition takes a noun-phrase argument to its right to produce a postnominal modifier. In the other direction, categories such as $np\backslash s$ would be assigned to both verb phrases and intransitive verbs: they look backward for a noun phrase to produce a sentence. Thus the category $(np\backslash s)/(np\backslash s)$ is a preverbal verb-phrase modifier, or in other words, an adverb. Similarly, $(np\backslash s)/np$ would be assigned to transitive verbs which look for an object noun phrase to the right and a subject noun phrase to the left, whereas $((np\backslash s)/np)/np$ will be assigned to ditransitive verbs that take two noun-phrase objects to their right to produce a verb phrase.

From now on, we will omit disambiguating parentheses within categories, taking the forward slash to be left associative and the backward slash to be right associative. Furthermore, we will assume that the backward slash binds more tightly than the forward slash. This gives us abbreviated categories such as the following:

(3) a. $A/B/C \stackrel{\text{def}}{=} (A/B)/C$
    b. $C \backslash A \stackrel{\text{def}}{=} C \backslash (B \backslash A)$
    c. $B \backslash A/C/D \stackrel{\text{def}}{=} ((B \backslash A)/C)/D$
    d. $(D \backslash C) \backslash B \backslash A/E \stackrel{\text{def}}{=} ((D \backslash C) \backslash (B \backslash A))/E$

It would be naive to assume that we could adequately characterize natural-language word order with only two directional-slash categories. Even English presents constructions requiring a more sophisticated word-ordering mechanism. My basic approach is compatible with several analyses that have been proposed for treating word order in the phrase-structure tradition (Gazdar, Klein, Pullum, and Sag 1985; Reape 1989) and in the categorial tradition (Hepple 1990a; Morrill 1994; Moortgat and Oehrle 1993, 1994). As it is not my purpose to develop an extensive syntactic theory and I will be using English for illustration, I will maintain a simple directional version of categorial grammar.

4.2 SEMANTIC DOMAINS

One of the basic tenets of categorial grammar is that the category assigned to an expression should express its semantic functionality directly. To this end, I assume that every basic category is assigned some higher-order logical type. From such a type assignment to basic types, I assign functor categories the obvious functional type, determined by the types of its argument and result categories.

DEFINITION: TYPE ASSIGNMENT We extend a *type assignment* function Typ: **BasCat** → **Typ** to functor categories as follows:

$$\text{Typ}(A/B) = \text{Typ}(B \backslash A) = \text{Typ}(B) \rightarrow \text{Typ}(A)$$

It is significant to note that our mapping from categories to types can be composed from our mapping from types to domains to produce a mapping from categories to the semantic domains over which they are interpreted. Note that as a result of this definition, every syntactic category is assigned a unique type. But the converse might not hold, because we are free to assign more than one syntactic category the same type. For my purposes in this chapter, I assume the following type assignment:

(4) *Category*   *Type*   *Description*
     np   **Ind**   noun phrase
     n   **Ind** → **Bool** noun
     s   **Bool**   sentence

Note that I have assigned a basic category, *n*, to a complex type, **Ind** → **Bool**. Also note that the category *np\s*, which we will use for verb phrases, has the same type as the category *n* of nouns.

4.3   CATEGORIAL LEXICONS

In the categorial-grammar formalisms we consider, the lexicon is taken to be a relation between the basic expressions of a language and the linguistic categories to which they are assigned. Categories, as I construe them here, consist not only of a syntactic category but also a meaning. Following standard practice in natural-language semantics, I choose to represent meanings with λ-terms. With our interpretation of λ-terms in models, we could directly associate expressions with domain elements in the frame of a higher-order model. In this way we can think of a λ-term as nothing more than a symbolic stand-in for the domain element it denotes in some model (possibly under an assignment if the term has free variables). This was, in fact, Montague's approach. But if we wish to implement a proof-theoretic approach for a computational application, then the terms rather than their denotations must be manipulated.

As is usual in formal grammars, I suppose that we have a finite set **BasExp** of *basic expressions*. For my purposes, **BasExp** will be some finite subset of English words, or possibly complex sequences of words that constitute a single lexical entry such as idiomatic and particle constructions.

DEFINITION: CATEGORIAL LEXICON   A *categorial lexicon* is a relation **Lex** ⊆ **BasExp** × (**Cat** × **Term**) such that if $\langle e, \langle A, \alpha \rangle \rangle \in$ **Lex**, then $\alpha \in$ **Term**$_{\text{Typ}(A)}$.

This constraint on lexical entries enforces the requirement that if the expression *e* is assigned syntactic category *A* and λ-term α, then the term α is of the appropriate type for the category *A*. As an abbreviatory measure, we use the following notation for lexical entries.

(5) $e \Rightarrow \alpha \colon A \overset{\text{def}}{=} \langle e, \langle A, \alpha \rangle \rangle$

4.4 PHRASE STRUCTURE

To begin, I present categorial grammar as a kind of *phrase-structure grammar* (PSG). I employ the term *phrase structure* in its usual syntactic sense (see Crabtree and Powers 1991) rather than in the more general sense employed in formal-language theory, where it typically refers to an unrestricted generative grammar (see Hopcroft and Ullman 1979). The formal-language sense of the term is rather misleading in that no structure can be assigned to phrases other than a derivational history. In linguistics, phrase-structure analyses are typically taken to categorize complex expressions compositionally in terms of the categorizations of their constitutents, and this is the sense in which I will use the term. In particular, phrase-structure approaches to natural languages assume lexical assignments to basic expressions and a set of phrase-structure rules that combine expressions to produce phrases purely on the basis of their syntactic categorization. For instance, the prototypical natural-language phrase-structure rule states that a subject expression can be concatenated to the left of a predicate expression to form a sentence. A typical formal-language rule states that an arithmetic expression can be formed by concatenating an arithmetic expression, a binary operator, and another arithmetic expression.

Categorial grammars are rather unique among linguistic theories in adopting an infinite set of categories and phrase-structure rules (although these are typically generated by a finite number of rule schemes). Usually, linguistic phrase-structure grammars allow only a finite set of rules, in which case they are known as *context-free grammars*. This terminology is misleading in that all phrase-structure grammars are context-free in the sense of not distinguishing distribution on the basis of the internal structure of an expression but rather expressing distributional variation solely in terms of the category assigned to the expression by the grammar. Even extended phrase-structure formalisms such as GPSG only employ finitely many syntactic categories. Their expressive power comes from their ability to schematize large classes of rules by underspecification. In HPSG only the categorial conception of subcategorization generates an unbounded number of potential syntactic categories. Although most applications of HPSG bound the number of categories lexically, as in Pollard and Sag 1994, Hinrichs and Nakazawa (1994) exploit the lack of bounds to explain word-order phenomena in Germanic languages. Luckily, the set of phrase-structure rules employed in categorial grammar is quite well behaved. In the case of the pure applicative categorial grammar, which we take up now, the set of phrase-structure rules can be derived as instances of two simple schemes based on functional application. In fact, only a finite number of instances of these schemes will ever be needed for a fixed finite lexicon, which means that the syntactic component of applicative categorial grammars, and hence the language of expressions generated, is context-free.

The reliance on phrase-structure rules guarantees a resulting theory that is purely concatenative and in which grammar rules have locally determined behavior. One of the fundamental distinctions between *transformational grammars* and phrase-structure grammars, and hence applicative categorial grammars, stems from the way in which these formalisms treat the related topics of category structure and locality. (The other primary difference between these approaches is the *monostratal* nature of phrase-structure grammars and the existence of *intermediate representations* in transformational theories.) Phrase-structure grammars are such that if there are derivations of two expressions as being of the same syntactic category, then they are intersubstitutable as instances of that category in any context in which expressions of that category are allowed. This is the sense in which they are context-free. Of course, lexical ambiguity might mean that the expressions are not freely substitutable in arbitrary contexts. Thus a rich set of categories must be postulated to account for distributional distinctions. If two expressions behave differently, they must be assigned distinct categories. On the other hand, transformational accounts of syntactic structure often allow analyses of obviously distributionally distinct expressions, like *Chris met* and *Chris met Dana*, to show up in phrase markers with the same root category, because in the first case, the object has been "moved" out of its usual position in the context of a larger derivation.

(6) a. [Chris [met [t_0]$_{NP}$]$_{VP}$]$_S$.
     b. [Chris [met [Dana]$_{NP}$]$_{VP}$]$_S$.

The distributional distinction between the two phrases is then accounted for on the basis of the internal structure of the phrase markers in (6); the first, (6a), contains an *empty category* or *trace* with the index 0, whereas the second, (6b), has a lexical noun phrase in object position. In categorial grammar, as in such phrase-structure approaches to syntax and semantics as GPSG (Gazdar, Klein, Pullum, and Sag 1985) and HPSG (Pollard and

Sag 1994), the distinction between *Chris met* and *Chris met Dana* is made categorially.

(7) a. [Chris [met $[t_0]_{NP|NP}]_{VP|NP}]_{S|NP}$
   b. [Chris [met $[Dana]_{NP}]_{VP}]_S$

In a manner reminiscent of categorial grammar, the category $X|NP$ is interpreted as an X with an NP gap in it (although the gap is not required to be peripheral). Thus the distributional differences between the examples in (7) can be accounted for solely in terms of the category assigned to the root of the derivation.

In categorial grammar, our phrase-structure rules follow our intuitive explanation of A/B as a forward-looking functor and $B\backslash A$ as a backward-looking functor.

DEFINITION: APPLICATION SCHEMES   The following phrase structure *application schemes* are assumed:

a. $\alpha: A/B, \beta: B \Rightarrow \alpha(\beta): A$ (Forward application)
b. $\beta: B, \alpha: B\backslash A \Rightarrow \alpha(\beta): A$ (Backward application)

I have written the phrase-structure schemes with a bottom-up orientation, as is common for categorial grammars. Reading the application schemes in the usual way, the forward scheme states that if e_1 is an expression of category A/B with meaning α and e_2 is an expression of category B with meaning β, then the expression $e_1 \cdot e_2$, consisting of e_1 concatenated to e_2, is an expression of category A with meaning $\alpha(\beta)$. The backward application scheme is read similarly. I provide a precise definition of this interpretation below.

A striking symmetry arises in categorial rule schemes. Backward and forward application form what is known as a dual pair, where we define the *dual* of a binary (or unary) rule to be the result of flipping the order of the daughters and flipping the direction of all of the slashes in both the daughters and the result, while leaving the semantics invariant. For all of the rules I introduce, we will have this form of directional duality.

I now turn to the task of providing a formal definition of how phrase-structure grammars relate expressions to categories. I begin with a denotational account that matches the intuitive description of what is going on with phrase structure. I will write $[\![e]\!]_{Lex}$ for the set of categories, consisting of a pair of a syntactic category and λ-term, assigned to the expression e. I use the subscript **Lex** because categorial grammar denotations are determined by the lexicon.

DEFINITION: PHRASE-STRUCTURE DENOTATION   The *phrase-structure deno-tation* function $[\![\cdot]\!]_{\mathbf{Lex}}$ is the least such that

a. $\alpha\colon A \in [\![e]\!]_{\mathbf{Lex}}$ *if* $e \Rightarrow \alpha\colon A \in \mathbf{Lex}$
b. $\alpha(\beta)\colon A \in [\![e_1 \cdot e_2]\!]_{\mathbf{Lex}}$ *if* $\alpha\colon A/B \in [\![e_1]\!]_{\mathbf{Lex}}$ *and* $\beta\colon B \in [\![e_2]\!]_{\mathbf{Lex}}$
c. $\alpha(\beta)\colon A \in [\![e_1 \cdot e_2]\!]_{\mathbf{Lex}}$ *if* $\beta\colon B \in [\![e_1]\!]_{\mathbf{Lex}}$ *and* $\alpha\colon B\backslash A \in [\![e_2]\!]_{\mathbf{Lex}}$

I will drop the subscript **Lex** when the lexicon under consideration is clear from context. Note that with $[\![e]\!]_{\mathbf{Lex}}$ I have provided denotations for expressions. The fact that I have provided expressions with denotations in this definition, rather than say, categories, is an arbitrary one; the purpose of the definition is to establish a ternary relation between expressions, meanings, and syntactic categories. In the categorial-grammar literature, it is more common to see syntactic categories given denotations as expression and meaning pairs. We can easily translate to such an arrangement by defining a denotation function $[\![\cdot]\!]'$ for categories.

(8) $[\![A]\!]'_{\mathbf{Lex}} \stackrel{\mathrm{def}}{=} \{ \langle e, \alpha \rangle | \alpha\colon A \in [\![e]\!]_{\mathbf{Lex}} \}$

Often the pairing of an expression and a meaning is referred to as a *linguistic sign*, after de Saussure 1916. Under this view, syntactic categories merely classify expression and meaning pairs.

It is important to note that these rule schemes are *type sound*. That is, if the types of the meanings of the constituents line up appropriately with their categories, then the result of the application will have a meaning of the appropriate type for the syntactic category of the result. I prove such a result at the end of section 4.6.

4.5   A CATEGORIAL LEXICON

We turn our attention now to providing an example of a lexicon for categorial grammar. As a first pass, I present a lexicon given as the simple list in figure 4.1. Note that I have assumed in figure 4.1 that the meanings assigned to all of the lexical entries are constants. Later we take some of these constants to be abbreviations for more complex terms, in the same way that we took **or** to be an abbreviation for $\lambda x.\lambda y.\mathbf{not}(\mathbf{and}(\mathbf{not}(x))(\mathbf{not}(y)))$ in higher-order logic. It should also be noted that we are not yet considering issues such as tense and aspect but will return to these topics in later chapters.

Before considering the lexical entries in detail, I first present an example of how derivations are performed in pure categorial grammar. Given our

$Sandy \Rightarrow$ **sandy**: np $runs \Rightarrow$ **run**: $np\backslash s$

$the \Rightarrow \iota_{\mathbf{Ind}}$: np/n $loves \Rightarrow$ **love**: $np\backslash s/np$

$kid \Rightarrow$ **kid**: n $gives \Rightarrow$ **give**: $np\backslash s/np/np$

$tall \Rightarrow$ **tall**: n/n $outside \Rightarrow$ **outside**: $(np\backslash s)\backslash np\backslash s$

$outside \Rightarrow$ **outside**: $n\backslash n$ $in \Rightarrow$ **in**: $(np\backslash s)\backslash np\backslash s/np$

$in \Rightarrow$ **in**: $n\backslash n/np$

Figure 4.1
A pure categorial-grammar lexicon

lexicon, we know that **sandy**: $np \in [\![sandy]\!]$ and that **run**: $np\backslash s \in [\![runs]\!]$. By the third case of the inductive definition of denotation, we conclude that **run(sandy)**: $s \in [\![Sandy\ ran]\!]$. Consider the following slightly more complicated derivation.

(9) a. **tall**: $n/n \in [\![tall]\!]$
   b. **kid**: $n \in [\![kid]\!]$
   c. **tall(kid)**: $n \in [\![tall\ kid]\!]$
   d. ι: $np/n \in [\![the]\!]$
   e. $\iota(\mathbf{tall(kid)})$: $np \in [\![the\ tall\ kid]\!]$
   f. **run**: $np\backslash s \in [\![runs]\!]$
   g. **run**$(\iota(\mathbf{tall(kid)}))$: $s \in [\![the\ tall\ kid\ runs]\!]$

The convention adopted in (9) is to list assumptions before they are used. For instance, from the analysis of *tall* and *kid*, we can provide an analysis of *tall kid*.

I now wish to discuss the particular significance of some of the choices I have made in the lexicon. First, note that I have treated names as picking out individuals. This move can be seen as an oversimplification by considering the fact that a name does not uniquely determine an individual. For instance, several people can be named *Sandy*. But a logical constant such as **sandy** must be assigned to a unique individual in a model. We consider some alternatives in section 7.8.

Next note that we have treated nouns as determining properties of individuals. This interacts appropriately with our assumption that *the* is treated semantically as corresponding to the description operator. An expression *the N* thus refers to the unique individual with property P corresponding to N. For instance, the semantics of *the kid*, $\iota(\mathbf{kid})$, refers to an individual that is the unique object having the property denoted by **kid**. Similarly, *the tall kid* refers to the unique individual that has the property of being a tall kid. I discuss the semantics of modifiers in the context of meaning postulates in section 4.7.4. But if there is no object that is a kid, or if there are several, our condition on the interpretation of ι in higher-order logic does not enforce any particular behavior. We consider some alternatives involving quantification in section 7.8.

The interpretation of verbs in the lexicon is straightforward. In particular, each verb corresponds to a curried relation. For instance, *runs* would have a function from individuals to truth values as its meaning, while *likes* would correspond to a function from individuals to a function from individuals to truth values. One benefit of this move is that it provides a type, namely **Ind** → **Bool**, for verb phrases and derives *ran* and *likes Sandy* as both being of this category. In transformational accounts, all lexical verbs are assigned to the category V^0, and type distinctions are enforced elsewhere in the grammars. In the case of *likes Sandy*, the meaning is **like(sandy)**, because **like** is a constant denoting a function from individuals to functions from individuals to truth values. Thus **like(sandy)** and **run** can be uniformly treated as properties. Ditransitive verbs such as *give* are similarly treated as functions from individuals into functions from individuals to functions from individuals to truth values, or in symbols, as functions of type **Ind** → **Ind** → **Ind** → **Bool**, the significance of which is that **give(dana)** and **like** are of the same type, as are **give(dana)(spot)**, **like(dana)**, and **run**.

4.6 TREE ADMISSIBILITY

Derivations in categorial grammar can most naturally be expressed by means of tree diagrams. I adopt the Steedman-style notation for phrase-structure trees, which has become the standard in categorial grammar (Ades and Steedman 1982). The leaves of the trees correspond to lexical entries, with the result of applying rules to pairs of categories listed below them. The analysis of the sentence in (9) can be displayed as a parse tree as in figure 4.2. The correspondence between Steedman's style of trees and logical deductions is not coincidental. One reason for the popularity of Steedman's notation for trees will become clear in the next chapter when I draw out the parallels between categorial grammar derivations and logical deductions. Another reason for their popularity is that they are both easy to typeset and natural to work with from a derivational point of

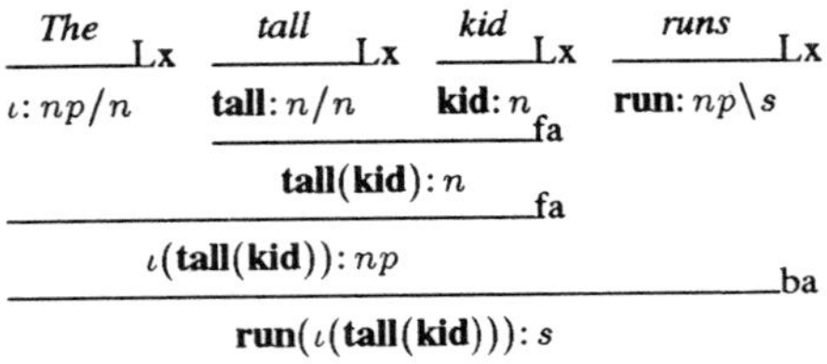

$$\frac{\quad The \quad}{\iota : np/n} \text{Lx} \quad \frac{\quad tall \quad}{\textbf{tall}: n/n} \text{Lx} \quad \frac{\quad kid \quad}{\textbf{kid}: n} \text{Lx} \quad \frac{\quad runs \quad}{\textbf{run}: np\backslash s} \text{Lx}$$

$$\frac{\textbf{tall}(\textbf{kid}): n}{\text{fa}}$$

$$\frac{\iota(\textbf{tall}(\textbf{kid})): np}{\textbf{run}(\iota(\textbf{tall}(\textbf{kid}))): s} \text{ba}$$

Figure 4.2
A derivation displayed as a tree

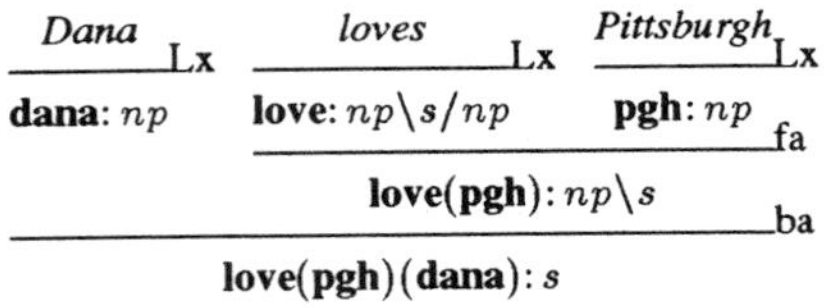

$$\frac{\quad Dana \quad}{\textbf{dana}: np} \text{Lx} \quad \frac{\quad loves \quad}{\textbf{love}: np\backslash s/np} \text{Lx} \quad \frac{\quad Pittsburgh \quad}{\textbf{pgh}: np} \text{Lx}$$

$$\frac{\textbf{love}(\textbf{pgh}): np\backslash s}{\text{fa}}$$

$$\frac{}{\textbf{love}(\textbf{pgh})(\textbf{dana}): s} \text{ba}$$

Figure 4.3
A derivation of *Dana loves Pittsburgh*

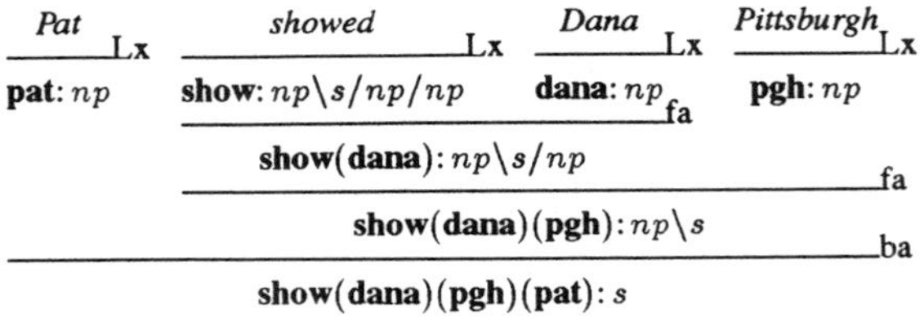

$$\frac{\quad Pat \quad}{\textbf{pat}: np} \text{Lx} \quad \frac{\quad showed \quad}{\textbf{show}: np\backslash s/np/np} \text{Lx} \quad \frac{\quad Dana \quad}{\textbf{dana}: np} \text{Lx} \quad \frac{\quad Pittsburgh \quad}{\textbf{pgh}: np} \text{Lx}$$

$$\frac{\textbf{show}(\textbf{dana}): np\backslash s/np}{\text{fa}}$$

$$\frac{\textbf{show}(\textbf{dana})(\textbf{pgh}): np\backslash s}{\textbf{show}(\textbf{dana})(\textbf{pgh})(\textbf{pat}): s} \text{ba}$$

Figure 4.4
A derivation of *Pat showed Dana Pittsburgh*

view. That is, starting with the lexical entries across the top line, derivations can be drawn out in a natural fashion. It is important to keep in mind the order of arguments I have assumed. Consider the derivations in figures 4.3 and 4.4. In the first example, we see that the meaning assigned to *Dana loves Pittsburgh* is **love**(**pgh**)(**dana**). The object is the first argument to which the verb is applied both syntactically and semantically. Similarly, the order of arguments in the semantics of *Pat showed Dana Pittsburgh* is the order in which they are attached syntactically, namely **show**(**dana**)(**pgh**)(**pat**). The choice of argument order in the λ-calculus is merely one of convenience. If I had assigned the category $\lambda x.\lambda y.\textbf{love}(y)(x): np\backslash s/np$ to *love*, the resulting semantics for *Dana loves*

Pittsburgh would be **love(dana)(pgh)**, rather than the other way around. I adopt the convention of attaching arguments semantically in the same order in which they are attached syntactically. The motivation for this choice is merely that it allows us to use simple constants in our lexicon.

In the applicative categorial grammar, selection can be made sensitive to the order in which arguments are specified. It seems, for instance, that there are two possibilities for assigning a category to a transitive verb:

(10) a. *likes* ⇒ **like**: $(np\backslash s)/np$
     b. *likes* ⇒ $\lambda y.\lambda x.\textbf{like}(x)(y): np\backslash(s/np)$

Both of these examples will allow sentences such as *Dana likes Pat* to be analyzed as **like(pat)(dana)**: *s*. In the applicative categorial grammar, we can actually make categories that are sensitive to this distinction in the order of arguments. For instance, we have only one of the following derivations.

(11) a. $A/((C\backslash B)/D), (C\backslash B)/D \Rightarrow A$
     b. $A/((C\backslash B)/D), C\backslash(B/D) \not\Rightarrow A$

Similarly, only (10a) allows us to employ verb-phrase modifiers in a simple categorial grammar. When we turn to the Lambek calculus in the next chapter, the lexical entries in (10) will be interderivable, and the distinction in (11) will disappear. But we will still be able to ensure that adverbs, auxiliaries, control verbs, and other items select for verb-phrase arguments, behaving asymmetrically with respect to subjects and objects.

One topic worth considering is the uniformity of matters such as word order within a language. For instance, English being a configurational language, intransitive verbs always take their arguments to the left, so all intransitive verb phrases with nominal arguments are assigned the category $np\backslash s$. Similarly, all other arguments occur to the right of the verb in English. We will not have cause to consider notions of freer word order, or even languages that do not adopt a subject-verb-object (SVO) ordering of the verb and its complements. Functionally, it makes sense that a language provide some way of indicating who did what to whom. Furthermore, it seems natural, for functional reasons ranging from language acquisition to parsing, that this be done in a relatively uniform manner. In English, word order (and in the case of pronouns, case markings), determine who did what to whom. In languages such as German or Japanese, case-marking morphology marks the role an argument plays with respect to the verb. With an increasing trend toward lexicalization in syntactic theories, a great deal of attention has been focused on the exact nature of the ordering and case-marking of verbal complements. Very often such studies focus on the correlation between the semantics of a verb—and in particular, *thematic* notions such as animacy, agentiveness, affectedness, and so on—and *grammatical roles*, such as subject, object, indirect object, and oblique complement (I take the *to* phrase in *give a book to Kim* to be an oblique complement rather than an indirect object). Perhaps most influential along these lines was work on Relational Grammar (RG) (Perlmutter and Postal 1983), which influenced almost every other theory of lexical structure currently under consideration. The notion arose that the more centrally agentive an argument was in the meaning of a verb, the less oblique it would be as a complement. Furthermore, work in RG reflected thematic structure and grammatical-role structure in relations between lexical entries, such as passivization, clefting, and causative constructions. Typically, an *obliqueness ordering* on grammatical roles makes subjects least oblique, objects next least oblique, indirect objects even more oblique, and oblique objects most oblique. Notions of obliqueness have been realized in categorial grammar in terms of the order in which arguments are consumed (Dowty 1982b, 1982c). In other theories, such as LFG (Bresnan 1982b), the notion of obliqueness is coded directly at the level of functional structure and linked directly to thematic structure (L. Levin 1987). In LFG, thematic structure is also used to relate different instances of verbs to one another in a uniform way (Bresnan 1982c). Notions of obliqueness have been used in HPSG (Pollard and Sag 1994) in order to define a thematically conditioned binding theory, which I will reproduce for reflexive binding in a type-logical setting in section 9.4. Dowty (1991) surveys several notions of thematic role that have been employed in the literature in an attempt to distill common semantic assumptions. We return to issues surrounding the structure of the lexicon in section 11.4.

It is common to directly define tree admissibility with respect to a phrase-structure grammar. I assume (see section A.6) that $\langle C, \langle T_1, \ldots, T_n \rangle \rangle$ is the tree *rooted* at category C with *daughter* trees $T_1, \ldots, T_n$, and that $\text{Root}(T)$ is the root of the tree T. I define the set of admissible trees with respect to an arbitrary collection **PSG** of phrase-structure rules of the form $C_1 \cdots C_n \Rightarrow C_0$, where the C_i are categories, and an arbitrary lexicon **Lex** with entries of the form $e \Rightarrow C$, where C is a category and e is a basic expression.

DEFINITION: TREE ADMISSIBILITY   The set of *admissible trees* with respect to a collection **PSG** of phrase structure rules is the least **AdmTree** such that

a. $\langle C, e \rangle \in$ **AdmTree** if $e \Rightarrow C \in$ **Lex**
b. $\langle C, \langle T_1, \ldots, T_n \rangle\rangle \in$ **AdmTree** if $T_1, \ldots, T_n \in$ **AdmTree**, and
   $\mathrm{Root}(T_1) \cdots \mathrm{Root}(T_n) \Rightarrow C \in$ **PSG**

Note that I have used the symbol C for categories, which in the case of applicative categorial grammars are pairs consisting of a syntactic category in **Cat** and a λ-term in **Term** of the appropriate type. The first clause of the definition says that any tree consisting of a category dominating an expression that is licensed by a lexical rule is admissible. The second clause says that a tree is admissible if its subtrees are admissible and its root C can be produced by a phrase-structure rule from the roots of its daughters.

The following theorem relates tree admissibility to our denotational definition of phrase-structure grammars. I write $\mathrm{Yield}(T)$ for the *yield* of a tree, which is made up of the leaves of the tree concatenated in order from left to right (see section A.6). The proof involves a simple constructive fixed-point argument in which the denotation of a category is constructed in finite stages.

THEOREM $C \in [\![e]\!]$ if and only if there is an admissible tree T such that $\mathrm{Root}(T) = C$ and $\mathrm{Yield}(T) = e$.

Proof   Let $\mathscr{T}$ be defined by induction as follows:

$$\mathscr{T}_0 = \{\langle C, e \rangle \mid e \Rightarrow C \in \mathbf{Lex}\}$$

$$\mathscr{T}_{n+1} = \mathscr{T}_n \cup \{\langle C, \langle T_1, \ldots, T_n \rangle\rangle \mid T_i \in \mathscr{T}_n, \mathrm{Root}(T_1) \cdots \mathrm{Root}(T_n) \Rightarrow C\}$$

$$T_\omega = \bigcup_{n \in \omega} \mathscr{T}_n$$

First, note that $\mathscr{T}_\omega = $ **AdmTree**. Clearly $\mathscr{T}_0 \subseteq$ **AdmTree**, and hence by induction, $\mathscr{T}_n \subseteq$ **AdmTree**. Thus $\mathscr{T}_\omega \subseteq$ **AdmTree**. Finally, note that $\mathscr{T}_\omega$ meets the conditions in the definition of **AdmTree**. Because **AdmTree** was defined to be the smallest set meeting its conditions and $\mathscr{T}_\omega$ meets the conditions on **AdmTree** and $\mathscr{T}_\omega \subseteq$ **AdmTree**, we have $\mathscr{T}_\omega = $ **AdmTree**.

Let $\mathscr{S}_n = \{\langle \mathrm{Yield}(T), \mathrm{Root}(T) \rangle \mid T \in \mathscr{T}_n\}$. A simple induction establishes that for all $n, \langle e, C \rangle \in \mathscr{S}_n$ only if $C \in [\![e]\!]$. By setting $[\![e]\!] = \{C \mid \langle e, C \rangle \in \mathscr{T}\}$, the conditions on $[\![\cdot]\!]$ are satisfied. As $[\![\cdot]\!]$ was defined to be minimal, the result follows. $\square$

Note that the proof proceeded by a standard induction on the depth of the tree. In effect, $\mathscr{T}_n$ is the set of trees of depth n.

We exploit the equivalence between derivations and denotations to establish the following:

THEOREM: TYPE SOUNDNESS   If $A\colon \alpha \in [\![e]\!]_{\mathbf{Lex}}$ then $\alpha \in \mathbf{Term}_{\mathrm{Typ}(A)}$.

Proof It suffieces to show that for every $T \in \mathbf{AdmTree}$, if $\mathrm{Root}(T) = \alpha\colon A$, then α is of type $\mathrm{Typ}(A)$. We proceed by induction on the depth of $T \in \mathbf{AdmTree}$. For lexical trees, the result holds by the definition of the lexicon. Now suppose that we have two trees T_1 and T_2 such that $\mathrm{Root}(T_1) = \alpha\colon A/B$, $\mathrm{Root}(T_2) = \beta\colon B$, and $\mathrm{Yield}(T_i) = e_i$. Then by induction α is of type $\mathrm{Typ}(A/B)$ and β is of type $\mathrm{Typ}(B)$. Hence tree $T = \langle \alpha(\beta)\colon A, \langle T_1, T_2 \rangle \rangle$ with yield $e_1 \cdot e_2$ is such that $\alpha(\beta)$ is of type $\mathrm{Typ}(A)$.   □

The significance of type soundness is that we only need to ensure that our lexical term assignments are well typed. The well-typedness of derived expressions and meanings follows from the type-soundness theorem. This situation is very much like the strict typing regime found in some programming languages such as ML; if a program is well typed statically (at compile time) then it will not lead to dynamic (run time) type errors.

4.7 AMBIGUITY, VAGUENESS, AND MEANING POSTULATES

In this section I treat a number of issues arising from our conception of grammar as assigning discrete meanings to expressions. In particular, I consider the contrast between ambiguity, which arises when an expression has multiple meanings, and vagueness, which occurs when a single meaning is underdetermined. Finally, I consider meaning postulates, which are nonlogical axioms characterizing particular nonlogical constants and their relations to one another.

4.7.1 Lexical Ambiguity and Vagueness

Nothing in the definition of a categorial lexicon rules out lexical ambiguity in either syntax or semantics. An expression is said to display *lexical syntactic ambiguity* if it has two lexical entries with differing syntactic categories. For example, the basic expression *kiss* is ambiguous between verbal and nominal interpretations. For now our lexicon remains a simple list, and such lexical ambiguities are indicated by multiple expressions having the same form. Relations between different syntactic entries and their corresponding lexical meaning shifts is an important topic in categorial grammar (see Carpenter 1992a for an overview of categorial approaches to structuring the lexicon).

An expression is said to be *lexically semantically ambiguous* if it has two or more distinct λ-terms assigned to the same syntactic category. The canonical example of such a semantic ambiguity, often referred to as a *sense ambiguity*, is the word *bank*, which can be used to refer to either a savings institution or the side of a river, among other things (for a tractor operator on the job, *bank* might be assumed to refer to a bank of earth or a bank of valves in the tractor). Again, we will simply treat sense ambiguities as being listed in the lexicon. The choice of when to treat a word as being semantically ambiguous is an interesting one. For instance, the term *sister-in-law*, which we might treat as a lexical entry, can be applied in English to either the sister of a spouse or the wife of a sibling. But nobody would claim that the term is ambiguous. Rather, it is what is referred to as *vague*. Another vague term is *glove*, which can be applied to either a right or left glove. Several diagnostics have been suggested to determine whether or not a given term is vague or ambiguous. For instance, the negation test is one such method for discriminating between ambiguity and vagueness. Consider the following minimal pairs:

(12) a. Gerry went to the bank.
 b. No he didn't, he went to the river.

(13) a. Robin is wearing a glove.
 b. No he isn't, that is a left glove.

In the first case, (12), you can negate a statement by claiming that the person used an ambiguous term in the wrong way. On the other hand, it is simply infelicitous to correct a vague term in the same way, as (13) indicates. Unfortunately, the negation test is not always clear. For instance, names might be naturally considered as either vague or ambiguous. An ambiguous treatment, which is forced upon us in the current setting by our assumption that the type of noun phrases is that of individuals, would incur a separate entry for every individual with a given name. But it is not clear that names are ambiguous in this way, as can be seen in the following examples:

(14) a. Terry is teaching that class.
 b. No he isn't, Terry Smith is.

Another popular test for ambiguity is the ellipsis test. When a verb phrase is elided, it must be read with the same sense as in the antecedent.

(15) a. Sandy has a brother-in-law, and Kim does too.
     b. Sandy knows Pat, and so does Kim.
     c. The banker went to a bank, and so did the riverboat pilot.

In the first case, (15a), Sandy and Kim might have brothers-in-law of different varieties (the brother-of-spouse reading versus the spouse-of-sister reading). In the second case, (15b), the Pat who is known must be the same for both Sandy and Kim. But notice that in (15c), there cannot be different kinds of banks, with the banker going to the savings variety and the riverboat pilot to the river bank. These tests provide a rough heuristic by which to classify expressions as vague rather than ambiguous, but such classifications are often tied up with other grammatical assumptions.

Of course, it is possible for a word to be syntactically ambiguous without assigning ambiguous meanings and vice versa. Syntactic ambiguity without corresponding semantic ambiguity can arise only in the situation where the two syntactic categories assigned to the expression are of the same type. For instance, we could postulate a noun of category n and verb phrase of category vp with the same meaning. How such moves might relate to nominalizations is a subtle matter (see Chierchia 1982 for a propositional account and Carpenter 1989 for an event-based treatment, both in a categorial setting).

4.7.2 Derivational Ambiguity

Consider the two admissible trees in figure 4.5 that can be derived for a noun followed by two prepositional phrases. In the first, the pyramid is both near the box and on the table. Under the second reading, the box is on the table and the pyramid is near the box. Clearly these properties are semantically distinct.

The examples in figure 4.5 display what is known as *structural ambiguity*, which is a kind of *derivational ambiguity*. Structural ambiguity arises when there are two distinct parse trees for the same set of words, having the same lexical entries. The kind of ambiguity displayed in figure 4.5 is even more pronounced in classic cases involving interactions with verb-phrase complements.

(16) a. I put the block in the box on the table.
     b. I saw the astronomer with the telescope.

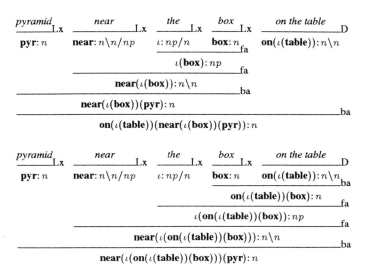

Figure 4.5
A derivation of ambiguity involving prepositional-phrase attachment

The first sentence is ambiguous as to whether the block was put into the box on the table or whether the block in the box was put on the table. The second sentence is also ambiguous and can be interpreted as meaning the astronomer with the telescope was seen by me or that I used a telescope to see the astronomer. Structural ambiguities of this variety are often referred to as *attachment ambiguities* because the site at which the modifier is attached causes the ambiguity. As can be seen from my intuitive glosses, English provides alternative ways to express the same idea without as much ambiguity in some cases.

An expression is said to be *lexically ambiguous* if there are derivations for it that use distinct lexical entries for one of its words. Lexical ambiguity can also contribute to structural ambiguity, as in the following classic examples.

(17) a. Visiting relatives can be dangerous.
      b. I forgot how good beer tastes.
      c. I saw that gas can explode.

In the previous examples in (16), I also postulate a lexical ambiguity because I provide prepositional phrases with different categories for verbal and nominal modification. Other theories may classify prepositions as being of a uniform class and thus not attribute any lexical ambiguity to the examples in (16).

4.7.3   Local and Global Ambiguity

An expression is said to be *locally ambiguous* if it has a subexpression that is ambiguous. For instance, there is local ambiguity in the two derivations of *The tall kid in pittsburgh ran,* due to the fact that *tall kid in pittsburgh* is itself ambiguous. Sometimes local ambiguity does not lead to global ambiguity. In some cases, ambiguous local analyses may not be consistent within the context in which they occur. For instance, the following well-known sentences are locally ambiguous but are not ambiguous.

(18) a. The horse raced past the barn fell.
      b. The cotton clothing is made with comes from Egypt.

The local ambiguity is so strong in these cases that they often produce what is known in the psycholinguistics literature as a *garden-path effect,* due to the fact that humans have a very difficult time coping with certain kinds of local ambiguity, especially without semantic priming (see Pritchett 1992 for an overview of garden-path effects). The tendency is to analyze the subexpression *the horse raced past the barn* as a complete sentence in and of itself. By the time the final verb is encountered, the required analysis is lost. The proper way to analyze these sentences is by analogy to the following.

(19) a. The horse ridden past the barn fell.
      b. The cotton with which clothing is made comes from Egypt.

In the first case, the local ambiguity arises from the possibility of analyzing *raced past the barn* either as a postnominal modifier, an $n\backslash n$ in categorial terms, or as a verb phrase. In the second case, the ambiguity stems from ambiguities between an adjectival and nominal reading of *cotton.* (For an account of the effect of semantics and context on garden-path effects, see Crain and Steedman 1985; Tannenhaus, Carlson, and Trueswell 1989.) Ambiguity in all forms is one of the primary bottlenecks in the computer processing of natural language, although humans are barely aware of any syntactic or semantic ambiguity during processing.

In applicative categorial grammars, structural ambiguity leads directly to a semantic ambiguity, in which there are two meanings assigned to the same expression. In the case of *red car in Pittsburgh,* the semantic ambiguity is between the scope of the adjective and the prepositional phrase. In one case the adjective applies to the noun before the prepositional phrase is attached, and in the second, the preposition applies before the adjective (see figure 4.6 below).

4.7.4   Meaning Postulates

In some cases we do not want structural ambiguity to lead to an ambiguity in meaning. Consider the consequences of making the following assumptions about the behavior of the constants **in** and **red**.

(20) a. **red** $\stackrel{\text{def}}{=} \lambda P.\lambda x.P(x) \wedge \textbf{red}_2(x)$
      b. **in** $\stackrel{\text{def}}{=} \lambda y.\lambda P.\lambda x.P(x) \wedge \textbf{in}_2(y)(x)$

Note that logical constants, such as conjunction, bind more tightly than abstraction and less tightly than predication. Further, note that for consistency, x and y must be individual variables of type **Ind** and P is thus a property variable of type **Ind** $\rightarrow$ **Bool**. Furthermore, we have two new constants, **red**$_2$ and **in**$_2$, which must be of types **Ind** $\rightarrow$ **Bool** and **Ind** $\rightarrow$ **Ind** $\rightarrow$ **Bool**, respectively.

Assumptions such as those in (20) are referred to as *meaning postulates*, following their introduction by Carnap (1947). Meaning postulates are used to constrain the interpretation of some constant, often by constraints expressible within the logic at hand. Model-theoretically, there are two ways to construe meaning postulates. The simplest method is to think of meaning postulates, such as the ones in (20), as introducing a notational shorthand, much as we did for the logical constants that were defined in terms of other logical constants. The second approach to meaning postulates is as restrictions on models. The defined symbols are taken to be actual parts of our language, rather than as abbreviations, but constrain attention to models that satisfy all of the meaning postulates. This latter strategy is common in the study of equational theories in abstract algebra, in which attention is often restricted to algebras satisfying several equational axioms. Which method we adopt is not significant, so I choose to think of meaning postulates simply as definitional in the cases where this is possible. But in some cases, which we will see later when I discuss plurality, meaning postulates are not equational but merely implicational, thus requiring the second interpretation, as constraints on models.

With the meaning postulates in (20), consider the derivations in figure 4.6. Even though there is structural ambiguity in the derivations, the terms assigned reduce to the same result after substituting the definitions of the constants.

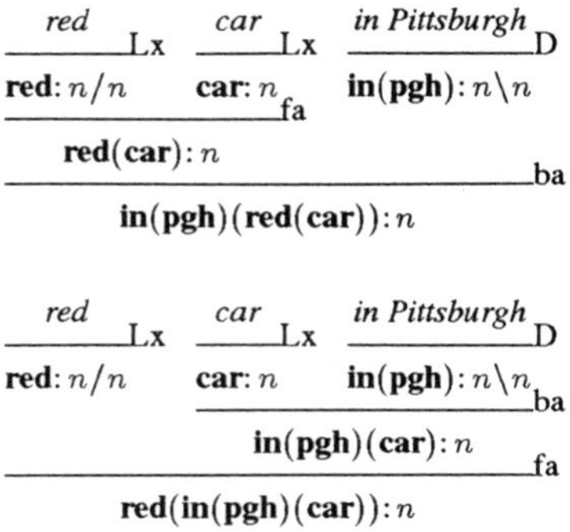

$$\frac{\dfrac{red}{\textbf{red}:n/n}\text{Lx} \quad \dfrac{car}{\textbf{car}:n}\text{Lx} \quad \dfrac{in\ Pittsburgh}{\textbf{in(pgh)}:n\backslash n}\text{D}}{\text{fa}}$$

$$\frac{\textbf{red(car)}:n}{\textbf{in(pgh)(red(car))}:n}\text{ba}$$

$$\frac{\dfrac{red}{\textbf{red}:n/n}\text{Lx} \quad \dfrac{car}{\textbf{car}:n}\text{Lx} \quad \dfrac{in\ Pittsburgh}{\textbf{in(pgh)}:n\backslash n}\text{D}}{\text{ba}}$$

$$\frac{\textbf{in(pgh)(car)}:n}{\textbf{red(in(pgh)(car))}:n}\text{fa}$$

Figure 4.6
A spurious attachment ambiguity

(21) a. $\textbf{red(car)} \equiv \lambda x.\textbf{car}(x) \wedge \textbf{red}_2(x)$
       b. $\textbf{in(pgh)(car)} \equiv \lambda x.\textbf{car}(x) \wedge \textbf{in}_2(\textbf{pgh})(x)$

Such structural ambiguities are said to be *spurious* because they do not lead to any semantic ambiguity. By the meaning postulates in (20), we have implicitly assumed that **red** and **in(pittsburgh)** behave as *intersective modifiers*. In other words, their semantic contribution to the nominal amounts to requiring an additional property to be added to that specified by the noun. The significance of treating modifiers as intersective is that they become semantically insensitive to order, thus providing an explanation for certain forms of spurious ambiguity. For instance, note that the following are equivalent by reassociating and commuting:

(22) a. $\textbf{red(in(pgh)(car))} \equiv \lambda x.((\textbf{car}(x) \wedge \textbf{in}_2(\textbf{pgh})(x)) \wedge \textbf{red}_2(x))$
       b. $\textbf{in(pgh)(red(car))} \equiv \lambda x.((\textbf{car}(x) \wedge \textbf{red}_2(x)) \wedge \textbf{in}_2(\textbf{pgh})(x))$

The term *intersective* arises from thinking of properties of type **Ind** $\rightarrow$ **Bool** as the characteristic functions of sets. In other words, a term of this type denotes a function from individuals to truth values, which picks out the set of individuals for which applying the function yields truth. In fact, the similarity in notation between $\lambda x.\phi$ and $\{x|\phi\}$ is not accidental: both are binding operations, and there is a natural isomorphism between sets and characteristic functions that relates them. Note that $\textbf{red}_2$ is also a property and can thus be thought of as a set. The intersection comes from the conjunction **and** because the denotation of the term $\lambda x.P(x) \wedge Q(x)$ yields truth when applied to an individual just in case the denotations of both P and Q yield truth when applied to the in-

$$
\frac{
\frac{Lee}{\textbf{lee}: np}\text{Lx} \quad
\frac{runs}{\textbf{run}: np\backslash s}\text{Lx} \quad
\frac{
\frac{in}{\textbf{in}: (np\backslash s)\backslash np\backslash s/np}\text{Lx} \quad
\frac{Chicago}{\textbf{chi}: np}\text{Lx}
}{\textbf{in}(\textbf{chi}): (np\backslash s)\backslash np\backslash s}\text{fa}
}{
\frac{\textbf{in}(\textbf{chi})(\textbf{run}): np\backslash s}{\textbf{in}(\textbf{chi})(\textbf{run})(\textbf{lee}): s}\text{ba}
}\text{ba}
$$

Figure 4.7
A derivation of *Lee runs in Chicago*

dividual. Thus the complex term $\lambda x. P(x) \wedge Q(x)$ corresponds to a set that is the intersection of the sets to which P and Q correspond. Not surprisingly, higher-order logic is powerful enough to directly express the intersection operation as a mapping from pairs of properties to properties.

(23) $\textbf{intersect} \stackrel{\text{def}}{=} \lambda P. \lambda Q. \lambda x^{\textbf{Ind}}. P(x) \wedge Q(x)$

Because we know the type of conjunction and have specified the type of the variable x in the above definition, we can determine that the intersection operator is of type $(\textbf{Ind} \rightarrow \textbf{Bool}) \rightarrow (\textbf{Ind} \rightarrow \textbf{Bool}) \rightarrow \textbf{Ind} \rightarrow \textbf{Bool}$. With this definition of **intersect** and our meaning postulate for **red**, we have the following logical equivalence:

(24) $\textbf{red}(\textbf{car}) = \textbf{intersect}(\textbf{red}_2)(\textbf{car})$

Just as with conjunction, we can write intersection in its usual notation as an infix operator:

(25) $P \cap Q \stackrel{\text{def}}{=} \textbf{intersect}(P)(Q)$

In section 6.1.1, I generalize the intersection construction to arbitrary boolean categories.

Before introducing a more sophisticated grammar formalism, I pause to consider the nature of prepositions in our grammar. I have assumed that the preposition *in* is assigned two distinct categories but is given the same semantic constant in each case. This move is possible because the categories $np\backslash s$ and n are of the same type, namely $\textbf{Ind} \rightarrow \textbf{Bool}$. We have already seen how such prepositions apply in the nominal case, but consider the verb-phrase modification in figure 4.7. Notice that with our meaning postulate for **in**, we have the following:

(26) $\textbf{in}(\textbf{chi})(\textbf{run})(\textbf{lee}) \equiv \textbf{run}(\textbf{lee}) \wedge \textbf{in}_2(\textbf{chi})(\textbf{lee})$

Such a statement will be true if Lee runs and Lee is in Chicago. Things become more complicated when tense is introduced, because an utterance of *Lee ran in Chicago* only entails that Lee was in Chicago when running and remains neutral as to Lee's present location. A related problem has to do with the subject-centeredness of this analysis; some verbs, when modified by prepositions, require their objects also to be in the stated location, or allow their subjects not to be in the stated relation, as in the following examples:

(27) a. Leslie talked to Kim in Chicago.
     b. Pat appeared on television.

The current offering is the closest we can come to the meaning of a preposition applied to a verb with our current semantic apparatus. We consider alternatives in section 11.1.6 and exercise 25 of chapter 12.

On the topic of prepositions, we would also like to consider the following contrast in their use:

(28) a. the picture of Robin
     b. the picture by Robin
     c. the picture on the table

In these noun phrases, the first preposition is being used to indicate that the picture depicts Robin, while the last indicates that the picture is physically located on the table. The middle case could either mean a picture created by Robin or a picture located somewhere near Robin. It has become common, following GPSG, to treat the first kind of use as an instance of *case marking*, in which the contribution of the preposition is simply to mark the argument. To handle this construction, GPSG applies an analysis similar to the following one:

(29) a. *picture* $\Rightarrow$ **picture**: n/np_{of}
     b. *of* $\Rightarrow \lambda x.x$: np_{of}/np_{obj}
     c. *Robin* $\Rightarrow$ **robin**: np_{obj}

Note that I have subcategorized our noun-phrase category into subtypes np_{obj} and np_{of}, where both have type **Ind**. We also need the type np_{sub} if we were going to account for subjects too. There is no deep significance to this interpretation of *of Robin* as being a noun phrase with case *of* rather than as a prepositional phrase of type *of*, as is done in GPSG; it is simply most convenient from the point of view of our type theory. An example of the kind of analysis these lexical entries allow for relational nouns is given in figure 4.8. Note that $\iota(\textbf{picture}(\textbf{robin}))$ in the derivation is equivalent to $\iota(\lambda x.\textbf{picture}(\textbf{robin})(x))$ by η-reduction. If we interpret $\textbf{picture}(y)(x)$ to be true if and only if x is assigned to a picture whose subject matter

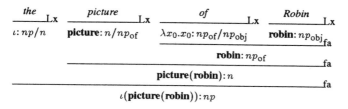

Figure 4.8
A relational derivation of *the picture of Robin*

is assigned to *y*, then we get the reading we are after. Nouns that take complements, such as *picture*, are said to be *relational nouns*. There is a large class of relational nouns, most of which take *of*-prepositional-phrase complements, such as *sister*, *department*, and so on. The objects of relational nouns can also be specified through possessives, as in *Sandy's picture*. Note that this latter expression is ambiguous and may also be interpreted as a picture standing in some other relation to Sandy, such as being owned, taken, or painted by. Both can occur at once, as in *Sandy's picture of Dana*. Some relational nouns take other prepositional complements, or even sentential complements. Consider the noun *belief*, which takes a complementized sentence as a complement, as in *belief that pigs can fly*, and can also take a prepositional genitive complement, as in *belief of Terry's*, although in a different sense. These possibilities multiply to allow the disambiguated *Terry's belief that pigs can fly*.

Exercises

1. Using the categories of the lexicon in figure 4.1, provide derivations for the following examples:
(a) Chris loves the kid.
(b) The tall kid in Pittsburgh loves Chris.
(c) Chris saw the woman with the telescope.
Are the examples structurally ambiguous?

2. From a newspaper, find some lexical and structural ambiguities that are local and some that are global.

3. Show that categorial grammars are weakly equivalent to context-free grammars. The direction showing that every categorial grammar defines a context-free language is straightforward once it is noted that the lexicon is finite and only subcategories of lexical categories occur in derivations. For the reverse direction, try putting the context-free grammar into Greibach normal form (see Hopcroft and Ullman 1979), so that every production is of the form $aA_1 \cdots A_n \Rightarrow A_0$, where

$n \geq 0$ and a is an expression and the A_i are all categories. Use a categorial lexical assignment of the form $a \Rightarrow A_0/A_n/ \cdots /A_1$, and prove the result by induction. (Bar-Hillel, Gaifman, and Shamir 1960)

4. Consider the following direct definition of $\overset{*}{\to}$, where we assume that the Γ_n are (possibly empty) sequences of categories and basic expressions.

(a) $\Gamma_1\Gamma_2\Gamma_3 \overset{*}{\to} \Gamma_1\Gamma_4\Gamma_3$ if $\Gamma_2 \Rightarrow \Gamma_4$

(b) $\Gamma \overset{*}{\to} \Gamma$

(c) $\Gamma_1 \overset{*}{\to} \Gamma_3$ if $\Gamma_1 \overset{*}{\to} \Gamma_2$ and $\Gamma_2 \overset{*}{\to} \Gamma_3$ for some Γ_2

Note that the first case is meant to encompass both lexical rewritings of the form $e \Rightarrow \alpha: A$ and also the forward and backward application schemes. Show that this definition in terms of rewriting is equivalent to the denotational one, so that $e_1 \cdots e_n \overset{*}{\to} \alpha: A$ holds if and only if $\alpha: A \in [\![e_1 \cdots e_n]\!]$.

5. Consider the addition of a lexical entry of the form $and \Rightarrow$ **intersect**: $n \backslash n/n$, where the definition of **intersect** is as given in (23). How would you define a lexical entry along similar lines for or? Use the entries for or and and to analyze the following examples:

(a) vegetarian and socialist

(b) vegetarian or socialist in Pittsburgh

(c) red car and toy

Use the meaning postulates given above to expand the semantics of your results. Does the grammar predict the correct semantic ambiguity for these examples?

6. Consider the subject relative pronoun who. Assume who is of the category **rel**: $n \backslash n/(np \backslash s)$. Provide a derivation of the following example:

(a) the kid who likes Chris.

Next, define an appropriate meaning postulate for the constant **rel**. Why is it not possible within the grammar I have presented so far to provide a reasonable category for the object relative pronoun $whom$?

7. Provide a definition of the constants **union** and **diff** for unions and binary set differences for sets of individuals. Recall that the difference of sets S_1 and S_2, indicated by $S_1 - S_2$, is defined to be those elements of S_1 that are not members of S_2.

For sets of individuals, provide a unary-set-complement operation using only the λ-calculus without any additional constants. Recall that the complement of a set S, usually written $\bar{S}$ or $\tilde{S}$, is taken to be the set of all elements in $\mathbf{Dom_{Ind}}$ that are not in S. (Hint: Define the set $\mathbf{Dom_{Ind}}$ using a λ-term.)

Provide a definition of **intersect**$_\tau$, which intersects sets of type τ. What are the types involved?

8. Provide a category for $Sandy's$ so that $Sandy's \ picture$ and $the \ picture \ of \ Sandy$ have the same meaning, $\iota(\mathbf{pict}(\mathbf{sandy}))$. Provide a category for $'s$ that combines with a noun phrase to its left and a relational noun to its right and derives the same meaning for the same two examples as above.

9. Provide lexical entries and meaning postulates relating *buy* and *sell* so that the following examples have the same meaning:

(a) Pat sold the book to Chris.

(b) Chris bought the book from Pat.

Treat *to* and *from* as case-marking prepositions.

10. Consider assigning the category $s/(np\backslash s)$ to subject noun phrases. What is the type assigned to this category? How can we use such a category to provide an analysis of quantified subjects and quantificational determiners? How might such an approach be extended to quantifiers in object position? (Steedman 1985, 1988)

Chapter 5

The Lambek Calculus

In this chapter we study the logical approach to categorial grammar introduced by Lambek (1958). Lambek extended the pure applicative categorial grammar according to a simple algebraic interpretation of the slashes. Lambek wanted an expression to be assigned to category A/B $(B\backslash A)$ if and only if when it was followed (preceded) by an expression of category B, it produced an expression of category A. This is a very natural interpretation of the meaning of a slash and of the assignment of slashed categories to linguistic expressions. However, applicative categorial grammar only respects one half of the biconditional. For instance, consider the verb *sampled*, of category $np\backslash s/np$, and the noun phrase *Pat*, of category np. With these lexical entries, whenever *Pat sampled* is followed by a noun phrase, a sentence results. But the applicative categorial grammar does not assign the category s/np to the expression, as Lambek's biconditional warrants. We will consider Lambek's logical approach to completing the applicative categorial grammar with dual rules for the other half of the biconditional.

Lambek's logical approach has deep significance both for the linguistic capability of categorial grammars and their logical and algebraic interpretations. Lambek's categorial grammars bear more than a passing resemblance to logics. Lambek followed the analogy between categories and propositions, with slashes acting as implications, and between logical deductions and grammatical categorization. I discuss several of Lambek's results, including the decidability of categorization and a cut-elimination result for the sequent presentation of the system.

Although Lambek's conception of grammar was purely syntactic, van Benthem (1983b) exploited the Curry-Howard correspondence, which I discuss at the end of this chapter, to associate λ-terms with derivations. These terms can be used to model the compositional derivation of meaning in natural language. For instance, reconsider the example from above, and note that if the noun phrase following *Pat sampled* has semantics y, the resulting sentence has semantics $\textbf{sample}(y)(\textbf{pat})$. The full category for *Pat sampled* is thus $\lambda y.\textbf{sample}(y)(\textbf{pat})$: s/np.

In this chapter we will explore Lambek's theory with an emphasis on its logical foundations. Its linguistic applications will also be illustrated, although many of these will not be exploited until subsequent chapters, when we will explore the interaction between the slashes and other constructors.

5.1   LAMBEK'S SEQUENT CALCULUS

In this section I introduce Lambek's categorial calculus using a Gentzen-style sequent presentation. In logical systems, sequents are usually of the form $\Gamma \vdash \phi$ and may be interpreted as stating that ϕ may be proven from Γ. In computational systems, sequents are usually of the form $P \Rightarrow a$ and are interpreted as stating that program P produces result a. In categorial grammar, sequents involve the rewriting relation, which I defined in the last chapter:

(1) $\mathscr{C}_1, \ldots, \mathscr{C}_n \Rightarrow \mathscr{C}_0$

Here the $\mathscr{C}_i$ are categories of the form $\alpha_i\colon A_i$, with α_i being a λ-term of the appropriate type for the syntactic category A_i. We interpret an admissible sequent as stating that a sequence of expressions e_i of categories $\mathscr{C}_i$ can be concatenated to produce an expression $e_1 \cdots e_n$ of category $\mathscr{C}_0$.

In adopting a sequent-based approach, we do not need to reconsider the notion of category or the mapping between categories and types. Rather, we simply assume as before that we have a fixed collection **BasCat** of basic categories and a collection **BasTyp** of basic types along with a function Typ mapping categories into (possibly complex) types. Furthermore, we adopt the same notion of a categorial lexicon, namely a simple relation **Lex** between basic expressions in a fixed domain **BasExp** and categories, where, as before, a category consists of a syntactic category in **Cat** and a λ-term of the appropriate type.

5.1.1   Applicative Fragment

In this section I recast our applicative categorial grammar in sequent notation to provide a launching point for further investigation. It is fairly straightforward to verify that the applicative sequent grammar admits exactly the same sequents as the phrase-structure approach. I first present the grammar and then provide an explanation of how it is to be understood.

DEFINITION: APPLICATIVE SEQUENT GRAMMAR   *Applicative sequent grammar* is defined by the following deduction schemes:

a. $\dfrac{\rule{2.5cm}{0.4pt}}{\alpha\colon A \Rightarrow \alpha\colon A}$ I

b. $\dfrac{\Gamma_2 \Rightarrow \beta\colon B \qquad \Gamma_1,\, \beta\colon B,\, \Gamma_3 \Rightarrow \alpha\colon A}{\Gamma_1,\, \Gamma_2,\, \Gamma_3 \Rightarrow \alpha\colon A}$ C

c. $\dfrac{\Delta \Rightarrow \beta\colon B \qquad \Gamma_1,\, \alpha(\beta)\colon A,\, \Gamma_2 \Rightarrow \gamma\colon C}{\Gamma_1,\, \alpha\colon A/B,\, \Delta,\, \Gamma_2 \Rightarrow \gamma\colon C}$ /L

d. $\dfrac{\Delta \Rightarrow \beta\colon B \qquad \Gamma_1,\, \alpha(\beta)\colon A,\, \Gamma_2 \Rightarrow \gamma\colon C}{\Gamma_1,\, \Delta,\, \alpha\colon B\backslash A,\, \Gamma_2 \Rightarrow \gamma\colon C}$ \L

As is standard in sequent systems, the sequents on top of the bar are the *assumptions* or *premises* and the sequent under the bar is the *conclusion*. The material to the left of a double arrow in a particular sequent is called the *antecedent*, whereas the material to the right of the double arrow is called the *consequent*. This terminology can become confusing, especially because premises or assumptions are often referred to as antecedents and the conclusions as consequents. The variables Γ_i and Δ indicate (possibly empty) sequences of category-meaning pairs. Unlike most logical systems, but like most computational systems, the order of categories on the left-hand side of a sequent is significant; the commas represent the concatenation of sequences rather than the union of sets.

As for the rules themselves, the I rule is the only axiom and represents reflexivity of rewriting. The C rule, known as the *cut rule*, enforces the transitivity of the derivation relation. It tells us that $\Gamma_1,\, \Gamma_2,\, \Gamma_3 \Rightarrow \alpha\colon A$ if $\Gamma_2 \Rightarrow \beta\colon B$ and $\Gamma_1,\, \beta\colon B,\, \Gamma_3 \Rightarrow \alpha\colon A$. Notice that the latter sequent is just the original sequent with Γ_2 replaced by $\beta\colon B$. These two rules are known as *structural rules*, because they do not make any reference to the logical constructors, which in this case are the slashes.

The two rules for the constructors, /L and \L, allow a slash to be eliminated from the left-hand side of a rewriting. In the sequent calculus, there is a standard method of assigning names to logical rules. Our rules are notated /L and \L because they govern the behavior of the forward and backward slash on the left-hand side of a sequent. The left rules reduce a derivation involving a slash on the left-hand side to one involving one fewer slashes. In particular, the forward left rule says that if we want to analyze a sequence with a forward category, Γ_1, $\alpha: A/B$, Δ, Γ_2, and we can find a subsequence Δ that rewrites to the correct argument category, $\beta: B$, then we can get the result from analyzing Γ_1, $\alpha(\beta): A$, Γ_2. Note that this latter result just involves replacing the subsequence $(\alpha: A/B, \Delta)$ with $\alpha(\beta): A$. The backward-slash rule works similarly. In the next section, we consider proofs with a slash on the right-hand side of the sequent.

As usual in such systems, a *proof* of a sequent involves constructing a tree each of whose local subtrees is an instance of one of the rule schemes (see section A.6 for definitions of terms involving trees).

DEFINITION: SEQUENT PROOF   A *sequent proof* consists of a finite tree $\mathscr{P}$ such that every local subtree matches one of the application schemes.

DEFINITION: DERIVABLE   A sequent $\mathscr{C}_1, \ldots, \mathscr{C}_n \Rightarrow \mathscr{C}$ is said to be *derivable* if and only if there is a sequent proof with no assumptions that is rooted at $\mathscr{C}_1, \ldots, \mathscr{C}_n \Rightarrow \mathscr{C}$.

We are primarily concerned with sequent proofs involving no assumptions. Such proofs must necessarily have all of their branches terminated by applications of the identity axiom scheme because it is the only scheme that does not require subproofs. Our linguistic theory is extensionally embodied in the set of derivable sequents. As we are dealing with a theory relating expressions to their meaning and nothing else, we place no stock on the form of the derivations, the number of possible derivations, and other structure that may depend on the presentation of the theory. For instance, in section 5.2, I will present a normalized natural-deduction method that generates the same sequents but eliminates the large number of redudant derivations.

The best way to illustrate the behavior of our sequent system is in terms of example proofs. Perhaps the simplest example possible is that of a noun phrase and a verb phrase, which I provide in figure 5.1. Note that this matches the definition of a proof because all three local subtrees match one of the rule schemes (one instance of \L and two of I). It is important to see how the rule \L was matched: we have taken $\Delta =$ **lee**: np and $\Gamma_1 = \Gamma_2 = \varepsilon$, the empty string. Further note how the identity schemes are required to ground the proof so that it does not depend on any assumptions.

Lexical expressions are linked to derived sequents by the lexicon.

$$\frac{}{\textbf{lee}: np \Rightarrow \textbf{lee}: np}I \qquad \frac{}{\textbf{run(lee)}: s \Rightarrow \textbf{run(lee)}: s}I$$
$$\frac{}{\textbf{lee}: np, \ \textbf{run}: np\backslash s \Rightarrow \textbf{run(lee)}: s}\backslash L$$

Figure 5.1
A derivation of *Lee runs*

$$\frac{}{\textbf{kid}: n \Rightarrow \textbf{kid}: n}I \qquad \frac{}{\iota(\textbf{kid}): np \Rightarrow \iota(\textbf{kid}): np}I$$
$$\frac{}{\iota: np/n, \ \textbf{kid}: n \Rightarrow \iota(\textbf{kid}): np}/L \qquad \frac{}{\textbf{run}(\iota(\textbf{kid})): s \Rightarrow \textbf{run}(\iota(\textbf{kid})): s}I$$
$$\frac{}{\iota: np/n, \ \textbf{kid}: n, \ \textbf{run}: np\backslash s \Rightarrow \textbf{run}(\iota(\textbf{kid})): s}\backslash L$$

Figure 5.2
A derivation of *The kid runs*

DEFINITION: LEXICAL LINKING   We write $e_1 \cdots e_n \Rightarrow \alpha: A$ if and only if $e_i \Rightarrow \alpha_i: A_i \in \textbf{Lex}$ for $1 \le i \le n$ and $\alpha_1: A_1 \cdots \alpha_n: A_n \Rightarrow \alpha: A$.

Thus the derivation in figure 5.1 establishes that *Lee ran* $\Rightarrow \textbf{run(lee)}: s$ under the assumption that our lexicon contains *Lee* $\Rightarrow \textbf{lee}: np$ and *ran* $\Rightarrow$ **run**: $np\backslash s$.

It is important to realize that in a sequent of the form $\Gamma \Rightarrow \alpha: A$, Γ is treated as a sequence. In other words, the elements of Γ are linearly ordered, may appear more than once, and so on. On the other hand, the sequent rules themselves do not have ordered premises. In particular, the cut rule is equivalently expressed in either of the following two forms:

(2) a. $\dfrac{\Gamma_2 \Rightarrow \beta: B \qquad \Gamma_1, \beta: B, \Gamma_3 \Rightarrow \alpha: A}{\Gamma_1, \Gamma_2, \Gamma_3 \Rightarrow \alpha: A} C$

   b. $\dfrac{\Gamma_1, \beta: B, \Gamma_3 \Rightarrow \alpha: A \qquad \Gamma_2 \Rightarrow \beta: B}{\Gamma_1, \Gamma_2, \Gamma_3 \Rightarrow \alpha: A} C$

The premises are order-independent because of how we construct proofs in the Lambek calculus. But keep in mind that the antecedents on the left-hand side of a sequent, such as $\Gamma_1, \beta: B, \Gamma_3$ and $\Gamma_1, \Gamma_2, \Gamma_3$, are taken to be ordered sequences.

I provide an analysis for the slightly more complex sentence *The kid runs* in figure 5.2, which involves both forward and backward slashes. Note that I have omitted the derivation of the noun phrase combined with the verb phrase, as it is the same as the one in figure 5.1. Rather

$$\frac{\qquad\qquad}{\textbf{kid}:n \Rightarrow \textbf{kid}:n}I \qquad \frac{\qquad\qquad\qquad\qquad}{\iota(\textbf{kid}):np,\ \textbf{run}:np\backslash s \Rightarrow \textbf{run}(\iota(\textbf{kid})):s}D}{\iota:np/n,\ \textbf{kid}:n,\ \textbf{run}:np\backslash s \Rightarrow \textbf{run}(\iota(\textbf{kid})):s}/L$$

Figure 5.3
A second derivation of *The kid runs*

than repeating derivations that I have already performed, I will simply employ the derived-rule schemes directly, using the symbol D. As can be seen from even the simple example in figure 5.2, sequent derivations become rather cumbersome and contain an enormous amount of redundant information. They also suffer from an extreme degree of structural ambiguity, in that there are usually many structurally distinct proofs for exactly the same sequent (with identical semantics), depending on the point at which the rules are applied. For instance, in the derivation of the sequent *The kid runs* $\Rightarrow$ **run**($\iota(\textbf{kid})$): *s*, we could have combined the determiner with its noun phrase in the first step and wound up with the same result, as shown in figure 5.3. Here we have used the /L scheme with $\Delta = \textbf{kid}:n$, $\Gamma_1 = \varepsilon$, and $\Gamma_2 = \textbf{run}:np\backslash s$. The degree of such spurious ambiguity increases rapidly when we introduce further sequent rules. Compounding the problems of spurious ambiguity, the cut rule actually admits infinitely many distinct derivations. For instance, we can trivially use a cut rule on a single category, combined with the identity scheme to rewrite the category to itself, to lengthen a derivation to one that is arbitrarily long. After completing Lambek's logic with the abstraction schemes in the next section, we are faced with infinitely many nontrivially distinct derivations. I wish to reinforce the notion that we do not draw any linguistic conclusions from the number of derivations; our theory is about the relationship between expressions and their meanings. It turns out that we can eliminate the spurious ambiguities arising from the cut, as we will see in section 5.1.3. Furthermore, the kinds of spurious ambiguity found in figure 5.3 are eliminated in the natural deduction presentation of the Lambek calculus, which I introduce in section 5.2.

5.1.2   Abstraction Schemes

In this section, I extend the applicative fragment to the full Lambek calculus. This is accomplished by adding rules that allow us to prove that a sequent derives a slashed category, and is thus of the form $\Gamma \Rightarrow \alpha: A/B$. These constitute the right rules for the constructors / and \ because they enable us to prove a sequent with a slash on the right side of the rewriting arrow. The right rules complete the proof-theoretic characterization of Lambek's interpretation of the slashes: a sequence will rewrite to category A/B if following it by a B produces an A (and dually for the backward slashes). In terms of semantics, the introduction rules for the slashes will correspond to abstraction rules in the semantic side of the category: a sequence will rewrite to $\lambda x.\alpha$ if following it by an x results in α.

I provide the Lambek (1958) calculus with the semantic term assignments established by van Benthem (1983b).

DEFINITION: LAMBEK CALCULUS   The *Lambek calculus* includes the rules of the applicative sequent grammar along with all instances of the following two schemes:

a.
$$\frac{\Gamma, x\colon A \Rightarrow \alpha\colon B}{\Gamma \Rightarrow \lambda x.\alpha\colon B/A} \, /R \qquad\qquad\qquad [x \text{ fresh}; \Gamma \text{ nonempty}]$$

b.
$$\frac{x\colon A, \Gamma \Rightarrow \alpha\colon B}{\Gamma \Rightarrow \lambda x.\alpha\colon A\backslash B} \, \backslash R \qquad\qquad\qquad [x \text{ fresh}; \Gamma \text{ nonempty}]$$

When applying the right rules, it is of utmost importance that each application of a rule involves a fresh variable x of the appropriate type for the category being introduced. This will prevent accidental variable capture, as we will see below. Note that like our elimination schemes, the introduction schemes form symmetric duals with one another. The backward introduction scheme is simply the forward scheme with the order reversed in the antecedents of sequents and the slashes reversed.

The introduction schemes extend the applicative fragment of the proof theory to the complete proof theory for the interpretation of categories given by Lambek. That this is so should be obvious from the definition of the introduction rules. The introduction rules increase the power of our formalism in that they allow us to prove sequents that did not hold in the simple applicative grammar. For instance, we can now prove that *Sandy likes* is of the category s/np, or in other words, is an expression that needs a noun phrase to its right to form a sentence. The derivation is given in figure 5.4 (recall the use of D for abbreviated derivations).

The grammar is powerful enough to derive abstractions over an unbounded stretch of intervening categories. For instance, consider the derivation in figure 5.5, with the category $np\backslash s/s$ assigned to *believes* (we return to the semantics of this category in section 11.1.2). The structurally unbounded nature of the introduction rules stems from the fact that the

$$\frac{\qquad\qquad\qquad I}{x\!:\!np \Rightarrow x\!:\!np} \qquad \frac{\qquad\qquad\qquad\qquad\qquad\qquad D}{s\!:\!np,\ \textbf{like}(x)\!:\!np\backslash s \Rightarrow \textbf{like}(x)(\textbf{s})\!:\!s}$$

$$\frac{s\!:\!np,\ \textbf{like}\!:\!np\backslash s/np,\ x\!:\!np \Rightarrow \textbf{like}(x)(\textbf{s})\!:\!s}{} L$$

$$\frac{s\!:\!np,\ \textbf{like}\!:\!np\backslash s/np \Rightarrow \lambda x.\textbf{like}(x)(\textbf{s})\!:\!s/np}{} R$$

Figure 5.4
A derivation of *Sandy likes*

$$\frac{\qquad\qquad\qquad\qquad\qquad D}{\begin{array}{l}t\!:\!np,\ \textbf{like}\!:\!np\backslash s/np,\ x\!:\!np\\ \Rightarrow \textbf{like}(x)(\textbf{t})\!:\!s\end{array}} \qquad \frac{\qquad\qquad\qquad\qquad D}{\begin{array}{l}l\!:\!np,\ \textbf{b}(\textbf{like}(x)(\textbf{t}))\!:\!np\backslash s\\ \Rightarrow \textbf{b}(\textbf{like}(x)(\textbf{t}))(\textbf{l})\!:\!s\end{array}}$$

$$\frac{l\!:\!np,\ \textbf{b}\!:\!np\backslash s/s,\ t\!:\!np,\ \textbf{like}\!:\!np\backslash s/np,\ x\!:\!np \Rightarrow \textbf{b}(\textbf{like}(x)(\textbf{t}))(\textbf{l})\!:\!s}{} L$$

$$\frac{l\!:\!np,\ \textbf{b}\!:\!np\backslash s/s,\ t\!:\!np,\ \textbf{like}\!:\!np\backslash s/np \Rightarrow \lambda x.\textbf{b}(\textbf{like}(x)(\textbf{t}))(\textbf{l})\!:\!s/np}{} R$$

Figure 5.5
A derivation of *Lee believes Terry likes*

$$\frac{\qquad\qquad\qquad\qquad D}{\textbf{r}\!:\!np,\ P\!:\!np\backslash s \Rightarrow P(\textbf{r})\!:\!s}$$

$$\frac{}{\textbf{r}\!:\!np \Rightarrow \lambda P.P(\textbf{r})\!:\!s/(np\backslash s)} R$$

Figure 5.6
An example of subject type raising

sequence $\Gamma, x\!:\!A$ is read as a string, so that the hypothetical assumption $x\!:\!A$ is simply concatenated to the sequence of assumptions Γ; the associative nature of concatenation entails that the assumption can attach at an arbitrary level of structural "embedding" so long as it remains on the right periphery of the derivation. In the rest of the development, I will frequently employ the abstraction schemes to produce derivations that are unavailable without them. I explore the utility of the unboundedness of abstraction in chapter 6.

Another interesting case is that of *type raising* (also known as *type lifting*), as illustrated by the derivation in figure 5.6. Type raising converts a noun phrase, *np*, which would normally be an argument to a verb phrase, $np\backslash s$, into a function looking forward for a verb phrase to produce a sentence, $s/(np\backslash s)$. Note that the semantics associated with the result, $\lambda P.P(\textbf{r})$, applies the verb-phrase argument as a property. Assigning the category $s/(np\backslash s)$ to a noun phrase is in keeping with Lambek's interpretation of categories; noun phrases are the kinds of expressions that

$$\frac{\qquad\qquad\qquad\qquad}{\mathbf{r}:np \Rightarrow \lambda P.P(\mathbf{r}):s/(np\backslash s)}\text{D} \qquad \frac{\qquad\qquad\qquad\qquad\qquad\qquad\qquad\qquad\qquad}{\lambda P.P(\mathbf{r}):s/(np\backslash s),\ \mathbf{run}:np\backslash s \Rightarrow (\lambda P.P(\mathbf{r}))(\mathbf{run}):s}\text{D}$$

$$\frac{\qquad\qquad\qquad\qquad\qquad\qquad\qquad\qquad\qquad\qquad\qquad\qquad\qquad}{\mathbf{r}:np,\ \mathbf{run}:np\backslash s \Rightarrow (\lambda P.P(\mathbf{r}))(\mathbf{run}):s}\text{C}$$

Figure 5.7
A spurious ambiguity involving cut and raising

when followed by verb phrases produce sentences. But note that type raising leads to further spurious ambiguity. We now have a derivation, as shown in figure 5.7, in which the noun phrase is raised before applying to the verb phrase, though after β-reduction the semantic result is the same. Here we match the cut scheme with $\Gamma_1 = \varepsilon$, $\Gamma_2 = \mathbf{r}:np$, and $\Gamma_3 = \mathbf{run}:np\backslash s$.

It is important to note that unlike the situation in most grammars, we have no need to stipulate grammatical rules. Instead, the right and left rules, embodying the logical interpretation of the slashes as representing concatenation, completely account for all the relevant possibilities. Rather than carrying out lexical type raising, as Montague did, or employing type raising as a phrase-structure scheme, as Steedman has, we simply derive type raising as in figure 5.6 from our general logic of the slash. Because a noun phrase can combine with a verb phrase to its right to form a sentence, our interpretation of the slash inevitably leads us to assign noun phrases to the category $s/(np\backslash s)$. This assignment is simply a consequence of our understanding of the meaning of the forward slash. One approach, suggested by Steedman's combinatory categorial grammars, is to disallow some instances of derivable rules. But to do so is to part company with the biconditional interpretation of the slash in terms of concatenation. In later sections we will see that it is just the seemingly unconstrained nature of our slash rules that allows us to derive a richer and more empirically appropriate set of meanings in many cases. Further, we do not find ourselves in the position of stipulating ad hoc or construction-specific rules as we go along. Of course, the question immediately arises as to the syntactic sensitivity of the resulting system. As I mentioned earlier, we lose several distinctions, such as that between $(np\backslash s)/np$ and $np\backslash(s/np)$. I hope to show that the distinctions we need remain. For instance, even though we can derive $s/(np\backslash s)$ from np, the converse does not hold. I exploit this basic fact to provide raising verbs with richer scoping possibilities than equi verbs in section 11.1.8. But there are cases of structural control about which I will have little to say, such as islands to extraction, the locality of

$$
\dfrac{\rule{3cm}{0.4pt}}{x:C \Rightarrow x:C}I \qquad \dfrac{\rule{5cm}{0.4pt}}{\alpha:A/B,\ \beta(x):B \Rightarrow \alpha(\beta(x)):A}D
$$

$$
\dfrac{\alpha:A/B,\ \beta:B/C,\ x:C \Rightarrow \alpha(\beta(x)):A}{\rule{6cm}{0pt}}/L
$$

$$
\dfrac{}{\alpha:A/B,\ \beta:B/C \Rightarrow \lambda x.\alpha(\beta(x)):A/C}/R
$$

Figure 5.8
Composition by abstraction

$$
\dfrac{\rule{3cm}{0.4pt}}{x:C \Rightarrow x:C}I \qquad \alpha(x):A \Rightarrow \beta:B
$$

$$
\dfrac{\alpha:A/C,\ x:C \Rightarrow \beta:B}{\rule{4cm}{0pt}}/L
$$

$$
\dfrac{}{\alpha:A/C \Rightarrow \lambda x.\beta:B/C}/R
$$

Figure 5.9
Isotonicity of results: value raising

reflexive binding, and phrasal constraints on word-order variation, which have played a pivotal role in contemporary syntactic theory. Instead, I refer the reader to other sources for discussions of locality (Morrill 1989a, 1994a), islands (Morrill 1992b, 1994a), word order (Moortgat and Oehrle 1994), and a general theory of structural sensitivity (Moortgat 1994, in press).

As another example of the power of the abstraction rules, consider the generic derivation of the functional composition of two categories in figure 5.8. As an example of this scheme, consider the result of composing a type-raised noun phrase with a transitive verb, a type-raised noun phrase with a sentential verb, or an adjective with a relational noun (all results have been β-reduced):

(3) a. $\lambda P.P(\mathbf{l}): s/(np\backslash s)$, **like**: $np\backslash s/np \Rightarrow \lambda x.\textbf{like}(x)(\mathbf{l}): s/np$
   b. **bel**: $np\backslash s/s$, $\lambda P.P(\mathbf{l}): s/(np\backslash s) \Rightarrow \lambda P.\textbf{bel}(P(\mathbf{l})): np\backslash s/(np\backslash s)$
   c. $\lambda P.\lambda y.P(y) \wedge \textbf{happy}(y): n/n$, **sis**: n/np
      $\Rightarrow \lambda x.\lambda y.\textbf{sis}(x)(y) \wedge \textbf{happy}(y): n/np$

Further instances of composition are provided as exercises.

The argument positions of the slashes behave with opposite polarity to one another when it comes to rewriting. One way in which this is reflected is in the *isotonicity* and *antitonicity* properties of the arguments, as established in figures 5.9 and 5.10. Note that these schemes depend on the assumption that $A \Rightarrow B$ holds. Combined with type raising, isotonicity of results allows us to convert an np/n into an $(s/(np\backslash s))/n$ and an $np\backslash s$ into

$$x:A \Rightarrow \beta:B \qquad \qquad \qquad \qquad \text{I}$$
$$\frac{\qquad \qquad \qquad \overline{\alpha(\beta):C \Rightarrow \alpha(\beta):C}}{\alpha:C/B, \ x:A \ \Rightarrow \ \alpha(\beta):C}\text{/L}$$
$$\frac{}{\alpha:C/B \ \Rightarrow \ \lambda x.\alpha(\beta):C/A}\text{/R}$$

Figure 5.10
Antitonicity of arguments: argument lowering

$$\frac{\vdots}{\qquad \qquad \qquad \qquad \qquad \qquad \qquad \qquad \text{D}}$$
$$\frac{x:np \quad \textbf{like}:np\backslash s/np \quad x:np \Rightarrow \textbf{like}(x)(x):s}{\textbf{like}:np\backslash s/np \quad x:np \Rightarrow \lambda x.\textbf{like}(x)(x):np\backslash s}\backslash\text{R}$$
$$\frac{}{\textbf{like}:np\backslash s/np \Rightarrow \lambda x.\lambda x.\textbf{like}(x)(x):np\backslash s/np}\text{/R}$$

Figure 5.11
Multiple and vacuous variable binding

$$\frac{\qquad \qquad \text{I}}{\frac{x:n \Rightarrow x:n}{\varepsilon \Rightarrow \lambda x.x:n\backslash n}\backslash\text{R}}$$

Figure 5.12
Empty antecedents

an $np\backslash((s/s)\backslash s)$. Dually, antitonicity of arguments combines with type raising to show that $(s/(np\backslash s))\backslash s \Rightarrow np\backslash s$. Isotonicity and antitonicity have familiar parallels in logic. Given $A \to B$, we infer $A \to C$ from $B \to C$, and we infer $C \to B$ from $C \to A$.

We now return to the side conditions placed on the right-rule schemes. First consider what would happen if we were to allow abstractions to be made twice on the same variable. An illustration of this situation is provided in figure 5.11. The problem with the resulting category should be obvious, because $\lambda x.\lambda x.\textbf{like}(x)(x)$ is the wrong term to assign to *like*. In applying this result to a subject and an object, the semantics of the object will be lost and the semantics of the subject will be used twice. Note that this is due to the logical equivalence of $\lambda x.\lambda x.\textbf{like}(x)(x)$ and $\lambda y.\lambda x.\textbf{like}(x)(x)$ by α-reduction, which can be applied because there are no free occurrences of x in $\lambda x.\textbf{like}(x)(x)$.

Now consider what would happen if we were to allow Γ to be empty in the right rule. For instance, consider the derivation in figure 5.12. The

$$\frac{s\colon np,\ \mathbf{like}\colon np\backslash s/np \Rightarrow \lambda x.\mathbf{like}(x)(\mathbf{s})\colon s/np \quad \lambda x.\mathbf{like}(x)(\mathbf{s})\colon s/np,\ \mathbf{d}\colon np \Rightarrow \mathbf{like}(\mathbf{d})(\mathbf{s})\colon s}{s\colon np,\ \mathbf{like}\colon np\backslash s/np,\ \mathbf{d}\colon np \Rightarrow \mathbf{like}(\mathbf{d})(\mathbf{s})\colon s}$$

Figure 5.13
A left-to-right derivation of *Sandy likes Dana*

problem here is that we produce a modifier category whose semantics is the identity function. Of course, there is no logical harm done in allowing Γ to be empty in an introduction rule. In fact, an application might be found for such a rule if we could find a category that took a modifier as an argument but would take the identity function as an argument if there were no modifier present. Otherwise, such a rule is rather harmless, but following standard practice, we filter out such trivial modifiers with a side-condition on the right rules. Typically, such empty categories have been ruled out on the basis of functor categories that take modifiers as arguments. For instance, *very* was often naively assumed to be assigned to the adjective-modifier category $n/n/(n/n)$, and the copula *be* to take adjectival objects, with the category $np\backslash s/(n/n)$. With the empty string deriving a modifier, we would consequently derive ungrammatical expressions such as **very kid* and **the kid is* (although the latter might arguably be grammatical, in which case we would coincidentally assign it the correct meaning in this way). But I uniformly escew any use of modifiers as arguments on independent, type-theoretical grounds having to due with purely semantic factors. I provide an alternative analysis of comparatives and intensifiers in section 7.12 and of the copula and predicative complements in section 6.2.4.

5.1.3   Associativity, Cut Elimination, and Decidability

The introduction schemes introduce a great deal of spurious ambiguity into the system, especially when coupled with the cut scheme. For instance, we can now analyze *Sandy likes Dana* by using cut and first deriving the category s/np for *Sandy likes* by the right rule for the forward slash and then applying the left rule for the forward slash to attach the object *Dana*, as shown in figure 5.13. But in my presentation of Lambek's calculus, spurious abstraction and then application only arises from the cut schemes. The right rules are constrained to require the whole string on the left to be consumed for the derivation. Lambek (1958) showed that the cut rule only multiplies the possible derivations for existing sequents but does not generate any new provable sequents.

THEOREM: CUT ELIMINATION If the sequent $\Gamma \Rightarrow \alpha: A$ is provable, then there is a cut-free proof of the sequent $\Gamma \Rightarrow \alpha': A$ where $\alpha \equiv \alpha'$.

Lambek (1958) proved the syntactic case, and H. Hendriks (1993) extended Lambek's results to van Benthem's (1983b) semantics. The proof of cut elimination is quite technical and involves a large number of subproofs to be established case by case. By induction on the depth of a proof, it is established that no matter how a cut is used in a derivation, the derivation can be reorganized to produce the same result with the cut occurring in a subderivation. Furthermore, Hendriks established that the semantic terms assigned were interderivable using β- and η-conversion.

The cut-elimination theorem has some important consequences, most notably the following:

THEOREM: FINITE DERIVATIONS For any sequence Γ and category A, there are at most finitely many provable sequents $\Gamma \Rightarrow \alpha: A$, and each sequent has a finite number of cut-free proofs.

Proof For any derivation, at most finitely many rule schemes will be applicable. Without the cut, each scheme strictly reduces the number of connectives in the sequents in its premises, and thus the depth of a cut-free sequent proof is bounded in the number of connectives in the sequent. □

A closely related fact concerning sequent derivations is that they satisfy the *subformula property*, which means that every category that occurs in the premises of the derivation of a sequent is a subcategory of a category that occurs in the resulting sequent. This result is obvious, given the structure of sequent derivations.

Lambek (1958) noticed that the finite-derivations theorem (without the semantic component) led to the decidability of sequent derivability.

THEOREM: DECIDABILITY The issue of whether $\Gamma \Rightarrow \alpha: A$ with respect to a finite lexicon **Lex** is decidable.

Proof Simply search backward from the sequent to be proven, applying all possible rule schemes. The finite-derivations theorem tells us that this procedure will terminate. □

Although it has been known for several decades that the Lambek calculus is decidable, Pentus's (1993) result provided much greater insight into its computational complexity and weak generative capacity:

THEOREM: CONTEXT-FREENESS The language generated by a finite lexicon under the rules of the Lambek calculus is context-free.

The proof is quite complex and involves the application of several deep theorems of logic that are well beyond the scope of this book. One interesting corollary to this result is the following:

COROLLARY: POLYNOMIAL COMPLEXITY   Given a fixed lexicon, the issue of whether a string is accepted under the lexicon in the Lambek calculus can be decided in polynomial time.

This involves a simple reduction to context-free parsing, the most efficient algorithm for which is asymptotically subcubic. But this only provides a grammar-specific-complexity result. At this writing, the complexity of the universal problem remains unknown. That is, when the input to the procedure is measured by combining the size of the grammar and the string, it is not known if a polynomial algorithm exists to decide whether the string is accepted by the grammar. Nor has the problem been proven to be NP-complete (for a definition of the class NP of nondeterministic polynomial problems, see Hopcroft and Ullman 1979). Further discussion of this issue, along with proofs of the polynomial recognizability of several subinstances of the universal problem, most notably the restriction to second-order categories, can be found in Aarts 1995.

One of the most startling properties of the Lambek calculus is its associativity. Lambek himself noticed that with the use of the cut scheme, derivations could be generated strictly from left to right. Lambek only considered the syntactic portion of the result, but the semantic result follows naturally. Suppose that we can derive the following sequent:

(4) $x_1: C_1, \ldots, x_n: C_n \Rightarrow \alpha: C_0$

By one application of the right rule for the forward slash, we have the following derivation:

(5) $x_1: C_1, \ldots, x_{n-1}: C_{n-1} \Rightarrow \lambda x_n.\alpha: C_0/C_n$

By $n-1$ applications of the abstraction scheme, we can derive the following:

(6) $x_1: C_1 \Rightarrow \lambda x_2.\ldots.\lambda x_n.\alpha: C_0/C_n/\cdots/C_2$

With the forward-slash left rule, we can now provide a purely left-to-right analysis of the input string by applying the first category to one argument at a time. Of course, no one would be so naive as to claim that this is a psychologically plausible model of human utterance processing, primarily because the space of possibilities for the first category to rewrite to is infinite in this system, each one corresponding to a possible grammatical continuation. Nevertheless, it might be interesting to consider systems of rewriting that fall somewhere between the "natural" ordering and the purely left-to-right ordering given above. Steedman has argued for a psychological interpretation of his combinatory categorial grammar, which lies somewhere between the applicative grammar and the full Lambek calculus in its derivations that do not mix order and lies beyond the Lambek calculus in cases where disharmonic composition (section 6.3.2) is allowed (Steedman 1988). It is well established that in humans semantic and syntactic processes interact on line during left-to-right processing. Although the precise granularity of this interaction is unknown, it is on the order of fractions of seconds. A further benefit of the categorial approach to grammar, as pointed out by Crain and Steedman (1985), is that it allows semantic interpretations to be derived from left to right in line with the syntactic derivations.

5.2   THE NATURAL-DEDUCTION LAMBEK CALCULUS

As can be seen from the derivations above, the sequent calculus is rather difficult to work with at the level of object derivations. Instead, it turns out to be much more perspicuous to use natural deduction for object-level derivations in our grammars.

5.2.1   Applicative Natural Deduction

I begin with the applicative fragment. I again present the grammar before explaining it.

DEFINITION: THE NATURAL-DEDUCTION APPLICATIVE FRAGMENT   The *natural-deduction applicative categorial grammar* consists of the following schemes:

$$\frac{\alpha\colon A/B \qquad \beta\colon B}{\alpha(\beta)\colon A}\,/\mathrm{E} \qquad \frac{\beta\colon B \qquad \alpha\colon B\backslash A}{\alpha(\beta)\colon A}\,\backslash\mathrm{E}$$

To read these rules, note that the vertical ellipses indicate a well-formed natural-deduction derivation with root as shown below the ellipses. A natural-deduction proof involves, in the derivation, a tree all of whose local subtrees match one of the schemes. The leaves of such a derivation represent the assumptions and are read in order from left to right. The definition allows a single category to count as a natural-deduction proof of itself from itself as an antecedent (thus matching the identity rule in the sequent calculus).

There is a straightforward correspondence between the natural-deduction presentation and an alternative sequent-based presentation (see Prawitz 1965). For the applicative fragment, the corresponding sequent rules are the following:

(7) a.
$$\frac{\Gamma_1 \Rightarrow \alpha : A/B \qquad \Gamma_2 \Rightarrow \beta : B}{\Gamma_1, \Gamma_2 \Rightarrow \alpha(\beta) : A}$$

    b.
$$\frac{\Gamma_1 \Rightarrow \beta : B \qquad \Gamma_2 \Rightarrow \alpha : B \backslash A}{\Gamma_1, \Gamma_2 \Rightarrow \alpha(\beta) : A}$$

This sequent characterization provides a precise definition of the natural deduction schemes, and the tree-based notation can be thought of as a readable shorthand for such derivations. The vertical ellipses in the natural-deduction schemes correspond to the assumptions Γ_i in the sequent schemes. Note that instances of these schemes are derivable in the sequent calculus by means of the cut. Also note that these schemes do not have the subformula property; nothing requires A/B or B to be sub-categories of the categories in Γ_1 or Γ_2. In some cases, cut can lead to shorter derivations. But admitting cut as a rule scheme undermines some of the more pleasant metatheoretical properties of the system. When we consider proof normalization in section 5.2.3, we will see how to recover the most important properties of the sequent system in the natural-deduction setting.

The naming of rules in natural deduction also follows an established pattern. The rules in the applicative fragment are instances of *elimination schemes*, because they combine subderivations and eliminate an occurrence of a connective. Of course, we have an elimination scheme for both slashes. Elimination is used in natural deduction in the same way that the left rules are used in the sequent system. Together, left rules and elimination rules are known as *rules of use*.

Note that these schemes and the conditions on a proof amount to nothing more than the locally-admissible-tree schemes from the phrase-structure presentation of the applicative categorial grammar. This fact establishes a deep connection between logical approaches and phrase-structure approaches, and this can be extended to the abstraction schemes.

Just as in the sequent calculus, we can insert lexical entries. This is much more easily notated in the natural-deduction setting, where we can simply allow the following scheme:

$$(8) \quad \frac{e}{\alpha:A} \, \text{Lx} \qquad\qquad [e \Rightarrow \alpha:A \in \textbf{Lex}]$$

Rather than providing example derivations using these schemes, I simply refer back to the parse trees given in the previous chapter, as they are all well-formed natural-deduction derivations. Just as parse trees can be used to represent equivalence classes of rewritings in phrase-structure grammars, natural-deduction derivations represent multiple sequent derivations. They do so by eliminating irrelevant ordering information encoded in a sequent derivation. If there is structural ambiguity in an applicative natural-deduction derivation, there will be an ambiguity in the semantic terms derived.

The sequent being proved in the natural-deduction setting is read off of a natural deduction scheme from left to right across the leaves of the proof tree, and the result is the root of the tree. Thus it is quite significant that the Lambek calculus is about ordered deductions. Other varieties of categorial grammar do away with the ordering inherent in Lambek's approach, some going so far as to close derivations under permutation (for discussion, see van Benthem 1986a; Moortgat and Oehrle 1994; Kurtonina and Moortgat, in press). In particular, we must order the derivation of the category A/B before the derivation of B in the case of forward-slash elimination, and similarly for the case of backward-slash elimination. Keep in mind that this is different than the case of premises in the sequent calculus. In the sequent presentation, the ordering of categories and expressions is represented in the sequents themselves, which are of the form $\Gamma \Rightarrow \alpha:A$, rather than in the structure of the proof. Finally, it should be noted that the identity scheme and the cut rule are implicit in the natural-deduction presentation and do not need to be explicitly stated with additional rules.

5.2.2   The Natural-Deduction Lambek Calculus

We can extend the natural-deduction presentation of applicative categorial grammar to capture the dual *rules of proof* in Lambek's calculus.

DEFINITION: NATURAL-DEDUCTION LAMBEK CALCULUS The *natural-deduction Lambek calculus* consists of the applicative natural deduction calculus along with the following two rule schemes:

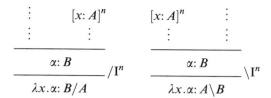

A few comments are in order concerning the notation in these rules, which follow the same basic pattern as natural-deduction rules for proving implications in propositional logic (see Prawitz 1965). First, as with propositional natural deduction, the brackets around the category at the top of the rule indicate an assumption that is introduced and then discharged at a later stage of the derivation. The assumption and the step at which it is discharged are coindexed with an integer n to mark the scope of the assumption. This means that the assumption category $x\!:\!A$ can be used in the derivation of $\alpha\!:\!B$, but is discharged at that point and cannot be used in any further inferences.

The natural-deduction introduction schemes can be understood as nothing more than notational variants of the right rules in the sequent calculus. The forward-slash scheme, for instance, uses a proof of $\alpha\!:\!B$ from some assumptions $\Gamma, x\!:\!A$ to establish a proof of $\lambda x.\alpha\!:\!B/A$ from the assumptions Γ. Here Γ corresponds to the assumptions indicated by the ellipsis in the actual rule. Further note that this last step eliminates the assumption $x\!:\!A$, which is why it is displayed in brackets; it is a real assumption insofar as the derivation of $\alpha\!:\!B$ was concerned, but thereafter it is no longer an assumption in the derivation of $\lambda x.\alpha\!:\!B/A$.

Next note that the rules are ordered in that the assumption of $\alpha\!:\!A$ in the forward (backward) introduction scheme is required to be the rightmost (leftmost) assumption used in the derivation of $\alpha\!:\!B$. Next, to fully match the sequent versions of the introduction schemes, we must satisfy the nonemptiness condition on the right rules; in the natural-deduction setting, this condition is expressed by requiring at least one assumption to be used in the derivation of $\alpha\!:\!B$ in addition to $\alpha\!:\!A$. Finally, as with the sequent rules, we must make sure that the variables used in the assumption are fresh, in the sense that they do not occur elsewhere in any other assumption in the derivation. As before, this will prevent the accidental capture of variables.

To illustrate the application of these rules, I provide some derivations in figures 5.14 and 5.15.

$$
\cfrac{
\cfrac{
\cfrac{
\cfrac{
\underset{\mathbf{l}:\,np}{\underline{\;Lee\;}}_{\text{Lx}}\quad
\underset{\mathbf{like}:\,np\backslash s/np}{\underline{\quad likes\quad}}_{\text{Lx}}\quad
[x\!:\!np]^0
}{\mathbf{like}(x):np\backslash s}\;/\text{E}
}{\mathbf{like}(x)(\mathbf{l}):s}\;\backslash\text{E}
}{\lambda x.\mathbf{like}(x)(\mathbf{l}):s/np}\;\backslash\text{I}^0
$$

Figure 5.14
A natural-deduction derivation of *Lee likes*

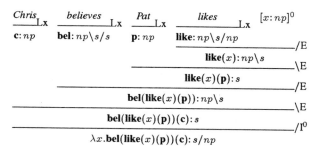

Figure 5.15
Another example of natural-deduction introduction

$$
\cfrac{
\cfrac{
\underset{\mathbf{r}:\,np}{\underline{\;Robin\;}}_{\text{Lx}}\quad
[P\!:\!np\backslash s]^0
}{P(\mathbf{r}):s}\;\backslash\text{E}
}{\lambda P.P(\mathbf{r}):s/(np\backslash s)}\;/\text{I}^0
$$

Figure 5.16
A subject type-raising derivation

There are a number of other cases in which the introduction schemes may be applied. For instance, consider the type-raising derivation in figure 5.16, which corresponds to the sequent derivation in figure 5.6. The next examples illustrate how seemingly odd arrangements of expressions can be assigned categories in the Lambek calculus. In particular, the derivation shown in figure 5.17 illustrates how two noun phrases can combine to produce a category looking backward for a ditransitive verb to produce a verb phrase. We will see how such a category can be used

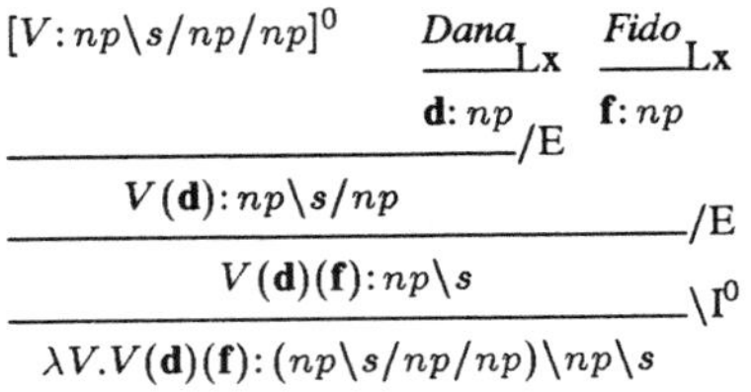

$$[V:np\backslash s/np/np]^0 \quad \underset{\textbf{d}:\,np}{\underline{Dana}}_{\text{Lx}} \quad \underset{\textbf{f}:\,np}{\underline{Fido}}_{\text{Lx}}$$

$$\frac{V(\textbf{d}):np\backslash s/np}{} /\text{E}$$

$$\frac{V(\textbf{d})(\textbf{f}):np\backslash s}{} /\text{E}$$

$$\frac{}{\lambda V.V(\textbf{d})(\textbf{f}):(np\backslash s/np/np)\backslash np\backslash s} \backslash\text{I}^0$$

Figure 5.17
A derivation of two noun phrases

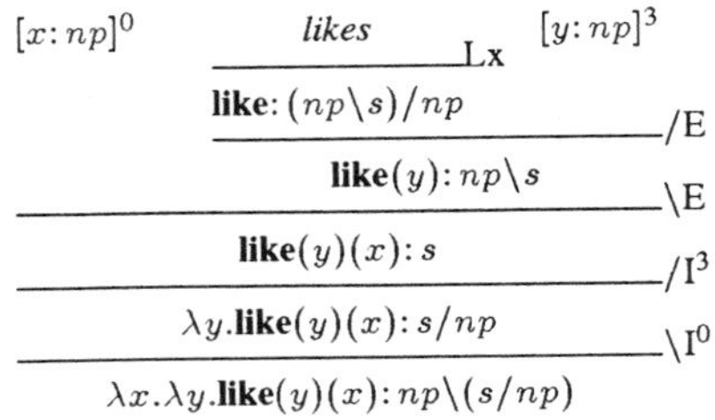

$$[x:np]^0 \quad \underset{\textbf{like}:\,(np\backslash s)/np}{\underline{likes}}_{\text{Lx}} \quad [y:np]^3$$

$$\frac{\textbf{like}(y):np\backslash s}{} /\text{E}$$

$$\frac{\textbf{like}(y)(x):s}{} \backslash\text{E}$$

$$\frac{\lambda y.\textbf{like}(y)(x):s/np}{} /\text{I}^3$$

$$\frac{}{\lambda x.\lambda y.\textbf{like}(y)(x):np\backslash(s/np)} \backslash\text{I}^0$$

Figure 5.18
An example of argument reordering

for coordination in the next chapter. For now I simply note that if we were to combine this analysis with a ditransitive verb, we would get the same result as if we had not done the type raising and simply done the application instead.

I will now show how the introduction schemes allow us to derive a number of well-known categorial grammar sequents. The first that we consider is that of argument permutation. In general, we can reorder forward and backward slashes with respect to one another using introduction. I show an example of such a derivation in figure 5.18. The next family of derivations falls under the general heading of *division* schemes, although they are commonly referred to as the *Geach rules* after their application by Geach (1972).

(9) a. $\alpha:A/B \Rightarrow \lambda y.\lambda x.\alpha(y(x)):A/C/(B/C)$
    b. $\alpha:B\backslash A \Rightarrow \lambda y.\lambda x.\alpha(y(x)):(C\backslash B)\backslash C\backslash A$

When coupled with simple application, the Geach rules admit one-step compositions. For instance, $A/B, B/C \Rightarrow A/C$ because $A/B \Rightarrow A/C/(B/C)$.

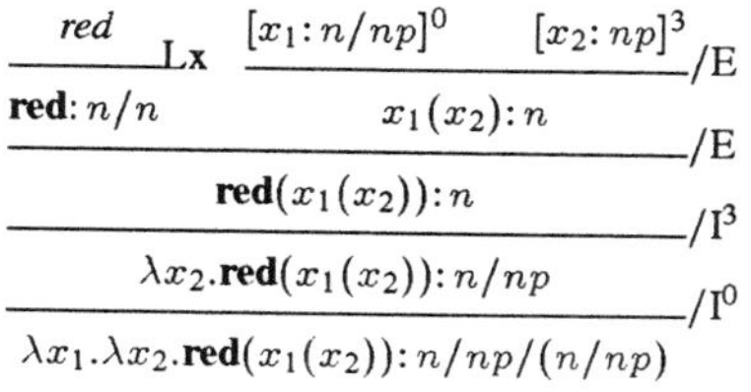

$$\cfrac{\cfrac{red}{\textbf{red}: n/n}\text{Lx} \quad \cfrac{[x_1 : n/np]^0 \quad [x_2 : np]^3}{x_1(x_2) : n}/\text{E}}{\cfrac{\cfrac{\textbf{red}(x_1(x_2)) : n}{\lambda x_2.\textbf{red}(x_1(x_2)) : n/np}/\text{I}^3}{\lambda x_1.\lambda x_2.\textbf{red}(x_1(x_2)) : n/np/(n/np)}/\text{I}^0}/\text{E}$$

Figure 5.19
A derivation of division

The previous schemes applied division to the functor, whereas the following divide out the result.

(10) a. $\alpha : A/B \Rightarrow \lambda P.\lambda x.P(\alpha(x)) : (C/A)\backslash C/B$
      b. $\alpha : B\backslash A \Rightarrow \lambda P.\lambda x.P(\alpha(x)) : B\backslash C/(A\backslash C)$

These forms of division allow for composition in the opposite order. We have $A/B, B/C \Rightarrow A/C$ in virtue of the division derivation $B/C \Rightarrow A/C\backslash(A/B)$. In figure 5.19, I show the natural-deduction derivation of an instance of (9a). I leave the other cases as an exercise. One consequence of the validity of the division schemes in the Lambek calculus is that there is no way to have a purely sentence-modifying adverbial that cannot also be analyzed as a verb-phrase modifier. This is because of the following valid instance of division.

(11) $\alpha : s\backslash s \Rightarrow \lambda V.\lambda x.\alpha(V(x)) : (np\backslash s)\backslash(np\backslash s)$

On the other hand, the converse derivation does not hold: a verb-phrase modifier cannot, in general, be recast as a sentential modifier.

The analysis of the division example shows how categories assumed during natural deduction may combine with each other before being eliminated. In general, division allows analyses involving functional composition. Composition itself is derivable, as I showed in figure 5.8; I leave the natural-deduction derivation as an exercise. Of course, backward composition is also derivable by a dual argument. Furthermore, all of the generalized versions of composition assumed by Ades and Steedman (1982), given below, are also directly derivable.

(12) $\alpha : A/B,\ \beta : B/C_1/\cdots/C_n$
      $\Rightarrow \lambda x_n.\ldots.\lambda x_1.\alpha(\beta(x_n)\cdots(x_1)) : A/C_1/\cdots/C_n$

Again, it is important to keep in mind that these derivations of the type-raising and division schemes are not additional assumptions but merely consequences of our understanding of the forward and backward slashes. As was the case in the sequent setting, there is a great deal of spurious semantic ambiguity in the natural-deduction system. For instance, a division or raising may be applied where a simple application would have sufficed. It is to a characterization of these cases that we turn in the next section.

5.2.3 Proof Normalization

In general, if we introduce a category and then immediately eliminate it, we are left with the same result as had we simply not done the introduction to start with. In this section I show how natural-deduction derivations can be normalized to a form in which there are no redundant subderivations. Normalization is closely linked to the notion of cut elimination in the sequent presentation in that we can set up a morphism from sequent proofs to their natural-deduction analogues; cut-free sequent proofs will correspond to normal derivations.

Proof normalization is characterized by two reduction schemes.

DEFINITION: PROOF NORMALIZATION   The *normalization* reductions are

a. β-normalization

$$
\cfrac{\cfrac{\begin{array}{cc} \vdots & [x\colon A]^n \\ \vdots & \vdots \end{array}}{\cfrac{\alpha\colon B}{\lambda x.\alpha\colon B/A}/\mathrm{I}^n \qquad \beta\colon A}{(\lambda x.\alpha)(\beta)\colon B}/\mathrm{E}} \quad \rightsquigarrow \quad \begin{array}{c} \vdots \quad \beta\colon A \\ \vdots \quad \vdots \\ \alpha[x \mapsto \beta]\colon B \end{array}
$$

b. η-normalization

$$
\cfrac{\cfrac{\alpha\colon A/B \qquad [x\colon B]^n}{\alpha(x)\colon B}/\mathrm{E}}{\lambda x.\alpha(x)\colon A/B}/\mathrm{I}^n \quad \rightsquigarrow \quad \alpha\colon A/B
$$

The normalization schemes are intended to be applied to a derivation to produce a simpler derivation of the same result. It should be obvious that the results of the derivations are the same, as this fact follows directly from the rules of β- and η-reduction in the λ-calculus. In fact, the normalization schemes correspond directly to the normalization schemes in the λ-calculus. A derivation is said to be *normal* if and only if it contains no subderivations that match the left-hand sides of the normalization reductions. A normal proof, in general, involves as little use of introduction rules as is possible for the derivation. Normal forms of categorial-grammar proofs have been exploited in computational applications of categorial grammar by Hepple (1990b), König (1989), and Carpenter (1994b). I later extend our normalization patterns to the new constructors I introduce in the following chapters, following the discussion in Morrill 1994.

Normalization in the proofs corresponds to normalization in the semantic terms because of a property known as *unique readability*. Suppose that we are dealing with a natural-deduction proof of the sequent $x_1: C_1, \ldots, x_n: C_n \Rightarrow \alpha: C$ in which every assumption is a variable. Then $\alpha = \lambda x. \beta$ if and only if the last step of the proof is an introduction. Similarly, $\alpha = \beta(\gamma)$ if and only if the last step is an elimination. This allows us to establish the following:

THEOREM: NORMALIZATION   If $\mathscr{D}$ is a normal-form derivation of $x_1: C_1, \ldots, x_n: C_n \Rightarrow \alpha: C$, then α is in β, η normal form.

Proof   If a subproof contains a β-redex, $(\lambda x. \alpha)(\beta)$, then the term arose by an elimination, the functor of which arose by introduction. In this case, the proof is not normal. Similarly, if a subproof contains an η-redex, $\lambda x. \alpha(x)$, then the entire term must have arisen by introduction over a derivation, the last step of which was an application of α to x. Again, such a proof could be normalized. Thus any proof containing a redex is not normal.   □

It is important to note that the sequent calculus and the natural-deduction proof system result in the same sequents being provable.

THEOREM   A sequent $\Gamma \Rightarrow \alpha: A$ is provable in the natural-deduction Lambek calculus if and only if it is provable in the sequent Lambek calculus.

Proof   ($\Rightarrow$) First note that every sequent provable with a cut is provable without the cut. Thus it will suffice to construct a natural-deduction proof for every cut-free sequent derivation. We proceed by induction on the depth of the sequent derivation of $\Gamma \Rightarrow \alpha: A$. If the identity axiom is used, the result is trivial. Assume that the left rule for forward slash was employed:

$$\frac{\Delta \Rightarrow \beta\colon B \qquad \Gamma_1, \alpha(\beta)\colon A,\, \Gamma_2 \Rightarrow \gamma\colon C}{\Gamma_1,\, \alpha\colon A/B,\, \Delta,\, \Gamma_2 \Rightarrow \gamma\colon C}/\mathrm{L}$$

By induction, we know that there is a natural-deduction derivation $\mathscr{D}_1$ of $\beta\colon B$ from Δ and a derivation $\mathscr{D}_2$ of $\gamma\colon C$ from $\Gamma_1, \alpha(\beta)\colon A, \Gamma_2$.

$$\frac{\begin{array}{c}\Delta\\ \vdots\end{array}}{\beta\colon B} \qquad \frac{\Gamma_1 \quad \alpha(\beta)\colon A \quad \Gamma_2 \\ \vdots}{\gamma\colon C}$$

Inserting the derivation $\mathscr{D}_1$ of $\beta\colon B$ to the right of $\alpha\colon A/B$ and applying forward elimination yields $\alpha(\beta)\colon A$. Inserting this proof above $\alpha(\beta)\colon A$ in $\mathscr{D}_2$ gives a natural deduction proof of the result.

$$\cfrac{\cfrac{\Gamma_1 \quad \alpha\colon A/B \quad \begin{array}{c}\Delta \quad \Gamma_2\\ \vdots\\ \beta\colon B\end{array}}{\alpha(\beta)\colon A}/\mathrm{E}}{\gamma\colon C\ \vdots}$$

The backward slash is symmetric. Now suppose that the right rule for the forward slash was used:

$$\frac{\Gamma,\, x\colon B \Rightarrow \alpha\colon A}{\Gamma \Rightarrow \lambda x.\alpha\colon A/B}/\mathrm{R}$$

By induction, we know that there is a natural-deduction derivation $\mathscr{D}_1$ of $\alpha\colon A$ from $\Gamma, x\colon B$. By treating $x\colon B$ as a hypothetical assumption on the right periphery of the derivation, it can be discharged at the next stage to yield a natural-deduction proof of $\lambda x.\alpha\colon A/B$ from Γ. A symmetric argument applies to the backward slash. Thus every sequent derivation has a natural-deduction derivation.

($\Leftarrow$) I now provide a sequent analysis for every natural-deduction derivation. I work by induction on the depth of the natural-deduction derivation. If the proof is of depth 0, it is just a single category $\alpha\colon A$, corresponding to the sequent $\alpha\colon A \Rightarrow \alpha\colon A$. This sequent is an instance of the identity scheme and hence is provable. Now suppose that the forward elimination scheme was used:

$$
\frac{\alpha: A/B \qquad \beta: B}{\alpha(\beta): A} /\mathrm{E}
$$

Let the left context be Γ_1 and the right context Γ_2, so that by induction, we have a sequent derivation of $\Gamma_1 \Rightarrow \alpha: A/B$ and of $\Gamma_2 \Rightarrow \beta: B$. Using the cut scheme, we have the following:

$$
\frac{\Gamma_1 \Rightarrow \alpha: A/B \qquad \dfrac{\Gamma_2 \Rightarrow \beta: B \qquad \dfrac{}{\alpha(\beta): A \Rightarrow \alpha(\beta): A}\mathrm{I}}{\alpha: A/B,\ \Gamma_2 \Rightarrow \alpha(\beta): A}/\mathrm{L}}{\Gamma_1,\ \Gamma_2 \Rightarrow \alpha(\beta): A}\mathrm{C}
$$

Thus by induction we have the sequent derivation. Now suppose that the forward introduction scheme was used:

$$
\frac{\begin{array}{c}[x: A]^n \\[4pt] \vdots \\[2pt] \alpha: B\end{array}}{\lambda x.\alpha: B/A}/\mathrm{I}^n
$$

By induction, we have a sequent derivation of $\Gamma, x: A \Rightarrow \alpha: B$. An application of the right rule then gives the result. This exhausts the possibilities for natural-deduction proofs. Thus every natural-deduction proof of a sequent is also provable in the sequent calculus. $\square$

The connection between sequents and natural deduction runs far deeper than we have yet explored; cut-free derivations in the sequent calculus will be mapped directly onto normal proof trees, and natural deduction proofs can be mapped directly onto cut-free derivations. We consider some of these properties in section 5.4.2. For now, consider the fact that there might be several cut-free sequent proofs that correspond to the same natural-deduction proof. Consider the following two sequent proofs and their natural-deduction analogue (I have omitted the semantics, which is the same in all cases).

(13) a.

$$\frac{}{C \Rightarrow C}\, \text{I} \qquad \frac{}{B \Rightarrow B}\, \text{I} \qquad \frac{}{A \Rightarrow A}\, \text{I}$$
$$\frac{}{A/B,\ B \Rightarrow A}\, /\text{R}$$
$$\frac{}{A/B,\ B/C,\ C \Rightarrow A}\, /\text{R}$$

b.

$$\frac{}{C \Rightarrow C}\, \text{I} \qquad \frac{}{B \Rightarrow B}\, \text{I} \qquad \frac{}{A \Rightarrow A}\, \text{I}$$
$$\frac{}{B/C,\ C \Rightarrow B}\, /\text{R}$$
$$\frac{}{A/B,\ B/C,\ C \Rightarrow A}\, /\text{R}$$

These both correspond to the following unique natural-deduction proof of the same result:

(14)
$$\frac{A/B \quad \dfrac{B/C \quad C}{B}\, /\text{E}}{A}\, /\text{E}$$

5.3 PRODUCTS

In Lambek's original presentation of his calculus, he introduced a binary category constructor to correspond to string concatenation.

DEFINITION: PRODUCT CONSTRUCTOR   The *product constructor* is defined as follows:

a. $A \cdot B \in$ **Cat** if $A, B \in$ **Cat**
b. $\text{Typ}(A \cdot B) = \text{Typ}(A) \times \text{Typ}(B)$

The intuitive understanding of this category is that an expression is to be assigned to $A \cdot B$ if and only if it is the concatenation of two expressions, one of category A followed by one of category B. I use products in the typing because we want a semantic object for an expression of category $A \cdot B$ to be a pair consisting of one semantic object of category A and another of category B. This type assignment extends the Curry-Howard morphism to conjunction, as we will see in section 5.4.2.

The sequent schemes for products are straightforward.

DEFINITION: SEQUENT SCHEMES FOR PRODUCTS   The sequent schemes for the product constructor are

$$\frac{}{\iota\colon np/n,\ \textbf{city}\colon n \Rightarrow \iota(\textbf{city})\colon np}\text{D} \qquad \frac{}{\textbf{a}\colon np,\ \textbf{like}\colon np\backslash s/np \Rightarrow \lambda x.\textbf{like}(x)(\textbf{a})\colon s/np}\text{D}$$
$$\frac{}{\iota\colon np/n,\ \textbf{city}\colon n,\ \textbf{a}\colon np,\ \textbf{like}\colon np\backslash s/np \Rightarrow \langle \iota(\textbf{city}),\lambda x.\textbf{like}(x)(\textbf{a})\rangle\colon np\cdot(s/np)}\text{·R}$$

Figure 5.20
A derivation with a product

$$\frac{}{\textbf{a}\colon np \Rightarrow \textbf{a}\colon np}\text{I} \quad \frac{}{\textbf{b}\colon np \Rightarrow \textbf{b}\colon np}\text{I} \qquad \frac{}{\textbf{give}_2(\langle \textbf{a},\textbf{b}\rangle)\colon np\backslash s \Rightarrow \textbf{give}_2(\langle \textbf{a},\textbf{b}\rangle)\colon np\backslash s}\text{I}$$
$$\frac{}{\textbf{a}\colon np,\ \textbf{b}\colon np \Rightarrow \langle \textbf{a},\textbf{b}\rangle\colon np\cdot np}\text{·R}$$
$$\frac{}{\textbf{give}_2\colon np\backslash s/(np\cdot np),\ \textbf{a}\colon np,\ \textbf{b}\colon np \Rightarrow \textbf{give}_2(\langle \textbf{a},\textbf{b}\rangle)\colon np\backslash s}\text{/L}$$

Figure 5.21
Verbal complements with products

a. $\dfrac{\Gamma_1,\ \pi_1(\alpha)\colon A,\ \pi_2(\alpha)\colon B,\ \Gamma_2 \Rightarrow \gamma\colon C}{\Gamma_1,\ \alpha\colon A\cdot B,\ \Gamma_2 \Rightarrow \gamma\colon C}\cdot\text{L}$

b. $\dfrac{\Gamma_1 \Rightarrow \alpha\colon A \qquad \Gamma_2 \Rightarrow \beta\colon B}{\Gamma_1,\ \Gamma_2 \Rightarrow \langle \alpha,\beta\rangle\colon A\cdot B}\cdot\text{R}$

For instance, we have the derivation in figure 5.20. The product allows us to take all of a verb's complements at once, as can be seen in figure 5.21. Compare the following lexical entries with respect to the constraint relating their semantics.

(15) a. *give* $\Rightarrow$ **give**: $np\backslash s/np/np$
      b. *give* $\Rightarrow$ **give**$_2$: $np\backslash s/(np \cdot np)$
      c. **give**$_2 \overset{\text{def}}{=} \lambda x.\textbf{give}(\pi_1(x))(\pi_2(x))$

Note that in the derivation in figure 5.21, we could have deduced the same result with the curried lexical entry in (15a) because **give**$_2(\langle \textbf{a},\textbf{b}\rangle) \equiv$ **give**(**a**)(**b**). In fact, the lexical entries in (15a) and (15b) are interderivable. For instance, consider the derivations of (15a) from (15b) and of (15b) from (15a) in figure 5.22. Now note that the derived results are equivalent, because by definition, **give** $\equiv \lambda x.\lambda y.\textbf{give}_2(\langle x,y\rangle)$. Thus there is neither a syntactic or a semantic distinction between the two lexical entries in (15). In general, we can freely curry and uncurry arguments by following this pattern. Linguistically, this result is significant in that it frees us from worrying about irrelevant distinctions, such as that between a function over tuples and its curried equivalent.

$$\frac{\textbf{give}_2: np\backslash s/(np\cdot np),\ x:np,\ y:np \Rightarrow \textbf{give}_2(\langle x,y\rangle): np\backslash s}{}\text{D}$$

$$\frac{\textbf{give}_2: np\backslash s/(np\cdot np),\ x:np \Rightarrow \lambda y.\textbf{give}_2(\langle x,y\rangle): np\backslash s/np}{}\text{/R}$$

$$\frac{}{\textbf{give}_2: np\backslash s/(np\cdot np) \Rightarrow \lambda x.\lambda y.\textbf{give}_2(\langle x,y\rangle): np\backslash s/np/np}\text{/R}$$

$$\frac{\textbf{give}: np\backslash s/np/np,\ \pi_1(x):np,\ \pi_2(x):np \Rightarrow \textbf{give}(\pi_1(x))(\pi_2(x)): np\backslash s}{}\text{D}$$

$$\frac{\textbf{give}: np\backslash s/np/np,\ x:np\cdot np \Rightarrow \textbf{give}(\pi_1(x))(\pi_2(x)): np\backslash s}{}\cdot\text{L}$$

$$\frac{}{\textbf{give}: np\backslash s/np/np \Rightarrow \lambda x.\textbf{give}(\pi_1(x))(\pi_2(x)): np\backslash s/(np\cdot np)}\text{/R}$$

Figure 5.22
The interderivability of product and slash

$$\frac{\alpha: A,\ x:B \Rightarrow \langle\alpha,x\rangle: A\cdot B}{}\text{D}$$

$$\frac{}{\alpha: A \Rightarrow \lambda x.\langle\alpha,x\rangle: A\cdot B/B}\text{/R}$$

$$\frac{\pi_1(\alpha): A/B,\ \pi_2(\alpha):B \Rightarrow \pi_1(\alpha)(\pi_2(\alpha)): A}{}\text{D}$$

$$\frac{}{\alpha: A/B\cdot B \Rightarrow \pi_1(\alpha)(\pi_2(\alpha)): A}\cdot\text{L}$$

Figure 5.23
Relating product and slash

We can derive further relationships between the product and the slash. For instance, consider the derivations in figure 5.23. But unlike the slash, the product is isotone in both of its arguments. Thus we have the following scheme, the derivation of which I leave as an exercise.

(16) $\dfrac{\pi_1(\alpha): A \Rightarrow \beta: C \qquad \pi_2(\alpha): B \Rightarrow \gamma: D}{\alpha: A\cdot B \Rightarrow \langle\beta,\gamma\rangle: C\cdot D}\text{D}$

Adding the product scheme does not disturb any of the logical properties we enjoy, such as cut elimination, decidability, or associativity. Furthermore, we have a theorem relating sequences to product categories and can directly prove the associativity of products, as represented by the following sequents (I leave the derivations as exercises).

(17) a. $\alpha: A\cdot(B\cdot C) \Rightarrow \langle\langle\pi_1(\alpha),\pi_1(\pi_2(\alpha))\rangle,\pi_2(\pi_2(\alpha))\rangle: (A\cdot B)\cdot C$
     b. $\beta: (A\cdot B)\cdot C \Rightarrow \langle\pi_1(\pi_1(\beta)),\langle\pi_2(\pi_1(\beta)),\pi_2(\beta)\rangle\rangle: A\cdot(B\cdot C)$

The product constructor can be treated via natural deduction, but the elimination scheme is rather complicated and involves a form of natural-deduction proof that we have not yet encountered.

DEFINITION: NATURAL-DEDUCTION SCHEMES FOR PRODUCT   The natural deduction schemes for the product constructor are the following:

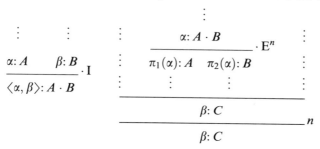

The introduction scheme is straightforward and simply allows us to derive a product $A \cdot B$ from derivations of A and B (remember that order matters here). The elimination scheme, on the other hand, eliminates $A \cdot B$, replacing it with separate occurrences of A and B. In such a derivation, it is important to note that the two results of the product elimination are ordered as shown and are not permutable. The semantics simply follows the components. What is perhaps more puzzling about this scheme is that the separate components of the product are treated as hypothetical arguments that are eliminated at the derivation of $\beta: C$. The reason for this seemingly redundant step is that we need to be able to determine the scope of the hypotheticals so that we can reconstruct the chain of reasoning that was carried out. In this way we can see how the product-elimination natural-deduction scheme corresponds to the left rule for the products. The left dots, the two hypothetical arguments, and the derivation of the first $\beta: C$ correspond to the antecedent sequent in the left-sequent scheme, whereas the left and right context, product, and final conclusion of $\beta: C$ correspond to the consequent sequent in the left-sequent scheme. As with other hypotheticals, they cannot be used outside of their hypothetical domain.

Just as with the other operators, we can normalize proofs involving paired uses of introduction and elimination as follows:

DEFINITION: PRODUCT NORMALIZATION   The schemes for normalization of products are as follows:

a.

$$
\begin{array}{c}
\vdots \\
\dfrac{\alpha\colon A\cdot B}{\dfrac{\pi_1(\alpha)\colon A \qquad \pi_2(\alpha)\colon B}{\dfrac{\langle \pi_1(\alpha),\pi_2(\alpha)\rangle\colon A\cdot B}{\langle \pi_1(\alpha),\pi_2(\alpha)\rangle\colon A\cdot B}\ n}\cdot \mathrm{I}}\cdot \mathrm{E}^n
\end{array}
\qquad \rightsquigarrow \quad \alpha\colon A\cdot B
$$

b.

$$
\dfrac{\begin{array}{cccc}
\vdots & \dfrac{\alpha\colon A \qquad \beta\colon B}{\dfrac{\langle \alpha,\beta\rangle\colon A\cdot B}{x\colon A \qquad y\colon B}\cdot \mathrm{E}^n}\cdot \mathrm{I} & \vdots \\
 & \vdots \qquad \vdots & \\
 & \gamma\colon C &
\end{array}}{\gamma[x\mapsto \pi_1(\langle\alpha,\beta\rangle)][y\mapsto \pi_2(\langle\alpha,\beta\rangle)]\colon C}\ n
$$

$$
\rightsquigarrow \qquad \dfrac{\alpha\colon A \qquad \beta\colon B}{\gamma[x\mapsto\alpha][y\mapsto\beta]\colon C}
$$

Note that the equivalences between the derived terms follow from our definitions of projection and tupling in the λ-calculus. In the normalization for $\cdot$ I followed by $\cdot$ E, I have introduced variables for the hypothethicals and then substituted for them when they are eliminated. This allows us to compare the results of the normal and nonnormal derivations, which are obviously equivalent. We could treat all hypothetical assumptions as introducing variables in this way, but I have opted for an abbreviated mode of presentation.

Furthermore, the natural-deduction schemes produce only one normal derivation for each semantically distinct reading; we derive results with semantic tupling only from $\cdot$ I and results with projections only from $\cdot$ E. Thus if we define a term to be normal just in case it does not contain any product or tupling reductions, then any derivation whose assumptions are variables or constants results in a category whose semantic term is in normal form.

5.4   CATEGORIAL GRAMMAR AS LOGIC

In this section we consider two connections between categorial grammars and implicational logics. We begin with the construal of categorial grammar as a substructural logic. We then see where this conception leads us via the Curry-Howard isomorphism.

5.4.1 Substructural Logic

To further understand the relation between logic and categorial grammar, it is necessary to recast logic in structural terms. In classical and intuitionistic logical systems, it is standard to assume that the premise of a sequent is structured as a set. But we may also think of it as a sequence, as long as we allow the following *structural rules*:

(18) *Permutation*   *Weakening*   *Contraction*

$$\frac{\Gamma, \phi, \psi, \Gamma' \vdash \xi}{\Gamma, \psi, \phi, \Gamma' \vdash \xi} \qquad \frac{\Gamma \vdash \psi}{\Gamma, \phi \vdash \psi} \qquad \frac{\Gamma, \phi, \phi, \Gamma' \vdash \psi}{\Gamma, \phi, \Gamma' \vdash \psi}$$

The first of these rules is known as *permutation*, the second as *weakening*, and the third as *contraction*. Together with the assumption that the antecedents form a sequence (and thus behave associatively), these structural rules allow us to treat the antecedents in a proof as forming a set. If we take the intuitionistic version of first-order logic and drop the rule of weakening, we are left with a version of what is known as *relevance logic*. In a relevance logic, each assumption must be used at least once in a derivation. The connection between linguistic deduction and substructural logics was developed independently by van Benthem (1983b) and by Morrill and Carpenter (1990). Morrill and Carpenter compare the fundamental logical assumptions of categorial grammar to other grammar formalisms, such as LFG, GPSG, and GB, from a logical perspective, relating them to the paradigm known as *type-driven translation*, introduced by Klein and Sag (1985). If we further drop the rule of contraction, we are left with what is known as (the implicational and multiplicative-conjunction fragment of) *linear logic*, which is the well-known logic closest to categorial grammar. For a thorough study of linear logic, including additional connectives beyond implication and multiplicative conjunction, see Girard 1987, Troelstra 1992. Linear logic, relevance logic, and their relatives form what are known as *substructural logics*, due to the fact that they drop one or more of the above structural rules from their proof systems (see Dŏsen and Schroeder-Heister 1993).

Lambek's categorial grammar descends even further in the hierarchy of substructural logics by eliminating the rule of permutation as well as the other structural rules. Along with this move, the notion of implication is divided into a leftward version and a rightward version, represented by our directional slashes. The variant of Lambek's categorial grammar in which the directional slashes are replaced by a single nondirectional implication (van Benthem 1986a) and the multiplicative fragment of linear logic have minor differences but are essentially the same. The nondirectional version of the calculus can be seen as the result of collapsing the leftward- and rightward-directed implications into a single instance by means of permutation.

At the lowest point in the standard hierarchy of categorial grammars is Lambek's (1961) nonassociative calculus, which further does away with the structural rule of associativity implicit in reading the premises of a sequent as sequences. (Moortgat and Morrill [1991] actually consider an even finer-grained logic that has directionally oriented nonassociative slashes.) In the nonassociative calculus, the sequence Γ in a sequent $\Gamma \Rightarrow \mathscr{C}$ must be read as a bracketed sequence rather than just as a string. In this setting, we could recover the associative version of Lambek's calculus by imposing an explicit structural rule of associativity. Recently there has been a great deal of interest in mixed systems that allow constrained applications of association, permutation, and other structural rules. Such control can be achieved by the addition of modalities to the forward- and backward-slash constructors, in addition to the structuring of antecedents in sequents. A general approach to mixed systems by means of structured sequents was developed for *display logic* (Belnap 1982), an early linguistic application of which can be found in Oehrle and Shi 1989. A very general, modal characterization of the substructural hierarchy involving permutation and association can be found in Kurtonina and Moortgat, in press; Moortgat 1994, in press. Linguistic applications, including some extensions to Lambek's constructors, can be found in Morrill 1994, Hepple 1990a, Moortgat and Oehrle 1994.

5.4.2 The Curry-Howard Isomorphism

The Curry-Howard isomorphism sets up a deep connection between well-typed terms in the simply typed λ-calculus and natural-deduction proofs in intuitionistic logic. Insofar as our categorial grammars are a kind of intuitionistic logic, the results will carry over to our setting. In particular, the Curry-Howard mapping can be seen to be at the root of van Benthem's (1983b) association of semantic terms with categorial derivations, and their extension by Morrill (1994a).

I begin by establishing the Curry-Howard isomorphism in the domain of intuitionistic logic and then turn to its instantiation in the Lambek calculus. The isomorphism is between well-typed terms in the simply typed λ-calculus and between proofs in intuitionistic implicational logic. The structure being preserved under the mapping is normalization of

The Lambek Calculus

Table 5.1
The Curry and Howard type-formula mapping

Type		Formula	
$\sigma \to \tau$	functions	$\phi \to \psi$	implications
$\sigma \times \tau$	products	$\phi \wedge \psi$	conjunctions
$\sigma + \tau$	sums	$\phi \vee \psi$	disjunctions

terms and the normalization (equivalently, cut elimination) of implicational proofs.

The notation I have used for types in the λ-calculus reflects their logical nature. This is the first step in constructing the mapping between terms and proofs, and is illustrated in table 5.1. Curry and Feys (1961) noticed the connection between the calculus of types in the simply typed λ-calculus and the proofs of intuitionistic implicational logic. Consider the rule of modus ponens, which allows us to conclude ψ from the assumptions ϕ and $\phi \to \psi$. This rule is strikingly similar to the rule of typing in the simply typed λ-calculus, which tells us that $\alpha(\beta)$ is of type τ if α is of type $\sigma \to \tau$ and β is of type σ. But the connection does not stop at modus ponens; hypothetical reasoning corresponds to λ-abstraction. In the λ-calculus, if x is a variable of type σ and α is a term of type τ, then $\lambda x.\alpha$ is a term of type $\sigma \to \tau$. This method of constructing terms of functional types is mirrored in logic by the implicaton-introduction rule, which tells us that if we can prove ψ from the assumption of ϕ, then we can prove $\phi \to \psi$ without that assumption. I provide the implicational fragment of the Curry-Howard mapping in table 5.2. I have chosen the sequent calculus for its perspicuity in establishing this correspondence, though the natural-deduction calculus can also be used for this purpose. Because we assume the propositional calculus is intuitionistic, we allow ourselves the structural rules of permutation, weakening, and contraction. Note that for each proof in the implicational calculus, we have a well-typed functional term in the λ-calculus. The typing schemes in sequent notation simply make explicit the recursive notion of typing in the simply typed λ-calculus.

Howard (1969) extended the connection to proofs involving conjunction and disjunction, which naturally correspond to products and sums in the typed λ-calculus. I provide the mappings for these in table 5.3. Note that there are two schemes for disjunction on the right. The left disjunction scheme is perhaps the most complex. Glossing its behavior, we

Table 5.2
Curry's mapping between implicational proofs and functional terms

Propositional proof	λ-term typing
$\dfrac{\Gamma \vdash \phi \qquad \Delta, \psi \vdash \xi}{\phi \to \psi, \Gamma, \Delta \vdash \xi}$	$\dfrac{\Gamma \vdash \beta:\sigma \qquad \Delta, \alpha(\beta):\tau \vdash \gamma:\rho}{\alpha:\sigma \to \tau, \Gamma, \Delta \vdash \gamma:\rho}$
$\dfrac{\Gamma, \phi \vdash \xi}{\Gamma \vdash \phi \to \xi}$	$\dfrac{\Gamma, x:\sigma \vdash \alpha:\tau}{\Gamma \vdash \lambda x.\alpha:\sigma \to \tau}$

Table 5.3
Howard's mapping between proofs with conjunctions and disjunctions and terms
with products and sums

Propositional proof	λ-term typing
$\dfrac{\phi, \psi, \Gamma \vdash \xi}{\phi \wedge \psi, \Gamma \vdash \xi}$	$\dfrac{\pi_1(\alpha):\sigma, \pi_2(\alpha):\tau, \Gamma \vdash \beta:\rho}{\alpha:\sigma \times \tau, \Gamma \vdash \beta:\rho}$
$\dfrac{\Gamma \vdash \phi \qquad \Delta \vdash \psi}{\Gamma, \Delta \vdash \phi \wedge \psi}$	$\dfrac{\Gamma \vdash \alpha:\sigma \qquad \Delta \vdash \beta:\tau}{\Gamma, \Delta \vdash \langle \alpha, \beta \rangle:\sigma \times \tau}$
$\dfrac{\Gamma, \phi \vdash \xi \qquad \Gamma, \psi \vdash \xi}{\Gamma, \phi \vee \psi \vdash \xi}$	$\dfrac{\Gamma, x:\sigma \vdash \alpha:\rho \qquad \Gamma, y:\tau \vdash \beta:\rho}{\Gamma, \gamma:\sigma + \tau \vdash (\gamma \to \lambda x.\alpha; \lambda y.\beta):\rho}$
$\dfrac{\Gamma \vdash \phi}{\Gamma \vdash \phi \vee \psi}$	$\dfrac{\Gamma \vdash \alpha:\sigma}{\Gamma \vdash \langle 1, \alpha \rangle:\sigma + \tau} \qquad \dfrac{\Gamma \vdash \beta:\tau}{\Gamma \vdash \langle 2, \beta \rangle:\sigma + \tau}$

see that if we can derive ρ from the assumption of σ and we can derive ρ from the assumption of τ, then we can derive ρ from the disjunction of σ and τ; the semantics is derived by assuming an x for σ, deriving α for ρ, and by assuming y for τ and deriving β for ρ. The final resulting semantics involves a choice based on the category γ of the disjunction; if it is of type σ, we apply the function abstracting x over α, and if it is of type τ, we apply the function abstracting y over β. By the definition of the choice function, these provide the same results as if we had simply used σ or τ directly. This latter property is significant, being at the heart of the duality between left and right usages of disjunction.

The primary result that can be established about the correspondences given tables 5.2 and 5.3 is that it is in fact an isomorphism:

THEOREM: CURRY-HOWARD ISOMORPHISM   The propositional proofs with implication, conjunction, and disjunction stand in a one-to-one relationship to the well-typed λ-terms with functions, products, and sums.

The isomorphism really comes down to the correspondence between cut elimination in the proof theory and λ-term normalization in the λ-calculus. The isomorphism can be extended to the natural-deduction calculus, where normalized proofs will correspond to normal-form λ-terms.

The connection between functions and intuitionistic logic was provided by Heyting (1956). He interpreted propositional formulas as the sets of their proofs, according to the following constructive understanding of proofs. A proof of a formula $\phi \rightarrow \psi$ is a function mapping a proof of ϕ to a proof of ψ; a proof of a formula $\phi \wedge \psi$ consists of a pair of proofs, one of ϕ and one of ψ; a proof of a disjunctive formula $\phi \vee \psi$ consists of the proof of either ϕ or ψ and an indication of which one. (It is really this last step of requiring a proof of a disjunction to prove one of the disjuncts that gives intuitionistic logics their constructive character.) Assuming proofs of basic formulas to be given, the Curry-Howard term association shows how to construct λ-term representations of constructive proofs according to Heyting's interpretation.

In our substructural setting, without the rules of weakening and contraction, the relationship is no longer total. By removing weakening, we require that every variable in the resulting term be bound and that there thus be no vacuous abstractions; the resulting logical system is a version of relevance logic. The Curry-Howard isomorphism can be restricted to λ-terms with no vacuous abstraction and to proofs in relevance logic. After we remove contraction, each variable may occur only once in a derivation, thus meeting the so-called *single-bind condition* of van Benthem (1983b). The resulting logic is a variant of the multiplicative fragment of linear logic, and the Curry-Howard isomorphism remains one-to-one and onto under this restriction. The variation simply involves the lack of empty antecedents in the categorial setting, which eliminates the well-formed term $\lambda x.x$. In our categorial setting, the mapping is no longer an isomorphism but is rather a homomorphism from our syntactic categories and natural-deduction derivations to λ-terms; both A/B and $B \backslash A$ will correspond to the same λ-term.

Besides setting up these handy correspondences, the Curry-Howard isomorphism preserves structure. The structure preserved is that of the normalization structure of proofs and the normalization of λ-terms. For every proof-normalization sequence, there is a corresponding λ-reduction.

What is more significant is that we can show the converse: for every λ-reduction of a term resulting from a proof, there is a corresponding normalization of a proof. For instance, if the term derived is the β-redex $(\lambda x.\alpha)(\beta)$, then there is only one way it can be derived. The λ-abstraction has to be the result of an introduction scheme, and the application the result of an elimination scheme. This is exactly the scheme that normalizes along with the term. The same holds for the η-cases; the only way to derive the term $\lambda x.\alpha(x)$ is by using an η-normalizable structure. In conjunction with the Church-Rosser theorem and the strong normalization theorem for the λ-calculus, the Curry-Howard morphism allows us to conclude the following:

THEOREM: STRONG NORMALIZATION FOR NATURAL DEDUCTION   If x_1: C_1, $\ldots, x_n$: $C_n \Rightarrow \alpha$: C has a natural deduction derivation $\mathscr{D}$, then every normalization sequence from $\mathscr{D}$ terminates in the unique normal derivation $\mathscr{D}'$, yielding the sequent x_1: $C_1, \ldots, x_n$: $C_n \Rightarrow \alpha'$: C, where α' is the normal form of α.

The reader who is interested in exploring the connection between types, λ-calculus, and intuitionistic logic should consult Thompson 1991 or Girard, Taylor, and Lafont 1989 for further details and references. Morrill 1994a discusses the correspondence in the categorial setting, as well as its extension to existential and universal quantifiers by means of dependent types.

Exercises

1. Prove that the sequent presentation of applicative categorial grammar yields the same rewriting relation as the phrase-structure presentation.

2. Prove that it is impossible to assign any expression to the category s/np using only the applicative sequent grammar, given the lexicon in figure 4.1. (Hint: Consider the result of an application as a subcategory of a lexical category.)

3. Consider the infinite set of sequents with one or two premises that are derivable in the Lambek calculus. Treat each of these sequents as a phrase-structure rule. Show that with a fixed lexicon, the resulting phrase-structure grammar yields the same notion of rewriting as is characterized by the Lambek calculus. (Hint: Proceed by induction on the length of the sequent derivation.) (Zielonka 1981)

4. Consider the following lexical entry for the reflexive pronoun *herself*:

(a) *herself* $\Rightarrow$?: $(np\backslash s/np)\backslash np\backslash s$

Consider the reflexive in examples such as the following, where subscripts have been used to indicate the intended antecedent:

(b) Sandy$_1$ likes herself$_1$.

Which closed pure λ-term should be assigned to the reflexive in this case? How can this category account for sentences such as these:

(c) Lee$_2$ showed Sandy himself$_2$.

(d) Lee$_3$ read the book near himself$_3$.

(e) Lee$_4$ kept the pen near himself$_4$.

Assume here that the prepositional phrase attaches to the noun in example (d) and to the verb phrase in example (e). What additional lexical entries are needed to account for reflexives in examples such as the following:

(f) Sandy$_2$ gave herself$_2$ the award.

(g) The photographer showed Sandy$_4$ himself$_4$.

What can you conclude in general about this approach to reflexives? Could this style of analysis be extended to examples such as the following?

(h) The pictures of herself$_1$ bothered Sandy$_1$.

(i) Lee showed Sandy$_2$ pictures of herself$_2$.

Show the semantic result of the derivation of $1: np \Rightarrow ?: (np\backslash s/np)\backslash np\backslash s$. Can quantifiers be assigned to a similar category, and if so, what semantics should they be given?

5. Show that in the presence of the cut, the forward and backward left rules can be reduced to the following applicative form without loss of derivable sequents:

$$\frac{}{\alpha: A/B,\ \beta: B \Rightarrow \alpha(\beta): A}/L' \qquad \frac{}{\beta: B,\ \alpha: B\backslash A \Rightarrow \alpha(\beta): A}/L'$$

6. Consider the following lexical entry for the object relative pronoun.

(a) $whom \Rightarrow \lambda P. \lambda Q. \lambda x. P(x) \wedge Q(x): n\backslash n/(s/np)$

Provide derivations for the following nominals:

(b) kid whom Lee liked

(c) city which Lee bought the ticket to

If *yesterday* is of category $s\backslash s$, why is it not possible to derive the following noun phrase in the Lambek calculus (assuming the category above for *which*, the usual transitive-verb entry for *liked*, the usual noun entry for *toy*, and the usual noun-phrase entry for *Lee*).

(d) toy which Lee liked yesterday

Is it ever possible to derive a relative clause in which the gap is either noninitial or nonfinal?

7. Provide a lexical entry for *if*, including both its syntactic category and a suitably defined logical term. Provide a derivation for the following:

(a) Lee ran if Brooke ran.

Can a similar lexical entry be used for the fronted version, as in the following (ignore the punctuation)?

(b) If Lee made the cake, Brooke made the pie.

8. Consider the following definition of *exponentiation* in the syntactic dimension.

(a) $A^B \overset{\text{def}}{=} B/(B\backslash A)$

Establish the following, which show that exponentiation is a kind of closure operation modulo rewriting.

(b) $A^B \Rightarrow (A^B)^B$

(c) $(A^B)^B \Rightarrow A^B$

9. Establish the following derived rules of inference, and provide their semantic-term assignments.

$$\frac{A, B \Rightarrow D}{A, B/C \Rightarrow D/C} \qquad \frac{A \Rightarrow B}{C \cdot A \Rightarrow C \cdot B}$$

10. Show that the identity scheme in the sequent calculus can be restricted to basic (nonfunctor) categories without losing any derivations. (Hint: Decompose applications of identities to connectives with /R and \R, and then reduce using /L and \L.) Next, show that if cut is not used and every identity scheme is applied only to atoms, then the derived term is in β, η long form.

Chapter 6

Coordination and Unbounded Dependencies

In this chapter we study two of the best known linguistic applications of categorial grammar: coordination and unbounded dependency. I introduce the fundamentally polymorphic categories required by coordinators such as *and* and *or*. With the associativity of the Lambek calculus, we are immediately able to coordinate arbitrary boolean categories, including both traditional constituents and categories not traditionally analyzed as forming constituents.

In section 6.2, I introduce boolean constructors for conjunction and disjunction into our type logic. These constructors have a natural logic related to the additive connectives of linear logic. Linguistically, they allow us to characterize lexical and derivational ambiguity logically. Even more important, they provide an elegant analysis of the so-called *coordination of "unlike" categories*.

Finally, in section 6.3, I introduce a further category constructor for unbounded dependency constructions—a move that can be seen as analogous to the separation of subcategorization and unbounded dependency information in HPSG (Pollard and Sag 1992). The unbounded dependency constructor acts like the slashes type-theoretically but is not restricted to operate at the left or right periphery of a derivation.

6.1 COORDINATION

Montague (1973) introduced a categorial notion of *coordination* into his grammars, and this construction was later generalized by Gazdar (1980), Keenan and Faltz (1985), and Rooth and Partee (1982; Partee and Rooth 1983). Steedman (1985) showed how the logic of categorial-grammar category assignments could be used to provide a syntactic basis for Gazdar's semantic conception. Coordination involves combining categories using coordinators like *and* and *or*, for example. A range of different categories may undergo coordination, as can be seen in the following examples:

(1) a. [$_s$ [Jo ran] and [Jo jumped]].
   b. Jo[$_{np\backslash s}$ [ran] and [jumped]].
   c. Jo[$_{np\backslash s}$ [hit Kelly] and [ran]].
   d. Every kid [$_{np\backslash s/np}$ [loved] or [hated]] the movie.
   e. Jo read the [$_n$ [book] or [magazine]].
   f. The kid [$_{n\backslash n/np}$ [in] or [on]] the box fell.
   g. The kid [$_{n\backslash n}$ [in the house] or [outside]] ran.
   h. Leslie [$_{np\backslash s/np/np}$ [sold] or [gave]] Jo the notes.

Our task is to provide a grammar that generates the appropriate readings for these examples and others like them. The coordinated expressions in brackets should be assigned the following semantics:

(2) a. **run**(**j**) $\wedge$ **jump**(**j**)
   b. $\lambda x.$**run**$(x) \wedge$ **jump**(x)
   c. $\lambda x.$**hit**(**kelly**)$(x) \wedge$ **ran**(x)
   d. $\lambda x.\lambda y.$**love**$(x)(y) \vee$ **hated**$(x)(y)$
   e. $\lambda x.$**book**$(x) \vee$ **magazine**(x)
   f. $\lambda x.\lambda P.\lambda y.$**in**$(x)(P)(y) \vee$ **on**$(x)(P)(y)$
   g. $\lambda P.\lambda x.$**in**$(\iota(\textbf{house}))(P)(x) \vee$ **outside**$(P)(x)$
   h. $\lambda x.\lambda y.\lambda z.$**give**$(x)(y)(z) \vee$ **sell**$(x)(y)(z)$

6.1.1   Boolean Coordination

I adopt a standard approach to coordination, in which two categories of the same boolean type may be coordinated (see Gazdar 1980, Keenan and Faltz 1985). A boolean type is simply one that eventually produces a boolean category after applying to all of its arguments.

DEFINITION: BOOLEAN TYPES   The set **BoolType** of *boolean types* is the least such that

a. **Bool** $\in$ **BoolType**,
b. $\tau \rightarrow \sigma \in$ **BoolType** if $\tau \in$ **Type** and $\sigma \in$ **BoolType**.

Thus a boolean type is of the following form, for arbitrary types σ_i.

(3) $\sigma_1 \rightarrow \cdots \rightarrow \sigma_n \rightarrow$ **Bool**

For instance, the types assigned to intransitive verbs are boolean, because $\text{Typ}(np\backslash s) = \text{Typ}(np) \rightarrow \text{Typ}(s) = \textbf{Ind} \rightarrow \textbf{Bool}$. Of course, nouns are also boolean types, because $\mathrm{Typ}(n) = \mathbf{Ind} \to \mathbf{Bool}$. In fact, any category producing a nominal or sentential result is boolean. Thus, adjectives, prepositions, prepositional phrases, transitive verbs, ditransitive verbs, and other verbs are all boolean categories. Of course, we can coordinate expressions of any of these categories, as we saw above.

Because I have not introduced quantifiers yet, I postpone further discussion of the following kinds of coordination involving quantifiers:

(4) a. [[Brett] or [some kid]] ran.
    b. Every [[man] and [woman]] ate.
    c. [Some] but not [all] kids ran.

When I introduce quantifiers in chapter 7, these coordinate structures will follow directly, because we assume that quantifiers are of a boolean type (see sections 7.4 and 7.6). On the other hand, we consider the following type of coordination to be of a rather different nature.

(5) Terry and Sandy met.

In fact, this kind of coordination is often referred to as *nonboolean conjunction* (Hoeksema 1989), a topic to which we return in section 8.8.

The notion of constituency is more flexible in categorial grammar than it is in theories such as GB or HPSG. In such theories the following examples are problematic because the expressions being coordinated do not form natural constituents.

(6) a. [[Chris hit] and [Jan kicked]] Morgan.
    b. Brett hit [[Chris yesterday] and [Morgan today]].
    c. Pat gave [[Robin Fido] and [Sal Tweety]].
    d. Sandy suspects [[Shawn will] but [Taylor won't]] pass the exam.

The ability to handle such "nonconstituent" coordination illustrates the flexibility with which the Lambek calculus is able to make category assignments both syntactically and semantically.

I consider the *subordinating conjunctions* in the following examples to be adverbials, and will lexically treat them as such in section 12.5.3.

(7) a. Terry will run *if* Brett runs.
    b. Brooke ate *before* he swam.
    c. Kelly eats *while* running.

As I have just illustrated, the fundamental principle of coordination is that any pair of boolean categories can coordinate to produce a result of the same category. The examples in (2) share the property that the coordinator appears as a boolean operator that has been distributed past the abstractions. Thus the semantics of coordination can be handled by means of a generalized form of coordination that applies pointwise to pairs of boolean terms of the same type. I define the generalized coordination combinator as follows, following Gazdar (1980) and Keenan and Faltz (1985).

DEFINITION: POLYMORPHIC COORDINATION COMBINATOR $\mathbf{Coor}_\sigma$ is of type $(\mathbf{Bool} \to \mathbf{Bool} \to \mathbf{Bool}) \to \sigma \to \sigma \to \sigma$, for $\sigma \in \mathbf{BoolType}$, and is defined recursively by

a. $\mathbf{Coor_{Bool}}(\alpha)(\beta_1)(\beta_2) \stackrel{\text{def}}{=} \alpha(\beta_1)(\beta_2)$
b. $\mathbf{Coor}_{\sigma \to \tau}(\alpha)(\beta_1)(\beta_2) \stackrel{\text{def}}{=} \lambda x^\sigma . \mathbf{Coor}_\tau(\alpha)(\beta_1(x))(\beta_2(x))$

Note that I am defining a family of combinators, one for each boolean type. We can thus think of $\mathbf{Coor}_\sigma$ as involving parametric polymorphism, where the parameter σ must be instantiated in order to determine a proper λ-term.

Consider the following base-case application of **Coor**, which assumes that **run** and **jump** are property terms, **t** and **f** are individual terms, and **and** is the ordinary higher-order logic binary conjunction.

(8) $\mathbf{Coor_{Bool}}(\mathbf{and})(\mathbf{jump}(\mathbf{t}))(\mathbf{run}(\mathbf{f})) \equiv \mathbf{and}(\mathbf{jump}(\mathbf{t}))(\mathbf{run}(\mathbf{f}))$

Note that $\mathbf{Coor_{Bool}}(\mathbf{and}) \equiv \mathbf{and}$ by expanding the definition and applying η-conversion twice. With the same type assignments, consider the following more complex example:

(9) $\mathbf{Coor_{Ind \to Bool}}(\mathbf{and})(\mathbf{run})(\mathbf{jump})$
$\equiv \lambda x . \mathbf{Coor_{Bool}}(\mathbf{and})(\mathbf{run}(x))(\mathbf{jump}(x))$
$\equiv \lambda x . \mathbf{and}(\mathbf{run}(x))(\mathbf{jump}(x))$
$\equiv \lambda x . \mathbf{run}(x) \wedge \mathbf{jump}(x)$

Boolean arguments of higher arity are treated similarly, by reducing their arity one argument at a time.

To analyze the basic syntax of coordination, we need coordinator categories of every boolean category, where a boolean category is simply a category whose type is a boolean type. This approach was adopted first by Steedman (1985) and later captured in a more general, polymorphic type logic by Emms (1990). It is now the standard approach to coordination in categorial grammars. Specifically, I will adopt the following infinite family of lexical entries:

(10) a. *and* $\Rightarrow \mathbf{Coor}_\sigma(\mathbf{and}): A\backslash A/A$ $[\mathrm{Typ}(A) = \sigma \in \mathbf{BoolType}]$
       b. *or* $\Rightarrow \mathbf{Coor}_\sigma(\mathbf{or}): A\backslash A/A$ $[\mathrm{Typ}(A) = \sigma \in \mathbf{BoolType}]$

$$\frac{\frac{Terry}{t:np}Lx \quad \frac{jumps}{\textbf{jump}:np\backslash s}Lx}{\textbf{jump}(\textbf{t}):s}\backslash E \quad \frac{\frac{and}{\textbf{Coor}_{\textbf{Bool}}(\textbf{and}):s\backslash s/s}Lx \quad \frac{Francis}{\textbf{f}:np}Lx \quad \frac{runs}{\textbf{run}:np\backslash s}Lx}{\textbf{run}(\textbf{f}):s}\backslash E}{\textbf{and}(\textbf{jump}(\textbf{t}))(\textbf{run}(\textbf{f})):s}D$$

Figure 6.1
A derivation of *Terry jumps and Francis runs*

$$\frac{\frac{Francis}{\textbf{f}:np}Lx \quad \frac{\frac{jumps}{\textbf{jump}:np\backslash s}Lx \quad \frac{\frac{and}{\textbf{Coor}_{\textbf{Ind}\to\textbf{Bool}}(\textbf{and})}{(np\backslash s)\backslash(np\backslash s)/(np\backslash s)}Lx \quad \frac{runs}{\textbf{run}:np\backslash s}Lx}{\lambda x.\textbf{and}(\textbf{jump}(x))(\textbf{run}(x)):np\backslash s}D}{}}{\textbf{and}(\textbf{jump}(\textbf{f}))(\textbf{run}(\textbf{f})):s}\backslash E$$

Figure 6.2
A derivation of *Francis jumps and runs*

The categories for other coordinators, such as *if* and *but*, can be defined similarly. As usual, the order of arguments is irrelevant here, because $A\backslash(A/A)$ and $(A\backslash A)/A$ are interderivable.

The simplest case of coordination is that of simple sentences, as illustrated in figure 6.1. Note that I have shortened the two-step application to one step and reduced the semantics, following (8). The next simplest case involves simple verb-phrase coordination, as shown in figure 6.2. As before, I use a derived scheme for the two elimination steps for the coordinator and reduce the semantics as in (9). Note that when the coordinated property is applied to the subject meaning, the constant **f** occurs twice in the result. This does not violate the single-bind condition on variables, which requires every variable to be bound once. The reason is that the single-bind condition is valid only if the lexical entries have constants as their meanings. Expanding constants according to meaning postulates allows arbitrary behaviors in the λ-terms as long as everything is well typed.

In the following exposition, I abbreviate the coordination categories and derived-rule applications to coordinators. Rather than writing $A\backslash A/A$, I will simply write *co* when the coordination category is clear from context. And I will simply write **and**$_\sigma$, or even simply **and**, for **Coor**$_\sigma$(**and**), and similarly for the other boolean connectives. To demonstrate our new

$$\frac{in}{\textbf{in}:n\backslash n/np}\text{Lx}\quad\frac{or}{\textbf{or}:co}\text{Lx}\quad\frac{on}{\textbf{on}:n\backslash n/np}\text{Lx}\quad\frac{the}{\iota:np/n}\text{Lx}\quad\frac{box}{\textbf{box}:n}\text{Lx}$$

$$\frac{}{\begin{array}{c}\lambda y.\lambda P.\lambda x.\textbf{or}(\textbf{in}(y)(P)(x)):n\backslash n/np\\(\textbf{on}(y)(P)(x))\end{array}}\text{D}\qquad\frac{}{\iota(\textbf{box}):np}\text{/E}$$

$$\frac{}{\lambda P.\lambda x.\textbf{or}(\textbf{in}(\iota(\textbf{box}))(P)(x))(\textbf{on}(\iota(\textbf{box}))(P)(x)):n\backslash n}\text{/E}$$

Figure 6.3
A derivation of *in or on the box*

$$\frac{Francis}{\textbf{f}:np}\text{Lx}\quad\frac{[V:np\backslash s]^1}{}\qquad\frac{and}{\textbf{and}:co}\text{Lx}\quad\frac{Brooke}{\lambda U.U(\textbf{b}):s/(np\backslash s)}\text{D}\quad\frac{studied}{\textbf{study}:np\backslash s}\text{Lx}$$

$$\frac{V(\textbf{f}):s}{}\backslash E$$

$$\frac{\lambda V.V(\textbf{f}):s/(np\backslash s)}{}/I^1$$

$$\frac{\lambda W.W(\textbf{f})\wedge W(\textbf{b}):s/(np\backslash s)}{}\text{D}$$

$$\frac{}{\textbf{study}(\textbf{f})\wedge\textbf{study}(\textbf{b}):s}\text{/E}$$

Figure 6.4
A derivation of *Francis and Brooke studied*

abbreviations, I show a slightly more complex example involving the coordination of prepositions in figure 6.3. Of course, this analysis would combine with a determiner and a noun phrase to produce the following result:

(11) *the dog in or on the box*
$$\Rightarrow \iota(\lambda x.\textbf{in}(\iota(\textbf{box}))(\textbf{dog})(x)\vee\textbf{on}(\iota(\textbf{box}))(\textbf{dog})(x)):np$$

6.1.2 Distributivity and Type Raising

The combination of general boolean coordination and the flexible type raising of Lambek categorial grammar allows the unbounded distribution of coordinate structures. Semantically, this can perhaps best be illustrated with quantifiers, as we will see in section 7.6. But even in the pure Lambek calculus with coordination we can find cases in which type raising allows the boolean coordination of apparently uncoordinable categories. For instance, consider the derivation in figure 6.4. Our logic of slashes generates exactly the category assigned to simple noun phrases as Montague (1973) lexically assumed. One of Montague's primary motivation's was to handle coordination of noun phrases, as in figure 6.4. Although Montague restricted attention to the disjunction of noun phrases, pre-

$$
\begin{array}{l}
[N:np/n]^2 \quad \underline{vegetarian}_{\ Lx} \quad [V:np\backslash s]^5 \quad \underline{and}_{\ Lx} \quad \underline{\qquad socialist \qquad}_{\ D} \\
\underline{\qquad\qquad\quad veg:n \quad}_{\ Lx} /E \qquad\qquad\quad and \qquad \lambda M.\lambda U.U(M(\mathbf{soc})) \\
\underline{\qquad N(\mathbf{veg}):np \qquad\qquad\qquad} \qquad\quad co \qquad (np/n)\backslash s/(np\backslash s) \\
\underline{\qquad\qquad V(N(\mathbf{veg})):s \qquad\qquad\qquad}\backslash E \\
\underline{\qquad \lambda V.V(N(\mathbf{veg})):s/(np\backslash s) \qquad}/I^5 \\
\underline{\lambda N.\lambda V.V(N(\mathbf{veg})):(np/n)\backslash s/(np\backslash s)}\backslash I^2 \\
\underline{\qquad\qquad\qquad\qquad\qquad\qquad\qquad\qquad\qquad\qquad\qquad}D \\
\quad \lambda L.\lambda W.W(L(\mathbf{veg})) \wedge W(L(\mathbf{soc})):(np/n)\backslash s/(np\backslash s)
\end{array}
$$

Figure 6.5
A derivation of *vegetarian and socialist*

sumably to avoid the problems of nonboolean coordination, his approach generalizes in the obvious way to conjunction. In contrast to Montague, we are able to assign a less complex lexical type to noun phrases, namely np, and then automatically generate the higher-order type $s/(np\backslash s)$. Note that the semantics of the raised noun phrase x is $\lambda P.P(x)$, which is its appropriate meaning as a generalized quantifier, as we saw in section 3.3.

Admitting type raising in its full generality through the logic of concatenation leads to a strong result concerning the distribution of coordinators over arbitrary contexts. For instance, consider the two contrasting readings of the following sentence (based on Keenan 1984).

(12) The vegetarian and socialist studied.

This sentence can be used to make the claim that one individual, who is both a vegetarian and socialist, studied. Alternatively, it can be used to make the claim that a vegetarian studied and a socialist studied. The latter reading may be facilitated by taking exclusive nouns such as *man* and *woman*. The single individual reading arises by coordinating the nouns directly. Because nouns are assigned a boolean type, the semantics of their coordination is exactly the same as the coordination of verb phrases, which are currently assigned the same type as nouns. As shown by Dowty (1988), the case where there may be two individuals arises by type raising the conjuncts, as shown in figure 6.5. These combine to provide the analysis of the entire string shown in figure 6.6. We will see similar examples when we study quantifiers, which more clearly illustrate some of the other cases. Note that in English, a conjoined noun phrase has plural agreement, rather than the singular agreement we expect and, in the case of disjoined noun phrases, find.

$$\frac{\displaystyle \frac{The}{\iota:np/n}\text{Lx}\quad \frac{\displaystyle \frac{\overline{vegetarian\ and\ socialist}}{\lambda N.\lambda V.V(N(\mathbf{veg}))\wedge V(N(\mathbf{soc}))}\text{D}}{(np/n)\backslash s/(np\backslash s)}\text{\textbackslash E}\quad \frac{studied}{\text{study}}\text{Lx}}{\displaystyle \frac{\lambda V.V(\iota(\mathbf{veg}))\wedge V(\iota(\mathbf{soc})):s/(np\backslash s)}{\mathbf{study}(\iota(\mathbf{veg}))\wedge \mathbf{study}(\iota(\mathbf{soc})):s}\text{/E}}$$

Figure 6.6
A derivation of *The vegetarian and socialist studied*

(13) a. {Sandy and Terry / The vegetarian and socialist} {*is / are}
    studying.
   b. {Sandy or Terry / The vegetarian or socialist} {is / *are}
    studying.

We have no explanation for the ungrammaticality of the singular case, but will be able to derive the plural case with the same meaning by employing a distributive reading over a nonboolean coordination (see section 8.8).

6.1.3   Nonconstituent Coordination

As I noted when introducing coordination, it is possible to coordinate expressions that do not form constituents in most grammatical theories. To achieve this effect with the grammar we have so far, it is necessary to combine the introduction rules and the coordination rule. First, recall that we can perform the following analyses, as was shown in figure 5.14.

(14) a. *Chris kicks* $\Rightarrow \lambda y.\mathbf{kick}(y)(\mathbf{c}):s/np$
   b. *Jo hits* $\Rightarrow \lambda x.\mathbf{hit}(x)(\mathbf{j}):s/np$

We can combine these two analyses to provide an analysis of cases of so-called *right-node raising*, as shown in figure 6.7. Recall the derivation of *Chris believes Pat likes* as an *s/np* in figure 5.15. This *s/np* can be used in the same way as the conjuncts in figure 6.7 to carry out the following analysis:

(15) *[Brett met] and [Chris believes Pat likes] Morgan*
    $\Rightarrow \mathbf{met}(\mathbf{m})(\mathbf{b})\wedge \mathbf{believe}(\mathbf{like}(\mathbf{m})(\mathbf{p}))(\mathbf{c}):s$

The derivation goes through because the coordinated expressions, indicated with brackets, can both be assigned the syntactic category *s/np*.

   In coordinating strings of modifiers, we can employ analyses parallel to those used for right-node raising (though in the case of postnominal and postverbal modifiers, it is really a case of left-node raising).

$$\frac{\overline{Chris\ kicks}}{\lambda y.\mathbf{kick}(y)(\mathbf{c}):s/np}D \quad \frac{\overline{or}}{\mathbf{or}:co}Lx \quad \frac{\overline{Jo\ hits}}{\lambda x.\mathbf{hit}(x)(\mathbf{j}):s/np}D \quad \frac{\overline{Francis}}{\mathbf{f}:np}Lx$$

$$\frac{\lambda z.\mathbf{or}(\mathbf{kick}(z)(\mathbf{c}))(\mathbf{hit}(z)(\mathbf{j})):s/np}{}D$$

$$\frac{}{\mathbf{or}(\mathbf{kick}(\mathbf{f})(\mathbf{c}))(\mathbf{hit}(\mathbf{f})(\mathbf{j})):s}/E$$

Figure 6.7
A derivation of *Chris kicks or Jo hits Francis*

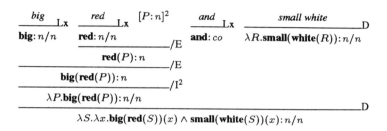

Figure 6.8
A derivation of *big red and small white*

Figure 6.9
A derivation of *in Pittsburgh yesterday and in Cleveland today*

(16) a. The [big red] and [small white] balloons are for sale.

  b. Jo ran [in Pittsburgh yesterday] and [in Cleveland today].

For these cases, composition can be used to analyze the coordinates. For instance, consider the coordinations in figures 6.8 and 6.9.

As another example of so-called "nonconstituent" coordination, consider the following case:

(17) *[Terry Fido] and [Jo Felix]*

$\Rightarrow \lambda V.\lambda x.\,V(\mathbf{t})(\mathbf{fido})(x) \wedge V(\mathbf{j})(\mathbf{felix})(x): (np\backslash s/np/np)\backslash np\backslash s$

Here we follow the analysis shown in figure 5.17 to assign the coordinated expressions to the boolean syntactic category $(np\backslash s/np/np)\backslash np\backslash s$. These can, of course, combine with a ditransitive verb and subject to produce the following:

(18) *Morgan sold [Terry Fido] and [Jo Felix]*
       $\Rightarrow$ **sell(t)(fido)(m)** $\land$ **sell(j)(felix)(m)**: s

This analysis is similar to the one proposed by Dowty (1988) in that the same syntactic category and semantic term is assigned to the sequence of two noun phrases in the coordinate structure. The only difference is that we employ the hypothetical reasoning of the Lambek calculus rather than the type raising of combinatory categorial grammar. Dowty's analysis is acceptable in our setting but is not a normal-form derivation. In general, arbitrary "nonconstituent" sequences such as these can be generated using the Lambek calculus. For instance, there is no problem in deriving cases where there are verbal modifiers attached to noun phrases in coordinations, such as the case in (6b). This generality actually leads to overgeneration as I have presented it. To correct this situation, it would be necessary to introduce finer-grained structural control to capture the islandhood of coordinate structures themselves and the constructions they interact with (see Morrill 1994a).

I leave further examples of coordination as exercises but return to the topic when we consider quantification, plurals, and intensional constructions involving control and phrasal embedding. All of these phenomena display interesting interactions with coordination.

With the addition of polymorphic categories for coordinators, it is no longer clear that the resulting grammar is decidable. Our decidability proof depended crucially on a finite search space for derivations, but with infinitely many lexical entries for coordinators, this proof no longer suffices. But by a slightly different method, we can recursively eliminate coordinators by reduction to derivations without coordinators.

THEOREM: DECIDABILITY WITH COORDINATION   Grammaticality is decidable with a finite lexicon extended with the infinitely many instances of polymorphic coordination of lexical entries.

Proof   The proof proceeds by inductively eliminating coordination steps. This can be achieved because $\Gamma, co, \Delta \Rightarrow C$ if and only if we can partition $\Gamma = \Gamma_1, \Gamma_2$ and $\Delta = \Delta_1, \Delta_2$ in such a way that $\Gamma_1, \Gamma_2, \Delta_2 \Rightarrow C$ and $\Gamma_1, \Delta_1, \Delta_2 \Rightarrow C$. Working forward, if we apply the coordination at category A, then we simply take Γ_2 and Δ_1 to be the two conjuncts. Because we must have $\Gamma_1, A, \Delta_2 \Rightarrow C$ and because $\Gamma_2 \Rightarrow A$ and $\Delta_1 \Rightarrow A$, the result holds. Conversely, if we can partition Γ and Δ appropriately, then we can apply coordination in conjunction with the right rules for slashes by noting that $\Gamma_2 \Rightarrow \Gamma_1 \backslash C / \Delta_2$ and $\Delta_1 \Rightarrow \Gamma_1 \backslash C / \Delta_2$. (I use the notation A/Γ as shorthand for $A/G_n/ \cdots /G_1$, where $\Gamma = G_1, \ldots, G_n$. The backward notation is defined analogously.) Finally, we can apply coordination at this category. Because there are only finitely many ways to partition a finite string, the search for a proof must eventually reduce to a finite number of searches for proofs in the Lambek calculus. $\qquad \square$

The somewhat different issue of whether there is some category at which two categories can be conjoined was proven to be decidable by Pentus (1994), following intermediate results of Roorda (1991), and is taken up in exercise 12.

6.2   CONJUNCTIVE AND DISJUNCTIVE CATEGORIES

In this section we consider the closure of categories under logical disjunction and conjunction. Logical category constructors were discussed by Lambek (1961) and were later studied by Kanazawa (1992) and Morrill (1989b, 1990c). My treatment follows Morrill 1994a.

6.2.1   The Conjunction Constructor

We begin with the constructor for conjunction and proceed to disjunction in the next section.

DEFINITION: CONJUNCTION CONSTRUCTOR   The *conjunction constructor* is as follows:

a. $A \wedge B \in \mathbf{Cat}$, if $A, B \in \mathbf{Cat}$
b. $\mathrm{Typ}(A \wedge B) = \mathrm{Typ}(A) \times \mathrm{Typ}(B)$

We think of an expression as being assigned to category $A \wedge B$ if it can be assigned to both category A and to category B. Semantically, we take a category $A \wedge B$ to be assigned to a pair, one element of which represents the semantics as an A and one as a B. This type assignment follows the Curry-Howard morphism in that the constructive representation of a proof for a conjunction contains a proof of each conjunct. I will assume that conjunction associates to the left and binds less tightly than the slash and other constructors. For instance, $s/np \wedge n/n$ is to be read as $(s/np) \wedge (n/n)$.

I characterize conjunction proof-theoretically as follows:

DEFINITION: CONJUNCTION SEQUENT SCHEMES   The sequent schemes for conjunction are the following:

a.
$$\frac{\Gamma \Rightarrow \alpha : A \qquad \Gamma \Rightarrow \beta : B}{\Gamma \Rightarrow \langle \alpha, \beta \rangle : A \wedge B} \wedge R$$

b.
$$\frac{\Gamma_1, \pi_1(\alpha) : A, \Gamma_2 \Rightarrow \beta : C}{\Gamma_1, \alpha : A \wedge B, \Gamma_2 \Rightarrow \beta : C} \wedge_1 L \qquad \frac{\Gamma_1, \pi_2(\alpha) : B, \Gamma_2 \Rightarrow \beta : C}{\Gamma_1, \alpha : A \wedge B, \Gamma_2 \Rightarrow \beta : C} \wedge_2 L$$

The right rule tells us that if Γ can produce an A with semantics α and the same Γ can produce a B with semantics β, then Γ can produce an $A \wedge B$, with a semantic term equal to the pairing of the terms α and β. The left rules for the conjunct allow us to use an $A \wedge B$ in our input either as an A or as a B, with semantics given by projecting the appropriate component. This logic captures both sides of the definition of conjunction: an expression is assigned category $A \wedge B$ if and only if it can be assigned both A and B.

It is important to note how the conjunctive scheme manages resources. In the right scheme, to deduce $A \wedge B$, we must use Γ to prove A and Γ again to prove B. The alternative is to split the resources and prove $A \wedge B$ from Γ, Δ by proving A from Γ and B from Δ. This would lead to a logic involving multiplicative products. The product is said to be a *multiplicative* connective in the terminology of linear logic, whereas conjunction is said to be *additive*.

Morrill (1994a) considers the assignment of items such as prepositions to conjunctive categories in order to capture the fact that prepositions have the same complement structure when used as sentential or nominal modifiers. For the sake of this example, I assume that verbal prepositions are assigned to the sentence-modifying category $s \backslash s / np$ rather than the verb-phrase-modifying category $(np \backslash s) \backslash np \backslash s / np$ (the latter can be derived from the former but not vice versa).

(19) $in \Rightarrow \lambda x. \langle \mathbf{in}_1(x), \mathbf{in}_2(x) \rangle : (n \backslash n \wedge s \backslash s) / np$

Note that $\mathbf{in}_1$ must be of type $\mathbf{Ind} \rightarrow (\mathbf{Ind} \rightarrow \mathbf{Bool}) \rightarrow \mathbf{Ind} \rightarrow \mathbf{Bool}$ and $\mathbf{in}_2$ of type $\mathbf{Ind} \rightarrow \mathbf{Bool} \rightarrow \mathbf{Bool}$. After application to the prepositional object, the result is a conjunctive category that can be used as either a nominal or sentential modifier, depending on which of the projections is chosen. Note that with the basic entry in (19) we are able to derive the ordinary nominal-modifier category for the preposition according to the general scheme in

$$\dfrac{\overline{\rule{1.5cm}{0.4pt}}^{\,I}}{x:C \Rightarrow x:C}$$

$$\dfrac{\dfrac{\dfrac{\overline{\rule{3.5cm}{0.4pt}}^{\,I}}{\pi_1(\alpha(x)):A \Rightarrow \pi_1(\alpha(x)):A}\,{\scriptstyle\wedge_1 L}}{\alpha(x):A \wedge B \Rightarrow \pi_1(\alpha(x)):A}\,{\scriptstyle /L}}{\dfrac{\alpha:(A \wedge B)/C,\ x:C \Rightarrow \pi_1(\alpha(x)):A}{\alpha:(A \wedge B)/C \Rightarrow \lambda x.\pi_1(\alpha(x)):A/C}\,{\scriptstyle /R}}$$

Figure 6.10
Conjunct-result distribution

figure 6.10. Logically, the derivation in figure 6.10 demonstrates half of the equivalence of $(\xi \to \phi) \wedge (\xi \to \psi)$ and $\xi \to (\phi \wedge \psi)$ (the other half is also derivable). When the first part of the derivation in figure 6.10 is applied to the preposition entry in (19), we obtain the following:

(20) $\lambda y.\langle \mathbf{in}_1(y), \mathbf{in}_2(y)\rangle: (n\backslash n \wedge s\backslash s)/np$
 $\Rightarrow \lambda x.\pi_1((\lambda y.\langle \mathbf{in}_1(y), \mathbf{in}_2(y)\rangle)(x)): n\backslash n/np$
 $\equiv \lambda x.\pi_1(\langle \mathbf{in}_1(x), \mathbf{in}_2(x)\rangle): n\backslash n/np$
 $\equiv \lambda x.\mathbf{in}_1(x): n\backslash n/np$
 $\equiv \mathbf{in}_1: n\backslash n/np$

The sentence-modifying category is derived in a similar fashion.

6.2.2 The Disjunction Constructor

The disjunction constructor is defined similarly to the conjunction one, but with the dual semantics.

DEFINITION: DISJUNCTION CONSTRUCTOR   The *disjunction constructor* is as follows:

a. $A \vee B \in$ **Cat** if $A, B \in$ **Cat**
b. $\mathrm{Typ}(A \vee B) = \mathrm{Typ}(A) + \mathrm{Typ}(B)$

Thus an object of type $A \vee B$ is either an object of type A (marked with a 1), or an object of type B (marked with a 2). This type assignment also follows the Curry-Howard morphism, where we associate disjunctive formulas with disjunctive-sum types in the typed λ-calculus. I assume that the disjunction constructor associates to the left and binds less tightly than our other constructors, including conjunction.

The logic of disjunction is simply dual to that for conjunction. The term assignment follows the Curry-Howard morphism.

DEFINITION: DISJUNCTION SEQUENT SCHEMES   The sequent schemes for disjunction are the following:

a. $\dfrac{\Gamma \Rightarrow \alpha \colon A}{\Gamma \Rightarrow \iota_1(\alpha) \colon A \vee B} \vee_1 \text{R}$ $\dfrac{\Gamma \Rightarrow \beta \colon B}{\Gamma \Rightarrow \iota_2(\beta) \colon A \vee B} \vee_2 \text{R}$

b. $\dfrac{\Gamma_1, \, x \colon A, \, \Gamma_2 \Rightarrow \alpha \colon C \qquad \Gamma_1, \, y \colon B, \, \Gamma_2 \Rightarrow \beta \colon C}{\Gamma_1, \, \gamma \colon A \vee B, \, \Gamma_2 \Rightarrow \gamma \rightarrow \lambda x.\alpha; \lambda y.\beta \colon C} \vee \text{L}$

Here the right rules split into two parts, because we can prove that an expression is of category $A \vee B$ if we can prove it is an A or if we can prove it is a B. The semantic marking with indices keeps track of which injection was used to map the domain of A or B into the domain of $A \vee B$. The left rule for disjunction is more complex. To use an $A \vee B$ in a context to produce a C, we must be able to use A in that context to produce a C and also use B in the same context to produce a C. This is a canonical example of what is known in logic as *reasoning by cases*. The choice function in the semantics of the result encodes the dependency on whether the term γ assigned to $A \vee B$ is instantiated as an A or as a B; if it is an A, so that $\gamma = \iota_1(\gamma')$, we must choose the first function and return $(\lambda x.\alpha)(\gamma')$, and similarly the second function for the B case. Note that this interpretation follows the standard constructive interpretation of disjunction, which provides the basis of the Curry-Howard morphism. In contrast to the classical setting, under the constructive understanding of provability, a disjunction can only be proved by proving one of its disjuncts. Under our semantic assignment, a term associated with a disjunctive category must consist of a term of one of the disjuncts along with an indication of which disjunct.

6.2.3   Natural-Deduction Conjunction and Disjunction

Before considering further examples, we pause to develop the natural-deduction version of the conjunctive and disjunctive sequent system. It is straightforward to encode the left conjunct rules and the right disjunct rules; they involve no special management of assumptions. On the other hand, encoding the right conjunct and left disjunct schemes strain the natural-deduction notation.

I begin with the schemes for the elimination (use) and introduction (proof) for categories involving conjunction.

DEFINITION: CONJUNCTION NATURAL-DEDUCTION SCHEMES   The natural deduction schemes for conjunction are the following:

a.
$$\frac{\alpha: A \wedge B}{\pi_1(\alpha): A}\wedge_1 E \qquad \frac{\alpha: A \wedge B}{\pi_2(\alpha): B}\wedge_2 E$$

b.
$$\Gamma \qquad [\Gamma]^n$$
$$\vdots \qquad \vdots$$
$$\frac{\alpha: A \qquad \beta: B}{\langle \alpha, \beta\rangle: A \wedge B}\wedge I^n$$

Note that the elimination rule is split into two components, depending on which side of the conjunct is eliminated. To have an introduction rule matching the right sequent rule, we require a more robust notation for discharging assumptions. This is because we need to be able to prove both A and B from exactly the same set of assumptions. In categorial grammar, we have to be careful both about the ordering and the number of occurrences of assumptions. I use the Γ notation to label a set of assumptions and $[\Gamma]^n$ to indicate that the whole sequence Γ of assumptions is eliminated at stage n in the derivation.

The schemes for disjunction resemble those for conjunction.

DEFINITION: DISJUNCTION NATURAL-DEDUCTION SCHEMES The natural deduction schemes for disjunction are the following:

a.
$$\frac{\alpha: A}{\iota_1(\alpha): A \vee B}\vee_1 I \qquad \frac{\beta: B}{\iota_2(\alpha): A \vee B}\vee_2 I$$

b.
$$\Gamma_1 \qquad \vdots \qquad \Gamma_2 \qquad [\Gamma_1]^n \qquad [y: B]^n \qquad [\Gamma_2]^n$$
$$\vdots \quad \frac{\gamma: A \vee B}{x: A}n \quad \vdots \qquad \vdots \qquad \vdots \qquad \vdots$$
$$\vdots \qquad \vdots \qquad \vdots \qquad \vdots \qquad \vdots \qquad \vdots$$
$$\frac{\alpha: C \qquad\qquad\qquad\qquad\qquad \beta: C}{\gamma \rightarrow \lambda x.\alpha; \lambda y.\beta: C}\vee E^n$$

Disjunction introduction splits into two halves, depending on which side of the disjunct the category occurs on. The elimination scheme, in order to match the left sequent scheme for disjunction, must employ identical contexts, one for each side of the disjunct being eliminated. In the natural-deduction disjunction-elimination scheme, the hypotheticals are all discharged at the elimination step n, including the hypothetical $x\colon A$, used in the proof of C, and the entire context of the right subderivation, $\Gamma_1, y\colon B, \Gamma_2$.

In the case of the disjunction constructor, we have a pattern of normalization like that for the product constructor.

DEFINITION: NORMALIZATION FOR DISJUNCTION   The *normalization scheme for disjunction* is the following:

$$
\cfrac{
  \cfrac{
    \cfrac{
      \Gamma_1 \quad \vdots \quad \cfrac{\delta\colon A}{\langle 1, \delta \rangle\colon A \vee B}\vee_1 I \quad \Gamma_2
    }{
      \vdots \quad x\colon A \quad \vdots
    }{}_n \qquad \vdots \qquad [\Gamma_1]^n \; [y\colon B]^n \; [\Gamma_2]^n
  }{
    \alpha\colon C \qquad\qquad\qquad \beta\colon C
  }\vee E^n
}{
  \langle 1, \delta \rangle \rightarrow \lambda x.\alpha; \lambda y.\beta\colon C
}
\qquad\leadsto\qquad
\cfrac{
  \Gamma_1 \quad \vdots \quad \delta\colon A \quad \vdots \quad \Gamma_2
}{
  \alpha[x \mapsto \delta]\colon C
}
$$

The semantic component of the reduction simply follows from β-reduction and the definition of the choice operator. More important, this normalization scheme preserves the Curry-Howard morphism in that the normalization of derivations in the grammar mirror the normalizations of the corresponding λ-terms. As usual in the sequent calculus, the analogue of the input to normalization is only derivable with the cut scheme.

There is a corresponding normalization scheme for conjunction:

DEFINITION: NORMALIZATION FOR CONJUNCTION   The *normalization scheme for conjunction* is the following:

$$
\cfrac{
  \cfrac{\alpha\colon A \wedge B}{\pi_1(\alpha)\colon A}\wedge_1 E \qquad \cfrac{[\alpha\colon A \wedge B]^n}{\pi_2(\alpha)\colon B}\wedge_2 E
}{
  \langle \pi_1(\alpha), \pi_2(\alpha) \rangle\colon A \wedge B
}\wedge I^n
\qquad\leadsto\qquad
\alpha\colon A \wedge B
$$

Thus any derivation that disassembles a conjunctive category only to immediately reassemble it can be simplified.

6.2.4 Copular Complements and Predicatives

The logical-category constructors lead to an interesting characterization of the lexicon in terms of conjunctive categories. I will illustrate the power of logical-category constructors by means of the complements to the copula. As we saw with prepositions, two lexical entries, $e \Rightarrow \alpha: A$ and $e \Rightarrow \beta: B$, can be combined into a common entry by means of the logical constructors. While this may appear to be a trivial application, its ramifications are quite significant.

Consider the following range of lexical entries for the copula *be*, setting aside matters of tense and agreement for the time being.

(21) a. *is* $\Rightarrow$ **eq**: $np\backslash s/np$
      b. *is* $\Rightarrow \lambda V. V: np\backslash s/(np\backslash s)$
      c. *is* $\Rightarrow \lambda V.\lambda x. V(\lambda y.\mathbf{true})(x): np\backslash s/(n/n)$
      d. *is* $\Rightarrow \lambda V.\lambda x. V(\lambda y.\mathbf{true})(x): np\backslash s/(n\backslash n)$

Semantically, there are three possibilities, depending on whether the complement is a noun phrase, a verb phrase, or a nominal modifier. In the case of a noun-phrase argument, as in (21a), the semantics is that of identity.

(22) *Jo is the mayor* $\Rightarrow$ **eq**$(\iota(\mathbf{mayor}))(\mathbf{j}): s$

When combining with a verb phrase, as in (21b), the semantics is that of function application (by η-conversion we have $\lambda V. V \equiv \lambda V.\lambda x. V(x)$). The copula takes two arguments, the verb phrase and the subject, and the resulting semantics is that of applying the verb phrase's semantics to that of the noun phrase.

(23) *Jo is running* $\Rightarrow$ **run**$(\mathbf{j}): s$

Russell had the following to say about the dual use of the copula: "It is a disgrace to the human race that it has chosen to employ the same word "is" for these two entirely different ideas—a disgrace which a symbolic logical language of course remedies," (1919, 168).

In addition to its application to identity and predication, the English copula also takes nominal modifiers as complements, as indicated by the lexical entries (21c) and (21d). Here the semantics is slightly more complex. The copula must combine a noun-phrase subject, of type **Ind**, with a nominal modifier n/n or $n\backslash n$ of type (**Ind** $\rightarrow$ **Bool**) $\rightarrow$ **Ind** $\rightarrow$ **Bool**. Following van Benthem (1991), I supply the extra term in the semantics, $\lambda x.\mathbf{true}$, to reduce the nominal modifier to type **Ind** $\rightarrow$ **Bool** to allow predication. Consider the following example:

(24) *Jo is male*
      $\Rightarrow (\lambda A.\lambda x. A(\lambda y.\mathbf{true})(x))(\lambda P.\lambda z. P(z) \wedge \mathbf{male}(z))(\mathbf{j}): s$

$$\dfrac{\overline{\quad\quad\quad\quad\quad\quad\quad\quad}\,D}{\pi_1(\alpha)\!:\!A/B,\ w\!:\!B \Rightarrow \pi_1(\alpha)(w)\!:\!A}{}_{\wedge_1 L} \qquad\quad \dfrac{\overline{\quad\quad\quad\quad\quad\quad\quad\quad}\,D}{\pi_2(\alpha)\!:\!A/C,\ y\!:\!C \Rightarrow \pi_2(\alpha)(y)\!:\!A}{}_{\wedge_2 L}$$

$$\dfrac{\alpha\!:\!A/B \wedge A/C,\ w\!:\!B \Rightarrow \pi_1(\alpha)(w)\!:\!A \qquad\quad \alpha\!:\!A/B \wedge A/C,\ y\!:\!C \Rightarrow \pi_2(\alpha)(y)\!:\!A}{}_{\vee L}$$

$$\dfrac{\alpha\!:\!A/B \wedge A/C,\ x\!:\!B \vee C \Rightarrow x \to \lambda w.\pi_1(\alpha)(w);\lambda y.\pi_2(\alpha)(y)\!:\!A}{\alpha\!:\!A/B \wedge A/C \Rightarrow \lambda x.(x \to \lambda w.\pi_1(\alpha)(w);\lambda y.\pi_2(\alpha)(y))\!:\!A/(B \vee C)}{}_{/R}$$

Figure 6.11
Conjunction, disjunction, and implication derivation

$$\equiv (\lambda x.(\lambda P.\lambda z.P(z) \wedge \mathbf{male}(z))(\lambda y.\mathbf{true})(x))(\mathbf{j})\!:\!s$$
$$\equiv (\lambda P.\lambda z.P(z) \wedge \mathbf{male}(z))(\lambda y.\mathbf{true})(\mathbf{j})\!:\!s$$
$$\equiv (\lambda z.(\lambda y.\mathbf{true})(z) \wedge \mathbf{male}(z))(\mathbf{j})\!:\!s$$
$$\equiv (\lambda y.\mathbf{true})(\mathbf{j}) \wedge \mathbf{male}(\mathbf{j})\!:\!s$$
$$\equiv \mathbf{true} \wedge \mathbf{male}(\mathbf{j})\!:\!s$$
$$\equiv \mathbf{male}(\mathbf{j})\!:\!s$$

Note that we have eliminated the **true** in the last line, because co-ordinating **true** with ϕ yields the same interpretation as ϕ; in symbols, **and**(**true**) $\equiv \lambda x^{\mathbf{Bool}}.x$. Similar semantic reductions apply in the case of backward directed nominal modifiers of category $n\backslash n$, such as relative clauses and nominal prepositional phrases.

Now consider combining these entries into one conjunctive category. We have the schematic derivation in figure 6.11. Applying this derivation to the case of the copula leads to the following sequent, after some β-conversion and projections.

(25) $\langle \mathbf{eq}, \lambda V.V \rangle\!:\!(np\backslash s/np) \wedge (np\backslash s/(np\backslash s))$
     $\Rightarrow \lambda C.(C \to \lambda x.\mathbf{eq}(x); \lambda W.W)\!:\!np\backslash s/(np \vee np\backslash s)$

Logically, we have an analogy to the equivalence of $(\phi \to \xi) \wedge (\psi \to \xi)$ and $(\phi \vee \psi) \to \xi$, which is established by a derivation dual to the one in figure 6.11. As established by Morrill (1990c, 1994a), this simple logical relationship provides a means for coordinating unlike complements of a category, some examples of which are as follows:

(26)   a. Jack is [a good cook] and [always improving].
     b. That man over there is either [the mayor] or [running for office].
     c. Jo was [exhausted yesterday] and [in a good mood last week].

In each example we must coordinate pairs of categories that share only the property of acting as complements to the copula. We can inject each of the categories being coordinated into a disjunctive category. But this is

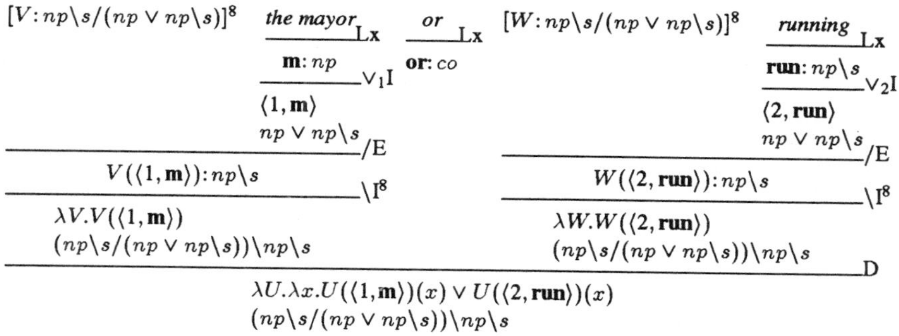

$$[V:np\backslash s/(np \vee np\backslash s)]^8 \quad \underset{\text{Lx}}{\text{\textit{the mayor}}} \quad \underset{\text{Lx}}{\text{\textit{or}}} \quad [W:np\backslash s/(np \vee np\backslash s)]^8 \quad \underset{\text{Lx}}{\text{\textit{running}}}$$

$$\cfrac{\cfrac{\cfrac{\cfrac{\mathbf{m}:np}{\langle 1,\mathbf{m}\rangle}V_1 I}{\cfrac{np \vee np\backslash s}{V(\langle 1,\mathbf{m}\rangle):np\backslash s}/E}}{\begin{array}{c}\lambda V.V(\langle 1,\mathbf{m}\rangle)\\(np\backslash s/(np\vee np\backslash s))\backslash np\backslash s\end{array}}\backslash I^8 \qquad \cfrac{\cfrac{\cfrac{\cfrac{\mathbf{run}:np\backslash s}{\langle 2,\mathbf{run}\rangle}V_2 I}{\cfrac{np \vee np\backslash s}{W(\langle 2,\mathbf{run}\rangle):np\backslash s}/E}}{\begin{array}{c}\lambda W.W(\langle 2,\mathbf{run}\rangle)\\(np\backslash s/(np\vee np\backslash s))\backslash np\backslash s\end{array}}\backslash I^8}{\begin{array}{c}\lambda U.\lambda x.U(\langle 1,\mathbf{m}\rangle)(x)\vee U(\langle 2,\mathbf{run}\rangle)(x)\\(np\backslash s/(np\vee np\backslash s))\backslash np\backslash s\end{array}}D$$

Figure 6.12
Coordination of "unlike" categories

not yet enough for coordination, as the result is not boolean. A further type raising allows the analysis to go through, as demonstrated in figure 6.12. Combining the analysis of the copula in figure 6.11 and the analysis of the coordination in figure 6.12, we get the following result by application:

(27) *is the mayor or running*

$$\Rightarrow (\lambda U.\lambda x.U(\langle 1,\mathbf{m}\rangle)(x)\vee U(\langle 2,\mathbf{run}\rangle)(x)):np\backslash s$$
$$(\lambda C.(C\to\lambda z.\mathbf{eq}(z);\lambda V.V))$$
$$\equiv \lambda x.(\lambda C.(C\to\lambda z.\mathbf{eq}(z);\lambda V.V))(\langle 1,\mathbf{m}\rangle)(x)$$
$$\quad\vee(\lambda B.(B\to\lambda z.\mathbf{eq}(z);\lambda V.V))(\langle 2,\mathbf{run}\rangle)(x):np\backslash s$$
$$\equiv \lambda x.(\langle 1,\mathbf{m}\rangle\to\lambda z.\mathbf{eq}(z);\lambda V.V)(x)$$
$$\quad\vee(\langle 2,\mathbf{run}\rangle\to\lambda z.\mathbf{eq}(z);\lambda V.V)(x):np\backslash s$$
$$\equiv \lambda x.(\lambda z.\mathbf{eq}(z))(\mathbf{m})(x)\vee(\lambda V.V)(\mathbf{run})(x):np\backslash s$$
$$\equiv \lambda x.\mathbf{eq}(\mathbf{m})(x)\vee\mathbf{run}(x):np\backslash s$$

The resulting semantics is what we would intuitively expect: it is the property of either being equal to the individual denoted by **m** or having the property denoted by **run**. Extending to any number of complements for the copula is straightforward, because the logical operations are associative and commutative and can thus be iterated.

The following examples, due to Milward (1994), show that polymorphism is not always desirable.

(28) a. Jo will drive and Sandy built the drive.
      b. *Jo [will] and [Sandy built the] drive.
      c. #Jo bored [the new hole] and [his fellow workers].
      d. ?Jo knows [Sandy] and [that it is raining].

If we allow the verbal and nominal uses of *drive* to coexist, we will be saddled with the coordination in (28b). Similarly, it is not clear what to make of Milward's example (28c), which involves two senses of the same category. In the last example, (28d), the verb *knows* is being used with both *np* and *s* complements, but the result seems more acceptable. Morrill (1994) suggests analyzing these cases as lexically ambiguous. Note that the lexical insertion scheme does not interact with the other derivation rules, thus neatly sidestepping the derivation of the problematic cases in (28).

But even without these cases, some strings remain rather difficult to coordinate. Some particularly problematic cases are the following:

(29) a. *The student [who likes] and [in] the library was studying.
   b. ?[I bought every red] and [Jo liked some blue] t-shirt.
   c. ?[The man who buys] and [the woman who sells] rattlesnakes met outside.
   d. *I saw [a friend of] and [the manufacturer of] Dana's handbag.
   e. *Sue saw the man [through the telescope] and [with the troublesome kid].

All of these examples will be derivable in our grammar as it stands. Example (29c) is due to Wexler and Culicover (1980), (29d) is attributed to Paul Dekker by Milward (1994), and (29e) is due to Milward (1994). Example (29d) is particularly opaque, because the possessive is structured in two ways:

(30) a. I saw [[a friend of Dana]'s] handbag.
   b. I saw the manufacturer of [Dana's] handbag.

Thus the bracketed constituents must be raised to consume the rest of the arguments one at a time, including the possessive, just as in the other examples. Enforcing island constraints through modal operators acting as barriers would likely eliminate the problematic cases of (29a) and (29c), both of which involve extraction through relative clauses, and (29d), which involves extraction through complex (possessive) nominals. It is unclear that (29b) is as bad as the others; not surprisingly, the literature is ambivalent about the islandhood of ordinary noun phrases. Unfortunately, (29e) remains problematic. To derive it, we can analyze the conjuncts as category $n\backslash(np/n)\backslash(np\backslash s/np)\backslash np\backslash s$.

Our treatment of copular complements can be improved upon in at least one dimension. Many of the complements to the copula are nominal modifiers. Such complements can always be interpreted as properties. Perhaps a more natural account than the one just given would be to introduce a new basic category, with the following definition.

(31) a. $pr \in \mathbf{BasCat}$
     b. $\text{Typ}(pr) = \mathbf{Ind} \to \mathbf{Bool}$

This approach is similar to the one adopted for LFG (Bresnan 1982b) and HPSG (Pollard and Sag 1987), and it is the one that we will adopt. With such a basic category, we can assume the following lexical entries:

(32) a. $is \Rightarrow \lambda P.\lambda x.P(x): np\backslash s/pr$
     b. $outside \Rightarrow \mathbf{outside}_2: pr$
     c. $in \Rightarrow \mathbf{in}_2: pr/np$
     d. $red \Rightarrow \mathbf{red}_2: pr$
     e. $whom \Rightarrow \lambda P.P: pr/(np\backslash s)$
     f. $Sandy \Rightarrow \lambda x.x = \mathbf{s}$

Until now, the only entries we had for such categories were as nominal modifiers. For instance, red was assigned the category $\lambda P.\lambda x.P(x) \wedge \mathbf{red}_2(x): n/n$. To achieve correct typing, our previous lexical entry for the copula had to apply it to the property $\lambda y.\mathbf{true}$ to derive the verbal predicate $\lambda x.\mathbf{true} \wedge \mathbf{red}_2(x)$, which is logically equivalent to $\mathbf{red}_2$. It is much more natural to derive the adjectival forms of predicatives from their predicative forms. If an expression has a lexical entry resulting in a predicative, it will also have a lexical entry as a nominal modifier. The semantics of a predicative modifier is the intersection of the predicative meanings. Lexical rules have been studied in a categorial grammar setting by Dowty (1979a), Ades and Steedman (1982), Bach (1983a), Keenan and Faltz (1985), Pollard and Sag (1987), and others. Carpenter (1992a) generalizes these approaches into a lexical metatheory, which is then applied to the distribution of predicative complements, albeit in a manner slightly different than that suggested here.

The introduction of a predicative category leaves open the possibility of analyzing participial verbs such as *running* also as predicatives. One benefit of such an analysis is that it would account for the use of participial verb phrases as nominal modifiers:

(33) The person [presenting the next tàlk] is brilliant.

Carpenter (1992a) provides a categorial treatment of such cases by providing lexical entries such as the following:

(34) *presenting* $\Rightarrow \lambda y.\lambda P.\lambda x.P(x) \wedge \mathbf{present}(y)(x): n\backslash n/np$

Carpenter also presents an analysis of modified versions of such predicatives, as in *person presenting the talk in the next room*, where *in the next room* is a modifier of *presenting* and thus has to be taken as the root of predication.

6.2.5 Incompleteness of Conjunction and Disjunction

The natural interpretation for conjunction and disjunction is as set intersection and union. For instance, an expression-meaning pair would be assigned $A \wedge B$ if and only if it were assigned both A and B. Similarly, the denotation of $A \vee B$ would be the union of the denotations of A and B. Our rules are incomplete with respect to this interpretation in the sense that there are pairs of categories that always have the same denotation but are not interderivable. This incompleteness is manifested in several ways. Perhaps the most obvious case is the inability to derive the distributive laws. For instance, we cannot derive the following sequent:

(35) $A \wedge (B \vee C) \Rightarrow (A \wedge B) \vee (A \wedge C)$

With the sequent calculus, the only fruitful rule scheme is the right rule for disjunction, with the only other possibility being an unhelpful application of the left rule for conjunction. This scheme requires a proof of either $A \wedge (B \vee C) \Rightarrow A \wedge B$ or $A \wedge (B \vee C) \Rightarrow A \wedge C$, neither of which is available. Dŏsen (1992) notes that such failures of distributivity are endemic to linear approaches to the connectives in which assumptions behave with at least as much structure as a multiset. I leave as an exercise the construction of a proof of the converse of (35). On a more optimistic note, Morrill (1994a) points out that linguistically, we only seem to need the rules of use for conjunctions and rules of proof for disjunctions.

Unlike the situation with the conjunction constructor, we do get distributivity of disjunction over the concatenation operator. For instance, we can derive the following.

(36) a. $(A \vee B) \cdot C \Rightarrow (A \cdot C) \vee (B \cdot C)$
    b. $(A \cdot C) \vee (B \cdot C) \Rightarrow (A \vee B) \cdot C$

This is because in the first case the left rule for the product allows us to decompose to a point where the left rule for the disjunction can apply. I leave the derivations as an exercise.

The incompleteness of the calculus arises because of my simplifying assumption that antecedents in sequents are sequences of categories. Using the approach developed for relevance logic, Restall (1994) shows how Dunn's (1973) logic of relevant conjunction and disjunction can be cast in Belnap's (1982) framework of *display logic*. The general logical technique is adapted to a categorial setting by Moortgat and Oehrle (1993; Moortgat 1994, in press). The basic idea is to encode in the antecedent information about whether decomposition was through a boolean category ($\land$ or $\lor$) or a concatenative category ($/$, $\backslash$, or $\cdot$).

6.3 UNBOUNDED DEPENDENCY CONSTRUCTIONS

Several families of natural-language constructions involve relationships among distant subexpressions within an expression. In fact, the following examples, which involve English relative clauses, show that the distance between a relative pronoun and the position it binds is in fact unbounded.

(37) a. kid who [Kelly likes ____]
      b. kid who [Kelly believes [Terry likes ____]]
      c. kid who [Kelly believes [Terry knows [Robin likes ____]]]

In English, unbounded dependencies also occur in questions, in topicalizations, in clefts and bare relatives, and in the complements to some predicates such as *easy*.

(38) a. Who does Kelly [believe [Robin voted for ____]]?
      b. That politician there, [Kelly believes [Terry voted for ____]].
      c. It is a Democrat that [Kelly believes [Robin voted for ____]].
      d. Who [Kelly believes [Terry liked ____]] is Francis.
      e. That theorem is easy [to believe [you thought [you proved ____]]].

The key to almost every contemporary theory of unbounded dependencies can be seen in the analysis of the complement of the relative pronoun as an incomplete sentence that could be completed by the insertion of a noun phrase at a particular point (indicated by an underscore). The mechanism by which these theories relate the vacant position and the relative pronoun varies greatly. Transformational theories, such as GB, postulate that the relative pronoun is initially found at the vacant position and then moved to its final position, leaving behind a *trace*, which shares some of the properties of the phrase being moved. Phrase structure theories, such as GPSG and HPSG, whether they postulate a trace or not, relate the position of the extraction to the binding relative pronoun by incrementally signaling the extraction of an element in each of the nodes dominating the vacant position. We will see that in our type-logical categorial grammar formalism, a third option is open to us.

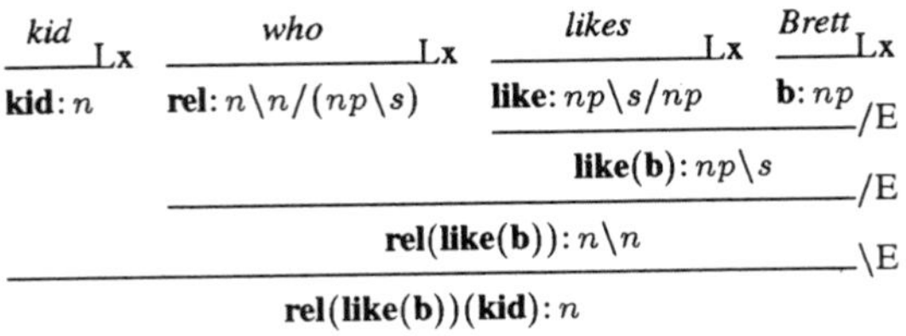

$$
\frac{\dfrac{kid}{\textbf{kid}:n}\text{Lx} \quad \dfrac{who}{\textbf{rel}:n\backslash n/(np\backslash s)}\text{Lx} \quad \dfrac{\dfrac{likes}{\textbf{like}:np\backslash s/np}\text{Lx} \quad \dfrac{Brett}{\textbf{b}:np}\text{Lx}}{\dfrac{\textbf{like}(\textbf{b}):np\backslash s}{}/\text{E}}}{\dfrac{\textbf{rel}(\textbf{like}(\textbf{b})):n\backslash n}{\textbf{rel}(\textbf{like}(\textbf{b}))(\textbf{kid}):n}\backslash\text{E}}/\text{E}
$$

Figure 6.13
A derivation of *kid who likes Brett*

6.3.1   The Lambek Calculus and Unbounded Dependencies

Within the pure Lambek calculus, it is tempting to assign categories such as the following to relative pronouns:

(39) a. *who* $\Rightarrow$ **rel**: $n\backslash n/(np\backslash s)$
      b. *whom* $\Rightarrow$ **rel**: $n\backslash n/(s/np)$
      c. **rel** $\overset{\text{def}}{=} \lambda V.\lambda P.\lambda x. V(x) \wedge P(x)$

Note that the semantic term assigned is simple set intersection, and it is of the appropriate type for both the object-relative and subject-relative pronouns. The first category, (39a), could be used for subject relatives, such as the following.

(40) a. kid who [hit Jo]
      b. kid who [believes Francis hit Jo]

In these cases there is no unboundedness, because the subject position is adjacent to the relative clause and the complement can be analyzed as a verb phrase. In fact, nothing more than the applicative categorial grammar is necessary. This can be seen in figure 6.13. Expanding the semantics gives us the following analysis:

(41) *kid who likes Brett* $\Rightarrow \lambda x.\textbf{like}(\textbf{b})(x) \wedge \textbf{kid}(x):n$

We can contrast this analysis with one in which the extracted element is made explicit, as shown in figure 6.14. Because of η-conversion, the resulting semantics is the same either way. With (39b) we can analyze the following examples by deriving the bracketed material as category s/np.

(42) a. store which [Kelly ran by]
      b. store which [Kelly ran by the corner of]
      c. store which [Kelly ran by the corner of the first floor of]

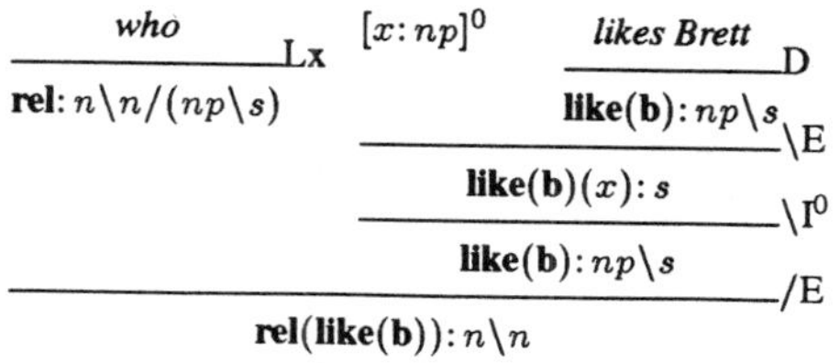
who
Lx
rel: $n\backslash n/(np\backslash s)$
$[x: np]^0$
likes Brett
D
like(b): $np\backslash s$
\E
like(b)(x): s
$\backslash I^0$
like(b): $np\backslash s$
/E
rel(like(b)): $n\backslash n$

Figure 6.14
A derivation of *who likes Brett*

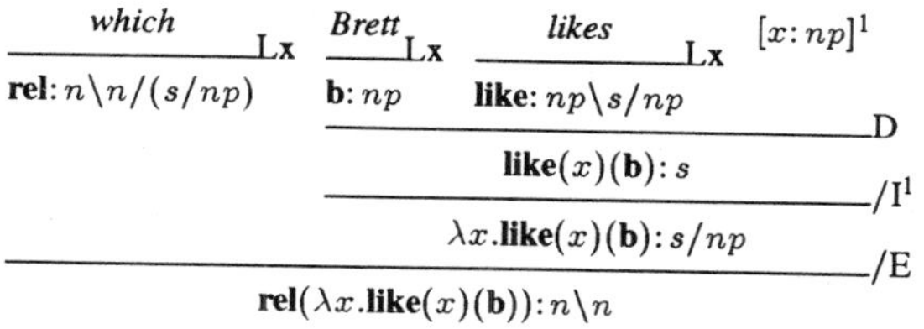
which
Lx
rel: $n\backslash n/(s/np)$
Brett
Lx
b: np
likes
Lx
like: $np\backslash s/np$
$[x: np]^1$
D
like(x)(b): s
$/I^1$
λx.like(x)(b): s/np
/E
rel(λx.like(x)(b)): $n\backslash n$

Figure 6.15
A derivation of *which Brett likes*

For instance, consider the derivation of the simple case in figure 6.15. Here the analogy to the derivation for the subject relative in figure 6.14 is obvious. When applied to a noun by application, we have the following analysis, after substituting the definition of **rel** and β-reducing.

(43) *city which Brett likes* $\Rightarrow \lambda x.\mathbf{city}(x) \wedge \mathbf{like}(x)(\mathbf{brett}): n$

Unfortunately, the categories assigned to the relative clause are not general enough. They do not account for cases, such as the following, in which the noun-phrase position bound by the relative is not peripheral in the complement sentence.

(44) a. kid who [Kelly liked ____ yesterday]
b. kid who [Jo believes ____ hit Brett]
c. kid who [Jo wanted ____ to mow the lawn]

This is because $np\backslash s$ is understood as making a sentence when combined with a noun phrase to its left, and similarly for s/np and a noun phrase to its right. Neither accounts for the internal case.

6.3.2 "Disharmonic" Combinations

Steedman (1985, 1987, 1988) allows a set of combinatorial possibilities that are underivable in Lambek's categorial grammar. Moortgat (1988b)

$$\frac{\textit{Jo hit}}{\lambda y.\mathbf{hit}(y)(\mathbf{Jo}):s/np}\ \mathrm{D} \qquad \frac{\textit{yesterday}}{\mathbf{yest}:s\backslash s}\ \mathrm{D}$$

$$\frac{}{\lambda x.\mathbf{yest}(\mathbf{hit}(x)(\mathbf{Jo})):s/np}\ *$$

Figure 6.16
A derivation under disharmonic composition

applied Steedman's scheme further to the study of morphology. Such schemes allow a directed s/np and $np\backslash s$ assignment for the complement of relative pronouns by deriving the category s/np even in cases of non-peripheral extraction. One combination scheme employed by Steedman is the following variant of composition:

(45) $\alpha: B/C,\ \beta: B\backslash A \Rightarrow \lambda x.\beta(\alpha(x)): A/C$

This allows analyses of nonperipheral extraction such as the that shown in figure 6.16 (where I ignore the semantics of *yesterday* for now).

Rules such as (45) are said to be *disharmonic*, in that they do not preserve the concatenative interpretation of the slashes. There are a total of sixteen such composition schemes involving categories of types $\sigma \to \tau$ and $\tau \to \rho$ (these result from four binary choices: the order of the first two arguments and the direction of the three slashes involved on the two arguments and the result). Only two of these, $A/B, B/C \Rightarrow A/C$ and $C\backslash B, B\backslash A \Rightarrow C\backslash A$, are derivable in the Lambek calculus. Steedman eliminates those in which the direction of the slash on the mother category is different than that on the daughter category. For instance, this methodology rules out $A/B, B/C \Rightarrow C\backslash A$ because the direction in which the C is sought has been lost. After this reduction, six disharmonic possibilities remain.

The disharmonic rules violate the interpretation of slashes as involving concatenation. Recall that an expression is assigned A/B if it can be concatenated to an expression of category B to form an expression of category A. Under such an interpretation, the disharmonic schemes are unsound. If e_1 is of category B/C and e_2 of category $B\backslash A$, this says nothing about $e_1 \cdot e_2$ being of category A/C. Furthermore, in the face of our logical schemes, even the admission of a single disharmonic-composition scheme results in a complete loss of sensitivity to order. For instance, with the scheme above, consider the derivation in figure 6.17. Steedman avoids this problem by limiting the applicability of some of his schemes to particular categories. For instance, Steedman might block the scheme in

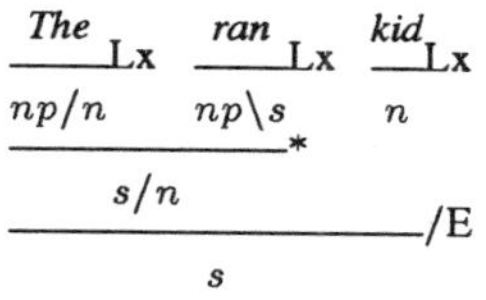

$$\dfrac{\dfrac{\textit{The}}{np/n}\text{Lx} \quad \dfrac{\textit{ran}}{np\backslash s}\text{Lx} \quad \dfrac{\textit{kid}}{n}\text{Lx}}{\dfrac{s/n}{s}\text{/E}}$$

Figure 6.17
Collapse of order under a disharmonic scheme

(45) from applying in the situation where $C = n$, thus blocking the derivation in figure 6.17. Rather than making such nonlogical restrictions on our proof theory, I turn to an alternative approach to unbounded dependencies.

6.3.3 Moortgat's Approach to Unboundedness

Rather than adopting the approach of the pure Lambek calculus to relative clauses and extraposition, I will adopt an alternative approach due to Moortgat (1988b, 1991). This analysis hinges on introducing an additional binary category constructor, $\uparrow$, which is used to construct categories of the form $A\uparrow B$. An expression is assigned to the category $A\uparrow B$ if it can be analyzed as an A with a B missing somewhere within it. For instance, $s\uparrow np$ is a sentence from which a noun phrase has been extracted. The category $s\uparrow np$ should be contrasted with s/np and $np\backslash s$, which indicate a sentence lacking a noun phrase on the right or left frontier, respectively.

DEFINITION: EXTRACTION CONSTRUCTOR   The construction and type rules for the *extraction constructor* are as follows:

a. If $A, B \in$ **Cat**, then $A\uparrow B \in$ **Cat**
b. $\text{Typ}(A\uparrow B) = \text{Typ}(B) \rightarrow \text{Typ}(A)$

Note that these clauses should be added to the recursive definition of types so that the extraction constructor can interact with the slashes in the construction of categories. Also note that the type of $A\uparrow B$ is the same as that of A/B and $B\backslash A$. The idea is that a relative pronoun will take an expression of category $s\uparrow np$ to produce a postnominal modifier.

The rule of proof for the extraction constructor is straightforward, and I first present it in sequent form. It is just like the right rules for the slashes, only the assumption corresponding to the extracted element is allowed to occur within the premises rather than peripherally.

$$\dfrac{\mathbf{k}\!:\!np,\ \mathbf{like}\!:\!np\backslash s,\ x\!:\!np,\ \mathbf{yest}\!:\!s\backslash s \Rightarrow \lambda x.\mathbf{yest}(\mathbf{like}(x)(\mathbf{k}))\!:\!s}{\mathbf{k}\!:\!np,\ \mathbf{like}\!:\!np\backslash s,\ \mathbf{yest}\!:\!s\backslash s \Rightarrow \lambda x.\mathbf{yest}(\mathbf{like}(x)(\mathbf{k}))\!:\!s{\uparrow}np}\ {\uparrow}\mathrm{R}$$
D

$$\dfrac{\mathbf{k}\!:\!np,\ \mathbf{bel}\!:\!np\backslash s/s,\ x\!:\!np,\ \mathbf{hit}\!:\!np\backslash s/np,\ \mathbf{b}\!:\!np \Rightarrow \mathbf{bel}(\mathbf{hit}(\mathbf{b})(x))(\mathbf{k})\!:\!s}{\mathbf{k}\!:\!np,\ \mathbf{bel}\!:\!np\backslash s/s,\ \mathbf{hit}\!:\!np\backslash s/np,\ \mathbf{b}\!:\!np \Rightarrow \lambda x.\mathbf{bel}(\mathbf{hit}(\mathbf{b})(x))(\mathbf{k})\!:\!s{\uparrow}np}\ {\uparrow}\mathrm{R}$$
D

Figure 6.18
Medial extraction using gap introduction

DEFINITION: EXTRACTION SEQUENT SCHEME   The sequent scheme for the
extraction constructor is the following:

$$\dfrac{\Gamma_1,\ x\!:\!A,\ \Gamma_2 \Rightarrow \alpha\!:\!B}{\Gamma_1,\ \Gamma_2 \Rightarrow \lambda x.\alpha\!:\!B{\uparrow}A}\ {\uparrow}\mathrm{R} \qquad\qquad [x\ \text{fresh}]$$

As with our other right rules, we must be careful to use a fresh variable x
of the appropriate type for A in the rule to avoid accidental variable
capture. As an example, consider the three problematic cases of nonfinal
extraction in (44) above, the analyses of the first two of which are shown
in figure 6.18.

The natural-deduction formulation of extraction introduction follows
the pattern of the slash-introduction schemes.

DEFINITION: NATURAL-DEDUCTION EXTRACTION INTRODUCTION   The natural deduction rule for *extraction introuction* is this:

$$\dfrac{\begin{array}{ccc} \vdots & [x\!:\!A]^n & \vdots \\ \vdots & \vdots & \vdots \\ & \alpha\!:\!B & \end{array}}{\lambda x.\alpha\!:\!B{\uparrow}A}\ {\uparrow}\mathrm{I}^n$$

The ellipsis notation here is meant to indicate that the assumption category can occur anywhere in the sequence of assumptions. Unlike the
other rules, we do not insist that there be additional assumptions, so we
will be able to derive $\lambda x.x\!:\!np{\uparrow}np$ from the empty string. Note that
this is the syntactic and semantic category assigned to traces (a kind of
category assigned to the empty string) in theories such as HPSG and
GPSG. This is because the argument of the extraction constructor, ${\uparrow}$,
serves the same purpose as the value of the feature "SLASH" in these

$$\frac{\vdots \qquad [x:B]^n}{\dfrac{\alpha:A/B}{\dfrac{\alpha(x):A}{\lambda x.\alpha(x):A{\uparrow}B}{\uparrow}I^n}}/E$$

Figure 6.19
Extractions from slashes

theories. The arguments of our directed slashes, $/$ and $\backslash$, can then be seen to correspond to the value of the "subcategorization" feature of HPSG. Pollard and Sag (1994) provide motivation in terms of feature agreement for subcategorizing the unified-slash feature used for unbounded dependencies in GPSG into three varieties: for questions, for relative clauses, and for extractions such as topicalizations. We could, of course, follow the same strategy and distinguish several variants of the $\uparrow$ constructor.

It should also be noted that with the extraction constructor we can derive $A{\uparrow}B$ anywhere we could derive A/B or $B\backslash A$. An object-level proof of this property for forward slashes is shown in figure 6.19. Note that $\lambda x.\alpha(x)$ and α are provably equivalent by η-reduction, given that we have chosen x to be a fresh variable. The dual result obviously holds for backward slashes. These derivations correspond to the rule proposed by Pollard and Sag (1994) for moving a category from the subcategorization list to the slash list, and thus eliminating traces from their analyses of unbounded dependencies.

With the extraction constructor at hand, all we need to analyze relative clauses is the following lexical entry:

(46) *who* $\Rightarrow$ **rel**: $n\backslash n/(s{\uparrow}np)$

Note that we have the same semantic type and have assigned the same semantic term as we did in slash-based lexical assignments in (39). The lexical assignment in (46) allows us to analyze not only the unbounded cases of relative clauses we saw above but also cases where the superordinate subject is what is missing in the complement sentence. For instance, consider the derivations in figure 6.20. Of course, the cases of medial extraction, shown in figure 6.18, serve as perfectly good complements for relative pronouns as well. Thus we are able to produce the following analyses:

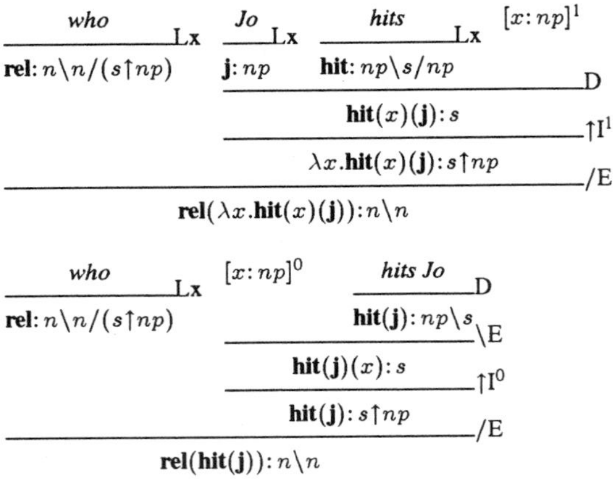

$$
\frac{
\frac{who}{\textbf{rel}: n\backslash n/(s{\uparrow}np)}\text{Lx}
\quad
\dfrac{
\frac{Jo}{\textbf{j}: np}\text{Lx}
\quad
\dfrac{
\frac{hits}{\textbf{hit}: np\backslash s/np}\text{Lx}
\quad
[x:np]^1
}{
\dfrac{
\dfrac{\textbf{hit}(x)(\textbf{j}): s}{\lambda x.\textbf{hit}(x)(\textbf{j}): s{\uparrow}np}{\uparrow}\text{I}^1
}{}
}\text{D}
}{}
}{\textbf{rel}(\lambda x.\textbf{hit}(x)(\textbf{j})): n\backslash n}
$$
/E

$$
\frac{
\frac{who}{\textbf{rel}: n\backslash n/(s{\uparrow}np)}\text{Lx}
\quad
\dfrac{
[x:np]^0
\quad
\dfrac{hits\ Jo}{\textbf{hit}(\textbf{j}): np\backslash s}\text{D}
}{
\dfrac{\textbf{hit}(\textbf{j})(x): s}{\textbf{hit}(\textbf{j}): s{\uparrow}np}{\uparrow}\text{I}^0
}\backslash\text{E}
}{\textbf{rel}(\textbf{hit}(\textbf{j})): n\backslash n}\text{/E}
$$

Figure 6.20
Examples of subject and object relative clauses

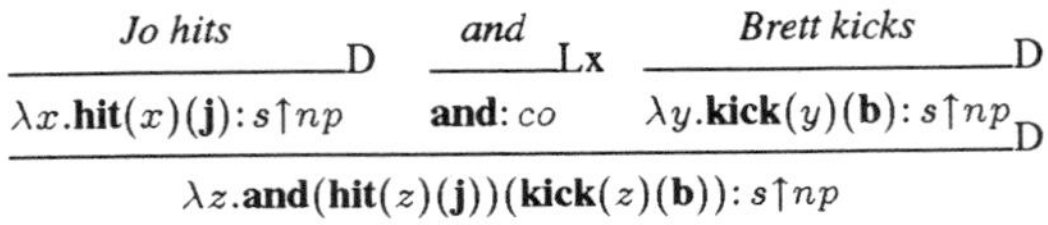

$$
\frac{
\dfrac{Jo\ hits}{\lambda x.\textbf{hit}(x)(\textbf{j}): s{\uparrow}np}\text{D}
\quad
\dfrac{and}{\textbf{and}: co}\text{Lx}
\quad
\dfrac{Brett\ kicks}{\lambda y.\textbf{kick}(y)(\textbf{b}): s{\uparrow}np}\text{D}
}{\lambda z.\textbf{and}(\textbf{hit}(z)(\textbf{j}))(\textbf{kick}(z)(\textbf{b})): s{\uparrow}np}\text{D}
$$

Figure 6.21
A derivation of *Jo hits and Brett kicks*

(47)   a. *who Jo belives hit Brett* $\Rightarrow$ $\textbf{rel}(\lambda x.\textbf{bel}(\textbf{hit}(\textbf{b})(x))(\textbf{j}))$

      b. *who Jo hit yesterday* $\Rightarrow$ $\textbf{rel}(\lambda x.\textbf{yest}(\textbf{hit}(x)(\textbf{j})))$

In fact, it should be obvious from the form of the rule for $\uparrow$ introduction that we can produce the category $s{\uparrow}np$ for any expression that we can analyze as an s by inserting an np. I leave further examples as exercises.

Note that coordination extends to the extraction constructor in the natural way. Thus we derive *across-the-board extraction*, so called because if something is extracted out of one side of a coordination, it must be extracted out of both sides. This constraint was first noted by Ross (1967). An example is shown in figure 6.21.

6.3.4   Islands and Extractability

It is well known that relative pronouns cannot be linked to arbitrary positions within a sentence. Some structures seem to block elements from being extracted from within them. For instance, consider the following examples, all of which are typically assumed to be ungrammatical (although judgements seem to vary fairly widely across speakers).

(48) a. *who [[Brett sneezed] and [Jo kicked ____]]
     b. *which [I read the news [without noticing ____]]
     c. *who [I believe [that [____ ran]]]
     d. *who [[the picture of ____] disturbed Brett]
     e. *which [Jo likes the director [who$_1$ ____$_1$ made ____]]
     f. *which [Jo holds [the belief that Francis likes ____]]

In each case, the context out of which we have extracted is problematic. In the first case, (48a), extraction is out of a coordinate structure. In the second case, (48b), the extraction is out of an adverbial modifier. In the third case, (48c), the position is that of the subject of an embedded complementized sentence. In the fourth case, (48d), extraction is out of a subject. In (48e), it is out of a relative clause (note the indicated linking of the embedded subject to the embedded relative). And in (48f), it is out of a complex noun-phrase complement. Such contexts have come to be known as *islands* to extraction, following their discovery and classification by Ross (1967).

In the logical categorial grammar I have presented, all of the examples in (48) will be derivable, contrary to the facts. The islandhood of these contexts has been addressed within the context of categorial grammar by means of modal constructors that act like locks and keys on extraction (Hepple 1990a; Morrill 1989a, 1992b, 1994a; Moortgat 1994a, in press). In other words, subconstituents such as relative clauses are locked, and the hypothesized noun phrase at the site of the trace does not have the key to get past this stage. Similar methods have been used to enforce locality on the binding of reflexive pronouns.

Although this logical categorial grammar generates all of the grammatical across-the-board extractions, it does not rule out coordinations in which extraction is not across-the-board, as in the following examples:

(49) a. *whom [$_{s/np}$ Jo liked Robin and Bill met ____]
     b. *whom [$_{s/np}$ Jo liked Robin and ____]

The derivations are straightforward, and I leave them for exercise 9. There are also unwanted instantiations of the coordination scheme that allow coordinators and other categories to coordinate, as in the following examples:

(50) a. *The $[_{n/n}$ [kid and] or [dog and]] cat ran.

   b. *Sandy ran $[_{s \backslash s/s}$ and or or] Kim jumped.

As shown by Morrill (1994a, 1995), such unwarranted coordinations can be blocked by a judicious use of island constraints on extractions.

6.3.5 Incompleteness of the Extraction Constructor

Clearly there is something missing on the logical side of the calculus for the extraction constructor. This can be seen by the lack of a left rule in the sequent calculus and an elimination rule in the natural-deduction presentation. That is, there is no rule governing the use of an expression assigned to category $A \uparrow B$. Intuitively, the rule of use should match the rule of proof. An expression of category $A \uparrow B$ should wrap around an expression of category B to produce an expression of category A. For instance, if *Jo met yesterday* is assigned $s \uparrow np$ and *Francis* is assigned np, we should be able to combine the two to analyze *Jo met Francis yesterday* as an s. But the reason this cannot be done soundly is that with our implicitly ordered sequents, we have no way to indicate the position at which the noun phrase was extracted out of the expression of category $s \uparrow np$. We can wrap *Jo met yesterday* around an np to produce a sentence only if the noun phrase is inserted between *met* and *yesterday*.

To get around these problems, Solias and Morrill (Solias 1992, Morrill and Solias 1993) proposed interpreting the expression associated with an $A \uparrow B$ be a pair $\langle e_1, e_2 \rangle$, with the result of wrapping around an expression e of category B being $e_1 \cdot e \cdot e_3$. Besides getting closer to the right logic of extraction, Solias and Morrill were able to handle cases such as the following:

(51) a. Jo hung the phone up.

   b. Jo gave Dana a hug.

In the first case, (51a), a particle verb like *hang up* can be assigned to the category $(np \backslash s) \uparrow np$ and analyzed as wrapping around its object to produce a verb phrase. Similarly, in (51b) we can attach the indirect object *a hug* first in *give Dana a hug* by assuming that *give a hug* wraps around *Dana* in the analysis just as in the case of the particle verb. This turns out to be useful in dealing with cases of reflexive pronoun binding, as we will see in section 9.4. This notion of wrapping as a mode of combination on a par with concatenation goes back to the Montagovian categorial grammar of Bach (1981a, 1984); Reape (1989) revived and generalized the operation of wrapping and applied it to Germanic word order in an HPSG setting.

In addition to these cases, Morrill and Solias treated instances of so-called *gapping*, a canonical instance of which is as follows:

(52) [Jo ate beans] and [Robin _____ toast].

They analyzed *Jo ate beans* as a pair consisting of a wrapper $\langle Jo, beans\rangle$ of category $s{\uparrow}(np\backslash s/np)$, representing a sentence with a transitive verb extracted. A transitive verb such as *ate*, can then be assigned its usual category $np\backslash s/np$ and then used as an argument around which $\langle Jo, beans\rangle$ is wrapped. The second conjunct is analyzed as $s{\uparrow}(np\backslash s/np)$ and the extracted transitive verb used in both contexts. Morrill and Solias were thus able to provide an interpretation within type-logical categorial grammar of Steedman's (1990) categorial methodology for gapping. Morrill (1994a, 1995) refines their approach even further in a multimodal categorial grammar that allows finer control over extraction. P. Hendriks (1995) also provides an analysis of gapping in the context of her analysis of comparatives.

Although such a refinement of the sorting of expressions assigned to categories allows a rule of use to be formulated for $\uparrow$, it is not as general as might be desired. For instance, it is not clear how to employ categories such as $n\backslash n/(s{\uparrow}np)$ when the argument expression $s{\uparrow}np$ is interpreted as a tuple or how to provide examples such as $s{\uparrow}np{\uparrow}np$ in which multiple extractions occur simultaneously. The issue of the completeness of the extraction constructor will arise again when we consider quantification.

Exercises

1. Provide a derivation to an equivalent semantics for each of the following sentences.

(a) [The ball in the box] or [the pyramid on the box] is hard.

(b) [The ball in] or [the pyramid on] the box is hard.

(c) The [ball in] or [pyramid on] the box is hard.

2. How many derivations are there in our grammar for the following relative clauses?

(a) professor who Jo likes the person who _____ knows _____

(b) professor who Jo likes the person who Francis talked to _____ about _____

Treat *talked* as taking two prepositionally case-marked *np* complements. Are all of the analyses appropriate readings for these sentences, and are there any appropriate readings of these sentences that are not derived?

3. Provide derivations for the following multiple nonconstituent coordinations.

(a) [[Jo showed] and [Brett sold]] [Francis the book] and [Robin the record].

(b) [[Jo drove] and [Brett biked]] [[the track on Monday] and [the road on Tuesday]].

(c) [[I liked] but [Brett disliked]] [[the red] and [the green]] t-shirts.

4. Consider how our analysis of unbounded dependencies can be extended to account for the semantics of so-called *parasitic gaps*, such as the following:

(a) papers which I file _____ if I read _____

(b) cities which kids in _____ hate _____

(c) kids which I show pictures of _____ to _____

(d) paper that the reviewer of _____ files _____ without reading _____

What is significant about these cases is that there are multiple extractions for one relative pronoun. It is probably best, for the sake of this exercise, to ignore the fact that one of the extractions in each of these examples is parasitic and cannot occur in isolation, as in the following:

(e)   magazines which I file _____ if I read *Vogue*

(f) *magazines which I file *Vogue* if I read _____

(g)   magazines which I file _____ if I read _____

(h)   cities which kids in London hate _____

(i) *cities which kids in _____ hate London

(j)   cities which kids in _____ hate _____

5. Extend our analysis of coordination to nonbinary coordination for cases such as these:

(a) man, woman, or child

(b) ran, jumped, and fell

Consider how the grammar can be extended to deal with noninfix coordinators such as *either-or* and *if-then* in examples such as the following:

(c) Jo either ran or jumped.

(d) Jo neither ran nor jumped.

(e) If Jo ran, then he jumped.

6. The lexical category $np\backslash s/(n/n)$ for the copula is not unproblematic. Show how the rules of proof for the slashes provide analyses for the following ungrammatical examples:

(a) *The block is $[big_{n/n}\ red_{n/n}]_{n/n}$.

(b) *Jo is $[[in\ the\ park]_{n\backslash n}\ [who\ Francis\ likes]_{n\backslash n}]_{n\backslash n}$.

Explain how this problem is solved by assuming that the complement of the copula is a predicative of category *pr* rather than either a forward-directed or backward-directed nominal modifier. (Milward 1994)

7. Provide a derivation of the following ill-formed example.

(a) *The [red] and [man in the] park sneezed.

What should we conclude from this concerning islandhood?

8. Provide a lexical entry for the possessive relative *whose*, and show how it can be used to derive the following examples:

(a) the student whose paper Brett liked

(b) the student whose paper upset Brett

9. Show how the across-the-board constraint violations in (49) can be generated using our grammar. (Hint: For (49b), the extracted noun phrase must be type-raised and coordinated with the object *Robin*.)

10. Show that there are two distinct analyses of the first sentence below, one of which is synonymous with the second sentence and one of which is synonymous with the third.

(a) Sandy didn't run and jump.

(b) Sandy didn't run or Sandy didn't jump.

(c) Sandy didn't run and Sandy didn't jump.

Assume the following lexical entry for negation.

(d) *didn't* $\Rightarrow \lambda V.\lambda x. \neg V(x): np\backslash s/(np\backslash s)$

(Hint: To derive a reading of the first sentence that is logically equivalent to the only reading of the third, raise the verb phrases of the first sentence to the syntactic category $(np\backslash s/(np\backslash s))\backslash np\backslash s$ before coordination.)

11. Using the sequent calculus, determine which of the directions of the following bi-implication are valid.

(a) $A \vee (B \wedge C) \Leftrightarrow (A \vee B) \wedge (A \vee C)$

Show the derivations of the distributivity of disjunction over concatenation.

(b) $A \cdot (B \vee C) \Leftrightarrow (A \cdot B) \vee (A \cdot C)$

12. Categories A and B are said to be *conjoinable* if there is a category C such that $A \Rightarrow C$ and $B \Rightarrow C$. Show that two categories A and B are conjoinable if and only if there exists a category D such that $D \Rightarrow A$ and $D \Rightarrow B$. (Hint: Following Pentus [1994], given C, set D to be $(A/C) \cdot C \cdot (C\backslash B)$; Lambek employed a more general category. A similar category can be found to establish the converse. Pentus [1994] also showed the notion of conjoinability to be definable, but the proof is rather complex and makes crucial use of group theory.)

Lambek (1958) defined the notion of category *equivalence* in the obvious way, by taking the minimal equivalence relation on categories containing the rewriting relation. This can be achieved by closing the rewriting relation under transitivity and symmetry (it is already closed under reflexivity). This amounts to defining $A \equiv B$ if and only if there are $C_1, \ldots, C_n$ such that $A = C_1$, $B = C_2$ and $C_i \Rightarrow C_{i+1}$ or $C_{i+1} \Rightarrow C_i$ for $0 < i < n$. Demonstrate that two categories are equivalent according to this definition if and only if they are conjoinable. (Hint: Using the above equivalence, redirect the rewrite arrows so that they all point in the same direction.) (Lambek 1958, Pentus 1994, Versmissen 1996)

13. By analogy to our entry for the definite *the* and to the relative pronouns, provide a lexical entry for the *free relative* pronoun *who* that derives the right meanings for the following sentences:

(a) [Who Jo likes ⎯⎯] is Francis.

(b) [Who Jo liked yesterday ⎯⎯] is Francis.

14. Provide a derivation of the following, and show the semantic result. (Hint: Use the derivation in figure 6.10.)

$$\alpha\colon (A \wedge B)/C \Rightarrow ?\colon (A/C) \wedge (B/C)$$

15. Consider generalizing negation to apply to arbitrary boolean categories as conjunction and disjunction were generalized. Which syntactic categories in English allow negation, and how can negation be realized in such cases (as the negative particle *not* or the prefix *non-*)? From this evidence, what is your conclusion concerning the utility of generalizing negation?

16. Recall the definition of the pointwise order $\leq$ on boolean domains introduced in exercise 14, chapter 3. Show that generalized conjunction and disjunction are just least upper bounds and greatest lower bounds with respect to $\leq$. Show that generalized negation (see the previous exercise) produces a unique element $\neg f$ such that $\neg f \wedge f = \bot$ and $\neg f \vee f = \top$, where $\bot$ and $\top$ are the least and greatest elements of their respective domains.

Chapter 7

Quantifiers and Scope

The purpose of this chapter is to provide a grammatical account of the contribution of quantified noun phrases to the meanings of phrases in which they occur. Logically, generalized quantifiers can be characterized as functions from properties to propositions, with determiners acting as functions from properties into generalized quantifiers. It remains to explain how quantifiers remain *in situ* yet take semantic scope around an arbitrary amount of surrounding material. As a minimal illustration, consider the following sentences with quantified subjects and objects.

(1) a. Every kid played with some toy.
    b. Some kid broke every toy.

These sentences provide the simplest possible example of *scope ambiguity*. The first sentence has two readings, distinguished by the *scope* of the quantifiers $\mathbf{every}^2(\mathbf{kid})$ and $\mathbf{some}^2(\mathbf{toy})$ (recall that the superscript 2 indicates a constant of generalized determiner type).

(2) a. $\mathbf{every}^2(\mathbf{kid})(\lambda x.\mathbf{some}^2(\mathbf{toy})(\lambda y.\mathbf{play}(y)(x)))$
    b. $\mathbf{some}^2(\mathbf{toy})(\lambda y.\mathbf{every}^2(\mathbf{kid})(\lambda x.\mathbf{play}(y)(x)))$

Under the first reading, (2a), every kid may have played with a different toy. In this reading, *every kid* is said to take *wide scope*, and *some toy narrow scope*. Under the second reading, (2b), there must be some toy such that every kid played with that toy. Thus the second reading, (2b), where the object quantifier takes wide scope over the subject quantifier, entails the first reading. From this fact alone, it might be tempting to claim that (2a) is the only relevant reading, as its truth is entailed by the truth of the other proposed reading. But now notice that although there is also an entailment between the two readings of (1b), it is the subject wide-scope reading that entails the object wide-scope reading. Similarly, by negating the predicate, any entailment relations between quantifier scopings will be reversed. Furthermore, with other quantifiers, such as *many* and *most*, there is no entailment relationship between the two relative scopings. It is simply not sufficient to provide a quantifier narrow scope at the point at which it can be thought to act as an argument.

In this chapter I extend the type-logical approach of the previous chapters to provide an adequate grammatical characterization of scoping phenomena. Before doing so, I first survey the two most historically significant approaches to quantifier scoping, Montague's quantifying-in scheme and Cooper's storage mechanism. I also briefly survey H. Hendriks' (1987) highly influential type-shifting approach to quantification. The first truly logical approach to quantification was provided by van Benthem (1986a), who introduced a variant of the Lambek calculus that allowed arguments (including quantifiers) to permute, thus allowing all possible quantifier scopings. Unfortunately, this system overgenerated in that it allowed the arguments to functions to be confused, deriving readings for sentences like *Every kid owned a dog* in which there is a single dog that owns every kid!

Following the work of van Benthem and Hendriks, Moortgat (1990a) introduced an elegant type-logical solution to the puzzle of scope by introducing a scoping constructor to account for the nonlocal semantic behavior of quantifiers in a compositional fashion. With Moortgat's scoping constructor, the permutability of quantifiers in terms of scope can be captured without losing sensitivity to which arguments go with which functions. The scoping constructor is intimately related to the extraction constructor ↑, also introduced by Moortgat, in that both enable binding at a distance. The grammatically distinguishing factor is that the binding quantifier itself remains *in situ*, marking the position of binding. In order to bind the position occupied by the quantifier, the scoping construct builds a derivation with an extracted element in much the same way as the extraction constructor ↑. Pereira (1990) independently introduced a similar deductive approach to quantifier scoping. Although Pereira was not working in the context of type-logical grammar, his approach was isomorphic to Moortgat's in the scope derivations it predicted for quantifiers scoping at the sentential level. But because Pereira did not introduce a general connective for quantifiers and did not integrate his approach into a general type logic for concatenation such as Lambek's categorial grammar, the resulting approach is somewhat less general. More recently, Dalrymple et al. (1995) have incorporated an approach similar to van

Benthem's and Pereira's into LFG. They synchronize functions and arguments by projecting LFG's syntactic representations into a set of linear-logic formulas, over which derivations in the style of van Benthem can be carried out without any danger of losing control of which arguments go with which functions. The multistratal LFG and linear-logic approach is almost identical to the method I adopt here in terms of the derivations it allows, although subtle differences arise because of the generality of linear logic relative to our type logics.

In this chapter we focus on singular quantifiers and determiners. Next, in chapter 8, I provide an account of plurality in which scope plays a crucial role. As we will see in chapter 9, the type-logical approach to scoping admits natural categorizations for other *in situ* binders, such as reflexive and reciprocal pronouns, as well as relative pronouns that participate in pied-piping.

7.1 QUANTIFYING IN

The most well known and widely studied approach to quantifier scoping phenomena is that of Montague, as embodied in his PTQ grammar (Montague 1973). In the PTQ fragment, Montague admits an infinite number of pronoun lexical entries. Below is a slight simplification of his scheme (he actually treated all noun phrases as denoting generalized quantifiers and type-raised pronoun entries accordingly).

(3) $he_n \Rightarrow x_n : np$

To account for quantifier scoping, Montague adopted a general scheme of *quantifying in*, the simplest case of which can be translated into our notation as follows (assuming an atomic category gq for generalized quantifiers with our standard extensional semantic typing).

(4) if $e \cdot he_n \cdot e'' \Rightarrow \phi : s$ and $e' \Rightarrow \alpha : gq$, then $e \cdot e' \cdot e'' \Rightarrow \alpha(\lambda x_n . \phi) : s$

(Quantifying in)

This rule can be illustrated by starting with the derivations in (5).

(5) a. he_5 *ran* $\Rightarrow$ **run**$(x_5) : s$
     b. *everyone* $\Rightarrow$ **every** : gq

We can now quantify (5b) into (5a) to produce the following result:

(6) *everyone ran* $\Rightarrow$ **every**$(\lambda x_5 . \mathbf{run}(x_5)) : s$

Here we matched the quantifying-in scheme with $e = \varepsilon$ (the empty string), $e' = everyone$, and $e'' = ran$.

By iteratively quantifying in, we can derive relative scope ambiguities. For instance, assume we have the following derived results:

(7) a. *he₄ likes him₇* $\Rightarrow$ $\mathbf{like}(x_7)(x_4)$
    b. *someone* $\Rightarrow$ $\mathbf{some}$: gq

Then by quantifying into (7a), we have the following derivations:

(8) a. *everyone likes he₇* $\Rightarrow$ $\mathbf{every}(\lambda x_4 . \mathbf{like}(x_7)(x_4))$: s,
    b. *everyone likes someone* $\Rightarrow$ $\mathbf{some}(\lambda x_7 . \mathbf{every}(\lambda x_4 . \mathbf{like}(x_7)(x_4)))$: s

(9) a. *he₄ likes someone* $\Rightarrow$ $\mathbf{some}(\lambda x_7 . \mathbf{like}(x_7)(x_4))$: s
    b. *everyone likes someone* $\Rightarrow$ $\mathbf{every}(\lambda x_4 . \mathbf{some}(\lambda x_7 . \mathbf{like}(x_7)(x_4)))$: s

In the first derivation, (8), we reduced the subject and then the object, giving the object widest scope. In the second derivation, (9), the order is reversed.

In chapter 9 we consider the full generality of Montague's quantifying-in scheme, which he also used to account for pronominal binding. There will also be ample opportunity to explore further consequences of the quantifying-in scheme, some of which are desirable and some of which are not, by way of comparison with the type-logical approach.

7.2   COOPER STORAGE

Before moving on to present the type-logical approach to scoping phenomena, I briefly describe the storage-based approach to scoping introduced and elaborated by Cooper (1975, 1979, 1983). One of Cooper's primary goals was to eliminate the operation of quantifying in from the syntactic domain, thus isolating the effects of quantification in the semantics.

Cooper generalized the notion of meaning along two dimensions. The first generalization enables quantifiers to apply nonlocally without modifying the structure of the syntactic derivations. That is, quantifier binding is transparent to the syntactic schemes that attach noun phrases as arguments. To achieve this effect, Cooper assumed that a meaning consisted not only of a semantic term of the appropriate type but also a record of quantifiers inherited through the derivation from subexpressions. More specifically, a meaning is taken to be a pair α; Q in which α is a λ-term of the appropriate semantic type (perhaps with free variables) and Q is

Table 7.1
Cooper's stored quantifiers for *Everyone likes someone*

Semantic term	Store
like$(y)(x)$	$x/$**every**, $y/$**some**
every$(\lambda x.\textbf{like}(y)(x))$	$y/$**some**
some$(\lambda y.\textbf{like}(y)(x))$	$x/$**every**
some$(\lambda y.\textbf{every}(\lambda x.\textbf{like}(y)(x)))$	ε
every$(\lambda x.\textbf{some}(\lambda y.\textbf{like}(y)(x)))$	ε

a (possibly empty) sequence of variable/quantifier pairs, known as the *store*. The variables paired with the quantifiers indicate which variables they bind.

For example, *everyone likes someone* is analyzed syntactically as a sentence, with the set of meanings in table 7.1. The first meaning has both quantifiers in storage, the next two have one of the quantifiers in storage, and the last two have no quantifiers in storage. Thus only the last two semantic terms count as readings of the sentence as a whole; the first three are incomplete with respect to the resolution of quantifier scope.

Cooper's second generalization was to associate each syntactic analysis not with a single meaning but with a set of meanings, each of which consisted of a term and a store, as above. This move is significant in that it allows a single phrase-structure scheme to behave nondeterministically, producing a set of results representing the possible ambiguities induced by quantification. With these two generalizations, Cooper was able to generalize the semantics attached to phrase-structure schemes so as to generate all of the readings in table 7.1 with a single syntactic analysis.

Cooper's grammar can be generated by starting with an ordinary phrase-structure grammar that associates single meanings with categories. Such a grammar can be extended to handle first stores and then sets of meanings. For illustration, I provide a pair of rules that construct a sentence out of a transitive verb and two arguments. These two rule schemes were first introduced by Montague (1973), albeit in a more general, intensional setting.

(10) a. $x: gq, \ y: vp \Rightarrow x(y): s$
    b. $x: tv, \ y: gq \Rightarrow x(y): vp$

These schemes illustrate the way in which both Cooper and Montague type-lift noun-phrase arguments to be quantifiers (and hence why

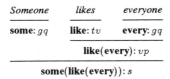

Figure 7.1
In situ quantifier binding

Montague's entries for pronouns *he$_n$* had to be assigned the type-raised quantifier term $\lambda P. P(x_n))$. The types can be induced from the terms and the type of generalized quantifiers; transitive verbs apply to their quantified objects to produce verb phrases, and subjects apply to verb phrases to produce sentences. Thus we have *vp* assigned type **Ind** $\rightarrow$ **Bool**, *gq* assigned (**Ind** $\rightarrow$ **Bool**) $\rightarrow$ **Bool**, and *tv* assigned ((**Ind** $\rightarrow$ **Bool**) $\rightarrow$ **Bool**) $\rightarrow$ **Ind** $\rightarrow$ **Bool**.

In this presentation of Cooper's grammar rule schemes, the daughter categories are assigned a variable semantics, and the mothers compound terms constructed out of the daughters' semantics. Enforcing this assumption in general leads to grammars that are wholly syntax-driven. That is, a rule can never fail to fire on the basis of its daughters' failing to match the input semantically. Furthermore, this form of rule allows the mother's semantics to be computed by variable substitution. For instance, with daughters $\alpha : gq$ and $\beta : vp$, the output produced by applying the scheme (10a) is $x(y)[x \mapsto \alpha][y \mapsto \beta] \overset{\text{def}}{=} \alpha(\beta)$, as is to be expected. Such a strategy follows Bach's (1989) notion of *rule-to-rule compositionality*, in which each grammar rule provides a combinator that computes the semantic term assigned to the mother as a function of the semantic terms assigned to the daughters. The combinator in the case of (10a) is $\lambda x. \lambda y. x(y)$; applying this to the terms assigned to the ordered sequence of daughters determines the semantics assigned to the mother.

As it stands, the phrase-structure schemes in (10) can only be used to scope quantifiers as they are consumed as arguments, as shown in figure 7.1. For extensional verbs such as *likes*, we have the meaning postulate in (11a), which was first introduced by Montague (1973).

(11) a. **like** $\overset{\text{def}}{=} \lambda Q. \lambda x. Q(\lambda y.\textbf{like}_p(y)(x))$

   b. **some**(**like**(**every**)) $\equiv$ **some**($\lambda x.\textbf{every}(\lambda y.\textbf{like}_p(y)(x))$)

Applying substitution and the postulate in (11a) leads to the reduction in (11b).

Cooper's first generalization extends rules such as those in (10) to allow for meanings that consist of term/store pairs. This is achieved as follows:

(12) if $x_1\colon C_1 \cdots x_n\colon C_n \Rightarrow \alpha\colon C_0$,
       then $x_1; Q_1\colon C_1 \cdots x_n; Q_n\colon C_n \Rightarrow \alpha; Q_1 \cdots Q_n\colon C_0$ (Percolation)

Here I have used Q_i as a variable ranging over sequences of variable/quantifier pairs. Note that the store associated with the mother category is simply the concatenation of the stores associated with the daughter categories. Further note that in a phrase-structure approach, the order of concatenation determines the order of quantifiers in the store, reflecting their linear order in the expression being analyzed. Cooper used this latter fact to prevent certain cases of backward-looking anaphora.

To extend the phrase-structure rules to sets, two important closure conditions are enforced. These two conditions allow quantifiers to be stored and retrieved. Percolating a quantifier in storage through the derivation to the point at which it is retrieved is already handled by (12). The first closure condition affects sets of meanings containing quantifiers. The second affects sets of meanings containing propositions.

(13) A set S of meanings is *closed* if and only if the following two
       conditions are satisfied:
       a. if $\alpha; Q \in S$, α of type (**Ind** $\rightarrow$ **Bool**) $\rightarrow$ **Bool**,
           then $\lambda P.P(x); x/\alpha \cdot Q \in S$ (Storage)
       b. if $\alpha; Q_1 \cdot x/\beta \cdot Q_2 \in S$, α of type **Bool**,
           then $\beta(\lambda x.\alpha); Q_1 \cdot Q_2 \in S$ (Scoping)

For example, by the storage condition, if S is closed and **every**; $\varepsilon \in S$, then $\lambda P.P(x); x/\textbf{every} \in S$ too. Furthermore, according to the scoping scheme, if $\textbf{run}(x); x/\textbf{every} \in S$ and S is closed, then $\textbf{every}(\lambda x.\textbf{run}(x)); \varepsilon \in S$. As usual, we can close an arbitrary set S of meanings by defining the function $\text{Close}(S) = T$ if and only if T is the least set such that $S \subseteq T$ and T is closed. Thus we can think of $\text{Close}(T)$ as freely applying quantifier scoping and storage.

Finally, to extend the phrase-structure rules that percolate stores to sets of meanings, we simply apply the rules pointwise to the input sets and close the result under the storage and scoping schemes.

(14) if $M_1\colon C_1 \cdots M_n\colon C_n \Rightarrow \Phi\colon C_0$,
       then $S_1\colon C_1 \cdots S_n\colon C_n \Rightarrow \text{Close}(\{\Phi[M_i \mapsto \alpha_i] \mid \alpha_i \in S_i\})\colon C_0$

Here I have used the variables M_i to range over term/store pairs and the variables S_i to range over sets of such term/store pairs. This scheme

Someone		_likes_	_everyone_	
$\lambda V.V(y)$;	$y/\textbf{some}$: gq	**like**: tv	$\lambda U.U(x)$;	$x/\textbf{every}$: gq
		like$(\lambda U.U(x))$;	$x/\textbf{every}$: vp	
$(\lambda V.V(y))(\textbf{like}(\lambda U.U(x)))$;		$y/\textbf{some} \cdot x/\textbf{every}$: s		

Figure 7.2
A Cooper storage derivation

basically says that a term/store pair appears in the mother category's meaning set if it can be derived by applying a rule to a sequence of meanings selected from the daughters' meaning sets. Furthermore, closure applies to generate new meanings by storage and scoping from this basic set of meanings; these derived meanings must also appear in the set of meanings assigned to the mother.

In figure 7.2, I provide a sample derivation where I have only included one member of the set of meanings at each node and have not performed any reductions on the terms. The storage-closure condition on quantifiers provided the derivations of the quantifiers. Given the meaning postulate for **like** in (11), the semantic term assigned to the sentential result in figure 7.2 reduces to **like**$_p(x)(y)$ by four applications of β-reduction. Application of the scoping-closure condition on propositions produces the remaining readings in table 7.1.

Cooper employed several filters on his closure conditions to prevent free variables and vacuous binding. We will explore some of these restrictions below when comparing Cooper storage to Moortgat's type-logical account of quantification. In that context I will discuss a more representative range of quantificational facts than can be captured by means of storage.

7.3 SCOPING CONSTRUCTOR

Many linguists seem to feel that if a semantic ambiguity has no distributional analogue, then its behavior should be characterized purely semantically. Because quantifiers share pretty much the same distribution as other noun phrases, issues of definiteness aside, Montague took the first opportunity to banish the syntactic distinction between quantifiers and other noun phrases. Because there seemed to be no syntactic distinction induced by the point at which a quantifier semantically applied, Cooper removed the syntactic structure associated with quantifying in, as well. Of course, I eschew this line of reasoning; in the type-logical approach, syntax is merely the vehicle by which expressions are associated with meanings. Thus it is not at all unnatural to find "syntactic" operations with "semantic" effects; they are merely two sides of the same coin.

As it turns out, the sequent presentation of the scoping constructor's rule of use bears a striking resemblance to Montague's quantifying-in scheme. Furthermore, the natural-deduction presentation of the logic is remarkably similar to Cooper storage. These similarities run so deep that the type-logical approach to scoping can be viewed as a rational reconstruction of the rather ad hoc approaches of Montague and Cooper (though, ironically, Moortgat's scoping constructor was intended as a logical reconstruction of H. Hendriks's [1987, 1993] type-shifting approach). In addition, the type-logical perspective on quantification sheds an enormous amount of light on what were once poorly understood connections between Cooper's storage mechanism and Montague's quantifying-in scheme. But the type-logical approach does not just rework earlier analyses in a logical light; throughout the rest of this chapter, I will demonstrate many ways in which the type-logical approach corrects serious shortcomings with both the quantifying-in and storage-based approaches to scoping. We will see examples in which quantifying in and Cooper storage lead to both overgeneration and undergeneration; several known holes in Montague's and Cooper's approaches have been patched by introducing further rules in the case of undergeneration and by introducing several kinds of filters in the case of overgeneration. The resulting analyses have neither the elegance nor the empirical adequacy of the type-logical approach. Not surprisingly, all of these shortcomings can be traced to the point at which Cooper storage and quantifying in break with the type-logical perspective.

Moortgat (1990a) introduced a binary connective to capture the behavior of quantifiers and other expressions that remain *in situ* syntactically while taking wider scope semantically. The use of such a connective is in keeping with the deductive tradition in type-logical grammars, in which category constructors are construed logically. Moortgat sought a logic in which the category $B \Uparrow A$ is assigned to expressions that act locally as Bs but take their semantic scope over an embedding expression of category A. For instance, a generalized quantifier will be given category $np \Uparrow s$ because it acts like a noun phrase *in situ* but scopes semantically to an embedding sentence. I will assume this interpretation of the scoping constructor, as further refined below.

DEFINITION: SCOPING CONSTRUCTOR   The *scoping constructor* ⇑ is such that

a. $B \Uparrow A \in \mathbf{Cat}$, if $A, B \in \mathbf{Cat}$,
b. $\mathrm{Typ}(B \Uparrow A) = (\mathrm{Typ}(B) \to \mathrm{Typ}(A)) \to \mathrm{Typ}(A)$.

I will assume that the scoping connective is not associative and binds more tightly than the slashes. The type assignment for such a scoping category is rather subtle. Intuitively, an expression of category $B \Uparrow A$ acts on an expression of category A in which it occurs as a B to produce an expression of category A. Thus the result should be the type of A, while the argument should be the type of an A with a B missing, namely $\mathrm{Typ}(B) \to \mathrm{Typ}(A)$. Note that for generalized quantifiers, we have the following:

(15) $\mathrm{Typ}(np \Uparrow s) = (\mathrm{Typ}(np) \to \mathrm{Typ}(s)) \to \mathrm{Typ}(s) = (\mathbf{Ind} \to \mathbf{Bool}) \to \mathbf{Bool}$

Thus the generalized quantifiers **every**, **no**, and **some** are constants of the type $\mathrm{Typ}(np \Uparrow s)$.

Now we turn to the logical rules for Moortgat's scoping constructor. But there is a problem with the interaction of associativity in the Lambek calculus and the need to mark locations of *in situ* binders. Unfortunately, no way has yet been found to provide a complete proof theory for the intended interpretation of a general *in situ* scoping constructor. Morrill (1994a) presents an alternative notion of quantification in a more refined logical setting, for which there is a complete proof theory, but we will not consider Morrill's approach here. I will be content to present Moortgat's proof theory and defer discussion of completeness until section 9.4. I begin with the sequent form of the rule of use:

DEFINITION: SCOPING SEQUENT SCHEME   The *scoping sequent* scheme is

$$\frac{\Delta_1, x{:}B, \Delta_2 \Rightarrow \beta{:}A \qquad \Gamma_1, \alpha(\lambda x.\beta){:}A, \Gamma_2 \Rightarrow \gamma{:}C}{\Gamma_1, \Delta_1, \alpha{:}B \Uparrow A, \Delta_2, \Gamma_2 \Rightarrow \gamma{:}C} \Uparrow \mathrm{L} \qquad [x \text{ fresh}]$$

As with our other schemes that involve hypothetical reasoning, we require the scoping scheme to choose fresh variables to avoid unwanted binding. This rule is most easily understood as involving two stages. The quantifier $\alpha{:}B \Uparrow A$ begins in the context of Δ_1, Δ_2, and it is over the material in Δ_1, Δ_2 that the quantifier scopes. First, we must establish the subgoal $\Delta_1, x{:}B, \Delta_2 \Rightarrow \beta{:}A$, where we substitute a hypothetical $x{:}B$ in the position originally occupied by the scope-taking element $B \Uparrow A$. Note that this is the same subderivation as would allow us to establish that

$$\frac{\overline{x\colon np,\ \mathbf{run}\colon np\backslash s \Rightarrow \mathbf{run}(x)\colon s}}{\mathbf{every}\colon np\!\Uparrow\!s,\ \mathbf{run}\colon np\backslash s \Rightarrow \mathbf{every}(\lambda x.\mathbf{run}(x))\colon s}\, ^{D}\quad \frac{}{\mathbf{every}(\lambda x.\mathbf{run}(x))\colon s \Rightarrow \mathbf{every}(\lambda x.\mathbf{run}(x))\colon s}\, ^{I}}{\mathbf{every}\colon np\!\Uparrow\!s,\ \mathbf{run}\colon np\backslash s \Rightarrow \mathbf{every}(\lambda x.\mathbf{run}(x))\colon s}\, {}_{\Uparrow L}$$

Figure 7.3
A derivation of *Everyone ran*

$\Delta_1, \Delta_2 \Rightarrow \lambda x.\beta\colon A{\uparrow}B$. This provides the deep connection between the right rule for $\uparrow$ and the left rule for $\Uparrow$, as was first pointed out by Moortgat (1991). In the second stage of the use of the quantifier, the entire context $\Delta_1, \alpha\colon B{\Uparrow}A, \Delta_2$ is replaced by $\alpha(\lambda x.\beta)\colon A$. This latter term is the result of applying the quantifier's semantic term to the result of the first sub-derivation with the hypothetical variable abstracted. Intuitively, the quantifier takes its scope at the level of the derivation of A from the Δs and the hypothetical B. The A is then used in the context between Γ_1 and Γ_2 to provide the final result. This latter substitution embodies the possibilities for employing the now quantified A in a further derivation; this also indicates how cuts can be incrementally eliminated from derivations involving $\Uparrow L$.

The simplest illustration of this rule in action can be found in figure 7.3. Note that we have used the generalized quantifiers **every** and **some** as instances of the category $np\,{\Uparrow}\,s$. In the derivation in figure 7.3, Γ_1, Γ_2, and Δ_1 are empty, and $\Delta_2 = \mathbf{run}\colon np\backslash s$. Given our definition of **every**, an utterance of *everyone ran* will be true if and only if the property denoted by $\lambda x.\mathbf{run}(x)$, which by η-reduction is equivalent to **run**, holds of every individual in the model.

In applying $\Uparrow L$, it is often the case that Γ_1 and Γ_2 are empty, and the second subderivation is carried out by the identity axiom, setting the result $\gamma\colon C = \alpha(\lambda x.\beta)\colon A$. In this case, we have the following derived inference scheme:

(16) $$\frac{\Delta_1,\ x\colon B,\ \Delta_2 \Rightarrow \beta\colon A}{\Delta_1,\ \alpha\colon B{\Uparrow}A,\ \Delta_2 \Rightarrow \alpha(\lambda x.\beta)\colon A}\, ^{D}$$

In fact, with cut, the derived scheme in (16) provides the same power as $\Uparrow L$. In addition, the derived instance of scoping in (16) illustrates most clearly the parallels between using $np\,{\Uparrow}\,s$ in Moortgat's system and quantifying in in Montague's grammar. One pleasant difference is that in the categorial setting, the pronominal lexical entries are not needed for marking the binding point of a quantifier. Instead, the form of the

$$\cfrac{\cfrac{\cfrac{}{x\!:\!np,\ \mathbf{break}\!:\!np\backslash s\!\!\not/np,\ y\!:\!np\ \Rightarrow\ \mathbf{break}(y)(x)\!:\!s}\ \text{D}}{x\!:\!np,\ \mathbf{break}\!:\!np\backslash s/np,\ \mathbf{every}\!:\!np\Uparrow s\ \Rightarrow\ \mathbf{every}(\lambda y.\mathbf{break}(y)(x))\!:\!s}\ \text{D}}{\mathbf{some}\!:\!np\Uparrow s,\ \mathbf{break}\!:\!np\backslash s/np,\ \mathbf{every}\!:\!np\Uparrow s\ \Rightarrow\ \mathbf{some}(\lambda x.\mathbf{every}(\lambda y.\mathbf{break}(y)(x)))\!:\!s}\ \text{D}$$

$$\cfrac{\cfrac{\cfrac{}{x\!:\!np,\ \mathbf{break}\!:\!np\backslash s/np,\ y\!:\!np\ \Rightarrow\ \mathbf{break}(y)(x)\!:\!s}\ \text{D}}{\mathbf{some}\!:\!np\Uparrow s,\ \mathbf{break}\!:\!np\backslash s/np,\ y\!:\!np\ \Rightarrow\ \mathbf{some}(\lambda x.\mathbf{break}(y)(x))\!:\!s}\ \text{D}}{\mathbf{some}\!:\!np\Uparrow s,\ \mathbf{break}\!:\!np\backslash s/np,\ \mathbf{every}\!:\!np\Uparrow s\ \Rightarrow\ \mathbf{every}(\lambda y.\mathbf{some}(\lambda x.\mathbf{break}(y)(x)))\!:\!s}\ \text{D}$$

Figure 7.4
A derivation of simple scope ambiguity

hypothetical antecedent directly takes care of that detail by replacing the quantifier with a variable of the appropriate category in the antecedent. By providing a proper sequent-based logic, we provide an explanation for the form of Montague's quantifying-in scheme.

Just as with quantifying in, the rule of use for the scoping constructor allows for the derivation of relative scope ambiguities. For instance, consider the derivations in figure 7.4, which make use of the derived scoping scheme in (16).

Three additional benefits of the type-logical approach will soon be apparent. First, the compositional form of the scope constructor in terms of a local category and a scoping category allows a natural generalization to other scoping phenomena. In the next two chapters I provide accounts of reflexives, reciprocals, pied-piped relative pronouns, and the plural operations of distribution and collection. Later we will see that quantificational adverbs can be treated along the same lines. Second, the scoping constructor provides a natural explanation of type raising from the perspective of both its logic and its range of application. As we will see in the next section, type raising is nothing more than the rule of proof for quantifiers. With type raising realized logically, we do not need to follow Montague's path of generalizing lexical entries to the worst possible case. Instead, we will be able to take simple lexical entries and derive their type-lifted forms automatically. Third, the logical basis of quantification provides a principled explanation of the interaction of quantification with other aspects of our grammar. This synergy between the slash constructors, the extraction constructors, coordination, and other quantifiers will be the topic of the rest of this chapter. Furthermore, we will see how the constructor-based approach to quantifiers allows a natural treatment of quantifiers occurring in free relative and possessive constructions. In later chapters we will see how quantifiers interact in the proper fashion with intensional verbs, including intensional transitive verbs, as well as with sentence-embedding propositional-attitude verbs and their control-based and clefted variants.

As with our previous analyses, it is most straightforward to work within the natural-deduction version of the scoping scheme.

DEFINITION: THE SCOPING NATURAL-DEDUCTION SCHEME   The natural deduction scheme for *scoping* is the following:

$$
\begin{array}{cccc}
\vdots & \vdots & \vdots & \qquad\qquad [x \text{ fresh}] \\
 & \dfrac{\alpha: B \Uparrow A}{x: B} \Uparrow \mathrm{E}^n & & \\
\vdots & \vdots & \vdots & \\
\vdots & \vdots & \vdots & \\
 & \beta: A & & \\
\hline
 & \alpha(\lambda x.\beta): A & & n
\end{array}
$$

The natural deduction scheme makes clear that we treat $B \Uparrow A$ locally as a B in the derivation of an A. Furthermore, these two stages of the derivation are coindexed in the natural-deduction scheme. It is important to note that the $\Uparrow \mathrm{E}$ scheme is intended to be read analogously to the sequent presentation in terms of scope. More precisely, it is intended to combine the following two independent derivations in the production of the final result.

$$
(17) \quad
\begin{array}{cccc}
\vdots & x: B & \vdots & \vdots \\
\vdots & \vdots & \vdots & \alpha: B \Uparrow A \\
\hline
 & \beta: A & &
\end{array}
$$

In particular, none of the assumptions in the derivation of $\alpha: B \Uparrow A$ are available for discharge in the derivation of $\beta: A$ from $x: B$ and the surrounding context. In section 7.5 we return to this issue and see why this structural understanding of the scope-elimination scheme is crucial in preventing some of the unpleasant consequences of Cooper's nonlogical, phrase-structure-based storage mechanism.

We can also gain insight into the behavior of the natural-deduction scoping scheme by considering its translation into sequent notation:

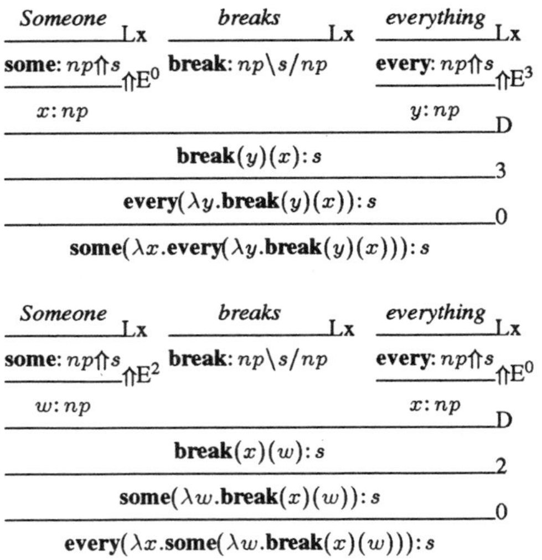

$$\frac{Someone}{\textbf{some: } np\Uparrow s}\text{Lx} \quad \frac{breaks}{\textbf{break: } np\backslash s/np}\text{Lx} \quad \frac{everything}{\textbf{every: } np\Uparrow s}\text{Lx}$$

$$\frac{\textbf{some: } np\Uparrow s}{x:np}\Uparrow\text{E}^0 \qquad\qquad \frac{\textbf{every: } np\Uparrow s}{y:np}\Uparrow\text{E}^3$$

$$\frac{}{\textbf{break}(y)(x):s}\text{D}$$

$$\frac{\textbf{break}(y)(x):s}{\textbf{every}(\lambda y.\textbf{break}(y)(x)):s}3$$

$$\frac{\textbf{every}(\lambda y.\textbf{break}(y)(x)):s}{\textbf{some}(\lambda x.\textbf{every}(\lambda y.\textbf{break}(y)(x))):s}0$$

$$\frac{Someone}{\textbf{some: } np\Uparrow s}\text{Lx} \quad \frac{breaks}{\textbf{break: } np\backslash s/np}\text{Lx} \quad \frac{everything}{\textbf{every: } np\Uparrow s}\text{Lx}$$

$$\frac{\textbf{some: } np\Uparrow s}{w:np}\Uparrow\text{E}^2 \qquad\qquad \frac{\textbf{every: } np\Uparrow s}{x:np}\Uparrow\text{E}^0$$

$$\frac{}{\textbf{break}(x)(w):s}\text{D}$$

$$\frac{\textbf{break}(x)(w):s}{\textbf{some}(\lambda w.\textbf{break}(x)(w)):s}2$$

$$\frac{\textbf{some}(\lambda w.\textbf{break}(x)(w)):s}{\textbf{every}(\lambda x.\textbf{some}(\lambda w.\textbf{break}(x)(w))):s}0$$

Figure 7.5
Two derivations of *Someone breaks everything*

(18) $\dfrac{\Gamma \Rightarrow \alpha: B\Uparrow A \qquad \Delta_1, x:B, \Delta_2 \Rightarrow \beta:A}{\Delta_1, \Gamma, \Delta_2 \Rightarrow \alpha(\lambda x.\beta):A}$

This makes clear the scope of the hypothetical assumption and how the hypothetical variable is bound, as illustrated in (17).

The natural-deduction schemes mimic the sequent rules in their effect, as can be seen in the alternative analysis of simple subject-object scope ambiguity in figure 7.5.

I have assumed that generalized quantifiers have the expected lexical entries:

(19) a. *everyone* $\Rightarrow$ **every**: $np\Uparrow s$
     b. *someone* $\Rightarrow$ **some**: $np\Uparrow s$

I make the standard categorial assumption that generalized determiners subcategorize for their nouns:

(20) a. *every* $\Rightarrow$ **every**^{2}: $np\Uparrow s/n$
     b. *some* $\Rightarrow$ **some**^{2}: $np\Uparrow s/n$
     c. *no* $\Rightarrow$ **no**^{2}: $np\Uparrow s/n$

Such an assumption follows the semantics in that determiners are relations between the property introduced by their nominal restriction and

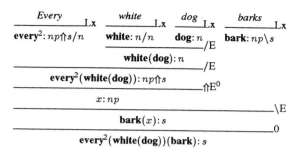

Figure 7.6
A derivation of *Every white dog barks*

that introduced by their scope. A derivation involving a generalized determiner can be found in figure 7.6. Note that I have η-reduced at the quantifier-elimination step, simplifying $\lambda x.\textbf{bark}(x)$ to **bark**. The bracketing in the semantic result on the root is as expected. Assuming that *white* is an intersective adjective, so that $\textbf{white} \overset{\text{def}}{=} \lambda P.\lambda x.(\textbf{white}_p(x) \wedge P(x))$, we generate the following analysis:

(21) *Every white dog barks* $\Rightarrow \textbf{every}^2(\lambda x.\textbf{white}_p(x) \wedge \textbf{dog}(x))(\textbf{bark}): s$

Given our interpretation of the generalized determiner $\textbf{every}^2$, an utterance of *Every white dog barks* will be true if and only if for every object x, if x is white and a dog, then x barks. In the remaining derivations, I will usually drop the superscript on generalized determiners when their type is clear from context.

The analogy between our elimination scheme for quantifiers and the operation of Cooper storage should be evident. The point at which elimination is effected corresponds to the point in Cooper's analysis in which a quantifier is replaced by a type-raised variable (Cooper's introduction of a variable type-raised to a quantifier rather than just the variable will be a consequence of the type-raising scheme we introduce in the next section). The point at which the quantifier is retrieved from storage corresponds to the stage at which a quantifier's hypothetical assumption is discharged and it applies semantically. Like Montague, we have a "syntactic" reflection of quantifier scoping, if we care to think of our various proof theories as syntactic theories in the traditional sense. The simple existence of two equivalent presentations with radically different structure demonstrates that a traditional syntactic presentation is unimportant in achieving the correct expression-meaning relation.

7.4   TYPE RAISING AND QUANTIFIER COORDINATION

In this section we turn our attention to a rule of proof for the scoping constructor. We have already seen Montague's solution to the discrepancy between the natural types assigned to names and to quantifiers, namely individual and generalized quantifier types. As in many other cases, Montague generalized to the worst case by lexically raising names and pronouns up to the type of generalized quantifiers. Lexically, the name *Jo* would be assigned to the category $\lambda P.P(\mathbf{j})$: *gq*. Because quantifiers are assigned to boolean categories, this allowed Montague to provide a grammar for the boolean coordination of arbitrary noun phrases, such as those in the following examples.

(22) a. [Jo] or [some tall kid] ran.
      b. Francis likes [Felix] and [every dog].

In these cases we have coordination of a proper name and a quantified noun phrase.

From our logical perspective, type raising is a reasonable rule of proof for the scoping constructor because it is sound with respect to our intuitive characterization of $B \Uparrow A$. By recognizing it as such, we avoid the ad hoc lexical character of Montague's use of lexical type raising, which turned out to be rather fragile and ill-suited to generalization. Furthermore, type raising allows us to generalize to the lexically best case, rather than the worst. As pointed out by H. Hendriks (1993), the worst case is often much worse than Montague envisaged when constructing his PTQ fragment. Instead of lexically type-raising whenever a higher type might be necessary, I will provide lexical entries of the lowest natural semantic type and allow the grammar to generate other categorizations freely according to the logic of the connectives. I am thus following the spirit of Hendriks's (1993) polymorphic approach to typing. Under Hendriks's approach, lexical entries are given the simplest appropriate semantic type and then are related to infinitely many other types via three schemes of type shifting, the semantic portion of which I provide as follows:

(23) a. Value raising

$$\frac{\alpha: \sigma_1 \rightarrow \cdots \rightarrow \sigma_n \rightarrow \mathbf{Ind}}{\begin{array}{l}\lambda x_1 \ldots \lambda x_n.\lambda P.P(\alpha(x_1)\cdots(x_n)): \\ \sigma_1 \rightarrow \cdots \rightarrow \sigma_n \rightarrow (\mathbf{Ind} \rightarrow \mathbf{Bool}) \rightarrow \mathbf{Bool}\end{array}} \text{VR}$$

b. Argument raising

$$\frac{\alpha\colon \sigma_1 \to \cdots \sigma_{n-1} \to \mathbf{Ind} \to \sigma_{n+1} \to \cdots \to \sigma_m \to \mathbf{Bool}}{\begin{array}{l} \lambda x_1 \ldots \lambda x_{n-1}.\lambda Q.\lambda x_{n+1} \ldots \lambda x_m.Q(\lambda x_n.\alpha(x_1)\cdots(x_m))\colon \\ \sigma_1 \to \cdots \sigma_{n-1} \to ((\mathbf{Ind} \to \mathbf{Bool}) \to \mathbf{Bool}) \to \sigma_{n+1} \to \cdots \\ \to \sigma_m \to \mathbf{Bool} \end{array}} \text{AR}$$

c. Argument lowering

$$\frac{\begin{array}{l}\alpha\colon \sigma_1 \to \cdots \sigma_{n-1} \to ((\mathbf{Ind} \to \mathbf{Bool}) \to \mathbf{Bool}) \to \sigma_{n+1} \to \cdots \\ \to \sigma_m \to \mathbf{Bool}\end{array}}{\begin{array}{l}\lambda x_1 \ldots \lambda x_{n-1}.\lambda x_n.\lambda x_{n+1} \ldots \lambda x_m. \\ \alpha(x_1)\cdots(x_{n-1})(\lambda P.P(x_n))(x_{n+1})\cdots(x_m)\colon \\ \sigma_1 \to \cdots \sigma_{n-1} \to \mathbf{Ind} \to \sigma_{n+1} \to \cdots \to \sigma_m \to \mathbf{Bool}\end{array}} \text{AL}$$

The first operation involved is *value raising*, which raises a category that produces an individual as a final result to one that produces the corresponding quantifier as a result. This is computed by simply distributing ordinary type raising through all of the arguments. The second operation is *argument raising*, and it involves replacing an individual argument to a function that produces a boolean result with a variable and applies the quantifier semantically by distributing through the arguments and binding the replacing variable. The third operation, *argument lowering*, replaces a quantifier argument in a function that produces a boolean result with an individual argument. The semantics is calculated by applying the original function to the type-raised version of the individual. Assuming that the individual results are noun phrases and the sentential results are sentences, all of these operations are derivable using our quantificational schemes; I leave this as exercise 9.

Hendriks motivates many more instances of these schemes than were applied lexically by Montague, and we consider many of his examples below. Fortunately, we do not need to postulate Hendriks's type-shifting operations directly. The approach I describe also differs from Hendriks's in that I maintain a single type for each syntactic category, whereas Hendriks associates each category with the (potentially infinite set of) types to which it can shift. Moortgat's introduction of the scoping constructor was, in fact, originally motivated by the desire to capture Hendriks's approach to quantification in a strict type-logical setting. As it turns out, Hendriks's semantic type shifts are all derivable in our approach from the simple quantifier rules of use and proof, when

$$\frac{\overline{\mathbf{j}: np \Rightarrow \mathbf{j}: np}^{\;\mathbf{I}}}{\mathbf{j}: np \Rightarrow \lambda V.V(\mathbf{j}): np \Uparrow s}\Uparrow \mathrm{R}$$

Figure 7.7
An example of noun-phrase type raising

combined with Lambek's existing rules for slashes (see exercise 9). Thus one way of viewing our approach is as providing a type-logical basis for the collection of operations proposed by Hendriks.

The sequent form of the rule of proof we will employ for the scoping constructor is as follows:

DEFINITION: SCOPE SEQUENT SCHEME   The *scope sequent scheme* is as follows:

$$\frac{\Gamma \Rightarrow \alpha: A}{\Gamma \Rightarrow \lambda x.x(\alpha): A \Uparrow B}\Uparrow \mathrm{R} \qquad\qquad [x \text{ fresh}]$$

Note that as with our other rules introducing variables, we must choose fresh ones for scope introduction. The simplest instance of this scheme allows us to produce generalized quantifiers from noun phrases, as shown in figure 7.7.

Before considering further applications of the rule of proof for the scope constructor, I provide it in natural-deduction format for ease of use.

DEFINITION: SCOPE-INTRODUCTION NATURAL DEDUCTION   The *scope intro-duction* natural deduction scheme is the following:

$$\frac{\begin{array}{c}\vdots\\ \alpha: A\end{array}}{\lambda x.x(\alpha): A \Uparrow B}\Uparrow \mathrm{I} \qquad\qquad [x \text{ fresh}]$$

I can now present a derivation of coordination of a noun phrase with a generalized quantifier. The derivation for a very simple example is given in figure 7.8. Note that we have raised the $\mathbf{j}: np$ category for *Jo* to a generalized quantifier, as in our sequent analysis. We have also performed relevant β-reductions, most notably in the application of the coordination. The reason this derivation goes through is that the generalized quantifier category, $np \Uparrow s$, is boolean and is thus allowed to participate in coordination, with the right results. I should also note that this scheme will allow us to coordinate two proper names, as in the following examples:

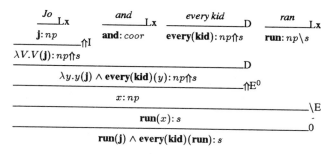

Figure 7.8
A derivation of *Jo and every kid ran*

(24) a. [Jo] and [Brett] ran yesterday.
     b. The teacher likes [Jo] but not [Brett].
     c. The painting of [New York] or [Chicago] was stolen.

It is sufficient to type-raise both names to generalized-quantifier categories and then scope the quantifiers, as usual. For instance, *Jo and Brett* can be analyzed as $\lambda V. V(\mathbf{j}) \wedge V(\mathbf{b}): np \Uparrow s$.

In general, it is always possible to raise a category using $\Uparrow$I and then eliminate it using $\Uparrow$E to derive the same result. With our slash connectives, we saw that we could eliminate this kind of spurious grammatical ambiguity. As with the slashes, we can simplify proofs involving spurious type raising. For quantifiers, we are not guaranteed to be left with normal terms, thought. This is one manifestation of the lack of generality of the rule of proof for quantifiers, as I discuss toward the end of section 9.4. For consistency, I still refer to the reduction operation as normalization.

DEFINITION: SCOPING NORMALIZATION   The normalization operation for the scope constructor is this:

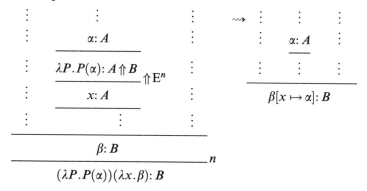

Note that the resulting terms are equivalent by two applications of β-reduction.

We will see below that the type-raising scheme derived by the scope introduction scheme has other uses in addition to type-raising names to allow them to coordinate with quantifiers. In particular, type raising will allow the proper interactions of quantifiers with expressions taking quantified arguments. Such expressions will include some intensional verbs, which take quantified subjects, and some auxiliaries, negation, and raising verbs, all of which take a quantifier as a controller. Furthermore, the same action of type raising lies at the root of certain other coordination phenomena, including some especially puzzling cases involving plurals.

7.5 EMBEDDED QUANTIFIERS

In this section we concentrate on occurrences of quantifiers embedded within other quantifiers. In particular, we consider quantifiers occurring as prepositional complements, as nominal complements, and within relative clauses. We first consider quantifiers occurring as objects of prepositional phrases, as illustrated in the following examples:

(25) a. Every kid in some class studied.
      b. Some kid in no class slept.

These sentences display quantifier-scope ambiguity. For instance, the first sentence, (25a), has a reading in which for some particular class, every kid in that class studied. It has a second reading that requires every kid who happened to be in some class or other to have studied. The second sentence, (25b), is analogous, although for some reason, negative or downward-entailing quantifiers seem much harder to scope widely than upward-entailing ones. Thus the reading in which there is no class such that some kid in that class slept is rather difficult to get without strong stress on *no class*. With the lexical entries I have provided for prepositions, which take noun-phrase complements, we are only able to derive the first of these readings, which I provide in figure 7.9.

Cooper's storage mechanism encounters a subtle problem when faced with embedded quantifiers. For instance, under any reasonable category assignment to nominal-modifying prepositions, the possibility for storage will generate the following kind of derivation.

(26) *every kid in some class passed*
   $\Rightarrow$ **pass**(x); $x/$**every**$($**in**$(y)($**kid**$))$, $y/$**some**$($**class**$)$: s

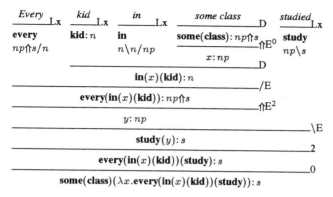

Figure 7.9
A derivation of *Every kid in some class studied*

This derivation is problematic because Cooper's scoping-closure condition, (13b), entails the existence of both of the following scope-resolved meanings, only the first of which is desirable.

(27) a. $\mathbf{some(class)}(\lambda y.\mathbf{every(in}(y)(\mathbf{kid}))(\lambda x.\mathbf{pass}(x)))$
b. $*\mathbf{every(in}(y)(\mathbf{kid}))(\lambda x.\mathbf{some(class)}(\lambda y.\mathbf{pass}(x)))$

The second derivation produces an unwanted free variable by scoping the quantifiers in nonnested order.

To circumvent this problem, Cooper (1979) restricted storage to apply only to quantifier meanings with an empty store. That is, Q is required to be the empty string in the storage-closure condition that requires $\lambda P.P(x); x/\alpha \cdot Q$ to be in a quantifier's meaning set if $\alpha; Q$ is. Thus the subject will be assigned a meaning set containing $\mathbf{every(in}(y)(\mathbf{kid}))$; $y/\mathbf{some(class)}$ but not $\lambda P.P(x); x/\mathbf{every(in}(y)(\mathbf{kid})), y/\mathbf{some(class)}$. It is this latter category that contributes to the undesirable free variable in (27b). Coincidentally, this restriction of storage to quantifiers with empty stores also prevents a quantifier that has already been stored from being stored again. This prevents a great deal of spurious ambiguity, which is eliminated in our system by means of derivation normalization. That is, we might find $\lambda P.P(x); x/\alpha$ in a meaning set without finding the redundant doubly quantified variant $\lambda R.R(y); y/\lambda P.P(x); x/\alpha$. Of course, our logic deals with the spurious ambiguity of type raising and then quantifying in by cut-elimination in the sequent setting and by normalization in the natural-deduction setting. Unfortunately, Cooper's restriction on

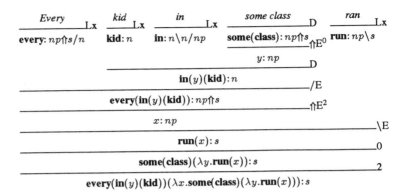

Figure 7.10
A nonderivation that violates independence

storage is not adequate. Although it prevents readings with unbound variables, it also blocks readings in which a quantifier and a quantifier nested within it outscope some other quantifier. For instance, this would arise in Cooper's grammars in the case of an object quantifier and a quantifier nested in the object not being allowed to outscope the subject. We should be able to derive the following:

(28) *someone likes every toy in some store*
$\Rightarrow$ **some**(**store**)($\lambda x.$**every**(**in**(x)(**toy**))($\lambda y.$**some**($\lambda z.$**like**(y)(z))))

But this requires both the quantifiers from the object and the embedded prepositional object to be stored simultaneously. Of course, the sequent in (28) is derivable in our system, just as it is in Cooper's system without the added restriction.

From the sequent presentation of our quantifier logic, it is clear that unbound variables cannot arise. In a derivation of Γ_1, $Q: np \Uparrow s$, $\Gamma_2 \Rightarrow Q(\lambda x.\alpha): s$ from a derivation of Γ_1, $x: np$, $\Gamma_2 \Rightarrow \alpha: s$, any free occurrences of x in α become bound in the result. Furthermore, the parallel between sequent derivations and natural-deduction ones, as indicated in (17), ensures that the same property holds. The assumption $B: x$, which introduces the free variable x, can only be used in the derivation of $\beta: A$, at which point the assumption is discharged and all free occurrences of x in β are bound. Because of the similarity of our natural-deduction characterization of scoping and Cooper storage, it is tempting to consider potential derivations such as that in figure 7.10. But the structure in figure

7.10 is not a derivation, because there is simply no way to match all of its rule applications to their respective schemes. The problem is that the subderivations are not independent in the sense required by the definition, as depicted in (17). Specifically, the quantifier elimination step $\Uparrow E^2$ is unwarranted because $\mathbf{some}(\mathbf{class})(\lambda y.\mathbf{run}(x)):s$ is not derived exclusively from the assumption $x:np$ and the remaining context $\mathbf{run}:np\backslash s$, as would be necessary for $\Uparrow E$ to be licensed. Finally, it should be noted that the sequent in (28), which is blocked by Cooper's restriction on storage, is generated by our approach.

From the previous analysis, we see that the essential problem for Cooper's approach is that it does not capture the structural relationship between the point at which a quantifier is stored and the point at which it is scoped. Moortgat's type-logical scheme for quantification, on the other hand, enjoys all of the pleasant properties of Cooper's storage mechanism with none of the unpleasant side effects, such as free variables in the case of the first version of the storage condition and undergeneration in the case of the second. The incorporation of further structure into Cooper's storage mechanism was independently proposed by Keller (1988) and Gerdemann and Hinrichs (1990). Their approach was to include an explicit indication of the nesting relations between quantifiers in the store. With such a marking, nesting quantifiers can be forced to apply before quantifiers nested inside them, thus capturing the appropriate scope restrictions. From our point of view, the maneuvering of Keller and of Gerdemann and Hinrichs can be explained by appeal to the logical structures of quantifier elimination; they have done nothing more than to encode the logical structure of quantifier derivations in a phrase-structure setting. Even though nonlogical theories such as Cooper's can occasionally be patched by building-in some of the logical structure, our theory not only avoids such patchwork but also explains a wide range of further interactions between the logical structures of quantification, complementation, unbounded dependency constructions, and coordination. In these cases, many of which we consider in the remainder of this chapter, it is not at all clear how even a logically reformulated version of Cooper storage will be able to generate the correct range of possible readings.

Although my system does not generate unwanted derivations with unbound variables, it still only generates one reading for each of the sentences in (25) with nested quantifiers. In the case of (25b), we should be able to generate the following analysis, where the prepositional-object quantifier is scoped *in situ*.

(29) *some kid in no class slept*

$\Rightarrow$ **some**$(\lambda x.\mathbf{kid}(x) \wedge \mathbf{no}(\mathbf{class})(\lambda y.\mathbf{in}(y)(x)))(\mathbf{sleep})$

A popular method for dealing with quantifiers that take scope at sub-sentential units is to provide additional rule schemes allowing quantifiers to scope within other boolean categories. For instance, Montague allowed quantifying in at the level of nouns and verb phrases, a move echoed by Cooper in his generalized scoping schemes. Furthermore, such extensions have been proposed in discourse-representation grammars (Roberts 1987a), and even in the government-binding theory of logical form (May 1985). The fundamental idea is the same as that of generalized coordination, namely that quantification can be distributed through arguments to boolean types. In a simple Montagovian setting, this would allow the following scheme:

(30) if $e \cdot he_k \cdot e'' \Rightarrow \phi\!: n$ and $e' \Rightarrow \alpha\!: gq$,

then $e \cdot e' \cdot e'' \Rightarrow \lambda y.\alpha(\lambda x_k.\phi(y))\!: n$ (Nominal quantifying-in)

The same semantic scheme would allow quantification within verb phrases (recall that nouns and verb phrases are assigned the type of properties).

Unfortunately, Montague's general scheme not only fails to generate the correct result but further allows the generation of incorrect readings. For instance, consider the following derivation:

(31) a. *kid in he₄* $\Rightarrow \mathbf{in}(x_4)(\mathbf{kid})\!: n$

   b. *kid in no class*

$\Rightarrow \lambda y.\mathbf{no}(\mathbf{class})(\lambda x_4.\mathbf{in}(x_4)(\mathbf{kid})(y))\!: n$

$\equiv \lambda y.\mathbf{no}(\mathbf{class})(\lambda x_4.\mathbf{kid}(y) \wedge \mathbf{in}_2(x_4)(y))\!: n$

The logical equivalence in (31b) follows from our definition of prepositional contents. Now notice that an individual a has the semantic property assigned to *kid in no class* if and only if there is no class b such that a is a kid and a is in b. But this holds trivially if a is not a kid. Of course, the nominal *kid in no class* denotes a property that only holds of kids; the prepositional phrase, even with a quantified object, is restrictive by nature. The problem with the nominal quantifying-in scheme is that the quantifier takes scope over not just the preposition's restrictive content but also over the restriction supplied by the common noun. Note that this result is not due to our meaning postulates for prepositions; no matter what kind of content is assumed for nominal modifiers, the situation in which an embedded quantifier outscopes the head noun's content will always arise.

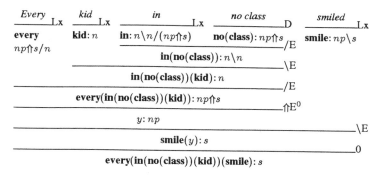

Figure 7.11
A derivation of *Every kid in no class smiled*

Within a type-logical approach, we are not free to postulate arbitrary, nonlogical rule schemes. Instead, if we want quantifiers to reduce within nominals, we could simply make the following kind of category assignment:

(32) *everyone* $\Rightarrow \lambda P.\lambda x.\mathbf{every}(\lambda z.P(z)(x)): np \Uparrow n$

This would mimic Montague's nominal quantifying-in scheme, allowing the derivation of (31b). But rather than following the errant path of allowing quantifiers to reduce within nominals, I instead isolate the problem in the lexical entry previously assigned to prepositions, as suggested by Cooper (p.c.). The revised lexical entries for prepositions, along with the meaning postulates reflecting their intersective nature, are exemplified as follows:

(33) a. *in* $\Rightarrow$ **in**: $n \backslash n/(np \Uparrow s)$
    b. **in** $\stackrel{\text{def}}{=} \lambda Q.\lambda P.\lambda x.P(x) \wedge Q(\lambda y.\mathbf{in_2}(y)(x))$

We are now in a position to generate a proper analysis of the narrow scope of an embedded quantifier, as shown in figure 7.11. Substituting the meaning of the preposition into the result, we have the following:

(34) **in**(**no**(**class**))(**kid**) $\equiv \lambda x.\mathbf{kid}(x) \wedge \mathbf{no}(\mathbf{class})(\lambda y.\mathbf{in_2}(y)(x))$

Although I have raised the object type for prepositions, I have done so for semantic reasons; quantified objects do not scope over the nominal modified by prepositions. It is worth noting that our original lexical entries for prepositions can be easily derived from that in (33a) by combining type raising and abstraction. Such a derivation for the case of *in* is

$$\frac{\dfrac{in}{\lambda Q.\lambda P.\lambda x.P(x) \wedge Q(\lambda y.\mathbf{in}_2(y)(x)):n\backslash n/(np\Uparrow s)}\,\text{Lx} \quad \dfrac{[z:np]^1}{\lambda R.R(z):np\Uparrow s}\,\Uparrow\text{I}}{\dfrac{\lambda P.\lambda x.P(x) \wedge \mathbf{in}_2(z)(x):n\backslash n}{\lambda z.\lambda P.\lambda x.P(x) \wedge \mathbf{in}_2(z)(x):n\backslash n/np}\,/\text{I}^1}\,/\text{E}$$

Figure 7.12
A derivation of a standard preposition lexical entry

shown in figure 7.12, with the semantic term for the preposition given in full. Thus lexical entries explicitly seeking a noun-phrase argument are no longer needed; they can be derived from the entries seeking quantified objects by hypothesizing a noun-phrase and raising it to a quantifier for the sake of the derivation. Analogous derivations may be carried out on any boolean category with a generalized quantifier argument. The general pattern is known as *argument lowering*. The combination of the logic of slashes and that of the scoping constructor generates all of the instances of argument lowering proposed by H. Hendriks (1987, 1993) as a purely semantic operation (see exercise 9).

Just as for modifying prepositions, we need to raise the categories assigned to relational nouns and case-marking prepositions:

(35) a. *picture* $\Rightarrow \lambda Q.\lambda x.Q(\lambda y.\mathbf{picture}(y)(x)):n/(np_{of}\Uparrow s)$
     b. *of* $\Rightarrow \lambda Q.Q:np_{of}\Uparrow s/(np\Uparrow s)$

Lexical entries of this form allow the following analysis purely by functional application.

(36) *picture of every kid* $\Rightarrow \lambda x.\mathbf{every}(\mathbf{kid})(\lambda y.\mathbf{picture}(y)(x))$

Note that these lexical entries are compatible with the assumption that quantifiers should be allowed to reduce within nominals in general. Of course, as with the modifying prepositions, the original lexical entries for these categories can be derived by argument lowering, given the type-raising possibilities for noun phrases. The semantic issues surrounding relational nouns are subtle; for one example of why this is the case, see exercise 28.

The other case of nominal modification that might involve quantification arises in relative clauses.

(37) a. Some kid who entered every event is tired.
     b. Every kid who entered some event received a ribbon.

c. Jo likes some movie which every student likes.

d. Every kid who is in some class passes every exam.

If quantifiers were allowed to freely scope out of relative clauses, we would have a large number of readings for these sentences. Although intuitions vary widely, it is usually assumed that relative clauses are so-called *scope islands*, in the sense that quantifiers embedded in an island cannot take scope outside of the island (Ross 1967, Rodman 1976). For instance, sentence (37a) is assumed to unambiguously mean that there is a particular kid, say x, such that x entered every event and is tired. Similarly, (37b) cannot mean that there is a particular event for which every student who entered it received a ribbon, but rather must mean that every kid who entered any event received a ribbon. Of course, in this second case, it may be a single ribbon that every kid received or a different ribbon for each kid; there is no restriction on how subject and object quantifiers scope with respect to one another.

If we wished to syntactically restrict quantifiers from scoping out of relative clauses, we would need to see how the quantifiers can be reduced within the relative clauses and also how they can be prevented from being reduced outside of the relative clauses in which they are found. The first of these issues is, in fact, already resolved. The scoping schemes already interact in the correct way with both the slash schemes and the extraction scheme. In the case of subject relative clauses, we can see how the slash-introduction scheme and the scope-elimination scheme cooperate to provide the correct result. The reduction of a quantifier within a verb-phrase complement to a subject-relative pronoun, as is required for (37a) and (37b), can be found in figure 7.13. The reduction of a quantifier within an unbounded dependency construction is similar, as can be seen in figure 7.14. Note that we have an η-reduction in the derivation at the quantifier-elimination stage. Inserting the definition of **rel** as set intersection, we have the following analyses:

(38) a. *student who likes every class*
$$\Rightarrow \lambda x.\mathbf{student}(x) \wedge \mathbf{every}(\mathbf{class})(\lambda y.\mathbf{like}(y)(x)):n$$
b. *movie which every kid likes.*
$$\Rightarrow \lambda x.\mathbf{movie}(x) \wedge \mathbf{every}(\mathbf{kid})(\lambda y.\mathbf{like}(x)(y)):n$$

Note that I have not performed the η-reduction of $\lambda y.\mathbf{like}(x)(y)$ to $\mathbf{like}(x)$, as was done in the derivation in figure 7.14.

While this explains how we can reduce quantifiers within expressions that are not full sentences, it does not explain why, in some cases, we

$$
\cfrac{
  \cfrac{
    \cfrac{\text{student}}{\textbf{student}: n}\text{Lx}
    \qquad
    \cfrac{
      \cfrac{who}{\cfrac{\textbf{rel}}{n\backslash n/(np\backslash s)}}\text{Lx}
      \qquad
      \cfrac{
        [x\!:\!np]^2
        \qquad
        \cfrac{
          \cfrac{\text{liked}}{\cfrac{\textbf{like}}{np\backslash s/np}}\text{Lx}
          \qquad
          \cfrac{\cfrac{\text{every class}}{\textbf{every(class)}}\text{D}}{\cfrac{\textbf{every(class)}}{np\!\Uparrow\!s}}
        }{ \cfrac{y\!:\!np}{} }\Uparrow\!\text{E}^3
      }{\ }
    }{\ }
  }{\ }
}{\ }
$$

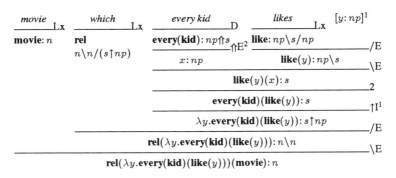

Figure 7.13
A derivation of *student who liked every class*

Figure 7.14
A derivation of *movie which every kid likes*

cannot extract quantifiers out of relative clauses. Although the data are subtle (see Cooper 1983), the type-logical approach lends itself to a highly elegant characterization of islands. To represent islands, we use a unary operator whose proof theory is that of a minimal modal logic. Details of such an account are presented in Morrill 1992b, 1994a; a general type-logical account of the logical possibilities for modalities can be found in Moortgat and Oehrle 1993 and Moortgat 1994. In these works a general solution to islandhood and its interaction with coordination, quantification, and unbounded dependencies is presented. Furthermore, the same kind of modal techniques that allow islands to be represented also show a great deal of promise for the treatment of word order (Moortgat and Oehrle 1994).

7.6 QUANTIFIERS AND COORDINATE STRUCTURES

One of the benefits of our categorial approach to complementation is the ease with which coordinate structures can be generated. Things are no different with the addition of quantifiers. We can generate the appropriate range of readings for a wide range of coordinated sentences with quantifiers. We have already seen that quantifiers themselves can be coordinated because $np \Uparrow s$ is a boolean category:

(39) a. [Some teacher] and [every student] ran.
     b. Jo hit [every student] or [some teacher].

There is no scope interaction between quantifiers when they are themselves coordinated. For instance, there is no reading of (39a) that has the universal and existential taking scope with respect to one another. But such scope interaction could be derived by first eliminating the quantifiers and then type-raising the hypothetical noun phrases; coordination can be carried out on the raised hypothetical noun phrases and the quantifiers scoped arbitrarily. Of course, this behavior is not desirable, and it is blocked by the categorial treatment of islands (Morrill 1992a, 1994a; Moortgat 1994). In general, Morrill's treatment of coordination prevents any kind of binding into a coordinate structure, thus preventing both extraction and quantification. In the remainder of this section I will continue to point out the locality enforced by coordination.

In the previous section we saw that there is no obstacle to quantifiers reducing within incomplete boolean constituents, such as verb phrases. Thus we will be able to derive the correct meanings for examples such as the following:

(40) a. Jo [likes every class] and [hates every assignment].
     b. [Every kid hates] but [every adult likes] a nap.
     c. The kid [in every track event] or [in some field event] ran.

The verb phrases in (40a) can be coordinated after being analyzed in the same way as the verb phrase containing a quantifier was analyzed in figure 7.13. When the conjunct is a nonstandard constituent, as in the s/np categories of (40b), the proper result is achieved in the same way. The analysis of the conjuncts proceeds as in the unbounded dependency analysis in figure 7.14 but with the /-introduction scheme being used to discharge the hypothesis rather than the ↑-introduction scheme. The coordinate structures in (40c) are simpler in the sense that they are derivable by simple application from the prepositional lexical entries that take quantified objects. In all of the cases in (40), the quantifiers cannot scope outside of their individual conjuncts, as is expected since coordinate structures are islands to dependencies. On the other hand, nothing will prevent quantifiers from reducing within an incomplete sentence if the missing elements can be hypothesized.

Some interesting cases of scope interaction arise between coordinate structures and quantifiers when the restriction or scope of the quantifier is coordinated.

(41) a. Every [kid] or [adult] just ran.
      b. Some [vegetarian] and [socialist] ran.
      c. Every kid [ran] or [jumped].
      d. Some kid [ran] and [jumped].
      e. [Jo likes] but [Brett hates] some class.

I claim that the first sentence is ambiguous, depending on whether or not everyone who is either a kid or an adult ran or whether it is enough that every kid ran or every adult ran. For the second reading, the disjunction is said to take wide-scope over the quantification. The availability of wide-scope disjunction has been challenged repeatedly, despite the fact that such usage is felicitous in many contexts. For instance, in the context of a series of races at a company picnic, the wide-scope reading of *or* in (41a) is more felicitous than the narrow reading. Dale Gerdemann (p.c.) pointed out that there is a Christmas carol with the following two lines, which are obviously meant to be read with wide scope coordinators.

(42) a. He's gonna find out who's naughty and nice.
      b. He knows if you've been bad or good.

To evoke wide-scope coordination readings in some situations, Partee and Rooth (1983, 1987) placed examples such as (41a) in the context of the continuation *but I don't know which*, by which the speaker expresses that the disjunction is distributed through the entire interpretation (although they argued that (41a) is not itself ambiguous in this way). H. Hendriks (1993) noted that such ambiguities are often possible if the entire sentence is embedded within a propositional-attitude context, say as the complement to a verb like *believe*. Following Hendriks, I allow all of the possi-

$$[Q_1: np{\Uparrow}s/n]^2 \quad \underline{\quad kid \quad}\text{Lx} \quad \underline{\quad or \quad}\text{Lx} \quad [Q_2: np{\Uparrow}s/n]^4 \quad \underline{\quad adult \quad}\text{Lx}$$

$$\cfrac{\cfrac{\textbf{kid}: n}{}\text{/E}}{\quad} \qquad \textbf{or}: coor \qquad \cfrac{\textbf{adult}: n}{}\text{/E}$$

$$\cfrac{Q_1(\textbf{kid}): np{\Uparrow}s}{\cfrac{\lambda Q_1.Q_1(\textbf{kid}): (np{\Uparrow}s/n)\backslash np{\Uparrow}s}{}}\backslash\text{I}^2 \qquad \cfrac{Q_2(\textbf{adult}): np{\Uparrow}s}{\lambda Q_2.Q_2(\textbf{adult}): (np{\Uparrow}s/n)\backslash np{\Uparrow}s}\backslash\text{I}^4$$

$$\cfrac{}{\lambda Q_3.\lambda P.Q_3(\textbf{kid})(P) \vee Q_3(\textbf{adult})(P): (np{\Uparrow}s/n)\backslash np{\Uparrow}s}\text{D}$$

Figure 7.15
a derivation of *kid or adult*

$$\underline{\quad Every \quad}\text{Lx} \qquad \underline{\qquad\qquad kid\ or\ adult \qquad\qquad}\text{D} \qquad \underline{\quad ran \quad}\text{Lx}$$

$$\textbf{every}: np{\Uparrow}s/n \qquad \lambda Q_3.\lambda P.Q_3(\textbf{kid})(P) \vee Q_3(\textbf{adult})(P) \qquad \textbf{run}: np\backslash s$$
$$(np{\Uparrow}s/n)\backslash np{\Uparrow}s$$

$$\cfrac{\lambda P.\textbf{every}(\textbf{kid})(P) \vee \textbf{every}(\textbf{adult})(P): np{\Uparrow}s}{}\backslash\text{E}$$

$$\cfrac{x: np}{}{\Uparrow}\text{E}^0$$

$$\cfrac{\textbf{run}(x): s}{}\backslash\text{E}$$

$$\cfrac{\textbf{every}(\textbf{kid})(\textbf{run}) \vee \textbf{every}(\textbf{adult})(\textbf{run}): s}{}\ 0$$

Figure 7.16
a derivation of *Every kid or adult ran*

bilities to be freely generated. Similar ambiguities are displayed by the remaining examples in (41). The narrowly scoped coordination analysis of (41a) is as usual; the nouns are simply coordinated as boolean categories and then are free to act as the complement to the quantificational determiner. The wide-scope disjunctive reading, on the other hand, arises by first lifting the nouns to functors over determiners and then coordinating at that level. Such an analysis is shown in figure 7.15. After we have the coordinate structure seeking a generalized determiner to its left and distributing it into both conjuncts, we can carry out the rest of the analysis as shown in figure 7.16. Analyses along similar lines are available to allow coordinate structures at any depth to be distributed to the top level (modulo any island constraints in a theory that is sensitive to them). For instance, the verb-phrase coordination in (41d) can occur at type $np\backslash s$, which allows the existential subject to take wide scope. Alternatively, we have the type-raised analysis in figure 7.17, in which the verb phrases undergo argument raising before being coordinated. Of course, a similar ambiguity can be found in the coordination of a subject and a transitive verb, as in (41e). Again, our grammar allows the coordinate structure to

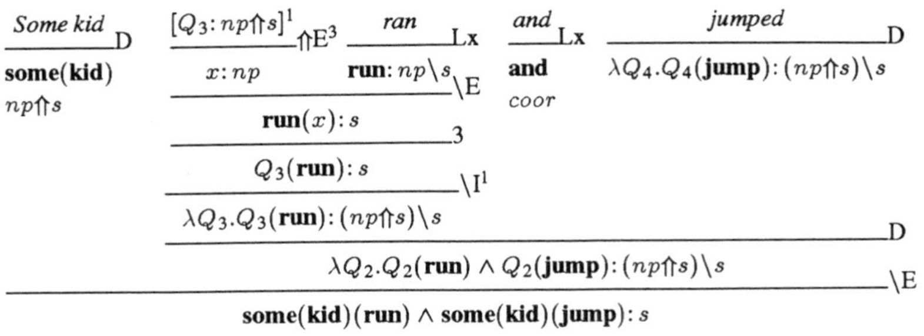

$$\cfrac{\cfrac{\cfrac{\cfrac{\cfrac{Some\ kid}{\begin{array}{l}\textbf{some}(\textbf{kid})\\ np{\Uparrow}s\end{array}}\text{D}\quad\cfrac{\cfrac{[Q_3:np{\Uparrow}s]^1}{x:np}{\Uparrow}\text{E}^3\quad\cfrac{ran}{\textbf{run}:np\backslash s}\text{Lx}}{\textbf{run}(x):s}\backslash\text{E}}{Q_3(\textbf{run}):s}3}{\lambda Q_3.Q_3(\textbf{run}):(np{\Uparrow}s)\backslash s}\backslash\text{I}^1\quad\cfrac{\cfrac{and}{\begin{array}{l}\textbf{and}\\ coor\end{array}}\text{Lx}\quad\cfrac{jumped}{\lambda Q_4.Q_4(\textbf{jump}):(np{\Uparrow}s)\backslash s}\text{D}}{\lambda Q_2.Q_2(\textbf{run})\wedge Q_2(\textbf{jump}):(np{\Uparrow}s)\backslash s}\text{D}}{\textbf{some}(\textbf{kid})(\textbf{run})\wedge\textbf{some}(\textbf{kid})(\textbf{jump}):s}\backslash\text{E}}$$

Figure 7.17
A derivation of *Some kid ran and jumped*

be analyzed as s/np or as $s/(np{\Uparrow}s)$, along the same lines as the analysis in figure 7.17. Further examples of the interactions between coordinate structures and quantifiers can be found in the exercises. I now simply note that examples such as the following can be provided with a range of correct readings.

(43) a. Every student [wrote some paper] and [read some book].
   b. Jo showed [someone every drawing] but [no one every painting].

The relevant fact for our flexible approach is that both relative scopings are available for both conjuncts.

7.7 QUANTIFICATION AND NEGATION

When quantifiers occur with negative particles, they may take scope either within or outside the negation, as can be seen in the following examples:

(44) a. Every student didn't study.
   b. Kim didn't pass every test.
   c. Kim didn't pass several tests.

The first example, (44a), has two readings. When the quantifier takes widest scope, the sentence states that no student studied. When the quantifier takes narrow scope, the sentence states that it is not the case that every student studied. The second example, (44b), has the same ambiguity (although the wide-scope-quantifier reading is perhaps better expressed with the negative polarity existential quantifier *any* with a narrow scope). With the third example, (44c), both readings are more evident. This example may mean that there are several tests that Kim did not pass or that it

$$
\begin{array}{ccc}
\dfrac{\textit{Brett}}{\text{Lx}} & \dfrac{\textit{didn't}}{\text{Lx}} & \dfrac{\textit{study}}{\text{D}} \\[4pt]
\dfrac{\mathbf{b}:np}{\lambda Q_1.Q_1(\mathbf{b}):np{\Uparrow}s}\,{\Uparrow}\text{I} & \begin{array}{c}\lambda V.\lambda Q_2.\neg V(Q_2)\\ (np{\Uparrow}s)\backslash s/((np{\Uparrow}s)\backslash s)\end{array} & \lambda Q_3.Q_3(\mathbf{study}):(np{\Uparrow}s)\backslash s
\end{array}
$$

$$
\dfrac{\lambda Q_2.\neg Q_2(\mathbf{study}):(np{\Uparrow}s)\backslash s}{}\,/\text{E}
$$

$$
\dfrac{\neg\mathbf{study}(\mathbf{b}):s}{}\,\backslash\text{E}
$$

Figure 7.18
A derivation of *Brett didn't study*

was not the case that Kim passed several tests (we return to plural noun phrases in the next chapter).

Although the sentences in (44) might suggest an analysis in which the negative particle takes scope, this is not the route that I will follow. A strong motivation for resisting such an analysis is that negatives only 'scope' with respect to quantifiers. That is, there is no scope ambiguity in expressions such as *probably didn't study*; the modal adverbial *probably* must outscope the negation (we return to modals in chapter 11). Instead of treating negative elements as scoping, I instead treat them as a kind of raising verb. Specifically, I will assume the following kind of entry for auxiliaries and negative particles (ignoring, for now, the delicate matter of tense and aspect).

(45) a. *did* $\Rightarrow \lambda V.V:(np{\Uparrow}s)\backslash s/((np{\Uparrow}s)\backslash s)$
     b. *didn't* $\Rightarrow \lambda V.\lambda Q.\neg V(Q):(np{\Uparrow}s)\backslash s/((np{\Uparrow}s)\backslash s)$
     c. *not* $\Rightarrow \lambda V.\lambda Q.\neg V(Q):(np{\Uparrow}s)\backslash s/((np{\Uparrow}s)\backslash s)$

Note that the complements of auxiliaries and negatives are not quite verb phrases but rather are like verb phrases but take quantified subjects instead. For Montague, and in many other theories, the introduction of the categories in (45) would necessitate a wholesale type lifting of all lexical verb phrases, adverbs, and so on, as Montague did in 1970a. From our logical vantage point, we can maintain our natural type assignments for verbs and simply raise their arguments to the appropriate level when necessary. For instance, the subject of a verb phrase like *ran* can be lifted as shown in figure 7.17. Similarly, we can raise noun phrases to quantifiers to act as subjects in such constructions. Thus an expression like *Brett didn't study* will be analyzed as $\neg\mathbf{study}(\mathbf{b})$, as shown in figure 7.18.

With the lexical entries we have, we can use type raising and slash introduction at the same time to produce the two readings of (44a), as shown in figure 7.19. The narrow-scope reading of the quantifier with

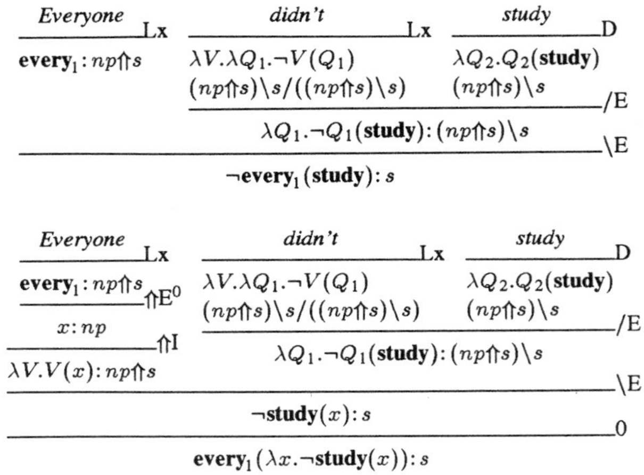

First derivation:

$$\dfrac{Everyone}{\mathbf{every_1}:np{\Uparrow}s}\text{Lx} \qquad \dfrac{\dfrac{didn't}{\substack{\lambda V.\lambda Q_1.\neg V(Q_1)\\ (np{\Uparrow}s)\backslash s/((np{\Uparrow}s)\backslash s)}}\text{Lx} \quad \dfrac{study}{\substack{\lambda Q_2.Q_2(\mathbf{study})\\ (np{\Uparrow}s)\backslash s}}\text{D}}{\dfrac{\lambda Q_1.\neg Q_1(\mathbf{study}):(np{\Uparrow}s)\backslash s}{}\text{/E}}\text{\backslash E}$$

$$\neg\mathbf{every_1}(\mathbf{study}):s$$

Second derivation:

$$\dfrac{\dfrac{\dfrac{Everyone}{\mathbf{every_1}:np{\Uparrow}s}\text{Lx}}{\dfrac{x:np}{\lambda V.V(x):np{\Uparrow}s}{\Uparrow}\text{I}}{\Uparrow}\text{E}^0 \qquad \dfrac{\dfrac{didn't}{\substack{\lambda V.\lambda Q_1.\neg V(Q_1)\\ (np{\Uparrow}s)\backslash s/((np{\Uparrow}s)\backslash s)}}\text{Lx}\quad\dfrac{study}{\substack{\lambda Q_2.Q_2(\mathbf{study})\\ (np{\Uparrow}s)\backslash s}}\text{D}}{\lambda Q_1.\neg Q_1(\mathbf{study}):(np{\Uparrow}s)\backslash s}\text{/E}}{\neg\mathbf{study}(x):s}\text{\backslash E}$$

$$\mathbf{every_1}(\lambda x.\neg\mathbf{study}(x)):s \quad 0$$

Figure 7.19
Two derivations of *Everyone didn't study*

respect to the negation, corresponding to the first analysis in figure 7.19, is derived naturally by application. The wide-scope reading of the quantifier is achieved by a combination of quantifier elimination and introduction. This is exactly the technique we used before to allow a quantifier to take wide scope out of a quantified argument position; the quantifier is eliminated and then immediately raised.

A further subtle case is encountered when higher-order modifiers such as *not* are nested.

(46) a. Everyone didn't not study.
    b. Everyone probably didn't study.

The examples in (46) are three-ways ambiguous with respect to quantifier scope. The quantifier can scope wide, between the two operators, or narrow with respect to both operators. The first and last possibility follow the same derivations as in figure 7.19; narrowest scope follows from application, and widest scope by eliminating the subject quantifier and then type-raising it before application. The intermediate case also follows by eliminating a quantifier and then raising it; only this time the relevant quantifier is a hypothetical, as shown in figure 7.20.

Many quantifiers can be modified by a negative particle, as in *not every student*, *not many students*, and *not more than three students*. Such cases of

$$
\begin{array}{cccc}
\dfrac{\textit{Every student}}{\begin{array}{l}\mathbf{every}(\mathbf{student})\\ np{\Uparrow}s\end{array}}\text{D} &
\dfrac{\textit{didn't}}{\begin{array}{l}\lambda V.\lambda Q_1.\neg V(Q_1)\\ (np{\Uparrow}s)\backslash s/((np{\Uparrow}s)\backslash s)\end{array}}\text{Lx} &
\dfrac{[Q_2:np{\Uparrow}s]^3}{\begin{array}{c}\dfrac{x:np}{\lambda U.U(x):np{\Uparrow}s}{\Uparrow}\text{I}\end{array}}{\Uparrow}\text{E}^5 &
\dfrac{\textit{not study}}{\begin{array}{l}\lambda Q_3.\neg Q_3(\mathbf{study})\\ (np{\Uparrow}s)\backslash s\end{array}}\text{D}
\end{array}
$$

$$
\dfrac{\neg\mathbf{study}(x):s}{\dfrac{Q_2(\lambda x.\neg\mathbf{study}(x)):s}{\dfrac{\lambda Q_2.Q_2(\lambda x.\neg\mathbf{study}(x)):(np{\Uparrow}s)\backslash s}{\dfrac{\lambda Q_1.\neg Q_1(\lambda x.\neg\mathbf{study}(x)):(np{\Uparrow}s)\backslash s}{\neg\mathbf{every}(\mathbf{student})(\lambda x.\neg\mathbf{study}(x)):s}\backslash\text{E}}\text{/E}}\backslash\text{I}^3}\backslash\text{E}}\text{5}
$$

Figure 7.20
A derivation of *Every student didn't not study*

quantifier negation can be handled semantically by generalized boolean negation. I assume the following lexical entry:

(47) *not* $\Rightarrow \lambda Q.\lambda V.\neg Q(V): np{\Uparrow}s/(np{\Uparrow}s)$

Thus an expression like *not every student* will be assigned to the category $\lambda P.\neg\mathbf{every}(\mathbf{student})(P): np{\Uparrow}s$. The infelicity of cases such as *not some student* is likely due to suppletion by *no student*. Similarly, *Not Jo ran* is more naturally expressed by *Jo didn't run*. Recall the discussion in section 3.3.2 of completeness and consistency for quantifiers derived from type-raising individuals, which explains the synonymy of verb-phrase and sentential negation for sentences with subjects that are names. We do see names negated in response to questions such as *Who ran?* which can be naturally answered with *Not Sandy*. Names can also be negated in coordinated contexts, such as *Francis and not Brett*.

7.8   QUANTIFICATION AND DEFINITE DESCRIPTIONS

In our current approach to quantification, it remains feasible to maintain our analysis of the definite determiner as being of the category $\iota: np/n$ (recall that ι is the description operator from higher-order logic). This assignment correctly generates the correct range of readings for sentences containing definites and quantifiers:

(48) a. The teacher scolded the unruly student.
  b. The teacher praised every student.
  c. The teacher in every class lectured.

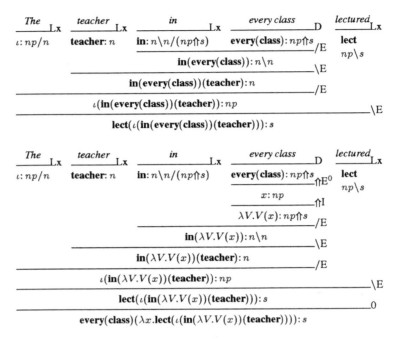

Figure 7.21
Two derivations of *The teacher in every class lectured*

    d. The collector from Cleveland with every comic book jumped at the deal.

The first example, (48a), which contains multiple definite determiners, is not ambiguous. In our grammar, it is assigned a unique reading; expressions of category np/n simply do not allow for scope ambiguities. Even though at the np stage a definite description such as *the teacher* may be raised to a quantifier, that quantifier will not participate in scope alternations. In the second example, (48b), the quantified object *every student* must be assigned scope. Even so, our grammar generates only one reading, in which the single teacher scolded every one of the students. In the last two examples, (48c) and (48d), a scope ambiguity arises with respect to whether the quantifier reduced within the nominal or escapes to take sentential scope. These two analyses are shown in figure 7.21. For the scoping of the quantifier within the prepositional phrase, simple application suffices. The resulting description, after substitution and reduction, is $\iota(\lambda x.\mathbf{teach}(x) \wedge \mathbf{every}(\mathbf{class})(\lambda y.\mathbf{in}_2(y)(x)))$. Such a term refers to the

$$
\cfrac{
\cfrac{
\cfrac{
\cfrac{\cfrac{\text{the}}{\iota:np/n}Lx \quad \cfrac{\text{rabbit}}{\textbf{rabbit}:n}Lx \quad \cfrac{\text{in}}{\textbf{in}:n\backslash n/np}Lx \quad \cfrac{\cfrac{\text{the}}{\iota:np/n}Lx \quad \cfrac{\text{hat}}{\textbf{hat}:n}Lx}{\iota(\textbf{hat}):np}{/E}}{\textbf{in}(\iota(\textbf{hat})):n\backslash n}{/E}
}{\textbf{in}(\iota(\textbf{hat}))(\textbf{rabbit}):n}{\backslash E}
}{\iota(\textbf{in}(\iota(\textbf{hat}))(\textbf{rabbit})):np}{/E}
}
$$

Figure 7.22
A derivation of *the rabbit in the hat*

unique individual who is a teacher and who is in every class. The more plausible reading in this case is the second, in which the description is $\iota(\lambda x.\textbf{teach}(x) \wedge \textbf{in}_2(y)(x))$. With the variable y bound by the wider universal, the term is free to denote a possibly different teacher in each class, as long as for each class there is a unique individual who is a teacher and is in that class.

While our definite-description operator produces the right kinds of readings for some sentences, it is not so clear that this is always the correct way to analyze definiteness. For instance, consider the following situation discussed by Haddock (1987). There are two rabbits, three hats, and one of the rabbits is in one of the hats, the other rabbit is not in a hat, and the other two hats are empty. In this context, it appears we can use a noun phrase such as *the rabbit in the hat*, which in our grammar has the unique analysis given in figure 7.22. With our meaning postulate for **in**, I derive the following sequent:

(49) *the rabbit in the hat* $\Rightarrow \iota(\lambda x.\textbf{rabbit}(x) \wedge \textbf{in}_2(\iota(\textbf{hat}))(x))$

The problem is that *the hat* can only be interpreted as $\iota(\textbf{hat})$, presupposing the existence of a unique hat. In fact, there is not a unique hat but merely a unique pair consisting of a rabbit and a hat such that the rabbit is in the hat. While our grammar does not predict what we feel is the correct interpretation here, I am aware of no suitable treatment of definites that can handle *the rabbit in the hat* properly.

It is worth noting that the way in which we have treated definites is not the only possible approach. For instance, Russell (1905) argued that the definite determiner *the* should be treated as a quantifier. For the examples in (48), a properly Russellian quantificational entry such as the following (with the semantics repeated from chapter 3, (45)) would generate the same range of readings as our nonquantificational entry.

(50) a. *the* ⇒ **the**: $np \Uparrow s/n$
      b. **the** $\overset{\text{def}}{=} \lambda P.\lambda Q.\textbf{some}(P)(Q) \wedge \textbf{definite}(P)$
      c. **definite** $\overset{\text{def}}{=} \lambda P.\textbf{some}(\lambda y.\textbf{every}(\lambda x.P(x) \leftrightarrow x = y))$

But how such readings are generated changes when we move from individual to quantified definites. For instance, in the case of a sentence with two definites, such as (48a), the grammar generates two cut-free (or normalized) derivations:

(51) a. *the teacher scolded the student*
      ⇒ **the**(**teach**)$(\lambda x.\textbf{the}(\textbf{stu})(\lambda y.\textbf{scold}(y)(x)))$: s
      b. *the teacher scolded the student*
      ⇒ **the**(**stu**)$(\lambda y.\textbf{the}(\textbf{teach})(\lambda x.\textbf{scold}(y)(x)))$: s

That these analyses are the same can be determined by substituting in the definition of **the**, the results of which are logically equivalent up to the order of existentials. Thus a spurious derivational ambiguity arises much as it does in the case of a pair of existentials or of adjectives and prepositional attachment. Similarly, the sentence in (48b) has the same ambiguous derivations as (48a). Here the readings are the same as long as there is at least one student. Otherwise, the analysis in which the universal is given wide scope could be trivially satisfied. Similarly, the scope ambiguities in (48c) and (48d) would have their usual analyses.

But matters are quite different when we consider the sentence that originally inspired Russell's analysis:

(52) The king of France is not bald.

If we treat the definite as a quantifier, then the analysis of (52) proceeds as in figure 7.19, which produces the following two results, as indicated in chapter 3, (46).

(53) a. **the**(**king_of_France**)$(\lambda x.\neg\textbf{bald}(x))$
      b. $\neg$**the**(**king_of_France**)(**bald**)

The key point here is that the first analysis, which Russell considered the primary analysis, only the verb phrase is negated, and the existence of a unique king of France is required for the interpretation to be true. Under the second analysis, in which the quantifier takes narrow scope under the negation, if there is no king of France, the sentence is automatically true.

Proponents of both the quantificational and referential approach to definiteness remain, and I leave the issue unresolved. I conclude by noting, as I did in section 3.5.3, that the debate between Strawson and Russell as to whether or not context plays a role in determining definiteness is orthogonal to the issue of whether the definite determiner behaves as a Russellian quantifier or a Strawsonian definite description. Further contextual restrictions on the interpretation of a noun can be encoded under either approach.

7.9   POSSESSIVES

In this section we consider the use of possessive noun phrases, as found in sentences such as the following:

(54) a. Chris stole Jody's hat.
      b. Every kid's toy broke.
      c. Sandy's student's machine is slow.
      d. Kim's student's computer's monitor's image is fuzzy.

These examples all involve a noun phrase, followed by 's. Morphologically, the 's is often treated as a *clitic*, where a clitic is understood simply as an expression that seems to attach itself to a word phonologically but has a wider scope semantically. For instance, in (54b), the subexpression *kid's* is often treated as a unit lexically. Instead of following this route, I will simply finesse the problem of surface representation and treat the 's as a lexical entry (but see Kraak 1995 for a type-logical analysis of clitic distribution).

(55) 's $\Rightarrow \lambda x.\lambda P.\iota(\lambda y.\mathbf{poss}(x)(y) \wedge P(y)): np\backslash(np/n)$

The first thing to note about this entry is that it treats possession as a definite relation. Such an analysis is appealing semantically, and can also be supported on syntactic grounds; possessive noun phrases can show up where referential noun phrases are required, as in copula complements and as apositive noun-phrase modifiers. Second, I have assumed a binary relation **poss** which holds between two objects if one possesses the other in some sense. For instance, the first sentence above is analyzed as in figure 7.23. Notice that I have chosen the lexical entry so that the combination of the possessive and its noun-phrase complement form a determinerlike category, which then applies to a noun in the ordinary way.

Of course, we also get cases of quantifiers showing up in the possessor slot, as in (54b). The proper readings of these sentences follow naturally

$$
\begin{array}{c}
\underline{\text{Chris}}_{\text{Lx}} \quad \underline{\text{stole}}_{\text{Lx}} \quad \underline{\text{Jody}}_{\text{Lx}} \quad \underline{\text{'s}}_{\text{Lx}} \quad \underline{\text{hat}}_{\text{Lx}}
\end{array}
$$

$$
\begin{array}{llll}
\mathbf{c}{:}\,np & \mathbf{steal} & \mathbf{j}{:}\,np & \lambda x.\lambda P.\iota(\lambda y.\mathbf{poss}(x)(y) \wedge P(y)) & \mathbf{hat}{:}\,n \\
 & np\backslash s/np & & np\backslash(np/n) &
\end{array}
$$

$$
\cfrac{
\cfrac{
\cfrac{
\cfrac{\lambda P.\iota(\lambda y.\mathbf{poss}(\mathbf{j})(y) \wedge P(y)){:}\,np/n}{
\iota(\lambda y.\mathbf{poss}(\mathbf{j})(y) \wedge \mathbf{hat}(y)){:}\,np}\;/\mathrm{E}
}{
\mathbf{steal}(\iota(\lambda y.\mathbf{poss}(\mathbf{j})(y) \wedge \mathbf{hat}(y))){:}\,np\backslash s}\;\backslash\mathrm{E}
}{}
}{
\mathbf{steal}(\iota(\lambda y.\mathbf{poss}(\mathbf{j})(y) \wedge \mathbf{hat}(y)))(\mathbf{c}){:}\,s}\;\backslash\mathrm{E}
$$

Figure 7.23
A derivation of *Chris stole Jody's hat*

$$
\begin{array}{c}
\underline{\text{Every kid}}_{\text{D}} \quad \underline{\text{'s}}_{\text{Lx}} \quad \underline{\text{toy}}_{\text{Lx}} \quad \underline{\text{broke}}_{\text{Lx}}
\end{array}
$$

$$
\begin{array}{llll}
\mathbf{every}(\mathbf{kid}) & \lambda z.\lambda P.\iota(\lambda y.\mathbf{poss}(z)(y) \wedge P(y)) & \mathbf{toy} & \mathbf{break} \\
np\Uparrow s & np\backslash(np/n) & n & np\backslash s
\end{array}
$$

$$
\cfrac{
\cfrac{\;}{x{:}\,np}\;\Uparrow\mathrm{E}^{0}
}{} \qquad
$$

$$
\cfrac{
\cfrac{
\cfrac{
\cfrac{\lambda P.\iota(\lambda y.\mathbf{poss}(x)(y) \wedge P(y)){:}\,np/n}{
\iota(\lambda y.\mathbf{poss}(x)(y) \wedge \mathbf{toy}(y)){:}\,np}\;/\mathrm{E}
}{
\mathbf{break}(\iota(\lambda y.\mathbf{poss}(x)(y) \wedge \mathbf{toy}(y))){:}\,s}\;\backslash\mathrm{E}
}{
\mathbf{every}(\mathbf{kid})(\lambda x.\mathbf{break}(\iota(\lambda y.\mathbf{poss}(x)(y) \wedge \mathbf{toy}(y)))){:}\,s}\;0
}{}
$$

Figure 7.24
A derivation of *Every kid's toy broke*

on my analysis, the one for (54b) being given in figure 7.24. Here we see that the analysis of quantification allows each kid to possess a different toy, though the toy must be unique for each kid.

Williams (1982) claimed that the relation between a possessive and the object "possessed" can be arbitrary. For instance, *Francis's car* can either mean the car Francis owns, the car Francis is standing next to, the one he's renting, and so on. To achieve this effect, we need only interpret the constant **poss** based on contextual factors. In contrast to Williams, Barker (1991) points out some interesting facts concerning the range of interpretations available for the possessive. For instance, consider the following expressions of part-whole relationships.

(56) a. the table's leg / #the leg's table

b. the box's cover / #the cover's box

c. the person's arm / #the arm's person

$$
\begin{array}{c}
\dfrac{Jo}{\mathbf{j}:np}\mathrm{Lx} \quad \dfrac{\text{'}s}{\lambda x.\lambda P.\iota(P(x)):np\backslash(np/(n/np_{\mathrm{of}}))}\mathrm{Lx} \quad \dfrac{picture}{\mathbf{picture}:n/np_{\mathrm{of}}}\mathrm{Lx}\\[2ex]
\dfrac{}{}\backslash\mathrm{E}\\[-1ex]
\dfrac{\lambda P.\iota(P(\mathbf{j})):np/(n/np_{\mathrm{of}})}{\iota(\mathbf{picture}(\mathbf{j})):np}/\mathrm{E}
\end{array}
$$

Figure 7.25
A derivation of *Jo's picture*

There is a conventional understanding in utterances of *the X's Y* that *Y* is a part of *X*. As usual, we will focus on the compositional contribution of the possessive rather than its fine-grained lexical semantics. The reader interested in other distributional facts and semantic analyses of the possessive is urged to consult Barker 1991.

In English, the possessive construction can also be used in some cases to fill the complement roles of a relational noun.

(57) a. the sister of Jo / Jo's sister
  b. the picture of Jo / Jo's picture
  c. Jo's picture of Francis / #Jo's sister of Francis
  d. the belief of Francis that Brett would retire
  e. Francis's belief that Brett would retire
  f. #that Brett would retire's belief of Francis

I claim that in the first two cases, (57a) and (57b), the *of*-marked prepositional object alternates with the possessive with the same effect. When both appear, as in (57c), the possessive must be read possessively because the only option for the *of*-phrase is as a complement. Of course, this leads to a pragmatic infelicity in the case of *Jo's sister of Francis*, because sisters aren't typically owned (although consider the situation in which Francis is a puppy with a lot of sisters, each owned by a different individual). The last cases, (57d–f), indicate that it is only *of*-complements that can be consumed by possessives. To handle such cases, we have two options. First, we could try to generalize the already highly contextualized notion of possession to filling argument roles. Alternatively, we could admit a second lexical categorization for the possessive that consumes a nominal complement that itself seeks a complement.

(58) $\text{'}s \Rightarrow \lambda x.\lambda R.\iota(R(x)):np\backslash(np/(n/np_{of}))$

An analysis of a noun phrase involving this entry can be found in figure 7.25. It is also interesting to note that an expression such as *Jo's picture* is ambiguous, due to the detransitivized lexical entry for *picture* (in general, any noun taking a complement also appears as a noun lacking an expressed complement but with its position bound off semantically by an existential quantifier).

(59) *picture* $\Rightarrow \lambda x.\mathbf{some}(\lambda y.\mathbf{picture}(y)(x)): n$

This entry allows a purely possessive reading of *Jo's picture*.

(60) *Jo's picture* $\Rightarrow \iota(\lambda x.\mathbf{some}(\lambda y.\mathbf{picture}(y)(x)) \wedge \mathbf{poss}(\mathbf{j})(x)): np$

   To further complicate matters, the possessive relation can be indicated by an *of*-marked complement, as long as the object of the preposition is itself possessive.

(61) a. the picture of {Jo / Jo's / his / him}
      b. the picture of Francis of {his / *him / Jo's / *Jo}

In the first example, (61a), the full range of complements is allowed, but with the possessives, the relationship is not depiction but ownership or some other form of possession. Similarly, when an explicit complement for the picture is given, as in (61b), we get the same pattern as in (57c). In exercise 11 we consider raising the type of possessives to take quantified complements to deal with expressions such as *every kid's favorite toy* used to refer to a single toy.

7.10   INDEFINITES

The behavior of noun phrases with the indefinite articles *a* and *an* stands in stark contrast both to that of noun phrases with quantifiers and to that of definite descriptions, although they share properties of both. As a first pass, we might try to analyze *a* as being synonymous with the existential determiner *some*. After all, the following sentences appear to have nearly identical truth conditions.

(62) a. A student studied.
      b. Some student studied.

But there are at least four ways in which indefinites differ from other quantifiers.

   First, indefinites pattern like definites in their ability to appear in contexts demanding so-called *referential noun phrases*, for instance, as a complement to *be* and in *appositive* constructions.

(63) a. Sandy is {a student / the best student / Terry's friend / no hero / some student / *every student}.
   b. Sandy, {a hero / the best student / *some student / *every student}, is our hardest worker.

These contrasts are perhaps not the strongest evidence, as it is not clear why *no hero* can appear as a complement to *be*, because negatives obviously fail to refer. Also, the pattern of the quantificational determiner *some* is confusing, perhaps because of its close connection with indefinites. There is also a reading with *some student* that can be interpreted as stating that Sandy is an impressive student.

The second point of departure concerns scope islands. Unlike other quantifiers, indefinites can penetrate islands on quantifiers to land in wide-scope positions. Consider the difference between the following examples (based on Fodor and Sag 1982 and Abusch 1994).

(64) a. Every student who is in {a / some} class I teach studied hard.
   b. Every teacher overheard the rumor that {a / some} student of mine had been called before the dean.
   c. If {a / some} student in the syntax class cheats on the exam, every professor will be fired.
   d. Each department head believes that it would be damaging for {a / some} professor in her department to quit.

In (64a), the relative clause forms an island from which ordinary quantifiers such as those with the determiners *some* and *every* cannot escape to take wide scope, whereas the indefinite clearly can. Similarly, in (64b), if *some* occurs, the rumor must be de dicto in the sense that the hearing was about some student or other; with the indefinite *a*, every teacher could have heard a specific rumor about the same student under the reading where the indefinite takes widest scope. In (64c), the antecedent clause of the conditional forms an island from which a quantified noun phrase cannot escape. Thus the claim is that with *some*, this sentence can only mean that every professor will be fired if any of the students cheat; with an indefinite, there is also a reading whereby there is a particular student such that if that student cheats, every professor will be fired. Example (64d) is similar to the previous three, with the island being an extraposed sentential subject (see section 11.1.4 for more details on sentential subjects and section 11.4 for an analysis of extraposition).

A third way in which indefinites differ from other determiners and pattern like definites is in their ability to induce generic readings, as we will see in section 7.11.

Like quantifiers, indefinites are not required to have scope over the clausal or sentential unit in which they appear. Indefinites can pattern just like existentials in contexts such as the following:

(65) Everyone in the U.S. drives {some / a} car.

It is apparent that either the indefinite or existential determiner can take narrow scope relative to *everyone* in such cases. This led Fodor and Sag (1982) to claim that indefinites are ambiguous between a reading in which they behave essentially like the existential *some* and a reading in which they behave like the demonstrative *that*, with the relevant "pointing" required by demonstratives going on in the mind of the speaker rather than in the context (I will discuss demonstratives in the context of indexicality in section 10.3). Such an analysis would generate either the restricted island-bound readings of a quantifier or would immediately move to the top level of the quantificational structure, like other demonstratives. Fodor and Sag's analysis prohibits *intermediate scopings* from being generated. For instance, in (64b), no reading is generated in which *a student of mine* escapes the relative-clause island while staying within the scope of the subject universal, a reading that is paraphrasable as stating that for each teacher, there was a particular student of mine such that the teacher overheard the rumor that the student had been called before the dean. King (1988) provides the putative counterexample (66a), claiming that an intermediate scoping is possible. Abusch (1994) agrees, citing the logical independence of the readings in the structurally identical (66b).

(66) a. Each author in the room despises every publisher who would
       not publish a book that was deemed pornographic.
     b. Every professor rewarded every student who read a book he had
       recommended.

The data is obviously quite subtle here. King's claim is that there is a reading where the book depends on the author, thus escaping the relative island but scoping within the universal subject. In any case, because I am not particularly concerned with islands here, I will turn to the most compelling reason for differentiating indefinites from existentials.

The fourth and perhaps most striking way in which indefinites differ from existentials is in their ability to be assimilated into quantifiers and conditionals. Consider the following examples of so-called *donkey sentences*, first noted by Geach (1962).

(67) a. Every farmer who owns a donkey beats it.
     b. If a farmer owns a donkey, he beats it.

The reading of (67a) that concerns us here is the one that is true if and only if for every pair consisting of a farmer and a donkey he owns, the farmer beats the donkey. There is a synonymous reading for (67b): if x is a farmer, y is a donkey, and x owns y, then x beats y. The puzzle that arises is how a basically existential determiner like *a* can behave universally in this way.

Lewis (1975) proposes a two-pronged solution to this problem. First, he assumes that indefinites are represented as free variables with restrictions on their interpretations. Abusch (1994) further develops the role of the restrictions, which I avoid for the time being. Lewis then proposes a new logical mechanism of *unselective binding*, in which a quantifier can bind all of the variables in its scope. He proposes notations $\forall\phi$ and $\exists\phi$, which he takes to bind all of the variables free in ϕ. This leads to the following definition:

(68) $[\![\forall\phi]\!]_{\mathcal{M}}^{\theta} = \begin{cases} \textbf{yes} & \text{if } [\![\phi]\!]_{\mathcal{M}}^{\theta'} = \textbf{yes for all } \theta' \sim_{\text{Free}_{(\phi)}} \theta \\ \textbf{no} & \text{otherwise} \end{cases}$

Recall that Free(ϕ) is the set of variables free in ϕ. The notation $\theta \sim_X \theta'$ is meant to indicate that θ agrees with θ' on every variable not in the set X. Thus in this case, $\forall\phi$ is true under an assignment if ϕ is true under every assignment that at most differs in the assignments to variables free in ϕ. $\exists\phi$ is handled in the same way. Lewis suggests that other operators also exploit unselective binding, mentioning as examples implications and quantificational adverbs (see section 12.5.8 for a discussion of quantificational adverbs). Lewis also points out that unselective binding does not introduce any new logical power above ordinary universal and existential quantifiers.

Lewis uses unselective binding to represent Geach's example (67a) as follows:

(69) $\forall((\textbf{farmer}(x) \wedge \textbf{donkey}(y) \wedge \textbf{own}(y)(x)) \rightarrow \textbf{beat}(y)(x))$

Such analyses are acceptable from a logical point of view for this case. Without unselective binding, we can approximate these readings by binding sequences of individuals, as in the following formula, which is logically equivalent to Lewis's (69).

(70) **every**$_{\mathrm{Ind} \times \mathrm{Ind}}$
$$(\lambda x.\mathbf{farmer}(\pi_1(x)) \wedge \mathbf{donkey}(\pi_2(x)) \wedge \mathbf{own}(\pi_2(x))(\pi_1(x)))$$
$$(\lambda x.\mathbf{beat}(\pi_2(x))(\pi_1(x)))$$

Although this logical expression appears to capture the meaning of the donkey sentence (67a), it is not at all clear how such meanings can be generated in a compositional fashion. There are also logical problems concerning binding from a higher clause: there has to be some mechanism to restrict the variables that unselective quantifiers bind. For instance, there should be a way to refine an expression such as $(\exists y)\forall\phi(x, y, z)$ so that y is bound by the selective existential and not the unselective universal. This problem was solved by the independent introduction of discourse-representation theory (DRT) by Kamp (1981) and file-card semantics by Heim (1982), theories that differed only in their notation. Both theories provide analyses of unselective quantification that allow binding to be more explicitly marked. The markers for scope are known as *discourse referents*, a construct introduced independently by Karttunen (1976) to address the related issues of presupposition and the potential for intersentential anaphora.

In addition to enabling scope to be marked, Heim and Kamp were able to uniformly treat indefinites as introducing discourse referents, which are essentially scope-marked variables with restrictive side conditions. This has allowed compositional syntactic/semantic theories to be developed (Carpenter 1989, Zeevat 1989, Muskens 1993). Discourse representation theories are also adept at handling constraints on intrasentential and intersentential anaphora, a topic to which we return in chapter 9.

To reconcile ideas from discourse-representation theory with more standard logical representations and the idea of discourse referents as being updated, Groenendijk and Stokhof (1991) introduced a system they call *dynamic predicate logic* (DPL). Roughly, the point of DPL is to treat the existential quantifier like an assignment statement in a programming language, threading such assignments from left to right through the evaluation of a conjunction. This dramatically changes the conventional notion of quantifier scoping. For instance, it becomes possible to interpret $((\exists x)\phi) \wedge \psi$ with the existential quantifier binding the occurrences of x in ψ, even though they are not properly within its scope. The way this is done is by treating the subterm $(\exists x)\phi$ as setting the value of x and passing this setting on to the evaluation of the second conjunct ψ. In classical first-order logic, such changes to assignments last only until the subterm over which the quantifier scoped was evaluated. With their notion of dynamic scoping, Groenendijk and Stokhof are able to treat indefinites as introducing existential quantifiers in the ordinary way. By interpreting the existentials differently, this allows the binding of an existential to survive beyond its usual scope limitations. Chierchia (1992) extends Groenendijk and Stokhof's logic to a higher-order intensional setting and discusses in detail the resulting possibilities for anaphoric binding.

I will not have much more to say concerning the logic of indefinites. Integrating their logic with the logic of other quantifiers remains an interesting open problem (however, see Kamp and Reyle 1993, Chierchia 1992).

7.11 GENERICS

In this section I discuss the semantics of so-called *generics*. My presentation closely follows that of Schubert and Pelletier's (1987) survey, and the interested reader is urged to consult that paper for further details. In the null context, the following sentences, drawn from Schubert and Pelletier (1987), will likely be interpreted generically.

(71) a. Snakes are reptiles.
    b. Telephone books are thick books.
    c. Guppies give live birth.
    d. Italians are good skiers.
    e. Frenchmen eat horsemeat.
    f. Unicorns have one horn.

As Schubert and Pelletier point out, these sentences are made true by different absolute numbers and ratios of instances of their subjects having the property introduced by the verb phrase. For instance, every snake is a reptile, but not every telephone book is a thick book. Only female guppies give live birth, and not all female guppies have that privilege. Although most Italians are not good skiers, there is a higher percentage of good Italian skiers than good skiers of other nationalities. And while few Frenchmen may eat horsemeat, the mere fact that some of them do seems enough to license (71e). And in the last case, note that there are no unicorns. This seems to prevent any kind of analysis of generics by means of a logical quantifier. Certainly *every* would be too strong, and the latter examples in (71) seem to argue against a weaker version with a quantifier like *most*.

Although the examples in (71) all involve *bare plurals* (see section 8.2) and are all in the present tense, generics may appear in any tense and with any kind of referential noun phrase. For instance, consider the following variants of (71a).

(72) a. Snakes are reptiles.
   b. A snake is a reptile.
   c. The snake is a reptile.

Thus the notion of a generic is not intrinsically linked to that of plurality. To see that the tense can vary for generic sentences, consider the following:

(73) a. Workers are not protected now.
   b. Workers were not protected last year.
   c. Workers will not be protected next year.

Thus an immediate puzzle raised by generics is how their genericity is signaled syntactically and semantically. In the rest of this section we consider the most well-known approaches that have been suggested for treating the semantics of generics.

In all of the approaches to the semantics of generics we discuss, there is a fundamental reliance on the notion of *kind*. Carlson (1977b), in his seminal work on generics, noted several phenomena that provide motivation for a kind-as-individual approach. First, some predicates appear to select generic complements, for instance *be extinct*, *be common*, and *be widespread*. Second, pronouns can have generic antecedents, as the following illustrates.

(74) Students are busy. They read and write.

Here the pronoun *they* is connected to a generic antecedent—something that is not possible with a quantified antecedent such as *every student*.

Carlson (1977b) introduced the notion of *kind* as a primitive, along with a relation between individuals and their kinds. He then interpreted generics as applying properties to these kinds. Thus (71a) might be represented as something like **reptile**$_g$(**snake**$_k$), where **snake**$_k$ is the kind of snakes and **reptile**$_g$ is the property that applies to kinds that are reptiles. Such an analysis is rather unsatisfying without further elaboration of the connection between the two kinds of predication, generic and ordinary. Carlson relates these by a *realization relation* **realize**$(k)(x)$, which holds if k refers to a kind of which x is an instance. Then the nongeneric interpretation of *snake* can be given by **realize**(**snake**$_k$), which is a property that holds of all individual snakes. But rather than locating the ambiguity in the noun phrase, Carlson notes examples such as the following and claims they are evidence for an approach where the distinction is made in the verb phrase.

(75) Snow is white and falling in my yard.

Thus Carlson locates the realization relation in the verb phrase because there is only one noun phrase in (75) and we need to read one verb phrase generically and the other referentially. But our type-logical approach allows us to analyze coordinations such as (75) with a realization operator that wold apply directly to the noun phrase by means of a technique I introduce in figure 8.7 in section 8.4. Carlson also provides a means of translating a predicate of individuals to a predicate of kinds. Further enriching his ontology, he introduces a third class of objects, which he calls *stages*. The idea is that an individual has various stages, such as Sandy during her 112th week of life and the tree outside Sandy's window for the next few minutes. Individuals are also related to their stages by a realization relation. The need for such operators to massage meanings into the appropriate forms present substantial obstacles to a compositional semantic analysis.

Chierchia (1982) elaborates, revises, and extends Carlson's theory by collapsing some of the type distinctions and showing how the theory can be applied to singular cases too. His analysis is based on a type theory in which polymorphic interpretation is the norm. An elaboration of this type theory would take us far afield, but the main idea is that some of the coercions needed by Carlson's theory are either assimilated to single coercions or dispensed with entirely.

Farkas and Sugioka (1983) provide an unselective quantifier-based approach to generics that can handle, in a natural way, sentences with multiple generics, such as the following:

(76) Dogs hate cats.

Generics also interact with other quantifiers, as can be seen in examples such as the following:

(77) a. Lions have a tail.
       b. Students entering college have to take a test.

These examples show that generics enter into standard scope alternations—a fact not taken into account by Farkas and Sugioka's theory.

Farkas and Sugioka also provide an analysis of so-called *restrictive if/when clauses*, the canonical example of which is (78a):

(78) a. Bears are intelligent {when / if} they have blue eyes.
      b. Canaries are popular when they are rare.

The principal idea is that there is a genericity to the conditional statement. Carlson, in contrast, analyzed these cases by assuming that the restrictive clause provided a restriction on the kind, which raises substantial problems for a compositional syntax/semantics interface.

There are two fundamental problems with all of these approaches. First, they obscure the syntax/semantics relation to such an extent that it is very difficult to see how to extend the analyses to interact properly with other phenomena, such as tense, quantification, anaphora, focus, plurality, embedded contexts like belief reports, modification, and even multiple generics. Just to take an example, consider the role of focus in the following two examples:

(79) a. It is beavers that build dams.
      b. It is dams that are built by beavers.

Although both of these cases involve two generically interpreted bare plurals and the same relation between them, their interpretations seem quite distinct in the cleft constructions in (79). With (79a), we are stating of dams that they are generically built by beavers; with (79b), we alternatively state that what beavers generically build are dams. Stressing the subject or object in the simple sentence *Beavers build dams* evokes readings synonymous with those in (79).

The second problem with the analyses we have discussed is that they do not even address the deep question of what it means for a kind to have a property or what the relationship is between a kind and a property in a nontrivial way. For instance, none of these analyses explain the problem raised by Schubert and Pelletier (1987) about the notion of regularity in the interpretation of generics. Schubert and Pelletier discuss a situation in which every child born in Rainbow Lake, Alberta, coincidentally happens to be right-handed, and they wonder about the status of the following sentence:

(80) Babies born in Rainbow Lake, Alberta, are right-handed.

It seems fairly clear that genericity is in some sense tied to regular, rule-governed phenomena, itself a notoriously tricky concept to analyze. Cohen (1994, 1996) presents a theory of generics based on Rooth's (1985,

1992) notion of focus and a measure of probability. For instance, the comparison class in (71b) would be the class of books, in (71c) it would be other individuals who give birth, and in (71d) and (71e) it would be other nationalities. In all cases, the generic item is statistically more likely to engage in the predicate it occurs with than the other members of the comparison class.

7.12   COMPARATIVES

In this section we consider the syntactic and semantic forms of *comparative* constructions. Comparison is realized in many different syntactic categories, including manner adverbs, temporal adverbs, adjectives, determiners, and prepositions. The most widely studied class consists of the *gradable adjectives*, which, like other gradable modifiers (see (82)), can be classified into four main constructions:

(81) a. Terry is tall.   (Positive)
      b. Terry is as tall as Chris.   (Equative)
      c. Terry is taller than Chris.   (Comparative)
      d. Terry is the tallest child.   (Superlative)

Comparatives in other categories include the following:

(82) a. Terry wrote more prosaically than Chris.   (Manner adverb)
      b. Terry arrived later than Chris.   (Temporal adverb)
      c. Terry is taller than Chris.   (Adjective)
      d. Terry wrote more papers than Chris.   (Determiner)
      e. Terry lives closer to school than Chris.   (Preposition)

In all of these cases, a gradable modifier (or determiner) is involved. Other categories also allow equative and superlative gradable forms. We begin our study with a brief survey of the semantics of gradability and comparison.

7.12.1   Gradability and Measurability

Fundamentally, comparison involves an ordering of a class of objects along a fixed dimension. Most abstractly, we can assume that the objects being compared form a preordering (a set with a binary relation that is transitive and reflexive; see section A.3 for full definitions). The reason I do not enforce linearity is that it might be the case that two objects cannot be compared along some dimension. For instance, in measuring how good a paper in linguistics is, many factors come into play, and it might not be possible to say that a given paper in phonology is better, worse, or even equally as good as another paper in pragmatics. Alternatively, we might compare the size of boxes and find some are longer but narrower than others; of course, if the scale is set to be volume, such comparisons become felicitous. Similarly, I do not enforce antisymmetry, because we might be able to compare two objects and find out they match on a scale. We might compare two different groups along the dimension of cardinality, such as practicing phonologists and nineteenth-century Romance-literature critics, and determine that they are identical in terms of their numbers of members. All we need to determine the truth of comparatives such as those in (81) is the ability to compare elements pairwise along some dimension. In general, we cannot be ensured that there will be a largest (or smallest) element in such a set, nor even in a finite subset of it.

Many, but not all, comparative constructions also allow *measure* or *degree* specifiers.

(83) a. Sandy is six feet tall.
     b. Sandy is fifty IQ points smarter than Terry.
     c. Sandy's time is the fastest by three seconds.

Here the expression *six feet* provides a specification of height in terms of the combination of the number *six* and unit *feet*. Similarly, *fifty IQ points* and *three seconds* provide a numerical specifier and an indication of the units of measure. Such specifiers can be *additive measures*, as in the previous examples, or *multiplicative measures*, as in the following.

(84) a. Sandy is three times as old as Terry.
     b. That route is half as fast as this one.

Note that additive measures occur with positive, comparative, and superlative constructions, whereas multiplicative measures occur with equatives. Further note that many dimensions of comparison do not allow measurement. Even though we may be able to determine that Sandy is a better writer than Terry, it is not clear that there are any objective standards, numerical or otherwise, by which to judge such matters. Notice that many multiplicative measures that do occur, such as *twice as smart* and *half as faithful*, are often meant metaphorically or hyperbolically rather than literally.

For measurable dimensions of comparison D, we can assume that there is a function $\text{Meas}_D: \mathbf{Obj} \rightarrow \mathbf{R}$ from the objects of comparison to real numbers in some fixed scale. Such a function determines a linear pre-ordering of the objects in the domain (with a linear preordering, every pair of objects has one is bigger than the other or they are the same size). We simply set $a \preceq b$ if and only if $\text{Meas}_D(a) \leq \text{Meas}_D(b)$. Viewed from the opposite perspective, a measure function is a homomorphism from the abstract ordering of objects to the real numbers. Other scales can be normalized to a single standard to allow comparison. For instance, meters, fathoms, hands, inches, and furlongs are all interconvertible, differing only by a linear multiple. It is also crucial to note that measurability is only determined relative to a scale. For instance, consider the following:

(85) Great Britain is larger than Australia (in terms of {population / area}).

If we are comparing populations, this is true, but if we are comparing land mass, it is false. The dimension of comparison is often supplied contextually, but can be made explicit with such phrases as *in terms of population*.

Even numerically scaled domains can have complex behaviors. For instance, the Richter scale for measuring the energy of earthquakes is logarithmic (base 60); an earthquake measuring 7 on the Richter scale generates 60 times as much energy as one measuring 6 on the Richter scale. Thus an expression such as *twice as big an earthquake* is highly ambiguous without a further specification such as *as measured on the Richter scale* or *in terms of the energy generated*. Other complexities arise from negative measures. For instance, the net worth of a person can be either positive or negative, depending on whether they have established net equity or net debt. It is rather unclear how we would use multiplicative measures to compare someone in debt to someone with net equity.

7.12.2 The Grammar of Comparatives

Over the years, several approaches to the syntax and semantics of comparatives have developed, with no clear consensus emerging. This is because certain comparative constructions involve predicative constructions with complicated word order and distribution, along with subtle interactions with unbounded dependencies respecting island constraints, ellipsis, quantificational force, negative-polarity items, vagueness, and cross-categorial similarities, in addition to a great deal of contextually supplied information that confounds the assignment of semantic types to syntactic categories. A fairly comprehensive survey of the syntactic issues and classification of syntactic constructions in transformational terms can be found in the seminal Bresnan 1973. Typological surveys of comparative constructions can be found in Ultan 1972 and Stassen 1985. A detailed study of comparatives in Dutch in a categorial setting, concentrating on gapping and coordination, can be found in Hendriks 1995.

Coupled with the rather complex nature of comparison and measure across multiple dimensions and subdomains, comparatives present a formidable puzzle for compositional-semantic treatments. Surveys of the key semantic issues can be found in von Stechow 1984 and Klein 1980. In this section we will concentrate on the core constructions involved in adjectival comparative constructions. Constructions in other syntactic domains are analogous, and we return to them in several exercises in later chapters after I introduce the relevant noncomparative analyses (exercise 21, chap. 8; exercise 21, chap. 9; and exercise 23, chap. 12).

I adopt an *extent*-based approach to comparison, following Seuren (1984). Under this theory, gradable adjectives such as *tall* will be interpreted as binary relations that hold of an individual and a degree if the individual has the quality (height) of that degree or more. Although the literature is rather silent on the matter of *polar opposites* of gradable adjectives, I will interpret *short* as a relation that holds between an individual and a degree if the individual has a height that is at most of that degree. Thus for the examples we will consider, I make the following definitions:

(86) a. **tall** $\overset{\text{def}}{=} \lambda d.\lambda x.\textbf{height}(x) \geq d$
     b. **short** $\overset{\text{def}}{=} \lambda d.\lambda x.\textbf{height}(x) \leq d$

Here we assume that **height** is a measure function mapping individuals into their heights measured in meters. Thus if **tall**$(d)(x)$ holds, then the individual denoted by x has a height of at least the degree denoted by d. Similarly, if **short**$(d)(x)$ holds, then x has at most height d. As will soon become evident, the extent-based approach has several advantages over an approach in which individuals are directly associated with unique heights; for explorations of the latter approach, see Cresswell 1976 and von Stechow 1984.

It will be important later to have other functions, such as **width**, which maps an individual to its width, and so on. It is important to note that width and height are *commensurable measures*, both given in meters. But not all measures are commensurate in this sense. This can be seen by noting the contrast in felicity created by the following examples, syntactic details of which are given after (114).

(87) a.   Sandy is wider than Terry is tall.
   b.   ?Sandy is a better runner than Terry is a jumper.
   c.   #Sandy is thinner than Terry is loyal.

When using commensurate degrees, the examples are fine. Perhaps (87b) can be interpreted as meaning that Sandy is in a higher percentile as a runner than Terry is as a jumper. Using percentile scores provides one way to make all comparisons commensurable. But when the gradable adjectives lack any kind of semantic or contextual connection, as in (87c), comparisons are less felicitous.

With an extent-based approach, we can provide a uniform semantic assignment to intensifiers that can be used with both upward and downward gradable adjectives. First note that in the interpretation of expressions such as *is tall* or *is very tall*, there is both vagueness and context dependency. Vagueness because it is not always clear what the boundary between tall and not-tall is, and context dependency because height is usually measured against some contextually given standard of comparison. We will represent the comparison class as a variable P denoting a set of individuals. A predicate such as *very tall* will be represented as applied to an individual variable y as $\mathbf{very}(P)(\mathbf{tall})(y)$, which holds if and only if $y \in P$ and there is a degree d such that $\mathbf{tall}(d)(y)$ and very few of the other elements $x \in P$ are such that $\mathbf{tall}(d)(x)$. Of course, what constitutes "very few" in an utterance of the intensifier is left vague. In this explanation of the intended meaning of *very*, note that there is an implicit quantification over degrees. We can codify this intuitive picture by defining the intensifier in terms of the vague determiner **few** as follows:

(88) $\mathbf{very} \overset{\text{def}}{=} \lambda P.\lambda G.\lambda y.P(y) \wedge \mathbf{some}(\lambda d.G(d)(y) \wedge \mathbf{few}^2(P)(\lambda x.G(d)(x)))$

In this term, P is the comparison class, G is a gradable adjective, and y is an individual of which the degree G is predicated relative to P. Note that the conjunct $P(y)$ ensures that y is a member of the comparison class P. The quantificational conjunct can be glossed as stating that there is some degree d to which y has G and to which few other members of P have G.

Now consider the intensified downward gradable adjective expression *very short*. The term $\mathbf{very}(P)(\mathbf{short})(y)$ will be true if and only if y is a member of the comparison class P and is at most some height d such that very few of the members of P are of at most height d.

For the bare predicate *tall*, we can introduce a predicate **pos** such that
pos$(P)(G)(y)$ is true of a gradable adjective G, comparison class P and
individual y if y is in P and there is a degree d such that $G(d)(y)$ and at
most half of the $x \in P$ are such that $G(d)(x)$. The positive case **pos** could
be defined in the same way as the intensifier **very**:

(89) **pos** $\overset{\text{def}}{=} \lambda P.\lambda G.\lambda y.P(y) \wedge \mathbf{some}(\lambda d.G(d)(y) \wedge \mathbf{most}^2(P)(\lambda x.G(d)(x)))$

We will need additional syntactic and semantic types to deal with
comparatives. To simplify the exposition, I will only consider the dimension of length, as expressed by such predicates as *tall, short, long*, and
wide. I will also assume that meters are the units of measurement; other
linear length scales can be mapped linearly to meters, as exemplified
below in my treatment of unit-denoting terms, such as *inches* and *fathoms*.
Thus we will not need to be concerned about vagueness with respect to
dimension, as in (85), nor about abstract comparison classes expressed
solely as partial orders. The categories I assume and their associated types
are as follows:

(90) *Category*   *Type*   *Description*
      num   **Real**   real number
      deg   **Real**   degree

I have simplified matters by assuming that we are dealing with a single
kind of degree measurable with real numbers. For a more general treatment, degrees need to include not only a numerical value but also an
indication of the *dimension* of comparison, such as weight, height, or land
speed. For nonmeasurable degrees, we could follow Cresswell (1976) in
representing degrees as equivalence classes of objects ordered by the
standard induced ordering (see section A.3). I also assume that the standard arithmetic operations of multiplication and addition interpret the
constants **times** and **plus**, which I will abbreviate with the standard infix
operators $\cdot$ and $+$.

I begin with an analysis of the following three predicative instances of
gradable adjectives, in both upward and downward polar varieties:

(91) a. Sandy is 160 centimeters {tall / #short}.
      b. Sandy is {tall / short}.
      c. Sandy is {very / extremely} {tall / short}.
      d. *Sandy is {160 cm very / very 160 cm} tall.

Unlike the positive gradable adjective *tall*, the negative *short*, though it
can be used bare or with a degree modifier, cannot be used with an

explicit degree (except in an ellided form in which it implies failure to reach some measure, as in *Sandy is 5 centimeters short of {two meters / her goal}*). This distribution could be coded straightforwardly with syntactic features. It is not at all clear why explicit degrees are infelcitous with negative gradable adjectives in the context of an extent-based theory. The property *160 centimeters short* would apply to an individual that is at most 160 centimeters tall. Below in the context of equative and comparative constructions, we will see further reasons to distinguish positive from negative gradable adjectives. Finally note that degree specifiers and intensifiers cannot co-occur, as will be reflected in our type assignments.

The following lexical entries generate the correct meanings for the positive instances of gradable adjectives, such as those in (91).

(92) a. *tall* $\Rightarrow$ **tall**: $deg \backslash pr$
 b. *short* $\Rightarrow$ **short**: $deg \backslash pr$
 c. *160* $\Rightarrow$ **160**: num
 d. *centimeters* $\Rightarrow$ $\lambda x.(\mathbf{0.01} \cdot x): num \backslash deg$
 e. *tall* $\Rightarrow$ $\mathbf{pos}(X)(\mathbf{tall}): pr$
 f. *very* $\Rightarrow$ $\mathbf{very}(X): pr/(deg \backslash pr)$

We employ two lexical entries for *tall*. In (92a), *tall* requires a degree specifier to produce a proposition indicating that its subject is at least as tall as the degree specifier. This usage is illustrated in figure 7.26. Note that the unit expression *centimeters* is assigned a lexical entry in (92d) in which it takes a numerical complement, such as the one in (92c), in order to produce a degree. I have ignored number agreement in the syntax: the singular-degree expression is appropriate for *one meter* and *one half meter*, whereas the plural-degree expression is found in *two meters* and *many meters*. The entry (92e) does not take a degree complement but

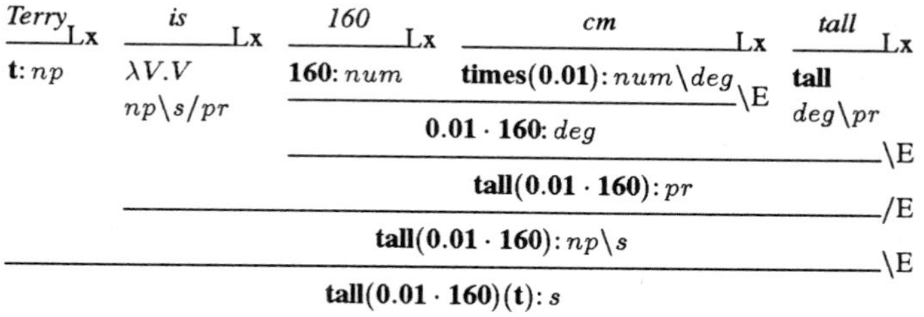

Figure 7.26
A derivation of *Terry is 160 cm tall*

$$
\frac{Sandy}{\text{s}:np}\text{Lx} \quad \frac{is}{\lambda V.V:np\backslash s/pr}\text{Lx} \quad \frac{tall}{\text{pos}(P)(\textbf{tall}):pr}\text{Lx}
$$
$$
\frac{}{\textbf{pos}(P)(\textbf{tall}):np\backslash s}/\text{E}
$$
$$
\frac{}{\textbf{pos}(P)(\textbf{tall})(\text{s}):s}\backslash\text{E}
$$

Figure 7.27
A derivation of *Sandy is tall*

$$
\frac{Sandy}{\text{s}:np}\text{Lx} \quad \frac{is}{\lambda V.V:np\backslash s/pr}\text{Lx} \quad \frac{very}{\textbf{very}(P):pr/(deg\backslash pr)}\text{Lx} \quad \frac{short}{\textbf{short}:deg\backslash pr}\text{Lx}
$$
$$
\frac{}{\textbf{very}(P)(\textbf{short}):pr}/\text{E}
$$
$$
\frac{}{\textbf{very}(P)(\textbf{short}):np\backslash s}/\text{E}
$$
$$
\frac{}{\textbf{very}(P)(\textbf{short})(\text{s}):s}\backslash\text{E}
$$

Figure 7.28
A derivation of *Sandy is very short*

merely specifies that the subject is above average relative to a contextually supplied class X, which I have indicated rather slopplily as a variable. An example derivation with this lexical assignment can be found in figure 7.27. In some cases, the contextually given comparison class can be indicated directly with expressions, such as *for a boy*, although the manner in which such a complement expresses a set is nontrivial (perhaps it involves a reference to kinds [see section 7.11]). In figure 7.28, I provide a derivation involving the intensifier lexical entry in (92f). Note that the derived meaning for an intensified gradable adjective also involves an implicit comparison class.

The categories I have assigned to intensifiers such as *very* will not iterate, and thus well-formed expressions such as *very very tall* and *really really short* are blocked. I claim that such occurrences should be treated by a lexical reduplication of some sort, for two reasons. First, many intensifiers do not iterate, as in **extremely extremely tall* or **quite quite quite tall*. Second, the intensifiers that do iterate do not mix, as shown by the infelicity of **very really very really tall* (the intensifier form of *really* should not be confused with the adverbial usage, as in *really very tall*, which is perfectly acceptable, in contrast to **very really tall*).

One issue worth considering at this point is the notion of *scalar implicature*, which is a kind of Gricean implicature having to do with scalars.

Grice's maxims explain why we prefer *Sandy is six feet tall* to *Sandy is five feet tall* if Sandy is in fact six feet tall. With an extent-based approach to gradable adjectives, the property of being six feet tall entails the property of being five feet tall, but not vice versa. In other words, although adjectives with degree specifiers provide only a lower bound, we are only being cooperative if we provide as tight a lower bound as possible. Of course, in some circumstances, the exact height may be irrelevant as long as it is above a certain minimum. For instance, we might say that *Sandy is four feet tall* if Sandy is in fact four feet, five inches tall and four feet is the minimum height required to ride a roller coaster at an amusement park. This completes our brief survey of the positive occurrences of gradable adjectives.

We turn now to the equative uses of gradable adjectives. We will be analyzing the following cases:

(93) a. Sandy is as {tall / short} as Terry.
     b. Sandy is {twice / half / two times} as {tall / ?short} as Terry.

I will treat the complement *as Terry* as a noun-phrase object, case-marked by *as*. In this case, we need to deal with multipliers rather than degrees. The following logical constant for multiplicative height relations will be useful.

(94) $\textbf{mult} \overset{\text{def}}{=} \lambda n.\lambda G.\lambda x.\lambda y.\textbf{every}^2(\lambda d.G(d)(x))(\lambda d.G(n \cdot d)(y))$

Thus $\textbf{mult}(n)(G)(x)(y)$ will hold if for every degree to which x is G, y has G to a degree at least n times that. Note that in multiplication, the forms of numerals vary; thus we find expressions like *twice* and *two times* rather than either bare numerals like *two* or degrees like *two inches*. To bring multipliers into the fold, I introduce the following category for multipliers:

(95) | *Category* | *Type* | *Description* |
| --- | --- | --- |
| *mlt* | **Real** | Multiplier |

The examples in (93) can be derived from the following lexical entries:

(96) a. $as \Rightarrow \lambda x.x\!: np_{as}/np$
     b. $as \Rightarrow \textbf{mult}(1)\!: pr/np_{as}/(deg\backslash pr)$
     c. $as \Rightarrow \textbf{mult}\!: mlt\backslash(pr/np_{as}/(deg\backslash pr))$
     d. $twice \Rightarrow 2\!: mlt$
     e. $times \Rightarrow \lambda n.n\!: num\backslash mlt$

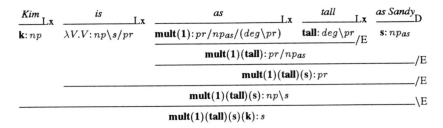

Figure 7.29
A derivation of *Kim is as tall as Sandy*

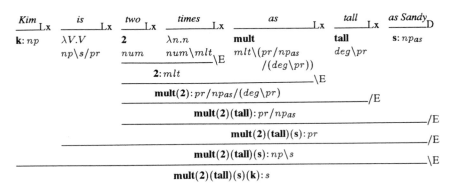

Figure 7.30
A derivation of *Kim is two times as tall as Sandy*

Derivations with and without an explicit numerical multiplier are given in figures 7.29 and 7.30. Note that the only difference is that the bare case has the constant **1** as an implicit multiplier.

Just as in the positive cases, the notion of scalar implicature explains why we want to provide as tight a bound as possible on someone's height. If Kim is 2.3 times as tall as Sandy, it is truthful to say that Kim is twice as tall as Sandy, but it is possible to be more informative if the situation warrants it. Such considerations are crucial in interpreting expressions involving fractional multipliers in equatives, such as the following:

(97) Kim is half as tall as Sandy.

Our grammar derives an interpretation that will be true if Kim is at least half as tall as Sandy. But again, if Kim were in fact exactly 75% as tall as Sandy, it would simply be more informative to assert that directly. Note that our analysis also accounts for negative occurrences, such as the following:

(98) Kim is not half as tall as Sandy.

Such a sentence can be uttered truthfully only if there is some degree d forming a lower bound on Sandy's height such that Kim is not half-of-d tall. Some uses of the negative case may be even more subtle in that we may be negating pragmatic conditions rather than semantic ones; that is, we might use the previous sentence if Kim and Sandy are the same heights, thus negating the scalar implicature. Matters are further complicated because sentences such as (98) can alternatively be phrased positively as *Sandy is less than half as tall as Sandy*. Negation and its interaction with discourse is a thorny issue, the best approach to which has been provided by Horn (1985, 1989).

Next, consider the equative uses of the polar opposites of gradable adjectives, with and without multiplicative specifiers.

(99) a. Sandy is as short as Terry.
　　 b. Sandy is {half / twice} as short as Terry.

In the nonspecific case, (99a), we derive a meaning in which every upper bound on Terry's height is also an upper bound on Sandy's height. Thus if Terry is at most five feet tall, then Sandy is also at most five feet tall. Although this interpretation seems perfectly natural, it is not at all clear, even at an intuitive level, how to interpret the cases in (99b) with multiplicative specifiers. But it is clear that our grammar assigns nonsensical meanings. In the case of *twice*, we derive an interpretation whereby every upper bound d on Terry's height is such that $2d$ is an upper bound on Sandy's height, thus allowing Sandy to be taller than Terry. The situation for *half* is no better. Perhaps such uses, when felicitous, are simply being used metaphorically or in terms of a positive percentile scale.

We now turn to the comparative uses of gradable adjectives. Consider the following examples:

(100) a. Sandy is taller than Terry.
　　　 b. Sandy is six centimeters taller than Terry.

Note that the operation applied to the explicit degree given in (100b) is addition. But for the bare case of (100a), we must have some number greater than 0 to rule out the case where Sandy and Terry are exactly the same height. This is yet another way in which the equative and comparative diverge semantically. The following logical constants will be used in the lexical specification of the positive comparative forms.

(101) a. **add** $\overset{\text{def}}{=} \lambda e.\lambda G.\lambda x.\lambda y.\textbf{some}(\lambda d.G(d+e)(y) \wedge \neg G(d)(x))$
      b. **addsome** $\overset{\text{def}}{=} \lambda G.\lambda x.\lambda y.\textbf{some}(\lambda e.\textbf{add}(e)(G)(x)(y))$

Note that in these terms e and d are degrees, G a gradable adjective, and x and y individuals in this term. Thus $\textbf{add}(e)(G)(x)(y)$ will hold if there is some degree d to which x has G to the degree $d+e$ but y does not have G even to the extent d. Thus x will have G to some degree at least e greater than y does. The term **addsome** simply existentially binds the degree argument of **add**.

In expressing the comparative, we find an alternation between the suffix *-er* and the syntactic modifier *more* (which also has a polar-opposite form, namely *less*, which we consider in exercise 25). The facts concerning the distribution of these two forms are subtle and depend at least on matters of morphological and metrical structure (stress and length, in particular). We treat the complement to the comparative as a *than*-marked noun phrase.

(102) a. *more* $\Rightarrow \lambda G.\lambda d.\textbf{add}(d)(G): deg\backslash(pr/np_{th})/(deg\backslash pr)$
      b. *-er* $\Rightarrow \lambda G.\lambda d.\textbf{add}(d)(G): (deg\backslash pr)\backslash deg\backslash(pr/np_{th})$
      c. *more* $\Rightarrow \textbf{addsome}: pr/np_{th}/(deg\backslash pr)$
      d. *-er* $\Rightarrow \textbf{addsome}: (deg\backslash pr)\backslash(pr/np_{th})$

These lead to derivations with explicit degrees, as in figure 7.31, and with existentially bound degrees, as in figure 7.32. Note that just like the

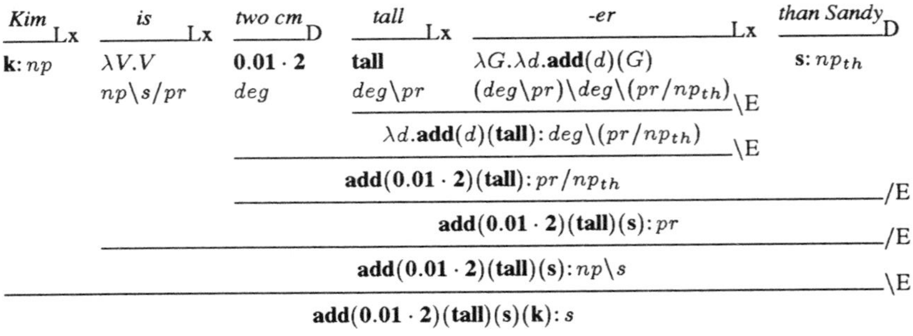

Figure 7.31
A derivation of *Kim is two cm taller than Sandy*

equative case, the meaning assigned to the comparative morpheme and modifier extends naturally to the downward gradable adjectives.

For cases of polar negative gradable adjectives, such as *short*, we can provide roughly the same kind of analysis. The one difference is that we use subtraction rather than addition in the underlying semantics of the comparative morpheme or modifier. Of course, this should be syntactically indicated in some way, but I will finesse that detail here. Consider the meanings that would be assigned under such a move:

(103) *Kim is 3 cm shorter than Sandy*
$$\Rightarrow \mathbf{some}(\lambda d.\mathbf{short}(d - \mathbf{3cm})(\mathbf{k}) \wedge \neg\mathbf{short}(d)(\mathbf{s}))$$

Similar readings would arise in the bare case by existentially quantifying over the degree of difference.

One further point to note about our analysis in terms of extents has to do with the boundary conditions. I defined extents in terms of the less-than-or-equal comparison. Unfortunately, in the case of comparatives, this rules out an "exact" reading of the degree of difference e. For instance, if we have $\mathbf{tall}(d + e)(\mathbf{s}) \wedge \neg\mathbf{tall}(d)(\mathbf{k})$, then Sandy cannot be exactly e taller than Kim, because of the negation. That is, Sandy is at least $d + e$ tall, but Kim is not even d tall. Although the difference is arbitarily small, it would perhaps be better to place the burden of extent-based reasoning on the comparative and equative predicates rather than on the gradable adjective. We explore such an alternative in exercise 31.

We now turn to an analysis of superlatives. The superlative construction is marked with either an *-est* suffix or the modifier *most*.

(104) a. Sandy is tallest.
       b. Sandy is most aggressive.

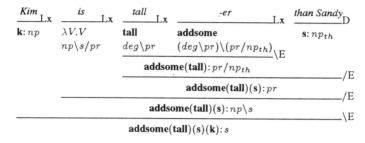

Figure 7.32
A derivation of *Kim is taller than Sandy*

These examples are rather stilted when used as predicates, but appear more natural when used as postnominal modifiers (see (107) below). The notion of superlative degree is that the individual in question is at the top of the scale, relative to some contextually supplied comparison class. The following constant can be defined to serve this function.

(105) **top** $\overset{\text{def}}{=}$ $\lambda P.\lambda G.\lambda x. P(x)$
$\wedge$ **some**$(\lambda d. G(d)(x)) \wedge$ **every**$(\lambda y. P(y) \wedge y \neq x)(\lambda y. \neg G(d)(y)))$

With this definition, **top**$(P)(G)(x)$ will be true if x is an individual in P such that there is some degree to which x is tall but no other member of P is that tall (we return to consider the superlative in the plural form, as in *tallest three boys*, in exercise 24, chapter 8). Note that this definition transfers appropriately to downward gradable adjectives like *short*. This is because having an upper bound on a height that no one else has makes one the shortest person.

We can now provide the lexical entries for the superlative suffix and modifier.

(106) a. *-est* $\Rightarrow$ **top**(P): $(deg\backslash pr)\backslash pr$
       b. *most* $\Rightarrow$ **top**(P): $pr/(deg\backslash pr)$

A sample derivation can be found in figure 7.33.

All forms of gradable adjectives can also be used as nominal modifiers, as the following examples illustrate:

(107) a.   (160 centimeter) tall student
       b.   *student tall
       c.   student 160 centimeters tall
       d.   student (twice) as tall as Sandy
       e.   (*six cm) taller student than Sandy
       f.   student (six cm) taller than Sandy
       g.   tallest student

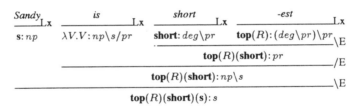

Figure 7.33
A derivation of *Sandy is shortest*

Note that there are subtle variations in word order. The positive construction can be used prenominally, with or without an explicit degree, as seen in (107a). The example in (107b) shows that a simple positive gradable predicate cannot appear postnominally, but (107c) appears better, although note the pluralization of the degree. The equative only appears postnominally, with or without a multiplier, as seen in (107d). The comparative can appear prenominally without an explicit degree, and postnominally with or without the degree specifier. The semantics of the modifier form is derived from the predicate form by intersection. I leave the specifics to exercise 21, chapter 8. The only semantic facts worth noting concern the contribution of the modified noun. By simply constructing intersective modifiers out of the predicate forms, we assume that the comparison class is always given contextually and need not be identified with the noun being modified. Following Pollard and Sag (1994), my claim that the other instances are just the natural intersective modifiers leads to the conclusion that the comparison class for the positive constructions is not required to be the interpretation of the noun being modified. They consider an example of a linguistics department recruiting intramural basketball players, during which time someone might say they were looking for a *good linguist* with the meaning that the linguist was a good basketball player and not necessarily a good linguist. Semantically, of course, it would be a simple matter to restrict the lexical entry so that the modified noun supplied the comparison class in the positive and superlative cases. Further note that there is an implication in (107e) that Sandy must be a student (in general, the comparative object must satisfy the property given by the modified noun); there is no such implication in (107f).

It is interesting to note that the extent-based constants we have used to derive meanings for the equative *as tall* and the comparative *taller* create a negative polarity environment for the object noun phrase. The downward monotonic environment is created by the negation of an extent-based degree predicate, as seen in the derivations of the equative, figure 7.29, and the comparative, figure 7.32, which expand as follows:

(108) a. *Kim is as tall as Sandy*
$$\Rightarrow \mathbf{some}(\lambda d.\mathbf{tall}(d)(\mathbf{k}) \wedge \neg\mathbf{tall}(d)(1 \cdot \mathbf{s})): s$$
  b. *Kim is taller than Sandy*
$$\Rightarrow \mathbf{some}(\lambda e.\mathbf{some}(\lambda d.\mathbf{tall}(d+e)(\mathbf{k}) \wedge \neg\mathbf{tall}(d)(\mathbf{s}))): s$$

For the superlative modifier, it seems that examples like *the best student who anyone has ever met* indicate that the whole of the noun and its relative-clause modifier should constitute a negative polarity context. This would argue that the comparison class be given lexically rather than contextually in the case of the superlative. On the other hand, it seems possible to interpret *the best student* as meaning the student who is best at basketball, for instance. So I leave open the issue of where exactly the comparison class is derived from, along with the dimension of comparison.

The final point I will address concerning the comparative has to do with its use in so-called *comparative deletion* and *comparative subdeletion* constructions (Bresnan 1973, 1975). The following are examples of comparative deletion (we return to comparative subdeletion below).

(109) a. Sandy is as tall as [Terry was ____ last year].
      b. Sandy is (6 centimeters) taller than [Terry was ____ last year].

Note that an entire predicate is missing following the copula *is*. Our analysis of these cases follows Larson (1988) in treating the complement as a quantifier. From a typed perspective, this makes sense, because the type of $s{\uparrow}pr$ is the same as that of $np{\Uparrow}s$, namely a generalized quantifier type. For instance, consider the derivation in figure 7.34, which shows that the sentence *Terry is* with a predicate extracted is synonymous with the proper name *Terry* raised to a generalized quantifier: both denote the set of Terry's properties. Setting aside matters of tense and aspect, *Terry is* receives the same translation as the name *Terry* raised to a quantifier category, as shown in figure 7.35. If we were to consider raising the equative and comparative complements to generalized quantifiers, we would have the following results:

(110) a. $as \Rightarrow \lambda G.\lambda n.\lambda Q.\lambda x.Q(\lambda y.\mathbf{mult}(G)(n)(x)(y))$
         $mlt\backslash(pr/(np_{as}{\Uparrow}s))/(deg\backslash pr)$
      b. $more \Rightarrow \lambda G.\lambda d.\lambda Q.\lambda x.Q(\lambda y.\mathbf{add}(d)(G)(y)(x))$
         $deg\backslash(pr/(np_{th}{\Uparrow}s))/(deg\backslash pr)$

$$
\begin{array}{c}
\dfrac{Terry}{t\colon np}{\scriptstyle\mathrm{Lx}} \quad \dfrac{is}{\lambda P.P\colon np\backslash s/pr}{\scriptstyle\mathrm{Lx}} \quad [R\colon pr]^0 \\[2ex]
\hline
\dfrac{R\colon np\backslash s}{}\ /\mathrm{E} \\[1.5ex]
\hline
\dfrac{R(\mathbf{t})\colon s}{}\ \backslash\mathrm{E} \\[1.5ex]
\hline
\lambda R.R(\mathbf{t})\colon s{\uparrow}pr\ {\uparrow}\mathrm{I}^0
\end{array}
$$

Figure 7.34
A derivation of *Terry is*

Such derivations follow the other argument raising cases we have considered. Note that the same kind of raising could be applied to the objects of the entries without explicit degrees and multipliers. But what is interesting is that these derived meanings are just what we need to provide lexical entries for the comparative deletion cases.

(111) a. $as \Rightarrow \lambda G.\lambda n.\lambda Q.\lambda x.Q(\lambda y.\textbf{mult}(n)(x)(y))$
$mlt\backslash(pr/(s{\uparrow}pr))/(deg\backslash pr)$

 b. $more \Rightarrow \lambda G.\lambda d.\lambda Q.\lambda x.Q(\lambda y.\textbf{add}(d)(G)(y)(x))$
$deg\backslash(pr/(s{\uparrow}pr))/(deg\backslash pr)$

The beauty of Larson's analysis of comparative deletion is that it interacts appropriately with quantifier scope. Consider the contrast in scope possibilities between the following two examples:

(112) a. Someone is taller than everyone.
 b. Someone is taller than everyone is.

In the first example, (112a), the object quantifier *everyone* can take wide or narrow scope. With the object given widest scope, (112a) means that for every person, there is someone who is taller than him; with the object scoped narrowly, it means that there is one person who is taller than everyone. These two scopes can be generated in the ordinary way using our quantifier-elimination schemes. The example (112b), on the other hand, does not have a reading in which the quantifier embedded in the $s{\uparrow}pr$ complement receives widest scope. This is to be expected because the sentential complement is an island to extraction, as noted by Chomsky (1977). The correct scoping is derived with the following analysis of the

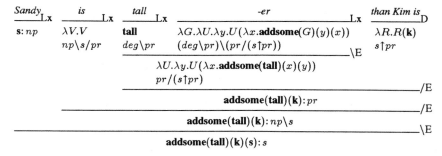

Figure 7.35
A derivation of *Sandy is taller than Kim is*

$$\cfrac{\cfrac{\cfrac{\cfrac{Sandy}{\text{s}:np}\text{Lx} \quad \cfrac{is}{\lambda V.V}\text{Lx} \quad [d:deg]^0 \quad \cfrac{tall}{\mathbf{tall}}\text{Lx}}{np\backslash s/pr} \qquad \cfrac{\mathbf{tall}}{deg\backslash pr}}{\cfrac{\cfrac{\mathbf{tall}(d):pr}{\mathbf{tall}(d):np\backslash s}/\text{E}}{\mathbf{tall}(d)(\mathbf{s}):s}\backslash\text{E}}}{\lambda d.\mathbf{tall}(d)(\mathbf{s}):s{\uparrow}deg}{\uparrow}\text{I}^0$$

Figure 7.36
A subdeletion derivation of *Sandy is tall*

complement, which proceeds along lines similar to the derivation of *every kid likes* in figure 7.14.

(113) *everyone is* $\Rightarrow \lambda P.\mathbf{every}(P):s{\uparrow}pr$

The wider scoping of the embedded quantifier is then blocked by whatever mechanism blocks other island violations (see Morrill 1992b, 1994a). The equative entries with clausal complements with extracted elements can be treated in the same way.

Unlike comparative deletion, *comparative subdeletion* involves only the omission of the degree modifier rather than the entire predicate.

(114) a. Sandy is (twice) as tall as [Terry is _____ wide].
       b. Sandy is (6 centimeters) wider than [Terry is _____ tall].

The complements will thus be given the category $s{\uparrow}deg$ of a sentence with a degree expression extracted. An example of a derivation of such a category can be found in figure 7.36. Subdeletion requires another lexical entry for both the equative and comparative morphemes and modifiers. These can be formulated as follows:

(115) a. *as* $\Rightarrow \mathbf{esd}: mlt\backslash(pr/(s{\uparrow}deg))/(deg\backslash pr)$
       b. $\mathbf{esd} \overset{\text{def}}{=} \lambda G.\lambda n.\lambda V.\lambda x.\mathbf{some}(\lambda d.G(d)(x) \wedge \neg V(n \cdot d))$

(116) a. *more* $\Rightarrow \mathbf{csd}: deg\backslash(pr/(s{\uparrow}deg))/(deg\backslash pr)$
       b. *-er* $\Rightarrow \mathbf{csd}: (deg\backslash pr)\backslash(deg\backslash(pr/(s{\uparrow}deg)))$
       c. $\mathbf{csd} \overset{\text{def}}{=} \lambda G.\lambda e.\lambda V.\lambda x.\mathbf{some}(\lambda d.G(d)(x) \wedge \neg V(e + d))$

The entries without explicit multiplier or degree complements can be defined as usual. In the case of equative *as*, we insert the constant **1**, and in the case of comparative *more*, we existentially quantify over the degree of difference:

$$\cfrac{\cfrac{\cfrac{\text{Sandy}}{\text{s}:np}\text{Lx} \quad \cfrac{\cfrac{\text{is}}{\lambda V.V}\text{Lx}}{np\backslash s/pr} \quad \cfrac{\cfrac{3\ cm}{0.03}\text{D}}{deg} \quad \cfrac{\cfrac{\text{wide}}{\textbf{wide}}\text{Lx}}{deg\backslash pr} \quad \cfrac{\cfrac{-er}{\textbf{csd}}\text{Lx}}{(deg\backslash pr)\backslash deg\backslash(pr/(s\uparrow deg))} \quad \cfrac{\text{than Terry is tall}}{\lambda d.\textbf{tall}(d)(\textbf{t})}\text{D}}{s\uparrow deg}}{}$$

Reading the derivation tree:

```
Sandy ―――Lx    is ―――Lx    3 cm ―――D    wide ―――Lx         -er ―――――――――――――――Lx   than Terry is tall ―――D
s: np           λV.V           0.03          wide      csd                                  λd.tall(d)(t)
                np\s/pr        deg           deg\pr    (deg\pr)\deg\(pr/(s↑deg))            s↑deg
                                                       ――――――――――――――――――――――――――――\E
                                                       csd(wide): deg\(pr/(s↑deg))
                                                       ――――――――――――――――――――――――――――\E
                                                       csd(wide)(0.03): pr/(s↑deg)
                                                       ――――――――――――――――――――――――――――――/E
                                                       csd(wide)(0.03)(λd.tall(d)(t)): pr
                                                       ――――――――――――――――――――――――――――――/E
                                                       csd(wide)(0.03)(λd.tall(d)(t)): np\s
――――――――――――――――――――――――――――――――――――――――――――――――――――――\E
csd(wide)(0.03)(λd.tall(d)(t))(s): s
```

Figure 7.37
A derivation of *Sandy is 3 cm wider than Terry is tall*

(117) a. *as* ⇒ **besd**: $pr/(s\uparrow deg)/(deg\backslash pr)$
  b. **besd** $\overset{\text{def}}{=} \lambda G.\lambda V.\lambda x.\textbf{some}(\lambda d.G(d)(x) \wedge \neg V(\mathbf{1} \cdot d))$

(118) a. *more* ⇒ **bcsd**: $pr/(s\uparrow deg)/(deg\backslash pr)$
  b. *-er* ⇒ **bcsd**: $(deg\backslash pr)\backslash(pr/(s\uparrow deg))$
  c. **bcsd** $\overset{\text{def}}{=} \lambda G.\lambda V.\lambda x.\textbf{some}(\lambda e.\textbf{some}(\lambda d.G(d)(x) \wedge \neg V(e + d)))$

A sample derivation involving a case of comparative subdeletion can be found in figure 7.37. Note that the same facts concerning scope possibilities arise for the subdeletion case as arise for deletion: the complement lacking a degree is an island, but quantifiers within it can be assigned narrow scope by reducing them within the clausal construction.

7.13 EXPLETIVES AND THE UNIT TYPE

In English, the words *it* and *there* in their nonpronominal incarnations do not provide a semantic contribution to meaning. First consider some uses of nonpronominal *it*:

(119) a. It is raining.
  b. It is Francis who Brett conspired with.
  c. It bothered Pat that Francis conspired with Brett.

The first example, (119a), involves a *weather predicate*. The second sentence, (119b), is an instance of *clefting*. The last example, (119c), is an instance of sentential subject *extraposition*. Next consider the use of *there*:

(120) a. There is a unicorn.
  b. There was a lion in the garden.
  c. There were 37 papers submitted.

Each of these examples involves an existential claim. These noun-phrase placeholders are known as *expletives, pleonastics*, or *dummies*. Their semantic analysis is puzzling from the perspective of compositional, type-logical approaches (Klein and Sag 1985, Morrill and Carpenter 1990).

The solution adopted in GPSG (Gazdar, Klein, Pullum, and Sag 1985) is to treat expletives as ordinary noun phrases whose denotation must be a special distinguished individual. Gazdar et al. attribute to Dowty the notion of treating the corresponding verbs as vacuously abstracting over their arguments. But expletives do not have any of the other properties of noun phrases, such as providing potential antecedents for pronouns or participating in scoping relations. Furthermore, the assumption of a distinguished individual in the domain of individuals is ontologically unmotivated and thus rather ad hoc.

Within a type-logical approach, there is a more appealing solution, which can be formulated by using the following standard addition to the type theory.

DEFINITION: UNIT TYPE   The *unit type*, written as $\mathbf{1}$, is associated with the singleton domain $\mathbf{Dom_1} \overset{\text{def}}{=} \{1\}$.

By assuming that we have a constant $\mathbf{1}$ of type $\mathbf{1}$, we can conclude the following for every model $\mathcal{M}$ (note that I am overloading our notation here).

(121) $[\![\mathbf{1}]\!]_{\mathcal{M}} = 1$

The reason $\mathbf{1}$ is called the unit type is because of its behavior as an identity (up to isomorphism) for both products and functions. More specifically, the elements of type $\mathbf{1} \times \sigma$ will all be of the form $\langle 1, a \rangle$, where a is an object of the domain of type σ. Thus the domain of $\mathbf{1} \times \sigma$ stands in a one-to-one relationship to the domain for σ. Because products are symmetric, the domain of $\sigma \times \mathbf{1}$ is also isomorphic to that of σ. For functions, note that the elements of $\mathbf{1} \to \sigma$ will be functions from the domain of type $\mathbf{1}$ to the domain of type σ. Because the domain of $\mathbf{1}$ is a singleton, each function in the domain of $\mathbf{1} \to \sigma$ only determines the image of the object 1. There is exactly one such function for each element of the domain of type σ. Thus the domains $\mathbf{1} \to \sigma$ and σ are isomorphic in the sense of standing in a one-to-one correspondence. The function type constructor is not symmetric. Indeed, the domain $\sigma \to \mathbf{1}$ consists of mappings from the domain of σ to the singleton domain of objects of type $\mathbf{1}$. Of course, there is only one such function, making $\sigma \to \mathbf{1}$ isomorphic to $\mathbf{1}$ itself. The

Curry-Howard morphism can be extended to the type **1** by associating this type with the denotation of the propositional constant **true**. That this extension is natural is evidenced by the domain equalities mentioned above. For instance, note that **true** $\wedge \phi$ and **true** $\rightarrow \phi$ are logically equivalent to ϕ. In exercise 14 we explore the related *zero type* **0**, whose domain is the empty set and which corresponds to the denotation of the propositional constant **false**.

For grammatical purposes, I assume two new basic categories:

DEFINITION: EXPLETIVE CATEGORIES AND TYPES   The *expletive categories* and corresponding types are the following:

a. $ex_t, ex_i \in$ **BasCat**
b. $\text{Typ}(ex_t) = \text{Typ}(ex_i) = \mathbf{1}$

The subscripts t and i are used to mark expletives corresponding to *there* and *it* respectively. With this definition we ensure that an expression of type ex_t or ex_i denotes 1, because that is the only element of the appropriate domain. I assume that the expletives are of these categories:

(122) a. *it* $\Rightarrow$ **1**: ex_i
      b. *there* $\Rightarrow$ **1**: ex_t

Because we take ex_t and ex_i to be basic categories, they may be connected with other categories. In the case of verbs taking expletive *it* as subject, the following category is appropriate:

(123) *rained* $\Rightarrow$ **rain**: $ex_i \backslash s$

This allows us to generate the following analysis by simple application.

(124) *it rained* $\Rightarrow$ **rain(1)**: s

Because **rain** is of type $\mathbf{1} \rightarrow$ **Bool**, it can be identified with an element of the domain of type **Bool**. The dummylike nature of *it* is thus naturally accounted for: syntactically, it acts like other subjects, but semantically, it is vacuous in that it makes no contribution.

Expletive subjects are also used in cases of so-called *it clefts*, which are a case of *extraposition* (the latter term being held over from transformational grammar). For *it* clefts, we can follow GPSG in locating the analysis on the various forms of the verb *be*. Assuming we have lexical entries of category $pr/(np\backslash s)$ and $pr/(s\uparrow np)$ for subject and object relative pronouns, we can employ the following category for the forms of *be* that involve extraposition.

$$\begin{array}{c}\dfrac{It}{}\text{Lx}\end{array}\quad \dfrac{is}{}\text{Lx}\quad \dfrac{Sandy}{}\text{Lx}\quad \dfrac{who}{}\text{Lx}\quad \dfrac{Terry\ likes}{}\text{D}$$

$$
\begin{array}{lllll}
1 & \lambda x.\lambda P.\lambda y.P(x) & \mathbf{s}:np & \lambda V.V & \lambda z.\mathbf{like}(z)(\mathbf{t})\\
ex_i & ex_i\backslash s/pr/np & & pr/(s{\uparrow}np) & s{\uparrow}np
\end{array}
$$

$$\cfrac{}{\lambda P.\lambda y.P(\mathbf{s}):ex_i\backslash s/pr}\ /\mathrm{E} \qquad \cfrac{}{\lambda z.\mathbf{like}(z)(\mathbf{t}):pr}\ /\mathrm{E}$$

$$\cfrac{}{\lambda y.\mathbf{like}(\mathbf{s})(\mathbf{t}):ex_i\backslash s}\ \backslash\mathrm{E}$$

$$\mathbf{like}(\mathbf{s})(\mathbf{t}):s$$

Figure 7.38
A derivation of *It is Sandy who Terry likes*

(125) a. *is* $\Rightarrow$ **ex**: $ex_i\backslash s/pr/np$
       b. **ex** $\overset{\text{def}}{=} \lambda x.\lambda P.\lambda y.P(x)$

The expletive receives a trivial denotation in the unit type, which is then semantically ignored by the meaning assigned to the verb. A simple example of a use of this lexical entry for extraposition can be found in figure 7.38. The standard account of extraposition in nontransformational theories is by means of a lexical rule. The extraposed cases in (119b) and (119c) are closely related to their nonextraposed variants.

(126) a. Francis is who Brett conspired with.
       b. Who Brett conspired with is Francis.
       c. That Francis conspired with Brett bothered Pat.

We consider sentential complements and subjects such as those in (119c) and (126c) in section 11.1.2. There are subtle relationships governing the behavior of extraposition, and these have been the object of intense syntactic scrutiny in a variety of frameworks. The lexical approaches of LFG (Bresnan 1982b) and HPSG (Pollard and Sag 1994) are compatible with the variety of type-logical grammar I develop here. By means of extraposition, the flow of information can be dynamically structured. Particularly relevant is the order of presentation of referential expressions, which has often been argued to follow from the status of a referent as *given* versus *new* in a discourse (Halliday 1967; Brown and Yule 1983, chapter 5). Such matters determine, for instance, the potential for anaphoric reference.

The case of expletive *there* is similarly straightforward. Perhaps the most obvious analysis is in terms of a predicate of existence.

(127) a. *is* $\Rightarrow$ **some$_2$**: $ex_t\backslash s/np$
       b. **some$_2$** $\overset{\text{def}}{=} \lambda x.\lambda y.\mathbf{true}$

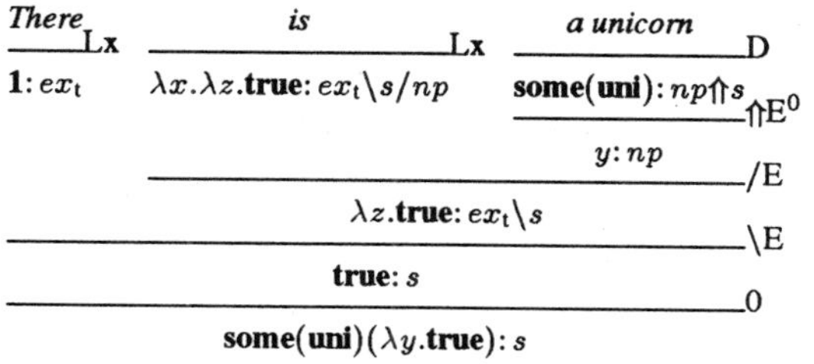

$$
\begin{array}{c}
\dfrac{\textit{There}}{1:\mathbf{ex}_t}\mathrm{Lx} \qquad
\dfrac{\textit{is}}{\lambda x.\lambda z.\mathbf{true}:\mathbf{ex}_t\backslash s/np}\mathrm{Lx} \qquad
\dfrac{\dfrac{\textit{a unicorn}}{\mathbf{some(uni)}:np\Uparrow s}\mathrm{D}}{y:np}{\Uparrow}\mathrm{E}^0 \\[2ex]
\end{array}
$$

A derivation of *There is a unicorn* (Figure 7.39)

The lines:

$$
\dfrac{\lambda z.\mathbf{true}:\mathbf{ex}_t\backslash s}{}\;/\mathrm{E}
$$

$$
\dfrac{\mathbf{true}:s}{}\;\backslash\mathrm{E}
$$

$$
\dfrac{\mathbf{some(uni)}(\lambda y.\mathbf{true}):s}{}\;0
$$

Figure 7.39
A derivation of *There is a unicorn*

$$
\dfrac{\textit{There}}{1:\mathbf{ex}_t}\mathrm{Lx} \qquad
\dfrac{\textit{is}}{\lambda x.\lambda y.\mathbf{true}:\mathbf{ex}_t\backslash s/np}\mathrm{Lx} \qquad
\dfrac{\textit{Sandy}}{s:np}\mathrm{Lx}
$$

$$
\dfrac{\lambda y.\mathbf{true}:\mathbf{ex}_t\backslash s}{}\;/\mathrm{E}
$$

$$
\dfrac{\mathbf{true}:s}{}\;\backslash\mathrm{E}
$$

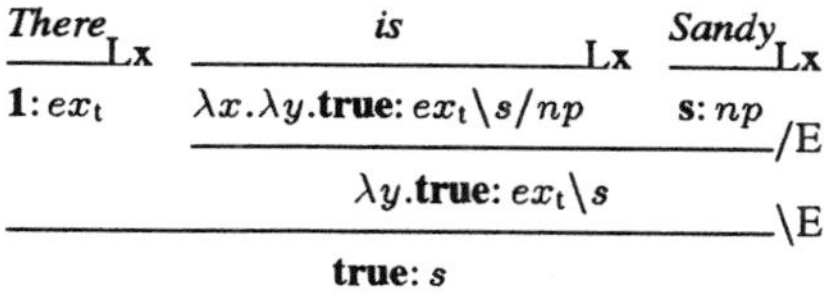

Figure 7.40
A derivation of *There is Sandy*

Consider the derivation in figure 7.39. Note that the meaning assigned in figure 7.39 asserts the existence of a unicorn. We return to the notion of existence in section 10.2.1, in the context of an intensional logic. Next consider the following analysis, which varies from that in figure 7.39 only in the meaning of the determiner.

(128) *There is no unicorn* $\Rightarrow$ $\mathbf{no(uni)}(\lambda x.\mathbf{true})$

Such a sentence can thus only be used truthfully if there are no unicorns.

Now consider the status of the following two examples, which are certainly infelicitous, if not ungrammatical, when used on their own.

(129) a. #There is Sandy.
      b. #There is every unicorn.

As answers to questions, these can both be acceptable; consider *Who can we get to deliver the letter?* to which (129a) is a perfectly reasonable answer. This is perhaps because in answering questions, we are interested in simply contributing referents to the discourse (see chapter 9). Note that the meaning assigned to the first example, (129a), is simply **true**, because the object's referent is discarded after application, as shown in figure 7.40. (Of course, there is a preferred reading of (129a) in which the subject *there* acts as a demonstrative locative pronoun.) Further, if we assume that interpretation is a dynamic process whereby noun-phrase referents are established before the noun phrases become complements to verbs, then (129a) could be understood as introducing a referent into the discourse. But the sentential meaning assigned to (129a) in figure 7.40 is trivially true. Similarly, the meaning assigned to (129b), **every**(**uni**)(λz.**true**), is also vacuously true.

Barwise and Cooper (1981) provide a semantic explanation for the infelicity of the examples in (129). Specifically, statements are not allowed to have readings that are degenerate in being always true or always false independent of the model. This principle clearly fails in general, as can be seen with perfectly acceptable examples such as *Francis is Francis*, or *Francis is tall, or Francis is not tall*. What remains interesting about Barwise and Cooper's approach is that they apply their general principle to provide a semantic characterization of when *there*-expletive sentences are infelicitous. They frame their story in terms of properties of determiners. A determiner D is said to be *positive strong* if $D(P)(P)$ is true for all P, and it is said to be *negative strong* if $D(P)(P)$ is false for all P. A determiner that is not strong is said to be *weak*. Barwise and Cooper noted that only weak determiners are appropriate objects for *there is*. For instance, *some* and *no* are interpreted as weak determiners, because **some**$(P)(P)$ is false if P is empty and true otherwise, and just the opposite holds for *no*. The plural cases—*three, exactly two, many*, and *few*—are weak. Quantificational plural determiners such as *most* are a bit trickier, because it is unclear whether sentences such as *Most unicorns are unicorns* can be uttered truthfully if there are no unicorns. Such an utterance would seem infelicitous at best. But if the sentence is actually false, then *most* is also a weak determiner. On the other hand, **every** is positive strong. Note that if we assume conservativity $(D(X)(Y) \equiv D(X)(X \cap Y))$, then a determiner is strong if and only if $D(X)(\lambda z.\textbf{true})$ holds for every X. This provides some clue as to why the quantifier $\lambda P.P(\textbf{j})$, derived from the individual **j**, is not an appropriate complement to *there is*.

Exercises

1. Provide a Russellian definition of the constant **the** used in a quantificational entry for the definite determiner:

the $\Rightarrow$ **the**: $np \Uparrow s/n$.

It should be defined so that *The kid ran* is true if and only if there is exactly one kid and that kid ran.

2. Does the Cooper-storage approach to quantifier scope lead to the same kinds of spurious ambiguity as nonnormal natural-deduction analyses?

3. Show how lexical entries of the kind illustrated in (32) can be used to produce the undesired result in (31).

4. How many readings are generated by our grammar for the following sentences, and does this match the empirical data?

(a) Every student [wrote some paper] and [read some book].

(b) Jo showed [someone every drawing] but [no one every painting].

(Hint: Try coordinating at the categories $(np \Uparrow s) \backslash s$ and $(np \backslash s / np / np) \backslash np \backslash s$, respectively.)

5. Explain why our approach to the copula, which is basically Montague's, provides a meaning for *Jo is a man* that is logically equivalent to the one suggested by Quine, namely **man(j)**. (Quine 1960, Montague 1973)

6. Explain the distinctions among the following examples with respect to the logical nature of the scope and unbounded-dependency constructors.

(a) Every person that Sandy took a [picture of ____] smiled.

(b) Every person that Sandy showed [a picture] [to ____] smiled.

(c) Every person that Sandy showed [____] [a picture] smiled.

Assume that *to* is a dative-marking preposition here.

7. What are the possibilities for scoping in the following example:

(a) A visiting professor who at least one student challenged every statement of collapsed.

8. Consider generalized-quantifier categories of the forms $(s/np) \backslash s$ and $s/(np \backslash s)$. Note that these categories are of the same type as $np \Uparrow s$. Using these categories, determine whether is it possible to generate the correct range of scope ambiguities in the following examples. (H. Hendriks 1987)

(a) Someone likes everyone.

(b) Someone showed everyone something.

9. Show how all of the examples in (23) can be derived on the assumption that the semantic terms all result in sentences and that each argument σ_i is either a forward or backward slash and that all of the quantifier arguments are of category $np \Uparrow s$. Show that the composition of argument raising and argument lowering is simply the identity function of the appropriate type. Why does composing in the opposite order not produce the identity function? (H. Hendriks 1987)

10. The quantificational element *only*, as it occurs in the following sentences, can be analyzed as a generalized quantifier with an individual argument.

(a) Only Jo likes Morgan.

Assuming a lexical entry for *only* of category **only** $: np \Uparrow s / np$ and assuming that the logical translation of this sentence is **only(j)(like(m))**, provide an appropriate definition of the constant **only**.

Jackendoff (1972) pointed out that there are truth-conditional differences that arise due to *focus*. For instance, consider the following standard examples, where the focused element is italicized. (Hint: If the difference in truth conditions is not clear, try reading them aloud with stress on the focused element.)

(b) Jo only introduced *Brett* to Sue.

(c) Jo only introduced Brett to *Sue*.

Using the quantificational constant **only** that you defined above, show how to represent the meanings of these two sentences.

The syntax and semantics of *only* is further complicated by both polymorphism and context sensitivity, as demonstrated by the following example (Rooth 1985).

(d) Jo only ran.

Show how such an example could be treated by generalizing your definition of **only** to a generalized quantifier of type $\tau \rightarrow (\tau \rightarrow \mathbf{Bool}) \rightarrow \mathbf{Bool}$ and instantiating τ to $\mathbf{Ind} \rightarrow \mathbf{Bool}$ in the above example.

As Rooth points out, even though the first argument may be determined by information such as syntactic attachment and focus, the quantification is still contextually restricted. Show how you could add an additional argument to the polymorphic **only** of type $\tau \rightarrow \mathbf{Bool}$ to provide a set of alternatives from which the second argument must be drawn. Alternatively, show how the same effect could be achieved by restricting the second argument itself.

11. Consider the ambiguity of the following sentence.

(a) Jo broke every kid's favorite toy.

Here *Jo* may be construed as having broken either the favorite toy of each kid or just one toy, which happened to be everyone's favorite. To provide a single lexical entry that accounts for both readings, Carpenter proposed a lexical entry with the following syntactic category:

(b) $'s \Rightarrow ?: (np \Uparrow s) \backslash np / n$

Provide an appropriate semantic term for the possessive that will allow for the following reading of *every kid's toy*:

(c) *every kid's toy* $\Rightarrow \iota(\lambda x.\mathbf{toy}(x) \wedge \mathbf{every}(\mathbf{kid})(\lambda y.\mathbf{poss}(y)(x))): np$

Use your lexical entry to provide both possible derivations for the ambiguous sentence (a) above. Further, show that your lexical entry derives the lexical entry in the text with the same semantics by means of argument lowering. (Carpenter 1994a, 1994c)

12. Show that possessives such as *Jo's* and *every kid's*, as we have defined them, are not permutation invariant in the sense of definition 8 in section 3.3.2. Next, show that determiners composed of lexical determiners and adjectives are not necessarily permutation invariant. For instance, consider such examples as *every blue*, which can be analyzed as being of the category of determiners, $np \Uparrow s / n$. (Keenan and Stavi 1986)

13. Show that if we assume n-tuple types σ^n for arbitrary types σ, then the unit type, $\mathbf{1}$, is isomorphic to σ^0 for any type σ.

14. Assume that we have a *zero type* $\mathbf{0}$, whose domain is the empty set. What does this imply for the domains of $\mathbf{0} \times \sigma$, $\sigma \times \mathbf{0}$, $\mathbf{0} + \sigma$, $\sigma + \mathbf{0}$, $\mathbf{0} \to \sigma$, and $\sigma \to \mathbf{0}$? Explain the extension of the Curry-Howard morphism to $\mathbf{0}$, under the assumption that $\mathbf{0}$ corresponds to the denotation of the propositional constant **false**.

15. Provide a category for the negative particle *not* that will account for the semantics of negated quantifiers, as in the following examples:

(a)   Not every student studied.

(b)   Not one student studied.

(c)   *Not {some student / Sandy} studied.

What is the range of quantifiers that *not* can apply to? Is there a difference in readings predicted between the first example above and *Every student did not study*?

16. Write a grammar that accounts for the distribution of negative-polarity determiners such as *any*, negative-polarity adverbials such as *ever*, and negative-polarity idioms such as *budge an inch*, as described in section 3.4. More specifically, assume that there is a binary feature on all basic syntactic categories that signifies whether or not an expression needs to be embedded inside of a negative-polarity context. Thus *ever ran* should be marked as requiring a negative-polarity context, but a simple verb phrase such as *ran* should be marked as not requiring a negative-polarity context. Keep in mind that the need to be embedded in a negative-polarity environment should propogate, and thus not only should *any kid* be marked as requiring a negative-polarity context but so should *likes any kid* and *teacher who likes any kid*. Negative-polarity-inducing elements such as the verb-phrase negation *not* and the negative determiner *no* should be marked with features so as to license arguments with negative polarity. But importantly, they do not produce results that need to be embedded in negative-polarity contexts. Finally, grammatical sentences will be the ones that do not require negative-polarity marking. (Sánchez Valencia 1991, Dowty 1994)

17. Partee introduced the following example, which highlights the *proportion problem* for unselective binding accounts of indefinites, as presented in section 7.10. (Partee 1984a, Kadmon 1985)

(a)   Most women who own a cat are happy.

For the sake of this exercise, assume that *most* is translated as a generalized determiner binding individuals with the obvious interpretation over finite domains (see section 8.6 for motivation). Explain why the unselective analysis is problematic in this case. (Hint: Consider a model in which there are a few women who own a varying number of cats.)

18. Provide the lexical entries required to derive the examples in (107). Be sure to capture the difference in properties attributed to the comparative object in (107e) and (107f).

19. Provide the derivations of *as* and *more* given in (111).

Provide the two derivations of (112a) and the one derivation of (112b) that do not violate island restrictions. (Note: The island-violating case of (112b) is also derivable because we have not enforced island constraints.)

20. Provide an analysis of a complement-taking comparative, such as the following:

(a) more [loyal to the home team] than Terry

Is such a scale measurable?

21. What is the meaning generated by our grammar for equatives with fractional multipliers, such as *half as tall* and *half as short*? How does this compare to those generated by *twice as tall* and *twice as short*? Be sure to discuss the interaction between the polarity of the comparative and the size of the multiplier.

22. Consider the use of *comparative free relatives*, as in the following example.

(a) Sandy grew {tall / three inches tall / three inches / however tall Terry grew}.

Provide appropriate lexical assignment(s) for *grow*. Then consider how the free-relative-version pronoun can be assigned a lexical entry that will interact with these.

23. Show that the expressions *taller than* and *not as short as* can be assigned synonymous meanings as binary relations of category pr/np. Note that you will need to assume the category pr/pr for *not* with the same meaning as it receives as category $s/np/(s/np)$. Is there also synonymy between *shorter than* and *not as tall as*?

24. Consider the modification of number-denoting terms such as the following:

(a) at {least / most} five feet tall

(b) {exactly / approximately} 1.5 meters tall

(c) almost five feet tall

Provide an analysis in which terms such as *at least*, *exactly*, and *almost* act as quantificational modifiers of numbers, of category $num\Uparrow s/num$. Use your category to generate two readings for the following example:

(d) Every student is [approximately 1.5] meters tall.

Does it make any difference that we chose the category $num\Uparrow s/num$ rather than the category $deg\Uparrow s/deg$?

25. Consider the term *less*, as used in examples such as the following:

(a) Sandy is less tall than Terry.

(b) Sandy is three inches less tall than Terry.

Provide an analysis of *less* along the lines of that given for *more* in (102). (Hint: Use subtraction rather than addition in the basic semantics.) How does the term *less tall* compare with *shorter*?

26. Consider nominalized forms of comparatives, as in the following:

(a) Jo's height is six inches.

Extend the semantics of the copula to handle this case, and consider the type that should be assigned to *height* and the possessive. Provide a derivation.

27. Bresnan (1973, 1975) and later Pollard and Sag (1994) discuss examples of nested comparison such as the following:

(a) This factory is [very many times / much] more productive than that one.

(b) Kim is much more productive than Dana.

(c) Kim is (three times) as much more intelligent than Sandy as Chris is more intelligent than Dana.

Can *very many times* and *much* in the first example be analyzed as a multiplier? Is there a way to extend our analysis of equatives to deal with the nesting in the second example above? (Hint: Consider the category $s{\uparrow}mlt$ for the complement *Chris is ___ more productive than Dana.*)

28. Show why the following example gets the wrong reading under our categorization of relational nouns as taking quantified complements.

(a) picture of no one

Contrast this with the similar expression *sister of no one*. This suggests that perhaps the correct lexical entry for *picture* would be something along the following lines:

(b) *picture* $\Rightarrow \lambda Q.\lambda x.\mathbf{pic}(x) \wedge Q(\lambda y.\mathbf{of}_2(y)(x)): n/(np{\Uparrow}s)$

Why does this entry not produce the same undesirable form of derivation as in the entry we gave in (59)? (Gerdemann, p.c.)

29. Consider the following *exceptive* constructions with *but*.

(a) Every student but Sandy studied.

(b) No student but Sandy studied.

Now consider the following possible lexical entry for *but*, and provide analyses of the sentences above.

(c) *but* $\Rightarrow \lambda y.\lambda P.\lambda x.P(x) \wedge x \neq y: n\backslash n/np$

Explain why this lexical entry does not require Sandy to be a student in either example and why it does not require Sandy to study in the second example.

Von Fintel (1993) provides a semantic term for the exceptive that reduces to the following semantic behavior in the singular case and would naturally be assigned the following syntactic category:

(d) *but* $\Rightarrow \lambda y.\lambda P.\lambda D.\lambda R.D(P - \{y\})(R)$
$$\wedge \mathbf{every}_{\mathbf{Ind} \rightarrow \mathbf{Bool}}(\lambda S.D(P - S)(R))(\lambda S.\{y\} \subseteq S):$$
$$n\backslash(np{\Uparrow}s/n)\backslash(np{\Uparrow}s)/np$$

By deriving the two sentences above, explain why the semantic terms assigned to them provide the correct entailments for the studenthood and study habits of Sandy in both cases. Next, explain how the semantics above accounts for the infelcity of conjoined exception clauses (as noted by Geis 1973) and exception clauses modifying an existential quantifier.

(e) #Every kid [but Sandy and but Terry] studied.

(f) #Some kid but Terry studied.

(Hint: It may help to derive the sentences above and consider the resulting semantic assignment.) (Geis 1973, Keenan and Stavi 1986, von Fintel 1993)

30. Consider the following *exceptive* constructions with *but*.

(a) Every student but Sandy studied.

(b) No student but Sandy studied.

Now consider the following possible lexical entry for *but*, and provide analyses of the sentences above.

(c) $but \Rightarrow \lambda y.\lambda P.\lambda x.P(x) \wedge x \neq y: n\backslash n/np$

What is the status of the studenthood of Sandy in these examples, and is it captured by this analysis? Does such an analysis license the following inference? (Hint: Consider the monotonicity of the quantifiers.)

(d) {Every / No} student but Sandy studied.

(e) {Every / No} student but Sandy and Terry studied.

   Von Fintel provides a richer analysis for the semantics of a construction such as "Det N *but* NP VP." In the case where D is the denotation of a determiner, P the property denoted by the head noun, X the set of exceptions denoted by the NP, and R the property denoted by the verb phrase, von Fintel provides the following definition:

(f) $D\,P\,\textbf{but}\,X\,R \stackrel{\text{def}}{=} D(P-X)(R) \wedge \textbf{every}(\lambda S.D(P-S)(R))(\lambda S.C \subseteq S)$

Does this analysis solve the problems mentioned above? How could this proposal be realized syntactically in a categorial grammar with a lexical entry for *but*? (Hint: Allow *but* to take as arguments all the components other than the verb phrase to produce a new quantifier.)

   Formulate a lexical entry for *except for*, the so-called *free exceptive*, and consider how it differs from *but*. Provide a lexical entry for *except* that captures this difference. (Hoeksema 1987, von Fintel 1993)

31. Provide an analysis along the lines of that given in section 7.12 in which gradable adjectives like *tall*, when occurring in comparative and equative constructions, are assigned meanings directly in terms of measures rather than in terms of extents. That is, *tall* would be assigned to the meaning $\lambda d.\lambda x.\textbf{height}(x) = d$, which involves equality rather than inequality. The burden of extent-based reasoning must now be placed on the basic predicates in the positive construction, and on the comparative and equative expressions in those constructions.

Chapter 8

Plurals

In this chapter I provide a type-logical account of plurality. From this perspective, the perplexing array of behaviors displayed by plural determiners, nominal modifiers, adverbials, conjunctions, and reciprocals can be classified and explained in a unified manner. I approach this task constructively, building a grammar as I motivate its various components. I conclude the chapter with a treatment of mass terms, which in many ways closely resemble groups in their behavior.

8.1 AN ONTOLOGY OF GROUPS

The semantics of plurality has engendered a vast literature concerning the fundamental ontological organization of referential expressions in natural language. Such considerations provide a natural starting point for a type-logical account of plurality. We begin with the simple observation that plural noun phrases can be construed in more than one way, as the following examples illustrate.

(1) a. Fifty kids sneezed. (Distributive)
    b. Fifty kids gathered outside. (Collective)
    c. Three kids moved the piano. (Ambiguous)

An example such as (1a) can be true only if each of the fifty kids sneezed individually. Such a construal of the subject is said to be *distributive*, because the property denoted by the verb phrase is distributed over the members of the set picked out by the subject. In contrast, (1b) can be true only if the fifty kids gathered as a group. Such readings are known as *collective*. An example such as (1c) might be used truthfully either way: three kids could have moved the piano individually, perhaps because each liked to have it in a different spot to practice, or the three kids could have acted collectively to move the piano. I take such distinctions to be lexical properties of verbs. Some verbs, like *sneeze*, only apply to individuals. Other verbs, like *gather*, apply only to groups. Still other verbs, like *carry*, can apply to both groups and individuals.

Such ambiguities between a distributive construal and a collective-construal of a plural noun phrase can interact with lexical properties of various predicates. Some nouns, such as *gang* and *committee*, pick out groups directly. In such cases, plural instances of the nouns will induce an ambiguity when coupled with predicates that apply to groups.

(2) a.   The gang dispersed.
    b.   The gangs dispersed.
    c.   #The kid dispersed.
    d.   #The committee sneezed.

For instance, in (2a) we have a group predicate with a singular. When such group nouns occur in the plural, an ambiguity arises, as can be seen in the two interpretations of (2b). Under a collective interpretation, the group of all the gangs dispersed, leaving open the possibility of the individual gangs remaining intact. With the distributive reading, the sentence is interpreted as stating that each of the gangs in the collection of gangs dispersed. It is important to note that whereas sets introduced by plural nouns may denote the group of which they form the members, it is not in general possible for a group to be automatically decomposed into its members. For instance, there is no reading of (2d) stating that each of the committee members sneezed. Because sneezing is a property attributable only to individuals, an infelicity arises. I consider this a pragmatic infelicity that comes about due to selection-restriction violations. Similarly, (2c) is infelicitous because dispersing is something only a group can do.

With this motivation, it is natural to seek a common domain in which to interpret individuals and groups. Following Link (1984), I simply assume that the type of groups is a subtype of the type of individuals:

(3) **Group ⊆ Ind**

This accounts naturally for the existence of group-denoting singular nouns like *team*, *committee*, and *group*, and of group-denoting noun phrases like *Parliament*. It also allows a natural type assignment to predicates like *carry*, which can apply to both individuals and groups. They will remain functions from individuals into propositions.

Because we need to be able to interpret plural noun phrases as groups whose members consist of the set denoted by the noun phrase, I provide a relation linking groups to their members.

(4) **group**: (**Ind** → **Bool**) → **Group** → **Bool**

I take **group**$(P)(x)$ to be true if and only if x denotes a group whose members are elements of the set denoted by P. I require every group to have a set of members, which can be expressed as follows:

(5) $\textbf{Dom}_{\textbf{Group}} = [\![\lambda x.\textbf{some}(\lambda P.\textbf{group}(P)(x))]\!]$ (Group membership)

This simple conception of groups leaves open a number of possibilities. First, nothing blocks us from having groups whose members are themselves groups. Consider the following example, due to Landman (1989a): the proletariat and the bourgeoisie are groups of people, the state is a group consisting of the proletariat and the bourgeois, and the states of Eastern Europe form a group consisting of the groups consisting of the proletariat and bourgeoisie of each state, and so on. Similarly, an expression such as *Bob and Carol and Ted and Alice* can be used to pick out a group consisting of two couples, each of which is a group consisting of two individuals (Kaplan 1973). Thus we can employ a group $g \in$ **Group**, where **group**$(\{c_1, c_2\})(g)$ holds, with c_1 and c_2 being the two couples. We would also have **group**$(\{b, c\})(c_1)$ and **group**$(\{t, a\})(c_2)$ holding, where the first couple, c_1, is a group composed of Bob and Carol and the second couple, c_2, is a group composed of Ted and Alice.

Without further restrictions on the interpretation of **group**, nothing prevents us from composing the same group out of two different sets of members. To avoid this possibility, we make the following assumption:

(6) $(\textbf{group}(P)(x) \wedge \textbf{group}(Q)(x)) \rightarrow P = Q$ (Unique membership)

While unique membership requires each group to have a unique set of members, nothing yet requires each set to determine a unique group. A typical example would be two committees which might be formed by the same members, such as the admissions committee and the computing committee. The committees do not appear to have the same properties in that an action taken by one committee is not taken by the others, for instance. The admissions committee's bringing a matter before the head of the department in an official capacity is a different affair than the computing committee's doing the same. Such arguments have motivated approaches in which two distinct groups are allowed to have the same members. Link (1983) points out that such a case is no different from the case of a gold ring, which might be quite new, whereas the gold out of which it is composed might be quite old, and the atoms composing the gold even older still. If it were desirable, we could legislate in our models a condition requiring groups with the same members to be identical:

(7) $(\textbf{group}(P)(x) \wedge \textbf{group}(P)(y)) \rightarrow x = y$ (Unique group)

The unique-group assumption prevents the existence of two different groups with the same members. Such an assumption was made by Link (1984), who postulated a function mapping sets to the groups they determined. Landman (1989a) encoded a similar distinction by directly modeling groups as sets within an extensional set theory (Landman [1989b] also proposed an alternative account, with individuals, including groups, having different properties under different guises).

Our relational treatment of groups opens another possibility, namely that there are sets that correspond to no groups. The following postulate requires every set to form a group.

(8) $\textbf{some}(\lambda x.\textbf{group}(P)(x))$ (Group comprehension)

It would be sensible to restrict the set P in this constraint to have at least two elements. The combination of the comprehension and unique-membership requirements introduces a paradox, given our assumption that every group is an individual. These assumptions together require the existence of a one-to-one embedding of $\textbf{Ind} \rightarrow \textbf{Bool}$ (the power set of individuals) into $\textbf{Ind}$ that picks out a group to be associated with each set (note that without the unique-group assumption, there may be more than one, but that is not relevant in terms of inducing a paradox). Unfortunately, there are no such functions, as was shown by Cantor (see section A.2 for a proof).

THEOREM: CANTOR'S THEOREM   For any set S, there is no one-to-one function $f : \mathscr{P}(S) \rightarrow S$.

Thus one of the assumptions, comprehension or unique membership, must be abandoned. In the standard axiomatic set theory of Zermelo and Fraenkel (ZF), general comprehension is sacrificed in favor of a weakened relativized version. Relative comprehension simply requires that if S is a set and ϕ is a proposition, then $\{x \in S \mid \phi(x)\}$ exists, which is the set of x in S that satisfy ϕ. In a group setting, this would amount to requiring every subset of members of an existing group picked out by some property to pick out a group.

(9) $(\mathbf{group}(P)(y) \wedge R \subseteq P) \to \mathbf{some}(\lambda x.\mathbf{group}(R)(x))$

(Relativized group comprehension)

Landman (1989a) employed the standard set-theoretic construction of ordinal recursion (Kunen 1980) in order to develop an extensional model of groups. Landman's model satisfies the unique-membership and relativized-comprehension, as well as unique-group, assumptions. Landman's model consists of a universe of individuals $\mathscr{U}$ constructed from a set **Atom** of atoms.

(10) a. $\mathscr{U}_0 = \mathbf{Atom}$
    b. $\mathscr{U}_{n+1} = \mathscr{U}_n \cup \mathscr{P}(\mathscr{U}_n)$
    c. $\mathscr{U}_\omega = \bigcup_{n \in \omega} \mathscr{U}_n$

Landman then takes the domain of predicates to be $\mathscr{U} = \mathscr{U}_\omega$. In set theory, this collection is known as the *hereditarily countable* sets generated by **Atom**. A set $x \in \mathscr{U}$ is taken to represent the group composed of the members of the set. Note that we get not only groups of atoms but also groups of groups of arbitrarily high finite order (infinite, though still bounded, orders would be possible if an ordinal larger than ω was used in the construction). Furthermore, in Landman's model, the following two closure conditions from classical set theory also obtain.

(11) a. if $x, y \in \mathscr{U}$, then $x \cup y \in \mathscr{U}$ (Finite closure)
    b. if $x \in \mathscr{U}$, then $\{x\} \in \mathscr{U}$ (Individual comprehension)

Note that neither of these closure conditions are entailed by relativized comprehension. Of course, Landman's construction could be carried out for limit ordinals other than ω, and the resulting domain of groups would still satisfy the unique-membership, relativized-comprehension, and unique-group assumptions. We could adopt the model of Landman, but there is no need to restrict ourselves to this possibility. It is only one of many models consistent with the grammar I will develop for plurals. In the rest of the chapter, I remain agnostic on these deep ontological issues underlying the semantics of groups. See Boolos 1984 for some further discussion of these issues.

8.2   A PLURAL GRAMMAR

To account for the syntax of plurals, as well as some semantic distinctions, I will need to introduce some additional categories for plural noun phrases and plural nouns. My analysis will be based on the type-logical assumption that ordinary plural noun phrases denote sets. I will then analyze distributive and collective readings by freely applying distributing and collecting operators to set-denoting plural noun phrases. I thus assume the following pair of additional nominal categories.

(12) a. np^*: **Ind** → **Bool**
      b. n^*: (**Ind** → **Bool**) → **Bool**

Note that elements in the domain of the type assigned to np^* will be sets, whereas elements in the domain of the type assigned to np will be individuals. Similarly, meanings assigned to category n^* will be sets of sets, and those assigned to n are simply sets. I further allow syntactic subcategorization into plural and singular varieties, which I will indicate with subscripts s and p. For instance, np^*_p is a syntactically plural noun phrase that denotes a set, whereas np_p is a syntactically plural noun phrase that denotes an individual. I will often suppress the syntactic subcategorization information in our derivations.

Our type assumptions in (12) are at odds with many proposals in the literature that carve up the categorial space in a very different way. For instance, many researchers have followed Link's (1983) analysis, in which individuals are conflated with singleton sets. I will argue that a strong type distinction is beneficial in predicting the correct range of distributive and collective possibilities for natural language, as well as their co-occurrence with certain overt elements such as determiners, adverbials, and reciprocals. We will return to consider Link's motivation for his type assignment in section 8.8 and see how it can be reconciled with the one given here.

Semantically, it is important to consider how plural nouns are related to their singular counterparts. To this end, we define an operator, **plu**, the purpose of which is to map a property of individuals to a property of sets. This is achieved by taking the powerset and discarding the empty set and the singletons.

(13) a. **plu**: (**Ind** → **Bool**) → (**Ind** → **Bool**) → **Bool**
      b. $\mathbf{plu} \stackrel{\text{def}}{=} \lambda P.\lambda Q.\mathbf{every}(Q)(P) \wedge \|Q\| \geq \mathbf{2}$

In general, $\|Q\|$ denotes the *cardinality* of the set denoted by Q (see section A.2). Thus the cardinality function $\|\cdot\|$ maps sets into numbers, which makes its type (**Ind** → **Bool**) → **Num** (see section 7.12 for a discussion of the type **Num**). Interpreting the arithmetic operators and numerals as usual, the formula $\|Q\| \geq \mathbf{2}$ will be true if and only if the cardinality of the set denoted by Q is greater than or equal to two. Hence **plu**$(P)(Q)$ will be true if and only if Q denotes a subset of P that contains at least two elements. In particular, an expression such as **plu**(**kid**) denotes a set of sets, each of which is a set of kids containing at least two elements, or in other words, the powerset of the denotation of **kid** with the singletons and empty set removed. I take **plu** to be the semantic component of the morphological operation of pluralization in English. As I do not wish to develop a theory of morphology here, I simply assume the following kinds of lexical entries:

(14) a. *kid* $\Rightarrow$ **kid**: n_s
      b. *kids* $\Rightarrow$ **plu**(**kid**): n_p^*

Those interested in categorial approaches to morphology should consult Bach 1983a, Dowty 1979a, Keenan and Stavi 1986, Hoeksema 1984, Moortgat 1988b, Carpenter 1992a, the latter two being the most compatible with the logical approach to categorial grammar taken here.

Standard intersective adjectival modifiers can be handled by raising their types:

(15) *red* $\Rightarrow \lambda P.\lambda X.P(X) \wedge$ **every**$(X)($**red**$_2)$: n_p^*/n_p^*

Here we assume that **red**$_2$: **Ind** $\rightarrow$ **Bool** is an ordinary property. In this way, we get analyses such as the following by simple application.

(16) *red boxes* $\Rightarrow \lambda X.$**plu**(**box**)$(X) \wedge$ **every**$(X)($**red**$_2)$: n_p^*

Nonintersective adjectives like *alleged* cannot be handled in this way. Instead, we need to be able to generate analyses where the plural morphology outscopes the modification, as in **plu**(**alleged**(**thief**)). In morphology, such cases are common and have come to be known in general as *bracketing paradoxes*, because the proper analysis of *alleged thieves* can be indicated by [[*alleged thief*]*s*], even though lexically, the plural noun *thiefs* appears to be a unit. A more familiar example would involve derivational morphology, as in the expression *categorial grammarian*, meaning a person who studies categorial grammar. This expression seems to be structured semantically as [*categorial grammar*]-*ian*. In exercise 15 we consider some solutions to the plural bracketing paradox. In the rest of this chapter I maintain the naive approach outlined above.

Although it may at first seem tempting to treat numerical modifiers as determiners, I will instead treat them as n_p^* modifiers.

(17) a. *five* $\Rightarrow$ **five**$_a$: n_p^*/n_p^*
      b. **five**$_a \overset{\text{def}}{=} \lambda P.\lambda X.P(X) \wedge \|X\| = 5$

In general, I will use a numeral subscripted with the letter a in the sense of the above definition. Note also that we have treated numerical modifiers as requiring an exact number of members. We thus have analyses such as the following:

(18) a. *five kids* $\Rightarrow$ **five**$_a$(**plu**(**kid**)): n_p^*

   b. **five**$_a$(**plu**(**kid**)) $\equiv \lambda X.\textbf{every}(X)(\textbf{kid}) \wedge \|X\| \geq \mathbf{2} \wedge \|X\| = \mathbf{5}$

As we will see shortly, the possibility of more than five kids sneezing in examples such as *Five kids sneezed* will derive not from a property of the modifier *five* but rather from the operation of distributivity (see the discussion following (27)).

Before leaving the topic of plural adjectives, consider the following:

(19) a.   the three big kids

   b.   *the big three kids

I believe this scoping is a result of a type-theoretic difference between "ordinary" singular adjectives, such as *big*, and properly plural adjectives, such as *three*. For an interesting semantics-based approach to the relative ordering of modifiers in general, see Crain and Hamburger 1992. I suggest a type-logical approach to this ordering in exercise 15. The basic idea is that ordinary adjectives are simply property modifiers and modify a plural noun within the scope of the plural operator, whereas the numerical plural modifiers must take scope outside of the plural operator. For the rest of this chapter, I stick to the direct approach in which plural nouns are treated as being of category n_p^*.

I begin our analysis of plural noun phrases with the bare plural. Note that in English, plural noun phrases can occur without a determiner, as so-called *bare plurals*.

(20) a.   Weeds overran the garden.

   b.   The weeds overran the garden.

   c.   *Tall weed overran the garden.

   d.   The tall weed overran the garden.

This is not possible for singular count nouns. The interpretation of a bare plural is very similar to that of an indefinite singular. For instance, both allow discourse reference and generic readings, and both carry existential import. But not everyone agrees about what exactly counts as a bare plural, the debatable cases being ones like *three kids*. There is even more disagreement concerning the relation between bare plurals and indefinites. A common alternative is to treat bare plurals as kinds or properties

$$\frac{\quad\quad\varepsilon\quad\quad}{\textbf{some}: np_{\text{p}}^{*}\Uparrow s/n_{\text{p}}^{*}}\text{Lx} \quad \frac{\quad kids \quad}{\textbf{plu}(\textbf{kid}): n_{\text{p}}^{*}}\text{Lx}$$
$$\frac{}{\textbf{some}(\textbf{plu}(\textbf{kid})): np_{\text{p}}^{*}\Uparrow s}\text{/E}$$

Figure 8.1
A derivation with a bare-plural existential determiner

(Carlson 1977a, McNally 1995). I restrict our attention to the existential-generalized-quantifier reading of the bare plural. The effect will be to quantify over sets in the plural-noun denotation.

To create a locus for the quantificational nature of the bare plural, I will introduce lexical entries with the empty string, ε, as their expression component. Up until now, we have only considered lexical entries with basic expressions in **BasExp**, but there is no obstacle to allowing arbitrary expressions from **Exp** $\overset{\text{def}}{=}$ **BasExp***, such as $\varepsilon \in$ **Exp**. Despite having a null expression component, they will otherwise function exactly like ordinary lexical entries in derivations (recall the definition of lexical linking, definition 3, from chapter 5).

For our analysis of bare plurals, I assume the following existential generalized determiner with the null string as its expression component.

(21) $\varepsilon \Rightarrow \textbf{some}_{\textbf{Ind}\rightarrow\textbf{Bool}}: np_{\text{p}}^{*}\Uparrow s/n_{\text{p}}^{*}$

Note that the constant is of the appropriate type for the syntactic category to which it is assigned. The existential generalized determiner **some$_{\textbf{Ind}\rightarrow\textbf{Bool}}$** quantifies over sets, or in other words, elements of type **Ind** $\rightarrow$ **Bool**. I will drop the type annotation when it is obvious from context. The empty category for the bare plural existential determiner allows us to carry out the derivation shown in figure 8.1. I have assumed that the empty bare-plural determiner is forward looking, in the same way as other determiners. But in general, for empty categories, there is not much of a distinction as to directionality, and we could have alternatively used an undirected version of the slash.

Having modeled the treatment of bare plurals on the treatment of existentials in the singular case, I will treat plural definites as a generalization of singular definites. Suppose that we tried simply to extend the description operator to the plural domain. In a model with just three kids, k_1, k_2, and k_3, *kids* picks out the set containing the elements $\{k_1, k_2, k_3\}$, $\{k_1, k_2\}$, $\{k_1, k_3\}$, and $\{k_2, k_3\}$. Obviously, this set is not a singleton, so directly applying the description operator is meaningless because of the failure of the uniqueness presupposition of the definite. Thus a more subtle approach is required.

To recover uniqueness for the definite determiner, Sharvy (1980) and Link (1983) assumed that the definite picked out the largest set in the denotation of its plural nominal complement. For instance, in the denotation of *kids* above, the definite would produce the set $\{k_1, k_2, k_3\}$ of all three kids. In our categorial setting, this leads to the following lexical entry:

(22) a. *the* $\Rightarrow$ **the**: np_p^*/n_p^*
  b. **the** $\overset{\text{def}}{=} \lambda Q.\imath(\lambda P. Q(P) \wedge \textbf{every}(Q)(\lambda X. \textbf{every}(X)(P)))$

Glossing this lexical entry, we pick out the unique P such that $P \in Q$ and every $X \in Q$ is such that $X \subseteq P$. In particular, note that the description operator $\imath$ used here maps sets of sets into sets; if the set of sets is a singleton, $\imath$ will return its unique member. This lexical entry provides the following kind of analysis, by application.

(23) *the kids* $\Rightarrow \imath(\lambda P. \textbf{plu}(\textbf{kid})(P) \wedge \textbf{every}(\textbf{plu}(\textbf{kid}))(\lambda X. \textbf{every}(X)(P))): np_p^*$

Note that now the $\imath$ applies not simply to **plu(kid)** but rather to the singleton set consisting of the maximum element of the set of sets Q, assuming there is one. Otherwise, it applies to the empty set, and the presupposition of the definite is violated. For instance, if *two kids* denotes the set containing the sets $\{k_1, k_2\}$, $\{k_1, k_3\}$, and $\{k_2, k_3\}$, then the value of *the two kids* is unconstrained, and a presupposition is violated. Of course, contextual factors can always be used to restrict the denotation of a noun, including a plural noun.

8.3 DISTRIBUTORS AND COLLECTORS

Our analysis so far has left us with plural noun phrases denoting sets. I will make the rather natural, yet nonstandard, assumption that both singular and plural verb phrases have the same denotation. In this approach, they receive the categories $np_s \backslash s$ and $np_p \backslash s$, both of which are associated with the type **Ind** $\rightarrow$ **Bool**.

My approach to the distributive and collective readings is to treat them as quantifiers over the sets introduced by the set-denoting plural noun phrase of category np_p^*. Treating distribution and collection as quantification was first proposed by Heim, Lasnik, and May (1991), who also treated the bare plural as an existential indefinite. Our lexical entries are as follows:

(24) $\varepsilon \Rightarrow \mathbf{every_{Ind}}: np_p^* \backslash np_p \Uparrow s$ (Distributor)

(25) $\varepsilon \Rightarrow \lambda P.\mathbf{some_{Ind}}(\mathbf{group}(P)): np_p^* \backslash np_p \Uparrow s$ (Collector)

The empty *distributor* takes a plural noun phrase denoting a set and produces a universal quantifier over the members of that set. The empty *collector*, on the other hand, takes a plural noun phrase denoting a set and produces an existential quantifier requiring the existence of a group composed of the elements of that set. Note that for the latter case, **some**(**group**(*P*)) is logically equivalent to **some**($\lambda x.$**group**(P)(x)) by η-reduction and that the semantics of the collector as a whole is equivalent to $\lambda P.\lambda Q.\mathbf{some_{Ind}}(\lambda x.\mathbf{group}(P)(x))(Q)$ by η-reduction. I have assumed that the distributors and collectors are backward looking functions for reasons that will become clear when we come to the treatment of coordination in section 8.4.

The easiest way to understand the distributor and collector is to consider them in action. Before doing this, recall that I assign plural verbs the same semantic types as their singular counterparts.

(26) a. *sneeze* $\Rightarrow$ **sneeze**: $np_p \backslash s$

b. *gather* $\Rightarrow$ **gather**: $np_p \backslash s$

Of course, verbs such as *gather* only apply to groups, whereas *sneeze* can only be applied to proper individuals. With these lexical entries, I show an application of distribution in figure 8.2 and the parallel operation of collection in figure 8.3. In the distributive analysis in figure 8.2, we see that there are two quantificational stages. First, the empty plural existential

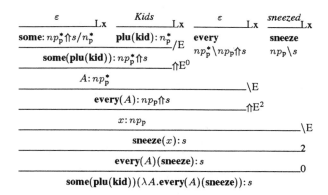

Figure 8.2
A distributive derivation of *Kids sneezed*

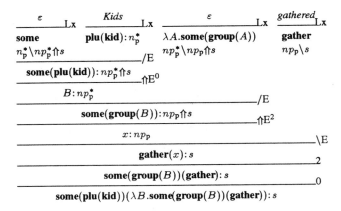

Figure 8.3
A collective derivation of *Kids gathered*

determiner combines with *kids* to produce a plural quantifier asserting the existence of a set of two or more kids. Then this quantifier is eliminated, leaving an np_p^* hypothesis to which the empty distributor applies. The distributor requires universal quantification over the set of kids. Next, the distributional quantifier is eliminated, leaving a hypothetical np_p to which the verb may apply. Finally, the quantifiers are given scope in nested order to produce the final reading. The collective analysis in figure 8.3 is nearly identical, the only difference being that the collector applies rather than the distributor, which requires the set of kids assumed to exist to form some group. As I mentioned earlier, there is nothing to prevent *Kids sneezed* from being interpreted collectively or *Kids gathered* from being interpreted distributively; such analyses simply violate selectional restrictions and can thus never be true.

It is important to note that even though there are two quantifiers in the analyses in figures 8.2 and 8.3, there is only one distributive reading and one collective reading. It is simply not possible, given our logical construal of quantification, for the quantifier introduced by the distributor or collector to outscope the quantifier introduced by the bare plural. This is because one quantifier is properly nested inside of the other.

Using exactly the same distributive and collective analyses as in figure 8.2, only with a numerical modifier, we get the following analyses:

(27) a. *Three kids sneezed* $\Rightarrow$ **some**$(\lambda P.\textbf{plu}(\textbf{kid})(P) \land \|P\| = 3)$
$$(\lambda R.\textbf{every}(R)(\textbf{sneeze})): s$$

b. *Three kids gathered* $\Rightarrow$ **some**$(\lambda P.\textbf{plu}(\textbf{kid})(P) \wedge \|P\| = 3)$
$(\lambda R.\textbf{some}(\textbf{group}(R))(\textbf{gather})): s$

Note that in both analyses in (27), the set R that is supposed to exist is taken to consist of exactly three kids. The distributive reading, (27a), allows the possibility that more than three kids sneezed. All that is required is that there is a set of exactly three kids, each of whom sneezed. The collective analysis, (27b), on the other hand, requires the existence of a group that gathered that has exactly three kids as members. Of course, if we believe (27b) is true in a situation where more than three kids gathered, we can employ the greater than or equal to relation rather than the strict equality in the term representing the semantics of the numerical modifiers. But I believe that examples such as *Three kids carried the box* indicate that the group denoted by a numerically modified plural noun must contain exactly the number of individuals indicated by the modifier.

Now consider the possibilities for the scoping of a plural subject relative to a quantified object.

(28) a. Three kids carried a box.

b. Three teachers marked six exams.

For the first example, the analysis involves three quantifiers; in the distributive case, we have **some**$(\textbf{three}_a(\textbf{plu}(\textbf{kid})))$ for the bare plural, **every**(K) for the distributor, and **some**$(\textbf{box})$ for the object. Only three of the six permutations of these quantifiers correspond to grammatical readings of the sentence; it is not possible for the distributor to outscope the bare plural.

(29) a. **some**$(\textbf{three}_a(\textbf{plu}(\textbf{kid})))$
$(\lambda K.\textbf{every}(K)(\lambda x.\textbf{some}(\textbf{box})(\lambda y.\textbf{carry}(y)(x))))$

b. **some**$(\textbf{box})(\lambda y.\textbf{some}(\textbf{three}_a(\textbf{plu}(\textbf{kid})))$
$(\lambda K.\textbf{every}(K)(\lambda x.\textbf{carry}(y)(x))))$

c. **some**$(\textbf{three}_a(\textbf{plu}(\textbf{kid})))$
$(\lambda K.\textbf{some}(\textbf{box})(\lambda y.\textbf{every}(K)(\lambda x.\textbf{carry}(y)(x))))$

Note that the second and third analyses yield logically equivalent results. If we had employed the collective rather than the distributive quantifier, we would get the same three analyses, only there would be three existential quantifiers, and all three readings would be logically equivalent.

The potential ambiguity is even more dramatic in the case of (28b). There are 4 ways in which 4 quantifiers can be introduced, depending on

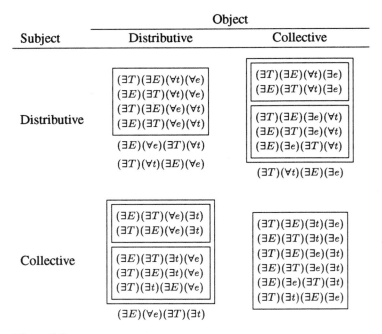

Figure 8.4
Equivalent quantifier prefixes for *Three teachers marked six exams*, indicated by
boxes

the choice of distributor and collector for the subject and object. With
each possibility yielding 24 permutations, apparently 96 possibilities for
scoping arise. But of these 96, only 24 obey the relative scoping restrictions requiring the distributor or collector to take narrow scope with
respect to the embedding bare plural. This leaves 24 grammatical possibilities, which I list by abbreviated quantificational prefix in figure 8.4. As
with the singular quantified object, there are many logical equivalences
between readings, again due to the commutation of pairs of universal or
existential quantifiers. These equivalences are represented by the innermost boxes in figure 8.4. If we further make the unique-group assumption,
so that for every set of objects, there is exactly one group that it forms, we
get the further reduction of the pairs of collective/distributive readings
indicated by the two outer boxes in figure 8.4. The result is exactly the
readings proposed pretheoretically by Davies (1989). Note the perhaps
unexpected reading in which the bare-plural existentials outscope both the
distributors, noticed by Gil (1982), who referred to it as the *strong sym-*

metric reading; it requires the existence of sets for the subject and object bare plurals, with distribution forcing a pairwise interpretation.

We get different analyses in terms of scope with the definites than we did with indefinites. For instance, consider the following sentences:

(30) a. The three boys carried a piano.
b. The three boys carried the three boxes.

In the first case, the same possibilities are generated as for the bare plural. There is one collective reading, and under a distributive analysis, the distributor can scope wide or narrow with respect to the existential object. For the second example, with a definite plural in both subject and object position, there are eight possibilities, depending on the choice of distributor and collector and their relative scopes. Of course, if both are universal or both collective, scope is irrelevant, and thus at most six of the readings are logically distinct. If we further assume a unique group for each set, the scope distinction between distributives and collectives collapses to produce only four distinct readings.

8.4 COORDINATION, NEGATION, AND ARGUMENT LOWERING

The following sentences provide a particularly puzzling use of plural noun phrases, especially for an approach such as ours, in which the distributive/collective distinction is centered on the noun phrase.

(31) a. Three kids met and sneezed.
b. The thirty students in our program drafted and signed a petition.

The first sentence can be interpreted truthfully if there are three kids who met as a group and who sneezed individually. The second example can be true if the students drafted the petition as a group but signed it individually. This phenomenon drove many researchers, such as Link (1983), to treat the distributive/collective distinction as a property of the verb phrase. The primary drawback to such a move is that all the properties of plurals in subject position must be duplicated in all nominal argument positions. Van der Does (1992) presents such a generalization for the unscoped distributive/collective distinction; presumably a lexicalized theory of quantification such as that of H. Hendriks (1993) would then be required to account for scoping.

Our type-logical analysis of plurals, within the general approach to complementation and coordination, provides a novel solution to the

$$[A:np_{\mathrm{p}}^{*}]^{0} \quad \cfrac{\cfrac{\varepsilon}{\mathbf{every}:np_{\mathrm{p}}^{*}\backslash np_{\mathrm{p}}\!\Uparrow\! s}\mathrm{Lx} \quad \cfrac{sneezed}{\mathbf{sneeze}:np_{\mathrm{p}}\backslash s}\mathrm{Lx}}{\cfrac{\mathbf{every}(A):np_{\mathrm{p}}\!\Uparrow\! s}{\cfrac{x:np_{\mathrm{p}}}{\cfrac{\mathbf{sneeze}(x):s}{\cfrac{\mathbf{every}(A)(\mathbf{sneeze}):s}{\lambda A.\mathbf{every}(A)(\mathbf{sneeze}):np_{\mathrm{p}}^{*}\backslash s}\backslash I^{0}}2}\backslash E}\Uparrow\! E^{2}}/E}$$

Figure 8.5
An argument-lowering derivation of *sneezed*

$$[B:np_{\mathrm{p}}^{*}]^{0} \quad \cfrac{\cfrac{\varepsilon}{\lambda A.\mathbf{some}(\mathbf{group}(A)):np_{\mathrm{p}}^{*}\backslash np_{\mathrm{p}}\!\Uparrow\! s}\mathrm{Lx} \quad \cfrac{gathered}{\mathbf{gather}:np_{\mathrm{p}}\backslash s}\mathrm{Lx}}{\cfrac{\mathbf{some}(\mathbf{group}(B)):np_{\mathrm{p}}\!\Uparrow\! s}{\cfrac{x:np_{\mathrm{p}}}{\cfrac{\mathbf{gather}(x):s}{\cfrac{\mathbf{some}(\mathbf{group}(B))(\mathbf{gather}):s}{\lambda B.\mathbf{some}(\mathbf{group}(B))(\mathbf{gather}):np_{\mathrm{p}}^{*}\backslash s}\backslash I^{0}}2}\backslash E}\Uparrow\! E^{2}}/E}$$

Figure 8.6
An argument-lowering derivation of *gathered*

analysis of these mixed predications. We can use the slash-introduction rules in conjunction with the quantifying-in schemes to lower arguments from type np_{p} to type np_{p}^{*} (somewhat counterintuitively, this is properly an instance of argument lowering because the quantifier scheme derives an np_{p} from an np_{p}^{*}). Consider the parallel analyses in figures 8.5 and 8.6. In the analysis of *sneezed*, I have used argument lowering to show how the category $np_{\mathrm{p}}\backslash s$ can be analyzed as being of category $np_{\mathrm{p}}^{*}\backslash s$. This requires the following sequence of operations: first, we assume there is an np_{p}^{*}, then apply the empty distributor to this hypothetical category, and finally apply slash introduction to eliminate the assumption. The resulting $np_{\mathrm{p}}^{*}\backslash s$ is seeking an np_{p}^{*}, which is construed distributively by quantifying over its elements. The analysis of the case of *gather* in figure 8.6 is almost identical, except that the empty collector is applied to the hypothetical category rather than the distributor. These derivations provide the motivation for the backward directionality of our distributor and collector

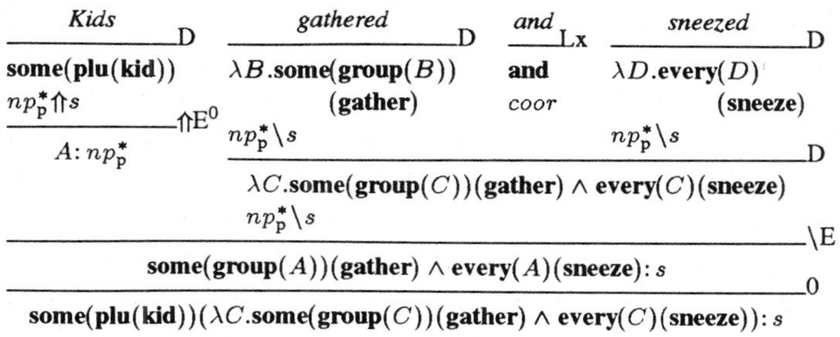

$$\frac{\begin{array}{c}Kids\\ \hline \textbf{some}(\textbf{plu}(\textbf{kid}))\\ np_p^*\Uparrow s\end{array}D \qquad \frac{\begin{array}{c}gathered\\ \hline \lambda B.\textbf{some}(\textbf{group}(B))\\ (\textbf{gather})\\ \hline np_p^*\backslash s\end{array}D \quad \begin{array}{c}and\\ \hline \textbf{and}\\ coor\end{array}Lx \quad \frac{\begin{array}{c}sneezed\\ \hline \lambda D.\textbf{every}(D)\\ (\textbf{sneeze})\\ \hline np_p^*\backslash s\end{array}D}{\lambda C.\textbf{some}(\textbf{group}(C))(\textbf{gather})\wedge\textbf{every}(C)(\textbf{sneeze})}D\\ np_p^*\backslash s}{}}{}$$

Kids — D

some(plu(kid))
$np_p^* \Uparrow s$

$\dfrac{}{A : np_p^*} \Uparrow E^0$

gathered — D
$\lambda B.$some(group(B))
(gather)
$np_p^* \backslash s$

and — Lx
and
coor

sneezed — D
$\lambda D.$every(D)
(sneeze)
$np_p^* \backslash s$

—————————— D
$\lambda C.$some(group(C))(gather) $\wedge$ every(C)(sneeze)
$np_p^* \backslash s$

——————————————————— \E
some(group(A))(gather) $\wedge$ every(A)(sneeze): s

——————————————————— 0
some(plu(kid))($\lambda C.$some(group(C))(gather) $\wedge$ every(C)(sneeze)): s

Figure 8.7
A derivation of *Kids gathered and sneezed*

lexical entries. Had they been forward functors, the noun would not have been the leftmost assumption, and hence could not have been abstracted.

With these two analyses in hand, we can coordinate them as shown in figure 8.7. Note that I have applied the bare plural to the subject and quantified into it to provide it with widest scope. A similar analysis can be constructed for other cases of "mixed" collective/distributive interpretations, such as those found in the following examples:

(32) a. Jody destroyed and rebuilt three cars.
      b. The kids who ran in the hall gathered in the principal's office.

The first sentence, (32a), on the reading where Jody destroyed the cars collectively but rebuilt them one at a time, can be analyzed along the same lines as the derivation in figure 8.7. The only difference is that the argument raised is the object rather than the subject. One way in which to view our analysis is as providing a deeper explanation for the operations introduced in a nonlogical manner by Link (1983) and extended by Roberts (1987a) and van der Does (1993). Instead of proposing type-shifting operations and synchronizing their application to verb phrases and noun phrases by lexical stipulation, I generate all the proper interactions through our simple schemes for complementation, coordination, and quantification.

Examples involving plural relative clauses, such as (32b), must be treated at the level of n_p^* modifiers. This can be achieved by treating the plural relatives as the set-modifying analogues of the singular relatives.

(33) a. *who* $\Rightarrow \lambda Q.\lambda R.\lambda X.Q(X) \wedge R(X): n_p^* \backslash n_p^* / (np_p^* \backslash s)$
      b. *that* $\Rightarrow \lambda Q.\lambda R.\lambda X.Q(X) \wedge R(X): n_p^* \backslash n_p^* / (s \uparrow np_p^*)$

If we employed a polymorphic λ-calculus (see Barendregt 1991), we could employ the same semantic term for both the singular and plural relatives; both act simply as intersection, the singular being the intersection of individual properties, whereas the plural acts as the intersection of properties of sets. We could also use a single syntactic entry if we had a polymorphic categorial grammar (see Emms 1990).

Note that with the availability of argument lowering, we can derive verb phrases of category $s{\uparrow}np_p^*$ or $np_p^*\backslash s$ from verb phrases of category $np_p\backslash s$. Simple application then derives sequents such as the following:

(34) *kids who sneezed* $\Rightarrow \lambda X.\mathbf{plu}(\mathbf{kid})(X) \wedge \mathbf{every}(X)(\mathbf{sneeze}): n_p^*$

Similar analyses allow us to analyze the unbounded cases necessary for relativization of positions other than the subject.

Along similar lines, the argument lowering schemes appear to provide a source for attributive adjectival modification, as found in the following examples:

(35) a. The competing candidates gave a speech.
      b. Mary noticed the sneezing students.

To handle these kinds of examples, the modifiers *competing* and *sneezing* have to be assigned to plural nominal modifiers of category n_p^*/n_p^*.

(36) a. *competing* $\Rightarrow \lambda P.\lambda Q.P(Q) \wedge \mathbf{some}(\mathbf{group}(Q))(\mathbf{compete}): n_p^*/n_p^*$
      b. *sneezing* $\Rightarrow \lambda P.\lambda Q.P(Q) \wedge \mathbf{every}(Q)(\mathbf{sneeze}): n_p^*/n_p^*$

Such entries are merely the intersective modifiers derived from the lowered verb phrases in figures 8.5 and 8.6.

It has been claimed by Verkuyl (1988) and Lønning (1989) that in the presence of negation, scope possibilities are more limited:

(37) a. Some boys did not share a pizza.   (Lønning 1989)
      b. Some of the girls did not lift the stone.   (Lønning 1989)
      c. The two men did not lift three tables.   (Verkuyl 1988)
      d. Francis could not lift three tables.
      e. Three kids didn't vote.

Lønning claims that both quantifiers cannot outscope the negation in (37a), and that there is no wide-scope collective interpretation of (37b). Furthermore, Verkuyl claims that (37c) does not display a distributive/ collective ambiguity in the object position. Rather, he assumes that this sentence would be true only if the two men did not lift the three tables together and also did not lift them one at a time. In other words, Verkuyl believes negation operates over both readings simultaneously, negating each of them. If such a reading is possible, I would claim that it is an instance of metasemantic, or pragmatic, negation (Horn 1985). I provide (37d) as an example that might be false for the distributive reading of the object but true under the collective one; that is, Francis might be able to lift three tables one at a time but not all three at once. Finally, note that our approach to quantification and negation generates three distributive readings for the last example, (37e).

(38) a. $\neg$**some**(**three**$_a$(**plu**(**student**)))($\lambda X.$**every**(X)(**vote**))
    b. **some**(**three**$_a$(**plu**(**student**)))($\lambda X.\neg$**every**(X)(**vote**))
    c. **some**(**three**$_a$(**plu**(**student**)))($\lambda X.$**every**(X)($\neg$**vote**))

These readings are generated by all possible scopings of the bare plural and the distributor or collector relative to the negation. Of course, the distributor/collector is always given narrow scope with respect to the bare plural, so the three readings in (38) exhaust the possibilities. These analyses are constructed analogously to the singular cases given in figure 7.20. I leave the derivations for exercise 5. The reading in which the distributor and the bare plural are split by the negation seems less plausible than the other two, but I claim that such readings are possible in general. As we will see below in (42), there are certainly clearer ways to express the reading in (38b). Further, if we assume that sets correspond to unique groups, then the reading in which the negation splits the bare-plural existential and the collector will be logically equivalent to the reading in which both quantifiers outscope the negation.

8.5 ADVERBIAL DISTRIBUTION

In English we find the distributive reading marked explicitly by the word *each* in the following examples:

(39) a. Each of the three kids carried a piano.
    b. The three kids each carried a piano.
    c. The three kids carried a piano each.

All of these examples mean roughly the same thing, namely that there is a set of three kids, and each of them carried a piano. The partitive in (39a) acts exactly like an explicit realization of the distributor. In the last two examples, *each* appears adjacent to the verb phrase, a phenomenon commonly referred to as *quantifier floating* (because *each* is often considered to be a kind of universal quantifier, like *every*). Following Dowty and Brodie (1984), I treat the preverbal occurrences of *each* adverbially. The postverbal occurrences appear to be more constrained in their distribution:

(40) a. *The three kids carried the piano each.
    b. *The three kids ran each.
    c. *The three kids carried a piano yesterday each.

In fact, the example in (40a) differs from (39c) only in the definiteness of the object determiner. The result is also ungrammatical if there is no object determiner, as indicated in (40b), or if the object is separated from the floated *each* by an adverbial, as in (40c).

The examples in (39) appear to act on the subject. But floated *each* appears to act on the indirect object in (41a, b), and on the dative object in (41c):

(41) a. The student gave his teachers an apple each.
    b. The student gave his teachers each an apple.
    c. The student gave an apple each to his teachers.
    d. *The student gave an apple to his teachers each.

First note that *each* can occur before or after *an apple* but not before *his teachers*. Further note the contrast between (41a) and (41b); even in the dative form in (41c), the floated *each* still applies to a less oblique position. An attempt to float further afield, as in (41d), leads to ungrammaticality. I will not handle these postverbal floatings. For some hints on how they might be dealt with, and the requisite analysis of word order and obliqueness in a categorial setting, see Morrill 1994a.

The following sentences also indicate an adverbial position for *each*:

(42) a. The kids did not each run.
    b. The kids each did not run.
    c. ?The kids did each not run.
    d. The kids probably each cheated.
    e. The kids each probably cheated.

In these examples, we see *each* appearing after auxiliary elements and other adverbials but remaining preverbal. Note that the readings of (42a) and (42b) are different, as are the readings of (42d) and (42e).

The behavior of *each* is not purely modificational, though. It has a substantial type-shifting effect, as can be seen in the following examples:

(43) a. *The kids each were each tired.
  b. *The kids each ran a mile each.
  c. *Each of the kids each ran.
  d. The students each gave their teachers an apple each.
  e. *The committee each ran.

In the first three examples, we see that *each* cannot be used redundantly. Sentence (43d) is grammatical only because the two occurrences of *each* must apply to the students and the teachers. The last example, (43e), shows that *each* cannot force distribution through a group. I feel that this is convincing evidence that distribution takes place over sets, rather than over groups.

To accomplish this, I will treat *each* as having the same effect as argument-lowering a verb by implicit distribution. Recall that argument lowering was used in figure 8.5 to derive the following sequent:

(44) *sneezed* $\Rightarrow \lambda P.\mathbf{every}(P)(\mathbf{sneeze}): np_p^*\backslash s$

Following Dowty and Brodie (1984), I treat *each* as explicitly coercing lexical *sneezed*, which takes an individual argument, into a distributive version, which takes a set argument and universally quantifies over it:

(45) *each* $\Rightarrow \lambda V.\lambda P.\mathbf{every}(P)(V): np_p^*\backslash s/(np_p\backslash s)$

A simple analysis involving *each* is given in figure 8.8. In this analysis, I have included the application of the empty bare-plural existential. Note that the occurrence of *each* simply forces the distributive reading. It is not possible to have a collective interpretation of the subject with *each*, because the subject must contribute an np_p^* rather than an np_p.

We could use an entry for *each* with semantics identical to the subject-centered postverbal adverbial used in (39c). But as we saw in (40), its

$$
\begin{array}{c}
\cfrac{
\cfrac{\text{\emph{Six kids}}}{\begin{array}{c}\mathbf{some}(\lambda A.\mathbf{plu}(\mathbf{kid})(A)\wedge \|A\|=6)\\ np_p^*\Uparrow s\end{array}}\,{}_{\text{D}}\qquad
\cfrac{\cfrac{\begin{array}{c}\text{\emph{each}}\\ \lambda V.\lambda C.\mathbf{every}(C)(V)\\ np_p^*\backslash s/(np_p\backslash s)\end{array}\ {}_{\text{Lx}}\quad \cfrac{\begin{array}{c}\text{\emph{scored}}\\ \mathbf{score}\\ np_p\backslash s\end{array}}{}_{\text{Lx}}}{\lambda C.\mathbf{every}(C)(\mathbf{score}): np_p^*\backslash s}\,{}_{/\text{E}}
}{\cfrac{B: np_p^*\quad\quad\quad\quad\mathbf{every}(B)(\mathbf{score}): s}{\ }}\,\Uparrow\!\mathrm{E}^0\ \backslash\mathrm{E}\\[20pt]
\hline
\mathbf{some}(\lambda A.\mathbf{plu}(\mathbf{kid})(A)\wedge \|A\|=6)(\lambda C.\mathbf{every}(C)(\mathbf{score})): s
\end{array}\ {}_0
$$

Figure 8.8
A derivation of *Six kids each scored*

properties are more like that of the floated non-subject-centered *each* seen in (41).

8.6   PLURAL QUANTIFICATION

I have already employed a quantifier over sets in our analysis of the bare plural. This empty category existentially quantifies over sets. We also have the negation of the existential, *no*.

(46) a. No three students could lift this desk.

     b. No competing candidates like each other.

In the first case, (46a), the assertion is that there is no set of three students that could lift the desk. The lifting can be understood distributively or collectively, and both are plausible for this example. For instance, the desk might be so heavy that even the three strongest students could not lift it. Or it might be heavy enough that two students could each lift it but the third strongest student is slightly too weak. Note that the second example, (46b), states that there is no set of candidates who are competing among themselves as a group and who also individually like each other (we return to the reciprocal *each other* in section 9.6).

The negative case can be treated with a lexical entry that is simply the negation of that assigned to the bare-plural empty category:

(47) *no* $\Rightarrow$ **no**: $np_{\mathrm{p}}^* \Uparrow s/n_{\mathrm{p}}^*$

The constant **no** is simply the generalized negative determiner over sets. An example of a derivation involving this lexical entry is given in figure 8.9.

Next, consider how quantification over sets arises in cases such as the following:

(48) a. Fewer than five students attended.

     b. More than five students wrote a paper.

Traditionally, expressions such as *fewer than five* have been analyzed as generalized determiners. But their behavior is actually much more subtle. For instance, (48b) involves a distributive/collective distinction, as well as the requirement that there be more than five students involved. In addition, we would like an analysis under which *fewer than five* behaves like a quantifier over numbers, as follows:

(49) *fewer than five* $\Rightarrow$ **no**$(\lambda n.n \geq 5)$: $num \Uparrow s$

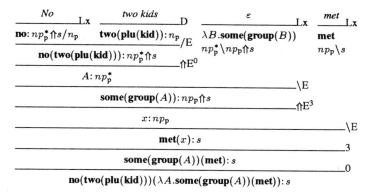

Figure 8.9
A derivation of *No two kids met*

Such a category can be used as the basis of our analysis of comparatives, as in *Sandy is fewer than five inches taller than Terry*. Now recall that any numeral expression assigned $k: num$ can act as a plural nominal modifier assigned to category $\lambda Q.\lambda P.Q(P) \wedge \|P\| = k: n_p^*/n_p^*$. Thus I will assume the following lexical entry for *fewer than*.

(50) *fewer than* $\Rightarrow \lambda k.\lambda V.\mathbf{no}(\lambda n.n \geq k)(\lambda n.V(\lambda Q.\lambda P.Q(P) \wedge \|P\| = n))$
$(n_p^*/n_p^*) \Uparrow s/num$

This leads to analyses such as the one in figure 8.10, in which the bare-plural existential and the empty distributor are applied. Note that the analysis in figure 8.10 allows that *Fewer than five kids sneezed* will be true if no students at all sneezed. We can provide similar lexical entries for other numerical quantifiers, such as *exactly five*, *approximately five*, *more than five* and for coordinations such as *more than five but less than ten*. We can also apply the collective operator. For instance, we will be able to derive analyses such as the following:

(51) *more than five students collaborated* $\Rightarrow$
$\mathbf{some}(\lambda n.n > 5)(\lambda n.\mathbf{some}(\lambda R.\mathbf{plu}(\mathbf{student})(R) \wedge \|R\| = n)$
$(\lambda X.\mathbf{some}(\mathbf{group}(X))(\mathbf{collab}))): s$

Here there is no upper bound on the number of students who may have collaborated, but there must be some collaboration among a group of more than five people, all of whom are students. Finally, note that our quantificational analysis of *fewer than* allows us to generate the proper ambiguity in the following sentence:

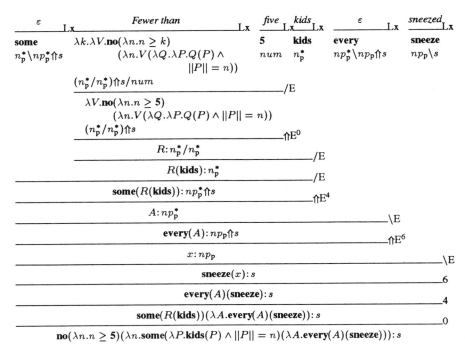

Figure 8.10
A derivation of *Fewer than five kids sneezed*

(52) Fewer than five students read a paper.

Here there might be a particular paper that fewer than five students read, or it might be the case that fewer than five students read any paper. With *any* in place of *a*, there is no ambiguity because the negative-polarity item *any* must fall within the scope of the negative-polarity context induced by the quantifier *fewer than*. Given our analysis of an example such as the following, there is no entailment of a meeting going on at all.

(53) Fewer than five kids gathered.

Empirically, it is very difficult to judge whether there is an entailment, or simply an implicature, that some group of less than five kids gathered. If we wished to treat it as an entailment, we could require that there is no number greater than or equal to five and some (positive) number less than five such that the property held. This would be the kind of analysis necessary for expressions such as *exactly five kids*; we must say that five kids have a given property, but no set of more than five kids have the property, and no set of less than five kids have the property. In all of these cases, the quantificational behavior of the numerals arises because of the bare-plural existential and the empty distributor and collector.

The status of other putative quantifiers over sets is less clear. For instance, *all* and *most* are quite limited as quantifiers:

(54) a. {Most / All} boys can carry the piano.
     b. {Most / All} baseball players earn a million dollars.
     c. Jody can carry {most / all} books.

In none of these cases does the plural appear to have a collective reading. I will assume that there are n_p categories for plural nouns, which are interpreted semantically as properties of individuals, just like their singular counterparts. We can then use the following lexical entry for *most*:

(55) *most* $\Rightarrow$ **most**: $np_p \Uparrow s/n_p$

This would allow analyses just like the singular cases:

(56) *Most students study* $\Rightarrow$ **most**(**student**)(**study**): s

Note that there is no longer any possibility of distributing or collecting; there is simply never an np_p^* category to distribute or collect. Such an assignment to *most* also blocks its co-occurrence with true plural modifiers such as numerals, which modify nouns, and *each*, which modifiers verbs.

(57) {*Most / All} fifteen students {passed / built a raft}.

While this appears correct for *most*, *all* seems to be felicitous in this context. Furthermore, *all* can also modify plural noun phrases.

(58) All the senators voted for the bill.

Further note that *all* differs from *most* in that it can take an adverbial-like position, in some ways similar to floated *each*:

(59) a. The senators probably all {voted for the bill / collaborated}.
     b. The senators all probably {voted for the bill / collaborated}.

On the basis of these examples, Dowty (1986a) argues that *all* contributes a participatory effect to the members of the set to which it attaches. He refers to this as distributing to the *subentailments* of a verb. For instance, voting does not ordinarily require participation by every member in a group, but with *all*, participation is mandatory. It remains unclear how to treat *all* grammatically and how to provide a term for the contributory semantic role of *all*.

Roberts (1987a) further notes that *all* and *most* do seem to quantify over limited quantities if there is some connection between the members.

(60) a. {Most / All} competing companies {dissolved / met / undercut each other}.
     b. {Most / All} identical twins {are smart / conferred / like each other}.

Note that these examples must allow quantification over sets in order to provide sets for distribution, collection, and reciprocation (see section 9.6 for an analysis of reciprocals). There does not seem to be a neat type-logical solution to this dilemma of limited quantification. Noticing that the cases in which such quantification can occur are highly restricted, Roberts (1987a) proposes a pragmatic approach. She treats *all* simply as a universal quantifier over sets, further assuming that such quantification is usually contextually restricted to singletons. Such a move is possible in her framework because Roberts adopts Link's approach in which individuals behave as singleton sets, and also allows singletons into the denotation of a plural, thus allowing *all* a direct distributive reading.

8.7   PARTITIVES AND PSEUDOPARTITIVES

Under our type-logical approach, a natural analysis of partitives and pseudopartitives is available. For instance, consider the range of partitives in the following examples:

(61) {Each / All / Most} of the five kids {sneezed / #met}.

I will analyze the complement to the partitives as an np_p^*, the result being a quantifier over individuals, $np_p \Uparrow s$. Semantically, *each* provides universal quantification, thus mimicking the behavior of the implicit distributor and the adverbial distributor.

(62) *each* $\Rightarrow$ **every**: $np_p \Uparrow s / np_p^*$

Note that this explicit distribution explains why the collective predicate *met* is pragmatically odd in (61). Also note that because partitives induce quantification over an np_p, they cannot co-occur in subject position with explicit distributors such as *each other* or floated adverbial *each*. I will assume that the particle *of* is semantically transparent; this can be achieved by treating it as an np_p^* modifier, with the identity function for its semantics. Of course, it contributes syntactic marking to the result, but I will not be concerned with this detail. The partitives play exactly the same

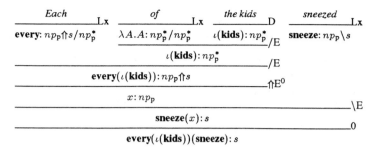

Figure 8.11
A derivation of *Each of the kids sneezed*

role as the empty distributors in derivations, as shown in figure 8.11. We can derive similar analyses for *none of the men* and *some of the men* under the assumption that *none* and *some* behave syntactically like *each* as a partitive but contribute the negative quantifier **no** and the existential quantifier **some** rather than the universal **every**.

Numerical partitives such as *three of the men, very few of the men,* and *at least sixteen of the men* are analyzed along lines similar to the numerical nominal modifiers. The primary difference is that they take an argument of category np_p^* rather than n_p^*. Further, the semantics involves the subset relation (here indicated by **every**). Thus we adopt the following lexical entry in the simple case.

(63) *three* $\Rightarrow \lambda P.\lambda R.\mathbf{every}(R)(P) \wedge \|R\| = 3 \colon n_p^*/np_p^*$

Note that the category assigned to *three of the students* is n_p^*. Now consider the analysis of the simple example in figure 8.12. Just as with the standard nominal-modifying numerals, it is clear how the partitive numerals are related to the underlying numerals. Thus such an analysis will extend to quantified numerals such as *fewer than three of the kids* in the same way as I analyzed *fewer than three kids*.

Our type assignment to the partitive *three* will be compatible with explicit distribution or collection, with a nominal specifier, an adverbial, or a reciprocal.

(64) a. All three of the kids sneezed.
      b. Three of the kids each sneezed.
      c. Three of the kids like each other.

We will also be able to have a definite in some cases, such as the following:

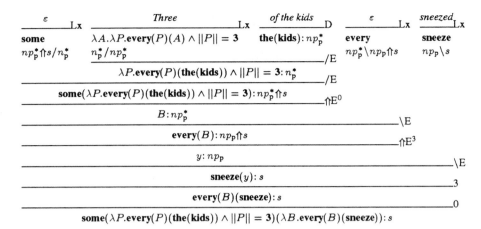

Figure 8.12
A derivation of *Three of the kids sneezed*

(65) a. ?The three of the students will get a prize.

b. The three of the students who wrote a paper will get a prize.

Our grammar generates both (65a) and (65b); I have no explanation for the relative infelicity of (65a). Of course, we can derive partitive complements that themselves have numerical content, as in *three of the five kids*. We can also account for more complex numeral partitives, such as *at least three* and *exactly three*. We can extend our analysis of simple numerals to numerical partitives in a fashion analogous to how we extended simple numerical nominal modifiers to deal with quantified numerals. Functionally, partitives differ from numerical modifiers in that the partitives take noun-phrase complements. Such noun phrases are typically definite and will have their usual presuppositions in this case. Thus we can use an expression such as *three of the five kids* if there are five kids who are salient in the discourse and we wish to pick out three of them. Note that our analysis of partitives also prohibits true plural quantifiers, such as *most men*, from acting as arguments, because of their type, which does not introduce a set-denoting noun phrase at any point. Thus we rule out *all of most men* on type-logical grounds.

Partitives can also behave quantificationally, as in *most of the six thousand students* and *none of the students*. Note that *most* in this case is a quantifier over a set, and that its complement denotes a set. Thus we simply need the following lexical assignment for *most*.

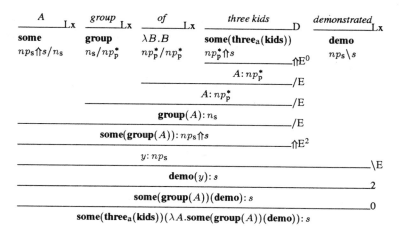

Figure 8.13
A derivation of *A group of three kids demonstrated*

(66) *most* ⟹ **most**: $np_p ⇑ s/np_p^*$

Again, *most of the students* behaves pretty much like *most students*, except with respect to the presupposition of a referent for *the students*.

The *pseudopartitives* are so called because they have a complement structure similar to ordinary partitives but do not have a part-of semantics. The following examples are based on examples of Jackendoff (1977), who refined and elaborated Selkirk's (1977) analysis.

(67) a.   {A / Every} group of {three kids / all the kids} demonstrateed.
     b.   Several groups of three men met.
     c.   *A group of most men met.
     d.   A group of three students greeted every visitor.

I analyze these type-theoretically by assuming that they produce nominal results rather than a quantifier or a set-denoting noun phrase. This accounts for the possibility of pluralization, as in (67b). Our lexical entry for *group* is as follows:

(68) *group* ⟹ **group**: n_s/np_p^*

Note that this is exactly the same constant **group** that I used to analyze the empty collector. This allows us to generate the proper readings of examples like (67a), one of which I provide in figure 8.13. Also note that we can generate the correct scope ambiguities for examples such as (67d).

This treatment of pseudo-partitives naturally covers the other cases in (67a). The analysis also naturally accounts for the pluralization of pseudo-partitive nominals, as in (67b); they are nothing more than nouns with a particular kind of plural complement. As with partitives, quantified complements, as in (67c), are blocked because they do not contribute an np^*_p. Finally, because of their nominal nature, pseudopartives in the singular are also blocked from implicit or explicit distribution and collection.

8.8   NONBOOLEAN COORDINATION

In this section we consider the meanings of plural noun phrases coordinated with *and*. Consider the following examples:

(69) a. Jody and Brooke met.
      b. Brooke is strong enough to carry Jody and Francis.
      c. The professors and the students met behind closed doors.

With such examples, we see that even singular noun phrases coordinated by *and* can be read collectively, as with the subject of (69a) and the object of (69b). The third example, (69c), displays an interesting ambiguity: either the professors met and the students met, or the students met the professors, or they all met together.

We have already seen that noun phrases can be coordinated by raising them to either the generalized quantifier category $np \Uparrow s$ or to a type-raised category such as $s/(np \backslash s)$ for subjects, $(np \backslash s/np) \backslash np \backslash s$ for objects, and so on. But in the examples in (69), this strategy does not provide appropriate meanings. For instance, boolean coordination is able to derive (69a) only as meaning **meet(j)** ∧ **meet(b)**. Furthermore, note that it is only the conjunct *and* that allows the kind of set/group coordination we see in the above examples and not any other kind of boolean coordinator, such as *or* or even the conjunctive *but*.

Instead of applying boolean coordination to these examples, what we need to do is to introduce a scheme allowing noun phrases to coordinate to produce sets, which can then be interpreted collectively or distributively. This scheme is complicated by the fact that the subject in example (69c), *the professors and the students*, can be interpreted either as a set whose members consist of the students and the professors or as a set consisting of a group of professors and a group of students. In addition, we need to be able to account for examples coordinating singular and plural noun phrases, such as the following:

(70) The professors and the dean met.

Here we can have either the group of professors meeting the dean or each of the professors meeting the dean or the group composed of the professors and the dean meeting as one large group.

We will treat nonboolean coordination using the following schematic lexical entry:

(71) *and* $\Rightarrow$ **gplus**: $np_\alpha \backslash np_p^* / np_\beta$

I will abbreviate applications of **gplus** as follows:

(72) $\mathbf{gplus}(x)(y) \overset{\text{def}}{=} x \oplus y$

The constant **gplus** is polymorphic and has four semantic instantiations, depending on whether the complement noun phrases are semantically singular or plural. The $\oplus$ operator can be defined as follows.

(73) $x \oplus y \overset{\text{def}}{=} \begin{cases} \{x\} \cup \{y\} & \text{if } x, y \in \mathbf{Term_{Ind}} \\ \{x\} \cup y & \text{if } x \in \mathbf{Term_{Ind}}, y \in \mathbf{Term_{Ind \to Bool}} \\ x \cup \{y\} & \text{if } x \in \mathbf{Term_{Ind \to Bool}}, y \in \mathbf{Term_{Ind}} \\ x \cup y & \text{if } x, y \in \mathbf{Term_{Ind \to Bool}} \end{cases}$

This entry allows us to coordinate, by simple application, singular noun phrases as in figure 8.14. This semantically and syntactically plural noun phrase can then participate in a collective or distributive predicate, just like any other np_p^*. Specifically, it can be collected into a group or distributed. Similarly, we can coordinate singular and plural, or pairs of plural, nouns, as shown in figures 8.15 and 8.16.

Our rule for plurals is sufficient to generate the correct readings for sentences such as the following:

(74) The dogs and the cats fought.

In addition to boolean coordination, there are ten nonboolean derivations available, even if we restrict our attention to the case where *fought* selects

$$\cfrac{\cfrac{\textit{Sandy}}{\text{s}: np}\text{Lx} \quad \cfrac{\cfrac{\textit{and}}{\mathbf{gplus}: np\backslash np_p^*/np}\text{Lx} \quad \cfrac{\textit{Terry}}{\text{t}: np}\text{Lx}}{\mathbf{gplus}(\text{t}): np\backslash np_p^*}\text{/E}}{\text{t} \oplus \text{s}: np_p^*}\backslash\text{E}$$

Figure 8.14
A derivation of *Sandy and Terry*

$$\frac{Sandy}{\text{s}: np}\text{Lx} \quad \frac{\dfrac{and}{\textbf{gplus}: np\backslash np_{\textbf{p}}^{*}/np_{\textbf{p}}^{*}}\text{Lx} \quad \dfrac{the\ three\ kids}{\textbf{the}(\textbf{three}(\textbf{kids})): np_{\textbf{p}}^{*}}\text{D}}{\textbf{gplus}(\textbf{the}(\textbf{three}(\textbf{kids}))): np\backslash np_{\textbf{p}}^{*}}/\text{E}}{\textbf{the}(\textbf{three}(\textbf{kids})) \oplus \text{s}: np_{\textbf{p}}^{*}}\backslash\text{E}$$

Figure 8.15
A derivation of *Sandy and the three kids*

$$\frac{\dfrac{the\ kids}{\textbf{the}(\textbf{plu}(\textbf{kid})): np_{\textbf{p}}^{*}}\text{D} \quad \dfrac{\dfrac{and}{\textbf{gplus}: np_{\textbf{p}}^{*}\backslash np_{\textbf{p}}^{*}/np_{\textbf{p}}^{*}}\text{Lx} \quad \dfrac{the\ teachers}{\textbf{the}(\textbf{plu}(\textbf{teacher})): np_{\textbf{p}}^{*}}\text{D}}{\textbf{gplus}(\textbf{the}(\textbf{plu}(\textbf{teacher}))): np_{\textbf{p}}^{*}\backslash np_{\textbf{p}}^{*}}/\text{E}}{\textbf{the}(\textbf{plu}(\textbf{teacher})) \oplus \textbf{the}(\textbf{plu}(\textbf{kid})): np_{\textbf{p}}^{*}}\backslash\text{E}$$

Figure 8.16
A derivation of the *kids and the teachers*

a group subject. Nine readings arise from treating the coordination collectively and either distributing or collecting *the cats* and *the dogs* or doing neither before the coordination. The tenth reading comes from treating both noun phrases collectively and then treating the result of coordination distributively. These do not all produce logically distinct readings, though, given the interpretation of collection, distribution, and nonboolean coordination. For instance, the animals could be engaged in a collective fight, which would be derived by coordinating at the $np_{\textbf{p}}^{*}$ stage. At the other end of the spectrum, each pair of animals consisting of a dog and a cat could be involved in a fight. This reading comes from treating both plurals distributively and coordinating at the $np_{\textbf{p}}$ level. Alternatively, we could interpret the noun phrases each collectively and coordinate at the $np_{\textbf{p}}$ level, which results in a reading where the group of dogs fought the group of cats. I provide a derivation for this case in figure 8.17.

This last possibility neatly accounts for Landman's (1989a, 1989b) examples, the point of which is to show that the constitution of a group has significance beyond the elementary atomic individuals that make it up (for arguments to the contrary, see Schwarzschild 1990).

(75) a. The cards above seven and the cards equal to or below seven were separated.

   b. The cards above three and the cards equal to or below three were separated.

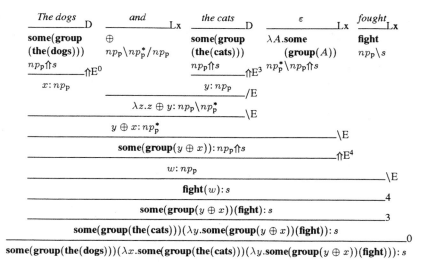

Figure 8.17
A derivation of *The dogs and the cats fought*

Given our semantic analysis, which generalizes Landman's approach, the subjects of the examples in (75) may denote distinct groups, because they are constituted of distinct groups. In utterances of the examples in (75), the subject of (75a) picks out a group with two members, the group of cards above seven and the cards equal to or below seven, whereas the subject of (75b) denotes a group consisting of different members, namely the group of cards above three and the group of cards equal to or below three. Nothing in our assumption about the identity of groups entails that the subjects of (75a, b) denote the same group.

The derivation in figure 8.17 illustrates how quantifiers can escape from one or both sides of a nonboolean conjunction. This flexibility is further motivated by examples such as the following, in which pronouns in one conjunct can have an antecedent in the other.

(76) Every student and his or her supervisor met.

But even with scoping out of nonboolean conjunction, our grammar is not sufficiently general to derive the appropriate readings of the following two sentences:

(77) a. Some men and women met outside in the rain.
    b. Three boys and girls met inside.

There is simply no way to coordinate the nouns in these examples in anything other than a boolean fashion, which obviously produces less than felicitous readings for these examples. Note that type raising is of no help in such cases. Rather, the fault seems to lie in the lack of generality in the operation of nonboolean coordination itself.

8.9   COMITATIVE COMPLEMENTS

Consider the following *comitative* uses of *with*:

(78) a. Francis built a contraption with Brett.
      b. The students frowned with the professors.
      c. Three students wrote a paper with Francis.
      d. Francis moved two boulders with his three coworkers.
      e. Francis and Wilma competed with Brett and Kelly.
      f. Three students wrote two papers with Brett.
      g. Every piece of useful mail arrives with two pieces of junk mail.
      h. Two guides must climb with novices.

In all of these cases, the subject is in some way accompanied by the object of *with*. In the case of (78a), there is a strong tendency to read the action of Francis and Brett as being collective. But in the case of (78b), with an individual action such as frowning, there is no such tendency (see exercise 8 for a discussion of related, more restricted examples in Russian). The third case, (78c), is ambiguous between a reading in which each of the three students independently wrote a paper with Francis and one in which all four parties collaborated on a single paper. Example (78d) illustrates that comitatives allow the full range of relative scope possibilities. The remaining examples show how the comitative interacts with other scope-taking elements.

Following our approach to non-boolean coordination, we can treat *with* as a variant realized as a preposition.

(79) $with \Rightarrow \lambda x . \lambda V . \lambda y . V(x \oplus y) : (np_p^* \backslash s) \backslash np_\alpha \backslash s / np_\beta$

Note that I have used α and β as subscripts on the category *np* to indicate an ambiguity between np_s and np_p. The simplest possible analysis with this category is illustrated in figure 8.18. But in addition to such simple uses, we also have all of the quantificational-scope ambiguities and distributive/collective ambiguities that we have with nonboolean conjunction. In general, singular quantifiers can quantify into either of the

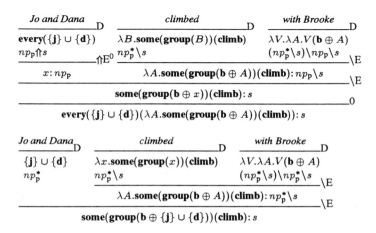

$$\frac{\textit{Francis}}{\mathbf{f}\colon np}\,\mathrm{Lx}\qquad \frac{\textit{met}}{\lambda A.\mathbf{some}(\mathbf{group}(A))(\mathbf{met})\colon np_{\mathrm{p}}^{*}\backslash s}\,\mathrm{D}\qquad \frac{\textit{with}}{\lambda x.\lambda V.\lambda y.V(x\oplus y)\colon (np_{\mathrm{p}}^{*}\backslash s)\backslash np\backslash s/np}\,\mathrm{Lx}\qquad \frac{\textit{Brooke}}{\mathbf{b}\colon np}\,\mathrm{Lx}$$

$$\frac{\lambda x.\lambda V.\lambda y.V(x\oplus y)\colon (np_{\mathrm{p}}^{*}\backslash s)\backslash np\backslash s/np \quad \mathbf{b}\colon np}{\lambda V.\lambda y.V(\mathbf{b}\oplus y)\colon (np_{\mathrm{p}}^{*}\backslash s)\backslash np\backslash s}\,/\mathrm{E}$$

$$\frac{\lambda A.\mathbf{some}(\mathbf{group}(A))(\mathbf{met})\colon np_{\mathrm{p}}^{*}\backslash s \quad \lambda V.\lambda y.V(\mathbf{b}\oplus y)\colon (np_{\mathrm{p}}^{*}\backslash s)\backslash np\backslash s}{\lambda y.\mathbf{some}(\mathbf{group}(\mathbf{b}\oplus y))(\mathbf{met})\colon np\backslash s}\,\backslash\mathrm{E}$$

$$\frac{\mathbf{f}\colon np \quad \lambda y.\mathbf{some}(\mathbf{group}(\mathbf{b}\oplus y))(\mathbf{met})\colon np\backslash s}{\mathbf{some}(\mathbf{group}(\mathbf{b}\oplus \mathbf{f}))(\mathbf{met})\colon s}\,\backslash\mathrm{E}$$

Figure 8.18
A derivation of *Francis met with Brooke*

$$\frac{\textit{Jo and Dana}}{\mathbf{every}(\{\mathbf{j}\}\cup\{\mathbf{d}\})\colon np_{\mathrm{p}}\Uparrow s}\,\mathrm{D}\qquad \frac{\textit{climbed}}{\lambda B.\mathbf{some}(\mathbf{group}(B))(\mathbf{climb})\colon np_{\mathrm{p}}^{*}\backslash s}\,\mathrm{D}\qquad \frac{\textit{with Brooke}}{\lambda V.\lambda A.V(\mathbf{b}\oplus A)\colon (np_{\mathrm{p}}^{*}\backslash s)\backslash np_{\mathrm{p}}\backslash s}\,\mathrm{D}$$

$$\frac{\mathbf{every}(\{\mathbf{j}\}\cup\{\mathbf{d}\})\colon np_{\mathrm{p}}\Uparrow s}{x\colon np_{\mathrm{p}}}\,\Uparrow\mathrm{E}^{0}\qquad \frac{\lambda B.\mathbf{some}(\mathbf{group}(B))(\mathbf{climb})\colon np_{\mathrm{p}}^{*}\backslash s \quad \lambda V.\lambda A.V(\mathbf{b}\oplus A)\colon (np_{\mathrm{p}}^{*}\backslash s)\backslash np_{\mathrm{p}}\backslash s}{\lambda A.\mathbf{some}(\mathbf{group}(\mathbf{b}\oplus A))(\mathbf{climb})\colon np_{\mathrm{p}}\backslash s}\,\backslash\mathrm{E}$$

$$\frac{x\colon np_{\mathrm{p}} \quad \lambda A.\mathbf{some}(\mathbf{group}(\mathbf{b}\oplus A))(\mathbf{climb})\colon np_{\mathrm{p}}\backslash s}{\mathbf{some}(\mathbf{group}(\mathbf{b}\oplus x))(\mathbf{climb})\colon s}\,\backslash\mathrm{E}$$

$$\frac{\mathbf{some}(\mathbf{group}(\mathbf{b}\oplus x))(\mathbf{climb})\colon s}{\mathbf{every}(\{\mathbf{j}\}\cup\{\mathbf{d}\})(\lambda A.\mathbf{some}(\mathbf{group}(\mathbf{b}\oplus A))(\mathbf{climb}))\colon s}\,0$$

$$\frac{\textit{Jo and Dana}}{\{\mathbf{j}\}\cup\{\mathbf{d}\}\colon np_{\mathrm{p}}^{*}}\,\mathrm{D}\qquad \frac{\textit{climbed}}{\lambda x.\mathbf{some}(\mathbf{group}(x))(\mathbf{climb})\colon np_{\mathrm{p}}^{*}\backslash s}\,\mathrm{D}\qquad \frac{\textit{with Brooke}}{\lambda V.\lambda A.V(\mathbf{b}\oplus A)\colon (np_{\mathrm{p}}^{*}\backslash s)\backslash np_{\mathrm{p}}^{*}\backslash s}\,\mathrm{D}$$

$$\frac{\lambda x.\mathbf{some}(\mathbf{group}(x))(\mathbf{climb})\colon np_{\mathrm{p}}^{*}\backslash s \quad \lambda V.\lambda A.V(\mathbf{b}\oplus A)\colon (np_{\mathrm{p}}^{*}\backslash s)\backslash np_{\mathrm{p}}^{*}\backslash s}{\lambda A.\mathbf{some}(\mathbf{group}(\mathbf{b}\oplus A))(\mathbf{climb})\colon np_{\mathrm{p}}^{*}\backslash s}\,\backslash\mathrm{E}$$

$$\frac{\{\mathbf{j}\}\cup\{\mathbf{d}\}\colon np_{\mathrm{p}}^{*} \quad \lambda A.\mathbf{some}(\mathbf{group}(\mathbf{b}\oplus A))(\mathbf{climb})\colon np_{\mathrm{p}}^{*}\backslash s}{\mathbf{some}(\mathbf{group}(\mathbf{b}\oplus \{\mathbf{j}\}\cup\{\mathbf{d}\}))(\mathbf{climb})\colon s}\,\backslash\mathrm{E}$$

Figure 8.19
Two derivations of *Jo and Dana climbed with Brooke*

noun-phrase positions in figure 8.18. Furthermore, plural quantifiers can also quantify into these positions. Finally, note that the combination can be done at either the np_{p}^{*} or the np_{p} levels, inducing further ambiguities. For instance, consider the two analyses in figure 8.19. In both analyses, I have collectivized the verb *climbed* by argument lowering. Note that at this stage I could also have distributed. The first analysis distributes the subject np_{p}^{*} and employs the corresponding instantiation of the polymorphic *with*. Applying the collective at this stage would be possible as well. Such an analysis would be needed to derive an interpretation of (78e) in which the competition was between the couples. The second analysis in figure 8.19 simply adds the comitative complement to the set introduced by the subject, using the $np_{\mathrm{p}}^{*}\backslash s$ complement instantiation of *with*. Thus there are a total of six readings for the sentence. Moving on to an even more dramatic case, consider the range of readings of (78h), in which both the subject and comitative object are bare plurals and there is an intervening deontic modal auxiliary *must*, which behaves grammatically in much the same way as negation (we return to modal auxiliaries in section 11.1.7). For this example, there are literally dozens of readings, with the scope of the two plurals interacting not only with themselves but with the comitative and the modal as well. Note that the range of readings would be the same if the subject and comitative object were reversed, due to the symmetry of *with*, of which they both can be arguments (of course, island and locality constraints might distinguish the possibilities for scope-taking elements in these positions).

8.10   MASS TERMS

Utterances of nouns and noun phrases in English can be characterized in terms of their *countability*. Most nouns have a strong lexical bias toward countability or uncountability. For instance, consider the following examples:

(80) a.   There are two pencils on the table.
   b.   *There is pencil on the table.
   c.   *There are snows on the ground.
   d.   There is snow on the ground.

The noun *pencil* is typically used as a *count noun*, whereas the noun *snow* is almost always used as a *mass noun*. At the root of the matter is the fact that we can count the number of pencils in a given situation, but we usually cannot count snow (of course, we can count snowflakes and snowfalls). Other concrete mass terms include *water, gold, space, dirt,* and *fruitcake*. Abstract nouns too are often uncountable, as evidenced by examples such as *applause, concentration,* and *happiness*. On the other hand, we can measure uncountable objects in several ways, typically expressed by means of partitives, mass determiners, and comparatives:

(81) a.   There are seven tons of gravel in the driveway.
   b.   There are five gallons of gas in the tank.
   c.   There is a lot of good will here.
   d.   Much concentration is needed to complete that task.
   e.   There is less space in the garden than dirt in that truck.

The notion of countability is complicated, though, by the ability of some terms to be *coerced* from their "usual" meanings into meanings of the other kind (see Lewis 1979, Partee and Rooth 1987, Moens and Steedman 1988, and Pustejovsky 1991 for discussion of the general topic of semantic coercion). For instance, consider the following examples:

(82) a. There is beer in the glass.
      b. There are three beers on the table.   (Packaging)
      c. There are three carrots on the table.
      d. There is carrot in the cake.   (Grinding)

These examples illustrate what Lewis (in Pelletier 1979) referred to as *packaging* and *grinding*. A term such as *beer*, which is canonically understood in a mass sense, can be understood as denoting a "package" or serving of beer. Such packaging can be carried out in several ways; for instance, *three beers* might also be understood as meaning three kinds of beer. Similarly, a term such as *carrot*, which is typically countable, can be understood as a substance or mass by means of "grinding."

The most well-known model of matter and its connection to mass terms was introduced by Link (1983), following the approach of the calculi of individuals introduced by Leonard and Goodman (1940) and Goodman and Quine (1947). More concretely, Link stipulated a domain of *material*, which is a part of the individual domain, with an ordering defined as corresponding to the *material part of* relation:

(83) a. **Mat** $\in$ **Typ**
      b. **Dom$_{\text{Mat}}$** $\subseteq$ **Dom$_{\text{Ind}}$**
      c. **part** $\in$ **Con$_{\text{Mat}\to\text{Mat}\to\text{Bool}}$**

I will employ the abbreviation $\alpha \sqsubseteq_m \beta$ for **part**$(\alpha)(\beta)$. Link (1983) enforces the condition that the interpretation of the material part of relation forms a complete boolean algebra over the domain of matter (see section A.8.2).

(84) $\langle$**Dom$_{\text{Mat}}$**, $[\![\sqsubseteq_m]\!]\rangle$ is a complete boolean algebra

With a boolean algebra defined in terms of an ordering, we can define several other useful operations and individuals. We will be particularly concerned with the join operation. I define the *material join* operation $\sqcup_m$ over pieces x and y of matter as usual, by taking $x \sqcup_m y$ to be the smallest piece of matter z such that $x \sqsubseteq_m z$ and $y \sqsubseteq_m z$. Intuitively, $x \sqcup_m y$ is just the combination of the matter making up x and y. Completeness of the boolean algebra is enforced to ensure that any quantity of matter can be combined to produce more matter, although we will only be concerned here with finite combinations. With a boolean algebra, we will also have a meet operation, written $x \sqcap_m y$, which can be interpreted as the greatest piece of matter common to both x and y, or in other words, the amount of matter overlapping in x and y. We also have complements, written $\neg_m y$, which is all the matter that is not part of a given piece of matter y. Finally, the existence of a least element and a greatest element in the ordering follow from the boolean condition. The least element $\mathbf{0}_m$ will be the null collection of matter, whereas the greatest element $\mathbf{1}_m$ will be the collection of all matter. The least element can be eliminated without loss of generality, as noted by Landman (1991). Besides guaranteeing the existence of meets, joins, complements, and greatest and least elements, the boolean axioms can be motivated by the fact that combining matter structurally behaves similarly to set union. Associativity and commutativity simply state that the combination of matter is not sensitive to order. Idempotence ensures that if some matter is "combined" with itself, the result is just the original matter. Distributivity ensures that if we look at the matter common to x and y and combine it with the matter common to x and z, the result is just the matter common to x and the result of combining y and z.

The assumption that the domain of matter forms a boolean algebra also guarantees that we have Landman's so-called *witness condition*. In the case of water, Landman states this condition thus: "If A is a body of water and B is a *proper* part of A, then there has to be some other part of A that does not overlap B" (1991, 314). This follows because in a boolean algebra, if $b \sqsubseteq_m a$ and $b \neq a$, then $a \sqcap_m \neg_m b \neq \mathbf{0}_m$. Simply note that $a \sqcap_m \neg_m b = \mathbf{0}_m$ if and only if $a \sqcap_m \neg_m b \sqcap_m b = \mathbf{0}_m \sqcap_m b$, which holds if and only if $a \sqcap_m \mathbf{0}_m = b$, which holds if and only if $\mathbf{0}_m = b$, which is a contradiction (assuming b is not the null element, as Landman does). The boolean assumptions concerning the structure of matter entail Landman's (1991) distributivity condition on matter, which requires that if $a \sqcup_m b = c$ and $d \sqsubseteq_m c$, then either $d \sqcap_m a \neq \mathbf{0}_m$ or $d \sqcap_m b \neq \mathbf{0}_m$ (see exercise 26).

As noticed by Quine (1960) and later developed logically by Bunt (1979), mass terms behave like countable plurals in that they both display what is known as *cumulative reference*. Thus if we have two distinct collections of carrots and combine them, the result is still a collection of carrots. Similarly, if we have two quantities of water and we put them together, the result is still water. It seems that this operation can be extended to arbitrary amounts of water. To capture the property of

cumulative reference, Link (1983) enforces the following meaning postulate on every property P denoting a mass term.

(85) $(P(x) \wedge P(y)) \rightarrow P(x \sqcup_m y)$ (Cumulative reference)

Thus if **water** is a mass property, substituting it for P in the above meaning postulate entails that if x and y are both masses of water, then $x \sqcup_m y$
is also a mass of water. Symbolically, if we have **water**$(\mathbf{x}) \wedge$ **water**$(\mathbf{y})$, then
we can conclude **water**$(x \sqcup_m y)$.

Although mass terms have the cumulative reference property, they
clearly do not have the following *homogeneity property*:

(86) $(P(x) \wedge y \sqsubseteq_m x) \rightarrow P(y)$ (Homogeneity)

This is due to the so-called *minimal-parts problem*, which arises for mass
terms such as water (see Bunt 1985). Clearly, there are parts of water that
are so small that they are no longer water but simply hydrogen atoms.
This problem is even more evident with the canonical example of fruit-
cake, which, once subdivided far enough, leaves only cake and pieces of
fruit.

Link elaborates his model in order to deal with the relationship
between nonmass nouns and the matter of which they are constituted. To
this end, he introduces a constant **matter**, of type **Ind** $\rightarrow$ **Mat**, the interpretation of which is a function from an individual to the mass of which it
is constituted. He then enforces meaning postulates on masses that have
roughly the following effects:

(87) a. **matter**$(x) = x$ if $x \in$ **Dom**$_{\text{Mat}}$
      b. **group**$(X)(x) \wedge$ **group**$(Y)(y) \wedge$ **every**$(X)(Y)$
         $\rightarrow$ (**matter**$(x) \sqsubseteq_m$ **matter**(y))

The first condition requires the matter making up a piece of matter to be
just itself. The second condition requires a group whose members are a
subset of the members of another group to have matter that is a material
part of the second group. Link models this latter condition by requiring
the matter function to be an order homomorphism from the domain of
sums to the domain of matter (see section A.3). This is only possible
because there is no distinct theory of groups as individuals in Link 1983.
Link also argues that the possibility of two individuals mapping onto the
same matter should be allowed. Link (1983) points out examples such as
this gold ring, which might refer to a new ring, whereas the gold that the
ring is composed of is likely to be much older. This argues for a separation of the gold and the ring. Similarly, two distinct groups might be

composed of the same individuals and thus have the same matter. Again similarly, Bach (1986) points out that a snowman may be new, whereas the snow that makes it up is slightly older. He argues that following Link (1983) in assuming a single function mapping objects to matter runs into trouble when the snowman example is examined a bit further. This is because it might be the case that the snow itself is made up of water that is even older than the snow, which is in turn made up of atoms that are older still.

Certain properties are *matter-invariant*, meaning that their being true or false of arguments can be determined solely by examining the matter composing their arguments (Link 1983). For instance, consider the following examples:

(88) a. The boys and the girls are heavy.
     b. The children are heavy.
     c. The cards above seven and the cards below seven are in the drawer.
     d. The cards above six and the cards below six are in the drawer.

The weight of the children does not depend on how they are arranged into groups, nor does it matter how the cards are separated when considering their containment in a drawer. More radically, Schwarzschild (1990, 1992) claims that all predicates that apply to groups are matter-invariant, concluding that the use of groups in natural-language semantics is misguided.

The grammar of mass terms is fairly straightforward, and can be developed along the same lines as our grammars of plurals. I first need to introduce a subcategory of nouns for mass terms that denote in the mass domain. This will allow syntactic selection for determiners, comparatives, partitives, and agreement to be sensitive to the count/mass distinction. The behavior of mass terms with a definite article is similar to the behavior of plurals with respect to maximality. The only other difference is that mass terms have agreement properties that mirror singular count nouns but can occur bare in much the same way as plural count nouns. One further point to notice about mass terms is that they occur in non-boolean-coordination constructions.

(89) Sandy drank champagne and orange juice.   (Mass collective)

Such conjunction can be carried out along the same lines as the non-boolean coordination of sets by using the $\sqcup_m$ operation. The conjunction of mass terms can also be read collectively, as evidenced by the following example of Landman's (1991):

(90) The water in the North Sea and the water in the IJssel Lake are separated by a dike.

But this will follow from the fact that the mass domain is simply a subset of the domain of individuals. Distribution to individual masses can be accomplished in the same way. On the other hand, it does not seem possible to distribute a predicate to the material parts of a mass term, even if we could avoid the problem of minimal parts in some way. Landman (1991) claims that distribution is possible for some predicates, such as *be whisky*, but it is just as likely that this is an extragrammatical effect due to cumulative reference working in reverse. As Landman (1991) points out for the following example, a mass can have a property that its parts do not have:

(91) The water in the North Sea carried a ship from England to Holland.

Exercises

1. Explain the ambiguity in the following sentences. (Dowty 1986a)

(a) The {trees / group of trees / forest} gets thinner in the middle.

2. Provide a lexical entry for the predicative *numerous*, as used in examples such as *The boys are numerous* (related examples include *few* and *plentiful*). Use the syntactic category $np_p^* \backslash s$. What is generated by such an entry, and are these analyses correct? (Carpenter 1994d)

3. Consider the advantages and drawbacks to lexically assigning dual nouns, such as *scissors* and *pants*, to the category n_p. Consider both semantically singular and plural usages. Perhaps *scissors* and *pants* behave like all nouns in languages that are unmarked for plurality. One possible account of these expressions would lexically analyze the plural categories n_p^* and np_p^* by generalizing to allow singular sets. How could such a maneuver be made for *scissors* and *pants* in English?

4. Link (1983) provided interpretations of singular noun phrases and set-denoting plural noun phrases as being elements of a complete atomic boolean algebra (see section A.8.2). Singular noun phrases were taken to denote atoms in the boolean algebra, whereas plurals were restricted to nonatomic elements. Given the correspondence between complete atomic boolean algebras and powersets (again, see section A.8.2), this move is tantamount to assigning the type **Ind** → **Bool** to both singular and plural noun phrases and assigning the type (**Ind** → **Bool**) → **Bool** to both singular and plural nouns. Lexically, we would assume that np_s always denoted a singleton, and that the properties denoted by a term assigned category n_s only held of singletons. Given these assumptions, show that the term provided for the definite determiner in (22b) can also be used for the singular case. How

does such a move simplify the semantic treatment of nonboolean conjunction? Are any type-logical complications introduced by Link's representation?

5. Derive the three analyses of (37e) yielding the readings given in (38).

6. Show that by further abstracting over the bare plural, we can derive readings for the following sentence that can be true in the case where there is a set of three kids who sneezed and a different set who coughed.

(a) Three kids sneezed and coughed.

Restrict your attention to the case where both the sneezing and coughing are read distributively.

7. Consider the following lexical entry for the distributor and collector.

(a) $\varepsilon \Rightarrow \lambda A . \langle \mathbf{every}(A), \mathbf{some}(\mathbf{group}(A)) \rangle : (np_p \Uparrow s) \wedge (np_p \Uparrow s) / np_p^*$

As an alternative to the argument-lowering analysis of "mixed coordination" given in (8.7), derive the same meaning using the lexical entry above and analyzing the verb phrases *gathered* and *sneezed* as being of the following syntactic category. (Morrill, p.c.)

(b) $(np_p \Uparrow s \wedge np_p \Uparrow s) \backslash s$

8. McNally (1993) noted that comitatives in Russian only allow a group reading of the subject and comitative object. Show how such a restriction could be built into the lexical entry for the comitative. (Hint: Consider an entry differing in type from the one we proposed for English.)

9. Consider the use of *with* in the following cases.

(a) Sandy mixed oil and water.

(b) Sandy mixed oil with water.

Argue for the position that the comitative *with* should be extended to deal with objects, or argue for the position that *mix* in this case is a ditransitive predicate that is symmetric between its two objects (compare the symmetric predicate *met* in exercise 27, chapter 9). (Oehrle, p.c.)

10. Redefine the empty collector using the constant **in_group** of type **Ind** → **Ind** → **Bool** such that **in_group**$(x)(y)$ if and only if x is a member of group y. (Hint: Use quantification.) Show how **in_group** can be defined in terms of **group** and vice versa. Provide a lexical entry for the empty collector in terms of **in_group**.

11. Discuss the possible analyses and provide derivations of the following examples.

(a) The groups of representatives each met before leaving their offices.

(b) At least five groups of three kids demonstrated.

(c) A group of five students met with every visitor.

12. Provide the derivations for the following three readings of *Two examiners marked six exams*:

(a) Each of the six exams was marked collectively by two examiners (and not necessarily the same two examiners).

(b) The six exams were collectively marked by the two examiners collectively.

(c) Each of the two examiners marked six exams (and not necessarily the same six).

13. Explain why our grammar cannot generate a reading for the following sentence in which the students of one department engaged in a fight with the students of another department. (Schwarzschild 1990, 1992)

(a) The students from the two departments fought.

14. Consider the following proposal for the semantics of the definite determiner:

(a) *the* $\Rightarrow \lambda Q. \bigcup Q: np_p^*/n_p^*$

Show how to type-theoretically define $\bigcup$, the union of a set of sets, in higher-order logic. Is this definition different than the one in (22)? Either prove that they are the same, or provide an example of where their results would vary.

15. The analysis of plural nouns as being of category n_p^* makes it impossible to analyze examples such as *fake trucks*, in which an intensional adjective applies to a plural noun. In particular, we want the analysis **plu(fake(truck))** rather than **fake(plu(truck))**. Define a grammar that lexically treats plural noun phrases as of category n_p of type **Ind** $\to$ **Bool**. Use a lexical entry with a null expression of category **plu**: n_p^*/n_p to achieve the semantic effect of pluralization. Provide a treatment of plural adjectives so that they are of type n_p/n_p and have the same semantic constants as their singular counterparts. Under this scheme, what syntactic type should be assigned to expressions such as *three*? Does this make the correct syntactic and semantic predictions? (Carpenter 1994d)

16. The following sentences were studied by Nerbonne (1994):

(a) Fewer than five kids ran or jumped.

(b) Fewer than five kids ran and jumped.

Show that there are two possible analyses for both of these cases, assuming distributive readings of all np_p^* categories. (Hint: Raise the category of *ran and jumped* to $np_p^* \backslash s$ for the case of wide-scope coordination, and to $np_p \backslash s$ for the case of narrow-scope coordination.)

17. Show how the categories assigned to plural relative pronouns in (33) allow us to analyze ambiguities in sentences such as the following:

(a) The kids who met sneezed.

(b) The kids who carried two boxes carried three bags.

How many ambiguities does your grammar predict for the second example? Does the number of readings depend on the islandhood of relative clauses?

18. Show how to derive the correct readings for the following nominals, which Link (1984) called *hydras*.

(a) big men or women

(b) men or women from Pittsburgh

Does this help us to analyze examples such as those in (77) and exercise 13?

19. Derive any three readings of the following sentence in which *the white dogs* is (1) coordinated after being distributed, (2) coordinated after being collected, and (3) coordinated at the np_p^* stage. You can assume that *the black cats* is read collectively in all cases and that the coordination is read collectively.

(a) The white dogs and the black cats fought.

20. Consider the numeral *zero*, which behaves quite differently from numerals denoting numbers greater than one.

(a) Zero students {sneezed / gathered}.

(b) *Zero students {each / all} carried a piano.

(c) *The zero students {met / sneezed}.

(d) ?At least zero students sneezed.

Provide a quantificational analysis of *zero* with a meaning similar to that of *no*, and determine whether or not this correctly captures the behavior of *zero*.

21. Provide appropriate lexical entries for *nominal comparative* examples such as the following:

(a) More students than professors attended the lecture.

The comparative determiner *more* should be assigned to the following syntactic category:

(b) *more* $\Rightarrow$?: $np_p \Uparrow s/n_p/n_p$

This assumes that the expression *than* is merely marking the case on the complement *than professors*, and that both complements, *professors* and *students*, are interpreted as semantically singular simple properties. As Keenan and Moss (1985) state, the resulting semantics will amount to a ternary quantificational determiner.

22. Provide terms for the meanings of the verb phrases in the following sentences:

(a) No three students read the same book.

(b) Fewer than six students read the same number of books.

What is the problem in assigning a meaning to the verb phrases in the following sentences that allows the whole sentence to be analyzed compositionally?

(c) Each student read a different book.

(d) Most of the students answered a different number of questions.

(e) Exactly two students support opposing political parties.

Keenan (1987) suggests treating such cases by means of ternary quantifiers. For instance, the first sentence above is translated as follows:

(f) **every_different**(**student**)(**book**)(**read**)

Provide an appropriate definition of **every_different**.

Is the ternary determiner **every_different** conservative on either of its arguments? Is it definable in terms of a pair of binary determiners (see exercise 25, chapter 3)? (Keenan 1987)

23. Consider decomposing expressions such as *fewer than five* into *numerical quantifiers*. For instance, we can assume the following.

(a) *at least five* $\Rightarrow \lambda V.\mathbf{some}(\lambda m.m \geq \mathbf{5})(V): num \Uparrow s$

Next consider the lexical relation between a numeral and a plural modifier, such as *five*.

(b) *five* $\Rightarrow \mathbf{5}: num$

(c) *five* $\Rightarrow \lambda Z.\lambda P.Z(P) \wedge \|P\| \geq \mathbf{5}: np_p^*/n_p^*$

Combining these two approaches, we are led to the following category for *fewer than*:

(d) *fewer than* $\Rightarrow \lambda k.\lambda V.\mathbf{no}(\lambda n.n \geq k)(\lambda n.V(\lambda Q.\lambda P.Q(P) \wedge \|P\| = n))$
    $(n_p^*/n_p^*) \Uparrow s/num$

Show that this category assignment, when combined with the bare-plural existential, generates the same readings as the lexical entry in (50).

24. Consider plural versions of the positive, equative, and comparative forms of gradable adjectives. Are there any problems in their pluralization? Consider the standard pluralization of the superlative *tall*, and show how the expression *the three tallest boys* can be derived. Is the meaning that results correct? If not, can a distinctly plural meaning be assigned to it that has the appropriate behavior? Show how an analysis similar to that of pseudopartitives can be provided for superlatives with explicit comparison classes, as in the following:

(a) The tallest of the kids is a bully.

25. Consider the *dual comparative*, the meaning of which is closely related to the superlative.

(a) Terry is the {taller / elder} child (of the two).

Provide a pair of lexical entries for the comparative marker *-er* that generates the appropriate meanings for the case with and without a complement. (Hint: Much like the argument of the preposition *between*, the complement *of*-phrase must denote a set with two members. It can be treated as the case-marked set-denoting noun-phrase category $np_{p,of}^*$.) (Oehrle, p.c.)

26. Prove that Landman's (1991) distributivity condition holds in any boolean algebra.

(a) if $a \sqcup_m b = c$, $d \sqsubseteq_m c$, and $d \neq \mathbf{0}_m$, then either $d \sqcap_m a \neq \mathbf{0}_m$ or $d \sqcap_m b \neq \mathbf{0}_m$.

27. Provide a grammar for mass nouns by analogy to our grammar for plurals. Introduce a new subcategory of nouns and noun phrases for mass terms. Be sure to handle the following phenomena:

a. singular agreement
b. nonboolean coordination by $\sqcup_m$
c. partitives with mass complements
d. the definite determiner as maximizer with respect to $\subseteq_m$ (and context)
e. mass determiners such as *much*

28. Consider the partitive noun phrase in *This is part of a Roman aqueduct* in the situation where there never was and never will be a complete Roman aqueduct of which the intended object is a part. The same phenomenon is found in the partitive in *This is part of a paper on natural-language metaphysics* if the paper in question is never completed. What is the puzzle presented by these examples for a compositional account of mass partitives? You might want to think of this in the context of the discussion of intensionality in chapter 11. (Bach 1986)

29. Show how our type-logical assumptions concerning plurals allow us to capture Hoeksema's (1987) generalization that the exceptive *but* selects only for objects that denote sets. Provide a lexical entry in addition to the one in exercise 29, chapter 7, that takes an np_p^* object. Show how this entry allows us to properly analyze the following examples:

(a) Every student but {Sandy and Terry / the slackers} studied.

Finally, provide a lexical entry for *but* that handles cases such as the following:

(b) All (of) the kids but Sandy and Terry studied.

(Hint: *All* is acting here as a universal quantifier with the set-denoting complement (*of*) *the kids*, so only the syntactic entry needs to change from the previous case.) (Hoeksema 1987; von Fintel 1993)

Chapter 9

Pronouns and Dependency

In this chapter, we consider the analysis of nonindexical, dependent pronouns. We begin with the Montagovian analysis of pronouns as variables. Then we consider Moortgat's treatment of reflexives as scoping operations. Next, we turn to the behavior of plural pronouns and of reciprocals such as *each other*. I also describe a categorial analysis of the pied-piping of relative pronouns, which involves a novel application of quantification. Finally, I provide an analysis of interrogative constructions.

9.1 PRONOUNS AND REFLEXIVES

In English, and in other languages of the world, pronominal elements come in a variety of flavors. One fundamental distinction is that between indexicals and nonindexicals. An *indexical* pronoun is one which takes its interpretation based solely on fixed components of the context of utterance. Examples of indexicals are *I, you,* and *now*. Consider some canonical examples of indexicals: the pronoun *I* always refers to the speaker, *you* to the listener, and *now* to the time of utterance. Such interpretation does not depend on structural position or how deeply embedded the indexical occurs. Of course, this only holds for uses of indexicals; in quoted contexts such as *Sandy said, "You mean me?"* expressions are mentioned rather than used (see section 11.3.2). I return to the analysis of indexicals in section 10.3.

In this chapter we consider only non-indexical pronouns such as *him*, *she*, and *itself* in the singular case, and such as *they* and *themselves* in the plural case. Furthermore, we will focus on the so-called *dependent* uses of pronouns. Dependent pronouns are characterized as having their interpretations depend on the interpretation of some other grammatically realized expression, known as the *antecedent*. There are many kinds of dependent elements in language. In the following examples, the dependent element is highlighted in italics and coindexed with its antecedent.

(1) a. Jody$_0$ believes *he*$_0$ will be famous.
   b. Jody bought a [green [t-shirt]$_0$]$_1$ and Brett also bought *one*$_1$, but Francis bought a red *one*$_0$.
   c. Jody [runs quickly]$_2$ and Brett *does*$_2$ too.

The first case is one of a simple pronoun depending on a proper name. The second example is rather more elaborate and involves so-called *one-anaphora*, in which the dependent nominal element *one* takes a noun as an antecedent. The final example involves so-called *verb-phrase ellipsis*, in which an entire verb phrase is replaced with some form of the *support verb do*.

Because of our focus on dependent pronouns, I will not have much to say about their *deictic* uses. Deictic pronouns receive their interpretation in a context-dependent manner but do not depend on linguistic context. For instance, *demonstrative pronouns* can receive their interpretation from pointing, as in the following examples:

(2) a. *There* is the book I've been looking for.
   b. I want *that*.

For an instance of a nondemonstrative but nevertheless deictic use of a pronoun, consider the following utterance in a situation in which an office worker is speaking to a late coworker who has just arrived.

(3) She's in a bad mood this morning.

Here the pronoun *she* could naturally be taken to refer to the boss of the office in question. It could just as easily refer to a cow that is about to be milked if the office context were replaced by one in a farmyard. In either case, there is no previous discourse to establish an antecedent for the pronoun. Deictic pronouns simply pick out a referent from context. There is not much to say about such pronouns from a type-logical perspective; they behave similarly to underspecified and context-dependent uses of names.

In the case of dependent pronouns, there is a fundamental distinction to be drawn between *reflexive* and *nonreflexive* pronouns, each of which has restrictions on its distribution and its relation to possible antecedents. Expressions such as *herself, itself,* and *themselves* are reflexive, while the other pronouns are nonreflexive. Nonreflexive pronouns are sometimes referred to as *personal pronouns*, even though they need not have anything to do with people. Consider the following examples, illustrating the difference in antecedence conditions on reflexives and personal pronouns.

(4) a. Jody likes him.
    b. Jody likes himself.
    c. Jody believes Francis likes him.
    d. Jody believes Francis likes himself.
    e. Jody gave pictures of him to Francis.
    f. Jody gave pictures of himself to Francis.

In the first pair of cases, we see the difference between reflexive and personal pronouns. In (4a), the nonreflexive *him* cannot be identified with the subject, while the only interpretation of the reflexive *himself* in (4b) is with the subject as its antecedent. In the second pair of examples, we see the same behavior in a nested setting; this time the nonreflexive *him* in (4c) can take the matrix subject as its antecedent, but the reflexive *himself* in (4d) must take the embedded subject. The last pair of examples, (4e) and (4f), shows how pronouns in the complement position to relational nouns are rather less restricted: the reflexive and nonreflexive can take either noun phrase as an antecedent.

We must be careful to distinguish the notion of a pronoun taking an antecedent from the notion of a pronoun being *coreferential*. Coreferentiality entails the existence of a referent, while a pronoun and its antecedent need not refer at all, even in a true utterance. For instance, consider pronouns in cases such as the following:

(5) a. Jody believes [a vampire]$_2$ likes his$_2$ casket.
    b. No one$_1$ believes he$_1$ is smart.

Clearly, there is no reference per se in these cases. Examples such as these have inspired theories in which a pronoun and its antecedent are interpreted as identical variables bound by a single operator.

It is significant that the theory of pronominals tied up with variable binding also predicts the restriction against intersentential uses of pronouns with quantified antecedents.

(6) [Every boy]$_0$ ran. #Then he$_0$ jumped.

It would not make sense, on a variable-binding approach, to allow a variable introduced by *he* to be the same as the one quantified by *every*, as we would be left with the following two interpretations.

(7) $(\forall x)(\textbf{boy}(x) \rightarrow \textbf{run}(x))$. $\textbf{jump}(x)$.

The intended binding of the x in **jump**(x) is not realized, with the result being an unbound variable in one of the clauses.

In contrast to the case of quantifiers illustrated in (6), it is perfectly natural to have coreference between the pronoun in the second sentence and the subject of the first in the following example:

(8) Jody₁ ran. Then he₁ jumped.

Such facts have led to the development of *discourse-representation theory* (DRT) by Kamp (1981), and the related theory of file-change semantics by Heim (1982). These theories are aimed at treating names and indefinites using implicit discourse-level quantification. They both provide the following semantics for (8).

(9) **name**(**Jody**, x) ∧ **run**(x).   **jump**(y) ∧ $x = y$.

The variables x and y are implicitly existentially quantified at the top level, allowing the x and y to be equated to represent antecedence without disturbing variable-binding conditions. The text by Kamp and Reyle (1993) presents a thorough introduction to DRT. Gamut (1991b) presents a concise overview of DRT in a higher-order-logic setting. Discourse representation structures have been integrated into categorial grammars by Calder, Klein, and Zeevat (1988; Zeevat, Klein, and Calder 1987) and by Carpenter (1989), and now into HPSG by Pollard and Sag (1994). As an alternative to DRT, Groenendijk and Stokhof (1991) have developed a novel approach to variable binding in first-order logic. In their system of *dynamic predicate logic* (DPL), expressions containing existential quantifiers such as $((\exists x)\textbf{run}(x)) \wedge \textbf{jump}(x)$ are interpreted in such a way that the second occurrence of x acts as if bound by the existential quantifier.

9.2   PRONOUNS AND AGREEMENT

Most languages display some kind of *agreement* system that restricts the potential for pronominal binding to those antecedents that share certain properties with the binder. Of course, there is also agreement between verb phrases and subjects in English, and with other objects in many other languages. Agreement is a particularly interesting issue from a cross-linguistic perspective, because languages vary greatly with respect to their agreement systems. Pollard and Sag (1992, 1994) claim that languages vary in terms of how they treat pronominal agreement on the syntactic, semantic, and pragmatic scale. For English, they propose an account in which agreement is at the level of discourse markers rather than at either a purely semantic or a purely syntactic level of representation. By way of contrast, Pollard and Sag note that case marking is a syntactic phenomenon, and hence must be preserved under conjunction. For instance, we cannot coordinate a nominative and an accusative, or find a nominative coordinated in an accusative argument position.

(10) a. *He and me ran.
     b. *Francis likes Sal and we.

On the other hand, number and gender agreement is at the level of intended reference. This is perhaps best illustrated with cases of metaphorical uses of noun phrases.

(11) a. [The ham and eggs at table 6]$_0$ wants *his*$_0$ check.
     b. [The volcano at table 7]$_1$ wants *his*$_1$ lunch.

The first example is a classic case of *reference transfer*, as studied by Nunberg (1977), while the second is a case of simple metaphor. Note that agreement for pronouns is similar to the animacy distinction shown with relative pronouns.

(12) a. the car {which / #who} I drive
     b. the person {#which / who} I met yesterday

Here we get agreement with the intended animacy (or personhood, in some dialects) of the referent. In cases of metaphor in general, and reference transfer in particular, we see agreement based on the intended referent.

Pollard and Sag (1993) also consider cases of specific *dual plurals* in English, such as *pants* and *scissors*. Such noun phrases can only refer to singular objects, but their syntactic agreement is plural.

(13) a. The scissors *are* on the table.
     b. I left my pants on the chair and better go back to get *them*.

The second case illustrates that pronouns with dual antecedents assume the plural form. Pollard and Sag's point was that these cases argue against a purely semantic analysis of agreement.

Before leaving the topic of agreement, I wish to point out some rather puzzling facts concerning the agreement of conjoined noun phrases.

(14) a. Jody and Brett {*is / are} tired.
     b. Jody or Brett {is / *are} tired.

In the case of plural conjunction with *and*, we have plural agreement at the verb level. On the other hand, with disjunction, we retain singular agreement. It would be natural to locate an account of such agreement on the nonboolean coordinator. Of course, this still does not explain the infelicity of the singular *is* with the conjoined subject, which is felicitous in the case of boolean conjunction.

9.3 PRONOUNS AS VARIABLES

Montague's approach to pronouns in PTQ (1973) was rather straight-forward. Syntactically, he treated pronouns as noun phrases, and semantically, he treated them as variables. There was some complication in the expression component of his treatment, but that will not concern us here. We might be tempted to carry over Montague's analysis by positing the following class of lexical entries for nonreflexive pronouns.

(15) *he* $\Rightarrow x : np$ $[x \in \mathbf{Var}_{\mathrm{Ind}}]$

Note that there will be infinitely many lexical entries for pronouns according to this scheme. In and of itself, this is not problematic. We have already assumed infinitely many lexical entries for coordinators. Unfortunately, there are a number of complications that arise from the use of free variables in semantic terms, which I will illustrate below. The interpretation of nonreflexive pronouns remains one of the outstanding puzzles faced by type-logical grammar.

In order to derive sensible readings for sentences involving pronouns, it is necessary to synchronize the variables bound by the antecedent quantifier and the variable in the pronominal entry. For instance, consider the derivation in figure 9.1 (see section 11.1.2 for a semantic analysis of

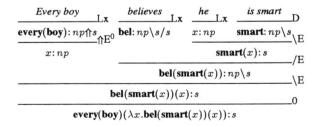

Figure 9.1
A Montagovian derivation of *Every boy believes he is smart*

believes). In order to derive a bound-pronoun reading, we must choose the variable in the pronoun's lexical entry, in this case x, to be the same as the variable bound by the quantifier intended to bind it. If we had chosen a different variable for the quantifier, say y, we would have derived a different result, such as the following:

(16) **every**(**boy**)($\lambda x.$**bel**(**smart**(y))(x))

The free variable y in this term is problematic because its interpretation, unlike any others we have considered, will depend on an assignment of variables to objects. On the syntactic side, nothing prevents us from deriving similar readings for nonreflexive pronouns in object position, as in *Everyone likes him*; Montague (1973) avoided this problem by finessing the expression component of his analyses in a decidedly noncompositional fashion in order to synchronize the gender, case, and form of a pronoun and its antecedents.

There are, unfortunately, even more serious drawbacks to Montague's approach. First, the quantifier-elimination step in figure 9.1 violates our requirement that hypothetical variables be fresh. To accommodate a treatment of pronouns as variables, the fresh-variable condition could be amended so as to ignore the variables introduced on pronouns. This is simply an ad hoc restriction on derivations rather than a consequence of the interpretation of our logical-category constructors.

To generate the proper bindings for pronouns with proper names as antecedents, we have two options. In the first, we can simply raise proper names to quantifiers and follow our analysis for quantifiers. I provide such an analysis in figure 9.2. Here I have taken the liberty of carrying out the β-reduction from $(\lambda P.P(\mathbf{j}))(\lambda x.\mathbf{bel}(\mathbf{smart}(x))(x))$ to $\mathbf{bel}(\mathbf{smart}(\mathbf{j}))(\mathbf{j})$ in the quantifier-application step. From a logical point of view, we can see

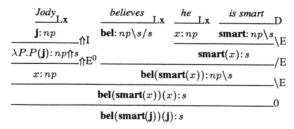

Figure 9.2
A Montagovian derivation of *Jody believes he is smart*

$$\cfrac{\cfrac{\cfrac{[x:np]^1 \qquad \textit{believes he is smart}}{\textbf{bel}(\textbf{smart}(x)):np\backslash s}\; \text{D}}{\textbf{bel}(\textbf{smart}(x))(x)}\; \backslash\text{E}}{\lambda x.\textbf{bel}(\textbf{smart}(x))(x):np\backslash s}\; \backslash\text{I}^0$$

Figure 9.3
A derivation of *believes he is smart*

that such a derivation is defective when we consider the result of normalization. In general, a quantifier-introduction step followed by a quantifier-elimination step should be reducible, as defined in the definition of scope normalization in section 7.4. But the only normal derivation of *Jody believes he is smart* yields the result $\textbf{bel}(\textbf{smart}(x))(\textbf{j})$, in which the variable x remains unbound.

Another alternative for generating a bound reading that we might consider would be to link the variable in a pronoun with that of a hypothetical antecedent. Consider the derivation of *believes he is smart* in figure 9.3. Here I have abstracted over the subject and, in so doing, associated the pronoun's variable with the variable of the hypothetical subject used, which then becomes bound on abstraction. This kind of analysis can apply to a simple name in subject position or to a quantified subject. But again, I have violated the condition on freshness for hypothetical variables and will face difficulty with unbound variables if I do not synchronize the choice of variables.

The variable-based approach to pronouns overgenerates by not enforcing syntactic constraints on coreference. For instance, *Everyone likes him* can be interpreted with the object pronoun being bound by the subject quantifier. And if we were to allow the same kind of entries for reflexives, we would not be able to enforce the locality condition. Instead, I introduce a quantificational approach to reflexives in section 9.4. Besides failing on these coarse-grained facts, a simple treatment of pronouns as variables fails to capture constraints on binding such as those arising from so-called *strong crossover* and *weak crossover* (see Postal 1971; Wasow 1972, 1977; Jacobson 1977). An example of strong crossover is the following:

(17) #He$_1$ likes [every boy]$_1$.

The "crossing over" at issue derives from a transformational analysis in which the object quantifier is moved to initial position, thus crossing over the pronoun that it binds. Although Chomsky (1976) characterized this condition by the actual ordering of the constituents, later versions of the theory have abandoned such notions in favor of structural descriptions (see Reinhart 1983). Within a transformational analysis based on structure, the following examples of weak crossover do not involve structural crossing.

(18) a. #His$_1$ mother likes [every boy]$_1$.
     b. #When he$_1$ gave his defense, [every student]$_1$ panicked.

In neither case can the pronoun be bound by the quantifier.

Another possibility for interpreting pronouns in the Montagovian tradition involves a quasi-logical sequent scheme. With a category *ana* for anaphors, which I do not associate with a domain of interpretation, we might imagine introducing the following rule scheme:

(19) $$\frac{\Gamma_1,\ \beta:np,\ \Gamma_2,\ \beta:np,\ \Gamma_3 \Rightarrow \alpha:A}{\Gamma_1,\ \beta:np,\ \Gamma_2,\ ana,\ \Gamma_3 \Rightarrow \alpha:A}\ ana$$

This rule allows us to identify an anaphoric element in the string being analyzed with any of the noun phrases occurring before it in the expression. We could just as easily allow the pronominal element to occur before its antecedent, in which case the connection between the variables is referred to as *cataphora*. This sequent-based method avoids the technicality of a lexical entry with variable syntax by introducing an entry with no semantic content. Such an analysis also rules out derivations in which there are unbound variables; any variables in β in (19) must eventually be bound. (Montague simply filtered results with unbound variables.) But under an approach such as the one in (19), there is no logical basis for the category *ana* and the rule scheme ana, rendering the combination nothing more than a stipulation of rewriting.

9.4   A QUANTIFICATIONAL APPROACH TO REFLEXIVES

Bach and Partee (1980) proposed a treatment of reflexives using a quantificational method wherein they are bound at the level of the verb phrase rather than the level of the sentence. The result of such binding is a verb phrase that associates the subject argument with both its own subject and that of its embedded reflexive. Moortgat (1991) made the type-logical analogue of this move in using his quantificational connective ⇑ to treat reflexivization. Recall that $B{\Uparrow}A$ is a category that behaves like a B in the derivation of an A, at which point its semantics applies to produce a new

$$\dfrac{\dfrac{Jody}{\mathbf{j}:np}\text{Lx} \quad \dfrac{likes}{\mathbf{like}:np\backslash s/np}\text{Lx} \quad \dfrac{\dfrac{himself}{\lambda V.\lambda x.V(x)(x):np\Uparrow(np\backslash s)}\text{Lx}}{y:np}\Uparrow E^0}{\dfrac{\dfrac{\mathbf{like}(y):np\backslash s}{\lambda x.\mathbf{like}(x)(x):np\backslash s}0}{\mathbf{like}(\mathbf{j})(\mathbf{j}):s}\backslash E}/E$$

Figure 9.4
A derivation of *Jody likes himself*

instance of category A with a meaning derived from the meaning of the expression of category $B\Uparrow A$ and the previous derivation of A depending on the hypothesis of a B. Standard generalized quantifiers quantify over sentences and are thus assigned the syntactic category $np\Uparrow s$.

With reflexives quantifying over verb phrases, Moortgat assigned them to the following category:

(20) *itself* $\Rightarrow \lambda V.\lambda x. V(x)(x): np\Uparrow(np\backslash s)$

As usual, the types of the variables can be inferred by the syntactic categories. The semantics of the reflexive simply takes a relation of two individual arguments into a unary relation that applies the original relation to the same argument twice. Such a category can be used in derivations such as the one in figure 9.4. In this derivation I have applied the following β-reduction at the quantifier stage.

(21) $(\lambda V.\lambda z.V(z)(z))(\lambda y.\mathbf{like}(y)) \Rightarrow \lambda z.\mathbf{like}(z)(z)$

With a quantificational subject, we have the analysis in figure 9.5.

A pleasant consequence of Moortgat's analysis is that it forces the reflexive to get a bound-variable reading (but see section 9.8 below for a discussion of rather subtle interactions with ellipsis). The same lexical entry can be used for subject-dependent reflexives in arbitrary positions within a verb phrase:

(22) a. Jody gave himself a nice present.
      b. Jody gave a nice present to himself.
      c. Jody is proud of himself.

An apparent shortcoming of the quantificational approach to reflexives as I have presented it is that the same lexical entry cannot be used for non-subject reflexive binding. For instance, consider the following contrast:

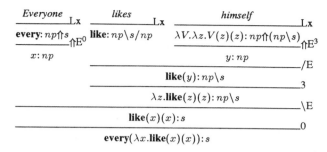

Figure 9.5
A derivation of *Everyone likes himself*

(23) a. Jody shows every boy himself.
      b. *Jody shows himself₁ [every boy]₁.

The sentence (23a) is ambiguous, allowing the reflexive to take either *every boy* or *Jody* as its antecedent. Not only does the subject-oriented lexical entry not generate the object-antecedent case, it is unclear how a lexical entry for the reflexive could be formulated that would allow such a reading. In some languages, there are distinct morphosyntactic forms for the object reflexives and the subject reflexives, motivating distinct lexical entries (see Morrill 1994a). With a concatenative approach to ditransitive verbs in an example like (23a), the verb *shows* attaches to the object *every boy* before attaching to *himself*. By the time *himself* attaches, it is too late to bind the argument position already filled by *every boy*. This same problem arose for the early categorial semanticists, and Bach (1981a) proposed a solution that involved analyzing verbs such as *show* in terms of wrapping. For example, in (23a), *shows ____ himself* can be analyzed as wrapping around *every boy* to form a verb phrase. Further note that this approach accounts for the infelicity of the pronoun-antecedent relation indicated in (23b). Morrill and Solias (1993) provided a type-logical foundation for Bach's wrapping operation, which Morrill (1994a) revised (the primary issue is keeping track of the insertion point for the wrapper). Of course, a separate lexical entry is required, and its semantics is used to reduce a ditransitive relation to a transitive one. An alternative approach, based on the notion of *headedness*, was provided by Moortgat and Morrill (1991).

While it appears that many of the relevant subject-oriented possibilities can be generated using Moortgat's approach to reflexives, it is equally clear that the approach does not respect the strong syntactic locality conditions introduced on reflexive binding. In particular, Moortgat's theory predicts ambiguity in cases such as the following:

(24) Jody believes Francis likes himself.

Here it would be possible for the reflexive to take as its antecedent either the matrix subject *Jody* or the embedded subject *Francis*. Morrill (1989a, 1990a) introduced modal operators into categorial grammar that have the ability to enforce locality restrictions (note that this approach is related, but not identical, to the modal approach to islands). I will not be concerned with islandhood, except to say that Morrill's approach is able to appropriately localize the range of bound reflexive readings. There is a technical problem with Moortgat's proof theory for quantification that is highlighted by the reflexive lexical entry. This problem, whose discovery Morrill (1994a) attributes to Herman Hendriks, is brought into focus with examples such as the following:

(25) Jody likes himself and every teacher.

The problem here is that it is not possible to conjoin the categories $np \Uparrow s$ and $np \Uparrow (np \backslash s)$, because they are not identical. It would be natural to convert the quantifier into the category of the reflexive, as follows:

(26) **every**(**teacher**): $np \Uparrow s \Rightarrow \lambda V. \lambda x.$**every**(**teacher**)$(V(x)): np \Uparrow (np \backslash s)$

If a category can serve as an *np* and reduce inside of a sentence, it should be able to serve as an *np* and reduce inside of a verb phrase. This indicates an incompleteness in the proof theory associated with the scoping constructor as I have presented it. More sophisticated approaches to the logic, such as Morrill's (1994a), do not suffer from this incompleteness. However, the rules for our scoping constructor do not generate (26). This failure stems from the lack of generality of the introduction rule for $\Uparrow$, which simply has no way of determining if something can behave like a scope operator. The underivability of this sequent highlights the incompleteness of the logic I have provided for the scoping operator $\Uparrow$, as this kind of derivation should go through according to the intended interpretation of $B \Uparrow A$. Intuitively, we want to classify an expression as being of category $B \Uparrow A$ if it can act as a B in a derivation of an A. In fact, a simple proof-theoretic inspection of the rule of use for the quantifier shows a striking asymmetry. With the rule of use, we can perform derivations as shown on the left and right of figure 9.6. In view of this understanding of the rule of use, the rule of proof for quantifiers should be strengthened to allow us to derive $C \Uparrow (B \backslash A)$ from $C \Uparrow A$ in general. It

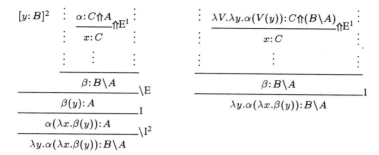

Figure 9.6
The incompleteness of ⇈

remains an open problem as to how to complete the logic for ⇈. An important insight due to Moortgat (1991) is that the scoping constructor ⇈ is related to the operations of infixing and wrapping. In particular, an expression of category B⇈A applies to an expression categorized as an A missing a B, by inserting itself into the missing B position while taking scope over the entire expression. Morrill (1994a) exploits this equivalence to provide a complete logic for ⇈ in terms of more primitive wrapping and infixing operators. Morrill (1995) introduces yet another logic for ⇈ based on a sorted algebra of strings and discontinuity that does derive the sequent in (26). Morrill's logic corresponds to our intuitive presentation of the scoping operator. In particular, it is possible to derive the following desirable sequent:

(27) *the autograph of some player*
$$\Rightarrow \lambda P.\textbf{some}(\textbf{play})(\lambda x. P(\iota(\textbf{autograph}(x)))): np \Upsilon s$$

In exercise 32, chapter 11, we consider a situation involving intensional transitive verbs where the underivability of this sequent in our simplified proof theory prevents us from deriving a valid reading. Finally, I note that Morrill has shown how to derive the correct reading for (25) without the derivation in (26) (see Exercise 2).

Some occurrences of reflexives fall outside of our analysis, such as the following:

(28) The picture of himself upset Terry.

Pollard and Sag (1992, 1994) provide an HPSG-based analysis of cases such as these that allows *himself* to be bound outside of the lexical predicate of which it is an argument if it is the least oblique argument of that predicate (recall the discussion of obliqueness in section 4.6). Otherwise, they require reflexives to be bound locally, in keeping with the traditional approach to binding. This forces *herself* in *Sandy likes herself* to have *Sandy* as an antecedent, but allows *himself* in (28) to be bound by *Terry*.

9.5   PLURAL PRONOUNS

In this section we consider the use of plural pronominals, such as the ones occurring in the following examples:

(29) a. Jody and Brett like themselves.
 b. The cranes hoisted themselves.
 c. Jody and Brett believe they can carry a piano.
 d. The three men met and then they sneezed.

Example (29a) has a reading in which Jody likes himself and Brett likes himself. In the next case, (29b), we see that the plural reflexive object pronoun *themselves* can take either a collective or distributive antecedent. This leads to a reading where the cranes collectively hoisted the cranes or a reading where each of the cranes hoisted itself. We can read the next sentence, (29c), in at least three ways. First, Jody might believe that Jody can carry a piano, and Brett might believe that Brett can carry a piano. Second, Jody and Brett might both believe that Jody and Brett can each carry a piano. Third, Jody and Brett might both believe they can carry a piano collectively. The last example also clearly shows a case in which the pronoun *they* is interpreted as taking *the three men* as its antecedent, with the pronoun interpreted distributively and the antecedent collectively. This evidence suggests that plural pronouns should be allowed to take antecedents of category np_p or np_p^*. In a Montagovian setting, this would provide the following entries:

(30) a. *they, them, themselves* $\Rightarrow x\!:\!np_p$ if $x \in \mathbf{Var_{Ind}}$
 b. *they, them* $\Rightarrow X\!:\!np_p^*$ if $X \in \mathbf{Var_{Ind \to Bool}}$

I leave a Moortgat-style quantificational analysis of plural reflexives such as *themselves* for exercise 12. An example of the use of a plural pronoun as an np_p can be found in figure 9.7. Note that I have used the sentential-complement verb *believe* in this example to allow nesting; I provide an intensional analysis of propositional-attitude verbs such as *believe* in section 11.1.2. Here we see the reading that Jody believes he sneezed and Brett believed he sneezed. We could also get a collective/collective inter-

$$\frac{\quad\quad \textit{Jody and Brett} \quad\quad}{\textbf{every}(\{\textbf{j}\} \cup \{\textbf{b}\}): np_p\Uparrow s}D \quad \frac{\textit{believe}}{\textbf{bel}: np_p\backslash s/s}\text{Lx} \quad \frac{\textit{they}}{x: np_p}\text{Lx} \quad \frac{\textit{sneezed}}{\textbf{sneeze}: np_p\backslash s}\text{Lx}$$

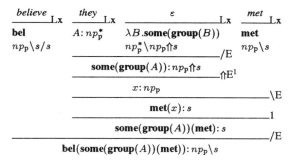

Figure 9.7
A derivation of *Jody and Brett believe they sneezed*

Figure 9.8
A group derivation of *believe they met*

pretation using an np_p lexical entry, but selectional restrictions prevent group beliefs. But consider the analysis of a sentence such as the following:

(31) [Jody and Brett]$_0$ convinced Francis that they$_0$ could carry the piano.

Here the convincing might be done by the group composed of Jody and Brett, with the carrying done by the same group. An analysis along these lines could be carried out as in figure 9.7, only with the group reading of the coordinated expressions being plugged in.

I provide an analysis in which the np_p^* entry is used for a pronoun in figure 9.8. This analysis of the verb phrase *believe they met* can combine with a plural subject in a number of ways. With a bare plural, the bare-plural existential can bind the variable introduced by the pronoun. With a coordinated structure, such as *Brett and Jody*, or with a definite noun phrase, such as *the three kids*, we need to type raise the introduced set of category np_p^* to quantify at the level of $np_p^*\Uparrow s$, and thus enable the pronominal variable to be bound.

(32) $\{\mathbf{j}, \mathbf{b}\}: np_p^* \Rightarrow \lambda P. P(\{\mathbf{j}, \mathbf{b}\}): np_p^* \Uparrow s$

In any case, the distributivity or collectivity of the subject is independent of the distributivity or collectivity of the dependent pronoun. While *belief* is not typically collective, this same kind of analysis works in cases such as the following:

(33) Jody and Brett convinced the coach they could make 3-point shots.

Here the convincing might be done collectively, while the 3-point shoot-ing is done individually. In addition to the readings given here, we have additional analyses in which the quantifiers for distribution or collection that are attached to the embedded pronoun take scope outside of the sentence in which they occur.

9.6   RECIPROCALS AND GENERALIZED QUANTIFICATION

In this section, we consider the use of the English *reciprocal* element *each other*. To begin, consider the following simple examples:

(34) a. [The three kids]₁ like [each other]₁.
     b. [Jody and Brett]₂ like [each other]₂.

In both of these cases the reciprocal occurs in object position and induces a form of distribution over the set introduced by the subject. I indicate the dependency of the reciprocal on an antecedent by means of subscripting. Clearly, such coindexing does not indicate coreference when applied to reciprocal/set dependency. Consider the first example, (34a), whose truth appears to require that each of the three kids must like each of the other kids. In the second example, Jody must like Brett, and Brett must like Jody. This kind of reciprocity in understanding, requiring the relationship to hold both ways, is where the reciprocal gets its name.

I wish to argue that the reciprocal acts in some ways like the distributor and in other ways like a dependent element. In particular, the reciprocal is dependent on a plural antecedent. The following evidence supports not only this claim but, with the third example, also supports the assumption that this plural antecedent must be of category np_p^*, an undiscriminated plural noun phrase denoting a set.

(35) a. *Jody₃ like [each other]₃.
     b. *[The committee]₄ like [each other]₄.
     c. *[Jody and Brett]₅ each like [each other]₅.

Our analysis requires a reciprocal reading between the antecedent position and the position of the reciprocal, quantifying over all of the elements in the antecedent set. Note also that it is not possible to derive collective readings of either the antecedent or the reciprocal, as can be seen with the following example:

(36) [Jody and Brett]$_6$ hoisted [each other]$_6$.

Here we must have Jody hoisting Brett and vice versa; any collective hoisting or being hoisted will not suffice.

I follow Bennett (1974) in assigning a semantic term to the reciprocator that relates a binary relation and a set.

(37) a. **each_other**: $(\mathbf{Ind} \rightarrow \mathbf{Ind} \rightarrow \mathbf{Bool}) \rightarrow (\mathbf{Ind} \rightarrow \mathbf{Bool}) \rightarrow \mathbf{Bool}$
     b. **each_other** $\overset{\text{def}}{=} \lambda V.\lambda P.\mathbf{every}(P)(\lambda x.\mathbf{every}(\lambda y.P(y) \wedge x \neq y)$
     $$(\lambda z.V(x)(z)))$$

The reciprocal applies to a relation and a set if and only if every pair of nonidentical members of the set stand in the relation (in both orders). We can use the reciprocator to provide a semantic term for (34b):

(38) **each_other**$(\mathbf{like})(\{\mathbf{j}, \mathbf{b}\})$

Note that this term is true if and only if Jody likes Brett and Brett likes Jody.

This syntactic analysis of the reciprocator is similar to Moortgat's (1991) analysis of the reflexive. I want to treat *each other* as a category that behaves locally as an individual-denoting plural noun phrase, and then reduces in the scope of a verb phrase to produce a result that seeks a set-denoting plural noun phrase. In symbols, I want *each other* to act like an np_p in a derivation of an $np_p \backslash s$, at which point the semantics applies to produce an $np_p^* \backslash s$. But this is not an effect we can achieve with a category of the form $B \Uparrow A$, because at the point of applying the reciprocator, the syntactic category and semantic type must also be shifted. Moortgat (1991) provided a generalization of the $\Uparrow$ constructor with which such behavior can be modeled. Moortgat noticed that there was a duplication of $\mathrm{Typ}(A)$ in the type assigned to $B \Uparrow A$.

(39) $\mathrm{Typ}(B \Uparrow A) = (\mathrm{Typ}(B) \rightarrow \mathrm{Typ}(A)) \rightarrow \mathrm{Typ}(A)$

This led Moortgat to introduce a new three-place category connective q. We interpret this constructor so that an expression of category $q(A, B, C)$ acts as a C in the derivation of a B, at which point its semantics applies to produce a result of category A.

DEFINITION: GENERALIZED SCOPING CONSTRUCTOR   The *generalized scoping constructor* is such that

a. $q(A, B, C) \in \mathbf{Cat}$ if $A, B, C \in \mathbf{Cat}$,
b. $\mathrm{Typ}(q(A, B, C)) = (\mathrm{Typ}(C) \to \mathrm{Typ}(B)) \to \mathrm{Typ}(A)$.

Moortgat generalized the sequent characterization of $\Uparrow$ in the natural way to allow the point of semantic application to shift types. The left rule for using the generalized scope constructor is as follows:

DEFINITION: GENERALIZED SCOPING SEQUENT   The left sequent scheme for *generalized scoping* is the following:

$$\frac{\Delta_1, x\colon C, \Delta_2 \Rightarrow \beta\colon B \qquad \Gamma_1, \alpha(\lambda x.\beta)\colon A, \Gamma_2 \Rightarrow \gamma\colon D}{\Gamma_1, \Delta_1, \alpha\colon q(A, B, C), \Delta_2, \Gamma_2 \Rightarrow \gamma\colon D} q\mathrm{L} \qquad [x \text{ fresh}]$$

Like the rule for $\Uparrow$, the rule for q has an application of cut built in. The natural-deduction scheme is the obvious analogue.

DEFINITION: THE GENERALIZED SCOPING NATURAL-DEDUCTION SCHEME   The natural deduction elimination scheme for *generalized scoping* is the following:

$$\begin{array}{ccc}
\vdots \quad \vdots & & \vdots \qquad [x \text{ fresh}] \\
\dfrac{\alpha\colon q(A, B, C)}{x\colon C} q\mathrm{E}^i & & \vdots \\
\vdots \quad \vdots & & \vdots \\
\end{array}$$

$$\frac{\beta\colon B}{\alpha(\lambda x.\beta)\colon A} i$$

Furthermore, we also retain the structural understanding of this scheme, requiring the derivation of $\beta\colon B$ to involve only $x\colon C$ and nothing from within the derivation of $\alpha\colon q(A, B, C)$.

   The first thing to note is that q is a generalization of $\Uparrow$. In fact, we can simply take $\Uparrow$ to be defined as follows:

(40) $B \Uparrow A \stackrel{\mathrm{def}}{=} q(A, A, B)$.

The logic for q is a proper generalization of that for $\Uparrow$; there is no way to directly simulate the behavior of $q(A, B, C)$ with any choice of $E \Uparrow D$. To fully capture the behavior of $\Uparrow$ in terms of q, we need a rule of proof for q.

DEFINITION: THE SEQUENT GENERALIZED SCOPING SCHEME The right sequent scheme for *generalized scoping* is the following:

$$\frac{\qquad\qquad\qquad\qquad}{\alpha: A \Rightarrow \lambda P.P(\alpha): q(B, B, A)} qR$$

In this case, the incompleteness of Moortgat's logic is even more evident; there is not even a way to introduce a category $q(A, B, C)$, where $A \neq B$. Just as with $B \Uparrow A$, there is no way to prove $\alpha: q(A, B, C) \Rightarrow \alpha: q(A, B, C)$ by decomposing the constructor q with the right rule. Compare this situation with that of $\alpha: A/B \Rightarrow \lambda x.\alpha(x): A/B$, which is derivable via the right rule for $/$ (see exercise 10, chapter 5). Morrill (1994a, 1995) solves these technical problems by decomposing q into wrapping, following a suggestion of Moortgat (1991).

Moortgat's connective q is just what we need to handle the reciprocal, which I provide with the following lexical entry:

(41) *each other* $\Rightarrow$ **each_other**: $q(np_p^*\backslash s, np_p \backslash s, np_p)$

Note that the definition of **each_other** is of the appropriate type. I show the behavior of q in the analysis of (34b) in figure 9.9.

The reciprocal has restrictions on the locality of its antecedent in much the same way as the reflexive.

(42) a. *[Jody and Brett]₁ believe that Francis likes [each other]₁.
     b. *[Jody and Brett]₂ believe that [each other]₂ ran.

The first example shows that reciprocals are subject to locality constraints when binding them to antecedents. The second example can be taken as evidence either of a kind of locality restriction on antecedents or of a restriction against reciprocals occurring in nominative-case position. But unlike reflexives, reciprocals are found as possessors in noun phrases.

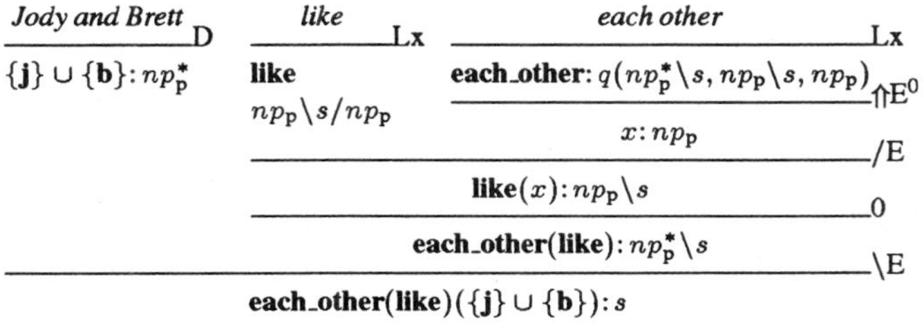

Jody and Brett D $\qquad$ $\dfrac{\textit{like}}{\begin{array}{l}\textbf{like}\\ np_p\backslash s/np_p\end{array}}$ Lx $\qquad$ $\dfrac{\textit{each other}}{\textbf{each\_other}: q(np_p^*\backslash s, np_p\backslash s, np_p)}$ Lx

$\{j\} \cup \{b\}: np_p^*$

$$\frac{\textbf{each\_other}: q(np_p^*\backslash s, np_p\backslash s, np_p)}{x: np_p}\Uparrow E^0$$

$$\frac{\textbf{like}\quad x: np_p}{\textbf{like}(x): np_p\backslash s}/E$$

$$\frac{\textbf{like}(x): np_p\backslash s}{\textbf{each\_other}(\textbf{like}): np_p^*\backslash s}0$$

$$\frac{\{j\}\cup\{b\}: np_p^* \qquad \textbf{each\_other}(\textbf{like}): np_p^*\backslash s}{\textbf{each\_other}(\textbf{like})(\{j\}\cup\{b\}): s}\backslash E$$

Figure 9.9
A derivation of *Jody and Brett like each other*

$$\dfrac{like}{\textbf{like}}\text{Lx}\qquad \dfrac{each\ other}{\textbf{each\_other}}\text{Lx}\qquad \dfrac{\text{'s}}{\lambda y.\lambda P.\iota(\lambda z.\textbf{poss}(y)(z))}\text{Lx}\qquad \dfrac{car}{\textbf{car}}\text{Lx}$$

$$np_{\text{p}}\backslash s/np \qquad \dfrac{q(np_{\text{p}}^{*}\backslash s,\ np_{\text{p}}\backslash s,\ np_{\text{p}})}{x:np_{\text{p}}}qE^{0} \qquad \dfrac{\wedge P(z)}{np_{\text{p}}\backslash(np/n)} \qquad n$$

$$\dfrac{\lambda P.\iota(\lambda z.\textbf{poss}(x)(z)\wedge P(z)):np/n}{\dfrac{\iota(\lambda z.\textbf{poss}(x)(z)\wedge\textbf{car}(z)):np}{\dfrac{\textbf{like}(\iota(\lambda z.\textbf{poss}(x)(z)\wedge\textbf{car}(z))):np_{\text{p}}\backslash s}{\textbf{each\_other}(\lambda x.\textbf{like}(\iota(\lambda z.\textbf{poss}(x)(z)\wedge\textbf{car}(z)))):np_{\text{p}}^{*}\backslash s}0}/\text{E}}/\text{E}}\backslash\text{E}$$

Figure 9.10
A derivation of *like each other's car*

(43) [Jody and Brett]₁ like [each other]₁'s {?car / cars}.

One puzzle arising from this sentence is the number attached to the dependent plural head nominal in the possessive. With a singular noun, such as *car* above, we are able to provide a derivation as in figure 9.10. But it seems that the sentence is more natural with the complement *cars* rather than *car*. Our grammar cannot generate the correct semantics with a plural entry; with a plural noun, each person is required to own several cars and like all of the cars of the other (either distributively or collectively). On the other hand, there is a strong reason to believe that the plural morphology found in (44) is an instance of a so-called *dependent plural*, in which the plurality marks agreement rather than independently marking semantic plurality.

(44) a. All {bicycles / unicycles} have wheels.
    b. From here, trains leave regularly for Amsterdam.

Chomsky's (1975) example, (44a), might be true with the noun *unicycles* even if each unicycle has only one wheel; thus the plural in *wheels* signals agreement rather than a true semantic plurality taking scope with respect to the subject. Similarly, deMey's (1981) example, (44b), can be true even if only one train leaves at a time; thus the plural *trains* is dependent on the adverb of quantification *regularly* (see section 12.5.8). Roberts (1987a) uses such dependent-plural behavior as evidence for a theory of plurals in which a plural noun can, in general, denote a singleton set. I leave the grammatical characterization of dependent plurals until exercise 15 (also see exercise 26).

Some of the more interesting uses of reciprocals involve embedded sentences and interactions with plural pronouns.

$$
\begin{array}{l}
\underline{\text{Jody and Brett}}\ \text{Lx} \qquad \underline{\text{told}}\ \text{Lx} \qquad \underline{\text{each other}}\ \text{Lx} \qquad \underline{\text{they}}\ \text{Lx} \qquad \underline{\text{sneezed}}\ \text{Lx}
\end{array}
$$

$$
\{j\} \cup \{b\} \qquad \textbf{tell} \qquad \textbf{each\_other} \qquad\qquad x:np_p \qquad \textbf{sneeze}
$$

$$
np_p^* \qquad np_p\backslash s/s/np_p \qquad \dfrac{q(np_p^*\backslash s,\, np_p\backslash s,\, np_p)}{}qE^2 \qquad\qquad \dfrac{np_p\backslash s}{}\backslash E
$$

$$
\dfrac{x:np_p}{\ }/E \qquad\qquad \dfrac{\textbf{sneeze}(x):s}{\ }
$$

$$
\dfrac{\textbf{tell}(x):np_p\backslash s/s}{\ }
$$

$$
\dfrac{\textbf{tell}(x)(\textbf{sneeze}(x)):np_p\backslash s}{\ }/E
$$

$$
\dfrac{\textbf{each\_other}(\lambda x.\textbf{tell}(x)(\textbf{sneeze}(x))):np_p^*\backslash s}{\ }2
$$

$$
\textbf{each\_other}(\lambda x.\textbf{tell}(x)(\textbf{sneeze}(x)))(\{j\}\cup\{b\}):s \quad \backslash E
$$

Figure 9.11
The *you* reading of *Jody and Brett told each other they sneezed*

(45) [Jody and Morgan]₃ told [each other]₃ that they should leave.

Here we have a plural subject, reciprocal object, and sentential complement with an embedded plural pronoun. Heim, Lasnik, and May (1991) claim that (45) is three-ways ambiguous and provide the following paraphrases (assume that Jody is male and Morgan female):

(46) a. Jody told Morgan that *he* should leave, and Morgan told Jody that *she* should leave.
   b. Jody told Morgan that *she* should leave, and Morgan told Jody that *he* should leave.
   c. Jody told Morgan and Morgan told Jody that they should leave.

They call these readings the *I reading*, the *you reading*, and the *we reading*, respectively, and refer to the problem of generating all of them as the *grain problem*. I claim that there is a further ambiguity stemming from a distributive/collective distinction in the *we* reading; Jody and Morgan could be leaving either separately or together. This is clearer in sentences such as the following:

(47) Jody and Morgan told each other they won.

Here the verb *won* can be interpreted either distributively or collectively.

Our grammar generates the *I*, *you*, and *we* readings noted by Heim, Lasnik, and May. It further generates a collective/distributive ambiguity in the *we* reading in examples such as (47). The *you* reading is illustrated in figure 9.11. Note that in the generation of the *you* reading, I used the np_p entry for the plural pronoun *they*. This picks up the same variable as is used for the reciprocal, leading to the *you* reading. We can also use the

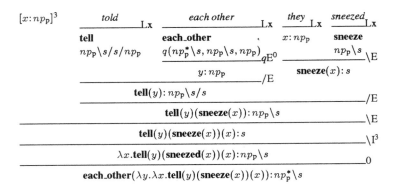

Figure 9.12
The *I* reading *of told each other they sneezed*

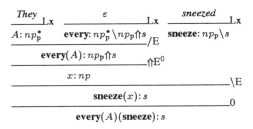

Figure 9.13
A derivation of *They sneezed*

np_p entry for *they* to generate the *I* reading. This time, it must be bound to the same variable as is bound by the subject. In the derivation in figure 9.12, I have displayed only the analysis of the verb phrase. It crucially involves abstracting over an np_p subject at the appropriate stage to provide an antecedent for the pronoun. The difference between the *I* and *you* readings is thus simply a matter of whether the pronoun takes the subject or object as its antecedent. Note that our impoverished approach to pronouns has no way of enforcing the requirement that the individual variable in figure 9.12 be bound by a plural antecedent.

Both the collective and distributive *we* readings are produced by using the np_p^* entry for *they*, which takes a set-denoting noun phrase as antecedent. In particular, we can analyze *they sneezed* as in figure 9.13. The analysis in figure 9.13 can then be used as a derived result to generate the distributive *we* reading of (45), given in figure 9.14.

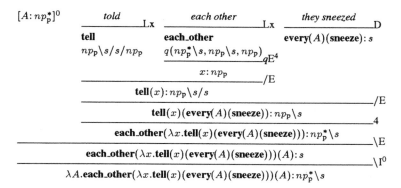

Figure 9.14
The *we* reading of *told each other they sneezed*

Our grammar for reciprocals, in addition to solving the so-called grain problem, as illustrated by the example in (45), also solves the so-called *scope problem*, illustrated in the following:

(48) Jody and Brett think they like each other.

Here the pronominal *they* can attach either as an np_p^* or as an np_p. In the np_p^* case, the reading is that both Jody and Brett think that they each like the other. In the np_p case, we find Jody thinking Jody likes Brett and Brett thinking Brett likes Jody, with nothing more required. In examples such as (48), it is not at all clear how to indicate dependency relations by means of coindexing, because reciprocity has to be kept separate from binding. The np_p entry for the plural pronoun provides a noncontradictory reading for the following example of Roberts's (1991).

(49) Joan and Morgan think they will defeat each other.

   Reciprocals in the least oblique argument position, like reflexives, can be bound nonlocally, as seen in the following example:

(50) Pictures of [each other]₅ disturbed [Jody and Morgan]₅.

In this example, we have pictures of Jody disturbing Morgan and vice versa as the only possible reading. Reciprocals that do not take subjects as antecedents present the same range of problems as do reflexives. Consider the following example due to Roberts (1991).

(51) I questioned them₅ about [each other]₅.

Here the reciprocation is with respect to the object *them* rather than the subject; because the pronominal is already attached at the point the reciprocal is used, the correct interpretation cannot be generated with our grammar. We find the same problem with the following example due to Heim, Lasnik, and May (1991).

(52) Their coaches think they will defeat each other.

The problem with this example is that the reciprocation must be with respect to the antecedent of *their*, but this antecedent is not available as part of the accessible meaning of *their*, which is a possessive pronoun of category np_p/n_p^* or np_p^*/n_p^*. This would not be a problem for very closely related examples such as the following.

(53) *Jody and Brett's coaches think they will defeat each other*
$\Rightarrow$ **each_other**$(\lambda x.\lambda y.$**think**$($**defeat**$(x)(y))(\iota($**coach**$(x))))(\{$**j**$,$ **b**$\})$: s

In this case, there is the constituent *Jody and Brett* for the reciprocal to work on. I leave the rather lengthy derivation as an exercise.

Our grammar appropriately predicts the distinction noticed by Mats Rooth (p.c. to Heim, Lasnik, and May 1991).

(54) a. The youngest three of the women each gave a lecture to the others.

b. The youngest three of the women gave lectures to each other.

In first example, (54a), there is an ambiguity as to whether the youngest three of the women gave lectures to the women older than themselves or to each other. The lack of ambiguity in the second example, (54b), is due to the fact that *each other* must reduce within an $np_p \backslash s$ category, and there is no way to generate such a category in this case. An analysis of *others* involves both linguistic dependency and nonlinguistic context. Ignoring the contextual component, we have the following:

(55) *others* $\Rightarrow \lambda P.\|P\| \geq \mathbf{2} \wedge (P \cap Q = \emptyset)$: n_p^*

Here the free variable Q must pick up an antecedent from context, with the result being sets of sets that are distinct from Q and have at least two elements. The context dependence stems from the fact that *others* also has a nominal dependence. In the case of (54a), we have a restriction to the set of women other than the three youngest. We could possibly account for this context dependence with another variable, by adding the restriction $P \subseteq R$ to the lexical entry, where R would also be dependent. In this case, R would pick up the set variable introduced by *the women* as an np_p^* or the variable associated with *the youngest of the women*. This distinction accounts for the ambiguity in (54a).

The reciprocation involved with *each other* is adequate to handle quantificational examples such as Roberts's (1991) example (46b), from chapter 8 above, repeated here along with another of her examples.

(56) a. No competing candidates like each other.
     b. No kids saw each other.

For instance, the second example can have only the following reading:

(57) **no**(**plu**(**kid**))($\lambda P.$**each_other**(**see**)(P))

Such a reading requires there to be no set of kids with at least two elements such that all pairwise seeings occurred. Note that these truth conditions are compatible with situations in which there are a lot of seeing relations between kids, as long as there are no mutual ones (any mutual seeing provides a doubleton set in the extension of *kids*).

Examples given by Langendoen (1978), Carlson (1980), and Fiengo and Lasnik (1973) suggest that the term assigned to reciprocators by Bennett is too strong. Consider the following examples:

(58) a. The plates are stacked on top of each other.
     b. The leaves of the tree are touching each other.
     c. The students know each other.

In these cases, it seems that total reciprocation is not necessary for the sentences to be true. If this is the case, we need to come up with a different definition for **each_other** that leaves a degree of vagueness in place of the universals in Bennett's term. One suggestion, due to Langendoen (1978), is the following, which he termed *weak reciprocity*.

(59) **each_other** $\overset{\text{def}}{=} \lambda P.\lambda V.(\forall x\colon P)(\exists y\colon P - \{x\})V(x,y)$
$\wedge\ (\forall x\colon P)(\exists y\colon P - \{x\})V(y,x)$

The notation $P - \{x\}$ is for the set P less the element x. Fiengo and Lasnik (1973) argue that weak reciprocity is still too strong for examples such as (58c), in which it is not even necessary for each of the students to stand in a knowing relationship.

In any case, everyone agrees that the reciprocal involves a relation between a set and a binary relation. The type-logical approach captures this fact lexically, with Moortgat's generalized quantifier approach providing the necessary power to generate the syntactic dependencies.

9.7   PIED PIPING

While not exactly a case of anaphora, we are now in a position to discuss Morrill's (1992b, 1994a, 1995) application of Moortgat's generalized scoping category to cases of so-called *pied piping*, such as the following:

(60) a. the table$_1$ [the leg of which$_1$]$_2$ Jody broke ——$_2$.
     b. the table$_1$ [behind which$_1$]$_2$ Jody stood ——$_2$.
     c. the student$_1$ [whose$_1$ thesis's title's spacing]$_2$ the committee found unacceptable ——$_2$.

The whimsical terminology reflects the fact that a relative pronoun, such as *which* in (60a), is able to carry along the rest of the phrase in which it is embedded, such as *the leg of which* in (60a), when appearing in a relative clause. The crucial thing to note about these examples is that there are multiple dependencies that must be resolved. The relative pronoun, in these cases *which* and *whose*, must be linked to the noun being modified, while the constituent of which *which* is a part fills a gap in the following sentence.

Morrill demonstrated how Moortgat's connective q could be used to provide an adequate generalization of our preliminary lexical entry for relative pronouns. He provided a polymorphic lexical entry for non-possessive pied-piping pronouns:

(61) *which* $\Rightarrow \lambda N.\lambda V.\lambda P.\lambda x.P(x) \wedge V(N(x)): q(n\backslash n/(s\uparrow A), A, np)$

In this schematic entry, A takes on values for the categories that can be pied-piped. Of course, we require that the type of the terms are appropriate, so that N is of type **Ind** $\rightarrow$ Typ(A) and V is of type Typ$(A) \rightarrow$ **Bool**, with P of type **Ind** $\rightarrow$ **Bool** and x of type **Ind**. It remains an open question as to exactly which categories should be allowed to instantiate A in the polymorphic version of *which*, though it should at least include singular and plural noun phrases, prepositionally case-marked noun phrases, and nominal- and verbal-modifying prepositional phrases. Lexical entries for the case of a singular noun phrase and the case of a preposition modifying a singular verb phrase are as follows:

(62) a. *which* $\Rightarrow \lambda N.\lambda V.\lambda P.\lambda x.P(x) \wedge V(N(x)): q(n\backslash n/(s\uparrow np), np, np)$
     b. *which* $\Rightarrow \lambda N.\lambda V.\lambda P.\lambda x.P(x) \wedge V(N(x)):$
        $q(n\backslash n/(s\uparrow((np\backslash s)\backslash np\backslash s)), (np\backslash s)\backslash np\backslash s, np)$

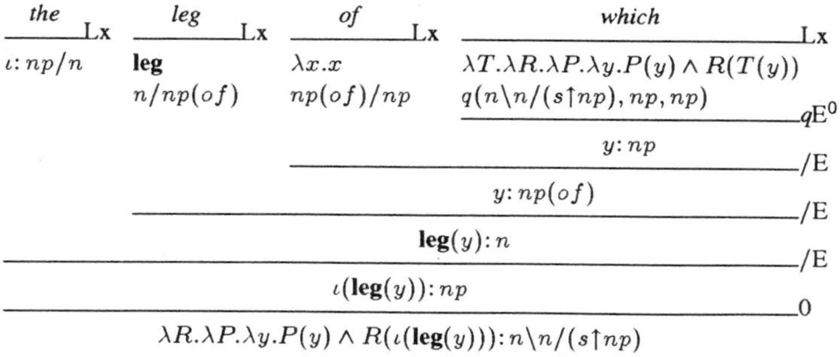

$$\cfrac{\cfrac{\cfrac{\cfrac{\cfrac{\cfrac{\cfrac{\text{the}}{\iota:np/n}\text{Lx} \quad \cfrac{\text{leg}}{\substack{\textbf{leg}\\ n/np(of)}}\text{Lx} \quad \cfrac{\text{of}}{\substack{\lambda x.x\\ np(of)/np}}\text{Lx} \quad \cfrac{\cfrac{\text{which}}{\substack{\lambda T.\lambda R.\lambda P.\lambda y.P(y)\wedge R(T(y))\\ q(n\backslash n/(s{\uparrow}np),np,np)}}\text{Lx}}{y:np}\text{qE}^0}{y:np(of)}\text{/E}}{\textbf{leg}(y):n}\text{/E}}{\iota(\textbf{leg}(y)):np}\text{/E}}{\lambda R.\lambda P.\lambda y.P(y)\wedge R(\iota(\textbf{leg}(y))):n\backslash n/(s{\uparrow}np)}\text{0}}$$

Figure 9.15
A derivation of *the leg of which*

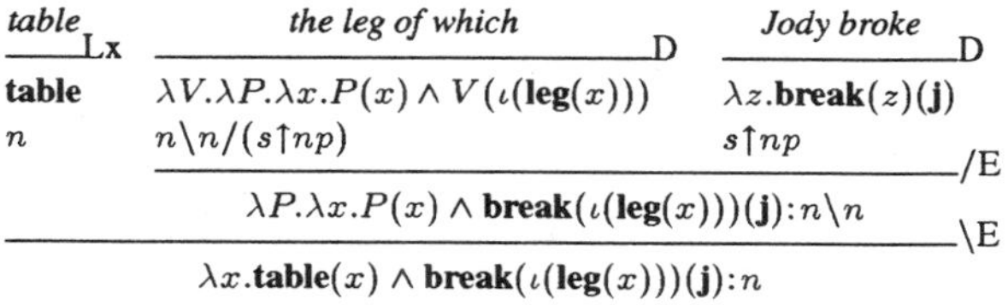

$$\cfrac{\cfrac{\cfrac{\text{table}}{\substack{\textbf{table}\\ n}}\text{Lx} \quad \cfrac{\text{the leg of which}}{\substack{\lambda V.\lambda P.\lambda x.P(x)\wedge V(\iota(\textbf{leg}(x)))\\ n\backslash n/(s{\uparrow}np)}}\text{D} \quad \cfrac{\text{Jody broke}}{\substack{\lambda z.\textbf{break}(z)(\textbf{j})\\ s{\uparrow}np}}\text{D}}{\lambda P.\lambda x.P(x)\wedge \textbf{break}(\iota(\textbf{leg}(x)))(\textbf{j}):n\backslash n}\text{/E}}{\lambda x.\textbf{table}(x)\wedge \textbf{break}(\iota(\textbf{leg}(x)))(\textbf{j}):n}\text{\\E}$$

Figure 9.16
A derivation of *table the leg of which Jody broke*

I provide an analysis of the pied-piped phrase in (60a) in figure 9.15. The rest of the nominal in (60a) is given in figure 9.16. The derivation in figure 9.15 first eliminates the prepositional-quantifier category by hypothesizing a noun phrase. This hypothetical noun phrase is then used in deriving a larger noun phrase, at which point the category for *which* is applied to produce a category just like that originally assigned to the relative pronoun. The rest of the analysis in figure 9.16 assumes the extraction category for *Jody broke*, the derivation of which we have seen many times, and proceeds by simple application. It is also evident that the semantics assigned to the nominal in figure 9.16 is the correct one.

I should also note that pied piping does not need to apply only in the case where the relative pronoun is phrase-final, as can be seen in the following noun phrase:

(63) the bicycle$_1$ [the wheel of which$_1$ with the broken axle]$_2$ Jody fixed $\underline{\hspace{1cm}}_2$.

The derivation of this example proceeds just as in figure 9.15, with the semantics of the relative pronoun taking scope in the bracketed constituent above. In addition, pied piping does not need to apply only to objects but can also apply to subjects, as follows:

(64) a. the table$_1$ [the leg of which$_1$] collapsed
      b. the thesis$_1$ [the lettering on the cover of which$_1$] was prescribed by the university

We do not need any additional lexical entires to derive these examples, as the verb phrase itself can be analyzed as $s{\uparrow}np$, and the rest of the derivation would go through just as in figure 9.16. On the other hand, an account of islands might introduce subject-object asymmetries in scope that could be captured by differentiating the subject and object cases of relative pronouns. The subject cases could be assigned lexical entries with complements of category $np{\backslash}s$ rather than $s{\uparrow}np$.

A further pleasant consequence of Morrill's analysis of pied piping is that the same lexical entry can be used for non-pied-piped cases. In particular, the relative-pronoun entry that allows pied piping can generate our previous lexical entry, as shown in figure 9.17. In this figure, the hypothetical noun phrase is immediately reduced by the scoping category into the same category I initially assigned to relatives. Thus we can effectively assume that the relative-pronoun entries provided by Morrill are the only ones available.

It seems that there are categories in addition to the ones I gave that undergo pied piping, as can be seen with the following examples:

(65) a. the person$_1$ [without whose$_1$ sage advice]$_2$
         [we would be lost ____$_2$]
      b. the table$_1$ [every leg of which$_1$]$_2$ [someone broke ____$_2$]

In particular, our type-logical account is powerful enough to capture the scope ambiguity in (65b). We consider the pied piping of quantifiers in

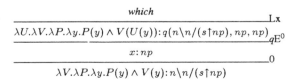

Figure 9.17
A derivation of *which*

exercise 16 and the existence of possessive relative pronouns in exercise 14.

It is instructive to compare the quantificational analysis of pied piping with those proposed for phrase-structure formalisms. In HPSG (Pollard and Sag 1992) and GPSG (Gazdar, Klein, Pullum, and Sag 1985), dependencies in relative clauses are percolated up a phrase-structure tree in much the same way as quantiifcational dependencies are passed via Cooper storage. By adopting Morrill's type-logical approach, we enjoy a logic that explains the similarity between these mechanisms: they all involve the same kind of hypothetical reasoning.

9.8   ELLIPSIS AND SLOPPY ANAPHORA

Geach (1962) first noticed that there was a systematic ambiguity in cases of *verb-phrase ellipsis*, such as the following:

(66) a. Jody loves his mother, and Brett does too.
      b. Jody believes he will win, and Brett does too.
      c. Jody likes himself, and Brett does too.

For instance, the first example, (66a), has a reading under which Brett loves Jody's mother and another reading under which Brett loves his own mother. Geach referred to these readings as being *strict* and *sloppy*, respectively. Similarly, there is a strict reading of (66b) in which Brett believes Jody will win, as well as a sloppy reading in which Brett believes that he (Brett) will win. The possibilities for a strict reading of (66c) are less clear, but a sloppy reading in which Brett likes himself (Brett) is clearly possible.

Geach also considered examples such as the following, which involve focusing expressions such as *only*.

(67) Only Jody believes he will win.

On a strict reading, (67) is interpreted as being true just in case Jody is the only person who believes that Jody will win. On a sloppy reading, (67) can be true if Jody is the only person x such that x believes x will win.

Carpenter (1989, 1994c) exploited the fact that the slash-introduction scheme from the Lambek calculus interacts in the appropriate way with the treatment of pronouns as variables in order to produce a verb-phrase meaning that can serve as an antecedent to the ellided verb phrase. Simply consider the example in figure 9.3. Here the verb-phrase meaning assigned to *believes he is smart* is $\lambda x.\mathbf{bel}(\mathbf{smart}(x))(x)$. In the reflexive case, the analysis I propose in section 9.4 will provide the reading $\lambda x.\mathbf{like}(x)(x)$ for *likes himself*, as is to be expected. These analyses allow us to generate an appropriate reading for the antecedent verb phrases in (66b) and (67).

Ellipsis has subtle interactions with quantifiers. In particualr, quantifiers must be allowed to reduce within the antecedents of ellided verb phrases, as the following example shows.

(68) Francis [saw at least three movies] and Brett did too.

An adequate grammar must allow for a reading of this sentence in which Brett saw a different set of three movies than Francis did. Following the analysis in figure 7.14, we can derive the antecedent verb phrase by hypothesizing a subject and reducing the quantifiers before the subject is abstracted again. The flexibility of Lambek's complementation schemes provides hope that we can maintain a purely anaphoric theory of ellipsis without recourse to either the kind of syntactic reconstruction postulated in early transformational accounts (Sag 1976) or the kind of semantic reconstruction employed by Dalrymple, Shieber, and Pereira (1991).

9.9 INTERROGATIVES

In this section, we consider the syntactic and semantic forms of *interrogative* constructions. We treat both the *polar* variety of interrogative, which can be answered with a simple *yes* or *no*, as well as the related issue of *wh-interrogatives*, which require richer answers. Typical examples of these constructions are as follows:

(69) a. Did Sandy study?
     b. {Who / Which student} studied?
     c. {What / Which topic} did Sandy avoid?

The first example, (69a), is a polar interrogative, whereas the others, (69b) and (69c), are subject-oriented and object-oriented *wh*-questions respectively. In this section I concentrate on questions about singular individuals, but in general, a question can be focused on just about any aspect of meaning. The examples in (70a) are centered on adverbial aspects of meaning, such as time, location, manner, motivation, and duration.

(70) {When / Where / Why / How / How long} did Sandy study?

We take up the topic of questions about time in exercise 21, chapter 12, after I provide a grammar for tense and aspect. It is also possible to ask questions about what activity is being performed, as in the following:

(71) What did Sandy do?

A further class of questions involves comparison, as the following examples illustrate.

(72) a. How many more students like Sandy than Terry?
      b. How tall is Sandy?
      c. How many inches taller than Sandy is Terry?
      d. How much taller than Sandy is Terry?
      e. How many times as tall as Terry is Sandy?

Comparative questions are a straightforward blend of our analysis of comparatives and our analysis of questions. Thus I have left their analysis as exercise 21. We also consider plural interrogatives in exercise 22.

In this section I adopt a rather naive extensional approach to the semantics of questions. In exercise 26, chapter 11, we consider a more finely articulated intensional semantics consistent with the development in this section. My approach follows the spirit of Searle's (1965) approach to speech acts, in which he claims that the denotations of interrogative constructions should also be assigned propositional content analogous to their noninterrogative counterparts. A significant benefit of this approach is that it allows us to preserve our truth-conditional semantics along with the rest of our grammatical apparatus. We reflect the speech act in the syntactic marking of the category assigned to questions, but not in their semantic content. I will assume that the semantics of a yes/no question is a proposition and that of a *wh*-question a property. Thus the meanings of the questions in (69) will be represented as follows:

(73) a. **study**(**s**)
      b. $\lambda x.\textbf{study}(x)$
          $\lambda x.\textbf{student}(x) \wedge \textbf{study}(x)$
      c. $\lambda x.\textbf{avoid}(x)(\textbf{s})$
          $\lambda x.\textbf{topic}(x) \wedge \textbf{avoid}(x)(\textbf{s})$

Polar interrogatives are thus assigned meanings just like their declarative counterparts. The meanings of *wh*-questions are closely related to the content of a noun modified by a relative clause. Such similarities will be reflected in the syntax, as well as in the semantics.

The meaning of a question is intimately connected to the issue of how it is going to be answered. This connection is brought out by the meanings assigned in (73). A polar interrogative presents a proposition. An appropriate answer is an indication of the truth value of the proposition. A *wh*-interrogative, on the other hand, presents an open proposition with one or sometimes more open variables. An answer to such a question is an indication of which values for the open variables make the resulting proposition true. Using higher-order logic, I have λ-abstracted the variables about which the questions are being made. Given the nature of conversational implicatures, there should be many ways to answer even a simple yes/no question with a more informative answer than a simple indication of truth value; in fact, polar interrogatives are very commonly used to make requests or to spark a description of why the proposition holds.

In exercise 26, chapter 11, we consider a commonly employed alternative to the simple semantics presented in (73) in which the meaning of a question is generalized to a set of propositions that the hearer is asked to classify into true and false instances (Hamblin 1958, Karttunen 1977). For (69b), the set of propositions would be the set of denotations of the term **study**(x) for all individuals x. Such an approach naturally extends to the semantics of interrogatives with multiple *wh*-elements, such as the following.

(74) a. To whom did Sandy give what?
      b. Who ran when?

Typically, such examples cannot be used in English except as so-called *echo questions*. That is, (74a) might follow an utterance of *Sandy gave Terry a book*. An alternative approach to multiple *wh*-questions would be to use unselective binding (see section 7.11). Interrogatives can also appear as embedded complements to propositional-attitude verbs (see section 11.1.3).

Syntactically, I will subcategorize sentences into three varieties: declarative, polar interrogative, and *wh*-interrogative. We assume new syntactic categories for the interrogative form of sentences and associate them with the following types:

(75) | *Category* | *Type* | *Description* |
|---|---|---|
| s | **Bool** | Declarative statement |
| s_y | **Bool** | Polar interrogative |
| s_w | **Ind $\rightarrow$ Bool** | *Wh*-interrogative |

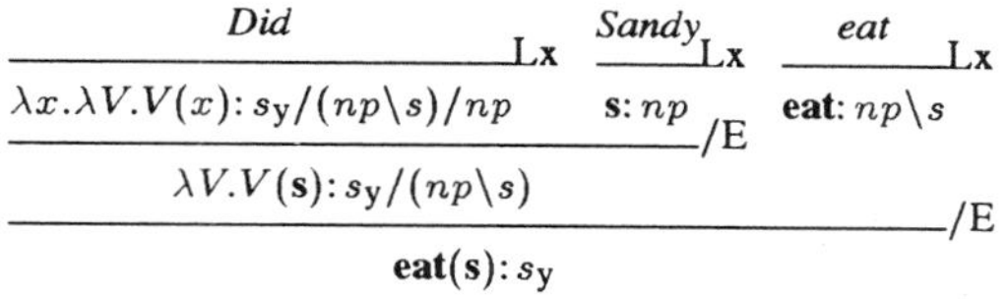

$$\frac{\quad\quad\text{Did}\quad\quad}{\lambda x.\lambda V.V(x): s_y/(np\backslash s)/np}\text{Lx} \quad \frac{Sandy}{s: np}\text{Lx} \quad \frac{eat}{\textbf{eat}: np\backslash s}\text{Lx}$$

$$\frac{\lambda V.V(\mathbf{s}): s_y/(np\backslash s)}{}\Big/\text{E}$$

$$\frac{}{\textbf{eat}(\mathbf{s}): s_y}\Big/\text{E}$$

Figure 9.18
A derivation of *Did Sandy eat?*

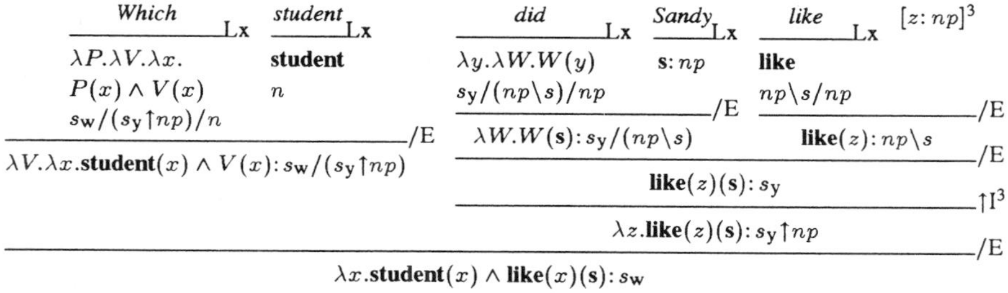

$$\frac{\quad\text{Which}\quad}{\begin{array}{l}\lambda P.\lambda V.\lambda x.\\ P(x)\wedge V(x)\\ s_w/(s_y\!\uparrow\! np)/n\end{array}}\text{Lx} \quad \frac{student}{\begin{array}{l}\textbf{student}\\ n\end{array}}\text{Lx}$$

$$\frac{}{\lambda V.\lambda x.\textbf{student}(x)\wedge V(x): s_w/(s_y\!\uparrow\! np)}\Big/\text{E}$$

$$\frac{\quad did\quad}{\begin{array}{l}\lambda y.\lambda W.W(y)\\ s_y/(np\backslash s)/np\end{array}}\text{Lx} \quad \frac{Sandy}{s: np}\text{Lx} \quad \frac{like}{\begin{array}{l}\textbf{like}\\ np\backslash s/np\end{array}}\text{Lx} \quad [z: np]^3$$

$$\frac{\lambda W.W(\mathbf{s}): s_y/(np\backslash s)}{}\Big/\text{E} \quad \frac{\textbf{like}(z): np\backslash s}{}\Big/\text{E}$$

$$\frac{\textbf{like}(z)(\mathbf{s}): s_y}{}\Big/\text{E}$$

$$\frac{}{\lambda z.\textbf{like}(z)(\mathbf{s}): s_y\!\uparrow\! np}\!\uparrow\! \text{I}^3$$

$$\frac{}{\lambda x.\textbf{student}(x)\wedge\textbf{like}(x)(\mathbf{s}): s_w}\Big/\text{E}$$

Figure 9.19
A derivation of *Which student did Sandy like?*

The readings in (73) can be generated from the following lexical entries:

(76) a. *did* $\Rightarrow \lambda x.\lambda V.V(x): s_y/(np\backslash s)/np$
      b. *who* $\Rightarrow \lambda V.V: s_w/(np\backslash s)$
      c. *which* $\Rightarrow \lambda P.\lambda V.\lambda x.P(x)\wedge V(x): s_w/(np\backslash s)/n$
      d. *whom* $\Rightarrow \lambda V.V: s_w/(s_y\!\uparrow\! np)$
      e. *which* $\Rightarrow \lambda P.\lambda V.\lambda x.P(x)\wedge V(x): s_w/(s_y\!\uparrow\! np)/n$

For instance, consider the polar interrogative derivation in figure 9.18. An analysis of a *wh*-interrogative is given in figure 9.19.

Questions interact with quantifiers in subtle ways, as the following simple examples illustrate.

(77) a. {Which professor / Who} liked every student?
      b. {Which professor / Who} did every student like?

These examples show how subject-oriented and object-oriented quantifiers differ in their scope possibilities. Both questions in (77) can be answered with a simple name such as *Sandy*. The second example, (77b), but not the first, (77a), can be answered with a list such as *Sandy likes Terry, Chris likes Jody,* ... or with a dependent answer such as *her*

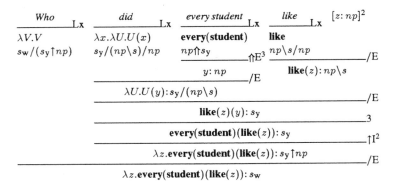

Figure 9.20
A derivation of *Who did every student like?*

supervisor. An analysis of (77b) is given in figure 9.20. Note that I have allowed quantifiers to take scope at polar-interrogative categories. The subject-oriented case in (77a) is analyzed similarly, the only difference being that a slash is introduced rather than an extraction.

Now consider the felicity of the following potential answers to these questions.

(78) a. Sandy.
      b. Her advisor.
      c. Sandy likes Terry, Chris likes Kim, ...

The standard judgement is that the subject-oriented (77a) is unambiguous in that an answer must consist of a single individual (in the singular case), which rules out answers such as (78b), which the pronoun *her* is bound by the quantifier, and (78c). The object-oriented example (77b), on the other hand, can be answered by any of the examples in (78).

In view of the meanings assigned to the questions in (77) by our grammar in (79), a semantic explanation of the scope possibilities is rather implausible.

(79) a. $\lambda x.\mathbf{every}(\mathbf{student})(\lambda y.\mathbf{like}(y)(x))$
      b. $\lambda x.\mathbf{every}(\mathbf{student})(\lambda y.\mathbf{like}(x)(y))$

In the literature, there have been several attempts to provide a syntactic account of the subject/object asymmetry displayed here. Perhaps the most compelling is the analysis of Chierchia (1993), which reduces the problem to that of weak crossover (see section 9.3). Such an analysis involves a kind of *reconstruction* in which we consider how the answer to a question would behave if it were substituted for the extracted element that is the focus of the question. Following Engdahl (1986), Chierchia assumes that the responses in (78b) constitute a functional response such as **mother_of**(x), where **mother_of** is a function from individuals to individuals returning their mothers and the variable x is bound by the *wh*-element. It might be more natural to view this as providing a definite description, such as $\iota(\textbf{mother}(x))$, where **mother** is the interpretation of the relational noun *mother*.

An alternative to the present treatment that was proposed in the transformational literature is to treat the semantics of *wh*-questions as involving question-forming operators that behave much like quantifiers (Higginbotham and May 1981, May 1985, Aoun and Li 1993). Thus rather than the terms in (73), the interrogatives in (69b) and (69c) would be represented as follows, where **whq**^{1} is the one-place question-forming operator and **whq**^{2} is its two-place equivalent.

(80) a. **whq**^{1}(**study**)
      whq^2(**student**)(**study**)
  b. **whq**^{1}($\lambda x.\textbf{avoid}(x)(\textbf{s})$)
      whq^2(**topic**)($\lambda x.\textbf{avoid}(x)(\textbf{s})$)

From a type-theoretic perspective, it is not clear what the resulting types assigned to questions should be if not propositional. One way of interpreting **whq**^{1} and **whq**^{2} would be to assume a meaning postulate that would reduce the terms in (80) to those in (73) (see exercise 25).

Exercises

1. Roberts (1987a) has noted some apparent violations of the principle that the intersentential binding of pronouns is possible only if the antecedent is not within the scope of a quantifier.

(a) If Jody bought [a book]$_1$, he'll be home reading it$_1$ by now. It$_1$'ll be a murder mystery.

(b) Terry courts [a girl]$_1$ at every convention. She$_1$ always comes to the banquet with him. She$_1$ is usually very pretty.

Roberts referred to this phenomena as *modal subordination*. Her theory is that in some contexts, later sentences in a discourse may be interpreted as falling under the scope of operators in previous sentences. Provide logical terms that capture the meaning of these sentences in terms of binding. Provide an example in which a modal adverb such as *might* or *could* in one sentence takes scope over the following sentence.

2. Derive the correct reading for (25) by analyzing both conjuncts as category $(np\backslash s/np)\backslash np\backslash s$. I repeat (25) here:

(a) Jody likes himself and every teacher.

Are there other coordination patterns involving reflexives for which such a structure might be useful? (Morrill 1994a)

3. Provide a derivation for the second example in (56), which I repeat here:

(a) No kids saw each other.

4. Prove by induction on the length of derivations that the anaphora-sequent system cannot result in any unbound variables.

5. Provide an analysis of *Every boy showed himself himself* in which both reflexives bind the subject.

6. How many readings are there for the following sentence?

(a) The committees convinced Francis that they met.

7. Extend our analysis of the possessive to account for plurals. Provide a derivation for (53), which I repeat here:

(a) Jody and Brett's coaches think they will defeat each other.

8. Explain how possessive pronouns like *his* and *their* can be analyzed as being assigned to category np/n in the singular case and np_p/n_p and np_p^*/n_p^* in the plural case. (Hint: Use the plural approach to definiteness to analyze the plural cases.) Then provide all possible analyses for the following sentence:

(a) Jody and Brett like their two coaches.

9. Generalize the category assigned to reciprocals and derive the example given in (50). Does this entry generate the appropriate analyses for the following example?

(a) Pictures of [them arguing with each other] disturbed Jody and Morgan.

You should treat the complement *them arguing with each other* as a sentential complement to *of*; you can ignore the present-participial form of *arguing* and simply treat it as a $np\backslash s/np$ for this exercise.

10. Heim, Lasnik, and May (1991) provide an analysis for reciprocals in which *each* and *other* contribute independent meanings. In particular, *each* gets its distributor reading, while *other* is assigned as follows:

(a) $other \Rightarrow \lambda x. P(x) \wedge x \neq y: n_p$

The variable P is assumed to anaphorically refer to the meaning of some np_p^* antecedent, while the variable y is also assumed to be taken anaphorically. Can you derive the correct form for reciprocal sentences using this entry? What conditions must be put on the antecedents of P and y?

11. Consider the following potential lexical assignment for reflexives, which differs from our ordinary entry in reducing at category s/np rather than at category $np\backslash s$.

(a) $himself \Rightarrow \lambda V. \lambda x. V(x)(x): np \Uparrow (s/np)$

Provide derivations for the following three sentences using this lexical entry.

(b) The picture of himself$_1$ upset Terry$_1$.

The data are very subtle here; replacing the relational noun *picture* with the similar relational noun *sister* leads to an infelitous binding. Further consider what kind of bindings, if any, would be possible with this lexical entry for the following two examples.

(c) Sandy showed Terry herself.

(d) Sandy showed herself Terry.

12. Provide a Moortgat-style quantificational characterization of the plural reflexive *themselves*. Demonstrate that it allows the collectivity and distributivity of the antecedent position and the reflexive position to vary independently, as well as allowing readings in which the individual introduced by the antecedent is bound by the reflexive. Thus you should generate six readings for the following example:

(a) Jody and Brett hoisted themselves.

(Hint: Consider both $np_\text{p} \Uparrow (np_\text{p} \backslash s)$ and $np_\text{p}^* \Uparrow (np_\text{p}^* \backslash s)$ entries, with the usual reflexive semantics.)

13. Provide derivations of the two readings of the following sentence:

(a) Every student doesn't like himself.

(Hint: For the wide-scope-negation case, use the quantificational version of negation combined with argument lowering; for the narrow-scope-negation case, use the quantificational version of negation and argument-raise its verb-phrase complement.)

14. Provide a semantic term for the pied-piping category assignment for possessive relative pronouns.

(a) *whose* $\Rightarrow$?: $q(n \backslash n/(s \uparrow A), A, np)/n$

Use your entry to provide an analysis of the following example:

(b) person$_2$ [the picture of whose$_2$ cat]$_1$ Jody bought ____$_1$

15. Which of the following plurals have a dependent-plural reading?

(a)   The boys had cars that had a steering wheel with a leather cover.

(b)   The boys had cars that had steering wheels with a leather cover.

(c) #The boys had cars that had a steering wheel with leather covers.

(d)   The boys had cars that had steering wheels with leather covers.

What kind of dependent plural readings are possible with transitive verbs, with locatives like *put*, and with ditransitive verbs (both double noun phrase and *to*-complement dative forms)? What does this say about obliqueness relationships and dependent plurals? (Roberts 1987a)

16. Show how Morrill's pied-piping category for relative pronouns can be used to generate the scope ambiguities in (65b) by taking $A = np \Uparrow s$ in the polymorphic

entry (61). (Hint: Analyze *someone broke* as being $s\uparrow(np\Uparrow s)$ with both scopes.) (Carpenter 1994a, 1994c)

17. Provide a lexical entry for *with* that will allow the generation of the following noun phrases involving predicate relatives.

(a) the student with Jody [annoying him]

(b) the student with Sandy [after him]

18. Consider the problems for the combination of quantification and anaphora that is posed by the following so-called *Bach-Peters sentence* (Bach 1968).

(a) [Every pilot who shot at it$_1$]$_2$ hit [some MIG that chased him$_2$]$_1$.

Without worrying about grammatical derivations, provide a first-order logical formula that captures the meaning of this example. Why is it unproblematic to interpret the following type of example using a Montagovian approach to pronouns?

(b) [Every pilot who shot at some MIG that chased him$_1$]$_1$ escaped.

19. Consider the following examples of so-called *antecedent-contained deletion*.

(a) Sandy greeted every student that Terry did.

(b) Sandy gave a book to every student that Terry did.

Independent of considerations of compositional grammar, what meanings should be assigned to these examples? Assuming, following Jacobson (1992), that the ellided element is a transitive verb phrase, show how the correct meanings can be derived? What syntactic argument could be used to support the hypothesis of transitive-verb ellision in these cases?

20. Extend the semantic approach to questions developed in section 9.9 to deal with pied-piped questions, such as the following:

(a)   To whom did Sandy talk?

(b)   In what city does Sandy live?

(c) *{Every / The} leg of which chair did Sandy break?

The last example illustrates that it only appears to be modificational and complement prepositional phrases that can be pied-piped for questions (other than embedded questions and echo questions).

21. Provide an account of the occurrences of adjectival comparatives in interrogatives, as in the examples in (72).

22. Show how our account of interrogatives can be coupled with our semantics of plurals to derive the appropriate meanings for examples such as the following:

(a) Which students studied?

(b) Which students wrote the paper?

(c) Which students does the professor favor?

(d) Which boys carried two boxes?

Be sure to concentrate on scope ambiguities and distributive/collective distinctions.

23. Provide an account of the following form of *cardinal interrogative*:

(a) How many students studied?

Can your approach be naturally extended to nominal comparative questions, such as the following?

(b) How many more students than professors studied?

24. Continuing on from Exercise 21 in the previous chapter, consider the following example, in which the *than* complement is extraposed.

(a) More students attended the lecture than professors.

Consider the following syntactic assignment, based roughly on Moortgat 1991.

(b) *more* $\Rightarrow$?: $q(s/n_p, s, np_p)/n_p$

What semantic term should be assigned to this category in order to derive the appropriate meaning? Next consider extending the analysis to cases of nominal comparative deletion:

(c) Sandy bought more books than Morgan sold records.

Combining the analyses of Moortgat (1991) and Hendriks (1991, 1995), show which semantic term should be assigned to the following in order to generate the correct reading for the previous example.

(d) *more* $\Rightarrow$?: $q(s/(s{\uparrow}(np_p/n_p)), s, np_p)/n_p$

25. Provide a meaning postulate for the question terms in (80) so that they reduce to those given in (73).

26. Assume the following lexical entry:

(a) *similar* $\Rightarrow$ **similar**: $np_p^*\backslash s$

Use this entry to provide analyses for the following examples:

(b) The three ties are similar.

(c) No students wore ties that were similar.

What is the problem in interpreting the second example? (Hint: Consider the fact that a student typically only wears one tie.) Explain why such an example would pose a problem for any analysis of the dependent plural that treated it as semantically singular. (E. Gettier p.c., reported in Partee 1975)

27. Discuss the relation between so-called *symmetric predicates* and their group and reciprocal analogues:

(a) Sandy met Terry.

(b) Sandy and Terry met.

(c) Sandy and Terry met each other.

Provide lexical entries that are suitable for each case. Next consider the case of more agentive predicates and their relation to reciprocals:

(d)   The car ran into the truck.

(e)   The car and the truck ran into each other.

(f)   The car ran into the tree.

(g) # The car and the tree ran into each other.

What can you conclude about the agentivity of the arguments to such non-symmetric predicates? Do these cases provide support for, or counterexamples to, our theory of reciprocals? (Dowty 1991)

Chapter 10
Modal Logic

In this chapter I introduce the notion of mode of truth (necessary, obligatory, past, etc.). I then develop first-order modal logic from both a model-theoretic and proof-theoretic perspective. Next we turn to first-order tense logics, where we consider both point-based and period-based models of time. After introducing these traditional systems, I integrate modal logic, tense logic, and higher-order logic into our type-theoretical setting. These logical developments serve as the underpinning of the approach to intensionality that I develop in the next chapter.

10.1 MODES OF TRUTH

At least since the time of Aristotle, it has been recognized that the meaning of a natural-language sentence involves more than a simple truth value. In contexts induced by certain higher-order verbs and modifiers, fine-grained distinctions in meaning among nouns, verbs, and noun phrases become apparent. But I have employed an extremely impoverished model of sentence meanings. As things stand, sentences denote one of two values, true or false; noun phrases denote individuals; nouns and verb phrases denote sets of individuals; quantifiers denote sets of sets; and so on. In this chapter I provide a more fine-grained model of meanings based on a richer notion of proposition than simple truth values. I begin with a survey of the motivating data. In the remainder of the chapter I develop the approach to these issues most commonly employed by linguists, namely modal and tense logics.

Aristotle, in *De Interpretatione*, provided a classification of sentences in terms of so-called *modes of truth* (the terminology was introduced later, as part of what has come to be known as *medieval logic*). For instance, a true sentence might be necessarily true, or merely contingent, as illustrated by the following examples (the first example, due to Plato, is not even true when considering the whole world).

(1) a. Humans are the only featherless bipeds.   (Contingent truth)
    b. The sum of the angles of any triangle is 180°.   (Necessary truth)

Aristotle developed syllogistic reasoning patterns involving the modes of *necessity* and *contingency*. For instance, any conclusion drawn from two necessary truths is also necessary. In contrast, any conclusion drawn from a necessary and a contingent truth is itself contingent. Modalities can be indicated explicitly in a sentence, as in the following examples involving necessity and possibility:

(2) a. Humans are necessarily featherless bipeds.
    b. Jo might have run to the store.

During the advent of modern logic, Frege (1892) was struck by the immediate failure of a compositional semantics that assigned sentences to simple truth values. When such sentences are embedded in certain contexts, such as the report of a belief, the substitution of sentences with the same truth value may change the truth value of an embedding sentence:

(3) a. The ancients believed [the morning star is the morning star].
    b. The ancients believed [the morning star is the evening star].

In these examples of Frege's, we have two embedded sentences, both of which are true in virtue of the fact that the morning star and the evening star are both the planet Venus, and hence identical to one another. Of the two sentences in (3), only (3a) is true. Similarly, consider the contrast in the following examples of Davidson's (1967a).

(4) Terry intentionally shot {the burglar / his best friend}.

If the burglar turns out to be Terry's best friend, then the sentence might only be true with the object *the burglar*.

Other contexts induce similar distinctions. Montague considered a special class of transitive verbs sensitive to the meanings of their complements.

(5) Sandy {wants to find / is seeking} {a dancer / a singer}.

We see here that *seeking* has roughly the same meaning as *wants to find* (a relationship I model in chapter 11). The intensionality comes from the fact that even if the set of singers and dancers turn out to be the same in that every singer dances and vice versa, the meaning of the two sentences is not the same.

Verbs and their modifiers also display intensionality. Davidson considered a class of adverbs that are sensitive to the description of an event.

(6) a. Morgan swam the channel quickly.
    b. Morgan crossed the channel slowly.

These sentences could be taken to describe the same physical actions of Morgan: a fast swimming may indeed be a slow crossing. Similar examples occur with nominal comparatives.

(7) Francis is a good Broadway {dancer / singer}.

It might just turn out that the set of Broadway singers and Broadway dancers are the same. Nevertheless, Francis might be good at one, but not at the other. Thus we need to distinguish comparison classes on the basis of more than just their extension.

Tense and aspect in natural language present another context that has come to be analyzed in the same way as the phenomena already discussed. For instance, we have a contrast between the following sentences in the past, present, and future.

(8) a. Jo scored a goal.
    b. Jo scores a goal.
    c. Jo will score a goal.

Similarly, we can see a contrast between the simple, progressive, and perfect aspects in the following past-tense examples.

(9) a. Jo built a house.
    b. Jo is building a house.
    c. Jo has built a house.

The most widely known approach to these issues is that of modal logic and its type-theoretical descendants. In this chapter I will focus on first-order modal logic. In such logics, sentential operators such as $\Box$ allow formulas such as $\Box\phi$ to be constructed, meaning that ϕ is necessarily true. Thus the modes are brought into the object language in order to characterize the logical relations between them. Modal logics were first introduced in their present syntactic form by C. I. Lewis (1914), and a wide range of axiomatic systems were consequently developed and examined. For instance, it is natural to assume the axiom $(\Box\phi) \rightarrow \phi$, which states that if ϕ is necessarily true, then it is also true. On the other hand, we would not want to be able to derive $\phi \rightarrow \Box\phi$, because not every true proposition is necessarily true. As an example of the versatility of the modal perspective, consider how tense logics can be modeled. We can adopt a modality $\mathbf{F}$ such that $\mathbf{F}\phi$ is taken to mean that ϕ will hold in the future. In the same way, knowledge and belief predicates could also be accommodated; for instance, $\mathbf{K}_s\phi$ could be interpreted as meaning that Sandy knows that ϕ. Of course, such systems are usually *multimodal* in the sense of mixing several modalities together. For instance, we might have a predicate $\mathbf{K}_s$ for Sandy's knowledge and $\mathbf{K}_t$ for Terry's knowledge. We can then begin to formulate logical questions such as whether knowledge is closed under logical consequence, or in symbols, whether $\mathbf{K}_s(\phi \rightarrow \psi)$ and $\mathbf{K}_s\phi$ should entail $\mathbf{K}_s\psi$. Similarly, we can note that a known fact must be true, a property known as *veridicality*; in symbols, $\mathbf{K}_s\phi$ entails ϕ. Note that this contrasts with belief: just because Sandy believes something does not make it true.

Kripke (1959, 1963b) revolutionized the study of modal logics by introducing a formal semantic model, based on set theory, of the traditional notion of *possible worlds*, which dates back at least to Leibniz. In a Kripke-style model, a possible world determines the truth or falsehood of every proposition, including modal ones. From the propositional perspective, this move amounts to modeling a proposition as a total function from possible worlds to truth values. As with most instances of type-shifting, these two perspectives are inextricably linked. It is natural to interpret necessity in such a system as meaning truth in every world and possibility to mean truth in some world. The usual notion of truth then reduces to truth in the actual world. Under an alternative conception of possible worlds, they can be taken to represent points of time. In such a system, propositions are functions from times to truth values. With a related notion of temporal precedence, defined as a relation over possible worlds, notions such beforeness and afterness, and hence tenses, can be modeled. Kripke's construction was general enough to encompass all of these logics, although we begin with a simplified version of Kripke's semantics that is in common use in natural-language semantics.

10.2   S5: A MODAL LOGIC OF NECESSITY

In this section I illustrate Kripke's general approach to modal logic with a very well-known example, the S5 logic of necessity. Montague's (1973) model of intensionality is basically a higher-order version of S5. As a result of Montague's seminal work, S5 has gained prominence as the most widely used modal logic in natural-language applications. In this section I introduce the language, the model theory, and finally the proof theory of a first-order version of S5. In the following section we consider Kripke's generalized notion of a possible-worlds model, of which the S5 model is an instance.

First-order modal logic employs exactly the same vocabulary of non-logical constants as standard first-order logics. In particular, I assume a collection **Con** of constants, collections **Fun**$_n$ of function symbols of arity n, and collections **Rel**$_n$ of relation symbols of arity n. Beyond first-order logic, modal logic provides an additional means of constructing compound formulas. We assume that if ϕ is a formula, then $\Box\phi$ is a formula, read *necessarily ϕ*, and $\Diamond\phi$ is a formula, read *possibly ϕ*. The necessity and possibility operators are allowed to apply recursively to produce formulas such as $(\Box\mathbf{R}(\mathbf{a})) \vee (\Diamond\neg\mathbf{R}(\mathbf{b}))$, or $\Box(\Diamond(\mathbf{P}(\mathbf{c}) \wedge \neg(\Box\mathbf{R}(\mathbf{a},\mathbf{b}))))$. I will assume that modals are right-associative and bind more tightly than the first-order connectives. Thus we read $\Diamond\Box\phi \rightarrow \psi$ as $(\Diamond(\Box\phi)) \rightarrow \psi$.

10.2.1 The Model Theory of S5

The only significant difference between models of first-order modal logic and those of standard first-order logic is in the interpretation of propositions. In the modal setting, we take propositions to be functions from possible worlds to truth values. Specifically, we interpret n-ary relations as functions from n-tuples of individuals into functions from possible worlds into truth values.

We also make a standard simplifying assumption that the set of individuals is the same in all worlds. Rather than treating $\forall x\phi$ as quantifying over the individuals in a particular world, we take it as quantifying over all individuals. Thus we will not distinguish between formulas such as $\exists x\Diamond\phi$ and $\Diamond\exists x\phi$, the former of which says that some individual possibly satisfies ϕ, and the latter of which says that it is possible that some individual satisfies ϕ. Scott (1970) argues that this is a reasonable simplification of modal logic even if we want to assume that different individuals exist in different worlds. To achieve this effect, we can introduce a unary existence predicate **E**, taking $\mathbf{E}(x)$ to mean that x exists in the world of evaluation. Thus we would translate the latter example as $\Diamond\exists x(\mathbf{E}(x) \wedge \phi)$ and the former as $\exists x(\mathbf{E}(x) \wedge \Diamond\phi)$. Scott's advice was heeded by Montague (1973), and a single domain of individuals was assumed for PTQ. An alternative to the assumption of a single set of individuals was provided by Kripke's (1959) original semantics, but even that system presupposed that the same individuals could exist in different worlds. Thus in Kripke's semantics, a statement like $\forall x \Box \mathbf{R}(x)$ would say that if x is an individual in the actual world, then x has the property $\mathbf{R}$ in every world. Yet another alternative was presented by Lewis (1968) under the name of *counterpart theory*. Lewis's idea was to have each world come with a distinct set of individuals, with the model providing a *counterpart relation* that linked individuals in one world to their counterparts in other worlds. Both Scott's solution involving an existence predicate and Kripke's models finesse the so-called problem of *transworld identity*. Quine (1960) discusses the transworld identity problem, concluding that the use of modalities in natural language is incoherent. I will have very little more to say about notions of transworld identity or counterpart theory but note that the issue is still highly controversial, even among those who accept the basic tenets of possible-worlds semantics.

We turn now to a special case of Kripke's (1961) semantics for modal logic, which provides a semantics for the logic known as S5.

DEFINITION: A POSSIBLE-WORLDS MODEL   A *possible-worlds model* is a tuple $\mathcal{M} = \langle \mathbf{Ind}, \mathbf{World}, [\![\cdot]\!] \rangle$ where $\mathbf{Ind}$ is a nonempty set of *individuals*, $\mathbf{World}$ is a nonempty set of *possible worlds*, and $[\![\cdot]\!]$ is an *interpretation function* such that

a. $[\![c]\!] \in \mathbf{Ind}$ if $c \in \mathbf{Con}$
b. $[\![f]\!] : \mathbf{Ind}^n \rightarrow \mathbf{Ind}$ if $f \in \mathbf{Fun}_n$
c. $[\![R]\!] : (\mathbf{World} \times \mathbf{Ind}^n) \rightarrow \mathbf{Bool}$ if $R \in \mathbf{Rel}_n$

Thus a model supplies a pair of basic domains for individuals and worlds and, in addition, an interpretation over these domains for the nonlogical constants. Note that our interpretation of function symbols and constants does not depend on a possible world, whereas the evaluation of a relation does. As before, $\mathbf{Bool}$ will be assumed to denote the set {**yes**, **no**} consisting of the truth values.

We can use this definition of a model to provide denotations for expressions in our logic, just as we have done before. We begin by assuming a countably infinite set $\mathbf{Var}$ of variables and treat an assignment as a function $\theta : \mathbf{Var} \rightarrow \mathbf{Ind}$ from variables to individuals. Note that we are able to make assignments independent of worlds because there is a single domain of individuals for all worlds. Because function symbols do not depend on worlds, we can interpret terms as in first-order logic. Formulas, on the other hand, have truth values relative to a possible world. In practical terms, this means adding a parameter to the denotation function for the world of evaluation. Another way of viewing this is as giving a formula a denotation consisting of a function from worlds to truth values.

DEFINITION: DENOTATION IN S5   The *denotation* of a term t relative to assignment θ in a model $\mathcal{M}$ is given as follows:

a. $[\![x]\!]_{\mathcal{M}}^{\theta} = \theta(x)$ if $x \in$ **Var**

b. $[\![c]\!]_{\mathcal{M}}^{\theta} = [\![c]\!]$ if $c \in$ **Con**

c. $[\![f(t_1, \ldots, t_n)]\!]_{\mathcal{M}}^{\theta} = [\![f]\!]([\![t_1]\!]_{\mathcal{M}}^{\theta}, \ldots, [\![t_n]\!]_{\mathcal{M}}^{\theta})$ if $f \in$ **Fun**$_n$ and $t_i \in$ **Term**

The *denotation* of a formula ϕ relative to an assignment θ, world w, and model $\mathcal{M}$ is given as follows:

a. $[\![R(t_1, \ldots, t_n)]\!]_{\mathcal{M}}^{\theta,w} = [\![R]\!](w, [\![t_1]\!]_{\mathcal{M}}^{\theta}, \ldots, [\![t_n]\!]_{\mathcal{M}}^{\theta})$

b. $[\![\phi \wedge \psi]\!]_{\mathcal{M}}^{\theta,w} = \begin{cases} \textbf{yes} & \text{if } [\![\phi]\!]_{\mathcal{M}}^{\theta,w} = \textbf{yes} \text{ and } [\![\psi]\!]_{\mathcal{M}}^{\theta,w} = \textbf{yes} \\ \textbf{no} & \text{otherwise} \end{cases}$

c. $[\![\neg\phi]\!]_{\mathcal{M}}^{\theta,w} = \begin{cases} \textbf{yes} & \text{if } [\![\phi]\!]_{\mathcal{M}}^{\theta,w} = \textbf{no} \\ \textbf{no} & \text{otherwise} \end{cases}$

d. $[\![\forall x\phi]\!]_{\mathcal{M}}^{\theta,w} = \begin{cases} \textbf{yes} & \text{if } [\![\phi]\!]_{\mathcal{M}}^{\theta[x:=a],w} = \textbf{yes} \text{ for all } a \in \textbf{Ind} \\ \textbf{no} & \text{otherwise} \end{cases}$

e. $[\![\Box\phi]\!]_{\mathcal{M}}^{\theta,w} = \begin{cases} \textbf{yes} & \text{if } [\![\phi]\!]_{\mathcal{M}}^{\theta,w'} = \textbf{yes} \text{ for all } w' \in \textbf{World} \\ \textbf{no} & \text{otherwise} \end{cases}$

The clauses for the definition of terms are just as in first-order logic. Formulas, on the other hand, are now evaluated with respect to a particular world. For the standard first-order connectives, the world parameter is simply passed down to be used in the evaluation of subformulas. For instance, $\neg\phi$ is true in a world w just in case ϕ is false at the same world w. Similarly, the quantifier-evaluation scheme simply passes the world argument to the evaluation of its scope. Thus $\forall x\phi$ is true in a world just in case ϕ is true in that world for all values of x. The last clause shows how necessity is interpreted as truth at all possible worlds. In words, $\Box\phi$ is true at a world w just in case ϕ is true at every world w'. Note that the world of evaluation is irrelevant for necessity statements because their truth depends on the truth of their embedded formula in every world. This is the identifying characteristic of S5 modal logics; in the next section, we consider modal logics in which the world of evaluation plays an important role in evaluating modal formulas.

I employed only the minimal collection of logical connectives. Connectives for disjunction, implication, and bi-implication can be defined as usual. Also, I have only provided a definition of the necessity operator. Following standard practice, I define a modality for possibility as the dual to the modality for necessity.

(10) $\Diamond\phi \overset{\text{def}}{=} \neg\Box\neg\phi$ (Possibility operator)

In words, a formula is possibly true if it is not necessarily false. In terms of Kripke's semantic treatment of $\Box$ and $\neg$, $\Diamond\phi$ is true at world w if and only if $\neg\Box\neg\phi$ is true at world w, which holds just in case $\Box\neg\phi$ is false in w, which holds just in case $\neg\phi$ is false in some world, which holds just in case ϕ is true in some world. Thus $\Diamond\phi$ adequately represents the notion of possibility as truth in some possible world in our models. This definition highlights the quantificational nature of the interpretation of necessity and possibility in Kripke's models of modal logic. Note that the duality between $\Box$ and $\Diamond$ is the same as that between $\forall$ and $\exists$ in first-order logic. This is because $\Box$ universally quantifies over worlds, whereas $\Diamond$ quantifies existentially.

With our models, a formula $\Diamond\phi$ can be true in a world w even though ϕ is false at w, as long as ϕ is true at some other world w'. Similarly, $\Box\phi$ can be false and ϕ simultaneously true at some world, including the actual world. Thus we have achieved a degree of intensionality in the possible-worlds setting: just because a statement is possible does not mean it is true, and just because a proposition is not necessary does not mean that it is not contingently true. In fact, we can define the modality of *contingency* by saying that ϕ is contingent if and only if $\Diamond\phi \wedge \Diamond\neg\phi$ is true. In words, ϕ is contingent if and only there is a world at which it is true and some other world at which it is false. Of course, even in the possible-worlds model, a proposition cannot be true and false at the same world, because our interpretation operator $[\![\cdot]\!]_{\mathcal{M}}^{\theta,w}$ is defined to be a function.

We define entailment in the usual way but have to be careful about the worlds of evaluation. If Φ is a set of formulas, we say that Φ *entails* ψ, written $\Phi \models \psi$, if and only if for every model $\mathcal{M}$, world w, and assignment θ, if every $\phi \in \Phi$ is true in $\mathcal{M}$ at w under θ, then so is ψ. We say that a formula ϕ is *valid*, written $\models \phi$, just in case it is entailed by the empty set, hence the notation. We write $\phi \equiv \psi$ if ϕ and ψ mutually entail one another. The deduction theorem will obviously hold, given the standard definitions of satisfaction and entailment. Specifically, if Φ is finite, we have $\Phi \models \psi$ if and only if $\models \bigwedge\Phi \to \psi$, where $\bigwedge\Phi$ is shorthand for the conjunction of the formulas in Φ; the order of linearization obviously does not matter, as conjunction is both commutative and associative under our definitions.

We begin by considering some of the characteristic entailments of S5. First of all, consider the number of semantically distinct modalities that can be defined in S5. Here a definable modality is taken to be a sequence of negations and necessity statements. These modalities apply to formulas to produce formulas. Syntactic modalities include $\Box$, $\Box\Box$, $\Box\neg$, $\neg\Box\neg$ (equivalently, $\Diamond$), $\neg\neg\neg$, and the empty string of modalities, which I will write as $\cdot$.

THEOREM: MODALITIES OF S5   The only distinct modalities of S5 are $\Box$, $\Diamond$, $\cdot$, $\neg\Box$, $\neg\Diamond$, $\neg$.

Proof We begin by showing that these modalities cover all of the possibilities. For each of the six modalities, we can show that prefixing $\Box$, $\Diamond$, or $\neg$ yields a modality logically equivalent to one of the original six. For instance, consider prefixing a modality to $\Box$. We have $\Box\Box\phi$, which is equivalent to $\Box\phi$, so that if ϕ is necessary, then it is necessary that it is necessary. This holds because $\Box\phi$ is true if and only if ϕ is true at every world w, while $\Box\Box\phi$ is true if and only if $\Box\phi$ is true at every world w, which holds just in case ϕ is true at every world w. Similar reasoning shows $\Diamond\Box\phi$ to be equivalent to $\Box\phi$. The modality $\neg\Box\phi$ is one of the originals. The other cases are similar.

To show uniqueness, we can easily construct models which distinguish any pair drawn from the six modalities. For instance, we can have a model in which ϕ is true and $\neg\phi$ false, which shows that $\cdot$ and $\neg$ are independent modalities; obviously any modality is distinct from its negation. Similarly, we see that ϕ and $\Box\phi$ are distinct, as we can have a model with worlds w_1 and w_2 such that ϕ is true in w_1 but false in w_2, in which case ϕ would be true at w_1 but $\Box\phi$ would be false at w_1. The other cases are similar.   □

Of course, there are entailments between the modalities, some of which we have already seen. It is fairly easy to relate necessity, possibility, and simple truth in S5, where we have the following:

(11) a. $\Box\phi \models \phi$
      b. $\phi \models \Diamond\phi$

In words, if ϕ is necessary, it must be true, and if ϕ is true, it must be possible. Similarly, we can argue by duality that $\neg\Diamond\phi$ entails $\neg\phi$, which in turn entails $\neg\Box\phi$.

It is somewhat more interesting to consider relations between implications and modalities in S5 in which distribution holds.

(12) $\Box(\phi \rightarrow \psi) \models \Box\phi \rightarrow \Box\psi$

Thus if it is necessary that ϕ implies ψ, then the necessity of ϕ entails the necessity of ψ. Note that the converse does not hold (see exercise 1). In other words, necessity distributes through implication. Notice that distribution fails if we substitute possibility for necessity. A related result, which follows directly from our treatment of individuals, is that necessity also distributes through quantification.

(13) a. $\Box\forall x\phi \models \forall x\Box\phi$
       b. $\forall x\Box\phi \models \Box\forall x\phi$ (Barcan formula)

Thus if it is necessary that ϕ holds for all x, then for all x, ϕ necessarily holds. I leave the proof of these results as an exercise, as they merely involve applying the definition of denotation. The formula $(\forall x\Box\phi) \rightarrow \Box\forall x\phi$, which corresponds to (13b), is the well-known *Barcan formula* (Barcan 1946). If we were to allow the individuals to vary at each world, we could produce models where the Barcan formula failed to hold. Of course, the converse of the Barcan formula would remain valid. Note that the Barcan formula indicates the position of S5 on the transworld identity problem. The general models that I define in section 10.4 and the modal logics integrated with higher-order logic that I provide in section 10.6 also satisfy the Barcan formula. Given Scott's method of introducing an existence predicate, we can distinguish the following nonequivalent formulas:

(14) $\forall x(\mathbf{E}(x) \rightarrow \Box\phi) \not\equiv \Box\forall x(\mathbf{E}(x) \rightarrow \phi)$

The first of these formulas states that every extant individual in the world of evaluation necessarily satisfies ϕ in every world, while the second states that in every world, every individual existing in that world satisfies ϕ.

10.2.2 S5 Proof Theory

After considering some of the entailments of S5, I will now turn to providing the standard complete proof theory of the logic of S5. I present it in an axiomatic format. As with other logical systems, I assume a collection of axioms and inference rules, interpreted in the usual way. I indicate some of the names assigned to these axioms in the modal logic literature to the right of the schemes themselves. As is traditional, I present the proof theory for modal logic in terms of implication, where as usual, $\phi \rightarrow \psi \overset{\text{def}}{=} \neg(\phi \wedge \neg\psi)$.

DEFINITION: AXIOMATIZATION OF S5   The axioms of S5 consist of all of the instances of the following schemes:

a. $\vdash \phi$, where $\vdash \phi$ is an axiom scheme of first-order logic (see section A.7.3)

b. $\vdash \Box\phi \to \phi$ (T)

c. $\vdash \Diamond\phi \to \Box\Diamond\phi$ (5)

d. $\vdash \Box(\phi \to \psi) \to (\Box\phi \to \Box\psi)$ (K)

The rules of inference for S5 consist of all instances of the following:

a. $\phi \to \psi, \phi \vdash \psi$ (Modus ponens)

b. $\phi \vdash \forall x\phi$ (Generalization)

c. $\phi \vdash \Box\phi$ (Necessitation)

Because I have defined the first-order connectives just as in first-order logic, the first-order axioms are obviously sound. They are clearly necessary for a complete logic. Notice that we now require the scheme to allow modal propositions as instances, which does not affect the truth of first-order theorems, because of their compositional nature. To take the rest of the axioms in turn, axiom T states that if a proposition is necessarily true, then it is also true simpliciter. As long as the set of worlds is nonempty, this axiom is obviously sound. Axiom 5, which is where S5 gets its name, says that if a proposition is possibly true, then it is necessary that it is possibly true. To see that this axiom is sound, notice that $[\![\Diamond\phi]\!]_{\mathcal{M}}^{\theta,w} = \textbf{yes}$ if and only if $[\![\phi]\!]_{\mathcal{M}}^{\theta,w'} = \textbf{yes}$ for some w'. We also have that $[\![\Box\Diamond\phi]\!]_{\mathcal{M}}^{\theta,w} = \textbf{yes}$ if and only if $[\![\Diamond\phi]\!]_{\mathcal{M}}^{\theta,w'} = \textbf{yes}$ for every world w', which holds just in case $[\![\phi]\!]_{\mathcal{M}}^{\theta,w''}$ is true at some world w'', and thus $\Diamond\phi \equiv \Box\Diamond\phi$. Finally, if $\Box(\phi \to \psi)$ is true, then at every world where ϕ is true, ψ must be true. Thus if $\Box\phi$ is true, then ϕ must hold at every world, and hence ψ must hold at every world, and hence $\Box\psi$ must be true. Hence axiom K is also sound. As for the inference schemes, recall that $\Phi \vdash \psi$ holds if the theoremhood of all the elements in Φ entails the theoremhood of ψ. Modus ponens and generalization behave just as in first-order logic. The necessitation scheme should be compared to the universal-quantification-introduction scheme, as its behavior is the same. In words, if ϕ is a theorem, then ϕ must be true at every world in every model, and hence $\Box\phi$ must also be true at every world in every model. Thus the axiomatization of modal logic here is sound. It is also complete.

THEOREM: SOUNDNESS AND COMPLETENESS OF S5 $\vdash \phi$ with the S5 axioms and rules of inference if and only if $\models \phi$ with respect to the S5 semantics.

Proof   See Hughes and Cresswell 1968, 121, 164–169.   □

10.3   INDEXICALITY

The same technique as was used in developing modal logics can be used to provide a general account of *indexicality*. As I pointed out in sections 1.2.4 and 9.1, indexical expressions have their interpretations fully determined by the context of utterance. Indexical expressions include personal pronouns such as *I*, *you*, and *we*, temporal expressions such as *now* and *yesterday*, and locative expressions such as *here*.

The standard account of indexicality, due to Bar-Hillel (1954), involves intensionality of the form found in Kripke's later models of modal logic. Just as we could add a possible-world parameter to the denotation function, so we can add parameters for the speaker, hearer, location, and so on. Then specific constants such as **speaker** can be taken to denote the value of the index when they are evaluated. For instance, assume that we have indices *s* and *h* for the speaker and hearer respectively. We then define denotations relative to a model $\mathcal{M}$, assignment θ, and indices *s* and *h*, just as we did in the modal case; the indices are simply passed down through the recursive clauses, and the indexical constants use them to determine their denotation. For instance, we have clauses such as the following:

(15) a. $[\![\mathbf{speaker}]\!]_{\mathcal{M}}^{\theta,s,h} \overset{\text{def}}{=} s$

   b. $[\![\mathbf{hearer}]\!]_{\mathcal{M}}^{\theta,s,h} \overset{\text{def}}{=} h$

   c. $[\![\phi \wedge \psi]\!]_{\mathcal{M}}^{\theta,s,h} \overset{\text{def}}{=} \begin{cases} \mathbf{yes} & \text{if } [\![\phi]\!]_{\mathcal{M}}^{\theta,s,h} = [\![\psi]\!]_{\mathcal{M}}^{\theta,s,h} = \mathbf{yes} \\ \mathbf{no} & \text{otherwise} \end{cases}$

In this case, the model determines the denotation of the constants, the assignment the denotation of variables, and the additional indices the denotations of indexicals.

This technique is quite general and can be used for any number of indices. Cresswell (1973) generalized this approach to involve a single context index *c* that encoded an arbitrary number of properties that could be retrieved by functions. For instance, there might be a function *speak*: **Context** → **Ind** that maps a context *c* to the individual *speak*(*c*) who is speaking.

10.4   GENERAL MODAL LOGICS

On the way to developing tense logics, I pause to introduce Kripke's general framework for possible-worlds semantics, of which the semantics for S5 is an instance. The difference between the general framework and the one for S5 is the introduction of the notion of *accessibility*, which is a notion of relativized possibility. Formally, we add to the set of possible worlds an *accessibility relation* A such that wAw' is taken to mean that world w' is possible relative to w, in which case we say that w' is *accessible* from w. The semantics is then changed so that a proposition is necessarily true in a world if it is true in all of the worlds accessible from that world. Possibility is defined as before, so that a proposition is possibly true in a world if it is true in some world accessible from that world.

DEFINITION: GENERAL MODAL MODELS   A *general possible-worlds seman-tics is* a tuple $\mathcal{M} = \langle \mathbf{Ind}, \mathbf{World}, A, [\![\cdot]\!] \rangle$ where **Ind** is a nonempty set of *individuals*, **World** is a nonempty set of *possible worlds*, $A \subseteq \mathbf{World} \times \mathbf{World}$ is an *accessibility relation*, and $[\![\cdot]\!]$ is an *interpretation function* such that

a. $[\![c]\!] \in \mathbf{Ind}$ if $c \in \mathbf{Con}$,
b. $[\![f]\!] : \mathbf{Ind}^n \to \mathbf{Ind}$ if $f \in \mathbf{Fun}_n$,
c. $[\![R]\!] : (\mathbf{World} \times \mathbf{Ind}^n) \to \{\mathbf{yes}, \mathbf{no}\}$ if $R \in \mathbf{Rel}_n$.

The pair $\langle \mathbf{World}, A \rangle$ consisting of the set of worlds and the accessibility relation is often referred to as a *(Kripke) frame*. Much of the structure of a general model derives from constraints on its frame, as we will see below. Note that I have again chosen to interpret individual constants and function symbols uniformly across worlds, though I wish to stress that this is not necessary but merely a standard simplifying assumption.

In general models, we define truth relative to a model, world, and assignment, just as we did in S5 models. Here I only provide the definition for denotations of modal statements, as the clauses for interpreting all other statements are just as in first-order logic (see section A.7.2).

DEFINITION: DENOTATION IN GENERAL MODELS   The denotation of terms and nonmodal formulas follows S5. For modal formulas, we take

$$[\![\Box \phi]\!]_{\mathcal{M}}^{\theta,w} = \begin{cases} \mathbf{yes} & \text{if } [\![\phi]\!]_{\mathcal{M}}^{\theta,w'} = \mathbf{yes} \text{ for all } w' \in \mathbf{World} \text{ where } wAw' \\ \mathbf{no} & \text{otherwise} \end{cases}$$

Notice that the only change is that we now interpret necessity relative to those worlds accessible to the world of evaluation. Thus $\Box \phi$ is true in a world if and only if it is true in all worlds accessible from the world of evaluation.

The notions of entailment, validity, and logical equivalence are defined just as for S5 models. In particular, we have $\Phi \models \psi$ if and only if for every model $\mathcal{M}$, assignment θ, and world w such that every formula in Φ is true with respect to $\mathcal{M}$, θ, and w, ψ is also true with respect to $\mathcal{M}$, θ, and w. It is also useful to have notions of entailment, validity, and logical equivalence with respect to a class of models **C**, whereby $\Phi \models \psi$ with respect to **C** if and only if for every model $\mathcal{M} \in \mathbf{C}$ and assignment θ and world w of $\mathcal{M}$ such that every formula in Φ is true, ψ is also true in $\mathcal{M}$ at w under θ.

It can now be seen that S5 models are nothing more than general models in which the accessibility relation A is taken to be **World** $\times$ **World**, so that wAw' for every $w, w' \in$ **World**. But the S5 models I provided are not the only class of generalized models that produce the set of formulas valid in S5. The class of models for which A is an equivalence relation produces the same set of entailments. I leave the verification of this fact as an exercise. In fact, axioms T and 5 can be seen as simply requiring A to be an equivalence relation: T enforces reflexivity, while 5 enforces both symmetry and transitivity.

10.4.1   Classifying Modal Logics

One method of studying general modal logic is to consider conditions on the accessibility relation. For instance, we saw above that S5 results from requiring the accessibility relation to be an equivalence. The alternative and historically prior method of studying modal logics is to consider various modal axiomatic systems. As there are literally hundreds of distinct modal logics that have been classified in various ways, we will consider only some of the more well-known ones. In fact, we will restrict ourselves to the following four conditions for now:

(16) a. wAw' for some w' (Seriality)
     b. wAw (Reflexivity)
     c. wAw' if $w'Aw$ (Symmetry)
     d. wAw'' if wAw' and $w'Aw''$ for some w' (Transitivity)

As usual, these conditions are implicitly universally quantified. Thus seriality says that for every world w, there is some world w' that is accessible from it, even if that world is only itself. Note that these conditions are unrelated except insofar as reflexivity implies seriality. We can classify a number of modal logics based on which of the conditions above they satisfy. I present this classification in table 10.1. Table 10.1 also classifies the modal logics in terms of the characteristic axioms they satisfy. These axioms are drawn from the following list:

Table 10.1
Classification of some modal logics

Logic	Conditions on A				Axioms
	Serial	Reflexive	Symmetric	Transitive	
K					a–b
D	√				a–c
T	√	√			a–d
B	√	√	√		a–e
S4	√	√		√	a–d, f
S5	√	√	√	√	a–g

(17) a. $\vdash \Box\phi$ if ϕ is a classical theorem
      b. $\vdash \Box(\phi \to \psi) \to (\Box\phi \to \Box\psi)$ (K)
      c. $\vdash \Box\phi \to \Diamond\phi$ (D)
      d. $\vdash \Box\phi \to \phi$ (T)
      e. $\vdash \phi \to \Box\Diamond\phi$ (B)
      f. $\vdash \Box\phi \to \Box\Box\phi$ (S4)
      g. $\vdash \neg\Box\phi \to \Box\neg\Box\phi$ (S5)

In all of these systems, we allow modus ponens, generalization, and necessitation. Note that I have also employed an alternative version of axiom S5, for ease of comparison with the other axioms stated in terms of necessity.

We will now consider interpretations of some of these logics. Logic K is the weakest modal logic and characterizes the class of general models. In other words, the axioms of K capture entailment with respect to the entire class of general models.

Logic D is a standard *deontic logic*, meant to characterize the notions of obligation and permission. Here we interpret $\Box\phi$ to mean that ϕ is obligatory and $\Diamond\phi$ to mean that ϕ is permissible. The characteristic axiom of D states that if an action is obligatory, then it must be permissible. System D has also been used to study a system of tense logic in which time is interpreted as being discrete.

Logic T, introduced by Feys (1937), is the simplest logic in which every world is possible with respect to itself. System T is often taken to be the minimal logic in which $\Box$ can be interpreted in terms of possibility and necessity, the so called *alethic modalities*.

Logic S4 is interesting when □ is read as "it is known that." Thus transitivity in this setting yields the notion of *positive introspection*, as indicated by the characteristic axiom scheme of S4, $\Box\phi \rightarrow \Box\Box\phi$. In other words, if it is known that ϕ, then it is known that it is known that ϕ. Furthermore, the reflexivity of the accessibility relation entails that whatever is known is actually true, because we have $\Box\phi \rightarrow \phi$. This last property is known as the *veridicality* of knowledge.

S4 is also closely related to intuitionistic logic. McKinsey and Tarski (1948, 13–14) provided a translation T of intuitionistic propositional formulas into equivalent S4 formulas. They then showed that $\vdash \phi$ was provable intuitionistically if and only if $\vdash T(\phi)$ was provable in S4.

Hintikka (1962) studied *epistemic* modal logics of both knowledge and belief. He applied S4 to knowledge, and introduced a closely related *doxastic logic*, a logic of belief. Here □ is read as "it is believed (by Sandy) that." He took the accessibility relation to be serial and transitive but not necessarily reflexive. This lack of reflexivity captures the fact that belief is not veridical in that it is possible to believe a sentence without its being true. A model violating seriality, so that it contains a world w such that there is no w' such that wAw', would be such that at world w, everything is trivially believed.

S5 is the logic I introduced earlier. Note that the axiomatization given in table 10.1, involving a sequence of 7 axioms, is equivalent to the one that I provided before. Furthermore, axiom (17g) is equivalent, by contraposition, to $\Diamond\Box\phi \rightarrow \Box\phi$:

(18) $\neg\Box\phi \rightarrow \Box\neg\Box\phi \equiv \neg\Box\neg\Box\phi \rightarrow \neg\neg\Box\phi \equiv \Diamond\Box\phi \rightarrow \Box\phi$

S5 has recently been applied in the area of knowledge representation for agents with *full introspection* (Parikh 1984). Recall that S4 yields *positive introspection*, where what is known is known to be known. S5 strengthens this theory when applied to knowledge by validating *negative introspection*, which is formally stated by the characteristic axiom of S5, (17g). Read epistemically, this axiom says that if ϕ is not known, then it is known to be not known.

A number of other axiomatizations of T, S4, and S5 are provided by Hughes and Cresswell (1968, 123–132). I will not prove the various completeness results for these logics but instead refer the reader to Hughes and Cresswell 1968 and Chellas 1980 not only for proofs for the systems mentioned here but also for a wealth of other modal systems and related philosophical discussion. The area of modal logic is a rich one and has not only been applied to philosophical logic, including natural-language semantics, but has also been used to develop theories of computation, including parallel computation (see van Benthem 1988 and Goldblatt 1987 for overviews).

10.5 STRICT IMPLICATION AND COUNTERFACTUALS

The study of modal logics is both historically and conceptually related to the study of implicational logics. The traditional point of view was that the interpretation of implication in first-order logic, which has been called the *material conditional*, is not adequate to capture the logic of conditional sentences in natural languages (see C. I. Lewis 1914). The perceived problem with the material conditional was that it was always true whenever the antecedent was false. But this does not seem to be the way that conditionals work in natural language. For instance, consider some examples from D. Lewis's (1973) survey of *counterfactual conditionals*, in which the antecedent is false.

(19) a. If kangaroos had no tails, they would topple over.
     b. If Chris behaved himself, he would be ignored.

In both of these examples, the antecedent is taken to be false, yet the sentences are still assumed to convey some meaning. For instance, it is possible that such a counterfactual sentence could be false, as we take the following to be.

(20) a. If cats had no tails, they would topple over.
     b. If I had used color pictures in this book, it would have sold 3,000,000 copies.

The other side of this argument is that a material conditional is true if the consequent is true, regardless of the antecedent.

(21) a. If there were no cats, cats would eat mice.
     b. If there were no dogs, cats would eat mice.

Here the first example seems to be false, even though the statementthat cats eat mice is clearly true in our world. But the second example seems perfectly acceptable.

Lewis (1973, 3) argues for a distinction in the approachs taken to *indicative conditionals* and to *subjunctive conditionals*, based on the following examples of Adams's (1970, 89–94).

(22) a. If Oswald did not kill Kennedy, then someone else did.

     b. If Oswald had not killed Kennedy, then someone else would have.

Adams's observation is that the first sentence, an indicative conditional, must be true, given that Kennedy was killed, but the second one, a subjunctive conditional, could obviously be false. Barwise (1989, 107) points out that the indicative correlate of (22b) should actually be the following:

(23) If Oswald has not killed Kennedy, someone else will have.

Barwise's argument is that if one of the conspiracy theories of Kennedy's assassination were true and the conspirators had lined up a number of would-be assassins, then one of those assassins could utter (23) just after the assassination of Kennedy by Oswald to provide the same information as would be provided by uttering (22b) years later.

    A natural modal approach to conditionals in natural language is to embed them within the scope of a necessity operator. Thus, rather than translating a natural-language expression of the form *if ϕ then ψ* as $\phi \rightarrow \psi$, we could translate it as $\Box(\phi \rightarrow \psi)$. We immediately get one of the properties we need for treating counterfactuals: the truth of $\Box(\phi \rightarrow \psi)$ at a world w is independent of the truth of ϕ at w. Thus even if ϕ is false in world w, and hence $\phi \rightarrow \psi$ is true at the world w, there might be another world w' in which ϕ is true and ψ is false, which thus makes $\Box(\phi \rightarrow \psi)$ false. Of course, if $\phi \rightarrow \psi$ is false at world w, then $\Box(\phi \rightarrow \psi)$ is false at any world from which w is accessible. The interpretation we get for $\Box(\phi \rightarrow \psi)$ is that for every world in which ϕ is true, ψ is also true. Usually, the notation $\phi \dashv \psi$ is used for so-called *strict implication*. In modal logic, it is natural to define strict implication as follows:

(24) $\phi \dashv \psi \overset{\text{def}}{=} \Box(\phi \rightarrow \psi)$

If we had taken $\dashv$ as a primitive, we could have used it to define $\Box$, because of the following.

(25) $\Box\phi \equiv \top \dashv \phi$

Here I have used $\top$ to represent a formula that is always true. For instance, we could define $\top$ as $\phi \vee \neg\phi$ for any formula ϕ. Thus it appears that strict implication is a suitable basis for the study of modal logic, at least as it appears here.

    Unfortunately, strict implication interpreted in an S5 model of possible worlds does not adequately capture the truth conditions of the conditional statements discussed above, as noted by Lewis (1973, 4–13). For instance, consider Lewis's first example, (19a). With the strict conditional, this would be read as saying that in every possible world where kangaroos do not have tails, they topple over. But the notion of possible worlds is rather unconstrained, as Lewis himself recognized. Suppose that there is a possible world in which kangaroos walk around on crutches (Lewis 1973, 9). In this case they would not topple over. Such a world is enough to ensure that the strict-implication reading of (19a) is false. Lewis's proposed solution to this problem is to define a notion of *similar* worlds, where, for instance, the counterfactual (19a) is interpreted as follows: "In any possible state of affairs [possible world] in which kangaroos have no tails, and which resembles our actual state of affairs as much as kangaroos having no tails permits it to, the kangaroos topple over" (Lewis 1973, 1). Lewis (1973, 6) makes this notion more precise in defining a number of different kinds of necessity, each of which corresponds to a different accessibility relation over the same set of worlds. For instance, *logical necessity* is the same as in S5, in which every world is accessible from every other world. *Physical necessity*, on the other hand, takes the accessibility relation to partition the set of worlds into those where the same laws of nature hold at each world in a partition. Another interesting kind of necessity defined by Lewis is the rather prosaic *necessity in respect of facts of such and such kind*. Formally, Lewis took this to be the logic for models in which the worlds accessible from w with respect to a set of statements Φ are all those worlds in which the statements in Φ hold. He also defined a notion of *fatalistic necessity*, where the only world accessible from a world w is w itself. In the fatalistic system, $\Box\phi$ and ϕ are logically equivalent. Lewis also defines other notions of accessibility, but the one he applies to counterfactuals is what he calls *overall similarity* (Lewis 1973, 10). More specifically, the worlds accessible from w are all those worlds similar to w up to a "certain degree."

There are a number of problems that immediately arise for Lewis's treatment of counterfactuals. Lewis's approach relies on degrees of similarity of worlds, but the notion of degree of similarity is rather slippery, and Lewis notes that it may have to be taken to be different for different counterfactual conditionals. For instance, consider Lewis's (1973, 10) well-known example (based on Sobel 1970).

(26) If Chris had come, it would have been a lively party; but if both Chris and Dana had come, it would have been a dreary party; but if Sal had come as well, it would have been lively; but ...

Lewis points out that the forms of these statements, as strict conditionals, are as follows:

(27) a. $\phi_1 \dashv \psi$
      b. $(\phi_1 \wedge \phi_2) \dashv \neg\psi$
      c. $(\phi_1 \wedge \phi_2 \wedge \phi_3) \dashv \psi$

Presumably, we could iterate this construction indefinitely. The problem is that if $\phi \dashv \psi$ holds with respect to accessibility relation A, then $(\phi \wedge \xi) \dashv \psi$ holds with respect to accessibility relation A. This leads Lewis (1973, 13–19) to defend a notion of *variably strict conditionals*, which allows different accessibility relations for different counterfactuals. Under his definition (1973, 13), a variably strict conditional is "as strict, within limits, as it must be to escape vacuity." Lewis (1973, 92), in discussing the foundations of possible-worlds semantics, admits that the notion of relative similarity of worlds is vague. In fact, he argues that it is vague in the same way as the statement *Seattle resembles San Francisco more closely than it does Los Angeles* is vague. Lewis claims that this depends on "whether we attach more importance to the surrounding landscape, the architecture, the dominant industries," etc.

Quine (1959, 15) introduced the following well-known example.

(28) a. If Bizet and Verdi had been compatriots, Bizet would have been Italian.
      b. If Bizet and Verdi had been compatriots, Verdi would have been French.

Quine doubts that the notion of assigning truth values to counterfactual conditionals is coherent. Under Lewis's theory, both sentences must be false, as they have the same antecedent and thus must both use the same notion of similarity. Yet, depending on one's point of view, it seems that either one of these statements might be used to convey information.

Another strong objection to the use of possible worlds is that they are rather difficult objects to get a handle on empirically. Lewis (1973, 84–91; 1986) defends the thesis that possible worlds are *real*, in that they exist just as do chairs and trees. One of his primary arguments is that because we refer to other possibilities in language and seem to believe that things might have been other than they are, other possible worlds must exist. The important consequence of this line of pursuit is that Lewis believes that there is a fact of the matter corresponding to statements about possible worlds. But it is very difficult to see how a scientist embedded in our actual world could ever draw conclusions about which possible worlds existed, much less about how similar they are to our actual world. What we would need is a so-called *vernoscope*, named after the science-fiction author Jules Verne, which is a device much like a telescope that allows one to peer into other possible worlds. If only such a device made sense conceptually, we would be home free in a possible-worlds theory. Stalnaker (1984) argues for a more pragmatic, mainstream view of the role of possible worlds in semantics. He contends that they are motivated by their utility in classifying the knowledge of agents with respect to facts in the world. For instance, an agent is assumed to make plans based on which possible worlds are desirable and which are not.

10.6   FIRST-ORDER TENSE LOGICS

In this section we move on to consider tense logics, which are a kind of modal logic wherein the possible worlds are considered to represent states of affairs at different points in time. Tense logics let us reason about natural-language-like tenses such as the future and the past. To this end, they extend first-order logics with sentential operators $\mathbf{F}$ and $\mathbf{P}$, where we read $\mathbf{F}\phi$ as asserting that ϕ will be true some time in the future and $\mathbf{P}\phi$ as stating that ϕ was true at some time in the past. We read just plain ϕ as the statement that ϕ is true now, where now is taken to be the current time of evaluation. In effect, we have what is known as a *multimodal logic*, in which we have two modalities: one for the future and one for the past.

Models for tense logics assume a set of times for their interpretation, along with a basic temporal ordering. Note that in the following definition, the exact nature of the times is not specified. Models of tense logic are standardly interpreted as dealing with points of time, which are often called *moments* or *instants*. But they can also be interpreted with the times being construed as extended *periods* rather than instantaneous points. I return to consider the exact nature of time after laying out the basic logical apparatus we will use in our investigation.

DEFINITION: A TENSE-LOGIC MODEL   A *model for tense logic* is a tuple $\mathcal{M} = \langle \mathbf{Ind}, \mathbf{Tim}, \prec, [\![\cdot]\!] \rangle$ where $\mathbf{Ind}$ is a nonempty set of *individuals*, $\mathbf{Tim}$ is a nonempty set of *times*, $\prec \subseteq \mathbf{Tim} \times \mathbf{Tim}$ is an arbitrary binary relation of *temporal precedence*, and $[\![\cdot]\!]$ is an *interpretation function* such that

a. $[\![c]\!] \in \mathbf{Ind}$ if $c \in \mathbf{Con}$,
b. $[\![f]\!] : \mathbf{Ind}^n \rightarrow \mathbf{Ind}$ if $f \in \mathbf{Fun}_n$,
c. $[\![R]\!] : \mathbf{Tim} \times \mathbf{Ind}^n \rightarrow \mathbf{Bool}$ if $R \in \mathbf{Rel}_n$.

The interpretation of tense logics follows that of general modal logics, where the accessibility relation is interpreted as temporal precedence. In particular, statements about the future and past are evaluated by quantifying over statements about the future or past with respect to the temporal ordering. The notation $\prec$, rather than $\preceq$, indicates that our temporal ordering is the strict notion of proper temporal precedence. Although I have not yet built any restrictions on $\prec$ into the definition of tense logic, I will do so shortly when we study classes of restrictions that have been suggested for the temporal ordering. Whether we take the times to be moments or extended periods will in part determine the behavior of the temporal-precedence relations.

DEFINITION: TENSE LOGIC DENOTATIONS   The nonmodal clauses are just as in S5. For the tense clauses, I assume the following:

a. $[\![\mathbf{F}\phi]\!]_{\mathscr{M}}^{\theta,t} = \begin{cases} \mathbf{yes} & \text{if } [\![\phi]\!]_{\mathscr{M}}^{\theta,t'} = \mathbf{yes} \text{ for some } t' \in \mathbf{Tim} \text{ with } t \prec t' \\ \mathbf{no} & \text{otherwise} \end{cases}$

b. $[\![\mathbf{P}\phi]\!]_{\mathscr{M}}^{\theta,t} = \begin{cases} \mathbf{yes} & \text{if } [\![\phi]\!]_{\mathscr{M}}^{\theta,t'} = \mathbf{yes} \text{ for some } t' \in \mathbf{Tim} \text{ with } t' \prec t \\ \mathbf{no} & \text{otherwise} \end{cases}$

Note that the clauses in the denotation definition mirror those in the general modal-logic definition. More specifically, if we take $\prec$ to be the accessibility relation and think of **Tim** (the set of all times) as playing the role of **World**, then we have treated **F** as $\Diamond$, with $\prec$ playing the role of the accessibility relation. In particular, $\mathbf{F}\phi$ is true at time t if there is a time t' such that $t \prec t'$ and ϕ is true at t'. But note that the past-tense operator, **P**, is evaluated with respect to the inverse of the temporal ordering. Loosely speaking, the accessibility relation is taken to be $\prec^{-1}$, so the past relation is interpreted as the inverse of the future relation. Tense logic does not quite fit into the scheme of general modal logics, because we have two different, though closely related, accessibility relations. In general, a modal logic in which there are multiple accessibility relations over the same set of worlds is said to be a multimodal logic. For each accessibility relation A, the universal and existential modalities interpreted with respect to A are usually indicated as $[A]$ and $\langle A \rangle$, respectively. As usual, we take $\langle A \rangle = \neg[A]\neg$. In our temporal setting, this amounts to the following:

(29) $\mathbf{F} = \langle \prec \rangle \qquad \mathbf{P} = \langle \succ \rangle$

The tense operators **F** and **P** are not interdefinable in a first-order modal setting, even though both are evaluated with respect to the same temporal-ordering relation. Instead, we have dual universal modalities for both the future and the past:

(30) a. $\mathbf{W}\phi \overset{\text{def}}{=} \neg\mathbf{F}\neg\phi$ (Always will)
     b. $\mathbf{H}\phi \overset{\text{def}}{=} \neg\mathbf{P}\neg\phi$ (Always has)

Thus $\mathbf{W}\phi$, read as ϕ *always will hold*, is true just in case in the future ϕ is never false, or equivalently, if ϕ holds at every future time. Similarly, $\mathbf{H}\phi$, read as ϕ *always has held*, is true just in case it was never true in the past that ϕ was not true, or in other words, if ϕ was true at every past time.

Even with the minimal assumptions I have made, the following formula is valid.

(31) $\mathbf{FH}\phi \rightarrow \phi$

To gloss this formula, we have that if at some time in the future a given proposition held at every time in the past, then the proposition holds now. Because of the symmetry of $\mathbf{F}$ and $\mathbf{P}$, we know that the *temporal dual* to (31), $\mathbf{PW}\phi \rightarrow \phi$, is also valid. In general, temporal duals merely involve the interchange of $\mathbf{F}$ and $\mathbf{P}$. Thus, as long as we make symmetric restrictions on $\prec$ and $\succ$, the dual of any valid formula will also be valid.

It is very often the case in dealing with tense logics that we are concerned with making sure that $\prec$ properly behaves like a temporal precedence relation. To begin, it is almost always assumed that the temporal precedence relation $\prec$ is transitive:

(32) $t \prec t''$ if $t \prec t'$ and $t' \prec t''$ (Transitive)

With the assumption of transitivity, we have the following valid formula:

(33) $\mathbf{FF}\phi \rightarrow \mathbf{F}\phi$

Now consider the notion of antisymmetry, which would be required of $\prec$ for it to be a partial order.

(34) $t = t'$ if $t \prec t'$ and $t' \prec t$ (Antisymmetric)

The notion of antisymmetry does not have a first-order modal characterization, as we have no way to make statements about the equality or inequality of worlds.

We can go further than requiring the temporal order to be transitive and in fact require times to be linearly ordered. The notion of linearity only makes sense if we are dealing with temporal instants, as extended periods will most naturally be allowed to overlap and thus not line up into a linear ordering. Linearity naturally factors into the temporally dual notions of left and right linearity. Left linearity allows time to branch into the future but requires that for each future point, there is a unique time line extending into the past. In other words, time is deterministic in the past relative to a given time but possibly branching into the future.

(35) if $t' \prec t$ and $t'' \prec t$, then $t' \prec t''$, $t'' \prec t'$, or $t'' = t'$ (Left linearity)

The notion of right linearity requires time to be deterministic into the future:

(36) if $t \prec t'$ and $t \prec t''$, then $t' \prec t''$, $t'' \prec t'$ or $t'' = t'$ (Right linearity)

Of course, the combination of right and left linearity requires time to fall in a line with respect to any given point in time. But just like S5, whose logic only required the sets of worlds to be partitioned into equivalence classes of mutual accessibility, the assumption of right and left linearity allows parallel time lines, as long as each line is linear. There is no way to logically characterize the notion of true linearity in the object language; we can only evaluate with respect to a given point of time. True linearity would correspond to the following restriction:

(37) $t \prec t'$ or $t = t'$ or $t' \prec t$ (Linearity)

But models that are truly linear have exactly the same first-order modal logic as those that allow parallel linear time lines. When, in chapter 12, we move to a temporal logic in which we allow quantification over times, we will be able to express linearity logically. For now we have to be content with the leftward and rightward versions. Montague (1973), who adopted a tense logic in his analysis of English semantics, required the temporal ordering to be a strict linear ordering, which thus obeyed linearity, transitivity, and antisymmetry.

Another natural restriction on times is that there is no initial or final point of time. These restrictions can be characterized by the following dual restrictions on temporal frames:

(38) a. For some t', $t' \prec t$ (No beginning)
      b. For some t', $t \prec t'$ (No end)

Note that like our other axioms, these are taken to be universally quantified. The lack of a final point of time gives us the following:

(39) $\phi \rightarrow \mathbf{FP}\phi$

Thus if a proposition is true now, there is a time in the future relative to which the proposition was true in the past. The lack of beginning point gives us the dual entailment from ϕ to $\mathbf{PF}\phi$.

An even stronger condition, though one that is not very natural from a linguistic point of view, is to require that the temporal-precedence relation be symmetric.

(40) $t \prec t'$ if $t' \prec t$ (Symmetry)

A transitive and symmetric view of time is circular: going in only one direction, it would always be possible to wind up at the starting point. A transitive, symmetric temporal ordering would simply reduce to a logic like S5, conflating **F** and **P**.

In addition to the lack of end and beginning points, we might also wish to require the temporal ordering to be *dense*. Density requires that for every two points of time, there is an intervening point, which corresponds to the following condition on frames:

(41) $t \prec t' \prec t''$ for some t' (Density)

For instance, the real numbers and the rational numbers are dense, but the natural numbers are not. Similarly, the set of subsets of a set can be ordered by inclusion but does not have a dense ordering. On the other hand, intervals drawn from the set of times and ordered by *complete precedence*, in which every time in one interval must precede every time in the other interval, do form a dense ordering.

A property closely related to density is that of *continuity*, which is a topological notion having to do with the existence of certain kinds of bounds or limits to ordered sequences of times. In a linear ordering, continuity can be characterized negatively in terms of *Dedekind cuts*: a continuous ordering will be one in which there are no such cuts. A Dedekind cut is a partitioning of the complete set of times into two disjoint sets T and T', where **Tim** $= T \cup T'$, such that every element of T is before every element of T', T has no latest time, and T' no earliest time. For instance, a cut of the rational number consists of $T = \{q \mid q < \sqrt{2}\}$ and $T' = \{q \mid q > \sqrt{2}\}$. Because $\sqrt{2}$ is not a rational number and the rationals are dense, there is no greatest rational number less than $\sqrt{2}$ and no least rational number greater than $\sqrt{2}$. Somewhat surprisingly, we can characterize continuity axiomatically, as I do below in (51). For instance, the set of real numbers is continuous under the ordinary ordering, because they cannot be cut. Although continuity is often misconstrued as a stronger requirement than density, it is in fact an orthogonal one. For instance, the natural numbers form a continuous ordering that is not dense.

In contrast to dense orderings, we can also consider the case of *discrete orderings*. In a discrete ordering, every time that has a predecessor has a

Table 10.2
Classification of some tense logics

Logic	Transitive	Left linear	Right linear	No beginning	No end	Dense	Symmetric, reflexive
Kt							
CR	√						
Kb	√	√					
CL	√	√	√				
SL	√	√	√	√	√		
PL	√	√	√	√	√	√	
PCr	√	√	√	√	√	√	√

latest such predecessor, and similarly for successors. In other words, for every time with a preceding time, there is a unique immediately preceding time such that every other preceding time is before the immediate predecessor. We can factor the notion of discreteness into dual leftward and rightward versions and express it as a condition on the interpretation of temporal precedence:

(42) a. If $t' \succ t$ for some t', then for some $s \succ t$, if $t'' \succ t$ then $t'' \succeq s$
                                                        (Right discreteness)
      b. If $t' \prec t$ for some t', then for some $s \prec t$, if $t'' \prec t$ then $t'' \preceq s$
                                                         (Left discreteness)

For instance, the set $\{0\} \cup \{1/2^n \mid n \in \omega\}$ is only left-discrete because 0 has no successor. On the other hand, the closely related set $\{1/2^n \mid n \in \omega\}$ is both left- and right-discrete. It turns out that like the case of antisymmetry, there is no way to characterize discreteness axiomatically.

Table 10.2 contains a classification of some well-known tense logics in terms of their properties on frames. Note that the combination of the conditions of symmetry, reflexivity, and transitivity imply all of the other conditions and leave us with **F** and **P** behaving just like possibility in S5, because these are just the conditions that constitute an equivalence relation.

We now turn to an axiomatization of the temporal logics that I have introduced. I present the axioms for the systems I have introduced in turn. To begin, the axioms of Kt, the minimal tense logic, are merely those of K, the minimal modal logic, along with two axioms to relate the modalities.

(43) a. $\vdash \phi$ if ϕ is a classical theorem

     b. $\mathbf{W}(\phi \rightarrow \psi) \rightarrow (\mathbf{W}\phi \rightarrow \mathbf{W}\psi)$ (K)

     c. $\mathbf{H}(\phi \rightarrow \psi) \rightarrow (\mathbf{H}\phi \rightarrow \mathbf{H}\psi)$ (K)

     d. $\phi \rightarrow \mathbf{HF}\phi$

     e. $\phi \rightarrow \mathbf{WP}\phi$

We have the same set of inference schemes as in general modal logic:

(44) a. $\phi \rightarrow \psi, \phi \vdash \psi$ (Modus ponens)

     b. $\phi \vdash \forall x \phi$ (Generalization)

     c. $\phi \vdash \mathbf{W}\phi$ (Future necessitation)

     d. $\phi \vdash \mathbf{H}\phi$ (Past necessitation)

The axiomatization I have just presented is complete with respect to arbitrary temporal frames. The only new axioms here are the dual pair relating the tenses. Consider $\phi \rightarrow \mathbf{HF}\phi$. This says that if ϕ is true at t, then at all times t' such that $t' \prec t$, we have $\mathbf{F}\phi$ true at t'. Of course, if $t' \prec t$, then we must have $\mathbf{F}\phi$ true at t' if ϕ is true at t. The other axiom relating the tenses is simply dual to this, and thus obviously sound. We will not consider the completeness results.

The set of theorems true in the system CR, which requires transitivity of the temporal ordering, is characterized by the axioms for Kt along with the following axiom:

(45) $\vdash \mathbf{FF}\phi \rightarrow \mathbf{F}\phi$

This axiom is obviously true in all transitive frames: if $\mathbf{FF}\phi$ is true at time t, then there is a time t' such that $t \prec t'$ and $\mathbf{F}\phi$ is true at t', which means that there is a time t'' such that $t' \prec t''$ such that ϕ is true at t''. But with transitivity, we must have $t \prec t''$, and hence $\mathbf{F}\phi$ is also true at t. For the same reason, $\mathbf{PP}\phi \rightarrow \mathbf{P}\phi$ is also true in transitive frames. The point is not that the transitivity axiom holds if and only if a frame is transitive, but rather that the set of theorems that hold in transitive frames can be derived from it.

The system Kb, which incorporates left linearity, or determination of the past, is characterized by the axioms of CR along with the following rather complex axiom:

(46) $\vdash (\mathbf{P}\phi \wedge \mathbf{P}\psi) \rightarrow ((\mathbf{P}(\phi \wedge \psi)) \vee (\mathbf{P}(\phi \wedge \mathbf{P}\psi)) \vee (\mathbf{P}(\mathbf{P}\phi \wedge \psi)))$

In words, if ϕ holds in the past and ψ holds in the past, then there must be a time in the past t at which (a) both hold, (b) ϕ holds and ψ holds before t, or (c) ψ holds and ϕ holds before t. This axiom is obviously sound in the case of left-linear frames. The system CL is characterized by the axioms of Kb along with the temporal dual of the axiom characteristic of Kb:

(47) $\vdash (\mathbf{F}\phi \wedge \mathbf{F}\psi) \rightarrow ((\mathbf{F}(\phi \wedge \psi)) \vee (\mathbf{F}(\phi \wedge \mathbf{F}\psi)) \vee (\mathbf{F}(\mathbf{F}\phi \wedge \psi)))$

This axiom can be seen to be sound in right-linear frames by an argument dual to the one given for the soundness of the Kb axiom.

The interpretations of the logic SL involve frames with no beginning point and no end point, along with all of the assumptions involved in CL, namely transitivity and right and left linearity. The logic of SL can be characterized axiomatically by the following dual pair of axioms:

(48) a. $\vdash \mathbf{W}\phi \rightarrow \mathbf{F}\phi$
     b. $\vdash \mathbf{H}\phi \rightarrow \mathbf{P}\phi$

The first of these is sound with respect to frames with no right end point: if ϕ is always going to be the case and there is no end point in the future, then there must be some point in the future at which ϕ holds. The axiom concerning no beginning is simply dual to the one for no end point.

The constraint of density, which characterizes the logic PL, along with the previous constraints, can be given axiomatically as the converse of transitivity:

(49) $\vdash \mathbf{F}\phi \rightarrow \mathbf{F}\mathbf{F}\phi$

To see that this axiom is sound in dense frames, consider the situation in which $\mathbf{F}\phi$ holds at t. Then there must be a point t' such that $t \prec t'$ and ϕ holds at t'. With the assumption of density, there must be a time t'' such that $t \prec t'' \prec t'$. This entails that $\mathbf{F}\mathbf{F}\phi$ must hold at t, as $\mathbf{F}\phi$ holds at t'' because ϕ was assumed to hold at t'. Note that this axiom enforces the same condition as its temporal dual, $\mathbf{P}\phi \rightarrow \mathbf{P}\mathbf{P}\phi$.

Finally, the degenerate tense logic PCr, where time is interpreted as being circular and transitive, can be derived from the axioms of Cr along with the following:

(50) a. $\vdash \mathbf{W}\phi \rightarrow \phi$
     b. $\vdash \mathbf{W}\phi \rightarrow \mathbf{H}\phi$

I leave the soundness of these axioms as an exercise.

I conclude our survey of axiomatic systems with the quite tricky axiom that characterizes continuity:

(51) $\vdash (\mathbf{W}\phi \wedge \mathbf{H}\mathbf{W}(\mathbf{W}\phi \rightarrow \mathbf{H}\mathbf{W}\phi)) \rightarrow \mathbf{H}\mathbf{W}\phi$

Because we are not particularly concerned with continuity as a linguistic axiom, I leave the verification of its soundness in continuous frames as an advanced exercise.

The question arises again in tense logic as to the variety of the definable temporal modalities. In the unrestricted system Kt, there are infinitely many tenses, because $F\phi$ is always distinct from ϕ in truth value in some model. In fact, there are no implications that hold between the tenses in Kt: every syntactically distinct string of tenses represents a distinct modality. In the transitive logic CR, we also do not have a logical equivalence between $F\phi$ and ϕ, in general, but we do, for instance, have the entailment from $FF\phi$ to $F\phi$ by transitivity. Even density is not enough to ensure that $FF\phi$ and $F\phi$ are logically equivalent, because there might be an end point on a time line. The logic PL has many intuitively natural properties, and we will consider the tenses that PL affords us. Consider the diagram in figure 10.1. The points indicate the 15 positive tenses of PL, and the arrows indicate the implications that hold between them. Figure 10.1 is drawn so that the dualities present in the tense logic are evident.

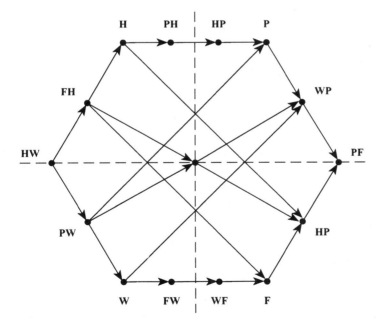

Figure 10.1
Positive PL tenses with dualities

Through the vertical dimension, we have the temporal dualities. For instance, **FH** and **PW** are related by swapping **F** for **P** and **W** for **H**. In the case of temporal dualities, three of the tenses are *self dual*, meaning they have themselves as their duals. For instance, **HW**ϕ is logically equivalent to **WH**ϕ in the logic PL and in fact means that ϕ always holds. Similarly, the empty modality, represented in the center of the diagram, is also self dual as it does not contain any modal operators. Through the horizontal dimension, we have modal duals. These are determined by exchanging **H** and **P** and exchanging **W** and **F**. For example, **FH** and **WP** are dual in this way. The only modally self-dual tense is the present, or empty tense. Reasoning by duality makes the verification of the soundness of the implications much more straightforward, as only one quadrant of the diagram needs to be verified. Just to take a few examples, we see that **HW**ϕ entails all other cases of $M\phi$ for positive modalities M. This is because **HW**ϕ is true if and only if ϕ is true at every point of time. Similarly, if **FH**ϕ is true at a time t, then there must be a time t' in the future with respect to t such that ϕ always held in the past with respect to t'. Since we have linear time lines in PL, this means that ϕ always held in the past with respect to t, and hence **H**ϕ must be true at t. The other implications can be verified in a similar fashion.

10.7   TENSE LOGIC AND NATURAL LANGUAGE

Tense logic was developed in part to provide a model of the *tenses* in natural language. In English, we can specify that an event occurred in the past, present, or future, as we saw in (8). It is natural to assume that tense logic would be useful in analyzing simple tenses, as follows:

(52) a. *Jo ran* $\Rightarrow$ **P run**(**j**)
     b. *Jo runs* $\Rightarrow$ **run**(**j**)
     c. *Jo will run* $\Rightarrow$ **F run**(**j**)

Note that each tense is realized as a (possibly null) modal operator applied to a proposition. I address the grammatical issues of how to generate such logical formulas in chapter 12, which can be carried out using control analogously to our treatment of negation.

With the power of tense logic at our disposal, we can even categorize propositions involving eternal past truth, by using the universal modality **H**.

(53) *Jo always liked Francis* $\Rightarrow$ **H like**(**j**, **f**)

As with most quantification in English, adverbs such as *always* are usually not intended literally and completely. For instance, before Jo and Francis were born, the issue is moot. It might also be argued that such sentences allow exceptions as well, such as a short period of time in which Jo did not like Francis. We will not consider such possibilities here but rather will focus on the basic logical structure of tenses.

For sentences such as *Everyone ran*, which involves a quantified subject and tensed verb, we have two representational possibilities: $(\forall x)\mathbf{P}\ \mathbf{run}(x)$ and $\mathbf{P}(\forall x)\mathbf{run}(x)$. The latter reading requires a particular time in the past at which everyone ran, whereas the former only requires that for every person, there is a time at which he ran. Of course, there would be no logical difference with an existential subject, as in *Someone ran*, because quantifiers in the definitions of modalities commute just like other quantifiers.

It is a significant generalization concerning natural-language tenses that they do not enter into relative scope relations. For a start, we do not find natural languages that allow the nesting of tenses at the morphological level, allowing, say, two past markers or a past and a future marker to attach to a verb stem. Even more strikingly, syntactic nesting does not lead to semantic nesting, as the following examples illustrate:

(54) a. Jo wanted to be in Paris now.
     b. Jo will discover that Francis ran.

For instance, even if we go beyond first-order logic, the first example cannot be translated as $\mathbf{P}\ \mathbf{want}(\mathbf{j}, \mathbf{in}(\mathbf{j}, \mathbf{paris}))$; the property of being in Paris is to be evaluated with respect to the current time. The first example also involves the indexical temporal modifier *now*, which is always interpreted relative to the present time. Note that #*Jo ran now* and #*Jo will run now* are infelicitous (although the second does appear to have an interpretation fully in the present, this is probably because the element *now* is so strictly indexical that the verb *will* is being used as a future tense relative to its utterance and *now* as a speech-time indexical at its time of utterance). In the second example, (54b), Francis must have run in the past relative to the speech time, not the time by which Jo makes his discovery.

Verbs are clearly subject to temporal interpretations. Nouns also appear to enter into temporal relations.

(55) a. Every admiral was once a cadet.
     b. Every president will face similar difficulties.

In the first example, (55a), due to Hinrichs (1986), a natural interpretation of the subject is in the present, whereas the object is naturally interpreted within the scope of the past-tense operator. This would lead to a reading such as $(\forall x)(\mathbf{admiral}(x) \rightarrow \mathbf{P}\ \mathbf{cadet}(x))$. The second example, (55b), seems most naturally to involve quantification over every future president, regardless of their time in office, and interprets the tenses in a dependent matter. Another natural interpretation would be over all current presidents.

In modal logics, nonlogical constants cannot be interpreted as possible worlds or times. In the case of worlds, this has often been cited as an advantage of Montague's basic type theory in which no expressions were typed to refer to possible worlds. But such a move is problematic for tenses, because it seems that there are at least two ways in which languages refer explicitly to times. First, we can place constraints on the time at which an event occurred.

(56) Jo ran at 5 p.m.

Expressions such as *5 p.m.* and *on Tuesday* can be incorporated as intersective propositional modifiers. For instance, suppose that the predicate $\mathbf{at}(\mathbf{5\ p.m.})$ is true only at times that are 5 o'clock in the afternoon. Then we can interpret the above sentence as $\mathbf{P}(\mathbf{run}(\mathbf{j}) \wedge \mathbf{at}(\mathbf{5\ p.m.}))$. Of course, subexpressions such as **5 p.m.** must denote in the domain of individuals because nonlogical constants cannot take denotations in the domain of times or possible worlds. In section 10.3 we consider how indexical expressions, including temporal instances such as *now* and *last Tuesday*, can be anchored contextually.

In addition to the time of an event, its duration may also be specified directly:

(57) a. Jo ran for an hour.
      b. Jo built a house in a year.

The proper treatment of such modification is truly beyond the tense-logical approach. For instance, we might analyze (57a) along the same lines as a quantificational adverb, requiring that there be an hour-long stretch at each time of which Jo was running. But such a move makes little sense in the case of (57b), which states that the whole building process was an event that lasted for a year. Such examples have led to the introduction of interval-based tense logics, in which points of time are replaced by intervals. In the case of the real numbers, such a move is straightforward: we can simply assume that the domain **Tim** of times contains intervals and that relations take a temporal argument that is an interval rather than a point of time. We will consider such a model in section 10.8.

10.8   TEMPORAL-PERIOD STRUCTURES

In this section we study the role of extended temporal periods from both logical and natural-language perspectives. The grounding of the semantics of tense and aspect in period-based semantics is fairly typical of serious studies of natural-language tense and aspect, as evidenced by the important work of Kamp (1979), van Benthem (1979), Dowty (1979a, 1982a), Bach (1980b, 1981b, 1986), Moens and Steedman (1988), Hinrichs (1988), and many others. The move to temporal periods allows us directly to account for a number of phenomena, such as duration adverbials like *for an hour* and inclusion intervals like *while Sandy sang*, as we will see in chapter 12. In this section we concentrate on the logical structure of temporal periods.

I begin by assuming a semantic domain of temporal periods.

(58) **Per ∈ BasTyp**

I further assume that there is a *temporal precedence* relation, which holds between periods of time just in case one is finished before the second begins, which is typically written using infix notation:

(59) $\prec \subseteq$ **Per** $\times$ **Per**   (Temporal precedence)

Temporal precedence is usually, but not necessarily, constrained to be a partial ordering. In addition to temporal precedence, two other temporal relationships are often adopted in models of periods. The first of these is the relation of *temporal overlap*.

(60) $\circ \subseteq$ **Per** $\times$ **Per**   (Temporal overlap)

As an alternative to taking precedence and overlap as primitives, van Benthem (1979) worked with temporal precedence and a relation of *temporal inclusion*:

(61) $\sqsubseteq \subseteq$ **Per** $\times$ **Per**   (Temporal inclusion)

In the rest of this section we explore the structure of models involving temporal periods in relations of precedence, overlap, and inclusion.

10.8.1   Constructing Periods from Moments

Perhaps the most straightforward way to build a model of periods is to take a collection of intervals over a structure of moments or instants under a temporal ordering. I begin our study with these concrete models of period structures in order to establish some intuitions. Over a linearly ordered set, such as the real numbers or the rationals, there are basically nine types of intervals, depending on whether they contain their endpoints and whether they are bounded or unbounded. But the notion of interval as the set of times that fall between two endpoints can be generalized to partially ordered sets of times. In what follows I assume that **Tim** is a set of temporal moments partially ordered by the $\prec$ relation. The relation $\preceq$ is defined as usual by assuming that $t_1 \preceq t_2$ holds if and only if $t_1 \prec t_2$ or $t_1 = t_2$.

DEFINITION: BOUNDED INTERVALS

a. $(t_1, t_2) \stackrel{\text{def}}{=} \{t \mid t_1 \prec t \prec t_2\}$ (Open bounded interval)

b. $[t_1, t_2] \stackrel{\text{def}}{=} \{t \mid t_1 \preceq t \preceq t_2\}$ (Closed bounded interval)

c. $[t_1, t_2) \stackrel{\text{def}}{=} \{t \mid t_1 \preceq t \prec t_2\}$ (Right semiopen interval)

d. $(t_1, t_2] \stackrel{\text{def}}{=} \{t \mid t_1 \prec t \preceq t_2\}$ (Left semiopen interval)

In these intervals, t_1 is said to be the *beginning point* and t_2 the *end point*. If an interval contains its beginning point (end point) it is said to be *closed* on the left (right). Otherwise, it is said to be *open*. Note that the *empty interval* is an instance of an open bounded interval in which the beginning and end points are the same, because $\emptyset = (t, t)$ for any moment t. We usually consider models without the empty interval. Further note that singleton intervals consisting of just the point t can be defined as the bounded closed interval $[t, t] = \{t\}$. Over a discrete ordering such as the natural numbers or integers, every open interval is also a closed interval and vice versa. This is not the case for the rational numbers or the real numbers, which are not discrete orderings. The *unbounded intervals* are similar to the bounded ones, but extend to infinity in one or both directions, and they may be closed or open on their bounded side.

DEFINITION: UNBOUNDED INTERVALS

a. $[t_1, \infty) \stackrel{\text{def}}{=} \{t \mid t_1 \preceq t\}$

b. $(t_1, \infty) \stackrel{\text{def}}{=} \{t \mid t_1 \prec t\}$

c. $(-\infty, \infty) \stackrel{\text{def}}{=} \{t \mid t \in \textbf{Tim}\}$

d. $(-\infty, t_2] \stackrel{\text{def}}{=} \{t \mid t \preceq t_2\}$

e. $(-\infty, t_2) \stackrel{\text{def}}{=} \{t \mid t \prec t_2\}$

We might consider adding distinguished temporal points ∞ and $-\infty$ ordered in the obvious way, in which case the unbounded intervals can be defined as open intervals with ∞ or $-\infty$ as endpoints.

Over a linear ordering, the intervals correspond exactly to the *convex sets*. But the notion of convexity is more general in that in arbitrary, nonlinear orderings, not every convex set is necessarily definable as an interval.

DEFINITION: CONVEX SET   A set $T \subseteq$ **Tim** is said to be *convex* if and only if for every $t_1, t_2 \in T$ and every $t \in$ **Tim** such that $t_1 \preceq t \preceq t_2$, we have $t \in T$.

In other words, a convex set contains any point that falls between any other two points in the set. The intervals are convex by definition. In standard two (or higher) dimensional Euclidean space, a set of points is said to be convex if for any two points in the set, every point on the line between them is also in the set. We are dealing with a generalization of convexity to orderings rather than to space.

With intervals, or in fact any set of subsets of **Per**, we can naturally define notions of precedence, overlap, and inclusion.

(62) a. $T_1 \prec T_2$ if and only if $t_1 \prec t_2$ for every $t_1 \in T_1$ and every $t_2 \in T_2$
                                                                                   (Precedence)
      b. $T_1 \circ T_2$ if and only if $T_1 \cap T_2$ is nonempty   (Overlap)
      c. $T_1 \sqsubseteq T_2$ if and only if $T_1 \subseteq T_2$ (Inclusion)

If our periods are built up from linear orderings of moments, the relations of inclusion and overlap are interdefinable.

(63) a. $T_1 \circ T_2$ if and only if there is some T such that $T \sqsubseteq T_1$ and $T \sqsubseteq T_2$
      b. $T_1 \sqsubseteq T_2$ if and only if for every T, if $T \circ T_1$ then $T \circ T_2$

Thus from the perspective of moments ordered like the reals or the rationals, either inclusion or overlap suffices as a semantic primitive.

10.8.2 Constructing Moments from Periods

So far we have only considered building periods out of sets of moments. In this section we consider the converse construction of a set of moments from a period structure. This idea has a long tradition in philosophy. Whitehead (1929) suggested that the notion of time itself is not primitive but rather is built up from the notion of events structured by temporal relations. Rather than viewing the members of the semantic domain **Per** as times, we thus might view them as events. Presumably not all such events are instantaneous; they might also be extended in duration. Whitehead's position raises the thorny metaphysical question of whether we should identify two events that occupy exactly the same stretch of time and space (see the essays in Davidson 1980 for discussion and further references). Russell (1956) sharpened Whitehead's position by adopting a realist posi- tion (see section 1.1.3) and arguing that claims about events and their temporal structure amount to empirical claims about the observable world. He argued that such observations are not instantaneous but extended in time. Such philosophical theorizing leads to the logical question of how the notion of a temporal moment, consisting of a durationless event, can be defined in terms of temporal periods and relations between them.

Several methods have been proposed for constructing moments from periods. We first consider Russell's (1956) construction, which builds moment structures out of period structures with overlap and precedence relations. To this end, I define the notion of a period structure on which I will base the construction. As usual, we take $T_1 \not\prec T_2$ if and only if it is not the case that $T_1 \prec T_2$.

DEFINITION: PERIODS WITH OVERLAP AND PRECEDENCE   A *temporal-period structure with overlap and precedence* is a tuple $\langle \mathbf{Per}, \prec, \circ \rangle$ such that for all $T_1, T_2, T_3, T_4 \in \mathbf{Per}$, we have the following:

a. $T_1 \prec T_2 \rightarrow T_2 \not\prec T_1$ (Antisymmetry)
b. $(T_1 \prec T_2 \wedge T_2 \prec T_3) \rightarrow T_1 \prec T_3$ (Transitivity)
c. $T \circ T$ (Reflexivity)
d. $T_1 \circ T_2 \rightarrow T_2 \circ T_1$ (Symmetry)
e. $T_1 \prec T_2 \rightarrow \neg T_1 \circ T_2$ (Proper precedence)
f. $T_1 \prec T_2 \vee T_1 \circ T_2 \vee T_2 \prec T_1$ (Linearity)
g. $(T_1 \prec T_2 \wedge T_2 \circ T_3 \wedge T_3 \prec T_4) \rightarrow T_1 \prec T_4$ (Consistency)

The first two axioms require the temporal precedence relation to be a strict ordering. The third and fourth axioms require the overlap relation to be reflexive and symmetric. The fifth axiom enforces the completeness of precedence by disallowing both the precedence and overlap relations to hold between two periods. The sixth axiom requires every pair of periods to either overlap or have one period precede the other, which provides a kind of linearity to the ordering. The last axiom is the most subtle; close inspection shows that it also enforces a kind of linearity of ordering with respect to overlap. It can easily be verified that the collection of nonempty intervals over a linear ordering satisfies these conditions. But this is not the only kind of set with two relations that satisfies the axioms. For instance, because all of the axioms are universal, any subset of intervals over a linear ordering would also satisfy all of these axioms, as would a number of other structures.

From a temporal-period structure with overlap, Russell (1956) provided a method of constructing a linearly ordered set $\langle \mathbf{Tim}, \prec \rangle$ of moments. The moments in **Tim** are constructed as maximal sets of pairwise overlapping periods. More formally, **Tim** consists of every $t \subseteq \mathbf{Per}$ such that the following two conditions are satisfied.

(64) a. $T_1, T_2 \in t$ only if $T_1 \circ T_2$ (Pairwise overlapping)
     b. If $T \circ T_1$ for every $T_1 \in t$, then $T \in t$ (Maximal)

These constructed moments are then ordered as follows:

(65) $t_1 \prec t_2$ if and only if $T_1 \prec T_2$ for some $T_1 \in t_1$ and $T_2 \in t_2$

Kamp (1979) established the following result:

THEOREM   The set of maximal pairwise overlapping periods derived from a period structure forms a strict linear ordering.

I leave the verification of this fact as an exercise. Kamp further demonstrated that if we begin with a rich enough linear ordering of moments and generate a period structure from its intervals, then the above construction results in an ordering isomorphic to the ordering of moments with which we began. Kamp further showed that no matter how we seed the process with a linear ordering or a period structure, the process of successively generating intervals and generating moment structures eventually stablizes at a fixed point so that applying the operations again results in an isomorphic ordering.

Van Benthem (1979) also provides a construction of moment orderings from a period structure, but he begins with precedence and inclusion relations. For his construction, van Benthem requires the temporal precedence relation and the inclusion relation to be partial orderings. He further requires greatest lower bounds over the inclusion ordering, so that for every pair of periods, there is (in the inclusion ordering) a largest period included in both of them.

(66) For every T_1 and T_2, there is a T, written $T_1 \sqcap T_2$, such that $T \sqsubseteq T_1$, $T \sqsubseteq T_2$, and for every T' such that $T' \sqsubseteq T_1$ and $T' \sqsubseteq T_2$, we have $T' \sqsubseteq T$ (Meets)

The period $T_1 \sqcap T_2$ is called the *meet* of T_1 and T_2. Meets give us a way of combining two periods to get a unique biggest period contained in both. From an event-based perspective, this is like allowing us to take any two events and construct an event consisting of the overlap between the two events. To relate inclusion and precedence, van Benthem enforced the following consistency principle:

(67) a. If $T_1 \sqsubseteq T_2$ and $T_2 \prec T_3$, then $T_1 \prec T_3$ (Left consistency)
　　 b. If $T_1 \prec T_2$ and $T_3 \sqsubseteq T_2$, then $T_1 \prec T_3$ (Right consistency)

An inclusion relation and overlap relation are said to be *consistent* if they are both left-consistent and right-consistent. We can then define a period structure in terms of inclusion and precedence as follows:

DEFINITION: PERIODS WITH PRECEDENCE AND INCLUSION   A tuple $\langle$**Per**, $\prec, \sqsubseteq \rangle$ is a *temporal period structure with precedence and inclusion* if $\prec$ is a partial ordering, $\sqsubseteq$ is partial ordering with meets, and $\prec$ and $\sqsubseteq$ are consistent.

Van Benthem provides a general construction in terms of which moments are constructed by means of *maximal filters*. A *filter* is a set of periods that is *upward closed* and *closed under meets*. Thus a set $t \subseteq$ **Per** of periods is a filter if and only if the following two conditions are met.

(68) a. If $T \in t$ and $T \sqsubseteq T'$, then $T' \in t$ (Upward closure)
　　 b. If $T_1, T_2 \in t$, then $T_1 \sqcap T_2 \in t$ (Meet closure)

A *maximal filter* is a filter that is not properly contained in any other filter.

Maximal filters can be construed as moments and ordered just as Kamp ordered his constructed moments:

(69) $t_1 \prec t_2$ if and only if $T_1 \prec T_2$ for some $T_1 \in t_1$ and $T_2 \in t_2$

Van Benthem was then able to establish the following fact about period structures and their induced moment structures.

THEOREM   If $\langle$**Per**, $\prec, \sqsubseteq \rangle$ is a period structure with precedence and inclusion and $\langle$**Tim**, $\prec \rangle$ is the induced moment structure of maximal filters, then the convex subsets of **Tim** form a period structure isomorphic to $\langle$**Per**, $\prec, \sqsubseteq \rangle$.

Van Benthem (1979) also investigates dozens of additional axioms that might constrict the relations of overlap, precedence, and inclusion. Obviously, we could enforce constraints such as linearity and density on intervals. For instance, we might want to assume that in addition to greatest lower bounds of pairs of periods, we also have least upper bounds of pairs of periods. He also considers requiring period orderings to be *well founded*, so that every decreasing sequence of periods contains a smallest period under the inclusion ordering. A related property is atomicity, which would require every period to have a minimal period included in it.

Van Benthem also considers a range of interesting properties concerning the homogeneity of the structure of time that reguires certain kinds of embeddings to hold among subintervals of the temporal structure. For instance, it is possible to require every nonempty open interval to be iso-morphic; the reals and rationals satisfy this constraint, but the integers do not.

10.8.3 Duration and Measure

One of the advantages of using real-valued intervals as periods is that they provide a natural way in which to measure time. Some metric is required to provide a semantics for sentences with explicit durations, such as the following:

(70) a. Sandy wrote her qualifying paper in two weeks.
    b. Terry has been writing for two years.
    c. Terry has been writing for longer than Sandy has been a student.

With a real-number line representing time, we can scale it in terms of hours, for instance, and then convert for other measures such as days, milliseconds, and so on, just as we did with other degrees in our study of comparatives (see section 7.12).

If we do not wish to assume that temporal periods are intervals of reals, we still have a number of options in terms of defining metrics. We could assume that the temporal periods are intervals over some more general *metric space*, as the term is understood in analysis and topology (Willard 1970). A *metric* in this sense is a function $d: \mathbf{Tim} \times \mathbf{Tim} \to \mathbf{Real}$ that provides a real number $d(t_1, t_2)$, known as the *distance* between any pair t_1 and t_2 of times. Metrics are typically required to satisfy the following constraints:

(71) a. $d(t_1, t_2) \geq 0$ (Positive measure)
    b. $d(t_1, t_2) = 0$ if and only if $t_1 = t_2$ (Extent)
    c. $d(t_1, t_2) = d(t_2, t_1)$ (Symmetry)
    d. $d(t_1, t_2) + d(t_2, t_3) \geq d(t_1, t_3)$ (Archimedean)

If our times are real numbers, the standard metric between two points is the distance between them, given by the absolute value of their difference, $d(t_1, t_2) = |t_2 - t_1|$. Other metrics can be defined corresponding to rela-tivistic time, the shortest walking distance between two points, and so on (see Willard 1970). Defining a metric on times allows us to measure the duration of an interval as the distance between its endpoints.

Even more abstractly, we might assume that temporal periods are not themselves modeled as intervals of reals, but that there is some measure function Dur: **Per** → **Real** from intervals to the real numbers. Such a measure function would have to respect certain principles in order to be a sensible measure. For instance, we would want a measure function to respect inclusion:

(72) If $T_1 \sqsubseteq T_2$, then $\mathrm{Dur}(T_1) \leq \mathrm{Dur}(T_2)$ (Measure inclusion)

Furthermore, if two periods are *neighbors* in the sense of one starting as soon as the other ended, then we want to be able to sum their durations. Two periods T_1 and T_2 are said to be *neighbors* if and only if they do not overlap, so $\neg T_1 \circ T_2$, and if there is no interval between them, so that there is no T_3 such that $T_1 \prec T_3 \prec T_2$. Now if $T_1 \sqcup T_2$ is the least interval containing both T_1 and T_2, we could enforce *additivity* (van Benthem 1979):

(73) $\mathrm{Dur}(T_1 \sqcup T_2) = \mathrm{Dur}(T_1) + \mathrm{Dur}(T_2)$ (Measure additivity)

In the absence of least upper bounds, we might simply require the following inequality:

(74) $\mathrm{Dur}(T) \geq \mathrm{Dur}(T_1) + \mathrm{Dur}(T_2)$ if $\neg T_1 \circ T_2$, $T_1 \sqsubseteq T$, and $T_2 \sqsubseteq T$
                                                                (Weak measure additivity)

This will at least guarantee some semblance of naturalness to the measure functions. In the remainder of this development, I will employ intervals constructed from real numbers under the standard distance metric.

10.9   HIGHER-ORDER MODAL LOGIC

There are two standard approaches to integrating modal extensions and higher-order extensions to first-order logic. The first method is simply to use higher-order logic with an additional index of evaluation for worlds or times. This was the approach introduced by Montague (1973), and followed by the standard semantics textbooks (Dowty, Wall, and Peters 1981; McCawley 1981; Chierchia and McConnell-Ginet 1990; Gamut 1991b). Morrill (1994a) provides an excellent introduction to Montague's intensional logic from a type-logical perspective, introducing categorial connectives to deal with abstraction and application over worlds. As I discuss in exercise 17, there are two primary drawbacks to simply intensionalizing higher-order logic. First, it complicates the behavior of λ-

abstraction, which interacts with the implicit abstraction over possible worlds. This is evidenced by the fact that β-conversion fails to hold in all contexts. Second and more significant, with an intensional approach to modalities there is no way for an object-language expression to directly refer to the world or time indices. While this deficiency can be remedied in some cases (see exercises 14 and 15), it is logically and conceptually much more straightforward to simply sidestep the problem.

Instead of employing an intensionalized version of higher-order logic, I follow Gallin (1975) in taking the domains of worlds and times to be basic types on a par with the domains of individuals and truth values. Gallin's approach is logically more straightforward, and it can be employed without loss of generality. Not only can Gallin's logic represent everything in Montague's logic; it is actually a good deal more flexible in allowing nonlogical constants to directly pick out possible worlds and times. Gallin's coding of Montague's grammar in this way is achieved by means of what is known as *correspondence theory*; we consider the first-order case in exercise 12. The remainder of this section will develop the notion of correspondence for the higher-order case. We will concentrate on integrating possible worlds, which we employ in the next chapter. We return to the integration of tense and higher-order logic in chapter 12.

Under the typed approach, worlds are treated on a par with other individuals, with a type **World** being introduced for possible worlds. The rest of higher-order logic is maintained as it stands; there are no further complications induced by additional types. But in addition to the type **Bool** of truth values, we have the richer type **World** $\rightarrow$ **Bool** of *propositions*, which I abbreviate as follows:

(75) **Prop** $\overset{\text{def}}{=}$ **World** $\rightarrow$ **Ind**

By adopting this approach, we can treat a proposition as providing a sense, and its corresponding boolean value at a world as providing a referent. This is consistent with Frege's (1892) view, sharpened by Carnap (1947) and Church (1951), that the sense of an expression should fully determine its referent.

We can lift our higher-order logical operations from **Bool** to **Prop**. For the simple logical operators, this merely involves distribution. For the modal operators, explicit quantification over worlds is required. I assume a simple S5-like behavior of the necessity operator □. I subscript the propositional variants of boolean operators with a "p."

DEFINITION: LOGICAL OPERATIONS ON PROPOSITIONS   For ϕ, ψ of type **Prop**, and P of type **Ind** $\rightarrow$ **Prop**, we make the following definitions:

a. $\phi \wedge_p \psi \overset{\text{def}}{=} \lambda w.\phi(w) \wedge \psi(w)$

b. $\neg_p \phi \overset{\text{def}}{=} \lambda w.\neg\phi(w)$

c. $\mathbf{every}_p(P) \overset{\text{def}}{=} \lambda w.\mathbf{every}(\lambda x.P(x)(w))$

d. $\Box\phi \overset{\text{def}}{=} \lambda w.\mathbf{every}_{\mathbf{World}}(\phi)$

Note that $\Box$ is defined simply by quantifying over worlds with the higher-order logic quantifier of the appropriate type. Further note that the abstracted world argument w in the definition is not bound; this provides an S5-like approach to necessity in which the denotation of a modalized formula $\Box\phi$ or $\Diamond\phi$ is the same for all worlds of evaluation. As before, we can define the existential duals of universal quantification and necessity as follows:

(76) a. $\mathbf{some}_p(P) \overset{\text{def}}{=} \neg_p\mathbf{every}_p(\lambda x.\neg_p P(x))$

       b. $\Diamond\phi \overset{\text{def}}{=} \neg_p\Box\neg_p\phi$

We will usually drop the subscript "p" on the propositional operators, as the types of their arguments will disambiguate them from the corresponding boolean connectives. It is straightforward to verify that this encoding is faithful in that the connectives have the same meaning as they would in a modal setting.

Exercises

1. Prove the distributivity of necessity over implication and universal quantification, given in (12) and (13). Provide a small finite model in which the converses fail.

2. Is there an entailment either way between the nonequivalent formulas in (14)?

3. Show that $\Phi \models \phi$ holds in S5 models if and only if it holds in all general models in which the accessibility relation A is an equivalence relation.

4. Contrast the notion of *instrumentalism*, the view that there is no correct logic, with the view that there is a correct logic. Noninstrumentalists can be split into two classes: the *monists*, who believe there is a single correct logic, and the *pluralists*, who believe there might be more than one correct logic. What might it mean for a logic to be correct in empirical terms? Keep in mind that logics only determine the behavior of logical operators, not the behavior of nonlogical constants.

5. Show that there are infinitely many distinct modalities with respect to general modal semantics. (Hint: Show that for an atomic formula ϕ, there are models

in which the truth of ϕ differs from that of $\diamond^n\phi$, where $\diamond^n$ is a sequence of n occurrences of $\diamond$.) Show that there are 14 distinct modalities in S4 (7 positive modalities and their negations). What are the implication relations between these modalities?

6. Show that the axioms of the temporal logic PCr are sound with respect to frames that are equivalence relations. Show that the continuity axiom is sound in continuous frames.

7. Consider Russell's (1905) solution to the puzzles posed by the examples of Frege's given in (3). Recall that Russell treats definites as quantificational, thus allowing two different scopes for the definite relative to the embedding verb phrase. Might it be possible to drive an analysis of examples such as (3) in this way? What would have to be done to the type of definites?

8. Consider an alternative treatment of discreteness applied to nonlinear orderings. We could require that for every time t, if there is a later time $t' \succ t$, then there is some later time $s \succ t$ such that there is no t'' such that $s \succ t'' \succ t$. Provide an ordering that is discrete in this sense but not discrete according to (42). Can you find an ordering that is discrete in the sense above but would not intuitively be considered discrete?

9. Often a model constitutes not only a set of possible worlds but also a distinguished world w, called the *actual world*, which provides a fixed initial world of evaluation. A tuple $\langle \mathbf{Tim}, \sqsubseteq, w \rangle$ is said to be an *actuated model* if w is a world in **Tim**. We then take validity in an actuated model as being truth in w. Show that the notion of entailment is the same in actuated models as in general models.

10. Derive the Barcan formula from the axiomatic presentation of S5. (Hughes and Cresswell 1968, 145)

11. Provide an intuitive explanation for the meaning of *McKinsey's axiom*:

(a) $\mathbf{WF}\phi \to \mathbf{FW}\phi$

Provide a condition on the temporal relations for transitive frames that captures McKinsey's axiom.

Show that a temporal relation that respects *Löb's axiom* must be transitive and a well-founded ordering.

(b) $\mathbf{H}(\mathbf{H}\phi \to \phi) \to \mathbf{H}\phi$

(Van Benthem 1983c)

12. *Correspondence theory* is a means of embedding modal logics into classical first-order or higher-order logics (van Benthem 1984b). Consider the function Cor mapping modal formulas into first-order ones.

(a) $\mathrm{Cor}(R(t_1, \ldots, t_n)) = R_c(w, t_1, \ldots, t_n)$

(b) $\mathrm{Cor}(\phi \wedge \psi) = \mathrm{Cor}(\phi) \wedge \mathrm{Cor}(\psi)$

(c) $\mathrm{Cor}(\neg\phi) = \neg\mathrm{Cor}(\phi)$

(d) $\mathrm{Cor}(\forall x\phi) = \forall x(\mathbf{Ind}(x) \to \mathrm{Cor}(\phi))$

(e) $\mathrm{Cor}(\Box\phi) = \forall w(\mathbf{World}(w) \to \mathrm{Cor}(\phi))$

An S5 model $\mathcal{M} = \langle \mathbf{Ind}, \mathbf{World}, [\![\cdot]\!]_{\mathcal{M}} \rangle$ can be translated into a first-order model $\mathcal{C} = \langle \mathbf{Ind} \cup \mathbf{World}, [\![\cdot]\!]_{\mathcal{C}} \rangle$ by the following:

(f) $[\![c]\!]_{\mathcal{C}} = [\![c]\!]_{\mathcal{M}}$ if $c \in \mathbf{Con}$

(g) $[\![f]\!]_{\mathcal{C}} = [\![f]\!]_{\mathcal{M}}$ if $f \in \mathbf{Fun}$

(h) $[\![R]\!]_{\mathcal{C}}(w, a_1, \ldots, a_n) = [\![R]\!]_{\mathcal{M}}(a_1, \ldots, a_n)(w)$ for $R \in \mathbf{Rel}$, $a_i \in \mathbf{Ind}$, and $w \in \mathbf{World}$

(i) $[\![\mathbf{World}]\!]_{\mathcal{C}}(a) = \begin{cases} \mathbf{yes} & \text{if } a \in \mathbf{World} \\ \mathbf{no} & \text{otherwise} \end{cases}$

(j) $[\![\mathbf{Ind}]\!]_{\mathcal{C}}(a) = \begin{cases} \mathbf{yes} & \text{if } a \in \mathbf{Ind} \\ \mathbf{no} & \text{otherwise} \end{cases}$

By induction, establish that the following translation is faithful.

(k) $[\![\mathrm{Cor}(\phi)]\!]_{\mathcal{M},\mathcal{C}}^{\theta[x:=w]} = [\![\phi]\!]_{\mathcal{M}}^{w,\theta}$

To go beyond S5, an accessibility relation can be included in the language of $\mathcal{C}$ and interpreted as in the modal model. Define the relevant correspondence for formulas and models, and prove that it is faithful.

13. Consider the following sentence and its two potential translations:

(a) Everyone ran.

(b) $\mathbf{P}(\forall x)\mathbf{run}(x)$

(c) $(\forall x)\mathbf{P}\ \mathbf{run}(x)$

Gloss the translations in English. Do the translations have the same truth conditions? Does one entail the other?

Perform the same exercise for the following sentence and its potential translations.

(d) Sandy didn't run.

(e) $\neg\mathbf{P}\ \mathbf{run}(\mathbf{s})$

(f) $\mathbf{P}\neg\mathbf{run}(\mathbf{s})$

14. Explain why the truth conditions of the following sentences cannot be expressed in a tense logic with operators $\mathbf{P}$ and $\mathbf{F}$.

(a) A child was born who will be king.

(b) One day, all persons alive now will be dead.

Note that the first example means that the child was born in the past relative to now and will be king in the future relative to now. Show how it is possible to represent the following closely related example, which only requires the child to be kinged some time after birth.

(c) A child was born who would be king.

Provide a representation in tense logic for this example.

Define a doubly indexed modal logic to account for the behavior of the English expression *now*. The basic idea is that denotations will be defined relative to two indices t and t_0, one of which, t, behaves as in tense logic, and one of which, t_0, is always the time of utterance. Kamp (1971) introduced a syncategorematic constructor **Now** with semantics as follows:

(d) $[\![\mathbf{Now}\phi]\!]^{t,t_0} \stackrel{\text{def}}{=} [\![\phi]\!]^{t_0,t_0}$

With this constructor, can either or both of the above sentences be given a logical translation?

15. Provide a semantic definition of the binary modal operators **S** ("since") and **U** ("until"), where $\mathbf{S}(\phi, \psi)$ holds at the present time if ϕ is true at some time before the present and ψ holds at every time between the time ϕ held and the present. **U** is the temporal dual of **S**, so that $\mathbf{U}(\phi, \psi)$ holds at the present time if ϕ is true at some time after the present and ψ holds at every time between the present and the future time at which ϕ holds. Next show how the connectives **P** and **F** can be defined in terms of **S** and **U**. (Hint: Use the constant **true**, which is always true, to define **H** and **W** first.) (Kamp 1960)

16. There are two well-known translations of modal logic into temporal logic. Under the Aristotelian approach, necessity corresponds to eternal truth. Under the approach of Diodorus, necessity corresponds to truth now and in the future. Provide such a translation of modal statements involving necessity into a tense logic using both these approaches. What is the translation of possibility, and is it still related to necessity as before? Show that if PL is our tense logic and we follow the Aristotelian translation, then the modal logic corresponds to S5. Show that if we take Cr as our tense logic and follow the translation of Diodorus, then we get the modal logic S4.

17. Montague (1973) combined modal logic with higher-order logic just as he added it to first-order logic. From a set **BasTyp** of basic types, the set **Typ** is the least superset of **BasTyp** such that $\sigma \to \tau, s \to \tau \in \mathbf{Typ}$ if $\sigma, \tau \in \mathbf{Typ}$. Model theoretically, constants of type σ are now assigned interpretations in $\mathbf{Dom}_{s \to \sigma}$ rather than in $\mathbf{Dom}_\sigma$ to reflect the intensionalization. Complex formulas are then evaluated as usual, where w is the world of evaluation, θ an assignment mapping variables to denotations of their given type, and $[\![\cdot]\!]_{\mathcal{M}}$ the interpretation function given by the model.

(a) $[\![c]\!]_{\mathcal{M}}^{\theta,w} = [\![c]\!]_{\mathcal{M}}(w)$

(b) $[\![x]\!]_{\mathcal{M}}^{\theta,w} = \theta(x)$

(c) $[\![\alpha(\beta)]\!]_{\mathcal{M}}^{\theta,w} = [\![\alpha]\!]_{\mathcal{M}}^{\theta,w}([\![\beta]\!]_{\mathcal{M}}^{\theta,w})$

(d) $[\![\lambda x.\alpha]\!]_{\mathcal{M}}^{\theta,w} = f$, where $f(a) = [\![\alpha]\!]_{\mathcal{M}}^{\theta[x:=a],w}$

Provide definitions for the logical constants of higher-order logic in this setting.

Montague defined operators $^\vee$ and $^\wedge$ as follows:

(e) $[\![^\vee \phi]\!]_{\mathcal{M}}^{\theta,w} = [\![\phi]\!]_{\mathcal{M}}^{\theta,w}(w)$

(f) $[\![^\wedge \phi]\!]_{\mathcal{M}}^{\theta,w} = f$ such that $f(w') = [\![\phi]\!]_{\mathcal{M}}^{\theta,w'}$

Show that $^\vee{}^\wedge\phi \equiv \phi$, and provide a counterexample showing why $^\wedge{}^\vee\phi \not\equiv \phi$. Is there a natural side condition under which the latter logical equivalence holds? Can this side condition be expressed syntactically over expressions of the object language?

Provide the denotation conditions for $\Box\phi$ in Montague's system. Is $\Box$ definable as a constant using higher-order logic? Provide an example that demonstrates that β-conversion is unsound in Montague's system. What is required to ensure that a β-contractum and its β-redex have the same denotation? Is η-conversion sound in this setting?

18. Show that every open, closed, and semiopen interval is convex. Provide a counterexample to the claim that every convex set is an open, closed, or semiopen interval.

19. Show that the moments consisting of maximal sets of pairwise overlapping periods form a linear ordering.

Chapter 11

Intensionality

I begin this chapter with a grammar of English covering a wide range of intensional constructions, including intensional verbs, control, quantificational and intensional adverbs, and individual concepts. I postpone issues surrounding tense and aspect until the next chapter. After considering the intensionalization of verbal categories, we consider raising the types assigned to noun phrases from simple individuals to individual concepts. Next we turn to issues involving the structure of the lexicon, especially as it pertains to related categorizations of the same word. I conclude the chapter with a discussion of several problems with, and alternatives to, the possible-worlds treatment of intensionality.

11.1   AN INTENSIONAL GRAMMAR

In this section I develop a possible-worlds approach to the semantic typing of English nominal and verbal constructions. I begin by considering the type assignments we will use. I then develop an extensive grammar fragment covering various intensional constructions in English.

11.1.1   Type Logic and Categorial Grammar

The primary motivation for introducing a more fine-grained notion of propositions is to address puzzles pertaining to the semantics of intensional natural-language expressions. We do not need to modify our grammatical apparatus. Rather, we simply lift our type assignments to basic categories by replacing **Bool** with **Prop**, which was defined as **Prop** $\overset{\text{def}}{=}$ **World** $\rightarrow$ **Bool**, where **World** is the type of possible worlds.

(1) a. $\text{Typ}(s) = $ **Prop**
     b. $\text{Typ}(np) = $ **Ind**
     c. $\text{Typ}(n) = $ **Ind** $\rightarrow$ **Prop**

Following the lead of modal logic, we type noun phrases as individuals rather than as functions from worlds to individuals. In a grammatical setting, this route was followed by Bennet (1974) but not by Montague (1973). We explore this choice more fully and contrast it with the alternative typing of *np* as **World** → **Ind**, so-called *individual concepts*, in section 11.2.

Under our new type regime, verb phrases of category *np\s* are still assigned to the same type as nouns. Our typing is nonstandard insofar as we treat nouns and verbs uniformly as mapping to propositions. The traditional type assignment of Montague would assign to nouns the type **World** → **Ind** → **Bool** rather than **Ind** → **World** → **Bool**. Of course, these domains are isomorphic, being related by simple permutation of arguments. Our typing is more convenient in that the proposition corresponding to a sentence can be constructed purely by application. It also leads to a more general perspective on models of intensionality, as I discuss in section 11.3.

A proposition produces a truth value only by application to a world. As in modal logic, I will assume that the actual world is a distinguished member of the domain of worlds. For convenience, I include the constant **actual_world** of type **World**. Thus the extension of a propositional formula ϕ in the actual world is the denotation of $\phi(\textbf{actual\_world})$, which is of type **Bool**. Similarly, the extension of a noun interpreted as a property P is $\lambda x.P(x)(\textbf{actual\_world})$. This highlights one distinctive feature of our type assignment: extensions are not directly generated by applying intensions to the actual world. Of course, such extensions can always be reconstructed by abstraction, as in the example above. I have assigned uniformly intensionalized types primarily for their pedagogical simplicity. Alternatively, I could have followed Morrill (1994a) in assigning intensional types only where semantically motivated, but this move will only work in the context of an intensional logic (see exercise 17, chapter 10) combined with a richer syntactic calculus to control intensionalization and extensionalization.

Our type-logical approach to categorial grammar remains unchanged. I still require the lexicon to assign expressions semantic terms of the appropriate types for their syntactic categories. So a derivation of *Francis ran* will now produce the meaning **run(Francis)**, and *Everyone ran* will produce **every$_\text{p}$(run)**, both of which are of type **Prop**. When these formulas are interpreted, they produce propositions; a truth value in the actual world is determined by application to the actual world. Thus

run(Francis)(actual_world) is a term of type **Bool**, and thus denotes a truth value.

11.1.2   Propositional Attitudes

I begin the construction of an intensional grammar with the propositional-attitude verbs. In this section I develop a Fregean treatment of propositional attitudes, using the logic introduced by Hintikka (1962) in a grammatical setting similar to that of Montague (1973). Such an analysis has provided one of the primary motivations for the application of possible worlds to natural-language semantics. Unfortunately, it also highlights a number of limitations of the possible-worlds approach.

With our type-logical approach to grammar, Frege's intuitions can be modeled with the following category assignments:

(2) a. *believe* ⇒ **bel**: $np \backslash s / s$
    b. *know* ⇒ **know**: $np \backslash s / s$

By application, we have analyses such as the following:

(3) *Francis believes Brooke cheated* ⇒ **bel**(**cheat**(**b**))(**f**): s

Under our type assignment, the constant **bel** is interpreted as a function mapping a proposition and an individual into a proposition. Because the domain of propositions is much more fine-grained than a simple pair of truth values, this category assignment neatly sidesteps the identification of a proposition with a truth value. For instance, it is now clear how sentences such as *Jan believes Brooke cheated* can be given a different truth value than *Jan believes Francis cheated*, even if the truth values of the embedded sentences, *Brooke cheated* and *Francis cheated*, are the same. This approach to the attitudes reflects Hintikka's (1962) modal approach to propositional attitudes. For instance, given a fixed individual **a**, the term $\lambda p . \mathbf{bel}(p)(\mathbf{a})$ behaves as a sentential operator that applies to a proposition p to produce a new proposition. Hintikka's approach was to introduce indexed modal operators of the form $\mathbf{B}_a$ and $\mathbf{K}_a$, reading $\mathbf{B}_a \phi$ as "a believes ϕ" and $\mathbf{K}_a \phi$ as "a knows ϕ." A number of Hintikka's logical assumptions concerning these operators are explored in exercise 2.

As I mentioned earlier, we can enforce the so-called *veridicality* of knowledge with the following meaning postulate:

(4) $\mathbf{know}(\phi)(x)(w) \to \phi(w)$

This postulate states that if x knows that ϕ at world w then ϕ must in fact hold at world w. Of course, this does not provide a complete characterization of human knowledge. For instance, we could take knowledge to simply be a belief that turns out to be true, as follows:

(5) $\mathbf{know}(\phi)(x) \equiv \mathbf{bel}(\phi)(x) \wedge \phi$

An interesting and insightful study of the application of possible worlds to problems of knowledge and belief can be found in Stalnaker 1984. This study revolves around an analysis of belief as a disposition to act and an analysis of dispositions as being toward possible outcomes, characterized as possible worlds.

The grammar I have presented for propositional-attitude verbs correctly captures the ambiguity of such verbs when taking complements containing a quantifier.

(6) a. Francis believes a student is shouting.
    b. Francis knows every student is smart.
    c. Francis knows every student solved a problem.
    d. Francis doesn't believe every student studied.

In the first example, (6a), we have two possible readings, as illustrated in figure 11.1. Under the first, known as the *de dicto* reading, Francis holds

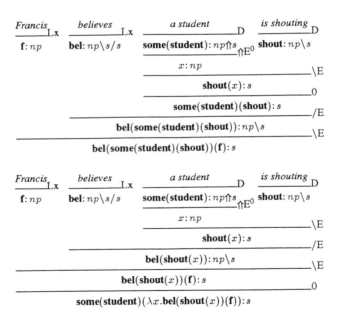

Figure 11.1
Two derivations of *Francis believes a student is shouting*

the nonspecific belief that there is a student who is shouting. The de dicto reading may be true even if Francis does not hold a belief about any particular student. Such a belief might come about after Francis hears someone celebrating the good grade they received on a paper but can't discriminate who the shouter is. A likely conclusion is that it is a student, though, because only students receive grades on papers. The alternative, known as the *de re* reading, states that Francis believes of a particular student that he or she is shouting. Such a belief might come about because Francis can see a specific person shouting and knows he is a student. The second example, (6b), discussed by Russell (1940), behaves similarly. In this case, it is possible for Francis to know for each student that the student is smart but not know that he has exhausted the complete set of students, and thus not know that every student is smart. With multiple quantifiers, the number of readings grows quickly. For instance, (6c) has six readings, depending on whether or not the quantifiers are resolved within the scope of the embedding verb. For the case where they are both scoped narrowly with respect to the attitude verb, there is a relative-scope ambiguity. For the case where both quantifiers outscope the embedding verb, there is also a relative-scope ambiguity. In (6d) the quantifier has three possible scopes: narrow, between the negation and the attitude verb, and wide.

11.1.3 Complementized Sentences

The occurrence of *that* in *Brooke believes that Francis schemed* is said to be a *complementizer*. Complementizers can be found on sentential subjects (see section 11.1.4 below) and are optional for most sentential complements. For instance, there appears to be no difference in meaning between *I believe that Francis schemed* and *I believe Francis schemed*. Following GPSG, I treat complementizers as feature markers, much like the prepositional case marker *of*, the comparative marker *than*, and the infinitival marker *to*. (I provide an explicit analysis of English verbal forms in section 12.5.1.) I will use the category s_c for complementized sentences and assign it the same semantic type as ordinary sentences. Without a treatment of the logic of features, such as that given in Morill 1994a, the fact that s_c and s look similar is inconsequential, because they are simply distinct basic categories. For the complementizers, I postulate the following lexical assignment:

(7) *that* $\Rightarrow \lambda x.x: s_c/s$

A lexical category for *believe* that takes a complementized complement would be $np\backslash s/s_c$ and would have the same semantic-term assignment as the instance of *believe* of category $np\backslash s/s$. With such a category, *believe* and *believe that* would have the same category in our grammar. While often alike in meaning, complementized and noncomplementized sentential objects often vary syntactically in terms of islandhood. The canonical example is the following from Perlmutter 1971.

(8) a.   Who$_1$ do you believe _____$_1$ ran?
   b. *Who$_1$ do you believe that _____$_1$ ran?

It appears that complementized sentences do not allow their subjects to enter into long-distance dependencies. Most theories of syntax try to provide an explanation of this fact, but I will not. Other complementizers in English are *whether* and *if*, though both of these appear to be closely related to interrogative constructions. They typically mark complements of attitude verbs such as *wonder* and *asked*.

(9) a.   Francis {wondered / asked / knew} if Brooke was bowling.
   b.   Francis {wondered / asked / knew} whether Brooke would get a high score.

Semantically, these cases can be treated in the same way as other complementizers. The same range of verbs also admit as complements sentential constructions resembling *wh-* questions

(10) a.   Francis {wondered / knew} what Brett wrote.
   b. *Francis {wondered / knew} what did Brett write?
   c.   Francis {wondered / knew} when it rained.
   d. *Francis {wondered / knew} when did it rain.

Note that there are syntactic distinctions between such embedded questions and ordinary questions.

Some propositional-attitude verbs take untensed complements, with or without a complementizer (Weeda 1981; Gazdar, Klein, Pullum, and Sag 1985).

(11) I {prefer / insist / desire} (that) the job be given to Lee.

This can be accounted for with features by simply subcategorizing complements as s_c and s, as I will do in our analysis of tense in chapter 12.

11.1.4   Sentential, Infinitival, and Gerundive Subjects

There are a range of verbs admitting sentential, infinitival, or gerundive subjects.

(12) a. That Francis schemes annoys Taylor.
     b. To run is fun.
     c. Shoveling snow can be dangerous.

The complementized sentential subject cases can be generated from lexical entries such as the following:

(13) *annoyed* $\Rightarrow$ **annoy**: $s_c \backslash s / np$

Thus for (12a) we derive the meaning **annoy**(**t**)(**scheme**(**f**)). The semantics is just as with other propositional attitudes; the only change is that the sentence is now the subject rather than the object of the attitude verb.

    Cases involving infinitival and gerundive subjects are equally straightforward. It appears that only predicatives take infinitival and gerundive subjects in English. For infinitival subjects, we have the following lexical entry (recall that *pr* is the category assigned to predicative complements of the copula).

(14) *fun* $\Rightarrow$ **fun**: $(np \backslash s) \backslash pr$

Assuming that the copula can also handle verb-phrase subjects (see the discussion of raising verbs in section 11.1.8), we will be able to analyze *is fun* as having the same meaning as *fun* and (12b) as **fun**(**run**): s.

11.1.5   Nominalization, Self-Reference, and Semantic Paradoxes

Within a simply-typed λ-calculus, such as the one we have employed, an integrated analysis of polymorphic subjects remains puzzling. In addition to examples such as *To run is fun*, we have parallel examples such as *Jan is fun*. One approach to predicatives like *fun* is to treat them as uniformly taking noun-phrase subjects and then *nominalizing* verb phrases. This requires a mapping from properties of type **Ind** $\rightarrow$ **Prop** to individuals of type **Ind**. As is well known from Cantor's theorem (see section A.2), such a function cannot be one-to-one. But verbs like *fun* need to be able to discriminate arbitrary properties from one another. One approach to this problem is to move to a monotyped λ-calculus, as proposed by Chierchia and Turner (1988). In such a theory, domains such as **Ind** $\rightarrow$ **Prop** are taken to contain not all total functions from individuals to propositions but only the subset of such functions that are continuous (in a well-defined topological sense). Models of the monotyped λ-calculus are beyond the scope of this volume; for details, see Barendregt 1984. Although the application of a monotyped λ-calculus to natural language provides a potentially useful approach to cases of nominalization, other problems are introduced, primarily having to do with partiality, negation, and quantification. Evidence weighing against a nominalization approach to infinitival subjects like *to run* in which they are analyzed as being of the same category as ordinary noun phrases is the infelicity of examples such as **Either Francis or to run is fun*. Inability to coordinate seems to require an analysis in which the subjects are not of the same type. Thus Chierchia and Turner (1988) reintroduce typing into the syntactic component of their grammars.

Next consider the possibilities of *self-application* of predicates, as illustrated by (15a) and (15b), and the type-logically related issue of *circular reference*, as shown in (15c).

(15) a. To be fun is fun.
      b. Being self-identical is self-identical.
      c. [[This sentence]₁ is false]₁.

Chierchia (1985) maintains that cases like (15a) and (15b) argue most strongly for true self-application. He believes that the two occurrences of *fun* in (15a) are semantically synonymous. Serious logical problems arise from cases of self-application, as shown by the classical problematic example (15c), known as the *liar's paradox*, in which the demonstrative subject is taken to refer to the embedding sentence. The paradox underlying such sentences is that if they are true, then their subject is false, and hence they are false. On the other hand, if they are false, then their subject is true, and hence they are true. Paradoxes of self-application rear their ugly heads in theories of sets and properties, such as Frege's (1879). For instance, Russell noted the paradox surrounding generalized comprehension, which allows the construction of the following set:

(16) $y = \{x \mid x \notin x\}$ (Russell's paradox)

The paradoxical issue here is whether $y \in y$; clearly if $y \in y$, then by definition $y \notin y$, and vice versa. Examples such as (16) led to the introduction of stratified theories of sets and properties by Whitehead and Russell (1910, 1912). The point of such theories is to block the construction of such paradoxes. Russell and Whitehead's solution is to enforce a condition on each stratum that restricts sets in that stratum to contain only members from lower strata. A set s such that $s = \{s\}$ is thus not stratified in this sense, as it contains a member of the same stratum, namely itself. Because it appeared that mathematics could be formalized in a stratified system, the idea was widely accepted. The idea of stratification is a foun-

dational cornerstone of the most popular axiomatic set theory, that of
Zermelo and Fraenkel, known as *ZF set theory*, and is embodied in the
axiom of foundation. Tarski's (1935) approach to truth embraced stratification, and simply disallowed self-reference. Kripke (1975) later developed
a theory of truth essentially involving a complex fixed-point construction,
which can be glossed as saying that a proposition is true only if it con-
verges to the truth in the limit. Paradoxical instances such as the liar sentence do not converge in this way but rather bounce back and forth in
truth value at each iteration in Kripke's construction. More recently, an
alternative set theory in which the axiom of foundation is replaced with
an *antifoundation axiom* was developed by Aczel (1988) and applied to
logical systems by Aczel (1980). Barwise and Etchemendy (1987) survey
Tarski's, Kripke's, and many other approaches to Russell's paradox and
then go on to develop their own situation-semantics treatment of these
paradoxes, based on Aczel's set theory.

11.1.6 Gerunds, Naked Infinitives, and Event-Based Semantics

An alternative account of the semantics of gerundive subjects is provided
by Parsons (1985, 1990), who considers the following examples:

(17) a. Every burning consumes oxygen.
   b. Morgan burned wood.
   c. Oxygen was consumed.

Parsons argued that the truth of (17c) follows from the truth of (17a) and
(17b) (modulo interpretative matters such as tense). The problem with
accounting for such entailments under the kind of type assignment I have
adopted is that there is no natural way to relate the gerundive use of
burning in (17a) and the verbal use in (17b). Parsons provides an intrigu-
ing analysis in terms of an event-based semantics along the lines of that
proposed by Davidson (1967a). The central idea is that the gerund *burning* represents a property of events in the same way that *kid* represents a
property of other kinds of individuals. Thus **burn** is a predicate such that
$[\![\mathbf{burn}]\!](e)$ is true if e is a burning event. Furthermore, sentences are also
taken to introduce properties of events. For example, (17b) is taken to
state a property of events, namely, burnings of wood by Morgan. This
might be represented by $\lambda e.\mathbf{burn}_3(e)(\mathbf{wood})(\mathbf{m})$, where $[\![\mathbf{burn}_3]\!](e)(x)(y)$ is
true if e is an event of y burning x. Of course, $\mathbf{burn}_3$ and **burn** must be
related, and the assumption of both Davidson and Parsons is that the
relation is existential, so that **burn** applies to an event just in case there

exists a burner and a burnee and the event is a burning of the burnee by the burner. Davidson took the truth conditions of a sentence to be determined by the existential quantification over the property of events denoted by the sentence. Parsons argued that the standard property-typed lexical entry for *burn* implicitly involves the existential quantification of the event-based entry, namely $\lambda x.\lambda y.\mathbf{some}(\lambda e.\mathbf{burn}_3(e)(x)(y))$. Since this entry is normally taken to be an atomic constant in theories such as ours, which type transitive verbs to curried binary relations, Parsons described his approach as *subatomic semantics*. The type-logical ramifications of such an event-based type assignment are studied in detail by Carpenter (1989). It is quite complicated and not unproblematic to integrate event-based analyses with natural logical operations such as negation and quantification.

Another application of event-based semantics is to so-called *naked infinitives*, such as the following:

(18) Francis saw Brooke cheat.

In such cases, it can be argued that there is not a propositional attitude being expressed. Rather, as argued by Barwise and Perry (1981, Barwise 1981), the infinitival complements of such verbs are extensional in nature, denoting an event. Such an analysis provides two benefits. First, it accounts for why alternative descriptions of the same event can be substituted without a change in truth conditions. For instance, if Brooke is the best pool player in town, then *Francis saw the best pool player in town cheat* would have the same truth conditions as (18). Furthermore, it is irrelevant whether or not Francis knows that Brooke is the best pool player in town. The second consequence of such an extensional analysis is that it explains the veridicality of such verbs; if (18) is true, then we can conclude that Brooke cheated. This latter fact follows on an event-based analysis because sentences such as *Brooke cheated* are analyzed, after Davidson (1967a), as making an existential claim about a cheating event by Brooke. Under a pure propositional-attitude-based account, it is not clear how to achieve the first of these effects. Note the contrast between the direct perception sentence in (18) and the indirect perception report produced by its complementized variant.

(19) Francis saw that Brooke cheated.

This example could be true even if Francis did not see Brooke in the act of cheating but rather noticed indirectly that Brooke had cheated. For instance, Francis might have observed that the cards Brooke had been using were marked.

Event-based semantics can also be used to provide a natural account of the similarity between nominal and verbal prepositions, as noted by Davidson (1967a) and developed grammatically by Parsons (1985, 1989, 1990). The preposition can be taken to modify a property by intersecting a further condition. For instance, consider the following meaning assignments.

(20) a. *kid in Pittsburgh* $\Rightarrow \lambda x.\mathbf{kid}(x) \wedge \mathbf{in}(\mathbf{pgh})(x)$
      b. *Sandy ran in Pittsburgh* $\Rightarrow \lambda e.\mathbf{run}(\mathbf{s})(e) \wedge \mathbf{in}(\mathbf{pgh})(e)$

In both cases, the property $\mathbf{in}(\mathbf{pgh})$ is intersected. We consider an alternative analysis of verb-phrase modifying prepositions in exercise 25, chapter 12.

11.1.7 Modal Adverbs and Modal Auxiliaries

A treatment of modal adverbs is straightforward under a possible-worlds account. They are given lexical entries analogous to those that I provided for negation. In the simplest case, we could assign categories like those below to the following alethic modalities:

(21) a. *necessarily* $\Rightarrow \lambda V.\lambda x.\Box V(x): np\backslash s/(np\backslash s)$
      b. *possibly* $\Rightarrow \lambda V.\lambda x.\Diamond V(x): np\backslash s/(np\backslash s)$

The abstraction of the individual variable x allows the subject noun phrase to act as a so-called *controller* of the verb-phrase complement to the modal adverb. The result is that the modal operator takes sentential scope. The following analysis comes about from simple application by substituting the definition of $\Diamond$ (recall definition (76) of chapter 10) and performing β-reduction.

(22) *Francis possibly ran* $\Rightarrow \lambda w_1.\mathbf{some}_{\mathbf{World}}(\lambda w_2.\mathbf{run}(\mathbf{f})(w_2)): s$

This analysis follows the analysis of possibility in modal logic in that Francis possibly ran in the actual world if and only if there is some world, perhaps even the actual one, in which Francis ran. Note that the abstraction of w_1 is vacuous. Thus the proposition is independent of the world at which it is evaluated, just as in the case of system S5 of modal logic.

Modal adverbs induce the same kinds of scope ambiguities as do negations. For instance, consider the two analyses of an occurrence with a quantified subject or object.

(23) a. Someone necessarily won.

     b. The judges will necessarily award someone a prize.

In (23a), the quantified subject can take either wide or narrow scope with respect to the modal adverb. The object in (23b) can also be scoped within or outside the modal adverb. The analysis of examples involving the subject, such as (23a), is exactly as in figure 7.19. To achieve such readings, we need to lexically lift the adverbs to allow for quantified subjects, as shown below for *necessarily*.

(24) *necessarily* $\Rightarrow \lambda V. \lambda Q. \Box V(Q) \colon (np \Uparrow s) \backslash s / ((np \Uparrow s) \backslash s)$

With these categories the reading in which the subject quantifier is inside the scope of the adverbial is derived by application, as in figure 7.19. The wide scope reading is achieved by applying the quantifier-elimination scheme and then type raising the resulting noun phrase. To account for verbal and sentential subjects, we need additional entries in our typed system. The simplest strategy to capture the similarity between such entries is to employ polymorphic entries such as the following:

(25) *possibly* $\Rightarrow \lambda V. \lambda X. \Diamond V(X) \colon A \backslash s / (A \backslash s)$

Here the category variable A should be allowed to range over np, $np \Uparrow s$, $np \backslash s$, s_c, the expletives ex_i and ex_t, and so on, with the semantic variable X instantiated as a variable of type $\mathrm{Typ}(A)$ and V as a variable of type $\mathrm{Typ}(A) \rightarrow \textbf{Prop}$.

    The range of modal adverbials in English includes instances such as *probably, certainly, accidentally, intentionally*, and so on. For cases such as *accidentally* and *intentionally*, clearly an analysis should rest on an analysis of propositional attitudes. But for the other cases, it is not so clear how to apply possible-worlds semantics.

    The *modal auxiliaries*, such as *should, might*, and *can*, semantically play much the same role as modal adverbs. The semantics of these expressions has been the subject of a number of studies of deontic logics, which also have been extended to verbs such as *allow* (von Wright 1951, 1963). Deontic logics typically endorse principles such as whatever is obligatory is possible, thus relating the modality of obligation and the modality of possibility. We consider the temporal aspects of finite auxiliaries such as the modals in chapter 12.

11.1.8   Control Verbs

There are a range of verbs in English, known as *control verbs*, that semantically parallel modal adverbs, negation, and auxiliaries. Control verbs involve untensed verb-phrase complements, the so-called *controlled predicate*, whose subject is understood to be another one of the complements of the control verb, the so-called *controller* (see the examples in (26)).

Control verbs are typically cross-classified along (at least) two dimensions. First, the controller can be either the subject or the object of the control verb. Subject-control verbs can be further divided into transitive and ditransitive cases, depending on whether or not there is an additional object besides the controlled-verb-phrase complement. Control verbs are also classified according to whether or not the controller itself plays a semantic role as an argument of the verb; if it does, the verb is known as an *equi control verb*, or simply *control verb*, and if it does not, the verb is said to be a *raising verb* (these names derive from transformations in early transformational grammar, namely raising and equi-NP deletion). Consider the following examples involving noun-phrase controllers, in which the controller has been emphasized.

(26) a. Francis persuaded *Brooke* to lie.   (Object equi)
      b. *Francis* promised Brooke to lie.   (Subject equi, ditransitive)
      c. *Francis* promised to lie.   (Subject equi, transitive)
      d. Francis wanted *Brooke* to lie.   (Object raising)
      e. *Francis* seemed to lie.   (Subject raising)

Syntacticians are primarily concerned with matters such as the relation between different categorizations of the same control verbs and their noncontrol counterparts; the possibility of expletive, sentential, and other types of controllers; and the domain of reflexive binding. As argued for by Brame (1976), nontransformational theories have converged on lexical accounts of such distributional issues (Bresnan 1982b; Shaumyan 1977; Perlmutter and Postal 1983; Dowty 1985; Gazdar, Klein, Pullum, and Sag 1985; Steedman 1988; Pollard and Sag 1994). Although categorial grammar is perhaps the most radically lexicalist grammatical theory, surprisingly little attention has been paid to the structure of the categorial lexicon. We turn to this issue in section 11.4. Here I will simply enumerate the range of lexical entries necessary to capture the distribution and meanings of control verbs.

I begin with the equi verbs, the subject- and object-control versions of which receive the same kind of lexical entry.

(27) a. *persuaded* $\Rightarrow$ **pers**: $np\backslash s/(np\backslash s)/np$
      b. *promised* $\Rightarrow$ **prom**: $np\backslash s/(np\backslash s)/np$

Syntactically, both verbs take a verb-phrase complement, as well as a noun-phrase object and subject. By simple application, we can generate the following analyses:

(28) a. *Francis promised Brooke to run* ⇒ **prom**(**b**)(**run**)(**f**)
    b. *Francis persuaded Brooke to run* ⇒ **pers**(**b**)(**run**)(**f**)

The fact that the subject acts as controller for *promise* and as object for *persuade* can be modeled in at least two ways. Dowty (1985) and later Chierchia (1988) adopted an approach in which the interpretation of the control predicates **prom** and **pers** is based on an understanding of which argument acts as the controller. For instance, **prom**(**b**)(**run**)(**f**) would be a true proposition if Francis promised Brooke that he (Francis) would run. Thus all of the necessary semantic components are assembled as arguments, and the controller is implicit in the interpretation of the matrix verb.

    An alternative approach, embodied in LFG (Bresnan 1982b) and HPSG (Pollard and Sag 1994), is to provide a propositional argument to promise. In these theories, such an effect is achieved by identifying the subject of the controlled verb and the controller. The semantic effects of such an approach can be enforced as follows:

(29) a. **prom** $\overset{\text{def}}{=} \lambda x.\lambda V.\lambda y.\textbf{prom}_2(x)(V(x))(y)$
    b. **pers** $\overset{\text{def}}{=} \lambda x.\lambda V.\lambda y.\textbf{pers}_2(x)(V(y))(y)$

There are two things to note here. First, the distinction between subject and object control is indicated in the argument to which the controlled verbal complement's meaning is applied. Second, the controller itself plays a role as an argument in the meaning. One semantic motivation for this is that we want to be able to directly relate the following examples to (26a) and (26b).

(30) a. Francis$_1$ promised Brooke (that) he$_1$ would run.
    b. Francis persuaded Brooke$_2$ (that) he$_2$ should run.

Here we have an explicit propositional complement, as would be found with the following lexical entries, which directly employ the constants **prom**$_2$ and **pers**$_2$.

(31) a. *promised* ⇒ **prom**$_2$: $np\backslash s/s/np$
    b. *persuaded* ⇒ **pers**$_2$: $np\backslash s/s/np$

With these entries, the examples in (30) and (26) are provided with the same meanings, modulo tense and aspect.

The range of controllers allowed by raising verbs is much greater than that of equi verbs.

(32) a. Francis wanted someone to speak.
     b. Francis wanted it to rain.
     c. Francis wanted there to be rain.
     d. That Francis is scheming seems to annoy Taylor.
     e. To rush matters seems to be a bad idea.

For instance, example (32a) may involve a de dicto desire on Francis's part for there to be some person who is speaking. In examples (32b) and (32c), an expletive object is perfectly natural. This shows that there is no semantic argument position assigned to the object by *want*. Note that in (32d) and (32e), sentential and verbal subjects are admissible. This range of behavior separates the raising cases from the equi cases, which do not display these possibilities.

(33) a.   Francis {promised / persuaded} everyone to read a paper.
     b. *Francis {promised / persuaded} it to rain.
     c. *Francis {promised / persuaded} there to be rain.
     d. *Brooke persuaded that Francis is scheming to annoy Taylor.
     e. *Brooke persuaded to rush matters to be a bad idea.

Only the first example is grammatical, and in this case, the quantifier *everyone* must receive wide scope over the matrix verb.

The range of possibilities for raising verbs can be characterized with the following polymorphic lexical entries.

(34) a. *want* $\Rightarrow \lambda x.\lambda V.\lambda y.\mathbf{want}(V(x))(y): np\backslash s/(A\backslash s)/A$
     b. *seem* $\Rightarrow \lambda V.\lambda y.\mathbf{seem}(V(y)): A\backslash s/(A\backslash s)$

From the examples in (32), we see that the range of polymorphism for *want* should at least admit instantiations of the controller A (and the type of the corresponding variables V and y) to the nominal categories np and $np\Uparrow s$, as well as the expletives ex_i and ex_t. In addition, *seem* allows complementized sentential and infinitival verbal subjects such as s_c and $np\backslash s$.

First we consider the quantificational possibilities. Consider the two analyses of (32a) given in figure 11.2. Note that I have derived the verb phrase *to study* as seeking a quantified subject. Expletive cases such as those in the object-raising example (32b) are derived analogously.

A subject-raising control verb like *seems* is assigned the same category as negation, auxiliaries, and adverbials. Control in such cases can be

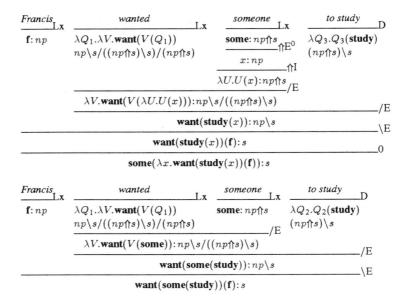

Figure 11.2
Two derivations of *Francis wanted someone to study*

arbitrarily deeply nested, as long as the complements are compatible at every stage of the derivation.

(35) a. It probably doesn't seem to be raining.
b. Francis apparently doesn't want it to appear not to be raining.
c. Francis might have persuaded Brooke to pretend to not be hungry.

Each control verb simply passes along its argument until it is finally applied as the controller of the embedded infinitival complement. For instance, consider the analysis in figure 11.3. At each stage the instantiation of the polymorphic subject is to ex_i, the category of the expletive *it*. The same sort of analysis would allow a quantifier in subject position to be embedded inside the scope of the sequence of verb phrases, just as in the analysis of *Every student didn't not study* in figure 7.20.

11.1.9 Control Predicatives

In addition to the ordinary control verbs, there are a range of predicate constructions that also involve control. Cases such as the following involve subject control of the predicate.

$$
\begin{array}{lllll}
\dfrac{It}{1:ex_i}\text{Lx} & \dfrac{probably}{\substack{\lambda V.\lambda x.\mathbf{prob}(V(x))\\ ex_i\backslash s/(ex_i\backslash s)}}\text{Lx} & \dfrac{doesn't}{\substack{\lambda U.\lambda y.\neg U(y)\\ ex_i\backslash s/(ex_i\backslash s)}}\text{Lx} & \dfrac{seem}{\substack{\lambda W.\lambda u.\mathbf{seem}(W(u))\\ ex_i\backslash s/(ex_i\backslash s)}}\text{Lx} & \dfrac{to\ be\ raining}{\substack{\mathbf{rain}\\ ex_i\backslash s}}\text{Lx}
\end{array}
$$

$$\cfrac{\qquad\qquad\qquad\qquad}{\lambda u.\mathbf{seem}(\mathbf{rain}(u)):ex_i\backslash s}/\mathrm{E}$$

$$\cfrac{\qquad\qquad\qquad\qquad}{\lambda y.\neg\mathbf{seem}(\mathbf{rain}(y)):ex_i\backslash s}/\mathrm{E}$$

$$\cfrac{\qquad\qquad\qquad\qquad}{\lambda x.\mathbf{prob}(\neg\mathbf{seem}(\mathbf{rain}(x))):ex_i\backslash s}/\mathrm{E}$$

$$\cfrac{\qquad\qquad\qquad\qquad}{\mathbf{prob}(\neg\mathbf{seem}(\mathbf{rain}(1))):s}\backslash\mathrm{E}$$

Figure 11.3
A derivation of *It probably doesn't seem to be raining*

(36) a. Francis is {eager / likely / willing / prone} to lie.
      b. It is {going / likely} to rain.
      c. That Francis lied is going to annoy Taylor.

Notice that even though predicatives such as *willing* and *likely* behave much like adverbs or main verbs, they have neither the distribution of adverbs nor the range of inflections of main verbs. Predicate control verbs can be given the following polymorphic predicative category, analogous to that of subject-control raising verbs.

(37) *likely* $\Rightarrow$ **likely**: $pr_A/(A\backslash s)$

For the predicatives in (36a), the controlled subject A must be a simple noun phrase, but in the case of predicatives like *going* and *likely*, it may also be an expletive, quantifier, sentence, or verb phrase. This distinction has a type-logical effect, so in addition to the category pr_{np} typed to **Ind** $\rightarrow$ **Bool**, we must also have pr_s, pr_{vp}, and pr_{ex} typed accordingly. This suggests that predicates might be decomposed to a marked form of verb phrase, as follows:

(38) $pr \overset{\mathrm{def}}{=} np\backslash s_{pr}$

This would naturally allow extensions to $ex_i\backslash s_{pr}$, $(np\Uparrow s)\backslash s_{pr}$, and $s_c\backslash s_{pr}$. Such a move would also allow us to analyze so-called *small clauses*, such as the following, as sentences of category s_{pr}.

(39) a. I consider [Francis a liar].
      b. I consider [Francis innocent].

Note that indefinite and definite noun phrases such as *a liar* and *the one for the job* may act as predicates.

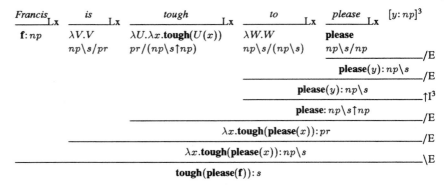

Figure 11.4
A derivation of *Francis is tough to please*

Like other predicatives, those with controlled nominal complements may also be used as nominal modifiers.

(40) a. The only person willing to lie is Francis.
     b. The person eager to get going is Francis.

The most widely studied form of predicative are instances of the so-called *tough-class*.

(41) a. Francis₁ is tough {to please ——₁/ *to please Taylor}.
     b. Francis is impossible to reason with ——.
     c. [The sonata]₂ is difficult to play ——₂ on your violin.

The first example shows that there must be an extraction in the controlled complement, and that this extracted element is controlled by the subject of the sentence. The nonlocal and nonperipheral position of the controlled extraction in (41b) and (41c), respectively, lead us to the following category assignment:

(42) *tough* $\Rightarrow \lambda V.\lambda x.\textbf{tough}(V(x)): np\backslash s/(np\backslash s\!\uparrow\! np)$

This lexical entry allows derivations of examples such as (41a), as shown in figure 11.4. Semantically, the constant **tough** is interpreted as a property of properties. For instance, in **tough**(**please**(**f**)), the argument **please**(**f**) is interpreted as the property of pleasing Francis. In such cases, the unexpressed argument of the property is interpreted generically. By using a *for* phrase as an explicit subject, the subject can be specified.

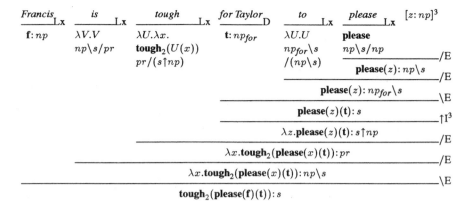

Figure 11.5
A derivation of *Francis is tough for Taylor to please*

(43) a. Francis is tough for Taylor to please.
    b. That sonata is difficult for you to play on your violin.

Here (43b) we employ a lexical entry such as the following:

(44) *difficult* $\Rightarrow \lambda P.\lambda x.\mathbf{tough}_2(P(x)): np\backslash s/(s\uparrow np)$

We must further assume that the infinitival *to* allows a *for*-marked subject to be expressed.

(45) *to* $\Rightarrow \lambda V.V: np_{for}\backslash s/(np\backslash s)$

An alternative would be to categorize *for* so that it takes an object noun-phrase complement and an infinitive verb-phrase complement to produce an infinitival sentence. There are also other uses of *for* phrases, as complements and as modifiers.

With the lexical entries in (44) and (45), we can perform derivations of examples such as (43a), as shown in figure 11.5. Here the reading is specific rather than generic, so that $\mathbf{tough}_2(\mathbf{please}(\mathbf{f})(\mathbf{t}))$ will be interpreted as true if the act of Francis pleasing Taylor is tough.

11.1.10   Nonobligatory Control and Purpose Clauses

In addition to the control verbs and predicates, there are related constructions that are much less rigid in their determination of controllers. For instance, consider the use of infinitival verb phrases as *purpose clauses.*

(46) a. Betty bought (Taylor) a car [(for Francis) to drive ____].
     b. Betty gave Taylor a car [(for Francis) to drive ____].
     c. The best vehicle [(for Francis) to ramble over hills in ____] is a Jeep.
     d. The best vehicle [to convince your mother you can safely ramble over hills in ____] is a Jeep.
     e. Jan bought (Morgan) a mirror [to look at {himself / herself} in ____].

Nishigauchi (1984) used examples like these to illustrate the flexible nature of the controller in such cases. The parenthetical noun phrases are optional, and if they occur, tend to act as the controller. The examples in (46c) demonstrate that such infinitivals modify a noun. Examples (46c) and (46d) suggest there is no bound on the distance from the infinitive to the missing noun phrase in its verb-phrase complement. But examples where the dependency is too distant or unconnected usually sound rather awkward. This observation leads us to the following lexical entries, where I locate the control on the infinitive marker *to*.

(47) a. $to \Rightarrow \lambda V.\lambda P.\lambda x.P(x) \wedge V(x)(y): n\backslash n/(np\backslash s\uparrow np)$
     b. $to \Rightarrow \lambda y.\lambda V.\lambda P.\lambda x.P(x) \wedge V(x)(y): n\backslash n/(np_{for}\backslash s\uparrow np)/np_{for}$

An alternative analysis to the two presented above might involve an empty relativizer. In the first entry, where there is no *for* clause, I have simply used a variable y for the controlled subject. Such a variable can be bound just like an ordinary pronoun or perhaps interpreted generically. In the second entry there is an explicit *for* clause, and the subject of the extracted infinitival complement is identified with the referent of the *for* clause.

The following examples, also based on Nishigauchi 1984, show variants in which there is no extraction.

(48) a. Man retains the ability [to deceive himself].
     b. Sobering up cured Morgan of the desire [to kill herself].

With such cases it is not clear that the infinitival verb phrase is not simply a complement of a relational noun. In fact, these nouns are related to the predicative *able* and the verb *desire*. These cases are further complicated by the difficulty of interpreting nominalizations in general. Further note that these examples do not admit *for* phrases as explicit subjects.

As well as nominal-modifying purpose clauses, there are those that clearly modify verb phrases.

(49) Francis practiced to defeat Brooke.

In order to enforce obligatory control on the subject, we could employ the following lexical entry.

(50) $to \Rightarrow \lambda P. \lambda R. \lambda x. \textbf{purpose}(R(x))(P(x)): (np \backslash s) \backslash np \backslash s / (np \backslash s)$

This would provide us with an analysis such as the following:

(51) *Francis practiced to defeat Brooke*
        $\Rightarrow \textbf{purpose}(\textbf{practice}(\textbf{f}))(\textbf{defeat}(\textbf{b})(\textbf{f}))$

The following examples, due to Ladusaw and Dowty (1988), show that matters of control are often more complex than I have assumed.

(52) a.   Francis asked Brooke [to shave {himself / him}].
      b.   Francis asked his mother [to go to the movies].
      c.   #Jan asked his mother [to behave himself].
      d.   Jan's mother was asked [to go to the movies].
      e.   He made such a favorable impression in his interview that he finally convinced the Parole Board to be allowed [to take an early parole].

The first example, (52a), shows that with a control verb like *ask*, we can have either subject or object control. But the examples (52b) and (52c) show that there is a subtle yet strong influence from the actual content of the controlled predicate. Jackendoff (1972), Nishigauchi (1984), and Ladusaw and Dowty (1988) provide a theory of controllers in terms of so-called *thematic roles*, which in some sense determine the kind of roles played by arguments across verbs. In (52c), the infelicity arises because asking only makes sense when the person asked has direct control over the action being requested. The last example, (52e), shows that the distance between the controller and the controlled complement is unbounded in terms of nesting. We could, of course, treat such cases as simply involving nonobligatory control in the sense of taking the controlled subject to behave like a pronoun.

11.1.11   Intensional Transitive Verbs

Consider the following examples involving transitive verbs with quantified objects.

(53) a. Sandy seeks a unicorn.
      b. Sandy wants every baseball card.

What is interesting about these sentences is that they induce quantifier-scope ambiguities despite only having a single transitive verb. For instance, the first sentence, (53a), has a reading in which Sandy is hoping to find a unicorn but is not seeking a specific unicorn. There is also a second reading in which there is a particular unicorn Sandy is seeking (although such a reading could not be true unless the unicorn in question exists). The first reading is de dicto, whereas the second is de re. In some sense, the de dicto reading has the object quantifier scoping inside the scope of the seeking. The de re reading, on the other hand, gives the object scope over the whole sentence. In this sense, it is interpreted referentially, like the sentence *There is a unicorn, and Sandy seeks it*. Similarly, the second sentence, (53b), can mean that Sandy wants a complete collection of baseball cards without knowing exactly which baseball cards there are. It can also mean that for each of the baseball cards, Sandy wants it. Note that this ambiguity can also be thought of as a scope ambiguity, as indicated by the paraphrases. The wide-scope reading is paraphrasable with an object pronoun, as in *Every baseball card is such that Sandy wants it*.

The possibility of object scope ambiguity, as in the examples in (53), must be encoded lexically in some fashion. This is because not every transitive verb exhibits this kind of scope ambiguity. For instance, (53a) is often contrasted with *Sandy found a unicorn*, which is unambiguous. Similarly, (53b) can be contrasted with the semantically unambiguous *Sandy owns every baseball card*.

The transitive verbs that produce scope ambiguities involving their objects are typically paraphrasable using control verbs. For instance, compare (53a) with the following sentence, especially in terms of its meanings, which are provided below.

(54) a. Sandy tries to find a unicorn.
   b. $\mathbf{try}(\mathbf{some}(\mathbf{uni})(\lambda x.\mathbf{find}(x)(\mathbf{s})))(\mathbf{s})$
   c. $\mathbf{some}(\mathbf{uni})(\lambda x.\mathbf{try}(\mathbf{find}(x)(\mathbf{s}))(\mathbf{s}))$

The first reading is clearly the de dicto version, whereas the second reading is de re. Several authors have exploited this purported synonymy. Quine (1960) suggested replacing uses of the problematic *seek* with its control-verb variant. Bach (1968) and McCawley (1970) treated verbs like *seek* by transforming them syntactically into *try to find*.

The analysis I adopt is a version of Montague's (1973) semantic approach and is related to the type-logical account of Morrill (1994a); I discuss the subtle distinctions in exercise 32. This involves treating the

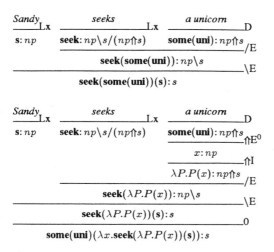

Figure 11.6
Two derivations of *Sandy seeks a unicorn*

object argument as a quantifier both semantically and syntactically, and providing a meaning postulate that relates the constant assigned to *seek* to the meaning of *try to find*. In type-logical grammar, Montague's type-theoretic proposal can be implemented with the following lexical entry (the meaning postulate follows in (56)).

(55) *seek* $\Rightarrow$ **seek**: $np \backslash s / (np \Uparrow s)$

For (53), the lexcial entry in (55) leads to the derivations in figure 11.6. The first derivation simply involves application, whereas the second involves scoping the quantifier and then type-raising the residual variable to provide an appropriate argument for *seek*. The derivations involving the type-raised constant **seek** are unusual in that it is not immediately clear how to interpret a predicate that is applied to a quantifier. With higher-order logic we are able to assign a meaning to *seek* that makes it synonymous with *try to find*, namely, the following meaning postulate:

(56) **seek** $\overset{\text{def}}{=} \lambda Q. \lambda z. \textbf{try}(Q(\lambda y. \textbf{find}(y)(z)))(z)$

Most significant, the results of the derivation in figure 11.6, with the definition of **seek** substituted, yield the results in (54). In exercise 31 we show how the lexical entry and meaning for *seek* can be derived from those for *try to find*.

It is important to work through our type assignments to see that we have the appropriate degree of intensionality. Explicitly by expanding the types, we have the following:

(57) $\text{Typ}(np \Uparrow s) = (\text{Typ}(np) \to \text{Typ}(s)) \to \text{Typ}(s)$
    $= (\textbf{Ind} \to \textbf{Prop}) \to \textbf{Prop}$
    $= (\textbf{Ind} \to (\textbf{World} \to \textbf{Bool})) \to (\textbf{World} \to \textbf{Bool})$

Thus the type assigned to generalized quantifiers is the type assigned to properties of properties. So it makes sense to have objects that are quantified with any kind of quantifier, including plural ones, as in *needs three reference letters*, or negative ones, as in *seeks no favors*, both of which are ambiguous in the same way as other quantified objects. The degree of intensionality displayed in (57) is necessary, because we need to be able to represent the distinction between *seek a unicorn* and *seek a vampire*, even though there might be neither unicorns nor vampires in the actual world.

Montague (1973), in order to have a uniform type assignment for transitive verbs, assumed that they all took a quantified object. He assigned meaning postulates to the "ordinary" transitive verbs so that the two derivations in figure 11.6 produced a semantic term logically equivalent with the meaning postulate. For instance, Montague used lexical assignments and meaning postulates such as the following for *found*.

(58) a. *found* $\Rightarrow$ **find**: $np \backslash s / (np \Uparrow s)$
    b. **find** $\overset{\text{def}}{=} \lambda Q . \lambda x . Q(\lambda y . \textbf{find}_2(y)(x))$

The resulting pair of derivations for *Sandy found a unicorn* are analogous to those in figure 11.6, but produce the same semantic term after normalization (see exercise 30). The type-logical approach to grammar allows us to simplify Montague's approach. Rather than raising to the worst case, we are able lower to the best case. The natural logic of our connectives allow type raising to be derived when needed, as in the derivations of Hendriks (1987, 1993), as noted by Morrill (1994a). In fact, the lexical entry in (58) can be derived from the category **find**$_2$: $np \backslash s / np$ (see exercise 30).

Some verbs, such as *worship* and *conceive* (*of*), appear to be be intensional to some degree but resist paraphrases involving control verbs. Although I remain neutral as to the kind of lexical entries appropriate for these cases, they could clearly be assigned to the same kind of category as *seek*; nothing forces transitive verbs with quantified objects to have semantic constants defined by meaning postulates relating them to the meanings of control verbs (see Bennet 1974; Dowty et al. 1981).

With either Montague's object-type-raised lexical entries or with our simpler lexical entries, we can properly analyze coordinations such as the following:

(59) I sought and found a fish.

Here we can even read the seeking as being de dicto and the finding as being de re. Such a reading is derived by raising *found* to the same category as is assigned lexically to *sought* and then coordinating. The case in which the seeking is de re can be analyzed in the same way by simply scoping the quantifier to the sentence level and using quantifier introduction to raise the noun phrase to the appropriate category. Of course, Montague also assumed generalized quantifiers as lexical entries for proper names; here we can simply type-raise an individual x to its properties of properties $\lambda P^{\mathbf{Ind}\to\mathbf{Prop}}.P(x)$. Thus there is only one logically distinct meaning assigned to *Sandy sought Terry*, because the wide-scope analysis, $(\lambda P.P(\mathbf{t}))(\lambda y.\mathbf{seek}(\lambda R.R(y))(\mathbf{s}))$, and the narrow-scope analysis, $\mathbf{seek}(\lambda P.P(\mathbf{t}))(\mathbf{s})$, both reduce to $\mathbf{try}(\mathbf{find}(\mathbf{t})(\mathbf{s}))(\mathbf{s})$.

11.1.12   Intensional Adjectives

A number of adjectives, such as *alleged*, *fake*, and *former*, are amenable to an intensional analysis. Because of our intensional type assignment to nouns, adjectives receive the following type:

(60) $\mathrm{Typ}(n/n) = \mathrm{Typ}(n) \to \mathrm{Typ}(n) = (\mathbf{Ind} \to \mathbf{Prop}) \to (\mathbf{Ind} \to \mathbf{Prop})$

Examples such as *former student* rely on more than the extension of the set of students at the current time. Instead, they say something about who was a student in the past. We consider such adjectives when we return to tense in chapter 12. Adjectives like *alleged*, on the other hand, are derived in some sense from verbs and have meanings that involve propositional attitudes. Assuming that the meanings are existential in nature, we have the following:

(61) *alleged* $\Rightarrow \lambda P.\lambda x.\lambda w.\mathbf{some}^1(\lambda y.\mathbf{allege}(P(x))(y)(w)): n/n$

Note that I have distributed the world of evaluation of the nominal to the embedded attitude predicate. Thus the individuals in the extension of *alleged thief* in a world must have been alleged by someone to be thieves in that world.

11.2   INDIVIDUAL CONCEPTS AND QUANTIFICATIONAL DEFINITES

In this section we consider two approaches to the treatment of definite descriptions and their interaction with intensional constructions. We begin by considering a quantificational approach to the definite determiner. Then we consider the possibility of raising the type of noun phrases to **World** → **Ind**, the type of so-called *individual concepts*.

11.2.1   Definite Descriptions and Scope

With a typing of noun phrases as simple individuals, $\text{Typ}(np) = \textbf{Ind}$, we have $\text{Typ}(np/n) = (\textbf{Ind} \rightarrow \textbf{Prop}) \rightarrow \textbf{Ind} = (\textbf{Ind} \rightarrow \textbf{World} \rightarrow \textbf{Bool}) \rightarrow \textbf{Ind}$. This typing is problematic because it is not obvious how to lift the type of the definite description operator ι, which, in higher-order logic, is given the type $(\textbf{Ind} \rightarrow \textbf{Bool}) \rightarrow \textbf{Ind}$. The constraint on ι is that it returns an individual when applied to the singleton set containing that individual. But now the argument is no longer a set but rather an intensional property. One possibility would be to fill the world argument with the actual world.

(62) $\iota_p \overset{\text{def}}{=} \lambda P.\iota(\lambda x.P(x)(\textbf{actual\_world}))$

With such an approach, Frege's examples remain puzzling.

(63) a. The ancients believed [the morning star is the evening star].
      b. The ancients believed [the morning star is the morning star].

This is because the noun phrase *the morning star* will be translated as $\iota(\lambda x.\textbf{morn\_star}(x)(\textbf{actual\_world}))$, which denotes the planet Venus, because Venus is the morning star in the actual world. Because the morning star and the evening star are the same in the actual world, the noun phrase *the evening star* also denotes Venus. Thus if we translate *is* as a transitive verb denoting the identity function (relativized to worlds), the two sentences in (63) receive the same meaning because their embedded sentences both denote the unique proposition true at every world.

One way out of this puzzle is to adopt Russell's (1905) quantificational approach to definite descriptions. We consider the alternative of intensionalizing the type of noun phrases in the next section. By treating *the* as a generalized determiner, we can distribute the worlds in a natural way.

(64) a. *the* ⇒ $\textbf{the}_p: np \Uparrow s/n$
      b. $\textbf{the}_p \overset{\text{def}}{=} \lambda P.\lambda Q.\lambda w.\textbf{the}(\lambda x.P(x)(w))(\lambda y.Q(y)(w))$
      c. $\textbf{the} \overset{\text{def}}{=} \lambda P.\lambda Q.\textbf{some}(P)(Q) \wedge \textbf{singleton}(P)$

As Russell suggests, the analysis of the examples in (63) can be achieved by treating them as instances of the de dicto/de re ambiguity. Because the ancients were ignorant of the fact that *the morning star* and *the evening star* both denoted Venus, clearly their attitudes toward them were de dicto in some sense. A thorny epistemological problem remains as to what exactly it means to have a de re belief. Russell, for instance, distinguished *knowledge by acquaintance* and *knowledge by description*. But the ancients in this sense were acquainted with the morning star and the evening star, if acquaintance is analyzed as a perceptual notion. To analyze the sentences in (63), we also need an intensional lexical entry for *is*:

(65) *is* $\Rightarrow \lambda x.\lambda y.\lambda w.x = y \colon np\backslash s/np$

Note that the world argument is simply vacuously abstracted: if the equality of individuals is true, it will be true at every world. With these lexical entries, the sentential complements in (63) would be translated as follows:

(66) a. $\mathbf{the_p}(\mathbf{morn\_star})(\lambda x.\mathbf{the_p}(\mathbf{ev\_star})(\lambda y.\lambda w.x = y)) \equiv$
          $\lambda w.\mathbf{the}(\lambda x.\mathbf{morn\_star}(x)(w))$
              $(\lambda x.\mathbf{the}(\lambda y.\mathbf{ev\_star}(y)(w))(\lambda y.x = y))$
      b. $\mathbf{the_p}(\mathbf{morn\_star})(\lambda x.\mathbf{the_p}(\mathbf{morn\_star})(\lambda y.\lambda w.x = y)) \equiv$
          $\lambda w.\mathbf{the}(\lambda x.\mathbf{morn\_star}(x)(w))$
              $(\lambda x.\mathbf{the}(\lambda y.\mathbf{morn\_star}(y)(w))(\lambda y.x = y))$

On the assumption that there are worlds in which the morning star as such is distinct from the evening star as such, the propositions in (66) will be distinct. In such a case, (66a) fails to hold at some worlds, but (66b) will hold at every world. Ironically, Russell would not have been happy with this solution, which uses his mechanism, because he did not countenance Fregean senses, which I have modeled as functions from worlds to truth values. It seems rather that Russell had something in mind like the structured meanings introduced by Carnap (see section 11.3.3). In the next section we consider an alternative, nonquantificational solution to Frege's puzzle.

11.2.2 Individual Concepts and Rigid Designation

Rather than typing noun phrases as individuals, Montague (1973) treated them as *individual concepts*, as follows:

(67) $\mathrm{Typ}(np) = \mathbf{IndConc} \overset{\text{def}}{=} \mathbf{World} \to \mathbf{Ind}$

Note that this leads to the following typing of verb phrases:

(68) $\text{Typ}(np\backslash s) = \textbf{IndConc} \rightarrow \textbf{Prop}$

Montague assigned nouns to the same type as verb phrases, but I will maintain our typing as $\text{Typ}(n) \stackrel{\text{def}}{=} \textbf{Ind} \rightarrow \textbf{Prop}$, which leads to the following type for the definite determiner category:

(69) $\text{Typ}(np/n) = (\textbf{Ind} \rightarrow \textbf{Prop}) \rightarrow \textbf{IndConc}$

Under such a typing, we can treat the definite determiner *the* as follows:

(70) *the* $\Rightarrow \lambda P.\lambda w. \imath(\lambda x. P(x)(w)): np/n$

This leads to an analysis of definite noun phrases such as the following:

(71) *the morning star* $\Rightarrow \lambda w. \imath(\lambda x.\textbf{morn\_star}(x)(w)): np$

In words, *the morning star* will denote a function from possible worlds to the individual that is the morning star in that world. Montague's lexical assignment to the copula can be captured in our system as follows:

(72) *is* $\Rightarrow \lambda x.\lambda y.\lambda w. x(w) = y(w): np\backslash s/np$

The subordinate sentences of Frege's examples from (63) would then be analyzed as follows:

(73) a. $\lambda w. \imath(\lambda x.\textbf{morn\_star}(x)(w)) = \imath(\lambda y.\textbf{ev\_star}(y)(w))$
       b. $\lambda w. \imath(\lambda x.\textbf{morn\_star}(x)(w)) = \imath(\lambda y.\textbf{morn\_star}(y)(w))$

Whereas the second example still denotes a necessary truth, the first example will not, as long as there are worlds in which the morning star and the evening star are not the same object. Modulo the possibility of presupposition failure, the result is the same as the meanings given in (66).

The use of individual concepts sheds some light on classic examples such as the following:

(74) a. The number of planets is odd.
       b. The number of planets is possibly not odd.
       c. The number of planets is necessarily odd.

First note that the definite description *the number of planets* will denote an individual concept whose extension might vary from world to world. Because there are nine planets in the solar system of the actual world, the sentence in (74a) can be used truthfully. If there are some possible worlds in which the number of planets is even, (74b) can be used truthfully. In this case (74c) must be false.

Typing noun phrases to be individual concepts also allows us to analyze examples such as the following, given that *rose* and *temperature* simply contribute logical constants **rise** and **temp** of the appropriate types.

(75) *the temperature rose* $\Rightarrow$ **rise**$(\lambda w.\imath(\lambda x.\textbf{temp}(x)(w))):s$

With the argument denoting an individual concept, once we extend our analysis to tense, it is clear how such a sentence could be treated: **rise** will apply to an individual concept if it denotes an increasing function of time over some contextually determined temporal period. Most verbs are more extensional than *rise* in that they take arguments that are truly individuals rather than individual concepts. To model this behavior, such "ordinary" verbs can be constrained to distribute their world argument to their individual concept argument. For instance, consider the following:

(76) *ran* $\Rightarrow \lambda x.\lambda w.\textbf{run}(x(w))(w):np\backslash s$

Here the constant **run** is of type **Ind** $\rightarrow$ **Prop**. With such a lexical entry, we will derive the following analysis:

(77) *the kid ran* $\Rightarrow \lambda w.\textbf{run}(\imath(\lambda x.\textbf{kid}(x)(w)))(w):s$

This proposition will be true at a world just in case the kid at that world ran at that world. Other argument positions of verbs could be treated analogously by distributing the world argument through.

The distinction between extensional verbs like *is* and intensional verbs such as *rise* accounts for the contrast noted by Partee between the following argument patterns:

(78) a. The temperature is 90 degrees.
      b. The temperature is rising.
      c. Therefore, 90 degrees is rising.

(79) a. The mayor is the best basketball player.
      b. Jan is the mayor.
      c. Therefore, the best basketball player is Jan.

Clearly, we want to license the conclusion of the last sentence in (79) from the first two, but not in the case of (78). The validity of the argument in (79) follows from extensional meaning postulates analogous to (76). Without assuming such a restriction on the interpretation of *rising*, the conclusion in (78) is rendered invalid. The invalidity arises because the copular sentence (78a) only entails that the extension of *the temperature* at the world of evaluation is the same as that of *90 degrees* at the world of

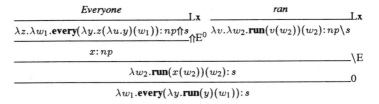

Figure 11.7
A derivation of *Everyone ran*

evaluation. For the conclusion (78c) to follow, the individual concepts would have to be identical (see exercise 24 for further discussion).

We now consider the ramifications of our individual-concept typing of noun phrases for generalized quantifiers and determiners.

(80) a. $\mathrm{Typ}(np \Uparrow s) = (\mathrm{Typ}(np) \to \mathrm{Typ}(s)) \to \mathrm{Typ}(s)$
$= (\mathbf{IndConc} \to \mathbf{Prop}) \to \mathbf{Prop}$

b. $\mathrm{Typ}(np \Uparrow s/n) = \mathrm{Typ}(n) \to \mathrm{Typ}(np \Uparrow s)$
$= (\mathbf{Ind} \to \mathbf{Prop}) \to (\mathbf{IndConc} \to \mathbf{Prop}) \to \mathbf{Prop}$

Lexically, we can treat generalized determiners and quantifiers as simply distributing their world arguments.

(81) a. *everyone* $\Rightarrow \lambda V.\lambda w.\mathbf{every}^{1}(\lambda x.V(\lambda w_2.x)(w)): np \Uparrow s$

b. *every*
$\Rightarrow \lambda P.\lambda V.\lambda w.\mathbf{every}^{2}(\lambda x.P(x)(w))(\lambda x.V(\lambda w_2.x)(w)): np \Uparrow s/n$

Note that in both cases we have distributed the propositional world argument through the quantifier, just as before. To account for the individual-concept-type assignment to noun phrases, I have vacuously abstracted a world over an ordinary individual. This vacuous abstraction converts x into a rigidly designating individual concept. This leads to analyses such as the following, which assumes the kind of extensional lexical entry for *run* given in (76), as shown in figure 11.7.

(82) *every kid ran* $\Rightarrow \lambda w.\mathbf{every}^{2}(\lambda y.\mathbf{kid}(y)(w))(\lambda x.\mathbf{run}(x)(w)): s$

Note that the resulting quantification is over individuals, rather than over individual concepts, and that the world of evaluation for the embedded verb is the same as that for the resulting sentence. The analysis of cases involving generalized determiners and nouns is similar. The fact that I have simply distributed the top-level world argument through to the nominal argument of the generalized determiner indicates why the following kind of example is rather odd.

(83) # Every temperature is rising.

There have been a number of approaches to the meanings of proper names. Consider the following pair of sentences:

(84) a. Cicero was Cicero.
      b. Cicero was Tully.

Even though *Cicero* and *Tully* are two names for the same orator, (84a) is tautologous, whereas (84b) presumably provides some informational content. Frege's (1879) first approach was to treat these examples as being about linguistic expressions, providing a meaning for the name *Cicero* as a definite description meaning the individual named *Cicero*. But as Searle (1958) points out, those who claim that Shakespeare was Bacon are not merely arguing about language. Later Frege (1892) simply assumed that the names *Cicero* and *Tully* differ in sense. Either of Frege's analyses could be captured in a semantics in which noun phrases denote individual concepts. Frege (1892) went on to suggest that the sense of a name is given as a kind of definite description. For instance, he claimed that the name *Aristotle* could stand for the description *the disciple of Plato and the teacher of Alexander the Great*. He also suggested that another description, namely "the Stagirite teacher of Alexander" would also suffice to pick out the same individual. Frege then attributed the nontautologous status of (84b) to the fact that not every speaker associates the same description to *Cicero*. This fact, according to Frege, is a shortcoming of natural language that should be remedied in a scientifically precise ideal language. Searle (1958) presents a version of Frege's approach in which names correspond to loose clusters of descriptions.

Another example amenable to treatment by a description-based theory of proper names is the following:

(85) Pegasus does not exist.

Russell (1905) provided an analysis of this sentence in which *Pegasus* is a shorthand for a definite description such as *the flying horse*. With Russell's analysis of descriptions as involving scope, (85) can be analyzed simply stating that there is no unique flying horse.

Kripke (1972), in contrast to Frege, Russell, and Searle, argued that names should be treated as so-called *rigid designators*, which are individual concepts that denote the same individual in each world. Frege argues that if we learn, for instance, that Alexander the Great was self-taught or perhaps had multiple teachers from Stagira, then we do not all of a sudden decide that the name *Aristotle* is nonreferential. As an alternative, Kripke puts forward his own *causal theory of names*, in which a chain of historical events relates a name back to the individual so named. For an approach to names in which they are individual concepts that behave as rigid designators, we can employ vacuous abstraction:

(86) *Francis* $\Rightarrow \lambda w.\mathbf{f}: np$

Here $\mathbf{f}$ is just an individual constant of type **Ind**. I have assumed for simplicity that expressions such as *nine* and *ninety degrees* are rigid designators in the sense of not having denotations that vary, depending on their world of evaluation.

If we adopt a rigid-designator approach to names, then we are left with a puzzle involving the names the Greeks gave to the morning star and the evening star, namely Hesperus and Phosphorus.

(87) a. Hesperus is Hesperus.
      b. Hesperus is Phosphorus.

Since Hesperus and Phosphorus are both names for the planet Venus, then because they are rigid designators, the meanings of the two sentences in (87) must be identical. But presumably the ancients believed (87a) but not (87b).

Putnam (1975), independently of Kripke, arrived at a theory of concepts in which they are also causally determined. For instance, the sense of *water* is taken by Putnam to be something along the lines of "a liquid identical (in some sense) to the first thing named water."

Another interesting puzzle concerning the use of definite descriptions is presented by Donnellan (1966), who considers the use at a party of an expression such as *the person drinking champagne*, intended to refer to someone who is in fact drinking ginger ale. Donnellan claims that the intentions of the speaker are crucial in determining the referent of a definite description. He argues that if there happens to be another person at the party who is drinking champagne, the utterance does not automatically refer to him. Following Kripke (1972), I take this latter problem to be one of pragmatics, rather than of semantics proper. Such uses of proper names were said to be *referential* by Donnellan. He contrasted the referential use of descriptions with their *attributive* uses. For instance, an expression such as *the next winner of the Nobel Peace Prize* might be used by a speaker who does not have a particular referent in mind. Motivated by a criticism of Kripke's causal theory of reference, Evans (1973) presents a theory of names based in part on the intentions of speakers.

11.3 ALTERNATIVES TO POSSIBLE WORLDS

In this section we consider some well-known flaws with a possible-worlds approach to intensionality, and we consider some alternatives.

11.3.1 Logical Omniscience and the Granularity of Propositions

As I mentioned in the previous section, there are a number of reasons to be concerned about the appropriateness of possible-worlds semantics for natural language. Besides the ontological questions about the existence of worlds and the epistemological problems of our knowledge of possible worlds and their holistic nature, there is cause for concern over their utility for adequately modeling propositional attitudes. The issue is the granularity of the identity conditions for propositions modeled as sets of possible worlds. Simply stated, two propositions are identified if they hold at the same possible worlds. The ramifications of this fact are highly problematic. For instance, if $2 + 2 = 4$ holds in every possible world and $\pi > 3.14$ holds in every possible world, then the following two sentences will have identical truth conditions.

(88) a. Jan knows $2 + 2 = 4$.
      b. Jan knows $\pi > 3.14$.

Both $2 + 2 = 4$ and $\pi > 3.14$ are necessary truths, which are propositions that are true in every possible world. Although such talk of mathematics is often met with suspicion and might perhaps be avoided by a more nominalistic stance toward numbers, arithmetic, and so on, the same problem can be seen in other cases. For instance, if ϕ is a necessary truth, then $\phi \wedge \psi \equiv \psi$ for all propositions ψ. We do not need to broach mathematics to find necessary truths; $\xi \vee \neg \xi$ is a perfectly natural example for any proposition ξ. In fact, any formulas ϕ and ψ that are logically equivalent in classical higher-order logic will denote the same proposition under a possible-worlds approach. This feature of possible-worlds approaches to propositional attitudes is known as *logical omniscience*. This means that the following two sentences would be identified truth conditionally, given that the tenses are fixed and all the names are fixed denotationally and the intended coordination is as indicated by brackets.

(89) a. Jan believes Francis ran.

  b. Jan believes Francis ran and [Brooke ran or Brooke did not run].

Under an intuitive conception of belief, Jan might not have any beliefs about Brooke's running or not running. Thus it seems that (89a) might be true and (89b) false. Further examples involve other laws of classical logic. For instance, De Morgan's laws tell us that $\neg(\phi \wedge \psi)$ and $\neg\phi \vee \neg\psi$ are logically equivalent, and by distribution, so are $\phi \wedge (\psi \vee \xi)$ and $(\phi \wedge \psi) \vee (\phi \wedge \xi)$.

The problem revolves around determining what kind of world is, in fact, possible. Unfortunately, such matters seem rather far removed from ordinary empirical investigation. Perhaps the issue of granularity could be solved by assuming that there are *impossible worlds*. In such an impossible world, it might be the case that $2 + 2 = 4$ does not hold or that $\phi \wedge \neg\phi$ holds. Of course, to construct such a model, a different approach to arithmetic and logical connectives must be taken. All of these examples stretch our intuitions concerning possible worlds to the point of breaking. In the rest of this section we consider a number of alternatives to possible-worlds semantics, all of which provide a more fine-grained individuation of propositional meanings.

11.3.2 Quotational Theories

Quotational theories of intensionality treat the complement to a propositional-attitude verb as an expression (see Davidson 1968, for example). Thus belief, for instance, is construed as a relation between individuals and expressions. One way of making sense of this relation is to assume that the sentence following the propositional-attitude verb is one to which the speaker would agree. A number of well-known problems present themselves under such an approach. First, consider the following pair of examples (from Chierchia and McConnell-Ginet 1990).

(90) a. Jan believes that it is raining.

  b. Jan crede che sta piovendo.

The second sentence, (90b), is the Italian translation of the first sentence, (90a). But clearly the words are different, and thus the sentences are different. The issue that arises is whether it would be possible for one sentence in (90) to be true without the other one being so. Clearly, these sentences have the same truth conditions. Recall that the Tarskian theory could assign them the same meaning by giving them the same T-sentence (see section 1.1.1). The possible-worlds theory sidesteps such problems of translation inherent in quotational theories. Synonymous sentences from different languages can pick out the same set of possible worlds at which they are true.

Problems also arise with respect to noun-phrase interpretation in quotational theories. Simply consider the behavior of demonstratives, pronouns, indexicals, and quantifiers.

(91) a. Sandy₁ believes she₁ is smart.
     b. Sandy doesn't believe that theory is correct.
     c. Sandy believes someone will finish the paper.

In all of these cases, the belief is not necessarily oriented toward the expression, such as *she* or *that theory*, but toward the individual to whom the pronoun or demonstrative is referring. And although we might try to rescue the quotational theory by claiming that pronouns reinsert their antecedents, note that the same problem arises for demonstratives. One problem is that sentences are uttered from the point of view of the speaker and are intended for the listeners. Thus terms might be used that the person to whom the belief is being attributed would not even be familiar with. Simply imagine two doctors using Latinate terminology to discuss the symptoms reported by a patient in plain English. Quantifiers present similar problems on their de re interpretations: if the embedded quantifier in (91c) receives wide scope, it is rather difficult to make sense of a quotational theory. Other problems facing quotational theories involve capturing the similarity between beliefs expressed with active versus passive sentences, because obviously the expressions will vary. More detailed arguments against the quotational theory of beliefs can be found in Partee 1973b and Thomason 1977.

11.3.3 Structured Meanings and General Intensional Models

In this section we consider two approaches that have their roots in Carnap's (1947) notion of *intensional isomorphism*. The key idea is to provide a more fine-grained notion of a proposition without succumbing to the obvious flaws of the quotational theory. In some sense, the theory is highly intensional and representational, but the constructors it uses are otherwise bona fide objects and relations with standard extensional identity conditions.

In the *structured meaning* theory of Cresswell (1985), the object of a propositional attitude is a "structure" built from otherwise meaningful components. In the simplest case, for instance, a sentence such as *Sandy studied* would be represented as $\langle [\![\mathbf{study}]\!], [\![\mathbf{s}]\!] \rangle$. It is crucial to note that I have employed the denotation of the objects rather than their symbolic representations. Just as important, I have not predicated the property of the individual but rather taken them together in a structure. This is important because it allows us to represent the sentence *The student studied* as $\langle [\![\mathbf{study}]\!], \langle [\![\mathbf{the}]\!], [\![\mathbf{student}]\!] \rangle \rangle$. Now even if $[\![\mathbf{the}]\!]([\![\mathbf{student}]\!])$ turns out to be the same individual as $[\![\mathbf{sandy}]\!]$, the structured tuples are not identical. The structured-meaning theory clearly avoids the pitfalls of the quotational theory. Variables can be assumed to operate in the usual way, and quantifying-in can be applied.

To assume a uniform, compositional translation of sentences, we need a way to recover the extension of a sentence from its structured representation by simple function application. We can map $\langle a, b \rangle$ to $a(b)$, thus retrieving a proposition (perhaps intensionalized with possible worlds still) or perhaps just a truth value from the structure.

A slightly less fine-grained approach to dealing with such "structured" propositions is to treat the meanings of sentences as elements in an algebra and to homomorphically map these elements to the boolean algebra of truth values (see section A.8.2). This is the approach to intensionality adopted by Keenan and Faltz (1985) and is related to the algebraic approaches of Thomason (1980) and Veltman (1984).

In possible-worlds semantics, a proposition is a set of worlds. The set of worlds forms a boolean algebra under the natural inclusion ordering. We let $\mathbf{0}$ represent the necessarily false proposition, which is false at every world, and $\mathbf{1}$ represent the necessarily true proposition, which is true at every world.

The simplest boolean approach to propositions is to allow propositions to be arbitrary elements of some boolean algebra. But to generate truth values for propositions, we must have some way of determining which elements of the algebra are true and which are false. In a possible-worlds semantics this is straightforward: we just inspect a set of worlds to determine if the real world is a member. The set of true propositions, $\{ W \subseteq \mathbf{Dom}_{\text{World}} \mid w \in W \}$, forms what is known as a *principal filter generated* by $\{w\}$; a principal filter is a set of elements in an ordering greater than or equal to a given element. In the possible-worlds case, the ordering is by set inclusion, and the generator of the filter is the proposition $\{w\}$

consisting of only the actual world. This is because a proposition is true if and only if $w \in W$, which holds if and only if $\{w\} \subseteq W$.

To generalize from the possible-worlds case, I follow Thomason (1980) in requiring a mapping TruthVal from elements of the boolean algebra to the truth values that is a homomorphism over the logical operators. Thus we insist on the following natural conditions for truth:

(92) a. TruthVal$(\phi \wedge \psi) = $ TruthVal$(\phi) \wedge$ TruthVal(ψ)
      b. TruthVal$(\phi \vee \psi) = $ TruthVal$(\phi) \vee$ TruthVal(ψ)
      c. TruthVal$(\neg\phi) = \neg$TruthVal(ϕ)
      d. TruthVal$(\mathbf{0}) = \mathbf{no}$
      e. TruthVal$(\mathbf{1}) = \mathbf{yes}$

Note that the operations and elements on the lefthand side are in the boolean algebra, and the ones on the right are the standard logical ones. Of course, the operation on propositions in the possible-worlds theory is such a homomorphism; in fact, this is how it was constructed.

By adopting the boolean axioms, though, our domain of propositions is left with a system of logical consequence that is perhaps too coarse-grained. Instead, it has been suggested on several occasions to loosen the axioms, say by leaving out true negation or distributivity in certain cases. By leaving out all such equivalences, we are left with a system resembling the structured meaning theory. For differing proposals on which axioms to leave out and which additional, weaker axioms to put in their place, see Veltman 1984, Landman 1986, and Thomason 1980. A common assumption is that propositions form a *Heyting algebra* rather than a boolean algebra (Veltman 1984, Landman 1986). Heyting algebras are models of intuitionistic propositional logic in the same sense that boolean algebras are models of classical propositional logic. Heyting algebras can be axiomatized in much the same way as boolean algebras, with the main difference being that they do not respect the *law of the excluded middle*.

(93) a. $x \vee \neg x = \mathbf{1}$ (Excluded middle)

Even weaker algebraic systems such as those underlying relevance logic or linear logic might also be taken as a basis for propositional logic.

11.3.4 Situation Semantics

The system of *situation semantics* (Barwise and Perry 1981, 1983) was developed with two primary goals. The first was to maintain some of the key ideas of possible-worlds semantics while loosening the restriction on the totality of worlds. Note that the equivalence of (89a) and (89b) follows from the fact that every proposition receives a truth value in a world. The second goal was to provide a semantic understanding of the notion of an event as employed in Davidsonian semantics. In situation semantics, a situation is understood ontologically much like a Davidsonian event: as a limited piece of reality that can stand in relation to other parts of reality. The important relations are those involving causality and the support of facts. Such limited situations might reflect the state of affairs during one inning of a particular baseball game in 1947. Such a situation would contain information about the pitcher, the batter, the number of balls, strikes, and outs, and so on. But it would provide no information about the goings on in the British parliament, the Amazonian rain forest, or on a particular Pacific ocean liner.

A standard assumption in situation semantics is that propositions are formed by evaluating a potential state of affairs against a situation. Thus evaluating a statement such as **sleep(j)** $\lor$ $\neg$**sleep(j)**, which is about Jan's sleeping, would not produce a truth value when evaluated with respect to a situation s in which Jan is not present. On the other hand, if the situation s does determine the truth of **sleep(m)**, then we can distinguish the statements **sleep(m)** and **sleep(m)** $\land$ (**sleep(j)** $\lor$ $\neg$**sleep(j)**).

In addition to actual situations in the world, situation semantics employs situations that are not realized, in order to deal with counterfactuals (Barwise 1989). Although such a model is promising, the details of such an analysis are far from clear. For instance, it is not at all clear how to deal with negation in situation semantics, nor is it obvious how to treat quantification. But these problems stem more from its event-based nature than from the partiality of situations.

11.3.5   Truth-Value Gaps and Partial Possible Worlds

There have been two key arguments for truth-value gaps in natural-language semantics. The first was made by Łukasiewicz (1920) in the context of statements about the future, which he claimed were indeterminate in terms of their truth values. The second argument was made by Strawson (1950) in the context of presupposition failure when he argued that utterances containing failed presuppositions, such as the following, should not be given determinate truth values.

(94) The king of France is bald, or the king of France is not bald.

The intuition here is that if there is no king of France, this sentence should not have a determinate truth value. But consider the following alternative, in which one of the disjuncts has a determinate value.

(95) The king of France is bald, or the earth is round.

Because the earth is round, we might argue that this example is true, even though one of its disjuncts involves a presupposition failure. In this section we will consider two semantic approaches, one of which makes this last sentence true and one of which gives it an unknown truth value.

Semantically, the most popular way to model truth-value gaps is by means of a three-valued logic in which the truth values correspond to truth, falsehood, and unknown. In general, a partial function $f: A \to B$ from A to B can be modeled by a total function $f': A \to B \cup \{\textbf{unknown}\}$, where $\textbf{unknown} \notin B$, such that $f'(a) = f(a)$ if $f(a)$ is defined and $f'(a) = \textbf{unknown}$ if $f(a)$ is undefined. (We could alternatively use the disjoint sum operation $B \oplus \{\textbf{unknown}\}$ for the target and thus dispense with the worry as to whether $\textbf{unknown} \in B$, but I will not take this approach here.)

Type-theoretically, we can capture the three-valued approach by taking the domain of truth values to contain three values. I use the type **Bool3** for this purpose, and assume the following:

(96) $\textbf{Dom}_{\textbf{Bool3}} \stackrel{\text{def}}{=} \{\textbf{yes}, \textbf{no}, \textbf{unknown}\}$

A three-valued logic was given by Łukasiewicz (1920), and two more widely used alternatives were later proposed in a recursion-theoretic setting by Kleene (1952). The first of these alternatives is as follows:

DEFINITION: KLEENE'S STRONG THREE-VALUED LOGIC   The truth conditions for Kleene's *strong three-valued logic* are as follows:

a. $[\![\neg\phi]\!]_{\mathcal{M}} = \begin{cases} \textbf{yes} & \text{if } [\![\phi]\!]_{\mathcal{M}} = \textbf{no} \\ \textbf{no} & \text{if } [\![\phi]\!]_{\mathcal{M}} = \textbf{yes} \\ \textbf{unknown} & \text{if } [\![\phi]\!]_{\mathcal{M}} = \textbf{unknown} \end{cases}$

b. $[\![\phi \wedge \psi]\!]_{\mathcal{M}} = \begin{cases} \textbf{yes} & \text{if } [\![\phi]\!]_{\mathcal{M}} = \textbf{yes and } [\![\psi]\!]_{\mathcal{M}} = \textbf{yes} \\ \textbf{no} & \text{if } [\![\phi]\!]_{\mathcal{M}} = \textbf{no or } [\![\psi]\!]_{\mathcal{M}} = \textbf{no} \\ \textbf{unknown} & \text{otherwise} \end{cases}$

c. $[\![\phi \vee \psi]\!]_{\mathcal{M}} = \begin{cases} \textbf{yes} & \text{if } [\![\phi]\!]_{\mathcal{M}} = \textbf{yes or } [\![\psi]\!]_{\mathcal{M}} = \textbf{yes} \\ \textbf{no} & \text{if } [\![\phi]\!]_{\mathcal{M}} = \textbf{no and } [\![\psi]\!]_{\mathcal{M}} = \textbf{no} \\ \textbf{unknown} & \text{otherwise} \end{cases}$

Note that the strong connectives display the same behavior on the classical truth values as the classical connectives. Disjunction could have been defined in the usual way in terms of negation and conjunction. Kleene's strong three-valued logic provides a kind of informational account of the behavior of **unknown**. In particular, $\phi \lor \psi$ will be true if ϕ is true and ψ is unknown because the truth value of ψ will not affect the truth of the disjunction.

The only way in which Kleene's strong system differed from that of Łukasiewicz is in the definition of implication, which Kleene defined as usual by taking $\phi \rightarrow \psi$ to be shorthand for $\neg(\phi \land \neg\psi)$. Thus under Kleene's interpretation, the truth value of $\phi \rightarrow \phi$ is **unknown** if the truth value of ϕ is unknown. In Łukasiewicz's system, $\phi \rightarrow \phi$ is always true.

It is unproblematic to create a quantificational logic along the line of Kleene's strong three-valued logic. We simply treat universal quantification as an infinite conjunction and existential quantification as an infinite disjunction. Thus $\forall x \phi$ will be true if ϕ is true for every value of x, false if ϕ is false for some value of x, and unknown otherwise. If we accordingly define $\exists x \phi$ as $\neg \forall x \neg \phi$, then $\exists x \phi$ will be true if there is some x for which ϕ is true, false if ϕ is false for every x, and unknown otherwise.

With Kleene's strong three-valued logic, if we are to model presupposition failure by assigning the truth value **unknown**, then (94) has an unknown truth value, but (95) is true. Kleene also defined a *weak three-valued logic* in which any proposition containing a component that is undefined would be undefined. Under Kleene's weak interpretation, $\phi \lor \psi$ would denote **unknown** even if ϕ was true and ψ was unknown. Thus a sentence such as (95) would have an unknown truth value.

Another well-known partial logic is that of van Fraassen (1969), who defined a logic in terms of so-called *supervaluations*. Under van Fraassen's approach, the truth value of a proposition involving unknown components would have a definite truth value t if every way of extending the unknown components to the determinate truth values **yes** or **no** led to the truth value t. Thus $\phi \rightarrow \phi$ would always be true under van Frassen's theory, as would $\phi \lor \neg \phi$; in either case, if ϕ is either true or false, the resulting proposition is true. Under van Fraassen's logic, (94) is true.

Although three-valued logics are fairly well behaved in a predicate-logic setting, matters are much more complicated in a higher-order setting. This is because we can no longer curry and uncurry functions at will. Inspecting the cardinality of the relevant domains shows why. If we assume that $\sigma \rightarrow \tau$ is the type of partial functions from the domain of σ to the domain of τ and, abusing notation somewhat, let $\|\sigma\|$ be the cardinality of the domain of σ, we have the following:

(97) $\|\sigma \rightarrow \tau\| = (\|\tau\| + 1)^{\|\sigma\|}$

Assuming products behave as usual, we have the following:

(98) a. $\|\sigma \rightarrow \rho \rightarrow \tau\| = (\|\rho \rightarrow \tau\| + 1)^{\|\sigma\|} = ((\|\tau\| + 1)^{\|\rho\|} + 1)^{\|\sigma\|}$
      b. $\|\sigma \times \rho \rightarrow \tau\| = (\|\tau\| + 1)^{\|\sigma \times \rho\|} = (\|\tau\| + 1)^{\|\sigma\| \times \|\rho\|}$

Clearly, the domains can have different cardinalities in general (consider the finite case) and thus there cannot be a one-to-one function between them. Of course, nothing would prevent us from using a model of propositions as being of type **World → Bool3**. It is just that currying and uncurrying functions would not behave as we might expect from reasoning by analogy to the case of partial functions.

To develop a model in which partial "worlds" could be treated type-theoretically, Muskens (1989a, 1989b) employed Orey's (1959) relational model of higher-order logic in which curried functions were uniformly replaced with relations. This allowed Muskens to provide a concrete model of relational λ-abstraction and relational application and thus regain the representational power of the λ-calculus. The main benefit of the partial possible-worlds approach from a semantic perspective is that it allows a model of propositional attitudes that is fine-grained enough to avoid the problem of logical omniscience. In particular, it provides the power to distinguish between cases such as (89a) and (89b). On the other hand, it leaves open as many ontological issues as it solves. For instance, what does it now mean to have a "world" in which some laws of arithmetic are true and some are of unknown truth value? Clearly, we need a better understanding of the epistemological nature of propositional attitudes and other intensional constructions in natural language.

11.4 LEXICAL RELATIONS

In this section we consider some of the relationships between different lexical entries. There are distributional facts concerning control verbs that pattern just like those of ordinary verbs. Consider the following examples:

(99) a. Francis promised Brooke to lie.
      b. Francis promised to lie.
      c. Francis ate a sandwich.
      d. Francis ate.

The relation between (99a) and (99b) is the same as that between (99c) and (99d). In both cases, an object is dropped and understood existentially. That is, for an utterance of *Francis ate* to be true, there must be

something that Francis ate, and for *Francis promised to lie*, there is someone to whom Francis made the promise. This phenomenon has typically
been analyzed with the lexical rule of *detransitivization*. This rule takes a
verbal lexical entry with at least one object, the most oblique object is
stripped off, and the position it occupied is existentially quantified. For
instance, the transformation of *ate* would be as follows:

(100) a. *ate* ⇒ **eat**: $np\backslash s/np$
       b. *ate* ⇒ $\lambda x.\textbf{some}(\lambda y.\textbf{eat}(y)(x)): np\backslash s$

For evidence that it is the most oblique object that is first removed, consider the following:

(101) a.   Francis gave Brooke the book.
       b.   Francis gave the book.
       c. #Francis gave Brooke.
       d.   Francis gave.

The third example, (101c), cannot mean that something was given to
Brooke. The last example, (101e), shows that a detransitivized verb can be
further detransitivized. But some verbs, such as *taught* and *served*, allow
either argument to be removed first (Dick Oehrle, p.c.).

(102) a. Francis taught Brooke logic.
       b. Francis taught Brooke.
       c. Francis taught logic.
       d. Francis taught.

Note that with *taught*, the objects can be marked with different prepositions, as in *taught logic to Brooke* and *taught Brooke about logic*, so it is
not immediately clear that it is not these prepositional forms of the verb
that are being detransitivized. There simply are no forms of *give Brooke
the book* in which the person something is being given to has a prepositional case marking, wherase it is possible to say *give the book to Brooke*.
     The following examples muddy the issue of whether detransitivization
existentially quantifies over the "missing" object.

(103) a. Francis kicked the ball.
       b. Francis kicked.

Parsons (1990) provides an event-based account of this difference in terms
of the thematic entailments of verbs.
     A construction closely related to detransitivization but also involving
intensionality is the *causative* construction. Consider the following pair:

(104) a. The window opened.
      b. Francis opened the window.

In the second case, it is understood that Francis caused the window to open. The lexical entries could be analyzed as follows:

(105) a. $open \Rightarrow$ **open**: $np \backslash s$
      b. $open \Rightarrow \lambda x. \lambda y. \textbf{cause}(\textbf{open}(x))(y)$: $np \backslash s / np$

Not every verb can partake in the causative construction. For instance, *Francis sneezed Brooke* does not mean that Francis caused Brooke to sneeze. The verb *to open* presents a further puzzle in terms of its change-of-state reading. Consider the contrast between the following two examples (Lakoff 1970a, Jackendoff 1972).

(106) a. The door opened.
      b. The door is open.

In the case of the first example, (106a), involving a simple past-tense verb, the door must have been closed in order for it to be opened. In the case of the second example, (106b), involving a predicative, the door could be open without ever having been closed. For instance, it might just have been built. These examples show that the relationship between verbs and their corresponding predicative adjectives is quite subtle. Furthermore, the following cases show that not all causative verbs are derived from underlying noncausative sources.

(107) a. Sandy {broke / cut} the glass.
      b. The glass {broke / #cut}.

But as with other lexical phenomena, the data is subtle: contrast the example above with *The glass is hard to cut* or with *The glass is so hard it doesn't cut* (Dick Oehrle, p.c.). B. Levin (1993) provides literally hundreds of classes of verbs that appear closely related semantically but can be distinguished in subtle ways that affect their argument structure.

As a further example of lexical relations, consider noncontrol instances of propositional attitudes and their variants involving control, for instance, the lexical category for *promise* in the following two cases:

(108) a. Francis$_1$ promised Brooke that he$_1$ would lie.
      b. Francis promised Brooke to lie.

The second example, (108b), is a case of subject equi control. This example shows where the term *equi-NP deletion* arose: two terms that refer to

Francis are in some sense reduced to one. But as with other lexical relations, the relationship is more subtle than one might imagine, as in the following examples involving object equi control (Dick Oehrle, p.c.).

(109) a. Francis persuaded Sandy to run.
b. Francis persuaded Sandy that she should run.

In the first example, (109a), Sandy's running is entailed. In the case of *that* complements, a tensed complement is required, and the modal *should* in (109b) allows the possibility that Sandy did not actually run, even though she was persuaded that she should. Note that it is simply not possible to use a simple-tensed complement such as *she will run* in place of the modal *she should run*.

Raising cases can also be related to their noncontrol counterparts; consider the relation between the following:

(110) a. Francis believed that Brett ran.
b. Francis believed Brett to run.

Lexical entries involving the expletive *there* are related to nonexpletive variants. In the transformational literature, this relationship has come to be known as *there insertion*. The following examples are due to McCawley (1988).

(111) a. Unicorns exist.
b. There exist unicorns.
c. A flagpole stood at the top of the hill.
d. There stood a flagpole at the top of the hill.
e. Yesterday a tragic event occurred.
f. Yesterday there occurred a tragic event.
g. An equal and opposite reaction corresponds to every action.
h. To every action there corresponds an equal and opposite reaction.

The nonexpletive subject can behave as an expletive object, with the expletive filling the subject position.

Expletive *there* serves the functional role in discourse of moving a subject to object position. In English, the subject/object distinction often corresponds to the so-called *given/new* distinction. Discourse referents that have already been introduced, or in other words given, tend to occur as subjects. New referents tend to be introduced into discourse using objects. This provides a functional explanation of why sentences with expletive-*there* subjects favor "indefinite" complements; indefinites are the means by which new individuals are introduced into a discourse. But there are clearly nonindefinite cases that are acceptable.

(112) a. No student is unhappy here.
     b. There is no student unhappy here.
     c. There was the biggest demonstration anyone had ever seen yesterday.

The functional perspective also explains the fact that expletive cases are resistant to generic interpretations, unlike their object counterparts. Consider the following examples of McCawley's (1988):

(113) a. Books are out of stock.
     b. There are books out of stock.

The same analysis of functionality seems to account for the lack of de re readings in embedded cases of expletive-*there* subjects. Again, the examples are McCawley's (1988).

(114) a. Sam believes that some drugs are in short supply.
     b. Sam believes that there are some drugs in short supply.

A functional role analogous to the expletive-*there* cases can be seen in cases of so-called *locative inversion*.

(115) a. Into the park strolled a minstrel.
     b. A minstrel strolled into the park.

Here either order for the locative preposition and noun phrase appears acceptable. A lexical, thematic account of such cases can be found in Bresnan and Kanerva 1989.

The next case we consider is that of *extraposed* variants of control verbs and control predicates.

(116) a. It is difficult to please Francis.
     b. Francis is difficult to please.

It is normally assumed that the extraposed variant, (116a), is derived from the nonextraposed version. We explore further cases of *extraposition* and its interaction with control in exercise 18.

There is a further class of related examples for which Pustejovsky (1991) has proposed a unified generative lexical account. These involve issues of modification, reference transfer, and certain forms of lexical vagueness. For instance, consider the vagueness in evidence in the contrast between the aperture/object construal of *door* in the following examples:

(117) a. Sandy went through the door.
     b. Sandy painted the door.

In the case of the first example, Sandy presumably went not through the physical door but through the aperture. In the second example, Sandy painted the door, understood as a physical object. A related example concerns the status of the argument in the following cases:

(118) Sandy baked {the cake / the potato}.

The act of baking a cake involves the actual creation of the object, whereas baking a potato merely requires heating an already extant object. Next consider the readings of modifiers such as *fast* and *red* when applied to different objects.

(119) a. the red pen
     b. a fast {typist / car / waltz / motorway}

A pen might be described as red if its casing is red or if the color of its ink is red. Similarly, a fast typist is a person who types quickly, a fast car is one that moves quickly, a fast waltz is one with a fast tempo, and a fast motorway is one on which traffic moves quickly. Other nominal complements lead to even more possible modes of being fast.

Finally, consider the following cases of *metonymy*, a figure of speech in which reference is transferred from one object to a related notion (see also Nunberg 1977).

(120) a. The bank called today.
     b. The bank raised its interest rates.
     c. The bank is next to the post office.

In the first case, it is a representative of the bank who called; in the second case, it is the institution that raised interest rates; and in the third case, a building is being picked out. In all of these cases Pustejovsky (1991) suggests generating the required meaning by means of default understandings of how particular classes of objects can participate in designated classes of events.

We have only scratched the surface of lexical semantics and, in so doing, have not strayed far from syntacitcally realized distinctions. Without understanding lexical meanings, the best compositional semantic systems will be of little use in understanding human language. Thus the amount of attention currently being devoted to lexical semantics is well deserved and will probably continue to grow in the future.

Exercises

1. Provide lexical entries to handle the verbs in the following examples:

(a) That Francis ran is possible.

(b) It is possible that Francis ran.

(c) That Francis ran is true.

(d) It is true that Francis ran.

2. Show that neither of the following examples entails the other in our grammar (Hintikka 1962).

(a) Francis doesn't believe Brooke is cheating.

(b) Francis believes Brooke is not cheating.

Provide a meaning postulate that guarantees an entailment from the first to the second. What happens if we substitute *know* for *believe*, maintaining the assumption of veridicality for knowledge?

   Carry out the same exercise for the following pair:

(c) Francis knows that Brooke cheated.

(d) Francis knows that he knows that Brooke cheated.

   Last, carry out the same exercise for this pair:

(e) Taylor knows that Brooke cheated and Francis cheated.

(f) Taylor knows that Francis cheated.

3. What problem for our theory of pronouns is presented by examples such as the following (Geach 1967).

(a) Sandy expects to get [the grant]$_1$ and intends to start a lab with it$_1$.

(b) Hob believes [a witch]$_1$ blighted his mare, and Nob believes she$_1$ blighted his corn.

4. Provide derivations of the readings of (6b-d).

5. Provide lexical entries for the propositional-attitude verbs in the following examples (Gazdar, Klein, Pullum, and Sag 1985).

(a) Jan {conceded / admitted} to the scientists that Jupiter has rings.

(b) I bet Jan five dollars that it would rain.

(c) I require of them that they be punctual.

6. Contractions provide an interesting puzzle for a general theory of verb phrase negation (Dick Oehrle, p.c.). Consider the interaction of ordinary and contracted negation and modal auxiliaries in the following cases.

(a) Sandy can run.

(b) Sandy can not run.

(c) Sandy can't run.

(d) Sandy can't not run.

Explain the distinction in meaning between the second and third examples and between the first and fourth examples. Why is it not possible to derive the correct meaning of *can't* by composing *can* and *not*? Provide a lexical entry for *can't* that allows the correct meaning of the examples involving *can't* to be derived.

7. Provide lexical entries for the verbs in the following examples (McCawley 1988).

(a) That Francis cheated proves that he is dishonest.

(b) For you to leave so soon would inconvenience us.

(c) That Francis quit his job surprised Susan.

Do these verbs allow extraposition with expletive *it*? Do they require a *that*?

8. Provide lexical entries for the following two control verbs (Chierchia and McConnell-Ginet 1990).

(a) Sandy signaled to the man standing at the corner to cross the road.

(b) Sandy recommended crossing the road to the man standing at the corner.

9. Consider the following cases of relativization:

(a) the person [_____ eating the sandwich]

(b) the person [Francis likes _____]

The first case is known as a *reduced relative*, whereas the second is known as a *thatless relative*. Provide a pair of empty categories that are able to combine the noun and the relative clause to derive the correct meanings for the results.

   Next consider the following cases of *infinitival relatives*:

(c) the person [to talk to _____]

(d) the person [for Francis to entertain _____]

Provide a pair of empty categories to handle these cases. For the second case, assume that *for* is a control verb that takes *Francis* and an infinitival verb phrase to produce an infinitival sentence. The empty relativizer should thus take complements that are either an infinitival verb phrase missing a noun phrase or an infinitival sentence missing a verb phrase.

10. Consider the following cases of extraposition, and provide the appropriate lexical entries for the predicative *help* (McCawley 1988).

(a) I can't help that I'm madly in love with Edith.

(b) I can't help it that I'm madly in love with Edith.

(c) For it to rain would be a disaster.

Consider generalizing the treatment of relatives to account for the following:

(d) The only thing that surprised me is that Sandy got so many votes.

Generalize the treatment of the pseudoclefting free relativizer *what* from exercise 13, chapter 6, to account for sentential complements such as the following:

(e) What I can't help is that I'm madly in love with Edith.

11. Consider the following examples and provide an appropriate polymorphic lexical entry for *seems* (Dale Gerdemann, p.c.). (Hint: The object is a predicative controlled by the subject.)

(a) Sandy seems {fun / tall / ?impossible}.

(b) To run seems {fun / *tall / impossible}.

(c) That Sandy solved that problem seems {*fun / *tall / impossible}.

12. Consider the de dicto and de re readings generated by our grammar for the following examples:

(a) That everyone failed is problematic.

(b) To know everyone is difficult.

Are both readings felicitous in both cases?

13. Consider the status of *conative* complements to verbs, which are expressed in English by means of the preposition *at*.

(a) Sandy waved the sword at Francis.

(b) Sandy threw the ball at Francis.

Next consider the status of *instrumentive* complements of verbs, which are expressed in English with the preposition *with*.

(c) Sandy buttered the toast with a knife.

(d) Sandy wrote with a pen.

What is the relation between sentences with such complements and those without? Is it only a subclass of verbs that can have such complements?

14. Consider the status of the adjectival, nominal, and prepositional predicates that occur in the following *resultatives* (Dowty 1979).

(a) Sandy pounded the dough {smooth / into a loaf}.

(b) Sandy painted the barn {blue / a reddish tint}.

(c) Sandy made her sculpture {tall / ugly}.

Provide lexical entries for the verbs that take predicate complements, and discuss their relation to the simple transitive versions of the verbs. Can you characterize the class of verbs that admits resultative complements?

15. Consider the following uses of control verbs with simple nominal objects, discussed by Dowty (1985).

(a)   Jan attempted the problem.

(b)   Jan wants an apple.

(c)   Jan finished the book.

(d)   Jan refused the drink.

(e)   Jan promised Morgan a book.

(f) *Jan persuaded Morgan a book.

Should examples such as these be read as implicitly involving a kind of ellipsis of a verbal meaning? And if so, what is the grammatical status of the argument with respect to the elided verb-phrase meaning? Pustejovsky (1991) goes so far as to suggest that there are typical meanings for such elisions, based on the semantics of the complement. He contrasts examples such as these:

(g) Jan finished the book.

(h) Jan finished the meal.

The first is typically understood as finished reading, whereas the second is understood as finished eating. Of course, both can mean other things, such as finished writing, finished editing for the former and finished cooking for the latter.

16. Consider the following intensional comparative constructions.

(a) Sandy is so tall that she cannot fit through the door.

(b) Sandy is too tall to fit through the door.

(c) Sandy is tall enough to reach the ceiling.

Provide lexical entries for *so*, *too*, and *enough* that generate predicatives with the appropriate semantics. Does the semantics you provide also work with the downard gradable adjective *short*?

17. Consider the difference between the following pairs of examples (Pustejovsky 1991).

(a) I forgot to run.

(b) I forgot that I ran.

(c) I promised (Sandy) to run.

(d) I promised (Sandy) that I would run.

In view of the change in veridicality in the first pair between the version with a complementized-sentence complement and the version involving subject equi control, what can you conclude about the generality of lexical relations?

18. Provide lexical entries for the extraposed variants of the following verbs:

(a) Francis is difficult to please

(b) It is difficult to please Francis.

(c) That Francis snores annoys Taylor.

(d) It annoys Taylor that Francis snores.

Use your categories to provide a derivation of the following:

(e) It doesn't seem to annoy Taylor that Francis snores.

19. Provide a meaning postulate that guarantees completeness of belief, so that for every proposition ϕ, an individual believes either ϕ or $\neg_p\phi$ (recall that $\neg_p \overset{\text{def}}{=} \lambda p.\lambda w.\neg p(w)$ is the propositional negation operator that distributes through the possible-worlds argument). Does such a meaning postulate make sense empirically?

20. The following examples are of a so-called *naked-infinitive verb of perception*:

(a) Francis saw Brooke run.

(b) Francis saw Betty's husband run.

(c) Francis saw his best friend run.

Barwise and Perry (1983) claim that unlike other propositional attitudes, perception reports are insensitive to differences in description. Why is such a theory so difficult to implement in a possible-worlds setting?

21. What sort of problems do fictional discourses present? For instance, how might names be dealt with in such a context? How might we account for the truth conditions of sentences such as *Santa Claus has a white beard* or *Santa Claus rides a sleigh*?

22. Quine had the following to say about ontological commitment in logical models: "Entities of a given sort are assumed by a theory if and only if some of them must be counted among the values of the variables, in order that the statements affirmed in the theory be true" (1961, 103). This is often translated as the slogan "to be is to be the value of a bound variable." Discuss Quine's point in relation to modal logic, and in particular, the status of the quantification induced by □.

Quine (1960, 176–186) introduced an operation that, he showed, could eliminate the need for singular terms. Recall the definition of the operation of *quining* from section 3.5.4, which I repeat here. The quining combinator $\mathbf{Q}$, of type $\mathbf{Ind} \rightarrow \mathbf{Ind} \rightarrow \mathbf{Bool}$, is defined as follows: $\mathbf{Q} \overset{\text{def}}{=} \lambda x.\lambda y.x = y$. Quine (1961, 13) says that "whatever we say with the help of names can be said in a language which shuns names altogether." How can quining, combined with a definite-description operator (or quantifier), eliminate the need for λ terms of type $\mathbf{Ind}$? How might we interpret Quine's ontological principles in the light of the quining operator, combined with variable-free, combinator-based logics?

23. Quine (1961) introduced another idea, which is captured by the slogan "no entity without identity." By this, Quine meant that to introduce an object or class of objects into a theory required a solid understanding of their identity conditions, or in other words, of the conditions by which such objects could be distinguished and/or identified. Discuss this concept in relation to the notion of possible worlds.

24. Dowty, Wall, and Peters (1981) attribute to Anil Gupta by way of Michael Bennett the following argument (which is invalid in Montague's [1973] grammar and logic).

(a) The temperature is necessarily the price.

(b) The temperature rises.

(c) Therefore, the price rises.

Do any of the analyses I have introduced for definite descriptions and intensional verbs like *rises* validate this argument?

25. How does a rigid-designator approach to proper names allow us to provide a possible-worlds analysis of counterfactuals such as the following (Gamut 1991b).

(a) If Dukakis had won the election in 1988, the president of the United States in 1989 would have been a democrat.

In particular, how does the assumption that names are rigid designators allow us to solve the transworld identity problem raised in section 10.2.1?

26. Hamblin (1958) introduced a semantics of questions based on so-called *answer spaces*, which was further articulated by Karttunen (1977). Consider the following interrogatives and their intended answer-space-based semantics.

(a) *Did Sandy study* $\Rightarrow \lambda p.p = \mathbf{study}(\mathbf{s})\colon s_y$

(b) *Which book did Sandy read* $\Rightarrow \lambda p.\mathbf{some}(\mathbf{book})(\lambda x.p = \mathbf{read}(x)(\mathbf{s}))\colon s_q$

Using the syntactic categories in (76), section 9.9, provide semantic terms that derive meanings such as those above for questions. With the lexical entries you provide, is it possible to provide an ambiguous interpretation for *disjunctive questions*, such as the following?

(c) Who likes Sandy or Terry?

(d) Who does Sandy or Terry like?

27. Several analyses have been put forward to handle Russell's (1905) famous example, in which a guest addresses a yacht owner with the following:

(a) *Guest*: I thought your yacht was larger than it is.

(b) *Yacht owner*: No, my yacht is not larger than it is.

Russell points out that the guest's utterance is ambiguous. Show that a natural intensionalization of the comparative provides an intuitive account of the contradictory construal of the guest's remark. Russell also pointed out there is a noncontradictory reading in which the actual size takes wide scope. Show how such an analysis would be possible by taking the phrasal complement with an extracted predicate, *than it is*, to be assigned to a quantifier, perhaps by assigning *that* to the category $np \Uparrow s/(s{\uparrow}pr)$. Can a noncontradictory reading be generated by assigning this quantifier widest scope?

An analysis that is perhaps more akin to the paraphrase Russell provided can be had by assigning the comparative *larger* to the syntactic category $(s/(np\backslash s))\backslash s/(s{\uparrow}pr)$. An appropriate semantics can be determined by considering the argument-raised version of *larger*. Two readings can then be generated for Russell's example, depending on whether the "subject" $s/(np\backslash s)$ is taken to be *I thought your yacht was* or *your yacht was*. Provide these two analyses. Do they generate the appropriate readings? Explain why these analyses do or do not generate the correct unambiguous meaning for the following related example.

(c) Your yacht is larger than I thought it was.

Discuss whether these analyses extend adequately to modal control ambiguities with comparatives, such as the following:

(d) Sandy could be taller than she is.

Can you think of other portions of the comparative complement that might be scoped out of the belief context in order to generate the right ambiguities for the above examples?

28. Prove that the following results hold in every boolean algebra (see section A.8.2 for definitions).

(a) $\neg \mathbf{1} = \mathbf{0}$ $\neg \mathbf{0} = \mathbf{1}$

(b) $\neg x$ is the unique element satisfying the inverse condition

(c) $\mathbf{0}$ and $\mathbf{1}$ are the unique elements satisfying the identity conditions

(d) $x \wedge x = x$ $x \vee x = x$

(e) $\neg \neg x = x$

(f) $x \wedge (x \vee y) = y$ $x \vee (x \wedge y) = y$

(g) $\neg (x \wedge y) = (\neg x) \vee (\neg y)$ $\neg (x \vee y) = (\neg x) \wedge (\neg y)$

(h) $\mathbf{0} \wedge x = \mathbf{0}$ $\mathbf{1} \vee x = \mathbf{1}$

29. Consider the intensional comparative construction involving *so*:

(a) Sandy was so tired that she fell asleep in class.

(b) So many flowers arrived today that Sandy had to stay home to arrange them.

(c) A man arrived who was so hungry that we had to order out for food.

(d) Our guest arrived so tired that we put her to bed.

(e) Dana learned calculus so long ago that he has forgotten it.

Ignoring the issue of the extraposition, explain how the meaning of the discontinuous *so ... that* construction can be represented.

30. Given the lexical entry in (58a) and the meaning postulate in (58b), show the two derivations of the following example:

(a) Sandy found a unicorn.

Given the meaning postulate above, show that the semantic terms resulting from these derivations normalize to the same result. Show that the lexical entry in (58) can be derived from the following lexical entry.

(b) *found* $\Rightarrow$ **find**$_2$: $np\backslash s/np$

31. Assume the lexical entry in (55) and the meaning postulate in (56) for *seek*, and assume that *try* is an ordinary object equi verb and that *find* is an ordinary transitive verb of category $np\backslash s/np$. Show that *seek* and *try to find* have the same two distinct semantic derivations of category $np\backslash s/(np\Uparrow s)$. (Hint: For all of the derivations, assume a left-peripheral noun phrase and a right-peripheral quantifier. For one derivation of the *try to find* case, reduce the quantifier inside the controlled verb phrase. For the other, reduce the quantifier at the topmost sentence level. Derive the cases involving *seek* in the same way as in figure 11.6.)

32. Explain why the incompleteness of the scoping operator $\Uparrow$, as I have presented it here, prevents us from deriving a de dicto reading of the quantifiers in the following examples:

(a) Sandy sought the autograph of some player.

(b) Sandy sought every player's autograph.

(Hint: Explain why the complement noun phrases cannot be analyzed as being of category $np\Uparrow s$.) How does the following lexical assignment, based loosely on that of Morrill (1994a), allow us to derive the the de dicto meaning?

(c) *seek* $\Rightarrow \lambda Q.\lambda x.\mathbf{try}(Q(\mathbf{find})(x))(x)$: $np\backslash s/((np\backslash s/np)\backslash np\backslash s)$

Finally, discuss why the above lexical entry allows us to derive the wrong reading for the following example:

(d) Jan sought Francis {in New York / last week}.

(Hint: Provide a derivation using composition in which the finding was in New York or yesterday rather than the trying.) (Note: Morrill [1994a] presents a solution to the second problem in terms of intensional modalities; he has also developed an unpublished solution to the problem of deriving a generalized quantifier from *the autograph of some player*.) (See Carpenter 1994c.)

Chapter 12

Tense and Aspect

In this chapter I will lay out a theory of the interpretation of tense, including tense morphology, auxiliaries, and temporal modifiers. In so doing, I build a theory of English aspect, covering both the progressive and the perfect, in addition to simple tenses.

The Priorean tense-operator approach, based on the modalities **F** and **P** of future and past, was seen in section 10.6 to be deficient along a number of lines. It did not allow expressions to refer to time, did not allow for embedded modifiers such as *now* to be interpreted properly, and had no way of accounting for the distinction between perfective, imperfective, and simple aspectual marking.

12.1 REICHENBACH'S APPROACH TO SIMPLE AND PERFECT TENSES

English is equipped with mechanisms to express the occurrence of events in the past, present, and future. The past and present tenses are expressed morphologically, whereas the future is expressed with the auxiliary *will*. English also has a morphologically expressed *subjunctive* form, used to express counterfactual or potential events. In addition to tense, English also makes an orthogonal distinction between perfective, progressive, and simple aspects. The traditional grammatical term *perfective* indicates a completion of the event in question, whereas *progressive* indicates an event in progress (which may never be completed). In English, simple tenses are used for events that have been completed. Aspect is expressed with a combination of tense morphology and special auxiliary verbs. Table 12.1 gives the pefect and simple cases in the past, present, and future (for third-person singular subjects). We return to progressives in section 12.5.5.

Reichenbach (1947) presented a theory of tense and aspect in which each phrase involved two temporal points of evaluation in addition to the

Table 12.1
Simple and perfect tenses in English

	Past	Present	Future
Simple	ate	eats	will eat
Perfect	had eaten	has eaten	will have eaten

Table 12.2
Reichenbach's constraints on event, reference, and speech times

Tense	Constraint	Aspect	Constraint
Past	$t_R < t_S$	Simple	$t_E = t_R$
Present	$t_R = t_S$	Perfect	$t_E < t_R$
Future	$t_R > t_S$		

Note: t_E = event time; t_R = reference time; t_S = speech time.

time of speech. The first temporal point is the *event time*, which is the time at which the event referred to by the verb is asserted to take place. For the examples in table 12.1, the event time would be the time of the eating. In addition, Reichenbach employed a *reference time*, which is the time from which the event is viewed. Reichenbach's theory of the perfect and simple tenses is quite straightforward. Past, present, and future tenses relate the reference time to the speech time, constraining it to be before, at, or after the time of speech respectively. In the simple tenses, reference time and event time are identified. Thus in simple tenses, the event time must be before, at, or after the speech time, depending on whether the tense is past, present, or future. The perfect tenses, on the other hand, requires the event time to be before the reference time. This provides an analysis of the notion of completion for the perfect aspect. Reichenbach's constraints are given diagrammatically in table 12.2. The distinction between a simple past, which requires that that $t_E = t_R < t_S$, and a past perfect, which requires that $t_E < t_R < t_S$, is that the past perfect requires two steps into the past. At the time of reference, which is before the speech time, the event has already been completed. For a simple present we have $t_E = t_R = t_S$, but for a present perfect we have $t_E < t_R = t_S$; in this case the shift in time is more dramatic because the reference time stays with the speech time but the event time is earlier. Note that for simple tenses, only two temporal periods are needed, because the event time and reference time are identified. Further note that the progressive and subjunctive forms of verbs fall outside the Reichenbachian system.

Åqvist (1976), Åqvist and Guenthner (1977), and Guenthner (1979) demonstrated that a Reichenbachian approach to tense and aspect could be represented by a multimodal logic with indices for reference times, speech times, and event times. Hinrichs (1988) extended their approach to intensional logic and showed how the approach could solve a number of outstanding problems having to do with the interaction of quantifiers, modifiers, and tense. I adopt a slightly different approach based on an alternative semantics of aspect.

12.2 TENSE AND DISCOURSE

Theories of discourse are often formulated in Reichenbachian terms. Hinrichs (1981, 1986), Dowty (1982a), Nerbonne (1986), and Partee (1984a), for instance, put forward theories in which narrative discourses typically require the reference time to move forward with each successive clause. These theories share the property of treating the reference time as a kind of anaphoric element at the discourse level. Such theories can account for discourse fragments such as the following:

(1) a. Sandy walked into the room. $t_E = t_R < t_S$
     b. She turned on the light. $t'_E = t'_R < t'_S$

(2) a. Sandy walked into the room. $t_E = t_R < t_S$
     b. He had turned on the light. $t'_E < t'_R < t'_S$

In the sequence of simple past tenses, as in (1), it is natural to interpret the light's being turned on as occurring after Sandy walked into the room. When the second utterance involves a perfective, as in (2), the natural interpretation is that the light had been turned on earlier. In both cases, the reference time can move along in the discourse independently of the time of the events being reported. These temporal discourse relations are realized by the constraint $t_R < t'_R$; in (1), this entails $t_E < t'_E$, but for (2), we can draw no conclusions about the relations between t_E and t'_E. Hinrichs (1986) elaborates a theory that accounts not only for sequences of two tenses indicated morphologically but also for interactions of (temporal) conjunction and adverbial modifiers.

As pointed out by Nerbonne (1986), it is not difficult to find cases in which this very strong constraint on sequencing reference times is violated. For instance, in the case where the second sentence involves a more static verb, the second sentence can be interpreted cotemporaneously with the first.

(3) a. Sandy walked into the room.
    b. The light was on.

Here we naturally interpret the walking into the room to occur while the light was on. In other kinds of discourse, further statements can be taken as *elaborations* of previous utterances.

(4) a. Sandy built a house.
    b. She laid out the plans, bought the materials, and acted as a general contractor.

Here the second sentence involves a sequence of clauses, each of which is interpreted in sequence as an elaboration of the first sentence. Such elaborations need not occur in order, either. Nerbonne concludes that the principle of reference-time sequencing should be taken as a pragmatic implicature, rather than as a strict implication. Dowty (1986b) also adopts a pragmatic view and allows explicit adverbials to override the implicated progression of reference times.

In computational implementations of discourse, it is often assumed that there is a kind of *discourse grammar* that classifies the possible relationships between discourse segments (Mann and Thompson 1988). These are often structured much like a phrase-structure grammar (Grosz and Sidner 1986). For instance, the elaboration in (4b) is taken to be subordinate to the initial statement in (4a), whereas the clauses in (4b) are analyzed as sisters. Other approaches eschew grammatical approaches to discourse structure and instead concentrate on possible coherence relations between utterances, given versus new information, and so on. But everyone agrees that there is a tight interconnection between the temporal interpretation of utterances and the way in which utterances are put together to form a discourse.

12.3   VENDLER'S VERB CLASSES

Vendler (1967) introduced an influential classification of verbs based on their event structure. There are many variants of Vendler's classifications; I adopt the version proposed by Carlson (1981) and modified slightly by Bach (1986), which has gained wide acceptance in the literature on aspectual structure. I reproduce a diagrammatic version of Bach's clas-

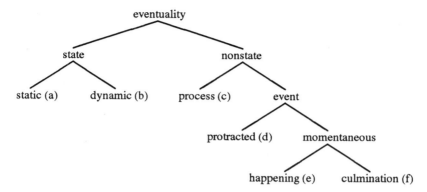

Figure 12.1
The Bach and Carlson classification of events

sification in figure 12.1. It is difficult, perhaps even impossible, to give necessary and sufficient conditions for classifying a verb utterance into one of these categories. As instances of these classes, Bach proposed the following examples in their typical uses.

(5) a. Static state: be drunk, be in New York, own x, love y, resemble z, . . .
   b. Dynamic state: sit, stand, lie (locative), . . .
   c. Process: walk, push a cart, be mean (agentive), . . .
   d. Protracted event: build x, walk to Boston, . . .
   e. Happening: recognize, notice, flash once, . . .
   f. Culmination: die, reach the top, . . .

The main divison is between statives and nonstatives, with statives lacking activity in comparison with processes. Often dynamic states are identified with processes and classifed as nonstatives. States are also *temporally homogeneous* in that if a state holds during a temporal period, it holds during all of its subperiods. For processes, like running, if the subperiods get small enough, it is no longer clear whether we can say that someone is running or not. The problem is analogous to mass nouns, such as *fruit-cake*, which I discussed in the context of the homogeneity constraint in section 8.10.

A sharp syntactic divide between the static states and other kinds of events is manifest in the infelicity of progressive variants of static states.

(6) a.   Sandy is walking.   (Process)
    b.   Sandy is sitting.   (Dynamic state)
    c. # Sandy is owning a car.   (Static state)

Within the nonstative categories, the division between processes and events is determined by whether there is a natural progression and culmination to the activity (an event), as opposed to a homogeneous structure followed by a simple stoppage of the activity (a process). To some extent, this division parallels the mass/count distinction in the noun system. Events are themselves broken down according to whether they occupy an extended period of time or are viewed as occurring at moments (such viewpoints can change in discourse, so what is considered a protracted event in one setting may be treated as momentaneous from a more distant perspective). Processes and states occur with the temporal preposition *for*, whereas events do not. Protracted events can be modified by the temporal preposition *in*, whereas no other class of utterances can be.

(7) a.   Terry walked {for / #in} an hour.   (Process)
    b.   Kim wrote a paper {#for / in} an hour.   (Protracted event)
    c.   Kim recognized Sandy {#for / #in} an hour.   (Happening)

To see that it is not verbs but rather uses of them that have to be classified, consider the following contrasts. First note that the arguments such as the object can play a role in determining the aspectual category of the result.

(8) a. Sandy walked.   (Process)
    b. Sandy walked to Squirrel Hill.   (Protracted event)

With a locative preposition, the verb *walk* usually behaves as a protracted event rather than as a process; the destination provides a natural culmination to the activity. We observe similar contrasts with mass-noun and count-noun objects in verbs like *drink*:

(9) a. Sandy drank {ε / beer}.   (Process)
    b. Sandy drank {a beer / several beers}.   (Protracted event)

With no object or with a mass object, drinking is a process; with a countable object, such as *a beer* or *three beers*, drinking is a protracted event. But even without modifiers or objects to coerce a verb to a particular temporal aspect, a single verb can give rise to several different temporal structures, as exemplified by Moens and Steedman (1988):

(10) a. Sandy sneezed [for an hour].
     b. Dana played the sonata [for eight hours].
     c. Kim left the room [for a few minutes].
     d. Chris reached the top of the mountain [in a day].

In (10a) through (10d), verbs that are typically interpreted as nonprocesses are interpreted as processes. In (10a), sneezing, which is typically a momentaneous happening, behaves as a process. It is understood as an iterative act of sneezing several times. In (10b), the protracted event of playing a sonata is naturally iterated to form a process of repeated sonata playing. Other coercions are more interesting. The act of leaving a room is typically momentaneous, but (10c) is naturally interpreted as meaning that Kim stayed out of the room for a few minutes, rather than as an iteration or a protracted single leaving event. In (10d), the momentaneous act of reaching the top of a mountain is modified by *in a day* with the understanding that the preparatory process of climbing extended throughout a day. Moens and Steedman present a range of similar examples, along with a collection of coercion operations that can be used to shift the aspectual type of an utterance. The complete range of coercion operators they consider are as follows:

(11) a. add a preparatory processes to a culmination
     b. view any eventuality as pointlike
     c. iterate a point to produce a process
     d. map a point to a culmination
     e. strip a culmination from a culminated process to produce a
        process
     f. add a culmination to a process to produce a culminated process
     g. convert a point into a habitual state
     h. convert a culmination into its consequent state
     i. convert a process to a progressive in-process state

They point out, as well, that these coercion operators can be composed. For instance, a point can be iterated into a process and then have a culmination added. Similarly, a culminated process can be mapped into a point and then iterated.

12.4 A SEMANTIC APPROACH TO ASPECT

Rather than strictly following Reichenbach's approach, I incorporate his insights into the semantics of Moens and Steedman (1988) and Passonneau

(1988). The key to these event-based approaches is to segment an event into three components, which Moens and Steedman refer to as the *nucleus* of the event. As they define it, a nucleus consists of three stages: a *preparatory process*, a *culmination*, and a *consequent state*. For instance, they break down the event of climbing Mount Everest into the preparation of climbing the mountain, the culmination of reaching the summit, and the consequent state of being at the top of the mountain.

Particular utterances of clauses are then assumed to refer to distinguished parts of the nucleus. For instance, a perfective such as *Sandy has eaten the cake* is assumed to refer to the consequent state of the cake having been eaten. This explains, among other things, the fact that perfective consequent states follow the events of which they are consequents. Thus in a present perfect sentence, the consequent state is going on presently, having followed the preparation and culmination. Reichenbach's reference time naturally corresponds to the time of the consequent state, whereas the event time corresponds to the preparation and culmination. Consider the following present perfect example:

(12) I have spilled my coffee.

This sentence can naturally be uttered soon after the coffee was spilled but is infelicitous if uttered the next day, for instance.

Turning to progressives, we can treat an example such as *Sandy is crossing the street* as referring to the preparatory process of street crossing. The key semantic fact concerning the progressive in most cases is that the event in question need not be culminated. Of course, not every event can be so naturally segmented into a preparatory process, culmination, and consequent state. In cases such as blinking and sneezing, Moens and Steedman point out that the more natural coercion to a state for *Sandy is sneezing* involves an iteration. We return to a detailed analysis of progressives in section 12.5.5.

Moens and Steedman also provide a decompositional approach to Vendler's event classification. First they set aside states. Nonstates are then subcategorized according to whether or not they have a culmination and whether or not they are extended in time. Mapping this onto the Bach and Carlson classification in figure 12.1, we see that processes are extended but not culminated, whereas a protracted event is both culminated and extended. The momentaneous events are not extended, with happenings having no culmination, and culminations consisting only of a culmination. Coercion operators such as iteration, culmination stripping, preparation addition, and so forth, can be used to move between event types.

12.5   A GRAMMAR OF TENSE AND ASPECT

In this section we develop a categorial grammar of English tense and aspect. Adopting Moens and Steedman's (1988) semantic approach to aspect allows us to get by with a single time index on verbs. But instead of an intensional approach, we follow the type-theoretic practice of incorporating a new basic type **Per** of semantic periods. Accompanying this domain are logical constants for complete temporal precedence, temporal overlap, and temporal inclusion. For the sake of concreteness, we can assume the domain of temporal periods is made up of intervals over the real numbers, with standard duration measures taken as primitive.

12.5.1   Verb Forms

We subcategorize verbs in the traditional way by classifying them according to whether they are finite or non-finite, and whether they involve simple or perfect tense. I postpone consideration of the progressive aspect until the next section. I achieve the desired syntactic effect by distinguishing the following kinds of sentences:

(13) *Category*	*Type*	*Syntax*	*Semantics*
s_b	**Per → Bool**	Base	Untensed
s_i	**Per → Bool**	Infinitive	Untensed
s_p	**Per → Bool**	Past participle	Perfect
s_g	**Per → Bool**	Present participle	Progressive
s_f	**Per → Bool**	Finite	Tensed

Note that each sentential category has the same semantic type, namely a function from times to truth values. There is nothing surprising in the interaction of tense and other types of intensionality, so I simplify matters here by assuming an extensional semantics. The temporal arguments will always correspond to the time of the eventuality being reported. Keep in mind that this simplification is possible because perfectives refer to consequent states of other, nonstative eventualities and progressives involve coercion of other eventualities to processes.

Syntactically, we do not need to change verbal lexical entries; verb phrases are still assigned the category $np\backslash s$. Semantically, we need to do a bit more work because we now have a time index to contend with. In the base form, no constraint is put on the point of evaluation.

(14) a. *run* ⇒ **run**: $np \backslash s_b$
      b. *like* ⇒ **like**: $np \backslash s_b / np$

Note that only sentences are marked for verb form; the form of a verb phrase is determined from that of its sentential-result category. We then interpret the constant **run** as a relation between an individual and a period such that $\llbracket \mathbf{run} \rrbracket (a)(t)$ is true if a is an individual that ran during period t. This English gloss of the meaning of *run* is rather vague. We have not specified, for instance, that the constant **run** picks out an eventuality of the process variety. It is plausible to derive Moens and Steedman's approach to aspect by assigning verbs lexically to a single aspectual category and then freely applying coercion operators to induce the desired range of polysemy. It remains unclear how to handle the range of lexical-argument frames for a verb like *run*, which can occur in contexts such as the following:

(15) a. Sandy ran.
      b. Sandy ran to the store.
      c. Sandy ran a mile.
      d. Sandy ran a mile from her house through the park to the store.

For instance, the expression *a mile* appears to act in some ways like an argument and in other ways like a locative modifier, whereas *to the store* is more clearly a modifier. Gawron (1986) provides a range of data on the forms of path modifiers that can apply to verbs of motion. There has been a great deal of attention paid to the kinds of alternations shown in (15) among those concerned with lexical semantics (Cruse 1986), excellent recent examples of which are Dowty 1991 and B. Levin 1993. From a categorial perspective, linking theories, such as that of L. Levin (1987) for LFG, could be employed to map underlying lexical semantic representations into categories and logical terms. I leave open the question of the extent to which issues of lexical semantics and coercion interact with syntax and pragmatics (see Pustejovsky 1991).

12.5.2   Simple Finite Verbs and Auxiliary Verbs

In this section we consider finite forms of verbs along with the finite-inducing auxiliary *do*, which is often referred to as a *support verb*. Our treatment of auxiliaries follows that of GPSG (Gazdar, Pullum, and Sag

1982). Under their analysis, the syntactic function of an auxiliary is to map a verb phrase of one type to a verb phrase of another type. With respect to their subjects, auxiliaries function like subject-raising control verbs such as *seem* and intensional adverbs like *possibly*. The contribution of the finite morphology is a restriction on the temporal interpretation. Auxiliaries can be classified according to the verb form of their argument: *be* takes progressive arguments, *do* and the modal auxiliaries like *will* and *should* take base-form arguments, and *have* takes perfective arguments. Auxiliaries are themselves marked for verb form and can be inflected much like other verbs, modulo their rather degenerate and exceptional paradigm structure, which both restricts and extends standard agreement patterns. For instance, the auxiliary forms of *do* and *be* do not have progressive forms. Forms of *be* are also more finely distinguished than forms of other verbs: consider the distinctions among *am*, *are*, and *is* in the present tense of *be*.

   I begin with the entries for the auxiliary *do*, which takes a base-form verb-phrase complement. I restrict attention to the third-person singular forms; the plural and non-third-person forms are analogous and introduce nothing new semantically. I will assume that the constant **now** is interpreted indexically as the time of utterance (see section 10.3).

(16) a. *does* $\Rightarrow \lambda V.\lambda x.\lambda t. V(x)(t) \wedge t = $ **now**$: np\backslash s_f/(np\backslash s_b)$
     b. *did* $\Rightarrow \lambda V.\lambda x.\lambda t. V(x)(t) \wedge t < $ **now**$: np\backslash s_f/(np\backslash s_b)$

This leads to analyses such as the following by simple application.

(17) *Sandy did run* $\Rightarrow \lambda t.\textbf{run}(s)(t) \wedge t < $ **now**$: s_f$

To generate a truth value for the sentence, we must existentially quantify over the temporal argument. In other words, *Sandy did run* is true if and only if there is some time t before now such that Sandy ran at time t. It is traditional to introduce this quantification directly into the meaning of the auxiliary, but this blocks a number of indefinite patterns of tense, as pointed out by Partee (1973a). First, it is natural to have intersentential binding of temporal pronouns like *then*, as in the following:

(18) a. Sandy went to the store yesterday.
     b. Terry went to the store then, too.

If the temporal index of the first sentence is bound off by a quantifier, it will not be accessible as an antecedent for *then*. Partee (1984a) provides the following example in support of the fact that simple tenses themselves can act pronominally.

(19) Sandy didn't turn off the stove.

Neither scoped reading generated by a tense logic suffices for the interpretation of such an example. The logical form $\mathbf{P}\neg\mathbf{turn\_off}(\imath(\mathbf{stove}))(\mathbf{s})$ implies that there was some time in the past at which Sandy did not turn off the stove, which is trivially true. The other possibility, $\neg\mathbf{P}\ \mathbf{turn\_off}(\imath(\mathbf{stove}))(\mathbf{s})$ is true only if Sandy never turned off the stove. Partee suggests that the temporal refernce in such a sentence should be interpreted like an indefinite, with the temporal point of evaluation being determined anaphorically in relation to the context. Next consider the parallel between generics and so-called *habituals*:

(20) a. A bear will attack if provoked.
       b. Sandy smokes after dinner.

In the first case, the indefinite *a bear* can be interpreted generically. Similarly, the second example can have the tense interpreted generically, thus inducing a habitual reading. Because I am not presenting a grammar for indefinites, I will provide an approximation in terms of λ-abstraction of the indefinitelike temporal point of evaluation. Partee (1984a) and Kamp and Reyle (1993) embed a theory of temporal interpretation in discourse-representation theory, which provides an excellent model of indefiniteness.

Finite verbs such as *ran* will be lexically characterized as synonymous with *did run*. Thus we have verbs inflected for past and present tense as follows:

(21) a. *ran* $\Rightarrow \lambda x.\lambda t.\mathbf{run}(x)(t) \wedge t \prec \mathbf{now}: np\backslash s_{\mathrm{f}}$
       b. *runs* $\Rightarrow \lambda x.\lambda t.\mathbf{run}(x)(t) \wedge t = \mathbf{now}: np\backslash s_{\mathrm{f}}$

Similar moves will be made for other subcategories of verbs, such as transitive, ditransitive, sentential complement, control verbs, and so on.

To return to present-tense verbs, note that the constraint induced by the finite morphology is $t = \mathbf{now}$. This proposal is difficult to distinguish from one in which the constraint is either $t \sqsubseteq \mathbf{now}$ or $t \circ \mathbf{now}$, because of the vagueness of interpreting $\mathbf{now}$ as an interval. The simple present tense is rather underutilized in everyday conversation. It has been called the *sportscaster's tense* because sports announcers are frequently in a position to use the present tense. Often present-tense forms are interpreted generically or habitually.

(22) a. She dribbles down the field and scores.
       b. Sandy runs.

In the first example, (22a), the present tense is used when the dribbling is done and as the score is made. In the second example, (22b), a natural interpretation in the null context would be a habitual use. The present tense is much more common when coupled with the perfective or progressive aspect.

The future "tense" is expressed in English with the modal auxiliary *will*. A simple tensed approach can be achieved with the following lexical entry, paralleling the past tense *did*.

(23) *will* $\Rightarrow \lambda V.\lambda x.\lambda t.V(x)(t) \wedge$ **now** $\prec t: np\backslash s_f / (np\backslash s_b)$

This modal auxiliary, and others such as *should, could,* and *might*, apply to base-form verb phrases to produce finite ones. The semantics of the other modal auxiliaries is intensional along dimensions other than tense.

Unfortunately, matters are not so simple. We can use the modal *will* not only to refer to events in the future but also ones in the present, as noted by Palmer (1974).

(24) I will write that paper now.

Moens and Steedman (1988) elaborate Boyd and Thorne's (1969) speech-act-based model by claiming that *will* applies if, at the time of speech, the speaker thinks that the proposition denoted by the argument will occur. They further claim that modal *must* is similar, modulo the lack of speaker orientation, and that *may* differs from *must* in the way that *possibly* differs from *necessarily*.

Further complicating the notion of future in English is the possibility of the so-called *tenseless future*. Leech (1971) noted that for a present-tense verb to be used in the future, an anchoring adverbial is needed.

(25) a.   Sandy leaves next Tuesday.
      b. # Sandy leaves.

Thus the bare case in (25b) cannot be used to refer to a time in the future.

12.5.3 Intersective Temporal Modifiers

Simple temporal modifiers such as *yesterday, at 5 p.m., on Tuesday, for two hours,* and so on, can be analyzed as intersective adverbials whose contribution is a restriction on the event time. I will treat them lexically as verb-phrase modifiers, but they can equally well be handled as sentence modifiers (see exercise 2).

(26) a. *yesterday* $\Rightarrow \lambda V.\lambda x.\lambda t. V(x)(t) \wedge \mathbf{yest}(t): (np\backslash s_\alpha)\backslash np\backslash s_\alpha$
    b. *at* $\Rightarrow \lambda y.\lambda V.\lambda x.\lambda t. V(x)(t) \wedge \mathbf{at}(y)(t): (np\backslash s_\alpha)\backslash np\backslash s_\alpha/np$

In the case of modifiers, we have used the subscript α to indicate that the categories are polymorphic over the possible instantiations of verb form. Note that the constant **yest** is indexical and always refers to the day before the speech time. In the preposition cases, the noun-phrase complement must be of the appropriate temporal type. For instance, *at* requires a point in time, *for* a measurable temporal period, *on* a referential time, and so forth. Further, they require the sentences they modify to also be of the appropriate type; we already saw that *for* cannot modify events, and *in* does not modify processes or states. The difference between *in* and *for* appears to be simply a matter of selectional restrictions; both restrict the temporal point of evaluation to an interval of length indicated by the object.

These entries lead to analyses such as the following by simple application.

(27) *Sandy ran at 5 p.m.* $\Rightarrow \lambda t.\mathbf{run}(\mathbf{s})(t) \wedge t \prec \mathbf{now} \wedge \mathbf{at}(\mathbf{5\ p.m.})(t): s_f$

Temporal modifiers simply add in their restriction to the time of the eventuality. Notice that this neatly avoids the problems of scoping of tenses and modifiers in cases such as the following:

(28) Terry ran yesterday.

Both the past tense and the indexical temporal adverbial *yesterday* contribute restrictions on the time of interpretation.

There are also subordinating conjunctions that are interpreted temporally, as in the following examples:

(29) a. Sandy ran after Terry jumped.
    b. Sandy stumbled while running.

This is another case where we should properly interpret the tense of the subordinate clause as an indefinite. This is because the speaker typically has in mind a particular event that he or she is picking out with the subordinate clause. I will approximate the indefinite approach by providing lexical entries that bind the time in the subordinate clause with existential quantification.

(30) a. *after* $\Rightarrow \lambda p.\lambda V.\lambda x.\lambda t. V(x)(t) \wedge \mathbf{some}(p)(\lambda t'.t' \prec t)$
       $(np\backslash s_\alpha)\backslash np\backslash s_\alpha/s_f$
    b. *while* $\Rightarrow \lambda U.\lambda V.\lambda x.\lambda t. V(x)(t) \wedge \mathbf{some}(U(x))(\lambda t'.t \sqsubseteq t')$
       $(np\backslash s_\alpha)\backslash np\backslash s_\alpha/(np\backslash s_g)$

Both of these subordinating temporal modifiers simply contribute a constraint on the temporal point of evaluation, just like the simple modifiers. Note that the adverbial *while* identifies the subject of the main clause with that of the subordinate clause. Thus by simple application we have derivations such as the following for the examples in (29) (I am presently ignoring the contribution of the progressive in (29b); its contribution is compositional).

(31) a. $\lambda t.\mathbf{run}(\mathbf{s})(t) \wedge t \prec \mathbf{now}$
      $\wedge \, \mathbf{some}(\lambda t'.\mathbf{jump}(\mathbf{t})(t') \wedge t' \prec \mathbf{now})(\lambda t'.t' \prec t)$
      b. $\lambda t.\mathbf{stumble}(\mathbf{s})(t) \wedge t \prec \mathbf{now}$
      $\wedge \, \mathbf{some}(\lambda t'.\mathbf{run}(\mathbf{s})(t') \wedge t' \prec \mathbf{now})(\lambda t'.t \sqsubseteq t')$

Subordinating adverbials with other lexical contents, such as *before*, can be treated similarly.

A particularly interesting temporal conjunction is *when*, because there is no relation other than proximity specified, as can be seen in the following examples of Moens and Steedman (1988):

(32) When they built the Thirty-Ninth Street Bridge,
      a. local architect drew up the plans.
      b. they used the best materials.
      c. they solved most of their traffic problems.

Such facts led Partee (1984a) and Hinrichs (1986) to propose that the *when* clause is merely supplying a kind of anaphoric anchor for the evaluation of the main-clause tense. Moens and Steedman sharpen this idea by noting that the time of the antecedent can be any of the stages that exist in the nucleus of the antecedent event (preparation, culmination, or consequent state). They further note that these facts interact with their notion of aspectual coercion. On one view, the preparation is the planning and the culmination is the building and the consequent is the bridge built, whereas on another view of the same event, the preparation is the building and the culmination is the completion itself. They further note that there must be some kind of connection between the antecedent and main-clause events, illustrating this point with (33):

(33) #When my car broke down, the sun set.

12.5.4   The Perfect

Semantically, I follow Moens and Steedman (1988) in treating the semantics of the perfect aspect as moving attention to the consequent state of an event. To this end, I assume that there is an operator **perf** of the sentential-modifying type $(\mathbf{Per} \rightarrow \mathbf{Bool}) \rightarrow \mathbf{Per} \rightarrow \mathbf{Bool}$ such that $\mathbf{perf}(\phi)(t)$ holds if and only if t is the time when the consequent state of ϕ holds (recall that ϕ is of type $\mathbf{Per} \rightarrow \mathbf{Bool}$ and thus does not directly specify its own time of evaluation). Our target in the simplest case is the following:

(34) *Sandy has run* $\Rightarrow \lambda t . \mathbf{perf}(\lambda t' . \mathbf{run}(\mathbf{s})(t'))(t) \wedge t = \mathbf{now}$

Note that the present tense is simply conjoined in as a constraint on the time of evaluation. Thus the sentence can be truly uttered if at the time of utterance, Sandy is in the consequent state of having run.

To develop a grammatical approach to the perfect aspect, we must decide whether its semantic content is contributed by the auxiliary (such as *has*) or by the participle (such as *eaten*). Clearly, we will want to treat the finiteness as arising from the inflection on the perfect aspect auxiliary *has*. It turns out that there are advantages and drawbacks to both approaches. It is not clear that an argument mapping times into truth values is the appropriate argument for the perfective; it would be more convenient to work directly from some kind of underlying lexical representation of an event. This would favor an approach in which the semantic contribution of a perfect such as *eaten* would be taken as primitive. In this case, the role of the auxiliary would simply be to convert to finiteness. But such an approach runs into problems with temporal modifiers, as in the following examples raised by Dowty (1979a) and later studied by Richards (1982) and Heny (1982).

(35) a. Sandy had eaten at 5 p.m.
       b. Sandy had eaten for two hours.
       c. Sandy had eaten a sandwich in two hours.

A standard Reichenbachian approach for (35a) and (35b) stipulates that temporal modifiers such as *at 5 p.m.* and *for two hours* can modify either the reference time or the event time (Reichenbach himself assumed adverbials always applied to the reference time). In our grammar, I have eliminated the notion of reference time, so the ambiguities displayed by the examples in (35) require another explanation. One natural solution, first proposed in a generative framework by Braroe (1974) and later argued for by Hornstein (1990) and Thompson (1994), is to allow the modifier to scope relative to the perfective marker. Thus for (35a) we would aim for the following two analyses:

(36) a. $\lambda t.\mathbf{perf}(\lambda t'.\mathbf{eat}(\mathbf{s})(t'))(t) \wedge t \prec \mathbf{now} \wedge \mathbf{at}(\mathbf{5\ p.m.})(t)$
    b. $\lambda t.\mathbf{perf}(\lambda t'.\mathbf{eat}(\mathbf{s})(t') \wedge \mathbf{at}(\mathbf{5\ p.m.})(t'))(t) \wedge t \prec \mathbf{now}$

This ambiguity is naturally generated if we treat the auxiliary *have* as introducing the perfective content, as in the following lexical entries:

(37) a. *eaten* $\Rightarrow$ **eat**: $np \backslash s_p$
    b. *have* $\Rightarrow \lambda V.\lambda x.\lambda t.\mathbf{perf}(V(x))(t): np \backslash s_b / (np \backslash s_p)$
    c. *has* $\Rightarrow \lambda V.\lambda x.\lambda t.\mathbf{perf}(V(x))(t) \wedge t = \mathbf{now}: np \backslash s_f / (np \backslash s_p)$
    d. *had* $\Rightarrow \lambda V.\lambda x.\lambda t.\mathbf{perf}(V(x))(t) \wedge t \prec \mathbf{now}: np \backslash s_f / (np \backslash s_p)$

Note that *have* has both base and finite forms, and in some instances also occurs in the progressive as *having*. The two readings in (36) are generated by application with the following two structures.

(38) a. Sandy [had eaten] [at 5 p.m.].
    b. Sandy had [eaten at 5 p.m.].

In the first case, the temporal modifier attaches to *had eaten*, whereas in the second, it applies to *eaten* and then *had* applies to the resulting meaning. Note that we have the same structural ambiguity in the case of *Sandy did eat at 5 p.m.*, but the two readings that result are logically equivalent. Also note that subordinate-clause temporal modifiers present the same range of ambiguities as the prepositional modifiers, as is to be expected.

    In general, we have an entailment from the perfective holding at a given time to the equivalent simple finite holding at an earlier time (but see exercise 8 for examples in which only the perfective is felicitous).

(39) a. Chris has eaten.
    b. Chris ate.

(40) a. Chris had eaten.
    b. Chris ate.

Thus both the present and past perfective entail the past version of a sentence, all else being the same. But direct entailments only go so far. Consider the future perfective case:

(41) a. Chris will have eaten.
    b. Chris ate, or Chris eats, or Chris will eat.

The second sentence follows from the first, but a disjunction is required because the time of a future perfect event relative to the speech time is indeterminate; the future moves the perspective forward, and the perfect aspect allows the event time to shift backward from there. This is quite natural in cases where we know, for instance, that Chris has been working on a paper and will finish it before the deadline on Friday. An utterance on Wednesday of *Chris will have written the paper by Friday* is true if Chris has been so diligent that she has already finished. Of course, to respect the Gricean maxims of quality and quantity (see section 1.3.1), we will use the future perfect only if we are uncertain as to whether Chris has finished or not.

To account for these entailments, we can constrain the interpretation of the perfect marker as follows:

(42) $\mathbf{perf}(p)(t) \rightarrow \mathbf{some}(\lambda t'.t' \prec t)(\lambda t'.p(t'))$

This will guarantee all of the entailments above.

12.5.5 The Progressive

In some ways, the progressive aspect is more straightforward than the perfect. Most important, it does not enter into any of the structural ambiguities displayed by the perfect. Semantically, I will assume a constant **prog** of the same type as **perf** that converts an event into a process. This sweeps the deep semantic issues under the rug. For instance, as Moens and Steedman (1988) pointed out, the determination of the progressive process is sensitive to context. For instance, *Sandy was blinking* is naturally interpreted as an iteration of a punctual event, whereas *Sandy was building a house* is most naturally interpreted as referring to the preparatory process of a house-building event. It is also rather unclear as to what constitutes satisfaction of a progressive description. For instance, if Sandy is buying paper and pencils in order to start drawing up plans, it seems a bit premature to say *Sandy is building a house*, but if she has bought all of the lumber and poured the foundation, then clearly the sentence can be uttered truthfully. In some ways, this is no more vague than other verbs, such as *run*, where it is also not clear exactly what constitutes a running event; for instance, we could ask at exactly what point walking becomes running. In many ways, these issues are highly pragmatically conditioned by the discourse purpose and other contextual factors.

It may appear that a simple intention is what is needed. For a sentence like *Sandy is crossing the street*, we might assume it can be uttered truthfully if Sandy starts to cross the street with the intention of getting to the other side. But intentional agents are not even necessary, as can be seen with examples such as *The roof was collapsing until it was reinforced*. Intuitively, the semantics of the progressive is similar to what is found in the nominal partitive *part of*, as in the following example of Bach's (1986).

(43) This is part of a Roman aqueduct.

The problem is the vagueness in the semantics of *part of*; clearly, not every pile of stones is part of a Roman aqueduct. Note that the partitive can also be expressed with noun compounding in English, as in *a Roman-aqueduct part*.

An influential possible-worlds treatment of the semantics of the progressive was proposed by Dowty (1979a), in which the semantics of the progressive bears a striking resemblance to the semantics of counterfactuals. In particular, Dowty assumes that a progressive sentence such as *Kim is building a house* is true if there are suitably closely related possible worlds, which he dubs *inertia worlds*, in which the house-building event is completed, regardless of whether the house is completed in the real world. Like many possible-worlds analyses, this simply begs the question as to what the proper inertia worlds are. Later analyses, such as that of Moens and Steedman (1988) and Parsons (1985, 1989, 1990), have assumed that the progressive can involve simply stripping off a culmination point, though no model-theoretic or proof-theoretic content is supplied to describe this operation. Progressives do not warrant the same kinds of entailments as perfect forms; semantically, they are complementary. The following pattern of entailments has come to be known as the *imperfective paradox*. In the case of events with culminations, entailments such as the following fail to go through.

(44) a. Sandy was building a house.
      b. Sandy built a house.

A progressive may hold of a preparatory activity even if the event is never completed. Processes, on the other hand, do license such entailments.

(45) a. Chris was running.
      b. Chris ran.

This pattern can be explained by the lack of a natural culmination for process verbs. In addition, it argues for a coercion-based approach to the progressive in which process verbs need no modification to become processes, whereas protracted events can have their culminations stripped, and any event can be iterated to form a process.

Progressives appear as present participles in English and serve as complements to the various forms of the auxiliary *be*.

(46) a. *running* $\Rightarrow \lambda x.\lambda t.\mathbf{prog}(\mathbf{run}(x))(t)$: $np\backslash s_{\mathrm{g}}$
    b. *be* $\Rightarrow \lambda V.V$: $np\backslash s_{\mathrm{b}}/(np\backslash s_{\mathrm{g}})$
    c. *is* $\Rightarrow \lambda V.\lambda x.\lambda t.V(x)(t) \wedge t = \mathbf{now}$: $np\backslash s_{\mathrm{f}}/(np\backslash s_{\mathrm{g}})$
    d. *was* $\Rightarrow \lambda V.\lambda x.\lambda t.V(x)(t) \wedge t \prec \mathbf{now}$: $np\backslash s_{\mathrm{f}}/(np\backslash s_{\mathrm{g}})$
    e. *been* $\Rightarrow \lambda V.V$: $np\backslash s_{\mathrm{p}}/(np\backslash s_{\mathrm{g}})$

Note that the auxiliary *be* is inflected in every verb form other than the progressive. A progressive form of *be* would be redundant, leading to expressions such as *is being running*, which can already be expressed as *is running*. In addition to progressive-verb-phrase complements, *be* can also be applied to passive verb phrases, as well as the range of predicative complements, such as adjectives, prepositions, and noun phrases. In these cases, the progressive form *being* can be used with its standard interpretation. For instance, we can contrast *is being unreasonable* with *is unreasonable*, the latter typically being understood as generic and the former as a claim about a particular moment or interval.

With the lexical entries in (46), we have the following analyses:

(47) a. *Sandy was reading* Beowulf
      $\Rightarrow \lambda t.\mathbf{prog}(\mathbf{read}(\mathbf{b})(\mathbf{s}))(t) \wedge t \prec \mathbf{now}$: s_{f}
    b. *Sandy will be reading* Beowulf
      $\Rightarrow \lambda t.\mathbf{prog}(\mathbf{read}(\mathbf{b})(\mathbf{s}))(t) \wedge \mathbf{now} \prec t$: s_{f}

More complex adverbial sequences are also generated with this grammar, as in the following example:

(48) *Sandy will have been reading* Beowulf
    $\Rightarrow \lambda t.\mathbf{perf}(\mathbf{prog}(\mathbf{read}(\mathbf{s})(\mathbf{b})))(t) \wedge \mathbf{now} \prec t$: s_f

To gloss our semantic analysis, this sentence can be uttered truthfully about a time t in the future if that time is part of the consequent state of Sandy's having been in the process of reading *Beowulf*. In the semantic term, there are actually three temporal points introduced: one for the constant **read**, another for the progressive, and the final one for the perfect. The ambiguities introduced by modification in this case is the subject of the second half of exercise 4.

12.5.6 Tense and Nominal Quantification

There are dramatic interactions between the semantics of tense and the semantics of nominal quantification. Consider the simplest possible case:

(49) Every student studied.

It is often assumed that there is an ambiguity in this sentence between the scope of the quantifier over students and the evaluation of the event time. Under one reading, every student studied at the same time, and under the other, there is a possibly different time of studying for each student. In a Priorean tense logic, we have the following two possibilities:

(50) a. $\mathbf{P}(\forall x)\mathbf{study}(x)$
     b. $(\forall x)\mathbf{P}\ \mathbf{study}(x)$

Unfortunately, this simple analysis cannot be reconstructed in the present approach, because there is no implicit quantification over times introduced by the past tense.

Under our current typing, quantifiers have lifted types analogous to those we studied for the possible-worlds approach to intensionality.

(51) $\mathrm{Type}(np \Uparrow s) = (\mathbf{Ind} \rightarrow \mathbf{Per} \rightarrow \mathbf{Bool}) \rightarrow \mathbf{Per} \rightarrow \mathbf{Bool}$

Here I have used s to stand in for all of the verb forms s_α; quantifiers must be allowed to reduce in contexts other than finite ones. If we simply distribute, as we did in the possible-worlds case, we arrive at the following lexical entry:

(52) $everyone \Rightarrow \lambda V.\lambda t.\mathbf{every}^1(\lambda x. V(x)(t)): np \Uparrow s$

But this would unambiguously derive times with wider scope than any quantifiers.

(53) $everyone\ studied \Rightarrow \lambda t.\mathbf{every}^1(\lambda x.\mathbf{study}(x)(t))$

One possibility is the following, which was explored by Carpenter (1989) in an event-based setting.

(54) $everyone$
$\Rightarrow \lambda V.\lambda t.\mathbf{every}^1(\lambda x.\mathbf{some}^2(\lambda t'.t' \sqsubseteq t))(\lambda t'. V(x)(t')): np \Uparrow s$

But with this lexical entry, we derive only the following reading:

(55) $everyone\ studied$
$\Rightarrow \lambda t.\mathbf{every}^1(\lambda x.\mathbf{some}^2(\lambda t'.t' \sqsubseteq t))(\lambda t'.\mathbf{study}(x)(t')): s$

This latter analysis is weaker than the first because $(\forall x)(\exists y)\phi$ is entailed by $(\exists y)(\forall x)\phi$. Another potential analysis would be to allow the tense expression itself to be given scope, in the same way as other indefinites.

Again, the solution to this problem appears to be best handled by an indefinite approach to tense in which indefinites can be absorbed into universal quantifiers or bound at a higher structural level, as in discourse-representation approaches to donkey sentences (Heim 1982, Kamp 1984, Clark and Keenan 1986). As I mentioned earlier, such an approach is adopted by Partee (1984a) and by Kamp and Reyle (1993), although these authors were not concerned with quantifiers interacting with tense. Hinrichs (1988) sidesteps this problem by using an operator-based approach to Reichenbachian temporal logic.

12.5.7   Tense, Nominals, and Quantification

Tensed expressions can show up as part of noun phrases, which I have not provided with temporal reference points. Consider the following example:

(56) The kid who ran three days ago will be walking next week.

Clearly, the times associated with events in relative clauses are independent of those of main clauses. But tenses and temporal indexicals within relative clauses are evaluated relative to speech time. In (56) the expressions *three days ago* and *next week* are independently evaluated relative to the speech time. To provide the correct readings for these sentences, I will existentially bind off the time argument within relative clauses.

(57) $who \Rightarrow \lambda V.\lambda P.\lambda x.P(x) \wedge \textbf{some}_{\textbf{Tim}}(V(x)): n\backslash n/(s{\uparrow}np)$

This leads to derivations such as the following:

(58) $kid\ who\ ran \Rightarrow \lambda x.\textbf{kid}(x) \wedge \textbf{some}(\lambda t.\textbf{run}(t)(x) \wedge t \prec \textbf{now})$

Another issue that needs to be addressed is the temporal nature of some nouns and adjectives:

(59) a. The former president attended the celebration.
      b. Sandy's former boss fired him.
      c. I will marry my former boss.

Temporal adjectives such as *former* seem to be evaluated with respect to the utterance time rather than with respect to the temporal point of evaluation of the sentence. That is, in a past-tense sentence, the formerness is still relative to the current time. This is supported by (59b), in which the person firing Sandy was his boss at the time of firing but is now his former boss. In (59c), even though the adjective is embedded within the verb phrase, the formerness of the boss seems relative to the utterance time.

But in some cases there does seem to be interaction, as displayed in example (60a) of Enç's (1986), the similar (60b), and Vlach's (1981) (60c).

(60) a. Every admiral was (once) a cadet.
    b. Every admiral commanded a cadet.
    c. Every fugitive is now in jail.

In (60a) we are likely dealing with current admirals, who at some point in the past were cadets. Enç also makes the dubious claim that there is a reading of this sentence in which we are quantifying over all admirals at all points in time (past, present, and future), stating that before they were admirals, they were cadets. Vlach (1981) noted that for (60c) to be interpreted reasonably, we must be referring to past fugitives who are currently in jail; clearly, if they are in jail, they are no longer fugitives.

One approach to this data would be to raise the type of nouns and noun phrases to include a temporal evaluation point, much as I did in the case of individual concepts in section 11.2. We take up this possibility in exercise 13. In most cases, this point would be set to the speech time, but in cases such as those above, it would be bound to the verb's temporal point of evaluation. Both Vlach (1981) and Enç (1986) argue that the temporal point of evaluation of nominals is anaphoric. We could certainly allow free variables for times, but there seems to be no point of coreference for the cases in (60). Most appealing, perhaps, would be an indefinite-based theory of tense, such as that presented by Partee (1984a); this would naturally account for the binding of nominal tenses by other times and also for their assimilation to universal quantifiers.

12.5.8 Adverbs of Quantification and Negation

The last topic we will consider in our survey of temporal phenomena is the puzzling issue of quantificational adverbs, exemplified as follows:

(61) a. Sandy sang frequently.
    b. Sandy ran three times last year.
    c. Sandy never ran.

In the case of modifiers like *frequently* and *three times*, a claim is being made about how many times an event is realized. As can be seen from (61b), the result of applying the modifier leaves a temporal point of evaluation for further modification and binding. I will assume the following lexical entries:

(62) a. *frequently*
$$\Rightarrow \lambda V.\lambda x.\lambda t.\mathbf{frequent}(\lambda t'.V(x)(t') \wedge t' \sqsubseteq t)\colon (np\backslash s_\alpha)\backslash np\backslash s_\alpha$$
    b. *three times*
$$\Rightarrow \lambda V.\lambda x.\lambda t.\|\lambda t'.V(x)(t') \wedge t' \sqsubseteq t\| \geq \mathbf{3}\colon (np\backslash s_\alpha)\backslash np\backslash s_\alpha$$

With this analysis, the time corresponding to the modified verb phrase will contain all of the times introduced by the quantifiers.

Our lexical entries for the adverbs of quantification lead to the following derivations:

(63) a. *Sandy ran frequently*
$$\Rightarrow \lambda t.\textbf{frequent}(\lambda t'.\textbf{run}(\textbf{s})(t') \wedge t' \prec \textbf{now} \wedge t' \sqsubseteq t): s_f$$
b. *Sandy ran twice on Friday*
$$\Rightarrow \lambda t.\|\lambda t'.\textbf{run}(\textbf{s})(t') \wedge t' \prec \textbf{now} \wedge t' \sqsubseteq t\| \geq \textbf{2} \wedge \textbf{on}(\textbf{fri})(t): s_f$$

Note that in the second case we have a reading in which on a given Friday t there are two instances of running. This could be contrasted with the analysis we would have if the order of modifiers were reversed:

(64) *Sandy ran on Friday twice*
$$\Rightarrow \lambda t.\|\lambda t'.\textbf{run}(\textbf{s})(t') \wedge t' \prec \textbf{now} \wedge t' \sqsubseteq t \wedge \textbf{on}(\textbf{fri})(t')\| \geq \textbf{2}: s_f$$

For this example, the two runnings are not necessarily on the same Friday. In the system I have established, the only way in which the two examples with alternatively ordered modifiers can be construed as synonymous is if the modifiers were allowed to extrapose, which is a not unreasonable assumption.

Although these analyses appear satisfactory at first glance, they leave open the issue of how events are to be counted. For instance, any running event has many subevents that are also running events. Thus we must assume that what is being counted is maximal stretches of running, not counting short breaks, as noted by Richards (1982). What is to count as a short break is left vague.

A more difficult puzzle concerning adverbs of quantification stems from the fact that temporal adverbials can bind unselectively in a way that is sensitive to facts concerning focus. Consider cases such as the following, introduced by Lewis (1975).

(65) a. Sandy usually sings when he is in the shower.
b. If a farmer owns a donkey, he usually beats it.
c. Usually, if a farmer owns a donkey, he beats it.
d. Riders on the Thirteenth Avenue line seldom find seats.

Example (65a) can be construed as meaning that usually, if Sandy is in the shower, he is singing. But it can also be construed as meaning that usually, if Sandy is singing, he is in the shower. Lewis (1975) argued that either the *when* clause or the matrix clause can act as the restriction on the adverbial quantifier *usually*. Note that the adverb *only* induces the same kind of ambiguity in this context; thus it is natural to try to apply the theory of focus developed by Rooth (1992) for *only* to cases of quantificational adverbs. Lewis (1975) used examples such as (65b) and (65c) to argue for an unselective binding approach to adverbs of quantification, since the sentence quantifies over farmer/donkey pairs that stand in the owning relation. A similar puzzle is raised by (65d), in which the quantification appears to be over the riders, not over times. In defense of this analysis, Lewis notes that (65d) may be uttered truthfully even if it is easy to find seats in the 22 hours outside of rush hour but 86 percent of the passengers ride during the two peak hours, at which time most of them ride seatless. Lewis thus concludes that adverbs of quantification range over cases rather than over times, where the cases may be parametric on any number of indefinites. Lewis applied his mechanism of unselective binding to this problem (recall the definitions in section 7.10. Adverbs of quantification interact with donkey sentences, as seen in (65b) and (65c). Here the adverb *usually* qualifies what would otherwise be a universal unselective quantification. Other quantificational adverbs, such as *often* and *infrequently*, behave in much the same way. A detailed analysis of quantificational adverbs as generalized quantifiers is proposed by de Swart (1991); she also provides a thorough survey of the relevant data and previous approaches to unselective binding and sensitivity to focus.

We now turn to negation, which I claim behaves as an adverb of quantification. The immediately obvious approach would be to simply distribute the temporal indices through negation, as done by the following lexical entry:

(66) *not* $\Rightarrow \lambda V.\lambda x.\lambda t. \neg V(x)(t): np\backslash s_\alpha/(np\backslash s_\alpha)$ $\qquad\qquad [\alpha \neq f]$

Note first that the negative particle can apply to any form of verb other than finite verbs. Consider the following analysis with this entry:

(67) *Sandy did not run* $\Rightarrow \lambda t. \neg \mathbf{run}(\mathbf{s})(t) \wedge t \prec \mathbf{now}$

Note in particular that the past tense contributes a restriction outside of the scope of the negation, in accord with Partee's intuitions concerning the indefinite nature of temporal evaluation.

But this simple entry is not sufficient to generate the relevant ambiguities for the following example:

(68) a. Sandy did not play until 5 p.m.
      b. Sandy did not stay out until dark.
      c. Sandy did not eat until 5 p.m.

In the case of (68a), a semantic ambiguity arises. This sentence can be true if Sandy did not have the property of playing until 5 p.m., or in other words, if there was some period just before 5 p.m. during which Sandy did not play. This is the natural reading of (68b) in the null context. But (68a) can also be true if Sandy did not play throughout the interval up until 5 p.m. This is the most natural interpretation of (68c) in the null context. Similar ambiguities arise in the case of modification by other temporal adverbials, such as *all day*. The two readings generated with the naive lexical entry for negation are as follows:

(69) a. $\lambda t.(\neg\mathbf{play}(\mathbf{s})(t)) \wedge \mathbf{until}(\mathbf{5\,p.m.})(t) \wedge t \prec \mathbf{now}$
      b. $\lambda t.\neg(\mathbf{play}(\mathbf{s})(t) \wedge \mathbf{until}(\mathbf{5\,p.m.})(t)) \wedge t \prec \mathbf{now}$

The first reading seems reasonable and corresponds to the case where Sandy did not play throughout the whole interval. But nothing would prevent such a reading from being true in the case where she played until 4:30 and then took a nap. The second analysis, (69b), would be trivially true because we can simply take a t that does not run up until 5 p.m.

Now consider an alternative for the semantics of negation in which it is treated as an adverb of quantification.

(70) $not \Rightarrow \lambda V.\lambda x.\lambda t.\mathbf{no}^2(\lambda t'.t' \sqsubseteq t)(\lambda t'.V(x)(t'))$
      $np\backslash s_\alpha/(np\backslash s_\alpha)$ $[\alpha \neq f]$

With this lexical entry, the following two readings are generated for (68a).

(71) a. $\lambda t.\mathbf{no}^2(\lambda t'.t' \sqsubseteq t)(\lambda t'.\mathbf{play}(\mathbf{s})(t') \wedge \mathbf{until}(\mathbf{5\,p.m.})(t')) \wedge t \prec \mathbf{now}$
      b. $\lambda t.\mathbf{no}^2(\lambda t'.t' \sqsubseteq t)(\lambda t'.\mathbf{play}(\mathbf{s})(t')) \wedge t \prec \mathbf{now} \wedge \mathbf{until}(\mathbf{5\,p.m.})(t)$

The first reading, derived by applying the negation to the verb phrase including the adverbial, will be true if there is a time before now such that there is no subperiod of that time at which Sandy's running until 5 p.m. took place. This reading is roughly analogous to the first reading we derived using the nonquantificational lexical entry for *not*. The second reading says that there is a time period before now that runs until 5 p.m. and throughout which Sandy did not run, which provides the second reasonable reading for the example. An alternative is considered in exercise 18 in which the duration adverb is considered quantificational rather than the negative particle.

Exercises

1. Provide at least four different realistic examples that illustrate how Moens and Steedman's (1988) coercion operators can be composed.

2. Provide lexical entries of category $s_\alpha \backslash s_\alpha / np$ for the simple temporal modifiers in (26), and show how the verb-phrase-modifier categories in (26) can be derived from the sentence-modifier category. (Hint: See the discussion of the division schemes in section 5.2.2.)

3. Develop a Reichenbachian grammar for some simple verbs, the auxiliaries *do* and *have*, and some restrictive temporal modifiers. Assume the semantic type of sentences of all verbal forms is **Per** → **Per** → **Bool**. Treat the first argument as the reference time and the second as the event time.

4. Show that there is no semantic ambiguity arising from attachment in the following example:

(a) Chris will be reading *Beowulf* at 5 p.m.

How many readings are there for the following sentence in our grammar?

(b) Sandy will have been reading the paper for two hours.

5. Consider the following example involving a present-tense perfect form.

(a) Sandy has swum this afternoon.

Can this sentence be uttered truthfully in the afternoon if Sandy only swam in the morning? What does our analysis in section 12.5.4 generate as possible meanings? Consider an analysis in which temporal modifiers of present perfects restrict both the event time and the utterance time. Does this move provide the correct results? (Dick Oehrle, p.c.)

6. What consequences would there be if subordinating temporal adverbials such as *while* used a definite description rather than an existential quantifier to bind the subordinate temporal point of evaluation? Provide a reasonable lexical entry for such an analysis.

7. Provide lexical entries for verbs and for the auxiliary forms of *be* that can handle the passive. Then show that the correct readings can be generated for the following examples:

(a) The building was built by Sandy.

(b) The building was being built by Sandy.

(c) The building will have been built by Sandy.

8. Consider the following two perfective forms for which the corresponding simple tense is infelicitous.

(a) Sandy {has been / ?was} to Fiji.

(b) Sandy {has had / ?had} it with computers

Why are these examples more natural with the perfective? Could lexical entries for the relevant verbs and/or auxiliaries be provided to make the simple tense forms marked with a question mark above ungrammatical while generating the correct meanings for the perfective forms? (Dick Oehrle, p.c.)

9. Consider a type assignment in which Typ(s) = **Bool** and lexical entries for simple tensed verbs are as follows:

(a) *ran* $\Rightarrow \lambda x.\textbf{some}(\lambda t.t \prec \textbf{now})(\lambda t.\textbf{run}(x)(t)): np \backslash s$

Show how such a lexical entry can be lexically raised to category $(np \Uparrow s) \backslash s$ to account for the ambiguity of scope in *Everyone studied*. What problems does such an approach raise for modification?

10. Discuss the causes for the contrast in felicity between the following cases:

(a) #Jo has eaten the apple for two weeks.

(b)   Dinosaurs have been extinct for millions of years.

11. Consider a scoping analysis of tense in which a tensed verb phrase is assigned the category $(np \backslash s) \Uparrow s$. This should allow derivations in which an existential tense takes scope over other elements in a sentence.

12. Provide lexical entries for subordinating conjunctions that allow for temporal arguments, such as the following:

(a) Sandy ran [two hours before] Terry ran.

What kinds of expressions can show up in the same position as *two hours* in this example?

13. Consider raising the type assignment to nominals as follows:

(a) $\text{Typ}(np) = \textbf{Per} \rightarrow \textbf{Bool}$

(b) $\text{Typ}(n) = \textbf{Ind} \rightarrow \textbf{Per} \rightarrow \textbf{Bool}$

Consider lexical entries for simple transitive and intransitive verbs, auxiliaries, nouns, and noun phrases. What are some of the possibilities for distributing or binding the temporal reference points in order to account for the facts described in section 12.5.7?

14. Provide a lexical entry for *never* and an analysis of the two derivations for the following example:

(a) Sandy never ran on Friday.

Is there semantic ambiguity in this sentence?

15. Our treatment of coordination carries over without modification to our typing of sentences for tense. Consider the two analyses of the following example. (Hint: One arises by raising the verbs over the adverbials before coordinating.)

(a) Sandy came and went {yesterday / on Friday}.

Is there semantic ambiguity in this sentence?

16. Extend our analyses of tensed negation to the category $(np \Uparrow s) \backslash s / ((np \Uparrow s) \backslash s)$ in order to allow subject quantifiers to scope relative to negation.

17. Consider how control verbs can be made to interact with tense in the following examples:

(a) Terry wants to study.

(b) Terry persuaded Sandy to study.

(c) Terry made Sandy study.

(d) Terry saw Sandy {build / building} a house.

(Hint: Apply the technique of distributing the temporal points of evaluation. Treat *to* as the identity function.)

18. Consider the results of treating adverbials such as *for two hours* as quantificationally stating that for every subinterval of the two hours, the event in question held. Formulate an appropriate lexical entry, and apply it to the following examples.

(a) Sandy did not run for two hours.

(b) Sandy has run for two hours.

In the first case, is a quantificational theory of the negative necessary to generate an appropriate ambiguity? (Richards 1982, Heny 1982)

19. Consider the following examples of Moens and Steedman (1988):

(a) Sandy took two hours to explain the problem.

(b) It took Sandy two hours to explain the problem.

Provide lexical entries for *take* that allow for the appropriate kind of temporal and nominal control in these examples.

20. Consider the following case of raising verbs used to indicate the future.

(a) Sandy is going to write a paper.

(b) Sandy is to be the main author.

Provide lexical entries for *going* and *is* that allow these examples to be generated. (Leech 1971, Palmer 1974, Moens and Steedman 1988)

21. Extend the approach to questions developed in section 9.9 to deal with the semantic contributions of auxiliaries. Are there any complications in such an extension? Next consider *wh*-questions that involve questions about time, such as the following:

(a) When did Sandy study?

(b) For how long did Sandy study?

Provide a lexical entry for the question-forming *when* that addresses the issue of tense. The second example involves both pied-piping and a complement-taking variant of *how*. Provide a lexical entry for *how* that accounts for this example and others like it.

22. Provide lexical entries for *started* and *finished* that will generate the correct meanings for the following example:

(a) Sandy started running before Terry finished swimming.

Why is a progressive complement functionally appropriate in this example?

23. Provide an analysis of comparative temporal modifiers, such as those used in the following examples:

(a) Sandy saw Terry early.

(b) Sandy saw Terry as early as me.

(c) Sandy saw Terry (2 hours) earlier than she saw me.

(d) Sandy saw Terry {first / (the) earliest}.

Do any special complications come up from the temporal nature of the examples?

24. Is there a difference between *progressive naked infinitives* and tenseless infinitives?

(a) Sandy saw Terry {eat / eating} a sandwich.

How should the tense of the complement be handled?

25. Extend the semantic typing involving tense to one involving both tense and location. How could such a typing be used to handle *locative prepositions*? Consider examples such as the following:

(a) Sandy ran in the park.

(b) Sandy saw Terry in the park.

(c) Sandy typed sentences into the computer.

Is there a difference in the way in which the locative is used in these cases?

Appendix A

Mathematical Preliminaries

In this appendix I introduce the basic mathematical notions required for understanding this book. While it may be helpful to browse through this section to get acquainted with notational conventions, it is neither necessary nor advisable to get bogged down in detail here.

I begin with a review of basic naive set theory and continue with the notions of function and relation. These topics form the backbone not only of semantics but of discrete mathematics in general. I then proceed to the related notion of ordering and proof by induction in the next two sections. I then move on to more linguistically oriented topics, including the basic tools of formal languages and trees. I conclude with a review of first-order logic and abstract algebra.

A.1 SET THEORY

A *set* can be thought of as a collection of objects that can be grouped together and considered as an object in its own right. For a given set S and object x, if x is an *element* or *member* of S, we write $x \in S$ and say x is *in* S or S *contains* x. We write $x \notin S$ if x is not an element of S. We write $\{x_1, \ldots, x_n\}$ for the set with exactly the members $x_1, \ldots, x_n$. We write $\emptyset$ for the unique set $\{\ \}$ with no members, which is called the *empty set*. A set with only one member is called a *singleton*. Where $\phi(x)$ is a formula or statement containing an occurrence of the variable x and S is a set, we write $\{x \in S \mid \phi(x)\}$ for the set of all objects $x \in S$ such that $\phi(x)$ is true. When S is obvious from context, I shorten this to $\{x \mid \phi(x)\}$.

For two sets S and T, we write $S \subseteq T$ and say S is a *subset* of T if for every element $x \in S$, we have $x \in T$. The notion of set is inherently *extensional*, which means that two sets S and T are identical if and only if they have exactly the same members. So we have $S = T$ if and only if

$S \subseteq T$ and $T \subseteq S$. If $S \subseteq T$ and $S \neq T$, we write $S \subset T$ and say that S is a *proper subset* of T. Two sets S and T are said to be *disjoint* if there is no x such that $x \in S$ and $x \in T$.

There are a number of useful operations over sets. The *intersection* of S and T is defined as follows:

(1) $S \cap T = \{x \mid x \in S \text{ and } x \in T\}$

The *union* of S and T is as follows:

(2) $S \cup T = \{x \mid x \in S \text{ or } x \in T\}$

The *difference* between S and T is given by the following:

(3) $S - T = \{x \mid x \in S \text{ and } x \notin T\}$

We can extend the definitions of union and intersection to operate over sets of sets. Suppose S is a set, all of whose members are sets. We define the union and intersection of the members of a nonempty set of sets S as follows:

(4) $\bigcup S = \{x \mid x \in T \text{ for some } T \in S\}$

(5) $\bigcap S = \{x \mid x \in T \text{ for every } T \in S\}$

Note that if we take $S = \emptyset$, then $\bigcup S = \emptyset$, but $\bigcap S$ would contain every element and thus lead to a paradox if it were assumed that the result is itself a set. Hence our restriction to nonempty S in general. I often use the abbreviation $\bigcup_{\phi(S)} S$ for the set $\bigcup \{S \mid \phi(S)\}$, and similarly for other operations defined over sets of sets. I use the related notation $\bigcup_{i \in I} S_i$ for $\bigcup \{S_i \mid i \in I\}$, in which case we say that $S = \bigcup_{i \in I} S_i$ is *indexed* by the elements of I. If $s \in S_i$ then we say that s has index i. Note that every element of an indexed set has at least one index.

I write $\langle x_1, \ldots, x_n \rangle$ for the *ordered n-tuple* of objects $x_1, \ldots, x_n$ with $n \geq 0$. We call an arbitrary n-tuple a *sequence*. We call an n-tuple an *ordered pair* if $n = 2$, an *ordered triple* if $n = 3$, and so on. An n-tuple $\langle x_1, \ldots, x_n \rangle$ and an m-tuple $\langle y_1, \ldots, y_m \rangle$ are identical if and only if $n = m$ and $x_i = y_i$ for each i such that $1 \leq i \leq n = m$. For sets $S_1, \ldots, S_n$, we define their *cross-product* as follows:

(6) $S_1 \times \cdots \times S_n = \{\langle x_1, \ldots, x_n \rangle \mid x_i \in S_i\}$

We use the standard vector notation and write $\vec{x}$ for $\langle x_1, \ldots, x_n \rangle$ where convenient. For a set S, we define its *n-fold product* as follows.

(7) $S^n = \{\langle s_1, \ldots, s_n \rangle \mid s_i \in S \text{ for } 1 \leq i \leq n\}$

Note that $S^0 = \{\langle \rangle\}$ and is thus a singleton and not the empty set. We will write $\langle \rangle$ as ε. We say that s_m is the mth *coordinate* of the n-tuple $\vec{s} = \langle s_1, \ldots, s_n \rangle$, for $1 \leq m \leq n$.

A dual notion to that of products is that of *disjoint sums*:

(8) $S \oplus T = (\{1\} \times S) \cup (\{2\} \times T)$

Thus an element of $S \oplus T$ is either a pair $\langle 1, s \rangle$, where $s \in S$, or a pair $\langle 2, t \rangle$, where $t \in T$. There are natural *injection* functions from S and T into $S \oplus T$, $\iota_1 : S \rightarrow S \oplus T$ and $\iota_2 : T \rightarrow S \oplus T$, given as follows.

(9) a. $\iota_1(s) = \langle 1, s \rangle$
    b. $\iota_2(t) = \langle 2, t \rangle$

That is, ι_1 produces an element of $S \oplus T$ from an element of S, and ι_2 does the same for elements of T. Elements can be mapped from $S \oplus T$ back into $S \cup T$ by simply dropping the tag and mapping $\langle n, x \rangle$ to x.

A.2 FUNCTIONS AND RELATIONS

An *n-ary relation* over $S_1, \ldots, S_n$ is any set $R \subseteq S_1 \times \cdots \times S_n$. If $n = 2$, we say that R is a *binary relation*, if $n = 3$, a *ternary relation*, and so on. Sometimes I use the shorthand $R(s_1, \ldots, s_n)$ for $\langle s_1, \ldots, s_n \rangle \in R$ and say that $\langle s_1, \ldots, s_n \rangle$ are *R-related* or *stand* in the relation R.

For two sets S and T, a *partial function* from S into T is a relation $f \subseteq S \times T$ such that for every $x \in S$ there is at most one $y \in T$ such that $\langle x, y \rangle \in f$. If f is a partial function from S into T, I use the notation $f : S \rightarrow T$ and say that S is the *domain* and T is the *range* of f. For a partial function f, we write $\mathrm{Dom}(f)$ for its domain and $\mathrm{Ran}(f)$ for its range. For a partial function $f : S \rightarrow T$, if $\langle x, y \rangle \in f$, we write $f(x) = y$ and say that y is the *image of x under f* and that f is *defined* for x. If f is not defined for x, we say that $f(x)$ is *undefined*. We allow the standard abuse of notation and define the image of a subset $U \subseteq \mathrm{Dom}(f)$ as follows.

(10) $f(U) = \{f(y) \mid y \in U\}$

If $f : S \rightarrow T$ is a partial function defined for every $x \in S$, we say that f is a *total function*, or just a *function*. I assume throughout that a function is total unless its partiality is explicitly specified. A (partial) function $f : S_1 \times \cdots \times S_n \rightarrow T$ is called an *n-ary (partial) function*, and we use the standard shorthand $f(s_1, \ldots, s_n)$ for $f(\langle s_1, \ldots, s_n \rangle)$. For two sets S and T, we write T^S for the set of total functions from S into T such that the following holds:

(11) $T^S = \{f \mid f: S \to T \text{ is total}\}$

A partial function $f: S \to T$ is said to be *one-to-one* or an *injection* if and only if for every $t \in T$, there is at most one $s \in S$ such that $f(s) = t$, and is said to be *onto* or a *surjection* if for every $t \in T$ there is at least one $s \in S$ such that $f(s) = t$. A one-to-one, onto total function is said to be a *bijection*. A total one-to-one function $\rho: S \to S$ is often called a *permutation* of S. Of course, every permutation is onto, as well. We let $\mathbf{I}_S$ denote the total *identity function* on S, where $\mathbf{I}_S(x) = x$ if $x \in S$.

We let ω be the set of *natural numbers*.

(12) $\omega = \{0, 1, 2, \ldots\}$

Set-theoretically, it is standard to represent the number 0 as the empty set, $\emptyset$. An arbitrary number $n \in \omega$ can then be uniquely represented as the set of (representations of) elements less than n. For instance, 2 would be represented as $\{0, 1\} = \{\emptyset, \{\emptyset\}\}$. A set S for which there is a one-to-one, onto function from (the representation of) some natural number $n \in \omega$ to S is said to be of *cardinality n*, and we write $\|S\| = n$. A set S is said to be *finite* if it has a cardinality $n \in \omega$ and is said to be *infinite* otherwise. If there is a one-to-one function from a set S into ω, then S is said to be *countable* or *enumerable*. If this one-to-one function is also onto, then S is said to have cardinality $\aleph_0$. In general, countable sets can be either finite or infinite. A set which is not countable is said to be *uncountable*; all uncountable sets are infinite. We say that a set S is of smaller cardinality than T, written $S \prec T$, if and only if there is a one-to-one function $f: S \to T$, but no one-to-one function $f': T \to S$.

The *hereditary membership* relation $\in^*$ between objects and sets is such that $x \in^* S$ if and only if either $x = S$, $x \in S$, or there is some set $T \in S$ such that $x \in^* T$. We say that a set has a property *hereditarily* if and only if all of its hereditary members have the property. For instance, a set is said to be *hereditarily finite* if it is finite and all of its members are either atomic elements or are hereditarily finite sets.

We write $\mathscr{P}(S)$ for the *powerset* $\{T \mid T \subseteq S\}$ of all subsets of S. In general, there is no one-to-one function from a powerset into a set. The proof involves an important mathematical technique known as *diagonalization*.

THEOREM: CANTOR'S THEOREM   For any set S, there is no onto function from S to $\mathscr{P}(S)$.

Proof   Suppose $f: S \to \mathscr{P}(S)$ is onto. Define the *diagonal* of f as

$$D_f = \{x \in S \mid x \notin f(x)\}.$$

Clearly, $D_f \in \mathscr{P}(S)$, because $D_f \subseteq S$. Because f is assumed to be onto, there must be some $y \in S$ such that $f(y) = D_f$. But $y \in D_f$ if and only if $y \notin f(y)$. This contradicts the assumption that an onto f exists. $\qquad \square$

Note that there is an onto function $f: S \rightarrow T$ if and only if there is some one-to-one $f': T \rightarrow S$. Supposing $f: S \rightarrow T$ is onto, we can construct an $f': T \rightarrow S$ by setting $f'(y) = x$ for some x such that $f(x) = y$. Similarly, if $f': T \rightarrow S$ is one-to-one, we can construct an onto $f: S \rightarrow T$ by taking $f(x) = y$ if $f'(y) = x$ and taking $f(x)$ to be any element of T if there is no y such that $f'(y) = x$. This relationship between one-to-one and onto functions expresses the *duality* of these two notions. Thus, as a corollary of Cantor's theorem, we conclude that there is no one-to-one function from $\mathscr{P}(S)$ into S.

For a relation $R \subseteq S_1 \times \cdots \times S_n$ we define its *characteristic function* to be the total function $C_R: S_1 \times \cdots \times S_n \rightarrow \{\text{yes}, \text{no}\}$ such that the following holds.

(13) $C_R(\vec{x}) = \begin{cases} \text{yes} & \text{if } \vec{x} \in R \\ \text{no} & \text{if } \vec{x} \notin R \end{cases}$

Conversely, for any total function $f: S_1 \times \cdots \times S_n \rightarrow \{\text{yes}, \text{no}\}$ we can define a relation $R_f \subseteq S_1 \times \cdots \times S_n$ such that $\vec{x} \in R_f$ if and only if $f(\vec{x}) = \text{yes}$. Usually, **yes** is coded as 1 and **no** as 0, so that $\{\text{yes}, \text{no}\}$ is coded as $\{0, 1\}$, which is just the coding of 2. This coding, coupled with the relationship between characteristic functions and sets, is why the powerset $\mathscr{P}(S)$ is often written as 2^S.

There are a number of *projection functions* over tuples in $X_1 \times \cdots \times X_n$, each of the form $\pi_m^n: (X_1 \times \cdots \times X_n) \rightarrow X_m$, with $\pi_m^n(\vec{s})$ defined to be the mth coordinate of the n-tuple $\vec{s}$.

(14) $\pi_m^n(\langle s_1, \ldots, s_n \rangle) = s_m$ if $1 \leq m \leq n$

A binary function $f: S \times S \rightarrow S$ is often referred to as an *operator* over S. It is standard to write operators in what is called *infix* notation (as opposed to the *prefix* notation I have used so far), writing $f(x, y)$ as $x f y$. An operator f over S is called *symmetric* if for all $x, y \in S$ we have the following:

(15) $x f y = y f x$ (Symmetry)

An operator f over S is said to be *associative* if the following holds for every $x, y, z \in S$:

(16) $(x f y) f z = x f (y f z)$ (Associativity)

I usually drop parentheses around associative operators and shorten
$(x\, f\, y)\, f\, z$ and $x\, f\, (y\, f\, z)$ to $x\, f\, y\, f\, z$. I also use infix notation where
convenient for binary relations as well as operators, writing xRy for
$\langle x, y \rangle \in R$.

For two relations $R \subseteq S \times T$ and $R' \subseteq T \times U$, we define their *composition* to be the relation $R' \circ R \subseteq S \times U$ such that $\langle s, u \rangle \in R' \circ R$ if and
only if there is some $t \in T$ such that $\langle s, t \rangle \in R$ and $\langle t, u \rangle \in R'$. It is important that if $f: S \to T$ and $g: T \to U$ are partial (total) functions, then
$g \circ f: S \to U$ is a partial (total) function with domain S and range U.

Suppose that we fix a set S along with a collection F of operations on
some set containing S. We say that the *closure* of S with respect to F is
the smallest set $\text{Close}_F(S)$ such that the following holds:

(17) a. $S \subseteq \text{Close}_F(S)$
     b. $f(s_1, \ldots, s_n) \in \text{Close}_F(S)$ if $f \in F$ is an n-place operation and
         $s_1, \ldots, s_n \in \text{Close}_F(S)$

For instance, closing the set $\{2\}$ under the binary operation of addition yields $\text{Close}_{\{+\}}(\{2\}) = \{2, 4, 6, \ldots\}$. Closing a set of prime numbers
under multiplication gives their products, so that $\text{Close}_{\{\times\}}(\{2, 3\}) =
\{2, 3, 4, 6, 8, 9, 12, 16, \ldots\}$.

For a relation $R \subseteq S \times T$, we define its *inverse* to be the relation
$R^{-1} \subseteq T \times S$ such that

(18) $R^{-1}(x, y)$ if and only if $R(y, x)$

If f is a partial function, then f^{-1} is a partial function if and only if f
is one-to-one, and it is total only if f is onto. If $f: S \to T$ is a total bijection, then for every $x \in S$, $f^{-1}(f(x)) = x$, and for $y \in T$, $f(f^{-1}(y)) = y$.
As notational shorthand, if we have a relation R such as $\subseteq$, we just turn
the symbol around and write $\subseteq^{-1}$ as $\supseteq$. Similarly, $\leq^{-1}$ is written $\geq$, and
so on.

There are a number of special types of relations. Suppose that we fix
a relation $R \subseteq S \times S$. We associate the following names with relation R
meeting the following conditions:

(19) a. $\langle x, x \rangle \in R$ for every $x \in S$ (Reflexive)
     b. $\langle x, y \rangle \in R$ if and only if $\langle y, x \rangle \in R$ (Symmetric)
     c. $x = y$ if $\langle x, y \rangle, \langle y, x \rangle \in R$ (Antisymmetric)
     d. $\langle x, z \rangle \in R$ if $\langle x, y \rangle, \langle y, z \rangle \in R$ (Transitive)

Note that if R is symmetric, then $R = R^{-1}$. If R is antisymmetric, then
$R \cap R^{-1} = \emptyset$. If R is transitive, then $R \circ R = R$.

A relation that is transitive, reflexive, and symmetric is said to be an *equivalence relation*. For any set S, we define the *identity* equivalence relation over S to be the identity relation $\{\langle x, x \rangle \mid x \in S\}$ and the *complete* equivalence relation over S to be $S \times S$. An example of a nontrivial equivalence relation would equate all people who have the same birthday, for instance. A standard mathematical example of an equivalence relation relates numbers that have the same remainder on division by n, or in other words, are identical modulo n. For instance, 5 mod 3 = 8 mod 3 = 2.

If R is an equivalence relation over a set S and $x \in S$, we define the *equivalence class* of x, written $[x]_R$, as follows:

(20) $[x]_R = \{y \mid \langle x, y \rangle \in R\}$

We say that x is a *representative* of $[x]_R$. For instance, 8 is a representative of the equivalence class $[8]_{\text{mod } 3} = \{2, 5, 8, 11, \ldots\}$ of numbers with remainder 2 on division by 3. Note that $\langle x, y \rangle \in R$ if and only if $[x]_R = [y]_R$. For a given set S and equivalence relation R over S, we define the *quotient* set, written $S/_R$ and read S modulo R, to be the set of equivalence classes of S with respect to R.

(21) $S/_R = \{[x]_R \mid x \in S\}$

For instance, the quotient of the natural numbers modulo 3 is $\omega/_{\text{mod } 3} = \{\{0, 3, 6, \ldots\}, \{1, 4, 7, \ldots\}, \{2, 5, 8, \ldots\}\}$.

A.3   ORDERINGS, WELL ORDERINGS, AND LATTICES

A transitive and reflexive binary relation over a set S is said to be a *preordering* of the set. We refer to the pair of the set and its ordering as a *preorder*. Thus a preorder is a pair $\langle S, \leq \rangle$ where the following holds:

(22) a. $a \leq a$ (Reflexive)
      b. $a \leq c$ if $a \leq b$ and $b \leq c$ (Transitive)

A preordering that is also antisymmetric is said to be a *partial ordering*. Thus a partial order satisfies the following additional constraint:

(23) $a = b$ if $a \leq b$ and $b \leq a$ (Antisymmetric)

It is common to write $<$ for the following relation:

(24) $a < b$ if and only if $a \leq b$ and $a \neq b$

Such a relation is said to be a *strict ordering*.

It is easy to turn an arbitrary relation R into a transitive relation by what is known as *transitive closure*. The transitive closure of a relation R, written R^+, is the least transitive relation such that $R \subseteq R^+$. We can characterize the relationship more constructively, though. Suppose that we let $R^1 = R$ and $R^n = R \circ R^{n-1}$. Then $R^+ = \bigcup_{n \in \omega} R^n$. Similarly, the *reflexive closure* of a binary relation R over the set S is given by $R \cup \{\langle x, x \rangle \mid x \in S\}$ (note that the set S is a crucial parameter for the reflexive closure but is not needed to compute the transitive closure). We use the standard notation R^* for the transitive and reflexive closure of R over S, which is the least relation over S that contains R and is both transitive and reflexive. Note that $R^* = R^+ \cup \{\langle x, x \rangle \mid x \in S\}$.

A partial ordering can be generated in a natural way from a preordering. In particular, if $\langle S, \leq \rangle$ is a preordering, we define an equivalence relation over S as the smallest relation $=_\leq$ such that the following holds.

(25) $a =_\leq b$ if $a \leq b$ and $b \leq a$

The partial ordering generated by the preorder $\langle S, \leq \rangle$ is over the set S modulo this equivalence relation, which we write $S/_{=_\leq}$. The natural ordering over $S/_{=_\leq}$ is given as follows:

(26) $[a]_{=_\leq} \preceq [b]_{=_\leq}$ if and only if $a \leq b$

It is straightforward both to verify that $=_\leq$ is an equivalence relation and that $\preceq$ is a partial ordering over $S/_{=_\leq}$.

Suppose that we have a partial ordering $\langle S, \leq \rangle$ and a subset $T \subseteq S$. An element $t \in S$ is said to be a *lower bound* for T if $t \leq t'$ for every $t' \in T$. Dually, an element $t \in S$ is said to be an *upper bound* for T if $t' \leq t$ for every $t' \in T$. An element t is said to be a *greatest lower bound* or *meet* for T, written $\sqcap T$, if t is the greatest element in S that is a lower bound for T. Thus $t = \sqcap T$ if t is a lower bound for t and every other lower bound t' for T is such that $t' \leq t$. The notion of *least upper bound* or *join* of a set T, written $\sqcup T$, is defined dually. Note that if a meet or a join exists for a set, it must be unique. A partial ordering is said to be a *join semilattice* if every nonempty, finite subset of the ordering has a least upper bound, and it is said to be a *meet semilattice* if every nonempty, finite subset of the ordering has a greatest lower bound. A partial ordering is said to be a *lattice* if every finite subset of the ordering has both a least upper bound and a greatest lower bound.

A partial ordering is said to be a *complete join semilattice* if every nonempty (possibly infinite) subset of the ordering has a least upper bound.

Complete meet semilattices are defined dually. Note that a complete join semilattice must have a maximum element, defined by the join of all the elements in the ordering. Dually, a complete meet semilattice must have a minimum element. A *complete lattice* is a partial ordering in which every subset of the ordering has both a least upper bound and greatest lower bound. Note that the join of the empty set is the minimum element in the ordering, and the meet of the empty set is the greatest element in the ordering.

Another important kind of partial ordering is a *linear ordering*, sometimes known as a *total ordering*, in which the following holds:

(27) $a \leq b$ or $b \leq a$ (Linearity)

A subset $T \subseteq S$ of a partial ordering is said to be a *chain* if the ordering on S is linear when restricted to T.

A partial order $\langle S, \leq \rangle$ is said to be a *well-founded ordering* or *well-ordered set* if and only if there is no infinite chain $T \subseteq S$ such that for every element $a \in T$ there is some strictly smaller $b \in T$ such that $b < a$. For instance, the set of positive integers is well ordered, but the set of negative integers is not. Similarly, the set of all finite sets is well ordered by the subset relation, but the set of all infinite sets is not.

Orderings can be related using standard mathematical methods. Suppose we have two orderings $\langle S, \leq \rangle$ and $\langle S', \leq' \rangle$. A function $h\colon S \rightarrow S'$ is said to be an *order homomorphism* from S to S' if $s \leq t$ implies $h(s) \leq' h(t)$. An order homomorphism that is one-to-one is said to be an *order embedding*. An *order isomorphism* is an order homomorphism $h\colon S \rightarrow S'$ such that $s_1 \leq s_2$ if and only if $h(s_1) \leq' h(s_2)$. The *if and only if* conditions are necessary to ensure that the three-element ordering $V = \{a, b, c\}$ with $a \leq b$ and $a \leq c$ is not considered isomorphic to the three-element ordering $U = \{d, e, f\}$ with $d \leq' e \leq' f$ by mapping $a \mapsto d$, $b \mapsto e$, and $c \mapsto f$.

A.4 PROOF BY INDUCTION

The most commonly known form of proof by induction is stated over the natural numbers. If we want to establish that every natural number has a property P, we can do so by proving the following pair of results:

(28) a. $P(0)$ holds   (Base case)
      b. $P(n + 1)$ holds if $P(n)$ holds   (Inductive case)

The *principle of induction* tells us that if the above conditions hold, then every natural number has the property P. The assumption that $P(n)$ holds, which is used in the proof of $P(n+1)$, is usually referred to as the *inductive hypothesis*. For instance, it is easy to prove by induction that equation (29) holds for all integers n.

$$(29) \quad \sum_{i=0}^{n} = \frac{n(n+1)}{2}$$

For the base case, with $n = 0$, the result is obvious:

$$(30) \quad \sum_{i=0}^{0} i = 0 = \frac{0(0+1)}{2}$$

We now consider the inductive step, where we will be trying to find the sum of the first $n+1$ integers.

$$(31) \quad \sum_{i=0}^{n+1} i = \sum_{i=0}^{n} i + (n+1)$$

I broke apart the summation so that we can apply the inductive hypothesis. Because we know our result holds for n, we continue the equations above as follows.

$$(32) \quad \sum_{i=0}^{n} i + (n+1) = \frac{n(n+1)}{2} + (n+1)$$

By creating a common denominator and multiplying through, we are left with the desired result for $n+1$.

$$(33) \quad \frac{n(n+1)}{2} + (n+1) = \frac{n^2+n}{2} + \frac{2(n+1)}{2}$$

$$= \frac{(n^2+3n+2)}{2} = \frac{(n+1)(n+2)}{2}$$

This completes the proof of (29) by induction.

In logic, linguistics, and computation, we are usually not dealing with natural numbers and thus need a more general form of induction. Induction over the natural numbers is often referred to as ω-induction, as it is induction over the set ω of natural numbers under their natural ordering. The reason that induction holds for the natural numbers is that ω is a well-ordered set. The principle of *generalized induction* provides a powerful method of establishing that a property P holds of every element of a well-ordered set $\langle S, \leq \rangle$.

(34) In a well-ordered set $\langle S, \leq \rangle$, if the fact that $P(b)$ holds for all $b < a$ entails that $P(a)$ holds, then P holds of every element in S.

This single conditional statement accounts for both the base case and the inductive cases in standard inductive proofs. The base case is included because if a is minimal, then there are no $b < a$, and thus to satisfy the antecedent of the conditional in the induction principle, we must simply establish that $P(a)$. In the case of the natural numbers, for which 0 is the only minimal element in the ordering, we must establish that $P(0)$ holds if $P(n)$ holds for all $n < 0$. Because there are no $n < 0$, we must establish $P(0)$ directly. For $n > 0$, we must establish that if $P(k)$ holds for all $k < n$, then $P(n)$ holds.

A special kind of generalized induction that we will be concerned with is that of *structural induction*. In structural induction, a set of terms is well ordered by means of the subterm relation. Specifically, we set $\alpha < \beta$ if α is a proper subterm of β. This relation well orders the propositional formulas because every expression has only a finite number of subexpressions. Structural induction can be used to show that every λ-term has a balanced set of parentheses (see section 2.2 for a definition of λ-terms) and that every λ-term receives a denotation (see section 2.3 for a definition of denotation for λ-terms).

A.5   FORMAL LANGUAGES

For any set S, the *Kleene star* of S, written S^*, is defined as follows:

(35) $S^* = \bigcup_{n \in \omega} S^n = \bigcup_{n \in \omega} \{ \langle s_1, \ldots, s_n \rangle \mid s_i \in S \}$

The elements of S^* are tuples of elements of S of arbitrary finite length, where the *length* of an n-tuple is taken to be n. Note that Kleene star is a closure operation; we can define it by $S^* = \text{Close}_{\{\cdot\}}(S)$, or in other words, the closure of S under string concatenation (see below).

Elements of S^* are often called *sequences*, and in the context of linguistics are usually called *strings*. I use the shorthand $s_1 s_2 \cdots s_n$ for $\langle s_1, s_2, \ldots, s_n \rangle$, omitting the angle brackets and commas. In particular, I often shorten the sequence $\langle c \rangle$ to c and write $\langle a, b \rangle$ as ab. For the case where $n = 0$, I write the unique 0-tuple $\langle \ \rangle$ as ε, which is called the *null-string*. The *concatenation* operator $\cdot$ over S^* is defined as follows:

(36) $\langle s_1, \ldots, s_n \rangle \cdot \langle t_1, \ldots, t_m \rangle = \langle s_1, \ldots, s_n, t_1, \ldots, t_m \rangle$

Of course, for any string σ, we have the following:

(37) $\sigma \cdot \varepsilon = \varepsilon \cdot \sigma = \sigma$ (Identity)

The concatenation operation is also associative. For any strings σ, τ, and π, we have the following.

(38) $(\sigma \cdot \tau) \cdot \pi = \sigma \cdot (\tau \cdot \pi)$

This being the case, I usually omit the parentheses around concatenations, as no ambiguity can arise. I also take the step of suppressing the concatenation symbol and abbreviate $\sigma \cdot \tau$ as $\sigma\tau$. For two strings σ and τ we say that σ is a *substring* of τ if there are (possibly empty) strings π and ρ such that $\tau = \pi\sigma\rho$. We say that the string σ is a *prefix* of the string τ if there is a string π such that $\tau = \sigma\pi$, and we say that σ is a *suffix* of τ if there is a string π such that $\tau = \pi\sigma$.

We call any subset $\mathscr{L} \subseteq S^*$ a (*formal*) *language over* S. Because formal languages are nothing more than sets, operations such as complementation, union, and intersection can be applied to them. As the elements of languages are sequences, we can extend string operations to sets. For instance, the concatenation of two languages is given as follows:

(39) $\mathscr{L}_1 \cdot \mathscr{L}_2 = \{x_1 \cdot x_2 \mid x_1 \in \mathscr{L}_1, x_2 \in \mathscr{L}_2\}$

A.6   TREES

Trees are often used in the definition of formal languages. They are also used in the definition of proof systems for some logics. We construct trees from a set **BasExp** of basic expressions as well as a set **Cat** of *categories*, which are used to classify expressions. Often the categories themselves will be structured objects rather than atoms, but that will not affect any of the definitions. The set **Tree** of *trees* over the set **BasExp** of basic expressions and the set **Cat** of categories is the least such satisfying the following:

(40) a. **BasExp** $\subseteq$ **Tree**
     b. $\langle C, \langle T_1, \ldots, T_n \rangle\rangle \in$ **Tree** if $n \geq 0$, $C \in$ **Cat**, $T_1, \ldots, T_n \in$ **Tree**

Note that as long as **BasExp** and **Cat** are nonempty, **Tree** is an infinite set each of whose members is a finite structure. Furthermore, if both sets are countable, then so is **Tree**.

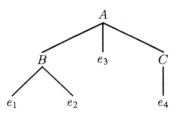

Figure A.1
Standard tree notation

Trees get their name due to the way in which they are drawn. For instance, the following tree, whose structure is rather undecipherable, would be graphically displayed as in figure A.1.

(41) $\langle A, \langle\langle B, \langle e_1, e_2 \rangle\rangle, e_3, \langle C, \langle e_4 \rangle\rangle\rangle\rangle$

Of course, the diagram in figure A.1 looks more like a tree growing upside down. Rather than display trees in this space-consuming fashion, two alternative graphical methods are standardly employed. The first method uses what are commonly known as *phrase markers*. This method is normally used within text for small examples and gives the following result for the tree in figure A.1.

(42) $[_A \, [_B \, e_1 \, e_2] \, e_3 \, [_C \, e_4]]$

We also display trees in a natural-deduction style, following Ades and Steedman (1982); using this notation, our example tree would be rendered as follows.

(43) $\dfrac{\dfrac{e_1 \quad e_2}{B} \quad e_3 \quad \dfrac{e_4}{C}}{A}$

Note that nothing in the definition of trees prevents a category from having no daughters (see the definition of daughterhood below).

There are a number of important components of trees, and these can be defined recursively as follows. The set Node(T) of (*internal*) *nodes* of a tree T is defined as follows:

(44) a. Node(e) $= \emptyset$ if $e \in$ **BasExp**
       b. Node($\langle C, \langle T_1, \ldots, T_n \rangle\rangle$) $= \{C\} \cup$ Node(T_1) $\cup \cdots \cup$ Node(T_n)

The set Leaf(T) of *leaves* of a tree T is defined as follows:

(45) a. Leaf$(e) = \{e\}$ if $e \in$ **BasExp**
     b. Leaf$(\langle C, \langle T_1, \ldots, T_n \rangle\rangle) = $ Leaf$(T_1) \cup \cdots \cup$ Leaf(T_n)

The *yield* of a tree T, Yield(T), is the expression derived from con-catenating the leaves in left-to-right order, given by the following:

(46) a. Yield$(e) = e$ if $e \in$ **BasExp**
     b. Yield$(\langle C, \langle T_1, \ldots, T_n \rangle\rangle) = $ Yield$(T_1) \cdots$ Yield(T_n)

The sample tree in figure A.1 above has a yield of $e_1 e_2 e_3 e_4$. We define the *root* of a tree as follows.

(47) a. Root$(e) = e$ if $e \in$ **BasExp**
     b. Root$(\langle C, \langle T_1, \ldots, T_n \rangle\rangle) = C$

The tree in figure A.1 above is rooted at A. The *depth* of a tree is defined in the following way.

(48) a. Depth$(e) = 0$ if $e \in$ **BasExp**
     b. Depth$(\langle C, \langle T_1, \ldots, T_n \rangle\rangle) = 1 + $ Max$_{1 \leq i \leq n}$Depth(T_i)

The tree in figure A.1 above has a depth of 2. The set SubTree(T) of *subtrees* of a tree is defined recursively as follows.

(49) a. SubTree$(e) = \{e\}$ if $e \in$ **BasExp**
     b. SubTree$(\langle C, \langle T_1, \ldots, T_n \rangle\rangle)$
        $= \{\langle C, \langle T_1, \ldots, T_n \rangle\rangle\} \cup$ SubTree$(T_1) \cup \cdots \cup$ SubTree(T_n)

Another useful notion is that of *local subtree*. A local subtree of a tree consists of a node in the tree and the roots of its immediate daughters.

(50) a. LocSubTree$(e) = \emptyset$
     b. LocSubTree$(\langle C, \langle T_1, \ldots, T_n \rangle\rangle)$
        $= \{\langle C, \langle$Root$(T_1), \ldots, $Root$(T_n) \rangle\rangle\}$
        $\cup$ LocSubTree$(T_1) \cup \cdots \cup$ LocSubTree(T_n)

The terminology here is standard but a bit misleading, because a local subtree is not necessarily a tree in the sense that I have defined it. In particular, a local subtree may be rooted at a category and have daughters that are simple categories rather than proper trees. For in-stance, $\langle A, \langle B, e_3, C \rangle\rangle$ is a subtree of figure A.1, but is not itself a tree. (Contrast this with $\langle A, \langle\!\langle B, \langle \rangle\rangle, e_3, \langle C, \langle \rangle\rangle\rangle\rangle$, which is a tree, although not a subtree or proper subtree of the tree in figure A.1.

   In a tree $T = \langle C, \langle T_1, \ldots, T_n \rangle\rangle$ we say that the category C is the *mother* of the trees $T_1, \ldots, T_n$ and conversely that $T_1, \ldots, T_n$ are the *daughters* of C. This genealogical terminology is extended to the roots of the daughters, so that if C is the mother of T, we also say that C is the mother of root(T). In this latter case, we also say that C *immediately dominates* the category or basic expression Root(T). The tree in figure A.1 above has A as the mother of C, e_3, and B; B is the mother of both e_1 and e_2. We use the term *descendant* for the transitive closure of the daughter-of relation and *ancestor* for the transitive closure of the mother-hood relation.

A.7   FIRST-ORDER LOGIC

In this section I lay out the basic language, proof theory, and model theory of first-order logic.

A.7.1   First-Order Terms and Formulas

I begin with the language of first-order logic, which is determined by a signature. A *first-order signature* consists of the following specifications of *nonlogical constants*.

(51) a. **Fun** $= \bigcup_{n \in \omega}$ **Fun**$_n$: a set of *function symbols* indexed by arity
     b. **Rel** $= \bigcup_{n \in \omega}$ **Rel**$_n$: a set of *relation symbols* indexed by arity

An element $f \in$ **Fun**$_n$ is said to be an *n-ary function symbol*; an $R \in$ **Rel**$_n$ is said to be an *n-ary relation symbol*. A 0-ary (nullary) function symbol is often referred to as a *constant*, and we use the notation **Con** $\stackrel{\text{def}}{=}$ **Fun**$_0$. A 0-ary relational symbol is also said to be a *propositional symbol*, and a 1-ary (unary) relational symbol is said to be a *property symbol*. We assume **Var** is a countably infinite set of variables. We assume that the sets of symbols for constants, functions, relations, and variables are pairwise disjoint. From the variables, function symbols, and constants, we construct the first-order terms as the least set **Term** satisfying the following conditions:

(52) a. **Var** $\subseteq$ **Term**
     b. $f(t_1, \ldots, t_n) \in$ **Term** if $f \in$ **Fun**$_n$ and $t_i \in$ **Term** for $1 \leq i \leq n$

We abbreviate $f(\ )$ as f for $f \in$ **Con** and note that **Con** $\subseteq$ **Term**. We use the collection of terms in defining the well-formed *formulas* of first-order logic, which are given by the least set **Form** meeting the following conditions:

(53) a. $R(t_1, \ldots, t_n) \in$ **Form** if $R \in$ **Rel**$_n$ and $t_i \in$ **Term** for $1 \leq i \leq n$
   b. $(\phi \wedge \psi) \in$ **Form** if $\phi, \psi \in$ **Form**   (Conjunction)
   c. $(\neg\phi) \in$ **Form** if $\phi \in$ **Form**   (Negation)
   d. $(\forall x)\phi \in$ **Form** if $x \in$ **Var** and $\phi \in$ **Form**   (Universal)

We drop parentheses where convenient if no confusion could arise. As many definitions range over terms and formulas, we use the term *expression* to refer to both. Furthermore, we define the following standard abbreviations.

(54) a. $(\phi \vee \psi) \overset{\text{def}}{=} \neg(\neg\phi \wedge \neg\psi)$ (Disjunction)
   b. $(\phi \rightarrow \psi) \overset{\text{def}}{=} \psi \vee \neg\phi$ (Implication)
   c. $(\phi \leftrightarrow \psi) \overset{\text{def}}{=} (\phi \rightarrow \psi) \wedge (\psi \rightarrow \phi)$ (Bi-implication)
   d. $(\exists x)\phi \overset{\text{def}}{=} \neg(\forall x)(\neg\phi)$ (Existential)

A.7.2 First-Order Model Theory

We begin by assuming that we have the set **Bool** $= \{$**yes**, **no**$\}$ of *truth values*. A *first-order model* is the pair $\mathcal{M} = \langle$**Ind**$_{\mathcal{M}}, [\![\cdot]\!]_{\mathcal{M}}\rangle$ with the following components.

(55) a. **Ind**$_{\mathcal{M}}$ is an arbitrary set of *individuals*
   b. $[\![\cdot]\!]_{\mathcal{M}}$ is an *interpretation function* such that
      1. $[\![f]\!]_{\mathcal{M}}:$ **Ind**$^n_{\mathcal{M}} \rightarrow$ **Ind**$_{\mathcal{M}}$ if $f \in$ **Fun**$_n$
      2. $[\![R]\!]_{\mathcal{M}}:$ **Ind**$^n_{\mathcal{M}} \rightarrow$ **Bool** if $R \in$ **Rel**$_n$

When the model $\mathcal{M}$ is clear from context, we drop the subscript. The set **Ind** is often referred to as the *domain* of a model. The function $[\![\cdot]\!]_{\mathcal{M}}$ interprets the nonlogical constants. Thus $[\![f]\!]_{\mathcal{M}}$ is said to be the *interpretation* of f. Note that for a constant $f \in$ **Con**, $[\![f]\!]$ is a mapping from **Ind**$^0 = \{\langle \rangle\}$ to **Ind**, and we abbreviate $f(\langle \rangle)$ as f in the usual way.

It is very important when working with logic to keep in mind the distinction between symbols, which are part of the language, and their interpretations, which are part of the model. Thus we should not refer to the function symbol f as a function, as it is only a symbol; $[\![f]\!]_{\mathcal{M}}$, on the other hand, is a function. Note that the interpretation of an n-ary function symbol is an n-ary function over the individuals, while the interpretation of an n-ary relation symbol is an n-ary relation.

We next extend $[\![\cdot]\!]_{\mathcal{M}}$ from function and relation symbols to arbitrary terms and formulas. First we need to introduce a mechanism to deal with variables. An *assignment* is a function $\theta:$ **Var** $\rightarrow$ **Ind** mapping variables to individuals in the domain of the model. With the model relating the nonlogical symbols for constants, functions, and relations to elements of the model's domain and the assignment linking variables to individuals of domain, we have enough machinery to connect our language with our models. For a model $\mathcal{M}$ and assignment θ we extend the *interpretation function* from functions and relations to a function $[\![\cdot]\!]^{\theta}_{\mathcal{M}}$ from terms and formulas to individuals and truth values.

(56) a. $[\![x]\!]^{\theta}_{\mathcal{M}} = \theta(x)$ if $x \in$ **Var**

b. $[\![f(t_1, \ldots, t_n)]\!]^{\theta}_{\mathcal{M}} = [\![f]\!]_{\mathcal{M}}([\![t_1]\!]^{\theta}_{\mathcal{M}}, \ldots, [\![t_n]\!]^{\theta}_{\mathcal{M}})$ if $f \in$ **Fun**$_n$

c. $[\![R(t_1, \ldots, t_n)]\!]^{\theta}_{\mathcal{M}} = [\![R]\!]_{\mathcal{M}}([\![t_1]\!]^{\theta}_{\mathcal{M}}, \ldots, [\![t_n]\!]^{\theta}_{\mathcal{M}})$ if $R \in$ **Rel**$_n$

d. $[\![\phi \wedge \psi]\!]^{\theta}_{\mathcal{M}} = \begin{cases} \textbf{yes} & \text{if } [\![\phi]\!]^{\theta}_{\mathcal{M}} = \textbf{yes} \text{ and } [\![\psi]\!]^{\theta}_{\mathcal{M}} = \textbf{yes} \\ \textbf{no} & \text{otherwise} \end{cases}$

e. $[\![\neg\phi]\!]^{\theta}_{\mathcal{M}} = \begin{cases} \textbf{yes} & \text{if } [\![\phi]\!]^{\theta}_{\mathcal{M}} = \textbf{no} \\ \textbf{no} & \text{otherwise} \end{cases}$

f. $[\![(\forall x)\phi]\!]^{\theta}_{\mathcal{M}} = \begin{cases} \textbf{yes} & \text{if } [\![\phi]\!]^{\theta[x:=a]}_{\mathcal{M}} = \textbf{yes} \text{ for all } a \in \textbf{Ind}_{\mathcal{M}} \\ \textbf{no} & \text{otherwise} \end{cases}$

The notation $\theta[x := a]$, defined as follows, indicates the assignment that maps x to a and otherwise agrees with θ.

(57) $(\theta[x := a])(y) = \begin{cases} a & \text{if } x = y \\ \theta(y) & \text{if } x \neq y \end{cases}$

If Ψ is a collection of formulas and ϕ is a formula, we say that ϕ is a *logical consequence* of Ψ, written $\Psi \models \phi$, if $[\![\phi]\!]^{\theta}_{\mathcal{M}} = \textbf{yes}$ for every model $\mathcal{M}$ and assignment θ such that $[\![\psi]\!]^{\theta}_{\mathcal{M}} = \textbf{yes}$ for every $\psi \in \Psi$. We say that a formula ϕ is *valid* if and only if $\emptyset \models \phi$. A formula ϕ is said to be *true* in a model under an assignment if its denotation is **yes**, and it is said to be *false* if its denotation is **no**.

Note that a formula is valid if and only if it is true in every model under every assignment. A dual notion is that of satisfiability: a formula ϕ is *satisfiable* if there is some model $\mathcal{M}$ and assignment θ in which ϕ is true. The duality stems from the fact that ϕ is unsatisfiable if and only if $\neg\phi$ is valid, or equivalently, that ϕ is valid if and only if $\neg\phi$ is unsatisfiable. The formulas ϕ and ψ are said to be *logically equivalent*, written $\phi \equiv \psi$, if and only if $[\![\phi]\!]^{\theta}_{\mathcal{M}} = [\![\psi]\!]^{\theta}_{\mathcal{M}}$ for every model $\mathcal{M}$ and assignment θ.

A.7.3 First-Order Proof Theory

In order to develop first-order proof theory, we need to define a few syntactic notions. The function Free maps formulas and terms to sets of variables as follows:

(58) a. Free(x) = \{x\} if $x \in$ **Var**
    b. Free($f(t_1, \ldots, t_n)$) = Free(t_1) $\cup \cdots \cup$ Free(t_n) if $f \in$ **Fun**$_n$
    c. Free($R(t_1, \ldots, t_n)$) = Free(t_1) $\cup \cdots \cup$ Free(t_n) if $R \in$ **Rel**$_n$
    d. Free($\phi \wedge \psi$) = Free(ϕ) $\cup$ Free(ψ)
    e. Free($\neg\phi$) = Free(ϕ)
    f. Free($(\forall x)\phi$) = Free(ϕ) $-$ \{x\}

A formula ϕ is said to be *closed* if it does not contain any free variables, or in other words, if Free(ϕ) = $\emptyset$. Note that Free(c) = $\emptyset$ if $c \in$ **Con**. A closed formula is often referred to as a *statement*. In general, we will translate natural-language sentences into statements, as we will not want any unbound variables.

We often want to consider what happens when the free occurrences of variables in a formula are replaced by some other term (possibly itself a variable). For any term $t \in$ **Term** and variable $x \in$ **Var**, we let $[x \mapsto t]$ stand for the *substitution* which replaces free occurrences of the variable x with the term t. We have to be careful in applying substitutions, as we do not want to perform substitutions on bound variables; only free variables will be affected. The effect of the *substitution* $[x \mapsto t]$ is defined as follows:

(59) a. $x[x \mapsto t] = t$ if $x \in$ **Var**
    b. $y[x \mapsto t] = y$ if $x \neq y \in$ **Var**
    c. $f(t_1, \ldots, t_n)[x \mapsto t] = f(t_1[x \mapsto t], \ldots, t_n[x \mapsto t])$ if $f \in$ **Fun**$_n$
    d. $R(t_1, \ldots, t_n)[x \mapsto t] = R(t_1[x \mapsto t], \ldots, t_n[x \mapsto t])$ if $R \in$ **Rel**$_n$
    e. $(\phi \wedge \psi)[x \mapsto t] = \phi[x \mapsto t] \wedge \psi[x \mapsto t]$
    f. $(\neg\phi)[x \mapsto t] = \neg(\phi[x \mapsto t])$
    g. $((\forall x)\phi)[x \mapsto t] = (\forall x)\phi$
    h. $((\forall y)\phi)[x \mapsto t] = (\forall y)(\phi[x \mapsto t])$ if $x \neq y$

Note that $c[x \mapsto t] = c$ if $c \in$ **Con**. Usually we want to make sure that none of the free variables in t are subsequently bound during a substitution, though this does not form part of the definition of substitution. Instead, we say that a term t is *free for x in a formula* ϕ if there are no variables in t that become bound when substituted for x in ϕ. We can define this notion by cases. We write FreeFor(t, x, ϕ) and say that the term t is *free for x in* ϕ if and only if one of the following cases applies:

(60) a. $\phi = R(t_1, \ldots, t_n)$
    b. $\phi = \psi \wedge \xi$ and FreeFor(t, x, ψ) and FreeFor(t, x, ξ)
    c. $\phi = \neg\psi$ and FreeFor(t, x, ψ)
    d. $\phi = (\forall y)\psi$ and FreeFor(t, x, ψ) and
       either $x \notin$ Free(ψ) or $y \notin$ Free(t)

For example, the term $f(x)$ is free for y in $(\forall z)R(y,z)$ and in $\neg R(y) \wedge P(y,z)$ but not in $(\forall z)(P(y) \rightarrow (\forall x)(R(y,z)))$. In the latter case, substituting $f(x)$ for y gives us $(\forall z)(P(y) \rightarrow (\forall x)R(f(x),z))$, where the x in $f(x)$ is bound by the embedded quantifier.

I provide an *axiomatic* presentation of first-order logic. We write $\Psi \vdash \phi$ if the formula ϕ is *provable* from the set of formulas Ψ. We use the shorthand $\vdash \phi$ for $\emptyset \vdash \phi$ to indicate that ϕ is a provable consequence of the empty set of formulas. The *axioms* for first-order logic consist of all instances of the following schemes (note that I have provided a presentation in terms of implication, which I have defined in terms of conjunction and negation).

(61) a. $\vdash \phi \rightarrow (\psi \rightarrow \phi)$
      b. $\vdash (\phi \rightarrow (\psi \rightarrow \xi)) \rightarrow ((\phi \rightarrow \psi) \rightarrow (\phi \rightarrow \xi))$
      c. $\vdash (\neg\phi \rightarrow \neg\psi) \rightarrow (\psi \rightarrow \phi)$
      d. $\vdash (\forall x)\phi \rightarrow \phi[x \mapsto t]$ [t is free for x in ϕ]
      e. $\vdash (\forall x)(\phi \rightarrow \psi) \rightarrow (\phi \rightarrow (\forall x)\psi)$ [$x \notin \text{Free}(\phi)$]

We add the following collection of *inference rules* to our axioms.

(62) a. $\{\phi, \phi \rightarrow \psi\} \vdash \psi$ (Modus ponens)
      b. $\{\phi\} \vdash (\forall x)\phi$ (Generalization)

With the axioms and inference rules in place, we move on to proofs. A *proof* of ϕ from Ψ is a sequence $\phi_0, \ldots, \phi_n$ such that $\phi = \phi_n$ and for every ϕ_i, either $\phi_i \in \Psi$ or else $\Phi \vdash \phi_i$ where $\Phi \subseteq \{\phi_0, \ldots, \phi_{i-1}\}$. Thus every step of a proof is either an assumption in Ψ, an axiom, or else follows by one of the inference rules from a subset of the formulas derived in the previous steps. Note that the axioms are incorporated as inference rules with empty antecedents. The $\vdash$ relation is typically overloaded, with $\Psi \vdash \phi$ representing inference rules, axioms, and more generally that there is a proof of ϕ from Ψ.

Two of the primary theorems of first-order logic have to do with the connection between the notion of provability and logical consequence. The first result tells us that provability preserves logical validity.

THEOREM: SOUNDNESS If $\vdash \phi$ then $\models \phi$.

Soundness is fairly straightforward to prove. It merely involves checking that each axiom scheme is valid and that the inference rules preserve truth.

The dual result, which is somewhat more surprising and a great deal more difficult to prove, tells us that every valid formula is also provable.

THEOREM: COMPLETENESS   If $\models \phi$ then $\vdash \phi$.

These results can be strengthened somewhat by relating the provability of an implication to the provability from an assumption. In doing so, we have to be careful about the application of the rule of generalization in our proofs, since we have proofs of the form $\phi \vdash (\forall x)\phi$, for which we do not have $\phi \models (\forall x)\phi$.

THEOREM: DEDUCTION   If $\Psi, \psi \vdash \phi$ and generalization has not been applied to a variable free in ψ, then $\Psi \vdash \psi \to \phi$. If $\Psi \vdash \psi \to \phi$, then $\Psi, \psi \vdash \phi$. $\Psi, \psi \models \phi$ if and only if $\Psi \models \psi \to \phi$.

The semantic portion of the deduction theorem is obvious from the definition of the modeling relation $\models$ and the truth conditions for implication. The first half of the syntactic part of the deduction theorem is also straightforward, but the second half must proceed by an induction on the structure of a proof of ϕ, which I will not provide here.

   An important theorem that characterizes the finiteness of the proof system has to do with deriving inconsistencies. A set Ψ of formulas is said to be *inconsistent* if and only if we can derive ϕ and $\neg\phi$ from Ψ for some ϕ. By completeness, a set of formulas is inconsistent if and only if it has no model. We can strengthen this result as follows:

THEOREM: COMPACTNESS   If a collection Ψ of formulas is inconsistent, there is a finite subset $\Psi' \subseteq \Psi$ that is inconsistent.

The compactness theorem is stated in terms of inconsistency, rather than in terms of consistency, for a very deep reason. There is a deep duality that tells us that ϕ is unsatisfiable if and only if $\neg\phi$ is valid. But note that the signs change in this context by the addition of negation. We have an axiomatic system for deriving validity, which gives us a method for deriving inconsistency. That is, our proof system can be used to enumerate all of the valid formulas, or equivalently, all of the unsatisfiable formulas. To determine if a formula is valid, we simply begin enumerating all of the valid formulas and wait to see if the formula in question shows up on the list. Even though this procedure will halt if the formula in question is valid, it will not halt if the formula is not valid, because there are infinitely many formulas that are valid. Now suppose that we had a mechanical method, for instance, in terms of a proof system, for enumerating the formulas that are not valid, or equivalently, those formulas that are satisfiable (recall that a formula is not valid if and only if its negation is satisfiable). This would give us a procedure that would halt whenever it was given an invalid formula. The combination of these two procedures would then give us a computational decision procedure to answer the question as to whether a formula was valid or not. We would simply turn on both machines and wait for one to halt with an answer. We could be sure that one would halt, because every formula is either valid or invalid. Unfortunately, first-order logic is too powerful, and it can be proved that there can be no such machine that halts if and only if it is given an invalid formula. I state this in the following theorem, which is often referred to as *Church's theorem*.

THEOREM: UNDECIDABILITY OF FIRST-ORDER LOGIC   There is no computational procedure that will decide whether or not a formula is valid.

This theorem can be proved by a reduction from the *halting problem* in the theory of computation, as can be seen in the very clear presentation of Boolos and Jeffrey (1980). The halting problem tells us that there is no way to write a computer program that takes an arbitrary program and an input for that program and decides whether or not the program halts on that input. We can directly code up an arbitrary computer program in first-order logic so that a formula is valid if and only if the program it encodes halts. Thus we are left in the unfortunate situation of having a problem for which we can enumerate the positive cases, here the valid formulas, but not the negative cases, here the invalid formulas. This is a serious obstacle for computational approaches to first-order logic. It might seem that things could not get much worse, but in the case of standard models of higher-order logic (see section 2.3), there is not even a computational system for enumerating the set of valid formulas.

A.8   ALGEBRAS AND EQUALITY

A.8.1   Algebras

An *algebra* is nothing more than the functional component of a first-order model. A *signature* for an algebra consists of a specification of constants **Con** and function symbols **Fun**. An algebra itself is just the domain **Ind** of individuals and the interpretations of the constants and function symbols. There are a number of interesting relationships between different algebras over the same signature. The most important of these notions is structural equivalence, expressed as follows. Two algebras $\mathscr{A}$ and $\mathscr{B}$ are said to be *isomorphic* if there is a one-to-one, onto function $h: \mathbf{Ind}_{\mathscr{A}} \rightarrow \mathbf{Ind}_{\mathscr{B}}$, called an *isomorphism*, such that the following hold:

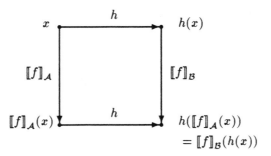

Figure A.2
Isomorphism

(63) a. $h(\llbracket c \rrbracket_{\mathscr{A}}) = \llbracket c \rrbracket_{\mathscr{B}}$ for every $c \in$ **Con**
 b. $h(\llbracket f \rrbracket_{\mathscr{A}}(x_1, \ldots, x_n)) = \llbracket f \rrbracket_{\mathscr{B}}(h(x_1), \ldots, h(x_n))$ for all $x_i \in$ **Ind**$_{\mathscr{A}}$

To gloss this definition in words, it tells us that for two algebras to be isomorphic, we must first be able to associate their domains in a one-to-one fashion, which establishes a correspondence between their objects. The second clause of the definition, (63a), says that if one algebra interprets a constant as x, then the second algebra must assign the constant to the element of the second algebra that corresponds to x. Finally, the third clause, (63b), tells us that if we take the image of a bunch of objects in the first domain under the interpretation of a function symbol in the first algebra, then the result of applying the interpretation of the same function symbol in the second algebra to the objects that correspond to the objects in the first algebra, we get the same result. In the case of a one-place function, it is natural to depict this condition graphically, as in figure A.2. It is a key feature of algebra that we are not concerned with differences between isomorphic structures, but only in their structure up to isomorphism.

An important algebraic notion is that of a substructure, which is the algebraic equivalent of a subset. In general, we require substructures to be closed under the application of algebraic operations. The algebra $\mathscr{N}$ is said to be a *subalgebra* of $\mathscr{M}$ if and only if the following hold:

(64) a. $\mathscr{N}$ and $\mathscr{M}$ are algebras over the same signature
 b. **Ind**$_{\mathscr{N}} \subseteq$ **Ind**$_{\mathscr{M}}$
 c. $\llbracket f \rrbracket_{\mathscr{N}}(a_1, \ldots, a_n) = \llbracket f \rrbracket_{\mathscr{M}}(a_1, \ldots, a_n)$ if $f \in$ **Fun**$_n$ and $a_1, \ldots, a_n \in$ **Ind**$_{\mathscr{N}}$
 d. $\llbracket f \rrbracket_{\mathscr{M}}(a_1, \ldots, a_n) \in$ **Ind**$_{\mathscr{N}}$ if $f \in$ **Fun**$_n$ and $a_1, \ldots, a_n \in$ **Ind**$_{\mathscr{N}}$

In words, an algebra $\mathcal{N}$ is a subalgebra of $\mathcal{M}$ if they are defined over the same signature, the domain of $\mathcal{N}$ is a subset of the domain of $\mathcal{M}$, functions in $\mathcal{N}$ are the same as the functions in $\mathcal{M}$ restricted to elements in the domain of $\mathcal{N}$, and finally, the domain of $\mathcal{N}$ is closed under all the functions. Note that by these definitions, a subalgebra is defined by its domain and the algebra of which it is a subalgebra. For example, in the algebra of integers under the addition function, the even positive integers form a subalgebra, as do the multiples of 7. On the other hand, in the algebra of integers under addition and unary negation, the positive integers do not form a subalgebra, as 5 is a positive integer but -5 is not. In the algebra of sets of natural numbers under union, the sets with greater than 5 elements form a subalgebra, as do the sets with greater than 5 elements and the empty set. On the other hand, these same subsets do not form subalgebras if we also consider intersection. Also, the set of all sets with an even number of members is not a subalgebra of the set of all sets under union, as $\{1, 2\} \cup \{2, 3\} = \{1, 2, 3\}$ demonstrates.

Any subset of the domain of an algebra $\mathcal{M}$ can be used to generate a subalgebra by closing it under the application of functions. If $\mathcal{M}$ is an algebra and $X \subseteq \mathbf{Ind}_{\mathcal{M}}$, we take $\mathbf{Ind}_X$ to be the least set meeting the following conditions:

(65) a. $X \subseteq \mathbf{Ind}_X$
      b. $[\![f]\!]_{\mathcal{M}}(a_1, \ldots, a_n) \in \mathbf{Ind}_X$ if $f \in \mathbf{Fun}_n$ and $a_1, \ldots, a_n \in \mathbf{Ind}_X$

The subalgebra with domain $\mathbf{Ind}_X$, written $[X]$, is said to be the subalgebra of $\mathcal{M}$ generated by X. For instance, the subalgebra of even numbered integers under addition and negation is generated by the set $\{0, 2\}$. Similarly, the subalgebra of the set of all integers under union consisting of finite sets of integers is generated by the collection of singletons along with the empty set.

If the subalgebra of $\mathcal{M}$ generated by X is $\mathcal{M}$ itself, then X is said to be a *generator* for $\mathcal{M}$. Furthermore, if there is no proper subset $Y \subset X$ that generates $\mathcal{M}$, then X is said to be a *prime generator* of $\mathcal{M}$. For instance, the set of all sets of finite sets of integers with two or fewer elements generates the algebra of all finite sets of integers, but is not prime. The notion of primality here is a natural generalization of prime numbers. The algebra of natural numbers under multiplication has the set of prime numbers as a prime generator. Generating sets are often finite, even though the algebras they generate are infinite. In this way, generators provide an important computational tool for representing algebras. For instance, in natural-language semantics we may often think of the set of available meanings as those generated by a set of *semantic primitives*, which form a prime generator of the set of all meanings.

A.8.2   Boolean Algebras

We can view a join semilattice $\langle S, \le \rangle$ as an algebra by defining a binary join operation as follows:

(66) $s \sqcup t \overset{\text{def}}{=} \bigsqcup\{s, t\}$

We can algebraically define the notion of join semilattice as a structure $\langle S, \sqcup \rangle$ meeting certain conditions on the binary operation $\sqcup$ (see Grätzer 1971). From an algebraic presentation of a lattice we can generate an ordering, as follows:

(67) $s \le t$ if $s \sqcup t = t$

We can similarly algebraicize meet semilattices and lattices.

A particular kind of lattice plays an important role in semantics, namely a *boolean algebra*. The lattice operations of meet and join are typically written as $\wedge$ and $\vee$ in boolean algebras, and additional operations are defined corresponding to complements and greatest and least elements. A boolean algebra is the tuple $\langle \mathbf{Prop}, \wedge, \vee, \neg, \mathbf{0}, \mathbf{1} \rangle$, where **Prop** is the set of propositions, $\wedge$ and $\vee$ are binary operations on **Prop**, $\neg$ is a unary operation on **Prop**, and $\mathbf{0}$ and $\mathbf{1}$ are elements of **Prop**, such that for all $x, y, z \in$ **Prop**, we have the following:

(68) a. $x \wedge (y \wedge z) = (x \wedge y) \wedge z$
           $x \vee (y \vee z) = (x \vee y) \vee z$ (Associative)
       b. $x \wedge y = y \wedge x$
           $x \vee y = y \vee x$ (Commutative)
       c. $x \wedge (y \vee z) = (x \wedge y) \vee (x \wedge z)$
           $x \vee (y \wedge z) = (x \vee y) \wedge (x \vee z)$ (Distributive)
       d. $\mathbf{0} \vee x = x$
           $\mathbf{1} \wedge x = x$ (Identities)
       e. $x \wedge \neg x = \mathbf{0}$
           $x \vee \neg x = \mathbf{1}$ (Inverses)

Given this algebraic definition, we see that $\mathbf{0}$ is interpreted as the least element and $\mathbf{1}$ as the greatest element in the ordering of elements in the boolean algebra.

The two best known boolean algebras are the ones underlying classical logic and set theory. The truth values **yes** and **no** form a boolean algebra under the classical logical operations (with $\mathbf{1} = \mathbf{yes}$ and $\mathbf{0} = \mathbf{no}$). The powerset of any set S also forms a boolean algebra by taking $\mathbf{1} = S$ and $\mathbf{0} = \emptyset$ and interpreting $\wedge$ as intersection, $\vee$ as union, and $\neg$ as set complement relative to S. I leave the verification of the axioms as a trivial exercise.

Classical propositional logic derives from the unique two-valued boolean algebra, which can be generated as the power set of a singleton set. The two elements are $\{\mathbf{0}, \mathbf{1}\}$, and if we think of $\mathbf{1}$ as representing truth and $\mathbf{0}$ falsehood, then $\wedge$ corresponds to classical conjunction, $\vee$ to classical disjunction, and $\neg$ to classical negation.

We can generate an ordering from a boolean algebra by setting $x \leq y$ if and only if $x \wedge y = x$, which holds if and only if $x \vee y = y$. We say that an object x is an *atom* if and only if $y \leq x$ implies $y = \mathbf{0}$ or $y = x$. A boolean algebra is said to be *atomic* if for every element $x \neq \mathbf{0}$, there is an atom y such that $y \leq x$. A boolean algebra is said to be *complete* if every set of objects S has a least upper bound $\bigvee S$. Of course, every finite boolean algebra is both atomic and complete. For a nontrivial example, any powerset algebra is atomic and complete. Least upper bounds are computed by union, and the atoms are the singleton sets. There is a deep *representation* theorem of complete atomic boolean algebras as powersets.

THEOREM: REPRESENTATION   A boolean algebra is complete and atomic if and only if it is isomorphic to the powerset of its atoms.

A proof of this result can be found in Stoll 1963. This result is based on the much more general *Stone representation theorem*, which says that any boolean algebra can be isomorphically embedded into a powerset algebra (Stone 1936; see also Davey and Priestley 1990).

A.8.3   First-Order Logic with Equality

The standard treatment of equality is to add equations as another kind of proposition to the first-order language, along with their natural interpretation as propositions. In particular, we assume the following additional rule for constructing formulas:

(69) $t_1 = t_2 \in \mathbf{Form}$ if $t_1, t_2 \in \mathbf{Term}$ (Equality)

We take $t_1 = t_2$ to assert that the two terms have the same denotation. This leads to the natural semantic clause for equality:

(70) $[\![t_1 = t_2]\!]^\theta_{\mathcal{M}} = \begin{cases} \textbf{yes} & \text{if } [\![t_1]\!]^\theta_{\mathcal{M}} = [\![t_2]\!]^\theta_{\mathcal{M}} \\ \textbf{no} & \text{otherwise} \end{cases}$

It should be obvious that equality forms an equivalence relation over the terms. In other words, equality is reflexive, symmetric, and transitive.

It is straightforward to provide a proof theory for equality. We only need to assert that any term is equivalent to itself and that like terms can be substituted in arbitrary contexts. The *equality axioms* are as follows:

(71) a. $\vdash t_1 = t_1$ (Reflexivity)
      b. $\vdash (t_1 = t_2) \rightarrow (\phi[x \mapsto t_1] \rightarrow \phi[x \mapsto t_2])$ (Substitution)

Obviously, any term is going to be equivalent to itself. The soundness of substitution should be obvious from the fact that our functions and relations are purely extensional in that they are defined solely in terms of their actions on inputs.

If we add equality to our language, and the equality axioms to our proof theory, the resulting system remains sound and complete.

THEOREM: SOUNDNESS AND COMPLETENESS WITH EQUALITY $\models \phi$ if and only if $\vdash \phi$.

Equality forms the cornerstone of algebra, where we are interested in establishing some equalities and restricting attention to models that satisfy those equalities. For instance, a *semigroup* is simply an algebra over the signature consisting of a binary operator $\cdot$, written in infix notation, which satisfies the associativity equation.

(72) $(x \cdot y) \cdot z = x \cdot (y \cdot z)$ (Associativity)

A *monoid* is an algebra over a binary sum operator with a constant e, for *identity*, such that the binary sum is associative, as in a semigroup, and in addition, we have the following:

(73) a. $e \cdot x = x$ (Left identity)
      b. $x \cdot e = x$ (Right identity)

For example, the set Σ^* of strings over a language, along with the binary operation of concatenation and the empty string as identity, form the canonical example of a monoid. This explains the close connection between monoids and formal language theory.

To carry this example further, a *group* is a monoid with an additional unary *inverse* operator, which, when applied to an object x, is written x^{-1}. The axioms are as follows:

(74) a. $x \cdot x^{-1} = e$ (Right inverse)
     b. $x^{-1} \cdot x = e$ (Left inverse)

Finally, a so-called *abelian* or *commutative* group satisfies the additional commutativity axiom:

(75) $x \cdot y = y \cdot x$ (Commutativity)

References

Aarts, E. 1995. Investigations in logic, language and computation. Ph.D. dissertation. University of Utrecht.

Abusch, D. 1994. The scope of indefinites. *Natural Language Semantics* 2:83–135.

Aczel, P. 1980. Frege structures and the notions of proposition, truth, and set. In J. Barwise, J. Keisler, and K. Kunen, editors, *The Kleene Symposium*. New York: North-Holland.

Aczel, P. 1988. *Non-Well-Founded Sets.* CSLI Lecture Notes, no. 14. Palo Alto: CSLI Publications.

Adams, E. 1970. Subjunctive and indicative conditionals. *Foundations of Language* 6:89–94.

Ades, A. E., and M. J. Steedman. 1982. On the order of words. *Linguistics and Philosophy* 4:517–558.

Ajdukiewicz, K. 1935. Die syntaktische Konnexität. *Studia Philosophica* 1:1–27.

Andrews, P. B. 1986. *An Introduction to Mathematical Logic and Type Theory: To Truth through Proof.* Orlando, Florida: Academic Press.

Aoun, J., and Y. A. Li. 1993. *Syntax of Scope.* Linguistic Inquiry Monograph, no. 21. Cambridge: MIT Press.

Åqvist, L. 1976. Formal semantics for verb tenses as analyzed by Reichenbach. In T. van Dijk, editor, *Pragmatics of Language and Literature*, 229–236. Amsterdam: North-Holland.

Åqvist, L., and F. Guenthner. 1977. Fundamentals of a theory of verb aspect and events within the setting of an improved tense logic. In F. Guenthner and C. Rohrer, editors, *Studies in Formal Semantics*. Amsterdam: North-Holland.

Austin, J. L. 1961. Performative utterances. In J. L. Austin, *Philosophical Papers*, J. O. Urmson and G. J. Warnock, editors. Oxford: Oxford University Press.

Austin, J. L. 1962. *How to Do Things with Words.* Revised second edition, 1975. Oxford: Oxford University Press.

Ayer, A. J. 1946. *Language, Truth, and Logic.* Second edition. London: Gollancz.

Bach, E. 1968. Nouns and noun phrases. In E. Bach and R. T. Harms, editors, *Universals in Linguistic Theory*, 91–122. New York: Holt, Rinehart and Winston.

Bach, E. 1979. Control in Montague grammar. *Linguistic Inquiry* 10:515–532.

Bach, E. 1980a. In defense of passive. *Linguistics and Philosophy* 3:297–341.

Bach, E. 1980b. Tenses and aspects as functions on verb-phrases. In C. Rohrer, editor, *Time, Tense, and Quantifiers*, 19–37. Tübingen: Niemeyer.

Bach, E. 1981a. Discontinuous constituents in generalized categorial grammars. In *Proceedings of the Eleventh Annual Meeting of the Northeastern Linguistics Society*, 1–12. Amherst: GLSA Publications.

Bach, E. 1981b. On time, tense, and aspect: an essay in English metaphysics. In P. Cole, editor, *Radical Pragmatics*, 63–81. New York: Academic Press.

Bach, E. 1983a. On the relationship between word-grammar and phrase-grammar. *Natural Language and Linguistic Theory* 1:65–89.

Bach, E. 1983b. Generalized categorial grammars and the English auxiliary. In F. Heny and B. Richards, editors, *Linguistic Categories, Auxiliaries, and Related Puzzles, II*, Dordrecht: Reidel.

Bach, E. 1984. Some generalizations of categorial grammars. In F. Landman and F. Veltman, editors, *Varieties of Formal Semantics: Proceedings of the Fourth Amsterdam Colloquium*. Dordrecht: Foris.

Bach, E. 1986. The algebra of events. *Linguistics and Philosophy* 9:5–16.

Bach, E. 1989. *Informal Lectures on Formal Semantics*. Albany: State University of New York Press.

Bach, E., and B. H. Partee. 1980. Anaphora and semantic structure. In J. Kreiman and A. E. Ojeda, editors, *Papers from the Parasession on Pronouns and Anaphora*, 1–28. Chicago: Chicago Linguistic Society.

Barcan, R. 1946. A functional calculus of first-order based on strict implication. *Journal of Symbolic Logic* 11:1–16.

Barendregt, H. P. 1981. *The Lambda Calculus*. Amsterdam: North-Holland.

Barendregt, H. P. 1991. Lambda calculi with types. In S. Abramsky, D. M. Gabbay, and T. S. E. Maibaum, *Handbook of Logic in Computer Science*, volume 2. Oxford: Oxford University Press.

Bar-Hillel, Y. 1950. On syntactical categories. *Journal of Symbolic Logic* 15:1–16.

Bar-Hillel, Y. 1953. A quasi-arithmetical notation for syntactic description. *Language* 29:47–58.

Bar-Hillel, Y. 1954. Indexical expressions. *Mind* 63:359–379.

Bar-Hillel, Y., C. Gaifman, and E. Shamir. 1960. On categorial and phrase structure grammars. *Bulletin of the Research Council of Israel* 9F:1–16.

Barker, C. 1991. Possessive descriptions. Ph.D. dissertation, University of California at Santa Cruz.

Barry, G., M. Hepple, N. Leslie, and G. Morrill. 1991. Proof figures and structural operators for categorial grammar. In *Proceedings of the Fifth Conference of the European Chapter of the Association for Computational Linguistics*. Morristown: ACL Publications.

Bartsch, R. 1973. The semantics and syntax of number and numbers. In J. P. Kimball, editor, *Syntax and Semantics*, volume 2. New York: Seminar Press.

Barwise, J. 1979. On branching quantifiers in English. *Journal of Philosophical Logic* 8:47–80.

Barwise, J. 1981. Scenes and other situations. *Journal of Philosophy* 78:369–397.

Barwise, J. 1989. *The Situation in Logic*. CSLI Lecture Notes, no. 17. Palo Alto: CSLI Publications.

Barwise, J., and R. Cooper. 1981. Generalized quantifiers and natural language. *Linguistics and Philosophy* 4:159–219.

Barwise, J., and J. Etchemendy. 1987. *The Liar: An Essay in Truth and Circularity*. Oxford: Oxford University Press.

Barwise, J., and J. Perry. 1981. Situations and attitudes. *Journal of Philosophy* 78:668–691.

Barwise, J., and J. Perry. 1983. *Situations and Attitudes*. Cambridge: MIT Press.

Barwise, J., and J. Perry. 1985. Shifting situations and shaken attitudes. *Linguistics and Philosophy* 8:103–161.

Becker, O. 1930. Zur Logik der Modalitäten. *Jahrbuch für Philosophie und Phänomenologische Forschung* 11:497–548.

Belnap, N. D. 1982. Display logic. *Journal of Philosophical Logic* 11:375–417.

Bennett, M. 1974. Some extensions of a Montague fragment. Ph.D., dissertation, University of California at Los Angeles.

Birkhoff, G. 1967. *Lattice Theory*. American Mathematical Society Colloquium Publications, no. 25. Providence, Rhode Island: American Mathematical Society.

Boole, G. 1854. *An Investigation of the Laws of Thought*. London.

Boolos, G. S. 1984. To be is to be a value of a variables (or to be some values of some variables). *Journal of Philosophy* 81:430–449.

Boolos, G. S., and R. C. Jeffrey. 1980. *Computability and Logic*. Second edition. Cambridge: Cambridge University Press.

Boyd, J., and J. Thorne. 1969. The semantics of modal verbs. *Journal of Linguistics* 5:57–74.

Brachman, R. J. 1979. On the epistemological status of semantic networks. In N. Findler, editor, *Associative Networks: Representation and Use of Knowledge by Computers*, 3–50. New York: Academic Press.

Brame, M. 1976. *Conjectures and Refutations in Syntax*. New York: Elsevier, North-Holland.

Braroe, E. 1974. *The Syntax and Semantics of English Tense Markers*. Ph.D. dissertation, University of Stockholm.

Bresnan, J. W. 1973. Syntax of the comparative clause construction in English. *Linguistic Inquiry* 4:275–343.

Bresnan, J. W. 1975. Comparative deletion and constraints on transformations. *Linguistic Analysis* 1:353–393.

Bresnan, J. W. 1982a. The passive in lexical theory. In J. W. Bresnan, editor, *The Mental Representation of Grammatical Relations*, 3–86. Cambridge: MIT Press.

Bresnan, J. W. 1982b. Control and complementation. *Linguistic Inquiry* 13:343–434.

Bresnan, J. W. 1982c. Polyadicity. In J. W. Bresnan, editor, *The Mental Representation of Grammatical Relations*, 149–172. Cambridge: MIT Press.

Bresnan, J. W., and J. Grimshaw. 1978. The syntax of free relatives in English. *Linguistic Inquiry* 9:331–391.

Bresnan, J. W., and J. Kanerva. 1989. Locative inversion in Chichewa: a case study in factorization in grammar. *Linguistic Inquiry* 20:1–50.

Brown, G., and G. Yule. 1983. *Discourse Analysis*. Cambridge: Cambridge University Press.

Bunt, H. 1979. Ensembles and the formal semantic properties of mass terms. In F. J. Pelletier, editor, *Mass Terms: Some Philosophical Problems*, 249–277. Dordrecht: Kluwer.

Bunt, H. 1985. *Mass Terms and Modeltheoretic Semantics*. Cambridge: Cambridge University Press.

Calder, J., E. Klein, and H. Zeevat. 1988. Unification categorial grammar: a concise, extendable grammar for natural language processing. In *Proceedings of the Twelfth International Conference on Computational Linguistics*, 83–86. Morristown: ACL Publications.

Carlson, G. 1977a. A unified analysis of the English bare plural. *Linguistics and Philosophy* 1:413–457.

Carlson, G. 1977b. *References to Kinds in English*. Ph.D. dissertation, University of Massachussets at Amherst. Revised version published by Garland, New York, 1980.

Carlson, L. 1980. Plural quantification. Unpublished manuscript. Massachusetts Institute of Technology.

Carlson, L. 1981. Aspect and quantification. *Tense and Aspect*. Syntax and Semantics, no. 14. New York: Academic Press.

Carnap, R. 1947. *Meaning and Necessity*. Second edition, 1956. Chicago: University of Chicago Press.

Carnap, R. 1952. Meaning postulates. *Philosophical Studies* 3:65–73.

Carpenter, B. 1989. Phrase meaning and categorial grammar. Ph.D. dissertation, Centre for Cognitive Science, University of Edinburgh.

Carpenter, B. 1991. The generative power of categorial grammars and head-driven phrase structure grammars with lexical rules. *Computational Linguistics* 17:301–314.

Carpenter, B. 1992a. Lexical rules, categorial grammar, and the English predicative. In R. Levine, editor, *Formal Grammar: Theory and Application*, Vancouver Studies in Cognitive Science, no. 2, 168–242. Oxford: Oxford University Press.

Carpenter, B. 1992b. Plurals as further motivation for Lambek's abstraction. Presented at the Third Mathematics of Language Conference, Austin, Texas.

Carpenter, B. 1994a. A deductive account of scope. In *Proceedings of the Thirteenth West Coast Conference on Formal Linguistics*, San Diego. Palo Alto: CSLI Publications.

Carpenter, B. 1994b. A natural deduction theorem prover for type-theoretic categorial grammars. Technical report. Laboratory for Computational Linguistics. Carnegie Mellon University. Pittsburgh.

Carpenter, B. 1994c. Quantification and scoping: a deductive account. Technical report. Institute for Speech and Language, University of Utrecht.

Carpenter, B. 1994d. Distribution, collection, and quantification: a type-logical account. Technical report. Laboratory for Computational Linguistics. Carnegie Mellon University.

Chellas, B. F. 1980. *Modal Logic: An Introduction*. Cambridge: Cambridge University Press.

Chierchia, G. 1982. Nominalization and Montague grammar: a semantics without types for natural languages. *Linguistics and Philosophy* 5:303–354.

Chierchia, G. 1984a. Topics in the syntax and semantics of infinitives and gerunds. Ph.D. dissertation, University of Massachusetts at Amherst. Published by Garland, New York, 1989.

Chierchia, G. 1984b. Anaphoric properties of infinitives and gerunds. In M. Cobler, S. MacKaye, and M. Westcoat, editors, *Proceedings of the Third West Coast Conference on Formal Linguistics*, 28–39. Palo Alto: CSLI Publications.

Chierchia, G. 1985. Formal semantics and the grammar of predication. *Linguistic Inquiry* 16:417–427.

Chierchia, G. 1988. Structured meanings, thematic roles, and control. In G. Chierchia, B. H. Partee, and R. Turner, editors, *Properties, Types, and Meaning, II*, 131–166. Dordrecht: Kluwer.

Chierchia, G. 1992. Anaphora and dynamic binding. *Linguistics and Philosophy* 15:111–183.

Chierchia, G. 1993. Questions with quantifiers. *Natural Language Semantics* 1:181–234.

Chierchia, G. 1995. *Dynamnics of Meaning: Anaphora, Presupposition, and the Theory of Grammar*. Chicago: Univesity of Chicago Press.

Chierchia, G., and S. McConnell-Ginet. 1990. *Meaning and Grammar: An Introduction to Semantics*. Cambridge: MIT Press.

Chierchia, G., and R. Turner. 1988. Semantics and property theory. *Linguistics and Philosophy* 11:261–302.

Chomsky, N. 1957. *Syntactic Structures*. The Hague: Mouton.

Chomsky, N. 1965. *Aspects of the Theory of Syntax*. Cambridge: MIT Press.

Chomsky, N. 1975. Questions of form and interpretation. In R. Austerlitz, editor, *The Scope of American Linguistics*. Lisse: Peter de Ridder.

Chomsky, N. 1976. Conditions on rules of grammar. *Linguistic Analysis* 2:303–351.

Chomsky, N. 1977. On 'wh'-movement. In A. Akmajian, P. Culicover, and T. Wasow, editors, *Formal Syntax*, 157–196. New York: Academic Press.

Chomsky, N. 1981. *Lectures on Government and Binding*. Dordrecht: Foris.

Chomsky, N. 1986a. *Barriers*. Cambridge: MIT Press.

Chomsky, N. 1986b. *Knowledge of Language: Its Nature, Origin, and Use*. New York: Praeger.

Chomsky, N. 1990a. Language and problems of knowledge. In A. P. Martinich, editor, *The Philosophy of Language*, second edition, 509–527, Oxford: Oxford University Press.

Chomsky, N. 1990b. On formalization and formal linguistics. *Natural Language and Linguistic Theory* 8:143–147.

Church, A. 1940. A formulation of a simple theory of types. *Journal of Symbolic Logic* 5:56–68.

Church, A. 1951. The need for abstract entities in semantic analysis. *American Academy of Arts and Science Proceedings* 80:100–113. Reprinted as "Intensional semantics" in A. P. Martinich, editor, *The Philosophy of Language*, second edition, 1990, 40–47. Oxford: Oxford University Press.

Clark, R., and E. Keenan. 1986. Absorption and universal grammar. *Linguistic Review* 6:113–136.

Cohen, A. 1994. Reasoning with generics. In H. Bunt, R. Muskens, and G. Rentier, editors, *Proceedings of the International Workshop on Computational Semantics*, 51–60. Tilburg: Tilburg University Department of Linguistics Publications.

Cohen, A. 1996. Think generic! Interpreting and reasoning with generics. Ph.D. dissertation, Carnegie Mellon University.

Collins, A. M., and M. R. Quillian. 1969. Retrieval time from semantic memory. *Journal of Verbal Learning and Verbal Behavior* 8:240–247.

Cooper, R. 1975. Montague's semantic theory and transformational syntax. Ph.D. dissertation, University of Massachusetts at Amherst.

Cooper, R. 1979. Variable binding and relative clauses. In F. Guenthner and S. Schmidt, editors, *Formal Semantics and Pragmatics for Natural Language*. Dordrecht: Reidel.

Cooper, R. 1982. Binding in wholewheat* syntax (* unenriched with inaudibilia). In P. Jacobson and G. K. Pullum, editors, *The Nature of Syntactic Representation*. Dordrecht: Reidel.

Cooper, R. 1983. *Quantification and Syntactic Theory*. Synthese Language Library, no. 21. Dordrecht: Reidel.

Crabtree, M., and J. Powers, editors. 1991. *Language Files: Materials for an Introduction to Language*. Fifth edition. Columbus: Ohio State University Press.

Crain, S., and H. Hamburger. 1992. Semantics, knowledge, and NP modification. In R. Levine, editor, *Formal Grammar: Theory and Application*, Vancouver Studies in Cognitive Science, no. 2, 372–401, Oxford University Press, Oxford.

Crain, S., and M. Steedman. 1985. On not being led up the garden path: the use of context by the psychological syntax processor. In D. R. Dowty, L. Karttunen, and A. M. Zwicky, editors, *Natural Language Parsing: Psychological, Computational, and Theoretical Perspectives*, 320–358. Cambridge: Cambridge University Press.

Cresswell, M. J. 1973. *Logics and Languages*. London: Methuen and Company.

Cresswell, M. J. 1974. Adverbs and events. *Synthese* 28:455–481.

Cresswell, M. J. 1976. The semantics of degree. In B. Partee, editor, *Montague Grammar*. New York: Academic Press.

Cresswell, M. J. 1985. *Structured Meanings: The Semantics of Propositional Attitudes*. Cambridge: MIT Press.

Cruse, D. A. 1986. *Lexical Semantics*. Cambridge: Cambridge University Press.

Curry, H. B. 1930. Grundlagen der kombinatorischen Logik. *American Journal of Mathematics* 52:509–536, 789–834.

Curry, H. B., and R. Feys. 1961. *Combinatory Logic, I*. Amsterdam: North-Holland.

Dalrymple, M., J. Lamping, F. C. N. Pereira, and V. Saraswat. 1995. A deductive account of quantification in LFG. In M. Kanazawa, C. J. Piñón, and H. de Swart, editors, *Quantifiers, Deduction, and Context*. Palo Alto: CSLI Publications.

Dalrymple, M., S. M. Shieber, and F. C. N. Pereira. 1991. Ellipsis and higher-order unification. *Linguistics and Philosophy* 14:399–452.

Davey, B., and H. Priestley. 1990. *Introduction to Lattices and Order*. Cambridge Mathematical Textbooks. Cambridge: Cambridge University Press.

Davidson, D. 1967a. The logical form of action sentences. In N. Rescher, editor, *The Logic of Decision and Action*. Pittsburgh: University of Pittsburgh Press.

Davidson, D. 1967b. Causal relations. *Journal of Philosophy* 64. Reprinted in D. Davidson, *Essays on Actions and Events*, 149–162. Oxford: Oxford University Press, 1980.

Davidson, D. 1967c. Truth and meaning. *Synthese* 17:304–323.

Davidson, D. 1968. On saying that. *Synthese* 19:130–146.

Davidson, D. 1980. *Essays on Actions and Events*. Oxford: Clarendon.

Davidson, D. 1989. The myth of the subjective. In M. Krausze, editor, *Relativism: Interpretation and Confrontation*, 165–166. Notre Dame, Indiana: University of Notre Dame Press.

Davies, M. 1989. 'Two examiners marked six scripts': interpretations of numerically quantified sentences. *Linguistics and Philosophy* 12:293–324.

De Saussure, F. 1916. *A Course in General Linguistics*. Reprinted in 1959. New York: McGraw Hill.

De Swart, H. 1991. Adverbs of quantification: a generalized quantifier approach. Ph.D. dissertation, University of Groningen.

DeMey, S. 1981. The dependent plural and the analysis of tense. In V. A. Burke and J. Pustejovsky, editors, *Proceedings of the Eleventh Meeting of the North Eastern Linguistics Society*. Amherst: University of Massachussets at Amherst Graduate Linguistics Student Association.

Donnellan, K. S. 1966. Reference and definite descriptions. *Philosohical Review* 75:281–304.

Dŏsen, K. 1992. A brief survey of frames for the Lambek calculus. *Zeitscrift für mathematische Logik und Grundlagen der Mathematik* 38:179–187.

Dŏsen, K., and P. Schroeder-Heister, editors. 1993. *Substructural Logics*. Oxford: Oxford University Press.

Dowty, D. 1978. Governed transformations as lexical rules in a Montague grammar. *Linguistic Inquiry* 9:393–426.

Dowty, D. 1979a. *Word Meaning and Montague Grammar*. Synthese Language Library, no. 7. Dordrecht: Reidel.

Dowty, D. 1979b. Dative 'movement' and Thomason's extensions of Montague grammar. In S. Davis and M. Methun, editors, *Linguistics, Philosophy, and Montague Grammar*, 153–222. Austin: University of Texas Press.

Dowty, D. 1982a. Tenses, time adverbs, and compositional semantic theory. *Linguistics and Philosophy* 5:23–55.

Dowty, D. 1982b. Grammatical relations and Montague grammar. In P. Jacobson and G. Pullum, editors, *The Nature of Syntactic Representation*. Dordrecht: Reidel.

Dowty, D. 1982c. More on the categorial analysis of grammatical relations. In A. Zaenen, editor, *Subjects and Other Subjects*. Bloomington: Indiana University Linguistics Club.

Dowty, D. 1985. On recent analyses of the semantics of control. *Linguistics and Philosophy* 8:291–331.

Dowty, D. 1986a. A note on collective predicates, distributive predicates, and 'all'. In F. Marshall, editor, *Proceedings of the Eastern States Conference on Linguistics, 1986*. Columbus: Linguistics Department, Ohio State University.

Dowty, D. 1986b. The effect of aspectual class on the temporal structure of discourse: semantics or pragmatics? *Linguistics and Philosophy* 9:37–62.

Dowty, D. 1988. Type-raising, functional composition, and non-constituent coordination. In R. T. Oehrle, E. Bach, and D. Wheeler, editors, *Categorial Grammars and Natural Language Structures*, 153–197. Dordrecht: Reidel.

Dowty, D. 1991. Thematic proto-roles and argument selection. *Language* 67:547–619.

Dowty, D. 1994. The role of negative polarity and concord marking in natural language reasoning. In *Proceedings of the Fourth Conference on Semantics and Linguistic Theory*. Ithaca: CLC Publications.

Dowty, D., and B. Brodie. 1984. The semantics of "floated" quantifiers in transformationless grammar. In M. Cobler, S. MacKaye, and M. T. Wescoat, editors, *Proceedings of the Third Annual West Coast Conference on Formal Linguistics*, 75–90. Palo Alto: CSLI Publications.

Dowty, D. R., R. E. Wall, and S. Peters. 1981. *Introduction to Montague Semantics*. Synthese Language Library, no. 11. Dordrecht: Reidel.

Dunn, J. M. 1973. A 'Gentzen' system for positive relevant implication (abstract). *Journal of Symbolic Logic* 38:356–357.

Eco, U., M. Santambrogio, and D. Violi, editors. 1989. *Meaning and Mental Representation*. Bloomington: Indiana University Press.

Emms, M. 1990. Polymorphic quantifiers. In G. Barry and G. Morrill, editors, *Studies in Categorial Grammar*, Edinburgh Working Papers in Cognitive Science, no. 5, 65–111. Edinburgh: Centre for Cognitive Science. Reprinted in M. Stokhof and L. Torenvliet, editors, *Proceedings of the Seventh Amsterdam Colloquium*, 139–163. Amsterdam: Institute for Logic, Language, and Information.

Emms, M. 1993. Parsing with polymorphism. In *Proceedings of the Sixth Conference of the European Chapter of the Association for Computational Linguistics*. Morristown: ACL Publications.

Enç, M. 1986. Towards a referential analysis of temporal expressions. *Linguistics and Philosophy* 9:405–426.

Engdahl, E. 1986. *Constituent Questions*. Synthese Language Library, no. 27. Dordrecht: Reidel.

Evans, G. 1973. The causal theory of names. *Aristotelian Society*, suppl. vol. 47:187–208.

Farkas, D., and Y. Sugioka. 1983. Restrictive 'if'/'when' clauses. *Linguistics and Philosophy* 6:225–258.

Fauconnier, G. 1985. *Mental Spaces*. Cambridge: MIT Press.

Feys, R. 1937. Les logiques nouvelles des modalités. *Revue Néoscholastique de Philosophie* 40:517–553.

Fiengo, R., and H. Lasnik. 1973. The logical structure of reciprocal sentences in English. *Foundations of Language* 9:447–468.

Fillmore, C. 1968. The case for case. In E. Bach and R. T. Harms, editors, *Universals in Linguistic Theory*. New York: Holt, Rinehart and Winston.

Fodor, J. A. 1975. *The Language of Thought*. Cambridge: Harvard University Press.

Fodor, J. D., and I. A. Sag. 1982. Referential and quantificational indefinites. *Linguistics and Philosophy* 5:355–398.

Frege, G., 1879. *Begriffsschrift*. Halle: Verlag Louis Nebert. English translation in J. van Heyenoort, editor, 1967, *From Frege to Gödel: A Sourcebook in Mathematical Logic 1879–1931*. Cambridge: Harvard University Press.

Frege, G. 1891. Function and concept. Translated by P. T. Geach. In P. T. Geach and M. Black, *Translations from the Philosophical Writings of Gottlob Frege*. London: Blackwell, 1952.

Frege, G. 1892. Über Sinn und Bedeutung. *Zeitschrift für Philosophie und Philosophische Kritik* 100:25–50. Translated by H. Feigl as "Sense and nominatum" in H. Feigl and W. Sellars, editors, *Readings in Philosophical Analysis*, 85–102. Atascadero, California: Ridgeview Publishing Company, 1949.

Gallin, D. 1975. *Intensional and Higher-Order Modal Logic*. Amsterdam: North-Holland.

Gamut, L. T. F. 1991a. *Logic, Language, and Meaning: Introduction to Logic*. Chicago: University of Chicago Press. First published in Dutch as *Logica, Taal en Betekenis*, volume 1. De Meern, Netherlands: Uitgeverij Het Spectrum, 1982.

Gamut, L. T. F. 1991b. *Logic, Language, and Meaning: Intensional Logic and Logical Grammar*. Chicago: University of Chicago Press. First published in Dutch as *Logica, Taal en Betekenis*, volume 2. De Meern, Netherlands: Uitgeverij Het Spectrum, 1982.

Gawron, J. M. 1986. Situations and prepositions. *Linguistics and Philosophy* 9:327–382.

Gawron, J. M., and P. S. Peters. 1990. *Quantification and Anaphora in Situation Semantics*. CSLI Lecture Notes, no. 19. Palo Alto: CSLI Publications.

Gazdar, G. 1980. A cross-categorial semantics for coordination. *Linguistics and Philosophy* 3:407–410.

Gazdar, G. 1981a. On syntactic categories. *Philosophical Transactions of the Royal Society*, series B 295:267–283.

Gazdar, G. 1981b. Unbounded dependencies and coordinate structure. *Linguistic Inquiry* 12:155–184.

Gazdar, G., E. Klein, G. Pullum, and I. Sag. 1985. *Generalized Phrase Structure Grammar*. Oxford: Basil Blackwell.

Gazdar, G., G. K. Pullum, and I. A. Sag. 1982. Auxiliaries and related phenomena in a restrictive theory of grammar. *Language* 58:591–638.

Geach, P. T. 1962. *Reference and Generality*. Ithaca, New York: Cornell University Press.

Geach, P. T. 1967. Intentional identity. *Journal of Philosophy* 64:627–632.

Geach, P. T. 1972. A program for syntax. *Synthese* 22:3–17.

Geis, M. 1973. 'If' and 'unless'. In A. Petrangeli and S. Saporta, editors, *Issues in Linguistics: Papers in Honor of Henry and Renée Kahane*. Urbana: University of Illinois Press.

Gerdemann, D., and E. W. Hinrichs. 1990. A unification-based approach to quantifier scoping. In L. Aiello, editor, *Proceedings of the Ninth European Conference on Artificial Intelligence*. Twente: ECCAI Publications.

Gil, D. 1982. Quantifier scope, linguistic variation, and natural language semantics. *Linguistics and Philosophy* 5:421–472.

Gillon, B. 1984. *The Logical Form of Plurality and Quantification in English.* Ph.D. dissertation, Massachusetts Institute of Technology.

Gillon, B. 1987. The readings of plural noun phrases in English. *Linguistics and Philosophy* 10:199–219.

Gillon, B. 1990a. Plural noun phrases and their readings: a reply to Lasersohn. *Linguistics and Philosophy* 13:477–485.

Gillon, B. S. 1990b. Bare plurals as plural indefinite noun phrases. In H. E. Kyburg Jr., R. P. Loui, and G. N. Carlson, editors, *Knowledge Representation and Defeasible Reasoning*, 119–166. Dordrecht: Kluwer.

Gillon, B. 1992. Towards a common semantics for English count and mass nouns. *Linguistics and Philosophy* 15:597–639.

Girard, J.-Y. 1987. Linear logic. *Theoretical Computer Science* 50:1–102.

Girard, J.-Y. 1995. Linear logic: a survey. In P. de Groote, editor, *The Curry-Howard Isomorphism*, Cahiers du centre de logique, Université catholique de Louvain, no. 8, 193–255, Louvain: Academia.

Girard, J.-Y., P. Taylor, and Y. Lafont. 1989. *Proofs and Types.* Cambridge Tracts in Theoretical Computer Science, no. 7. Cambridge: Cambridge University Press.

Gödel, K. 1931. Über formal unentscheidbare sätze der *Principia Mathematica* und verwandter systeme I. *Monatshefte für Mathematik und Physik* 38:173–198.

Gödel, K. 1933. Eine Interpretation des intuitionistischen Aussagenkalküls. *Ergebnisse eines mathematischen Kolloquiums* 4:34–40.

Goldblatt, R. 1987. *Logics of Time and Computation.* CSLI Lecture Notes, no. 7. Palo Alto: CSLI Publications.

Goodman, N., and W. V. O. Quine. 1947. Steps toward a constructive nominalism. *Journal of Symbolic Logic* 12:105–122.

Grätzer, G. 1971. *Lattice Theory: First Concepts and Distributive Lattices.* San Francisco: W. H. Freeman and Company.

Greibach, S. A. 1965. A new normal form theorem for context-free phrase structure grammars. *Journal of the ACM* (Association for Computing Machinery) 12:42–52.

Grice, H. P. 1975. Logic and conversation. In P. Cole and J. L. Morgan, editors, *Speech Acts*, Syntax and Semantics, no. 3, 41–58. New York: Academic Press.

Groenendijk, J., and M. Stokhof. 1984. Studies in the semantics of questions and the pragmatics of answers. Joint Ph.D. dissertation, University of Amsterdam.

Groenendijk, J., and M. Stokhof. 1990. Dynamic Montague grammar. In L. Kálmán and L. Pólos, editors, *Papers from the Second Symposium on Logic and Language*, 3–48. Budapest: Akadémiai Kiadó.

Groenendijk, J., and M. Stokhof. 1991. Dynamic predicate logic. *Linguistics and Philosophy* 14:39–100.

Grosz, B., and C. Sidner. 1986. Attention, intention, and the structure of discourse. *Computational Linguistics* 12:175–204.

Guenthner, F. 1979. Time schemes, tense logic, and the analysis of English tenses. In F. Guenthner and S. J. Schmidt, editors, *Formal Semantics and Pragmatics for Natural Languages*, 201–222. Reidel: Dordrecht.

Gunter, C. 1992. *Semantics of Programming Languages*. Cambridge: MIT Press.

Haack, S. 1978. *Philosophy of Logics*. Cambridge: Cambridge University Press.

Haddock, N. J. 1987. Incremental interpretation and combinatory categorial grammar. In *Proceedings of the Tenth International Joint Conference on Artificial Intelligence*, 661–663. Somerset, N.J.: IJCAI Publications.

Halliday, M. 1967. Notes on transitivity and theme in English, part 2. *Journal of Linguistics* 3:199–244.

Hamblin, C. L. 1958. Questions. Australasian Journal of Philosophy 36:159–168.

Heim, I. 1982. The semantics of definite and indefinitie noun phrases. Ph.D. dissertation, University of Massachusetts at Amherst. Published by Garland, New York, 1989.

Heim, I., H. Lasnik, and R. May. 1991. Distributivity and reciprocity. *Linguistic Inquiry* 22:63–101.

Hempel, C. G. 1950. Problems and changes in the empiricist criterion of meaning. *Revue International de Philosophie* 4:41–63.

Hendriks, H. 1987. Type change in semantics: the scope of quantification and coordination. In E. Klein and J. van Benthem, editors, *Categories, Polymorphism, and Unification*, 95–120. Edinburgh: Centre for Cognitive Science.

Hendriks, H. 1990. Flexible Montague grammar. In Deliverable R1.2.A of DYANA: Dynamic Interpretation of Natural Language. ESPRIT Basic Research Action BR3175. Centre for Cognitive Science, Edinburgh.

Hendriks, H. 1993. Studied flexibility: categories and types in syntax and semantics. Ph.D. dissertation, University of Amsterdam.

Hendriks, P. 1991. Subdeletion and the Lambek calculus. In P. Dekker and M. Stokhof, editors, *Proceedings of the Eighth Amsterdam Colloquium*, 233–252. Amsterdam: Institute for Logic, Language, and Information.

Hendriks, P. 1995. Comparatives and categorial grammar. Ph.D. dissertation, University of Groningen.

Henkin, L. 1950. Completeness in the theory of types. *Journal of Symbolic Logic* 15:81–91.

Heny, F. 1982. Tense, aspect, and time adverbials, part II. *Linguistics and Philosophy* 5:109–154.

Hepple, M. 1987. Methods for parsing combinatory grammars and the spurious ambiguity problem. M.Sc. thesis, University of Edinburgh.

Hepple, M. 1990a. The grammar and processing of order and dependency: a categorial approach. Ph.D. dissertation, University of Edinburgh.

Hepple, M. 1990b. Normal form theorem proving for the Lambek calculus. In *Proceedings of the Thirteenth International Conference on Computational Linguistics*. Morristown: ACL Publications.

Hepple, M. 1992. Chart parsing Lambek grammars: modal extensions and incrementality. In *Proceedings of the Fourteenth International Conference on Computational Linguistics*. Morristown: ACL Publications.

Hepple, M., and G. Morrill. 1989. Parsing and derivational equivalence. In *Proceedings of the European Chapter of the Association for Computational Linguistics*. Morristown: ACL Publications.

Herskovits, A. 1986. *Language and Spatial Cognition: An Interdisciplinary Study of the Prepositions in English*. Cambridge: Cambridge University Press.

Heyting, A. 1956. *Intuitionism*. Amsterdam: North-Holland.

Higginbotham, J., and R. May. 1981. Questions, quantifiers, and crossing. *Linguistic Review* 1:41–80.

Hindley, J. R., and J. P. Seldin. 1986. *Introduction to Combinators and λ-Calculus*. London Mathematical Society Student Texts, no. 1. Cambridge: Cambridge University Press.

Hinrichs, E. 1981. Temporale Anaphora im Englishchen. Staatsexamen thesis, University of Tübingen.

Hinrichs, E. 1986. Temporal anaphora in discourses of English. *Linguistics and Philosophy* 9:63–82.

Hinrichs, E. 1988. Tense, quantifiers, and contexts. *Computational Linguistics* 14:3–14.

Hinrichs, E., and T. Nakazawa. 1994. Linearizing finite AUX in German verbal complexes. In J. Nerbonne, K. Netter, and C. Pollard, editors, *German in Head-Driven Phrase Structure Grammar*, 11–38. Palo Alto: CSLI Publications.

Hintikka, J. 1961. Modality and quantification. *Theoria* 27:110–128.

Hintikka, J. 1962. *Knowledge and Belief: An Introduction to the Logic of the Two Notions*. Ithaca, New York.: Cornell University Press.

Hintikka, J. 1963. The modes of modality. In *Modal and Many-Valued Logics*, Acta Philosophica Fennica, no. 16, 65–81. Helsinki: Suomalaisen Kirjallisunden Kirjapaino.

Hintikka, J. 1974. Quantifiers vs. quantification theory. *Dialectica* 27:329–358. Reprinted, *Linguistic Inquiry* 5 (1974): 153–177.

Hobbs, J. R., and S. M. Shieber. 1987. An algorithm for generating quantifier scopings. *Computational Linguistics* 13:47–63.

Hoeksema, J. 1983a. Plurality and conjunction. In A. ter Meulen, editor, *Studies in Modeltheoretic Semantics*, Groningen-Amsterdam Studies in Semantics, no. 1, Dordrecht: Foris.

Hoeksema, J. 1983b. Negative polarity and the comparative. *Natural Language and Linguistic Theory* 1:403–434.

Hoeksema, J. 1984. *Categorial Morphology*. Ph.D. dissertation, University of Groningen. Published by Garland, New York, 1985.

Hoeksema, J. 1986. An account of relative clauses with split antecedents. In *Proceedings of the Fifth West Coast Conference on Formal Linguistics*. Palo Alto: CSLI Publications.

Hoeksema, J. 1987. The logic of exception. *Proceedings of the Fourth Eastern States Conference on Linguistics*, 100–113. Ithaca: CLC Publications.

Hoeksema, J. 1989. The semantics of non-boolean 'and'. *Journal of Semantics* 6:19–40.

Hopcroft, J., and J. Ullman. 1979. *Introduction to Automata Theory, Languages, and Computation*. Reading, Massachusetts: Addison-Wesley.

Horn, L. 1985. Metalinguistic negation and pragmatic ambiguity. *Language* 61:121–174.

Horn, L. 1989. *A Natural History of Negation*. Chicago: University of Chicago Press.

Hornstein, N. 1990. *As Time Goes By*. Cambridge: MIT Press.

Howard, W. A. 1969. The formulae-as-types notion of construction. In J. R. Hindley and J. P. Seldin, editors, *To H. B. Curry: Essays on Combinatory Logic, Lambda Calculus, and Formalism*. New York: Academic Press.

Hughes, G. E., and M. J. Cresswell. 1968. *An Introduction to Modal Logic*. London: Methuen and Company.

Hurford, J. R. 1975. *The Linguistic Theory of Numerals*. Cambridge: Cambridge University Press.

Jackendoff, R. 1972. *Semantic Interpretation in Generative Grammar*. Cambridge: MIT Press.

Jackendoff, R. 1977. *X-Bar Syntax: A Study of Phrase Structure*. Linguistic Inquiry Monographs, no. 2. Cambridge: MIT Press.

Jackendoff, R. 1983. *Semantics and Cognition*. Cambridge: MIT Press.

Jacobson, P. 1977. *The Syntax of Crossing Coreference*. Ph.D. dissertation, University of California at Berkeley. Published by Garland, New York, 1979.

Jacobson, P. 1992. Antecedent contained deletion in a variable free syntax. In C. Barker and D. Dowty, editors, *Proceedings of the Second Conference on Semantics and Linguistic Theory*, 193–213. Columbus, Ohio: Department of Linguistics, Ohio State University.

Kadmon, N. 1985. The discourse representation of noun phrases with numerical determiners. In S. Berman, J.-W. Choe, and J. McDonough, editors, *Proceedings of the Fifth Meeting of the Northeastern Linguistic Society*. Amherst: GLSA Publications.

Kamp, H. 1960. *Tense Logic and the Theory of Linear Order*. Ph.D. dissertation, University of California at Los Angeles.

Kamp, H. 1971. Formal properties of 'now'. *Theoria* 37:227–273.

Kamp, H. 1975. Two theories about adjectives. In E. L. Keenan, editor, *Formal Semantics of Natural Language*, 123–155. Cambridge: Cambridge University Press.

Kamp, H. 1979. Events, instants, and temporal reference. In R. Bäuerle, U. Egli, and A. von Stechow, editors, *Semantics from Different Points of View*, 376–417. Berlin: Springer Verlag.

Kamp, H. 1981. A theory of truth and semantic representation. In J. A. G. Groenendijk, T. Janssen, and M. Stokhof, editors, *Formal Methods in the Study of Language*. Amsterdam: Amsterdam Mathematisch Centrum, University of Amsterdam. Reprinted in J. A. G. Groenendijk, T. Janssen, and M. Stokhof, editors, *Truth, Interpretation, and Information*, 1–41. Dordrecht: Foris, 1984.

Kamp, H. 1984. A theory of truth and semantic representation. In J. Groenendijk, T. M. Janssen, and M. Stokhof, editors, *Truth, Interpretation, and Information: Selected Papers from the Third Amsterdam Colloquium*. Dordrecht: Foris.

Kamp, H., and U. Reyle. 1993. *From Discourse to Logic*. Dordrecht: Kluwer.

Kanazawa, M. 1992. The Lambek calculus enriched with additional connectives. *Journal of Logic, Language, and Information* 1:141–171.

Kaplan, D. 1964. Foundations of intensional logic. Ph.D. dissertation, University of California, Los Angeles.

Kaplan, D. 1973. Bob and Carol and Ted and Alice. In J. Hintikka, J. M. E. Moravcsik, and P. Suppes, editors, *Approaches to Natural Lnaguage: Proceedings of the 1970 Stanford Workshop on Grammar and Semantics*, 490–518. Dordrecht: Reidel.

Kaplan, D. 1977. Demonstratives: an essay on the semantics, logic, metaphysics, and epistemology of demonstratives and other indexicals. Manuscript. University of California, Los Angeles.

Kaplan, D. 1978. Dthat. In P. Cole, editor, *Pragmatics*, Syntax and Semantics, no. 9, 221–253. New York: Academic Press.

Kaplan, D. 1979. On the logic of demonstratives. In P. A. French, T. E. Uehling Jr., and H. K. Wettstein, editors, *Contemporary Perspectives in the Philosophy of Language*, 401–412, Minneapolis: University of Minnesota Press.

Kaplan, R., and Bresnan, J. 1982. Lexical-functional grammar: a formal system for grammatical representation. In J. Bresnan, editor, *The Mental Representation of Grammatical Relations*, 173–281. Cambridge: MIT Press.

Karttunen, L. 1976. Discourse referents. In J. McCawley, editor, *Notes from the Linguistic Underground*, Syntax and Semantics, no. 7. New York: Academic Press.

Karttunen, L. 1977. The syntax and semantics of questions. *Linguistics and Philosophy* 1:3–44.

Karttunen, L. 1984. Features and values. In *Proceedings of the Tenth International Conference on Computational Linguistics*, 28–33. Morristown: ACL Publications.

Katz, J. 1966. *The Philosophy of Language*. New York: Harper and Row.

Katz, J. 1972. *Semantic Theory*. New York: Harper and Row.

Katz, J. 1981. *Language and Other Abstract Objects*. New York: Harper and Row.

Katz, J., and J. A. Fodor. 1963. The structure of a semantic theory. *Language* 39:170–210.

Keenan, E. L. 1984. A boolean approach to semantics. In J. A. G. Groenendijk, T. M. Janssen, and M. Stokhof, editors, *Truth, Interpretation, and Information: Selected Papers from the Third Amsterdam Colloquium*. Dordrecht: Foris.

Keenan, E. L. 1987. Unreducible *n*-ary quantifiers in natural language. In P. Gärdenfors, editor, *Generalized Quantifiers and Logical Approaches*, 109–150. Dordrecht: Reidel.

Keenan, E. L., and L. M. Faltz. 1985. *Boolean Semantics for Natural Language*. Synthese Language Library, no. 23. Dordrecht: Reidel.

Keenan, E. L., and L. Moss. 1985. Generalized quantifiers and the expressive power of natural language. In J. van Benthem and A. ter Meulen, editors, *Generalized Quantifiers in Natural Language*, 73–126. Dordrecht: Foris.

Keenan, E. L., and Y. Stavi. 1986. A semantic characterization of natural language determiners. *Linguistics and Philosophy* 9:253–326.

Keller, W. R. 1988. Nested Cooper storage: the proper treatment of quantification in ordinary noun phrases. In U. Reyle and C. Rohrer, editors, *Natural Language Parsing and Linguistic Theories*, 432–447. Dordrecht: Reidel.

King, J. 1988. Are indefinite descriptions ambiguous? *Philosophical Studies* 53: 417–440.

Kleene, S. C. 1936. λ-definability and recursiveness. *Duke Mathematical Journal* 2:340–353.

Kleene, S. C. 1952. *Introduction to Metamathematics*. Amsterdam: North-Holland.

Klein, E. 1980. A semantics for positive and comparative adjectives. *Linguistics and Philosophy* 4:1–45.

Klein, E. 1982. The interpretation of adjectival comparatives. *Journal of Linguistics* 18:113–136.

Klein, E. 1991. Comparatives. In A. von Stechow and D. Wunderlich, editors, *Semantics: An International Handbook of Contemporary Research*, 673–691. Berlin: de Gruyter.

Klein, E., and I. A. Sag. 1985. Type-driven translation. *Linguistics and Philosophy* 8:163–201.

König, E. 1989. Parsing as natural deduction. In *Proceedings of 27th Meeting of the Association for Computational Linguistics*, 272–279. Morristown: ACL Publications.

Kraak, E. 1995. French object clitics: a multimodal analysis. In G. Morrill and D. Oehrle, editors, *Proceedings of the Conference on Formal Grammar*. European

Summer School in Logic, Language, and Information. Amsterdam: FOLLI Publications.

Kripke, S. A. 1959. A completeness theorem in modal logic. *Journal of Symbolic Logic* 24:1–14.

Kripke, S. A. 1963a. Semantical analysis of intuitionistic logic, I. In J. N. Crossley and M. A. E. Dummett, editors, *Formal Systems and Recursive Functions.* Amsterdam: North-Holland.

Kripke, S. A. 1963b. Semantical considerations on modal logic. *Acta Philosophica Fennica* 16:83–94.

Kripke, S. A. 1972. *Naming and Necessity.* Cambridge: Harvard University Press.

Kripke, S. A. 1975. Outline of a theory of truth. *Journal of Philosophical Logic* 72:690–716.

Kuhn, T. 1962. *The Structure of Scientific Revolutions.* Chicago: University of Chicago Press.

Kunen, K. 1980. *Set Theory.* Studies in Logic and the Foundations of Mathematics, no. 102. Amsterdam: North-Holland.

Kurtonina, N. 1994. Frames and labels: a modal analysis of categorial inference. Ph.D. dissertation, University of Utrecht.

Kurtonina, N., and M. Moortgat. In press. Structural control. In P. Blackburn and M. de Rijke, editors, *Logic, Structure, and Syntax.* Dordrecht: Kluwer.

Ladusaw, W. A. 1979. Polarity sensitivity as inherent scope relations. Ph.D. dissertation, University of Texas at Austin. Distributed by Indiana University Linguistics Club.

Ladusaw, W. A. 1982. Semantic constraints on the English partitive construction. In D. P. Flickinger, M. Macken, and N. Wiegand, editors, *Proceedings of the First West Coast Conference on Formal Linguistics.* Palo Alto: CSLI Publications.

Ladusaw, W. A., and D. R. Dowty. 1988. Toward a non-grammatical account of thematic roles. In W. Wilkins, editor, *Thematic Roles,* Syntax and Semantics, no. 21. New York: Academic Press.

Lakoff, G. 1970a. Linguistics and natural logic. *Synthese* 22:151–271.

Lakoff, G. 1970b. *Irregularity in Syntax.* New York: Holt, Rinehart and Winston.

Lakoff, G. 1987. *Women, Fire, and Dangerous Things: What Categories Reveal about the Mind.* Chicago: University of Chicago Press.

Lakoff, G. 1989. Cognitive semantics. In U. Eco, M. Santambrogio, and D. Violi, editors, *Meaning and Mental Representation.* Bloomington: Indiana University Press.

Lakoff, G., and M. Johnson. 1980. *Metaphors We Live By.* Chicago: University of Chicago Press.

Lambek, J. 1958. The mathematics of sentence structure. *American Mathematical Monthly* 65:154–169.

Lambek, J. 1961. On the calculus of syntactic types. In R. Jakobson, editor, *Structure of Language and Its Mathematical Aspects: Proceedings of Symposia in Applied Mathematics*, 166–178. Providence, Rhode Island: American Mathematical Society.

Landman, F. 1986. *Towards a Theory of Information: The Status of Partial Objects in Semantics*. Dordrecht: Foris.

Landman, F. 1988. Groups, plural individuals, and intensionality. In J. A. G. Groenendijk, M. Stokhof, and F. Veltman, editors, *Proceedings of the Sixth Amsterdam Colloquium*, 197–217. Amsterdam: Institute for Logic, Language, and Information.

Landman, F. 1989a. Groups, I. *Linguistics and Philosophy* 12:559–605.

Landman, F. 1989b. Groups, II. *Linguistics and Philosophy* 12:723–744.

Landman, F. 1991. *Structures for Semantics*. Studies in Linguistics and Philosophy, no. 45. Dordrecth: Kluwer.

Langacker, R. W. 1987. *Foundations of Cognitive Grammar*. Volume 1. Palo Alto: Stanford University Press.

Langendoen, T. 1978. The logic of reciprocity. *Linguistic Inquiry* 9:177–197.

Larson, R. K. 1988. Scope and comparatives. *Linguistics and Philosophy* 11:1–26.

Lasersohn, P. 1987. Collective nouns and distributive determiners. In B. Need et al., editors, *Proceedings of the 23rd Annual Meeting of the Chicago Linguistics Society*. Chicago: Chicago Linguistics Society.

Lasersohn, P. 1989. On the readings of plural noun phrases. *Linguistic Inquiry* 20:130–134.

Lasersohn, P. 1990. Group action and spatio-temporal proximity. *Linguistics and Philosophy* 13:179–206.

Leech, G. N. 1971. *Meaning and the English Verb*. London: Longman.

Leonard, H. S., and N. Goodman. 1940. The calculus of individuals and its uses. *Journal of Symbolic Logic* 5:45–55.

Lesniewski, S. 1929. Grundzüge eines neues Systems der Grundlagen der Mathematik. *Fundamenta Mathematicae* 14.

Levin, B. 1993. *English Verb Classes and Alternations: A Preliminary Investigation*. Chicago: University of Chicago Press.

Levin, L. 1987. *Toward a Linking Theory of Relation Changing Rules in LFG*. Report CSLI-87-115, Center for the Study of Language and Information, Stanford University, Palo Alto.

Levinson, S. 1983. *Pragmatics*. Cambridge: Cambridge University Press.

Lewis, C. I. 1914. A new algebra of strict implication. *Mind* 23:240–247.

Lewis, D. 1968. Counterpart theory and quantified modal logic. *Journal of Philosophy* 65:113–126.

Lewis, D. 1970. General semantics. *Synthese* 22:18–67.

Lewis, D. 1973. *Counterfactuals.* Cambridge: Harvard University Press.

Lewis, D. 1975. Adverbs of quantification. In E. L. Keenan, editor, *Formal Semantics of Natural Language.* Cambridge: Cambridge University Press.

Lewis, D. 1979. Scorekeeping in a language game. In R. Bauerle, U. Egli, and A. von Stechow, editors, *Meaning, Use, and Interpretation of Language.* Berlin: de Gruyter.

Lewis, D. 1986. *On the Plurality of Worlds.* Oxford: Basil Blackwell.

Link, G. 1983. The logical analysis of plurals and mass terms: a lattice-theoretical approach. In R. Bäuerle, C. Schwarze, and A. von Stechow, editors, *Meaning, Use, and Interpretation of Language*, 302–323. Berlin: de Gruyter.

Link, G. 1984. Hydras: on the logic of relative constructions with multiple heads. In F. Landman and F. Veltman, editors, *Varieties of Formal Semantics: Proceedings of the Fourth Amsterdam Colloquium.* Dordrecht: Foris.

Link, G. 1987a. Generalized quantifiers and plurals. In P. Gärdenfors, editor, *Generalized Quantifiers and Logical Approaches*, 151–180. Dordrecht: Reidel.

Link, G. 1987b. Algebraic semantics for event structures. Technical report, Seminar für Philosophie, Logik and Wissenschaftstheorie, Universität München.

Link, G. 1991. Plural. In H. Wunderlich and A. von Stechow, editors, *Handbook of Semantics.* Berlin: de Gruyter.

Lønning, J. T. 1987. Collective readings of definite and indefinite noun phrases. In P. Gärdenfors, editor, *Generalized Quantifiers and Logical Approaches*, 203–235. Dordrecht: Reidel.

Lønning, J. T. 1989. Some aspects of the logic of plural noun phrases. Cosmos Report, no. 11, Department of Mathematics, University of Oslo.

Lønning, J. T. 1991. Among readings: some comments on 'Among Collections'. In J. M. van der Does, editor, *Quantification and Anaphora, II*, DYANA Deliverable 2.2b. Edinburgh: Centre for Cognitive Science.

Łukasiewicz, J. 1920. Many-valued systems of propositional logic. Translated in S. McCall, editor, *Polish Logic.* Oxford: Oxford University Press, 1967.

Mann, W. C., and S. A. Thompson. 1988. Rhetorical structure theory: towards a functional theory of text organization. *Text* 8:243–281.

Martinich, A. P. 1996. *The Philosophy of Language.* Third edition. Oxford: Oxford University Press.

Massey, G. 1976. Tom, Dick, and Harry, and all the king's men. *American Philosophical Quarterly* 13:89–107.

May, R. 1985. *Logical Form.* Linguistic Inquiry Monographs, no. 12. Cambridge: MIT Press.

McCawley, J. D. 1970. Where do noun phrases come from? In R. Jacobs and P. Rosenbaum, editors, *Readings in English Transformational Grammar*, 166–183, Waltham, Massachusetts: Ginn and Company.

McCawley, J. D. 1981. *Everything That Linguists Have Always Wanted to Know about Logic But Were Ashamed to Ask*. Second edition, 1993. Chicago: University of Chicago Press.

McCawley, J. D. 1988. *The Syntactic Phenomena of English*, Volumes 1 and 2. Chicago: University of Chicago Press.

McKinsey, J. C. C., and A. Tarski. 1948. Some theorems about the sentential calculi of Lewis and Heyting. *Journal of Symbolic Logic* 13:1–15.

McNally, L. 1993. Comitative coordination: a case study in group formation. *Natural Language and Linguistic Theory* 11:347–379.

McNally, L. 1995. Bare plurals in Spanish are properties. In G. Morrill and D. Oehrle, editors, *Proceedings of the Conference on Formal Grammar.* European Summer School in Logic, Language, and Information. Amsterdam: FOLLI Publications.

Milner, R. 1978. A theory of type polymorphism in programming. *Journal of Computer and System Sciences* 17:348–375.

Milner, R., M. Tofte, and R. Harper. 1991. *The Definition of Standard ML*. Cambridge: MIT Press.

Milward, D. 1994. Non-constituent coordination: theory and practice. In *Proceedings of the Fifteenth International Conference on Computational Linguistics*, 935–941. Morristown: ACL Publications.

Moens, M. 1987. Tense, aspect and temporal reference. Ph.D. dissertation, University of Edinburgh.

Moens, M., and M. Steedman. 1988. Temporal ontology and temporal reference. *Computational Linguistics* 14:15–28.

Moltmann, F. 1992. On the interpretation of three-dimensional syntactic trees. In C. Barker and D. Dowty, editors, *Proceedings of the Second Conference on Semantics and Linguistic Theory*. Working Papers in Linguistics, no. 40. Ithaca: CLC Publications.

Montague, R. 1970a. English as a formal language. In B. Visentini et al., editors, *Linguaggi nella Spocietà e nella Tecnica*. Milan: Edizioni di Communità. Reprinted in R. Thomason, editor, *Formal Philosophy*, 188–221. New Haven: Yale University Press.

Montague, R. 1970b. Universal grammar. *Theoria* 36:373–398. Reprinted in R. Thomason, editor, *Formal Philosophy*, 222–246. New Haven: Yale University Press.

Montague, R. 1973. The proper treatment of quantification in ordinary English. In J. Hintikka, J. Moravcsik, and P. Suppes, editors, *Approaches to Natural Language: Proceedings of the 1970 Stanford Workshop on Grammar and Semantics*. Dordrecht: Reidel. Reprinted in R. Thomason, editor, *Formal Philosophy*, 247–270. New Haven: Yale University Press.

Moortgat, M. 1987. Compositionality and the syntax of words. In J. A. G. Groenendijk, D. de Jongh, and M. Stokhof, editors, *Foundations of Pragmatics and Lexical Semantics*. Dordrecht: Foris.

Moortgat, M. 1988a. Mixed composition and discontinuous dependencies. In R. T. Oehrle, E. Bach, and D. Wheeler, editors, *Categorial Grammars and Natural Language Structures.* Dordrecht: Reidel.

Moortgat, M. 1988b. *Categorial Investigations.* Dordrecht: Foris.

Moortgat, M. 1990a. The quantification calculus: questions of axiomatization. In Deliverable R1.2.A of DYANA: Dynamic Interpretation of Natural Language. ESPRIT Basic Research Action BR3175. Centre for Cognitive Science, Edinburgh.

Moortgat, M. 1990b. Cut elimination and the elimination of spurious ambiguity. In M. Stokhof and L. Torenvliet, editors, *Proceedings of the Seventh Amsterdam Colloquium.* Amsterdam: Institute for Logic, Language, and Information.

Moortgat, M. 1991. Generalized quantification and discontinuous type constructors. Technical report, Institute for Language and Speech, University of Utrecht. To appear in W. Sijtsma and A. van Horck, editors, *Discontinuous Constituency.* Berlin: de Gruyter.

Moortgat, M. 1994. Residuation in mixed Lambek systems. Paper presented to the Deduction and Language Workshop, London. To appear in *Bulletin of the Interest Group in Propositional Logic.*

Moortgat, M. 1996. Categorial type logics. In J. van Benthem and A. ter Meulen, editors, *Handbook of Logic and Language.* New York: Elsevier.

Moortgat, M., and G. Morrill. 1991. Heads and phrases: type calculus for dependency and constituent structure. To appear in *Journal of Logic, Language, and Information.*

Moortgat, M., and R. Oehrle. 1993. Categorial grammar: logical parameters and linguistic variation. Course notes for the Fifth European Summer School in Logic, Language, and Information, Lisbon.

Moortgat, M., and R. Oehrle. 1994. Adjacency, dependency, and order. In P. Dekker and M. Stokhof, editors, *Proceedings of the Ninth Amsterdam Colloquium.* Amsterdam: Institute for Logic, Language, and Information.

Morrill, G. 1988. Extraction and coordination in phrase structure grammar and categorial grammar. Ph.D. dissertation, University of Edinburgh.

Morrill, G. 1989a. Intensionality, boundedness, and modal logic. Research paper EUCCS/RP-32, Centre for Cognitive Science, Edinburgh.

Morrill, G. 1989b. Grammar as logic. Research paper EUCCS/RP-34, Centre for Cognitive Science, Edinburgh.

Morrill, G. 1990a. Intensionality and boundedness. *Linguistics and Philosophy* 13:699–726.

Morrill, G. 1990b. Rules and derivations: binding phenomena and coordination in categorial logic. In Deliverable R1.2.D of DYANA: Dynamic Interpretation of Natural Language. ESPRIT Basic Research Action BR3175. Centre for Cognitive Science, Edinburgh.

Morrill, G. 1990c. Grammar and logical types. In M. Stokhof and L. Torenvliet, editors, *Proceedings of the Seventh Amsterdam Colloquium*, 429–450. Amsterdam: Institute for Logic, Language, and Information.

Morrill, G. 1992a. Type-logical grammar. Report de Recerca LSI-92-5, Departament de Llenguatages i Sistemes Informàtics, Universitat Politècnica de Catalunya, Barcelona.

Morrill, G. 1992b. Categorial formalisation of relativisation: pied piping, islands, and extraction sites. Report de Recerca LSI-92-23, Departament de Llenguatages i Sistemes Informàtics, Universitat Politècnica de Catalunya, Barcelona.

Morrill, G. 1994a. *Type Logical Grammar*. Dordrecht: Kluwer.

Morrill, G. 1994b. Clausal proof nets and discontinuity. Report de Recerca LSI-94-21, Departament de Llenguatages i Sistemes Informàtics, Universitat Politècnica de Catalunya, Barcelona.

Morrill, G. 1995. Discontinuity in categorial grammar. *Linguistics and Philosophy* 18:175–219.

Morrill, G., and B. Carpenter. 1990. Compositionality, implicational logics, and theories of grammar. *Linguistics and Philosophy* 13:383–392.

Morrill, G., N. Leslie, M. Hepple, and G. Barry. 1990. Categorial grammar and structural operations. In G. Barry and G. Morrill, editors, *Studies in Categorial Grammar*, Edinburgh Working Papers in Cognitive Science, no. 5, 65–111. Edinburgh: Centre for Cognitive Science.

Morrill, G., and T. Solias. 1993. Tuples, discontinuity, and gapping in categorial grammar. In *Proceedings of the Sixth Meeting of the European Association for Computational Linguistics*, 287–297. Morristown: ACL Publications.

Mostowski, A. 1957. On a generalization of quantifiers. *Fundamenta Mathematicae* 44:12–36.

Muskens, R. 1989a. A relational formulation of the theory of types. *Linguistics and Philosophy* 12:325–346.

Muskens, R. 1989b. Meaning and partiality. Ph.D. dissertation, University of Amsterdam. Revised version appeared under same title in the series Studies in Logic, Language, and Information. Palo Alto: CSLI Publications, 1995.

Muskens, R. 1993. A compositional discourse representation theory. In P. Dekker and M. Stokhof, editors, *Proceedings of the Ninth Amsterdam Colloquium*, 467–486. Amsterdam: Institute for Logic, Language, and Computation.

Nagel, E. 1944. Logic without ontology. In Y. H. Krikorian, editor, *Naturalism and the Human Spirit*. New York: Columbia University Press.

Nerbonne, J. 1986. Reference time and time in narration. *Linguistics and Philosophy* 9:83–96.

Nerbonne, J. 1994. A semantics for nominal comparatives. In P. Dekker and M. Stokhof, editors, *Proceedings of the Ninth Amsterdam Colloquium*, 487–506. Amsterdam: Institute for Logic, Language, and Information.

Nishigauchi, T. 1984. Control and the thematic domain. *Language* 60:215–250.

Nunberg, G. 1977. The pragmatics of reference. Ph.D. dissertation, City University of New York, Graduate Center. Distributed by Indiana University Linguistics Club.

Nunberg, G., I. Sag, and T. Wasow. 1994. Idioms. *Language* 70:491–538.

Oehrle, R. T. 1988. Multi-dimensional compositional functions as a basis for grammatical analysis. In R. Oehrle, E. Bach, and D. Wheeler, editors, *Categorial Grammars and Natural Language Structures*, 349–389. Dordrecht: Reidel.

Oehrle, R. T., and Shi Zhang. 1989. Lambek calculus and preposing of embedded subjects. In C. Wiltshire et al., editors, *Papers from the 25th Annual Meeting of the Chicago Linguistic Society*, CLS no. 25, 328–341. Chicago: Chicago Linguistic Society.

Orey, S. 1959. Model theory for the higher order predicate calculus. *Transactions of the American Mathematical Society* 92:72–84.

Palmer, F. 1974. *The English Verb*. London: Longman.

Parikh, R. 1984. Logics of knowledge, games, and dynamic logic. In M. Joseph and R. Shyamasundar, editors, *Foundations of Software Technology and Theoretical Computer Science*, Lecture Notes in Computer Science, no. 181. Berlin: Springer Verlag.

Parsons, T. 1977. Type theory and ordinary language. In S. Davis and M. Mithun, editors, *Linguistics, Philosophy, and Montague Grammar*, 127–151. Austin: University of Texas Press.

Parsons, T. 1985. Underlying events in the logical analysis of English. In E. LePore and B. P. McLaughlin, editors, *Actions and Events: Philosphical Perspectives on the Philosophy of Donald Davidson*. Oxford: Basil Blackwell.

Parsons, T. 1989. The progressive in English: events, states, and processes. *Linguistics and Philosophy* 12:213–241.

Parsons, T. 1990. *Events in the Semantics of English: A Study in Subatomic Semantics*. Current Studies in Linguistics, no. 19. Cambridge: MIT Press.

Partee, B. 1973a. Some structural analogies between tenses and pronouns. *Journal of Philosophy* 70:601–609.

Partee, B. 1973b. The syntax and semantics of quotation. In S. R. Anderson and P. Kiparsky, editors, *A Festschrift for Morris Halle*. New York: Holt, Rineheart and Winston.

Partee, B. 1975. Comments on Fillmore's and Chomsky's papers. In R. Austerlitz, editor, *The Scope of American Linguistics*. Lisse: Peter de Ridder.

Partee, B. 1984a. Nominal and temporal anaphora. *Linguistics and Philosophy* 7:243–286.

Partee, B. 1984b. Compositionality. In F. Landman and F. Veltman, editors, *Varieties of Formal Semantics: Proceedings of the Fourth Amsterdam Colloquium*. Dordrecht: Foris.

Partee, B. 1985. Some thoughts about quantifier scope ambiguities. Unpublished manuscript. University of Massachusetts at Amherst.

Partee, B., and E. Bach. 1981. Quantification, pronouns, and VP-anaphora. In J. A. G. Groenendijk, T. Janssen, and M. Stokhof, editors, *Formal Methods in the Study of Language*. Amsterdam: Mathematical Centre. Reprinted in J. A. G. Groenendijk, T. Janssen, and M. Stokhof, editors, *Truth, Interpretation, and Information*. Dordrecht: Foris, 1984.

Partee, B., and M. Rooth. 1983. Generalized conjunction and type ambiguity. In R. Bäuerle, C. Schwarze, and A. von Stechow, editors, *Meaning, Use, and Interpretation of Language*. Berlin: de Gruyter.

Partee, B., and M. Rooth. 1987. Noun phrase interpretation and type shifting principles. In J. A. G. Groenendijk, D. de Jongh, and M. Stokhof, editors, *Studies in Discourse Representation Theory and the Theory of Generalized Quantifiers*, Groningen-Amsterdam Studies in Semantics, no. 8. Dordrecht:Foris.

Passonneau, R. 1988. A computational model of the semantics of tense and aspect. *Computational Linguistics* 14:44–60.

Pelletier, F. J., editor. 1979. *Mass Terms: Some Philosophical Problems*. Dordrecht: Kluwer.

Pentus, M. 1993. Lambek grammars are context free. *Proceedings of the Eighth Annual IEEE Symposium on Logic in Computer Science*, 429–433. Los Alamitos, Calif.: IEEE Computer Society Press.

Pentus, M. 1994. The conjoinability relation in Lambek calculus and linear logic. *Journal of Logic, Language, and Information* 3:121–140.

Pereira, F. C. N. 1990. Categorial semantics and scoping. *Computatonal Linguistics* 16:1–10.

Perlmutter, D. M. 1971. *Deep and Surface Structure Constraints in Syntax*. New York: Holt, Rinehart and Winston.

Perlmutter, D. M., and P. Postal. 1983. The relational succession law. In D. M. Perlmutter, editor, *Studies in Relational Grammar*, vol. 1, 30–80. Chicago: University of Chicago Press.

Perry, J. 1986. From worlds to situations. *Journal of Philosophical Logic* 15:83–107.

Pollard, C. J. 1988. Phrase-structure grammars and categorial grammars: an excursion on the syntax-semantics frontier. In R. T. Oehrle, E. Bach, and D. Wheeler, editors, *Categorial Grammars and Natural Language Structures*. Dordrecht: Reidel.

Pollard, C. J., and I. A. Sag. 1987. *Information-Based Syntax and Semantics*, volume 1, *Fundamentals*. CSLI Lecture Notes, no. 13. Palo Alto: CSLI Publications.

Pollard, C. J., and I. A. Sag. 1992. Anaphors in English and the scope of binding theory. *Linguistic Inquiry* 23:261–303.

Pollard, C. J., and I. A. Sag. 1994. *Head-Driven Phrase Structure Grammar*. Chicago: University of Chicago Press.

Postal, P. 1971. *Crossover Phenomena*. New York: Holt, Rinehart and Winston.

Postal, P. 1974. On certain ambiguities. *Linguistic Inquiry* 5:367–424.

Prawitz, D. 1965. *Natural Deduction: A Proof-Theoretical Study*. Uppsala, Sweden: Almqvist and Wiksell.

Prior, A. N. 1967a. *Past, Present, and Future*. Oxford: University of Oxford Press.

Prior, A. N. 1967b. The correspondence theory of truth. In P. Edwards, editor, *The Encyclopedia of Philosophy*, volume 2, 223–232. New York: MacMillan Publishing Co. and Free Press.

Pritchett, B. 1992. *Grammatical Competence and Parsing Performance*. Chicago: University of Chicago Press.

Pullum, G. 1989. Formal linguistics meets the Boojum. *Natural Language and Linguistic Theory* 7:137–143.

Pustejovsky, J. 1991. The generative lexicon. *Computational Linguistics* 17:409–441.

Putnam, H. 1970. On properties. In H. Putnam, *Mathematics, Matter, and Method*, vol. 1 of *Philosophical Papers*. Cambridge: Cambridge University Press.

Putnam, H. 1973. Meaning and reference. *Journal of Philosophy* 70:699–711.

Putnam, H. 1975. The meaning of 'meaning'. In K. Gunderson, editor, *Language, Mind, and Knowledge*, 131–193. Minneapolis: University of Minnesota Press.

Putnam, H. 1988. *Representation and Reality*. Cambridge: MIT Press.

Quine, W. V. O. 1953a. Reference and modality. In W. V. O. Quine, *From a Logical Point of View*, 139–159. Second edition, 1961. Cambridge: Harvard University Press.

Quine, W. V. O. 1953b. Two dogmas of empiricism. In W. V. O. Quine, *From a Logical Point of View*. Second edition, 1961. Cambridge: Harvard University Press.

Quine, W. V. O. 1959. *Methods of Logic*. Revised edition. New York: Holt, Rinehart and Winston.

Quine, W. V. O. 1960. *Word and Object*. Cambridge: MIT Press.

Quine, W. V. O. 1980. *Set Theory and Its Logic*. Revised edition. Cambridge: Harvard University Press.

Reape, M. 1989. A logical treatment of semi-free word order and bounded discontinuous constituency. In *Proceedings of the Fourth Conference of the European Chapter of the Association for Computational Linguistics*, 103–115. Morristown: ACL Publications.

Reichenbach, H. 1947. *Elements of Symbolic Logic*. New York: Macmillan.

Reinhart, T. 1983. *Anaphora and Semantic Interpretation*. London: Croon-Helm.

Rescher, N., and A. Urquhart. 1971. *Temporal Logic.* New York: Springer Verlag.

Restall, G. 1994. A useful substructural logic. *Bulletin of the Interest Group in Propositional Logic* 2:137–148.

Revesz, G. 1988. *Lambda-Calculus, Combinators and Functional Programming.* Cambridge Tracts in Theoretical Computer Science, no. 4. Cambridge: Cambridge University Press.

Reynolds, J. C. 1970. Transformational systems and the algebraic structure of atomic formulas. In D. Michie, editor, *Machine Intelligence*, 135–151. Edinburgh: Edinburgh University Press.

Richards, B. 1976. Adverbs: from a logical point of view. *Synthese* 32:329–372.

Richards, B. 1982. Tense, aspect, and time adverbials, part I. *Linguistics and Philosophy* 5:59–107.

Roberts, C. 1987a. Modal subordination, anaphora, and distributivity. Ph.D. dissertation, University of Massachusetts at Amherst.

Roberts, C. 1987b. Plural anaphors in distributive contexts. In *Proceedings of the Sixth West Coast Conference on Formal Lingusitics.* Palo Alto: CSLI Publications.

Roberts, C. 1987c. Distributivity. In J. A. G. Groenendijk, M. Stokhof, and F. Veltman, editors, *Proceedings of the Sixth Amsterdam Colloquium*, 291–309. Amsterdam: Institute for Logic, Language, and Information.

Roberts, C. 1991. Distributivity and reciprocal distributivity. *Proceedings of the First Semantics and Linguistic Theory Conference.* Ithaca: CLC Publications.

Rodman, R. 1976. Scope Phenomena, "Movement Transformations," and Relative Clauses. In B. Partee, editor, *Montague Grammmar*, 165–176. New York: Academic Press.

Roorda, D. 1991. Resource logics: proof theoretical investigations. Ph.D. dissertation, University of Amsterdam.

Roorda, D. 1992. Lambek calculus and boolean connectives: on the road. Working Paper OTS-WP-CL-92-004, Institute for Speech and Language, University of Utrecht.

Rooth, M. 1985. Association with focus. Ph.D. dissertation, University of Massachusetts at Amherst.

Rooth, M. 1992. A theory of focus interpretation. *Natural Language Semantics* 1:75–116.

Rooth, M., and B. H. Partee. 1982. Conjunction, type ambiguity, and wide scope 'or'. In D. P. Flickinger, M. Macken, and N. Wiegand, editors, *Proceedings of the First West Coast Conference on Formal Linguistics.* Palo Alto: CSLI Publications.

Rorty, R. 1979. *Philosophy and the Mirror of Nature.* Princeton: Princeton University Press.

Rorty, R. 1989. The contingency of language. In R. Rorty, *Contingency, Irony, and Solidarity.* Cambridge: Cambridge University Press.

Rosch, E., W. Gray, D. Johnson, and P. Boys-Braem. 1976. Basic objects in natural categories. *Cognitive Psychology* 8:382–439.

Ross, J. R. 1967. Constraints on variables in syntax. Ph.D. dissertation, Massachusetts Institute of Technology.

Russell, B. 1903. *Principles of Mathematics.* Second edition, 1938. New York: Norton.

Russell, B. 1905. On denoting. *Mind* 14:479–493.

Russell, B. 1919. Descriptions. In B. Russell, *Introduction to Mathematical Philosophy,* 167–180, London: Allen and Unwin.

Russell, B. 1940. *Inquiry into Meaning and Truth.* London: Allen and Unwin.

Russell, B. 1956. On order in time. In B. Russell, *Logic and Knowledge.* London: Allen and Unwin.

Russell, B. 1959. Mr. Strawson on referring. *Mind* 66:385–389.

Sag, I. A. 1976. Deletion and logical form. Ph.D. dissertation, Massachusetts Institute of Technology.

Sag, I. A., and C. J. Pollard. 1991. An integrated theory of complement control. *Language* 67:63–113.

Sánchez Valencia, V. 1991. Studies on natural logic and categorical grammar. Ph.D. dissertation, Department of Philosophy, University of Amsterdam.

Scha, R. J. H. 1981. Distributive, collective, and cumulative quantification. In J. A. G. Groenendijk, T. M. Janssen, and M. Stokhof, editors, *Formal Methods in the Study of Language,* volume 1. Amsterdam: Mathematical Centrum. Reprinted in J. A. G. Groenendijk, T. M. Janssen, and M. Stokhof, editors, *Truth, Interpretation, and Information: Selected Papers from the Third Amsterdam Colloquium,* Dordrecht: Foris, 1984.

Schank, R. C., and R. P. Abelson. 1977. *Scripts, Plans, Goals, and Understanding.* Hillsdale, New Jersey: Lawrence Erlbaum.

Schönfinkel, M. 1924. Über die Bausteine der mathematischen Logik. *Mathematische Annalen* 92:305–316.

Schubert, L. K., and F. J. Pelletier. 1987. Problems in the representation of the logical form of generics, plurals, and mass nouns. In E. LePore, editor, *New Directions in Semantics,* 385–451. New York: Academic Press.

Schwarzschild, R. 1990. Against groups. In M. Stokhof and L. Torenvliet, editors, *Proceedings of the Seventh Amsterdam Colloquium,* 475–493. Amsterdam: Institute for Logic, Language, and Information.

Schwarzschild, R. 1992. Types of plural individuals. *Linguistics and Philosophy* 15:641–675.

Scott, D. 1970. Advice on modal logic. In K. Lambert, editor, *Philosophical Problems in Logic,* 143–174. Dordrecht: Reidel.

Searle, J. R. 1958. Proper names. *Mind* 67:166–173.

Searle, J. R. 1965. What is a speech act? In M. Black, editor, *Philosophy in America*, 221–239. Ithaca, New York: Cornell University Press.

Searle, J. R. 1969. *Speech Acts*. Cambridge: Cambridge University Press.

Searle, J. R. 1975. Indirect speech acts. In P. Cole and J. L. Morgan, editors, *Speech Acts*, Syntax and Semantics, no. 3, 59–82. New York: Academic Press.

Searle, J. R. 1979. Metaphor. In A. Ortony, editor, *Metaphor and Thought*, 92–123. Cambridge: Cambridge University Press.

Selkirk, E. O. 1977. Some remarks on noun phrase structure. In P. W. Culicover, T. Wasow, and A. Akmajian, editors, *Formal Syntax*. New York: Academic Press.

Seuren, P. 1984. The comparative revisited. *Journal of Semantics* 3:109–141.

Sharvy, R. 1980. A more general theory of definite descriptions. *Philosophical Review* 89:607–624.

Shaumyan, S. K. 1977. *Applicational Grammar as a Semantic Theory of Natural Language*. Edinburgh: Edinburgh University Press.

Sobel, J. H. 1970. Utilitarianisms: simple and general. *Inquiry* 13:394–449.

Simons, P. M. 1987. *Parts: A Study in Ontology*. Oxford: Oxford University Press.

Smith, E. E., and D. L. Medin. 1981. *Categories and Concepts*. Cambridge: Harvarad University Press.

Sobel, J. H. 1970. Utilitarianism: simple and general. *Inquiry* 13:394–449.

Solias, T. 1992. Gramáticas categoriales, coordinación generalizada y elisión. Ph.D. thesis, Departamento de Lingüística, Lógica, Lenguas Modernas y Filosofía de la Ciencia, Universidad Autónoma de Madrid.

Sperber, D., and D. Wilson. 1986. *Relevance: Communication and Cognition*. Cambridge: Harvard University Press.

Stalnaker, R. 1984. *Inquiry*. Cambridge: MIT Press.

Stalnaker, R. 1986. Possible worlds and situations. *Journal of Philosophical Logic* 15:109–123.

Stassen, L. 1985. *Comparison and Universal Grammar*. Oxford: Basil Blackwell.

Steedman, M. 1977. Verbs, time, and modality. *Cognitive Science* 1:216–234.

Steedman, M. 1985. Dependency and coordination in the grammar of Dutch and English. *Language* 61:523–568.

Steedman, M. 1987. Combinatory grammars and parasitic gaps. *Natural Language and Linguistic Theory* 5:403–439.

Steedman, M. 1988. Combinators and grammars. In R. Oehrle, E. Bach, and D. Wheeler, editors, *Categorial Grammars and Natural Language Structures*. Dordrecht: Reidel.

Steedman, M. 1990. Gapping as constituent coordination. *Linguistics and Philosophy* 13:207–236.

Steedman, M. 1991. Structure and intonation. *Language* 67:262–296.

Steedman, M. 1992. Surface structure. Technical report MS-CIS-92-51/LINC LAB 229. Computer Science Department, University of Pennsylvania.

Stoll, R. R. 1963. *Set Theory and Logic*. San Francisco: W. H. Freeman and Co.

Stone, M. H. 1936. The theory of representations for boolean algebras. *Transactions of the American Mathematical Society* 40:37–111.

Stoy, J. E. 1977. *Denotational Semantics: The Scott-Strachey Approach to Programming Language Theory*. Cambridge: MIT Press.

Strawson, P. F. 1950. On referring. *Mind* 59:320–344.

Tait, W. W. 1967. Intensional interpretations of functionals of finite type. *Journal of Symbolic Logic* 32:198–212.

Tannenhaus, M. K., G. Carlson, and J. T. Trueswell. 1989. The role of thematic structures in interpretation and parsing. *Language and Cognitive Processes* 4:211–234.

Tarski, A. 1935. Der Wahrheitsbegriff in den formalisierten Sprachen. *Studia Philosophica* 1:261–405. English translation, The concept of truth in formalized languages, in A. Tarski, *Logic, Semantics, Metamathematics*. Oxford: Clarendon Press, 1956.

Tarski, A. 1944. The semantic conception of truth. *Philosophy and Phenomenological Research* 4:341–375.

Taylor, I., and M. M. Taylor. 1990. *Psycholinguistics: Learning and Using Language*. Englewood Cliffs, New Jersey: Prentice Hall.

Thomason, R. H. 1977. Indirect discourse is not quotational. *Monist* 60:340–354.

Thomason, R. H. 1980. A model theory for propositional attitudes. *Linguistics and Philosophy* 4:47–70.

Thomason, R. H., and R. C. Stalnaker. 1973. A semantic theory of adverbs. *Linguistic Inquiry* 4:195–220.

Thompson, E. 1994. The structure of tense and the syntax of temporal adverbs. In R. Aranovich, W. Byrne, S. Preuss, and M. Senturia, editors, *The Proceedings of the Thirteenth West Coast Conference on Formal Linguistics*, 499–514. Palo Alto: CSLI Publications.

Thompson, S. 1991. *Type Theory and Functional Programming*. Reading, Massachusetts: Addison Wesley.

Troelstra, A. 1992. *Lectures on Linear Logic*. CSLI Lecture Notes, no. 29. Palo Alto: CSLI Publications.

Turner, D. 1986. An overview of Miranda. *ACM SIGPLAN Notices* 21:156–166.

Ultan, R. 1972. Some features of basic comparative constructions. Stanford Working Papers on Language Universals, no. 9, 117–162. Palo Alto: Stanford University, Department of Linguistics.

Van Benthem, J. 1979. Points and periods. In C. Rohrer, editor, *Time, Tense, and Quantifiers*, 39–57. Tübingen: Niemeyer.

Van Benthem, J. 1983a. Determiners and logic. *Linguistics and Philosophy* 6:447–478.

Van Benthem, J. 1983b. The semantics of variety in categorial grammar. Report 83–29, Department of Mathematics, Simon Fraser University, Vancouver. Reprinted in W. Buszkowski, J. van Benthem, and W. Marciszewski, editors, *Categorial Grammar*, Linguistic and Literary Studies in Eastern Europe, no. 25, 37–55. Amsterdam: John Benjamins, 1986.

Van Benthem, J. 1983c. *The Logic of Time*. Synthese Library, no. 156. Second edition, 1991. Dordrecht: Kluwer.

Van Benthem, J. 1984a. Questions about quantifiers. *Journal of Symbolic Logic* 49:443–466.

Van Benthem, J. 1984b. Correspondence theory: the connection between intensional and classical logic. In D. Gabbay and F. Guenther, editors, *Handbook of Philosophical Logic*, volume 2, 167–247. Dordrecht: Reidel.

Van Benthem, J. 1986a. *Essays on Logical Semantics*. Dordrecht: Reidel.

Van Benthem, J. 1986b. Categorial grammar and lambda calculus. In V. Skordev, editor, *Druzhba Summer School in Applied Logic*. New York: Plenum Press.

Van Benthem, J. 1987. Semantic type change and syntactic recognition. In G. Chierchia, B. Partee, and R. Turner, editors, *Categories, Types, and Semantics*. Dordrecht: Reidel.

Van Benthem, J. 1988. *A Manual of Intensional Logic*. Second edition. CSLI Lecture Notes, no. 1. Palo Alto: CSLI Publications.

Van Benthem, J. 1989. Polyadic quantifiers. *Linguistics and Philosophy* 12:437–464.

Van Benthem, J. 1991. *Language in Action: Categories, Lambdas, and Dynamic Logic*. Amsterdam: North-Holland.

Van den Berg, M. H. 1990. A dynamic predicate logic for plurals. In M. J. B. Stokhof and L. Torenvliet, editors, *Proceedings of the Seventh Amsterdam Colloquium*. Amsterdam: Institute for Logic, Language, and Information.

Van der Does, J. 1991. Among collections. In J. van der Does, editor, *Quantification and Anaphora, II*, DYANA Deliverable 2.2b, 1–35. Edinburgh: Centre for Cognitive Science.

Van der Does, J. 1992. Applied quantifier logics. Ph.D. dissertation, University of Amsterdam.

Van der Does, J. 1993. Sums and quantifiers. *Linguistics and Philosophy* 16:509–550.

Van Eijck, J. 1983. Discourse representation theory and plurality. In A. ter Meulen, editor, *Studies in Modeltheoretic Semantics*. Dordrecht: Foris.

Van Fraassen, B. 1969. Presuppositions, supervaluations, and free logic. In K. Lambert, editor, *The Logical Way of Doing Things*. New Haven: Yale University Press.

Van der Linden, E. 1993. A categorial, computational theory of idioms. Ph.D. dissertation, Katholieke Universiteit Brabant.

Veltman, F. 1984. Data semantics. In J. A. G. Groenendijk, T. M. Janssen, and M. Stokhof, editors, *Truth, Interpretation, and Information: Selected Papers from the Third Amsterdam Colloquium*. Dordrecht: Foris.

Vendler, Z. 1967. *Linguistics in Philosophy*. Ithaca, New York: Cornell University Press.

Verkuyl, H. 1981. Numerals and quantifiers in X′-syntax and their semantic interpretation. In J. A. G. Groenendijk, T. Janssen, M. Stokhof, editors, *Formal Methods in the Study of Language*, volume 1. Amsterdam: Mathematical Centrum.

Verkuyl, H. 1988. Aspectual asymmetry and quantification. In V. Ehrich and H. Vater, editors, *Temporalsemantik: Beiträge zur Linguistik der Zeitreferenz*, 220–259. Tübingen: Niemeyer.

Verkuyl, H. 1992. Some issues in the analysis of multiple quantification with plural noun phrases. Technical report OTS-WP-TL-92-5, Institute for Speech and Language. To appear in F. Hamm and E. Hinrichs, editors, *Plural Quantification*. Dordrecht: Kluwer.

Verkuyl, H. 1993. Distributivity and collectivity: a couple at odds. In M. Kanazawa and C. J. Piñón, editors, *Dynamics, Quantification, and Polarity*. CSLI Lecture Notes, no. 48. Palo Alto: CSLI Publications.

Verkuyl, H. J., and J. van der Does. 1991. The semantics of plural noun phrases. Technical report LP-91-07, Institute for Logic, Language, and Information, University of Amsterdam. To appear in J. van der Does and J. van Eyck, editors, *Generalized Quantifier Theory and Applications*. Chicago: University of Chicago Press.

Versmissen, K. 1993. Lambek calculus, modalities, and semigroup semantics. In *Proceedings of the Sixth Conference of the European Chapter of the Association for Computational Linguistics*. Morristown: ACL Publications.

Versmissen, K. 1996. Grammatical composition: modes, models, modalities. Ph.D. dissertation, University of Utrecht.

Vlach, F. 1981. La semantique du temps et de l'aspect en Anglais. Translated by F. Nef. *Language* 64:65–79.

Vlach, F. 1993. Temporal adverbials, tenses, and the perfect. *Linguistics and Philosophy* 5:231–283.

Von Fintel, K. 1993. Exceptive constructions. *Natural Language Semantics* 1:123–148.

Von Stechow, A. 1980. Modification of noun phrases: a challenge for compositional semantics. *Theoretical Linguistics* 7:57–110.

Von Stechow, A. 1984. Comparing semantic theories of comparison. *Journal of Semantics* 3:1–77.

Von Wright, G. H. 1951. Deontic logic. *Mind* 60:1–15.

Von Wright, G. H. 1963. *Norm and Action*. London: Routledge and Kegan Paul.

Wasow, T. 1972. Anaphoric relations in English. Ph.D. dissertation, Massachussets Institute of Technology.

Wasow, T. 1977. Transformations and the lexicon. In P. Culicover, T. Wasow, and A. Akmajian, editors, *Formal Syntax*. New York: Academic Press.

Wasow, T., G. Nunberg, and I. Sag. 1994. Idioms. *Language* 70:491–538.

Weeda, D. 1981. Tenseless 'that'-clauses in generalized phrase structure grammar. In *Papers from the Seventeenth Regional Meeting of the Chicago-Linguistics Society*, 404–410. Chicago.

Westerståhl, D. 1987. Branching generalized quantifiers and natural language. In P. Gärdenfors, editor, *Generalized Quantifiers and Logical Approaches*, 269–298. Dordrecht: Reidel.

Westerståhl, D. 1988. Quantifiers in formal and natural languages. In D. Gabbay and F. Guenthner, editors, *Handbook of Philosophical Logic*, volume 4. Dordrecht: Reidel.

Wexler, K., and P. Culicover. 1980. *Formal Principles of Language Acquisition*. Cambridge: MIT Press.

White, A. R. 1967. The coherence theory of truth. In P. Edwards, editor, *The Encyclopedia of Philosophy*, volume 2, 130–133. New York: MacMillan Publishing Co. and Free Press.

Whitehead, A. N. 1929. *Process and Reality*. Cambridge.

Whitehead, A. N., and B. Russell. 1910, 1912. *Principia Mathematica*. Volumes 1 and 2. Second edition, 1925. Cambridge: Cambridge University Press.

Willard, S. 1970. *General Topology*. Reading, Masachusetts: Addison Wesley.

Williams, E. 1982. The NP cycle. *Linguistic Inquiry* 13:277–295.

Williams, E. 1991. Reciprocal scope. *Linguistic Inquiry* 22:173–192.

Wittgenstein, L. 1953. *Philosophical Investigations*. New York: Macmillan.

Wolfram, S. 1991. *Mathematica: A System for Doing Mathematics by Computer*. Second edition. Redwood City, California: Addison-Wesley.

Wood, M. M. 1993. *Categorial Grammars*. London: Routledge.

Zeevat, H. 1989. A compositional approach to discourse representations. *Linguistics and Philosophy* 12:95–131.

Zeevat, H., E. Klein, and J. Calder. 1987. Unification categorial grammar. In N. Haddock, E. Klein, and G. Morrill, editors, *Categorial Grammar, Unification Grammar, and Parsing*, Edinburgh Working Papers in Cognitive Science, no. 1, 195–222. Centre for Cognitive Science, Univerisity of Edinburgh. Reprinted in *Lingua e Stile* 26:499–527.

Zielonka, W. 1981. Axiomatizability of Ajdukiewicz-Lambek calculus by means of cancellation schemes. *Zeitscrift für mathematische Logik und Grundlagen der Mathematik* 27:215–224.

Index